Economics and Climate Emergency

This book explores a series of connected themes focused on the role economics and other influential forms of theory and thinking have played in creating the current predicament and the scope for alternatives and how they might be framed.

Thirty years have passed since the inception of the United Nations Framework Convention on Climate Change (UNFCCC) and the beginning of policy on climate change. Thirty wasted years. To most politicians, long-term collective interest has been denominated in meaningless units of time, a never and forever that has continually delayed action. From complacency has come potential disaster, and we are now living in a time of climate emergency and ecological breakdown. The next decade is a pivotal period requiring fundamental change. But numerous impediments remain. Continual material, energy and economic growth on a planetary scale are manifestly impossible, and yet economic theory takes these as a given and political leadership and policy seem unwilling to accept brute reality. Instead, they offer a series of implausible commitments and pledges rooted in technofixes, without addressing the fundamental drivers of the problems the world faces.

This edited volume explores the issues and offers a variety of ways to think through the problems at hand, from postgrowth, degrowth and social ecological economics to policy assemblage and transversalism.

The chapters in this book were originally published in the journal *Globalizations*.

Barry Gills is Editor in Chief of *Globalizations* and Professor of Global Development Studies at the University of Helsinki, Finland. He has written widely on World System theory, neoliberalism, globalization, global crises, democracy, resistance and transformative praxis.

Jamie Morgan is Professor of Economic Sociology at Leeds Beckett University, UK. He is the co-editor of the *Real-World Economics Review* with Edward Fullbrook. He has published widely in the fields of economics, political economy, philosophy, sociology and international politics.

Rethinking Globalizations

Edited by

Barry K. Gills, *University of Helsinki, Finland* and Kevin Gray, *University of Sussex, UK.*

This series is designed to break new ground in the literature on globalization and its academic and popular understanding. Rather than perpetuating or simply reacting to the economic understanding of globalization, this series seeks to capture the term and broaden its meaning to encompass a wide range of issues and disciplines and convey a sense of alternative possibilities for the future.

Why Globalization Matters
Engaging with Theory
Edited by Barrie Axford

Re-Globalization
New Frontiers of Political, Economic and Social Globalization
Edited by Roland Benedikter, Mirjam Gruber and Ingrid Kofler

Labour Conflicts in the Global South
Edited by Andreas Bieler and Jörg Nowak

Time, Climate Change, Global Racial Capitalism and Decolonial Planetary Ecologies
Edited by Anna M. Agathangelou and Kyle D. Killian

Globalizations from Below
The Normative Power of the World Social Forum, Ant Traders, Chinese Migrants, and Levantine Cosmopolitanism
Theodor Tudoroiu

Economics and Climate Emergency
Edited by Barry K. Gills and Jamie Morgan

Global Political Leadership
In Search of Synergy
Małgorzata Zachara-Szymańska

For more information about this series, please visit: https://www.routledge.com/Rethinking-Globalizations/book-series/RG

Economics and Climate Emergency

Edited by
Barry Gills and Jamie Morgan

Routledge
Taylor & Francis Group

LONDON AND NEW YORK

First published 2023
by Routledge
4 Park Square, Milton Park, Abingdon, Oxon, OX14 4RN

and by Routledge
605 Third Avenue, New York, NY 10158

Routledge is an imprint of the Taylor & Francis Group, an informa business

British Library Cataloguing-in-Publication Data
A catalogue record for this book is available from the British Library

ISBN13: 978-1-032-00566-9 (hbk)
ISBN13: 978-1-032-00567-6 (pbk)
ISBN13: 978-1-003-17470-7 (ebk)

DOI: 10.4324/9781003174707

Typeset in Minion Pro
by codeMantra

Publisher's Note
The publisher accepts responsibility for any inconsistencies that may have arisen
during the conversion of this book from journal articles to book chapters, namely the
inclusion of journal terminology.

Disclaimer
Every effort has been made to contact copyright holders for their permission to reprint
material in this book. The publishers would be grateful to hear from any copyright
holder who is not here acknowledged and will undertake to rectify any errors or
omissions in future editions of this book.

Contents

Citation Information

The chapters in this book were originally published in various issues of the journal *Globalizations*. When citing this material, please use the original citations and page numbering (or DOIs) for each article, as follows:

Introduction
Economics and climate emergency
Barry Gills and Jamie Morgan
Globalizations, volume 18, issue 7 (2021) pp. 1071–1086

Chapter 1
'The economy' as if people mattered: revisiting critiques of economic growth in a time of crisis
Clive L. Spash
Globalizations, volume 18, issue 7 (2021) pp. 1087–1104

Chapter 2
What does degrowth mean? A few points of clarification
Jason Hickel
Globalizations, volume 18, issue 7 (2021) pp. 1105–1111

Chapter 3
What does Degrowth mean? Some comments on Jason Hickel's 'A few points of clarification'
Ted Trainer
Globalizations, volume 18, issue 7 (2021) pp. 1112–1116

Chapter 4
Economics and the climate catastrophe
James K. Galbraith
Globalizations, volume 18, issue 7 (2021) pp. 1117–1122

Chapter 21

Climate and food inequality: the South African Food Sovereignty Campaign response
Vishwas Satgar and Jane Cherry
Globalizations, volume 17, issue 2 (2020) pp. 317–337

Chapter 22

The global south, degrowth and The Simpler Way movement: the need for structural solutions at the global level
Sarah Mackay
Globalizations, DOI: 10.1080/14747731.2021.2015103

Chapter 23

Climate justice and sustained transnational mobilization
Paul Almeida
Globalizations, volume 16, issue 7 (2019) pp. 973–979

Chapter 24

Deep Restoration: from The Great Implosion to The Great Awakening
Barry Gills
Globalizations, volume 17, issue 4 (2020) pp. 577–579

For any permission-related enquiries please visit:
http://www.tandfonline.com/page/help/permissions

Notes on Contributors

Pam Alldred is Professor in the Social Work, Social Care and Communities Department at Nottingham Trent University, UK. She researches sexualities, parenting and sex education, and has lead two large international projects on gender-related violence and then on sexual violence.

Paul Almeida is Professor and former Chair of Sociology at the University of California, Merced, USA. Almeida's research centers on the efficacy of collective action at the local, national and global levels of social and political life.

James Anderson is Emeritus Professor of Political Geography at Queens University Belfast, Northern Ireland, and Visiting Professor in the University's Senator George J. Mitchell Institute for Global Peace, Security and Justice. He publishes regularly on issues of imperialism, geopolitics and ecological change.

Salvi Asefi-Najafabady is an atmospheric scientist currently working as a senior consultant/ climate scientist at Environmental Resources Management in Washington, DC, USA.

Jana Bacevic is Assistant Professor in the Department of Sociology at Durham University, UK. Her work is in social and political theory, sociology of knowledge and political economy of knowledge production.

Saturnino M. Borras, Jr, is Professor of Agrarian Studies at the International Institute of Social Studies (ISS) at Erasmus University Rotterdam, The Hague, Netherlands, and Adjunct Professor at the College of Humanities and Development Studies at China Agricultural University, Beijing, China. He is also Fellow at the Transnational Institute (TNI).

Hubert Buch-Hansen is a political economist and Associate Professor in the Department of Organization at Copenhagen Business School, Denmark.

Jane Cherry is Executive Manager at the Cooperative and Policy Alternative Centre. Through COPAC, Jane has been involved in the South African Food Sovereignty Campaign and the Wits Food Sovereignty Centre, and has co-developed various campaigning tools.

Gareth Dale teaches politics at Brunel University, UK. His last books were on Karl Polanyi and on green growth; his next book is on revolutions in the neoliberal era (co-edited with Colin Barker and Neil Davidson).

Jonas Egmose is Associate Professor in the Department of People and Technology, and teaches in action research, participation and social learning in the context of sustainability planning. His research concerns how the democratization of knowledge creation can help enable ecological practices and sustainable ways of living.

Nick J. Fox is Professor of Sociology at the University of Huddersfield, UK. He has researched and written widely on materialist social theory as applied to health, embodiment, sexuality, creativity and emotions, and is currently working on issues in political sociology including citizenship, governance and policy.

Jennifer C. Franco is a political sociologist and research associate in the Agrarian and Environmental Justice and the Myanmar in Focus programs of the Transnational Institute (TNI), Amsterdam, the Netherlands. She is also Adjunct Professor at the College of Humanities and Development Studies at China Agricultural University, Beijing, China.

Stefan Gaarsmand Jacobsen is Associate Professor in the Department of Communication and Arts and teaches global history and climate politics. His research addresses climate justice, social movement history, eco-social transformation and political economy.

James K. Galbraith holds the Lloyd M. Bentsen Jr Chair in Government-Business Relations at the Lyndon B. Johnson School of Public Affairs at the University of Texas at Austin, USA.

Barry Gills is Editor in Chief of *Globalizations* and Professor of Global Development Studies at the University of Helsinki, Finland. He has written widely on World System theory, neoliberalism, globalization, global crises, democracy and resistance.

James Goodman is Professor and Director of the Climate Justice Research Centre at the University of Technology Sydney, Australia. He researches and teaches in global and climate politics and has coauthored six books, including *Beyond the Coal Rush: A Turning Point for Global Energy and Climate Policy?* (2020).

Henrik Hauggaard-Nielsen is Professor in the Department of People and Technology where his research addresses climate and environmental issues in food production connected to bioenergy solutions, plant nutrition, crop use, soil fertility, nutrient conservation and soil carbon sequestration, using participatory methods with a great emphasis on actor involvement.

Jason Hickel is an economic anthropologist whose research focuses on global inequality, political economy and ecological economics. He is the author of a number of books, most recently *Less Is More: How Degrowth Will Save the World* (2020). He is Fellow of the Royal Society of Arts.

Lars Hulgård is Professor in the Department of People and Technology doing research, teaching and consultancy in solidarity economy, social innovation, social policy, social economy, social entrepreneurship, public service, social enterprise, civil society and transformation of the welfare state. He is Co-Founder and former President of EMES International Research Network.

Steve Keen is Distinguished Research Fellow at the Institute for Strategy, Resilience and Security at University College London, UK; specialist on Minsky's Financial Instability Hypothesis (1995); and the author of *Debunking Economics* (2011).

Max Koch is sociologist and Professor of Social Policy at Lund University, Socialhögskolan.

Kristen Lyons is a public intellectual with over twenty years' experience in research, teaching and service that delivers national and international impacts on issues that sit at the intersection of sustainability and development, as well as the future of higher education.

Sarah MacKay is an independent social researcher in world-system analysis, global inequality and Middle East studies.

Jamie Morgan is Professor of Economic Sociology at Leeds Beckett University, UK. He is the co-editor of the *Real-World Economics Review* with Edward Fullbrook. He has published widely in the fields of economics, political economy, philosophy, sociology and international politics.

Peter Newell is Professor of International Relations at the University of Sussex, Brighton, UK. His recent research focuses on the political economy of low-carbon energy transitions. He is Co-Founder and Research Director of the Rapid Transition Alliance and sits on the board of directors of Greenpeace UK.

Pedram Rashidi worked for over 12 years in the Iranian and Australian energy industries, both in research and in practice, before commencing a PhD on global environmental governance.

Vishwas Satgar is Associate Professor of International Relations at the University of the Witwatersrand, Johannesburg, South Africa. He is principal investigator for the Emancipatory Futures Studies project, and he is the editor of the *Democratic Marxism* book series.

Clive L. Spash is economist holding the Chair of Public Policy & Governance at WU in Vienna, Editor-in-Chief of Environmental Values and former President of the European Society for Ecological Economics. He has published widely in the fields of economics, political economy, social psychology, project and policy evaluation, environmental policy, philosophy and ethics.

Will Steffen is Emeritus Professor at the Fenner School of Environment and Society at the Australian National University (ANU), Canberra, Australia.

Olivia Taylor is a doctoral researcher at the School of Global Studies at the University of Sussex, UK. Her research focuses on the political economy of climate change adaptation, in particular disaster risk financing and insurance.

Ted Trainer is retired Lecturer from the School of Social Work at the University of New South Wales, Australia. He has written numerous books and articles on sustainability and is developing Pigface Point, an alternative lifestyle educational site near Sydney.

Laura Villegas-Ortiz is an environmental and development economist working as researcher for the World Resources Institute in Washington, DC, USA.

INTRODUCTION

Economics and climate emergency

Barry Gills and Jamie Morgan

ABSTRACT
In this essay we provide introductory comment for the collection of solicited essays on Economics and Climate Emergency. In the first section we suggest that recent critique of the climate movement has broader systemic significance and this is indicative of issues that bear on the collected essays. In the following section we rehearse some of the standard arguments leading to complacency and delay to action on climate change and ecological breakdown. In the last section we set out the broad themes of the essays.

Introduction: pushback, complacency and delay

This collection of essays in *Globalizations* has been commissioned to critically address the relationship between economics, especially mainstream economics, though with some comment on the history of political economy, current international political economy and tensions in heterodox positions, and the global climate emergency. That emergency, of course, is one aspect of a broader ecological breakdown crisis now facing humanity. The stakes are extremely high: the future well-being, and possibly even survival of the human species, and myriad other species on our planet is now in question (Amen et al., 2008; Fullbrook & Morgan, 2019; Gills, 2008, 2020; Gills & Morgan, 2020a; IPBES, 2019; Oosthoek & Gills, 2005).[1] Just posing this possibility of existential threat provokes pushback. There is, for example, currently a concerted effort to delegitimise Extinction Rebellion. Critics have seized on internal dissent, disruptions created by protest (and differences over the effectiveness of these) and on some of the purported claims regarding bleak futures to suggest the movement has been captured by extremists with political agendas that have little to do with the climate issue. It is important, however, to place this critique in proper context and this, as we shall see, bears on the purpose of the essays collected here. How to adequately express the seriousness of a situation, how to create awareness, how to persuade and what to propose are never simple matters when the very terms of debate suggest the problems are urgent and *systemic*.

Still, there is no lack of evidence regarding the fundamental systemic tendencies and there is now scientific consensus that we have *entered* a global climate emergency. These points are conjoint. Current evidence does not indicate countries are collectively tending to significantly 'dematerialise' their economies. They are not achieving absolute 'decoupling' between material and energy use and scale of economy, measured by GDP (Fletcher & Rammelt, 2017; Hickel & Kallis, 2019; Parrique et al., 2019; Schröder & Storm, 2020). There has been and remains an underlying tendency for material and energy use to increase as economies grow (for context see Wiedmann et al., 2015) and for carbon emissions to also grow. This has had and continues to have consequences. The 'Alliance of World Scientists' suggests that we risk 'ecocide' if radical transformations are not implemented very soon (Ripple et al., 2020). Leading systems analysts and climate scientists argue that we have in fact already exceeded, or are now fast approaching, the threshold for 9 tipping points in the global climate system, and this is set within other broader environmentally destructive trends (Lenton et al., 2020). According to the IPCC *Global Warming of 1.5°C* report (IPCC, 2018), and the UNEP 9th 'Emissions Gap' report (UNEP, 2018), global carbon emissions need to fall by 45% by 2030, from the 2017 level of 53.5 Gigatonnes CO_2 equivalent ($GtCO_{2e}$).[2] That is, if we are to have some reasonable possibility of limiting average temperature rises over this century and into the next based on the goals of Article 2 of the Paris Agreement. However, the nature of those goals and achieving them remains problematic (Anderson et al., 2020; Morgan, 2016; Newell & Taylor, 2020; Spash, 2016). According to the 10th Emissions Gap report, global emissions actually *increased* from the 2017 level, to reach 55.3 $GtCO_{2e}$ in 2018 (UNEP, 2019). Both levels were record highs. According to a UNEP 10-year summary report, emissions 'show no signs of peaking' and current emissions policy is not sufficient to offset the 'key drivers' of 'economic growth and population growth' (Christensen & Olhoff, 2019, p. 3). Moreover, according to the 10th Emissions Gap report, based on the current 'implementation deficit' in COP member 'nationally determined contributions' (NDCs), emissions are projected to *continue* to increase to 59 $GtCO_{2e}$ by 2030.[3] By contrast, the report states a need for emissions to be reduced by 7.6% per annum from 2020 to 2030, in order to get back on track with Paris goals (rising to 15% if we delay sufficient action until 2025).

We are on the clock and that is obvious. Time is of the essence, and it is important to bear in mind that the planet as a complex dynamic system evolves through time. What our species (some more than others in some places more than others)[4] has been doing has brought an avoidable possible future into the present. We are already experiencing increasingly erratic weather and an increase incidence of extreme events. Average global temperatures are approximately 1 degree higher since the beginning of the industrial revolution and each year this century has been amongst the hottest since records began. Human activity now shapes the majority of land and affects much of the oceans and the very make-up of the air we breathe (e.g. IPBES, 2019; IPCC, 2019). So, from an 'emergency' point of view the future is 'now' because of what we have done, but what we do now and what we are observably continuing to do will also shape the planet for hundreds and perhaps thousands of years.

As Julia Steinberger notes, we have not just brought the future into the present, our future is also a kind of accelerated pathway to a dangerous past. In a recent piece on the 'planetary climate clock', she suggests we have affected 'planetary time' on a human timescale of little more than one long lifetime (Steinberger, 2020). A human unit of 1,000 years is about 40 generations, 12,000 years takes us back to the end of the last ice age and the beginning of the 'Holocene' period. Conditions in the Holocene have been highly conducive to the development of civilization. Drawing on recent earth systems research in *Nature* (Vega et al., 2020) she notes that we have in the last hundred years or so increased atmospheric CO_2 from an average 304 parts per million (ppm) to 415 ppm and rising.[5] This takes us out of the normal range for the Holocene and is considerably higher than the 360 ppm of the Pliocene, 3.3 million years ago when average temperature was 3 degrees higher and sea levels 20 m higher. So, whilst acknowledging uncertainty and some variation, it is reasonable to infer this is the future that is *now* feeding through in the coming decades and over this century and the next. Moreover, based on current trends in emissions we are heading towards GHG levels not seen since the Miocene (15 million years ago) and perhaps the

Eocene (50 million years ago), when a devastating set of volcanic events (which may have set off a cycle of methane release) induced warming of 5 degrees. We simply do not know whether our farming systems and complex and specialized long supply chain based civilizations can adapt to these changes (and bear in mind this is not just temperature and sea level effects, it is ecological breakdown). The beginning of the Eocene was recently recognized as an additional likely mass extinction period in the fossil record.

Of course, we may still prevent a continuing acceleration of temperature changes and other effects *if* we reduce emissions. Some future effects are 'baked-in', but that is no reason to continue to feed the fire. And to be clear, 2030 is *not* a cliff edge, failure to fully reduce emissions by that date in accordance with goals or address broader ecological problems should not be taken as a signal that further action has become pointless. Failure to act with urgency, however, cannot be considered as anything other than reckless and irrational given the weight of evidence (see also Hansen et al., 2017; Steffen et al., 2018, 2015; Wunderling et al., 2020).[6] It is with this in mind that one should read any critique of the climate movement. The overwhelming goals of the climate movement are to create awareness, induce *concern* and motivate immediate action. It would, then, be absurd to suggest that overall and given the direction of travel suggested by the evidence, the main intent amounts to 'scaremongering'. Perhaps the more pertinent question to ask regarding the criticism is why critics focus on and seek to accentuate division at this time?

There is, of course, growing media attention to the consequences of climate change and ecological breakdown – this has become impossible to ignore now. It is now common for reporting to have some connective thread – the recognition of climate change and so on. But this is not quite the same as the emergence of a common narrative where continuous coverage holds governments to *account*, which places critical pressure on those with the immediate power to create policy, directing criticism towards *them*. The IPCC and UNEP are not radical organizations, but they are now calling for mobilization equivalent to wartime and yet governments are manifestly *not* responding with urgency. It is for this reason that organizations like Extinction Rebellion, Greenpeace, Stay Grounded and many others are so important.[7] Their very existence is a signal of civilizational failure. Civil society organizations are rarely perfect, but again, there is another issue here, where does the burden of proof really lie for whether in fact current policy is adequate and whether in fact there is sufficient urgency? Surely it lies primarily with the relatively small number of corporations and governments responsible for the vast majority of emissions?

But there is also the systemic issue. The 'political agendas' of climate movement activists encompass a broad spectrum of systemic critiques of capitalism because capitalism is *the* dominant framework of economy and society in the world. Capitalism is in the main the system in which consequences have been and continue to be produced. This too is important to bear in mind when considering pushback. To suggest that a campaigning organization that criticizes corporations and governments has been 'captured' by political agendas that have little to do with the climate issue implies either that the climate issue is somehow separate from the systemic features of economy and society (domestic and global) within which those issues have arisen or that the system itself is giving rise to timely solutions to the problems that are arising. The latter is clearly false and the former is manifestly contradictory. The main question that should be asked and answered here is one that is more appropriately *directed* at corporations and governments: does the evidence suggest that the scale and intensity of our economies are compatible with the ecological and climate balance on which we depend? If we think of an economy as a material subsystem operating within an earth system, then we must recognize that the kinds of economies we have created exhibit structurally *inscribed tendencies* which affect that earth system. These are not somehow separate matters.

As such, the 'political agendas' of climate activists are not 'capture' they are highly relevant (if sometimes contentious) sources of insight and critique regarding the sources of tendencies.[8]

The point we are driving at here is that pushback on the climate movement, and most recently focused on Extinction Rebellion, is itself indicative of something systemic. Climate emergency does not just invite us to explain the material features of our economic systems that produce consequences, it invites inquiry regarding how it is that we have found ourselves in such a position of emergency. We have agency, we are reflexive, but as Marx noted, we do not choose the conditions in which we choose because we are born into societies that pre-exist us as individuals. There is nothing intrinsically subversive or radical about stating this, it is just another way of saying conscious social beings do not experience the world as though they were encountering it anew from moment to moment (creatures like us and civilization itself would be impossible if that were so). Every system has its socialisations, its system serving, interest bearing and belief inculcating features, its information, persuasion and knowledge practices. These may be complex, evolving and multi-faceted, but some are more influential than others. This brings us to the purpose of this collection of essays. Ecological economists and critical social scientists have been arguing for many years that mainstream economics and especially its sub-disciplinary theory of the environment, is falsely posed, and that it fosters dangerous complacency and delay (e.g. Dale, 2018; Daly, 2015, 1997, 1974; Hickel, 2018). Though mainstream economics has not been the only source of complacency and delay (see e.g. Dale, 2012; Lamb et al., 2020; Stevenson, 2020) it has been an important source.[9] It has played a prominent role as a source of concepts, theory, policy and education and many other issues and disciplines are influenced by it. It contrasts sharply with ecological economics. Ecological economics takes as its point of departure the key insight that an economy is a subsystem that depends on and mutually influences broader biophysical systems (for range in relation to this core commitment see Spash, 2020b, p. 2017). Using concepts such as throughput and metabolic flow ecological economics seeks to assess the relationship between systems. As such its basic insight is that an economy is a material processes involving entropy and waste creation. This is quite different than a mainstream focus on processes of value creation through the exchange of goods and services (see Daly & Morgan, 2019; O'Neill, 2007). With this in mind it is worth rehearsing some of the mainstream archetypal arguments for delay, since awareness of those arguments helps to make sense of the significance of the essays.

Mainstream archetypal arguments for delay

Let us consider the influence mainstream economics precepts have had when translated via the mainstream sub-disciplinary concerns of 'environmental economics'. They form a set of policy arguments and attitudes whose general direction of travel has always erred on the side of delay (a distorted idea of caution dictates 'do not intervene and prevent the system doing its thing'). The cumulative effect has been systematic complacency. As more historically-minded and older readers may know the 1970s was a period of 'oil shocks' and growing concern over resource security and environmental damage. Mainstream economic theorists of the environment began to argue that forecasts and warnings about the trends and consequences of expanding economies across the globe (scale and intensity) were expressions of unwarranted hysteria, lacking proper data and correct appreciation of economic mechanisms; that there is, in any case, plenty of time to solve environmental problems, by taxing externalities to make markets more efficient or by creating property rights to turn problems into assets that can be traded away, and more fundamentally by harnessing market processes of competition. Beginning in the 1970s, several standard lines of argument (and assumption) have emerged drawing from the mainstream economic framework:[10]

- 'Dynamic efficiency' in the form of induced technological progress will mainly take care of emissions via 'price signalling' and the profit motive.
- We can always find some 'backstop substitute' for whatever resource we use up.
- It is counterproductive to prevent economic activity now when future societies will be wealthier and more able to solve the problems we bequeath them.
- Pollution and environmental damage necessarily reduce as societies become wealthier.
- There are some economic benefits to climate change in some places and these may offset the economic costs or problems created elsewhere.
- One person's (or country's) waste is another person's (or country's) opportunity, so environmental profligacy and damage in one place may actually produce economic development elsewhere, leading to aggregate dynamic efficiency.
- Not all sectors of an economy are affected equally by climate change, and so economic activity can incrementally transfer from one to the other.
- There is no limit to human ingenuity, and there is, therefore, no *necessary* limit to how we grow into the environment we occupy and depend on (what seems like a major problem being created now will not seem so in the future …).

The serious weaknesses and flaws in these ('Panglossian') claims are now well documented (Spash, 2017). Fundamentally these claims involve two basic problems of perspective. First, they treat an aggregate globally connected cumulative problem of increasing collective scale and intensity of human interventions in myriad natural systems as if it were merely a localized set of individually manageable circumstances. Second, the claims all relate to a notional, i.e. imagined and 'utopian' future. That optimized future is conceived of as being the site where all serious tensions concerning the environment will be reconciled, i.e. where the problems being created now will all be solved (thus generating an attitude of deferral, delay, and complacency in the present). This logic suppresses the significance of the mounting empirical scientific evidence of current and past climate change and ecological problems, and tacitly or even explicitly counsels *against* prohibitions or major change of direction (rejecting or deferring these in favour of facilitating current trends and activity in practice). Taken together these arguments are appropriately characterized as being: implicitly system supportive; policy permissive; and, as evidence has now accumulated, historically reckless. Nevertheless, they have been basic to policy for the last forty years, and have become familiar as the 'business as usual' stance (a stance that is now increasingly being challenged, albeit mainly as green growth agendas). To non-economists, these conventional mainstream claims clearly violate the 'precautionary principle'.[11]

It is important to bear in mind that there is a 'market conforming' rationale behind each of these claims that sits comfortably within the mainstream framework of economic reasoning: price signals provide information that communicates to us that it is time to stop doing some things (e.g. it has become too expensive based on resource exhaustion and environmental or social damage) and that it is time to start doing other things (the state of the world induces investment in alternative ways of doing things and in resolving the problems created, and there is always the next period in which this can happen). Mainstream economic theory has no fundamental roots in earth system dynamics, material process or biophysical boundary states, but even though mainstream economic theory lacks these, there is a presupposition that our economic signalling system will divert us away from any seriously problematic biophysical limits. It is, for example, typically assumed we will avoid 'tipping points' even though measurement of these is not intrinsic to mainstream economics (hence no *necessary* limits need be imposed now to the economy).

The key point is that mainstream economic thinking has conveyed the central idea that even severe environmental problems being produced today can simply be thrown into the future, and that we can trust (have faith) that in the end all will be well. Moreover, it is continually assumed that the economic 'costs' are limited to some lost growth within *continued* growth and that innovation and technological change ('progress') will be sources of solutions to any given environmental problem. This perspective produces a frame of mind similar to Voltaire's famous jibe in Candide against the ridiculous optimism purveyed by some thinkers in his own day, i.e. that this economic theory and system perpetually (re)produces 'The best of all possible worlds'! This is despite ever increasing evidence to the contrary. This has been and remains (albeit increasingly in tension) a permanent drag on recognizing the urgency of our situation and the necessity of radical transformation. Moreover, it continues to instil 'faith' in market mechanisms and the logic of capitalism in the form of an expansionary capital accumulation system. By default it leads to a de-emphasis of the positive or even necessary role for prohibitions, large scale state intervention, government planning, and regulation, in halting and reversing material expansion. Moreover, it entirely ignores radical social change organized 'from below' (substituting for this the green consumer).

In environmental economics, one of the first times these arguments were played out was in *the American Economic Review* in 1974. In that year the *Review* published Robert Solow's Ely Lecture, and in the same issue a special section of papers by Herman Daly, William Nordhaus and others (Daly, 1974; Solow, 1974). In 1972, the Club of Rome report *Limits to Growth* (Meadows et al., 1972) was published, and as noted the 1970s generally started to bring issues of finite resource supply and resource security to the fore. Against this background Daly makes the case for a 'steady-state' economics in his 1974 essay. The basic premise is that a rational economic system must develop a set of measurements of its economic activity that ensure it stays within really existing environmental limits, and that it requires a set of systematic institutional mechanisms to ensure that this is achieved. In his Ely Lecture, Solow, a future Swedish Bank 'Nobel' Prize winner and seminal figure in mainstream economic growth modelling, covers the same issues. What is notable, however, is that he translates the whole into a mainstream context. Solow does not reference Daly, and for Solow, Daly's type of concerns are reduced to the relative emphasis different economic theorists put on markets or the state in a mixed economy. As such, he shifts the grounds of debate away from the problem of material expansion and the issue of evidence regarding long term trends. Whilst he initially makes some reference to work on the limits to growth (via a 1931 essay, and alluding to Meadows et al., 1972), he dismissively refers to *Limits* as 'doomsday' and 'cosmic', not unimportant, but not a serious matter for economists. Instead, he affirms his confidence in economics as a discipline that can guide our thinking, and discusses 'backstop technologies and resources' (the argument that there can be continuous and infinite substitution of one resource for another, including the environment itself). Though Solow notes that the real world might differ from textbook economics, he does not take this as a signal that the fundamentals that shape his attitude to both states and markets might be in error. For Solow, the problem is one of more or less faith in market processes and in different kinds of imperfections (failures).[12] Though Nordhaus pays closer attention to Meadows et al., he does not refer to Daly, and he starts from the assumption of 'stimulated competitive markets', efficient pricing, and allocation of energy resources over the long term. He recognizes however that this is not very 'realistic', and notes that there is a further problem of possible 'environmentally unacceptable' atmospheric carbon levels.

and yet he also (re)states (the faith) that 'with sufficient time and money – emissions can be brought into conformity with any reasonable set of standards', essentially through technology (Nordhaus, 1974, p. 25). No need to worry then, or to take radical urgent action, nor to change the dominant paradigm of economics in theory or practice.

In any case, both Solow and Nordhaus's arguments entirely miss Daly's central point. The ecologically-informed argument is rooted in the growing realization that a disastrous ecological future was obviously built into the general observed tendencies: i.e. the (increasingly globalized) spread of industrialization, urbanization, and consumption-heavy lifestyles, as well as the secular trend of targeting high economic growth (an economic system predicated on compound growth in GDP and attendant material expansion). This insight was by no means restricted to Daly in the 1970s (see e.g. Schumacher, 1993/1973 and Ivan Illich, discussed Samerski, 2018). Moreover, the central ecological argument was not actually about the relative merits of future technologies, nor whether we opt for more 'state' or more 'market' per se. The central point was that it made very good sense to *avoid* rather than have to retrospectively manage the foreseeable negative consequences of a material *growth* system.[13]

However, for decades everything about the mainstream framework counselled 'wait and see' and this became a continual drag on organizational responses through the 1980s and 1990s and into the new Millennium. To be clear, however, the mainstream framework has not been entirely antithetical to limited state intervention, but it has been blind to the concept of *absolute limits*. And it would be disingenuous to suggest that mainstream economics in general or environmental economics in particular have remained unchanged since the 1970s, or that they lack internal concerns and criticism (perhaps most notably from Nicholas Stern, e.g. Stern, 2013). What we want to emphasize is that environmental economics has evolved through mainstream economics, and mainstream economics may have changed as a consequence, but it has not been transformed (see Mearman et al., 2018a, 2018b; Morgan, 2015; Røpke, 2020; Söderbaum, 2018).

Mainstream economics has not yet addressed the fundamental points made by ecological economists. It has not yet been restructured around a full recognition and internalization of the realities of material processes, their consequences and (planetary) limits. Its primary focus remains a system of exchange values, price signals, and induced efficiencies, predicated on the (unlimited and perpetual) dynamism of growth. Issues of 'discount rates', energy intensity measures of $GDP, debates over absolute and relative decoupling, for example, have not led mainstream economists to accept the ecological economics position – even though sometimes the two can seem superficially similar, such as modern abatement analysis and use of integrated assessment models.[14] Complacency and delay have been and continue to be the dominant mainstream response. In the meantime, problems have continued to mount (carbon emissions, temperature rises, extreme events, species extinctions, plastic levels etc.), and so 'business as usual' frameworks have started to shift towards a language of more fundamental change in the form of green new deals (GNDs) and some versions of these are more radical than others. The more radical versions of GNDs emphasize climate crisis as an opportunity to address the cumulative pathologies of neoliberal economies and so tend to be critical of mainstream economics. These GNDs, for example, embrace alternatives such as Modern Monetary Theory (MMT) or post Keynesian finance theory and place greater emphasis on equalizing wealth and income, full employment and improving infrastructure and welfare services whilst greening the economy and society. Laudable though this is there is a still a question mark against the green growth aspect of these GNDs. In any case, mainstream economics typically opposes the financing proposals of radical GNDs and remains deeply problematic as a source of constructive theory, policy and education in the context of our climate emergency.

The essays

The IPCC is best known for its collation of findings of models on trends in emissions of greenhouse gases, but its various panels do not just report emissions trends and related forecast scenarios. Material is produced on socio-economic consequences, impacts on GDP and on 'adaption' and 'mitigation pathways'. These issues inform policy frameworks and the IPCC and the UNEP, like governments in general, look to mainstream economists and their models to inform this aspect of their work – depending, for example, on integrated assessment models developed by Nordhaus (and it was mainly for this he received the 2018 Swedish Bank 'Nobel' Prize). There has always been a disjuncture between the impacts in climate and earth system models and mainstream economic models use of those impacts (and more critical mainstream economists have recognized this, see Stern, 2013). In recent years, climate and earth system scientist IPCC panel members have become increasingly vocal (especially when speaking in a personal capacity) regarding the need for action on climate change and increasingly concerned about the drag on such action, so the difference between the climate science and the economics has become more obvious over time.

The IPCC and UNEP, of course, are acutely aware that climate change is a politically sensitive issue and that governments around the world operate under different sets of pressures, but always with a core concern for the economy. And, of course, mainstream economics is an established 'quantitative science' and carries disciplinary legitimacy. As a consequence, there has always been institutional reluctance to formally criticize the economics. Criticisms, however, have abounded. One major focus has been the 'discount rates' environmental economists apply to their models. Since impacts occur in the future, but are avoided through action taken in the present, economists apply discount rates as a way to distribute in time the economic costs against the benefits. The higher the discount rate then the greater weight placed on the present compared to the future. This implies numerous things, such as less pressure to reduce emissions now and lower likely immediate investment in mitigation or abatement. Behind this stands the whole array of arguments for delay we listed earlier. The UK Stern review of 2006, for example, used a relatively low average discount rate whilst Nordhaus has advocated a higher rate.[15] In our essay collection, Steve Keen (2020) goes much further and provides a comprehensive critique of mainstream economic modelling and evidence use.

According to Keen, assumptions and estimates used to calibrate integrated assessment models have been deeply dubious and these have underpinned the claim that climate change will merely reduce by some small proportion the growth of economies. Looking across the whole array of Nordhaus's work and the work that has mainly followed it, he notes much of economic activity (up to 90%) is assumed to be unaffected by climate change because it occurs in 'controlled environments'. Moreover, based on the observation of differences in output in relation to geographic temperature (a cross sectional observation i.e. of places and not changes in time), models assume that there will be benefits for economic activity in some places and costs in others as average temperatures rise *in the future* (i.e. an inference is drawn for complex processes in time). This facilitates the conclusion that climate change will be net beneficial, with the underlying implication that climate change does not prevent *continual* economic growth, and that there is an 'optimal' level of global warming. Concomitantly, Nordhaus has 'consistently reduced the value of parameters' in his 'damage function', meaning that values used to calculate the impact of global warming on GDP have *reduced* over time. Clearly, this can influence findings for net benefits and Nordhaus's optimal warming in his Nobel lecture is *4 degrees* – quite at odds with the concerns of climate science, which one might otherwise think would inform his work. According to Keen, the whole enterprise lacks realism, it misinterprets climate and earth system science, cannot adequately deal with feedback and tipping points and marginalizes the expressed opinion of scientists, whilst placing great weight on mainstream economic 'expert' opinion about climate science. Keen suggests that the socio-economic consequences might be mis-specified by an order of magnitude. As everything we have said in the previous sections indicates, not least based on the sharp contrast with ecological economics, mainstream economic expertise is profoundly problematic.

Keen's paper illustrates how mainstream economics has worked against calls for early and decisive action to prevent climate change and ecological breakdown. James Galbraith (2020) explores a parallel argument. Economics has consistently treated the problem of climate and ecological limits with 'derision' and offered deeply unrealistic policy proposals. He states:

> economics must be adjusted to the peculiar circumstances of the planet Earth, surrounded as it is by a fragile sheath of light gases, one of which has the annoying habit of trapping heat. The ability to withstand the heating of the atmosphere imposes a global limit, against which there is no appeal. An economics oriented toward the long term survival of human society in tolerable form must be adjusted to the reality of that limit, in which the terminal constraint is not the availability of carbon in the ground, but the necessity to restrict the concentrations in the air. (Galbraith, 2020)

Galbraith also notes the tremendous challenge we now face, since decarbonization requires use of *existing capital, rooted in carbon energy resources* to produce a decarbonized future. Even if decarbonized technology is possible it does not follow that a transition at equivalent levels is feasible and this has basic implications for the scale of economies, consumption and waste.[16] This raises a whole set of issues regarding the nature of economies and the role of economists in theorizing and legitimating those economies and this is the subject of two essays by Clive Spash. Spash is a prominent advocate of social ecological economics and in 'Apologists for growth' (Spash, 2020c) he argues that 'growthism' ('productivism', 'extractivism' etc.) is not just a mainstream economics issue. Many heterodox economists – including some post Keynesians – are critical of neoliberal economies, but advocate solutions which do not come to terms with the problem of scale and the commitment to material expansion (they are more concerned with solving income distribution problems and managing aggregate demand with the goal of producing full employment in a renewed industrial economy and tend to lack clarity on whether this is in fact compatible with material use etc.). Moreover, some proponents of staying within planetary boundaries are also inconsistent on this issue and Spash looks particularly at the work of Tim Jackson and Kate Raworth. In his second essay, Spash generalizes his growthism point and uses the Covid-19 pandemic to highlight the structural fragility of capitalist economies and the tendency to respond to crisis through policies intended to induce more demand and thus get growth 'going' (Spash, 2020a). For Spash, there are fundamental issues with capitalist accumulation. This remains the case as 'business as usual' evolves, since green growth does not come to terms with its basic material commitments within structures of accumulation and based on real biophysical limits.

The issue of biophysical limits also informs Gareth Dale's essay (Dale, 2020). Paralleling Spash, Dale ties together theory which fails to consider the fundamental structural tendencies of economic systems, Raworth's position and a longer history of economic thought beginning with the Physiocrats (Dale, 2020). The fundamental problem of material growth associated with economic growth and critique of growthism also lies behind the degrowth movement. Jason Hickel is a well-known advocate of degrowth and his essay sets out to clarify the meaning of the term, since it is a term easily misunderstood (Hickel, 2020a). He distinguishes degrowth from recession. Degrowth is a coordinated and designed reduction in scale involving redirection of activity, resource use and priorities. It focuses on provisioning, livelihoods, welfare and care and thus quality of life. Degrowth is not about sacrifice, cuts and austerity in a neoliberal context, but rather is an alternative to that context and this includes also the exploitative 'development' relations between the global North and South. This focus on reducing and reorienting economies also informs the concept of postgrowth and there is considerable overlap between postgrowth and degrowth. Max Koch and Hubert Buch-Hansen have written extensively on degrowth and postgrowth. With this in mind their essay argues that critical political economy needs to do more to assimilate the insights of ecological economics and in order to avoid emulating the errors of mainstream economics. The varieties of capitalism literature, for example, tends to neglect an ecological perspective. They suggest:

> Within the emerging and diverse political economy of and for the postgrowth era, the Marxian tradition, with its simultaneous focus on historically specific economic categories, social relations and modes of consciousness, is capable of playing a constructive part. And some of the concepts of contemporary critical political economy approaches such as regulation theory may give a hint into the further particulars of an analysis of this new epoch. Like growth economies, postgrowth economies will have institutions that may be understood in terms of 'institutional forms'. (Koch & Buch-Hansen, 2020)

This line of argument raises basic issues regarding transitions and the scope for constructive change, which is the subject of James Goodman and James Anderson's essay (Goodman & Anderson, 2020). Clearly, no one acts for or speaks on behalf of capitalism in general and this means that cumulative changes to capitalism based on climate issues experience complex feedback, which in turn leads to new political pressures. According to Goodman and Anderson, and following on from the general theme of sources of complacency and delay, 'drivers' for climate action from within capitalism have been relatively weak, but there is notably growing scope for 'deepening politicization and socialisation'. Nick Fox and Pam Alldred bring a new materialist perspective to this issue in terms of competing policy propositions (Fox & Alldred, 2020). According to Fox and Alldred, economics plays a different role in different policy assemblages and they suggest there is an opportunity for selection and synthesis to overcome apparent incommensurability. They state that in conjunction with practical actions one might assemble:

> From the *liberal environmentalist* policy, a focus on environmental protection and efforts to change individual and collective human behaviour to lower energy and fossil fuel use, reduce consumption of other resources and the production of waste. From the *United Nations* policy assemblage, action to redistribute income locally and globally, recognising that poverty is one of the drivers of environmental destruction. From the *green capitalism* assemblage: support for technological innovation to limit and remove greenhouse gases from the environment. From the *no-growth* policy, action to limit economic growth and wasteful competition. These provide the foundation for incremental actions locally, nationally and globally to address the physical, biological, social, economic and political affects within the climate change event-assemblage. (Fox & Alldred, 2020)

Ultimately, if socialization is significant and strategy matters, then the role of education also matters. In 'Teaching climate complacency', we explore the role of the mainstream economics textbook as a source of complacency and delay (Gills & Morgan, 2020b). Our essay focuses mainly on the negative – what the textbooks omit, how mainstream economics informs environmental economics and how this framing produces complacency. We highlight what needs to be unlearned and suggest some ways to transform economics. Finally, Jana Bacevic reminds us that there are additional complicating factors in any attempt to transform the conditions of knowledge production (Bacevic, 2020). According to Bacevic, 'any attempt to think about the future that is *not* capitalist or extractive-colonial faces the seemingly impossible task of undoing its own conditions of possibility'. The implication is that change 'requires undoing not only of modes of production (capitalism) *or* habits of thought (Occidentalism, Eurocentrism) that have arisen as a consequence of this history, but the modes of production *of* thought that are, themselves, its product'. Clearly, this *is* a challenge (structural, ideational etc.), but Bacevic is not a pessimist. The apparently 'impossible' is not really insurmountable. If it were then the critical faculties used to question conditions of possibility would, in turn, be either impossible or irrelevant. This brings us back to where we began when we suggested, how to create awareness, how to persuade, what to propose are never simple matters when the very terms of debate suggest the problems are urgent and *systemic*. We recommend the essays in this collection to our readers, and we trust that in them you may find not only the basis of a powerful critique of mainstream economics, but also sources of inspiration for the radical reconstruction of our understanding of economics and its ecological and social context, ideas that go to the roots of the crisis and lead us to new ways through.

Conclusion

The Covid-19 global pandemic has intervened in the trajectory of 2020 and (temporarily) induced cuts in global greenhouse gas emissions (particularly carbon dioxide). A global debate is now in motion about how to construct a post-Covid 'green recovery' while simultaneously undertaking deep reductions in global emissions. Yet despite increasingly urgent warnings from the scientific community, the underlying conclusion has been that 'not enough' is yet being done. There has been delay at every turn. This habit of delay and deferral of action seems set to continue, despite increasingly alarming scientific reports and widespread recognition of the urgency of radical action to reduce emissions and arrest ecological destruction. Indifference and complacency continue to abound in 'official circles' of corporate and government power. The situation is now extremely urgent, and with each delay becomes more so. However, hopelessness and nihilism cannot be our response. It is in this context that the contributors to our collection examine the relationship between the economics discipline and the causes of these existential global crises of our time.

Some uncomfortable truths about the reality of the situation facing the world community today seem fairly clear: aggregate annual global greenhouse gas emissions must fall rapidly, rather than continue to increase year on year as at present. The cumulative level of CO_2 and other greenhouse gases in the atmosphere must fall globally, and do so rapidly, rather than continue to increase year after year. The global rate of biodiversity loss and species extinctions must decrease significantly, and ecological restoration must become a central aim of policy, including at local, national, regional and global policy levels. The fundamental drivers of global extractivism, ecocide, and climate catastrophe must be addressed: with new radical ideas and transformations, not by short term system supporting technical fixes intrinsic to the dominant growth economy. Faith in the market mechanism and the corporate-finance private sector to deliver the type of radical transition necessary should not only be questioned, but abandoned. We need a new paradigm of development, drawing on just transitions, degrowth, postgrowth, social ecological economics, ecofeminism and many other resources (e.g. Büchs & Koch, 2017; Hickel, 2020b; Kallis et al., 2020; Liegey & Nelson, 2020; Newell & Simms, 2020; Spash, 2020b, 2017). Given the scale and intensity of the crises we are facing, it seems clear a profound transformation in how the field of economics is conceptualized, taught, and practiced will be absolutely essential if humanity is to successfully combat the global climate emergency and arrest on-going ecological destruction across the planet (Røpke, 2020). The mainstream economics that has been dominant for so long, and which continues to drive profound existential crises today, must once and for all be scientifically discredited, academically delegitimised, and socially rejected. The real task now is to collectively construct a viable radical alternative paradigm fit for purpose: and that purpose is to profoundly arrest an accelerating set of global processes leading us to ecological destruction and gross future human insecurity. It is time to 'overturn economics' in its conventional mainstream form.

Notes

1. Note the 2020 UNEP Convention on Biological Diversity *Global Biodiversity Outlook 5* report highlights progress made and opportunities that still exist despite the underlying scale of problems of loss of biodiversity and threatened extinctions etc. highlighted by the IPBES.
2. The UNEP report calls for a 55% reduction by 2030 in its introductory summary. To be clear, the IPCC calls for reduction of 45% on 2010 levels (IPCC, 2018, p. 12) and the UNEP for 55% on 2017 levels (UNEP, 2018, p. xv).
3. Though one should note China augmented its commitments in September 2020, committing to carbon neutrality by 2060 and peak GHG emissions in the coming decade. Policy detail and real commitment are, of course, what will ultimately matter (the nature of 'net', the difference between 'carbon' and all GHGs for some metrics etc.).
4. As Jason Moore notes, the influence of climate on socio-economic change is not unique to the present, but the current situation is perhaps better understood as capitalist produced ('Capitalocene') rather than more generically an 'Anthropocene' – though he argues the term is not meaningless as geological Anthropocene (see e.g. Moore, 2015). Class and capitalism, not man and nature are the appropriate context for Moore. So, whilst larger global population is not irrelevant, what matters more is the spread of industrialization and of a consumption model within an asymmetrical capital accumulation system. It is important to note a simple focus on population as 'overpopulation' tends to distract attention from issues arising from a capital accumulation system and shift responsibility from the relatively few producing much of the problem (Fletcher et al., 2014). According to a recent Oxfam and Stockholm Environment Institute report, between 1995 and 2015: 'The richest 10% of the world's population (c.630 million people) were responsible for 52% of the cumulative carbon emissions – depleting the global carbon budget by nearly a third (31%) in those 25 years alone; The poorest 50% (c.3.1 billion people) were responsible for just 7% of cumulative emissions, and used just 4% of the available carbon budget; The richest 1% (c.63 million people) alone were responsible for 15% of cumulative emissions, and 9% of the carbon budget – twice as much as the poorest half of the world's population' (Gore, 2020, p. 2). Moreover, World Bank data clearly indicates that emissions closely track GDP ranking and that the top 10 countries by GDP produce the majority of emissions. China accounts for about 30%, USA 15% and the EU collectively 10%. Note, figures can vary using per capita measures and consumption measures rather than production measures, but the *general* relation between GDP and emissions remains similar and the fact a *few* countries are responsible for the majority of emission remains the same. As Goodman and Anderson (2020) note, 65% of global emissions 1751–2010 were produced by 90 entities (of which two thirds were corporations), and 71% of emissions 1988–2015 were produced by 100 corporate and state entities See Heede (2014) and Griffin (2017). For a useful graphical summary of emissions contributions see https://www.vox.com/energy-and-environment/21428525/climate-change-west-coast-fires-cause-charts.
5. She begins from 304 ppm in 1921; preindustrial levels for the Holocene typically report 180 to 280 ppm Hansen et al. (2017), argue that Paris notwithstanding it makes more sense to target a return to less than 350 ppm. Note also that (1) a ton of carbon equates to about 3.7 tons of carbon dioxide in the atmosphere (2) ppm measures can vary globally and *model* estimates for ppm associated warming effects have also varied and are subject to readjustment as observations change. For example, 450 ppm has previously been used as a trigger for 2 degrees warming (which seems to be an underestimation). This, however is an issue of general evidence trends under rational uncertainty rather than spurious precision.
6. Note, Wunderling et al., 2020 had not yet completed review at the time of writing.
7. For example, Stay Grounded campaigns for a just transition reduction in aviation as a necessary aspect of real decarbonization to mid-century (e.g. Smith, 2019).
8. The point, of course, does not condone the personal dynamics of conduct and intra-organizational struggles involving matters of identity, recognition respect etc. It merely highlights the use made of division to undermine a movement.

9. There are many other subjects one might focus on, such as the work of Bjorn Lomborg.
10. The concept of an externality is, of course, much older. We are highlighting the prominence given to some standard lines of argument and suggesting readers should find this familiar and that each is a source of complacency and delay.
11. Principle 15 of the 1992 Rio Declaration states: 'In order to protect the environment, the precautionary principle shall be widely applied by the States [UN members] according to their capabilities. Where there are threats of serious or irreversible damage, lack of full scientific certainty shall not be used as a reason for postponing cost-effective measures to prevent environmental degradation.' The cost effec- tive' clause is, however, obviously open to problematic abuse.
12. For a critique of mainstream economic thought as a belief system, see George and Sabelli (1994).
13. To be clear, not all ecological economists are anti-capitalist, nor do they reject the idea of price signals. The shared commitment is that adequate theorization of a sustainable economic system must start from material processes and their consequences, rather than simply assume these are taken care of by exchange values. Most ecological economists also place strong emphasis on distribution, justice, fair- ness and alternatives to commodified and consumerist versions of identity.
14. Integrated assessment models, such as the Dynamic Integrated Climate-Economy (DICE) model, are *very* different, but when explained to a layperson they can seem to be covering the same ground as eco- logical economics in so far as they pay lip service to climate systems. See later and also Keen (2020).
15. Though it is worth noting that even mainstream economists when surveyed think low discount rates are more appropriate – at around 2% – and, of course, the whole endeavour ignores proper context of impacts etc. (Drupp et al., 2020).
16. There are, for example, issues regarding transport transition and electric cars (Morgan, 2020) and con- tradictory assumptions about future policy and matters of income and wealth inequality (Morgan, 2017).

Acknowledgements

The authors would like to confirm that they are joint and equal co-authors of this article.

Disclosure statement

No potential conflict of interest was reported by the author(s).

References

Amen, M., Bosman, M. M., & Gills, B. K. (2008). Editorial: The urgent need for global action to combat cli- mate change. *Globalizations*, 5(1), 49–52. https://doi.org/10.1080/14747730701850886
Anderson, K., Broderick, J., & Stoddard, I. (2020). A factor of two: How the mitigation plans of 'climate pro- gressive' nations fall far short of Paris-compliant pathways. *Climate Policy*, https://doi.org/10.1080/14693062.2020.1728209
Bacevic, J. (2020). Unthinking knowledge production: From post-Covid to post-carbon futures. *Globalizations*, 18(7), 1206–1218. https://doi.org/10.1080/14747731.2020.1807855

Büchs, M., & Koch, M. (2017). *Postgrowth and wellbeing. Challenges to sustainable welfare.* Palgrave Macmillan.

Christensen, J., & Olhoff, A. (2019). *Lessons from a decade of emissions gap assessments.* UNEP.

Dale, G. (2012). The growth paradigm: A critique. *International Socialism, 134,* 55–88. https://isj.org.uk/the-growth-paradigm-a-critique/

Dale, G. (2018, October 12). The Nobel Prize in climate chaos. *The Ecologist.* https://theecologist.org/2018/oct/12/nobel-prize-climate-chaos-romer-nordhaus-and-ipcc

Dale, G. (2020). Rule of nature or rule of capital? Physiocracy, ecological economics, and ideology. *Globalizations, 18*(7), 1230–1247. https://doi.org/10.1080/14747731.2020.1807838

Daly, H. (1974). The economics of the steady-state. *American Economic Review, 64*(2), 15–20. https://www.jstor.org/stable/1816010

Daly, H. (1997). Forum, Georgescu-Roegen vs. Solow/Stiglitz. *Ecological Economics, 22*(3), 261–266. https://doi.org/10.1016/S0921-8009(97)00080-3

Daly, H. (2015). *Essays against growthism.* WEA/College Books.

Daly, H., & Morgan, J. (2019). The importance of ecological economics: An interview with Herman Daly. *Real-World Economics Review, 90,* 137–154.

Drupp, M., Freeman, M., Groom, B., & Nesje, F. (2020). Discounting disentangled. *American Economic Journal: Economic Policy, 10*(4), 109–134. https://doi.org/10.1257/pol.20160240

Fletcher, R., Breitling, J., & Puleo, V. (2014). Barbarian hordes: The overpopulation scapegoat in international development discourse. *Third World Quarterly, 35*(7), 1195–1215. https://doi.org/10.1080/01436597.2014.926110

Fletcher, R., & Rammelt, C. (2017). Decoupling: A key fantasy of the post-2015 sustainable development Agenda. *Globalizations, 14*(3), 450–467. https://doi.org/10.1080/14747731.2016.1263077

Fox, N. J., & Alldred, P. (2020). Economics, the climate change policy-assemblage and the new materialisms: towards a comprehensive policy. *Globalizations, 18*(7), 1248–1258. https://doi.org/10.1080/14747731.2020.1807857

Fullbrook, E., & Morgan, J. (Eds.). (2019). *Economics and the ecosystem.* World Economic Association Books.

Galbraith, J. K. (2020). Economics and the climate catastrophe. *Globalizations, 18*(7), 1117–1122. https://doi.org/10.1080/14747731.2020.1807858

George, S., & Sabelli, A. (1994). *Faith and credit.* Penguin.

Gills, B. K. (2008). Climate change: A global call to action. *Globalizations, 5*(1), 83–87. https://doi.org/10.1080/14747730701587371

Gills, B. K. (2020). Deep restoration: From the great implosion to the great awakening. *Globalizations, 17*(4), 577–579. https://doi.org/10.1080/14747731.2020.1748364

Gills, B. K., & Morgan, J. (2020a). Global climate emergency: After COP24, climate science, urgency, and the threat to humanity. *Globalizations, 17*(6), 885–902. https://doi.org/10.1080/14747731.2019.1669915

Gills, B. K., & Morgan, J. (2020b). Teaching climate complacency: Mainstream economics textbooks and the need for transformation in economics education. *Globalizations, 18*(7), 1189–1205. https://doi.org/10.1080/14747731.2020.1808413

Goodman, J., & Anderson, J. (2020). From climate change to economic change? Reflections on 'feedback'. *Globalizations, 18*(7), 1259–1270. https://doi.org/10.1080/14747731.2020.1810499

Gore, T. (2020, September 21). Confronting carbon inequality. *Oxfam.*

Griffin, M. (2017). *Carbon Majors report.* CDP and Climate Accountability Institute.

Hansen, J., Sato, M., Kharecha, P., von Schuckmann, K., Beerling, D. J., Cao, J., Marcott, S., Masson-Delmotte, V., Prather, M. J., Rohling, E. J., Shakun, J., Smith, P., Lacis, A., Russell, G., & Ruedy, R. (2017). Young people's burden: Requirement of negative CO_2 emissions. *Earth System Dynamics, 8*(3), 577–616. https://doi.org/10.5194/esd-8-577-2017

Heede, R. (2014). Tracing anthropogenic carbon dioxide and methane emissions to fossil fuel and cement producers, 1854–2010. *Climatic Change, 122*(1–2), 229–241. https://doi.org/10.1007/s10584-013-0986-y

Hickel, J. (2018, December 6). The Nobel prize for climate catastrophe. *Foreign Policy.*

Hickel, J. (2020a). What does degrowth mean? A few points of clarification. *Globalizations, 18*(7), 1105–1111. https://doi.org/10.1080/14747731.2020.1812222

Hickel, J. (2020b). *Less is more: How degrowth will save the world.* Penguin Random House.

Hickel, J., & Kallis, G. (2019). Is green growth possible? *New Political Economy, 25*(4), 469–486. https://doi.org/10.1080/13563467.2019.1598964

IPBES. (2019, May). *Summary for policy makers of the global assessment report on biodiversity and ecosystem services of the intergovernmental science-policy platform on biodiversity and ecosystem services.*

IPCC. (2018, October). *Global warming of 1.5°C: Summary for policymakers.*

IPCC. (2019, August). *IPCC special report on climate change, desertification, land degradation sustainable land management food security and greenhouse gas fluxes in terrestrial ecosystems.*

Kallis, G., Paulson, S., D'Alisa, G., & Demaria, F. (2020). *The case for degrowth.* Polity Press.

Keen, S. (2020). The appallingly bad neoclassical economics of climate change. *Globalizations, 18*(7), 1149–1177. https://doi.org/10.1080/14747731.2020.1807856

Koch, M., & Buch-Hansen, H. (2020). In search of a political economy of the postgrowth era. *Globalizations, 18*(7), 1219–1229. https://doi.org/10.1080/14747731.2020.1807837

Lamb, W., Mattioli, G., Levi, S., Roberts, J., Capstick, S., Creutzig, F., Minx, J., Muller-Hansen, F., Culhane, T., & Steinberger, J. (2020). Discourses of climate delay. *Global Sustainability, 3*(e17), 1–5. https://doi.org/10.1017/sus.2020.13

Lenton, T., Rockstrom, J., Gaffney, O., Rahmstorf, S., Richardson, K., Steffen, W., & Schellnuber, H. (2020, November 28). Climate tipping points too risky to bet against. *Nature, 575*(7784), 592–595. https://doi.org/10.1038/d41586-019-03595-0

Liegey, V., & Nelson, A. (2020). *Exploring degrowth: A critical guide.* Pluto Press.

Meadows, D., Meadows, D., Randers, J., & Behrens, W. (1972). *The limits to growth.* American Library [Club of Rome].

Mearman, A., Berger, S., & Guizzo, D. (2018a). Whither political economy? Evaluating the CORE project as a response to calls for change in economics teaching. *Review of Political Economy, 30*(2), 241–259. https://doi.org/10.1080/09538259.2018.1426682

Mearman, A., Berger, S., & Guizzo, D. (2018b). Is UK economics teaching changing? Evaluating the new subject benchmark statement. *Review of Social Economy, 76*(3), 377–396. https://doi.org/10.1080/00346764.2018.1463447

Moore, J. (2015). *Capitalism in the web of life.* Verso.

Morgan, J. (2015). Is economics responding to critique? What do the UK QAA 2015 subject benchmarks for economics indicate? *Review of Political Economy, 27*(4), 518–538. https://doi.org/10.1080/09538259.2015.1084774

Morgan, J. (2016). Paris COP21: Power that speaks the truth? *Globalizations, 13*(6), 943–951. https://doi.org/10.1080/14747731.2016.1163863

Morgan, J. (2017). Piketty and the growth dilemma revisited in the context of ecological economics. *Ecological Economics, 136*, 169–177. https://doi.org/10.1016/j.ecolecon.2017.02.024

Morgan, J. (2020). Electric vehicles: The future we made and the problem of unmaking it. *Cambridge Journal of Economics, 44*(4), 953–977. https://doi.org/10.1093/cje/beaa022

Newell, P., & Simms, A. (2020). How did we do that? Histories and political economies of rapid and just transitions. *New Political Economy,* https://doi.org/10.1080/13563467.2020.1810216

Newell, P., & Taylor, O. (2020). Fiddling while the planet burns? COP 25 in perspective. *Globalizations, 17*(4), 580–592. https://doi.org/10.1080/14747731.2020.1726127

Nordhaus, W. (1974). Resources as a constraint on growth. *American Economic Review, 64*(2), 22–26. https://www.jstor.org/stable/1816011

O'Neill, J. (2007). *Markets, deliberation and environment.* Routledge.

Oosthoek, J., & Gills, B. K. (2005). Humanity at the crossroads: The globalization of environmental crisis. *Globalizations, 2*(3), 283–291. https://doi.org/10.1080/14747730500409454

Parrique, T., Barth, J., Briens, F., Kerschner, C., Kraus-Polk, A., Kuokkanen, A., & Spangenberg, J. H. (2019, July). *Report: Decoupling debunked: Evidence and arguments against green growth as a sole strategy for sustainability.* European Environmental Bureau. https://mk0eeborgicuypctuf7e.kinstacdn.com/wp-content/uploads/2019/07/Decoupling-Debunked.pdf.

Ripple, W., Wolf, C., Newsome, T., Barnbard, P., Moomaw, W., & 11,258 signatories (2020). World scientists' warning of a climate emergency. *BioScience, 70*(1), 8-12. https://doi.org/10.1093/biosci/biz152

Røpke, I. (2020). Econ 101—In need of a sustainability transition. *Ecological Economics, 169*, article 106515. https://doi.org/10.1016/j.ecolecon.2019.106515

Samerski, S. (2018). Tools for degrowth? Ivan Illich's critique of technology revisited. *Journal of Cleaner Production, 197*(Part 2), 1637–1646. https://doi.org/10.1016/j.jclepro.2016.10.039

Schröder, E., & Storm, S. (2020). Economic growth and carbon emissions: The road to 'hothouse earth' is paved with good intentions. *International Journal of Political Economy*, 49(2), 153–173. https://doi.org/10.1080/08911916.2020.1778866

Schumacher, E. (1993). *Small is beautiful: A study of economics as if people mattered*. Vintage. (Original work published 1973)

Smith, T. (Ed. for the collective). (2019). *Degrowth of aviation: Reducing air travel in a just way*. Stay Grounded. https://stay-grounded.org/new-study-measures-to-reduce-air-travel-in-a-just-way/

Solow, R. (1974). The economics of resources or the resources of economics. *American Economic Review*, 64 (2), 1–14. https://www.jstor.org/stable/1816009

Söderbaum, P. (2018). *Economics, ideological orientation and democracy for sustainable development*. WEA Books.

Spash, C. (2016). This changes nothing: The Paris Agreement to ignore reality. *Globalizations*, 13(6), 928–933. https://doi.org/10.1080/14747731.2016.1161119

Spash, C. (Ed.). (2017). *Routledge handbook of ecological economics: Nature and society*. Routledge.

Spash, C. (2020a). The economy as if people mattered: Revisiting critiques of economic growth in a time of crisis. *Globalizations*, 18(7), 1087–1104. https://doi.org/10.1080/14747731.2020.1761612

Spash, C. (2020b). A tale of three paradigms: Realising the revolutionary potential of ecological economics. *Ecological Economics*, 169, article 106518. https://doi.org/10.1016/j.ecolecon.2019.106518

Spash, C. (2020c). Apologists for growth: Passive revolutionaries in a passive revolution. *Globalizations*, 18(7), 1123–1148. https://doi.org/10.1080/14747731.2020.1824864

Steffen, W., Richardson, K., Rockstrom, J., Cornell, S. E., Fetzer, I., Bennett, E., Biggs, R., Carpenter, S., de Vries, W., de Wit, C., Folke, C., Gerten, D., Heinke, J., Mace, G. M., Persson, L. M., Ramanathan, V., Reyers, B., & Sorlin, S. (2015). Planetary boundaries: Guiding human development on a changing planet. *Science*, 347(6223), 736–746. https://doi.org/10.1126/science.1259855

Steffen, W., Rockström, J., Richardson, K., Lenton, T. M., Folke, C., Liverman, D., Summerhayes, C. P., Barnosky, A. D., Cornell, S. E., Crucifix, M., Donges, J. F., Fetzer, I., Lade, S. J., Scheffer, M., Winkelmann, R., & Schellnhuber, H. J. (2018). Trajectories of the earth system in the Anthropocene. *Proceedings of the National Academy of Sciences of the USA*, 115(33), 8252–8259. https://doi.org/10.1073/pnas.1810141115

Steinberger, J. (2020, July 10). Cogs in the climate machine: A short course in planetary time, for planetary survival. *Climate Conscious*, Blogged, https://medium.com/climate-conscious/cogs-in-the-climate-machine-167cf16750dd

Stern, N. (2013). The structure of economic modelling of the potential impacts of climate change: Grafting gross under-estimation of risk onto already narrow science models. *Journal of Economic Literature*, 51 (3), 838–859. https://doi.org/10.1257/jel.51.3.838

Stevenson, H. (2020). Reforming global climate governance in an age of bullshit. *Globalizations*, 18(1), 86–102. https://doi.org/10.1080/14747731.2020.1774315

UNEP. (2018, November). *Emissions gap report 2018* (9th ed.).

UNEP. (2019, November). *Emissions gap report 2019* (10th ed.).

Vega, E., Chalk, T., Wilson, P., Bysani, R., & Foster, G. (2020). Atmospheric CO_2 during the mid-piacenzian warm period and the M2 glaciation. *Nature*, 10(11002), https://doi.org/10.1038/s41598-020-67154-8

Wiedmann, T., Schandl, H., Lenzen, M., Moran, D., Suh, D., West, J., & Kanemoto, K. (2015). The material footprint of nations. *Proceedings of the National Academy of Sciences*, 112(20), 6271–6276. https://doi.org/10.1073/pnas.1220362110

Wunderling, N., Donges, J., Kurths, J., & Winkelmann, R. (2020). Interacting tipping elements increase risk of climate domino effects under global warming. *Earth System Dynamics*, https://doi.org/10.5194/esd-2020-18

'The economy' as if people mattered: revisiting critiques of economic growth in a time of crisis

Clive L. Spash

ABSTRACT

Coronavirus (COVID-19) policy shut down the world economy with a range of government actions unprecedented outside of wartime. In this paper, economic systems dominated by a capital accumulating growth imperative are shown to have had their structural weaknesses exposed, revealing numerous problems including unstable supply chains, unjust social provisioning of essentials, profiteering, precarious employment, inequities and pollution. Such phenomena must be understood in the context of long standing critiques relating to the limits of economic systems, their consumerist values and divorce from biophysical reality. Critical reflection on the Coronavirus pandemic is combined with a review of how economists have defended economic growth as sustainable, Green and inclusive regardless of systemic limits and multiple crises – climate emergency, economic crash and pandemic. Instead of rebuilding the old flawed political economy again, what the world needs now is a more robust, just, ethical and equitable social-ecological economy.

1. Introduction

Prioritising financial interests and economic growth over human life is nothing new, and has long been evident in the polluted state of the environment with its related morbidity and mortality. There are good longstanding social and ecological reasons why an economic crisis should be taken as an opportunity for redirecting the means of basic social provisioning away from stock markets, financiers, bankers, corporate interests and profiteering, while reconsidering what is provide, to whom and for what. However, there are also powerful lobbies, organisations and institutions forming the social structures and mechanisms that operate to prevent any substantive change and cover-up the social and ecological failures.

Gills and Morgan (2019) have explained why the Global Climate Emergency demands a profound historical transformation of our civilisation but also how this has been prevented and what could be done about this. As they note (Gills & Morgan, 2019, p. 13),

> it is manifestly the case that the main impediment to change is our system of capital accumulation with its commitment to material growth of economies. This, as the evidence so obviously shows, creates both an escalating problem to solve and a whole set of interests continuously working to slow down solutions.

Gills (2020) points out that humanity now faces a 'triple conjuncture' of global crises: climate change and ecological breakdown; a systemic crisis of global capitalism and neoliberal economic globalisation; and the current global Coronavirus pandemic.

The Coronavirus pandemic of 2020 provides a dramatic example of how modern economic systems are precariously structured to achieve financial returns. They are not robust in the face of sudden changes in demand, whether increases (e.g. panic buying) or decreases (e.g. not flying), or interruptions to supply. Financially motivated moves to change supply have involved avoiding physical stocks, increasing global outsourcing of production and elongating supply chains. The result has been international dependencies making the system more susceptibility to collapse. More than this, the primary capital accumulating motive, encapsulated in the economic growth imperative, means an inability of the system to pause even for a week, let alone a month or two, without economic and social crisis.

Success under capitalism is measured by accumulating money to reinvest to accumulate more money, with a precarious link to the qualitative state of the real material economy and production. That such a growth economy is divorced from the material reality upon which it depends, an unsustainable utopia and devastatingly harmful socially and environmentally, has long been noted by ecological economists (Daly, 1973; Georgescu-Roegen, 1971). Capitalism uses money to trade things (e.g. goods, services, commodities, property rights) to generate money flows through exchange. When exchange breaks down the money stops flowing: people are laid-off, interest on debts are not paid, investments fail, firms go bankrupt, banks go under, savings are lost, runs on banks start. Economic growth is all about keeping the exchange cycle of money growing as fast as possible and accumulating capital to increase the capacity to do so. The biggest worry for politicians in the global North is then to maintain such a financially oriented growth system when its basic means of operation fail, and to this end protecting 'the economy' has become a priority above all else.

In Austria the ski areas of the Tyrol had been identified by other nations (e.g. Iceland) as centres responsible for spreading the virus via international tourism, but information was supressed because tourism was booming (up 11% on the previous year) and business leaders closely allied to the ruling conservative party were against restrictions (Traill & Schocher, 2020). The UK government, concerned about its expanding airline and tourist business, was advising that trips to Italy were generally safe after the Italian lockdown started, and similarly for Spain, and on the 12th March stated 'It's not the current position of the UK, based on medical and scientific advice, that we should halt flights' (Stewart et al., 2020). Four days later they started doing exactly that. As the virus spread and death toll rose governments were forced to take action. However, many governments when initiating action were reluctant, slow and ill-prepared (e.g. UK, France, USA) or refused to implement any strong compulsory restrictions (e.g. Brazil, Sweden, the Netherlands), which later appeared to contribute to their relatively high per capita death rates.[1]

From the start of the Coronavirus outbreak in Europe and America politicians were balancing the impacts on 'the economy' of taking action against mortality and morbidity.[2] Official announcements emphasised only that ill and old people were dying, as if this were not really something about which most people should be worried. In a capital accumulating society, where production and productivity are at least rhetorically at the fore, losing the old and sick means 'the economy' might actually be healthier afterwards, because a group of unproductive financial dependents is removed.

Protecting economic interests was deemed consistent with advocating 'herd immunity' with its associated acceptance of high deaths rates. The idea of 'herd immunity' is to allow a virus infection to spread throughout an animal population with members either obtaining natural immunity or dying. Until mid-March 2020 this approach was official UK policy supported by the Prime Minster

Boris Johnston (Stewart et al., 2020). The policy was defended by the UK's chief medical officer, Chris Whitty (Stewart et al., 2020), and chief scientist, Patrick Vallance (Stewart & Busby, 2020). Whitty explained that it would require 80% of the population to become infected (if or how the remaining 20% would remain uninfected was unclear), and the death rate would be 1%, i.e. similar to normal seasonal flu. This meant accepting over 540,000 deaths in Britain. However, the chiefs had ignored the World Health Organisation (WHO) estimate of a 2% death rate in January as well as the update on the 3rd March when the WHO Director-General stated that: 'Globally, about 3.4% of reported COVID-19 cases have died'.[3] This would involve a worst case scenario of over 1.8 million deaths, and if the virus eventually spread to the whole UK population then 2.3 million.

The policy was dropped by the UK when it moved to lockdown but maintained in the Netherlands where social distancing formed the main policy response. Similarly, long after general government U-turns, the Swedish were also avoiding strict isolation measures. Both governments ignored the resulting relatively high per capita death rates (see footnote 1). Andreas Hatzigeorgiou, CEO at the Stockholm Chamber of Commerce stated that:

> We have to combine looking at minimising the health effects of the virus outbreak and the economic impacts of this health crisis […] The business community here really thinks that the Swedish government and the Swedish approach is more sensible than in many other countries. (Savage, 2020)

Meanwhile, an article in the *Wall Street Journal* entitled 'Coronavirus vindicates capitalism' tried to claim that the high Italian death rate was due to their government's health system and the America corporate capitalist model would respond far better (Strassel, 2020). Shortly after the USA accelerated into global pole position for both infections and deaths. Even as the general inadequacy of initial government policy led to global lockdown the primary aim was already to reassure stock markets, get 'the economy' back to normal and re-establish 'growth'. Supposedly non-interventionist, 'free-market', pro-corporate, anti-government business executives, billionaires and politicians united in supporting public policy packages offering trillions to save 'the economy'.

Again there is nothing new here. Generally capitalism has adapted to use all crises to increase returns to the richest and those in power (Klein, 2007). The neoliberal thought collective successfully used the 2008 financial crisis to their own advantage (Mirowski, 2013) and this saw billions in bailouts go to those who created the crisis while those at the bottom got less. A neoliberal capitalist system structured around corporate profits has meant cost cutting and austerity politics in the global North, notably impacting public service provision (e.g. health care), reducing protection of the poorest and increasing inequalities.

The richest nations and the most powerful corporations keep others subordinated to their interests – employing structural adjustment, military intervention, sanctions and support for authoritarian regimes. Social exploitation appears in precarious employment, unsafe working conditions and environmental degradation impacting health. The systematic exploitation of resources and peoples of the global South leaves them unable to react to crises such as a pandemic. In much of the Middle East, Africa, Latin America and Asia the prevalence of informal work and unpredictable daily wages mean self-isolation is impossible, because it would mean starvation (Hanieh, 2020). The extent to which the global North can avoid the same threat to those at the bottom is also limited, e.g. an estimate 1.5 million people were soon short of food in the UK (Lawrence, 2020b). The uneven ability of nations and peoples' within nations to respond to crises is a reflection of the structure of the globalised political economy.

In this paper I start by drawing-out some of the more general lessons that can be learnt from the Coronavirus crisis about the structure of the dominant economic system. I then relate this to how economists have promoted the idea of soft reformulation of capitalist economies in the face of crises and specifically the environmental crisis. The correlation between economic growth and environmental degradation is an empirically straight forward fact, as shown by pollution reduction due to the Coronavirus policies stopping economic activity. However, most economists have, since the 1970s, persistently denied the associated limits to economic growth. They recommend 'Greening' economies, using price incentives (i.e. internalising externalities), in order to maintain growth in the face of environmental degradation and ecosystem decline and loss. I review economists' defensive arguments and raise two specific problems with their account: how prices and value operate in actual capitalist economies, and the biophysical basis of any economy. The paper concludes by returning to the policy reaction to the Coronavirus pandemic and why attempts to re-establish economic growth, driven by self-serving vested interests, will fail to prepare humanity for future crises and indeed will help create them and make them worse.

2. Lessons from the Coronavirus crisis

When nation States ordered their populations to 'stay home', normal economic activity was frozen. In several countries hoarding occurred as people prioritised what they regarded as basic necessities (e.g. toilet roll, sanitary towels, pasta and rice). Profiteers sought to make money by trading on other peoples misfortunes, e.g. brokers speculating on the rising price of orange juice as Spain suffered high death rates and lockdown (Harper, 2020), airlines hiking prices on rebooking cancellations (Brignall, 2020), middlemen auctioning medical ventilators to the highest bidding public authorities (Greve & McCarthy, 2020). Meanwhile, nationalism and competitive self-interest appeared in the international fight with the USA over deliveries of face masks (DW Akademie, 2020b), and President Trump's offer of a billion dollars to biopharmaceutical company CureVac, based in Tübingen Germany, to secure its (under development) virus vaccine exclusively for the USA (The Guardian, 2020). While the latter was blocked by the German government, therein lies the true potential of the system of private property rights over public interest. In a competitive market economy obtaining property rights over resources for exclusive use ensures a competitive advantage. Germany disliked what has been common practice of corporations and the global North in the global South to secure supply lines under capitalism. Yet the globalised economy remains precariously supplied.

Critical supply disruption can arise for numerous reasons including war, sanctions, profiteering, natural disasters and human perturbation of ecological systems (e.g. human induced climate change). The Coronavirus epidemic exposed the structure of global supply chains and their fragility. Outsourcing to save costs and 'make money' has meant moving production to countries with low environmental and labour standards, poor welfare systems and public health care, making workers vulnerable. Increased international dependency has been built around fossil-fuel intensive transportation. Cost minimisation has removed the holding of large stocks as a buffer. Over the last forty years supermarkets in the global North moved to 'just in time' supply chains dependent upon regular delivery services for restocking. Simultaneously, consumer choice was expanded along with 'lifestyle' marketing to create brand loyalty and product differentiation to segment markets and enable price discrimination. For example, in the UK supermarkets have been offering more than 40,000 lines from around the world, including a permanent summertime of fresh fruits and vegetables (Lawrence, 2020a). This market system is designed for profiteering.

Under responses to the Coronavirus the excess provision of differentiated products for profiteering became recognised as a burden, not a benefit, and something that had to be addressed as an inefficient resource waste reducing ability to supply. Thus, excess demand stimulated by panic buying in the UK led supermarkets to stop supplying so many products to meet the same basic need (e.g. 60 types of sausages), and within a week of government restrictions they were cutting product lines, e.g. bakery lines from 17 to 7 and 20 types of pasta to 6 (Jack, 2020). Packaging needed to be streamlined not differentiated. Government policy had unintentionally stimulated a reappraisal of how public needs are supplied and exposed an important distinction. Social provisioning for the needs of all is not the same as corporate supply for profit maximisation – expansion of 'choice' in the market place, tailoring products to meet individual consumer preferences, highly specialised inflexible production lines and product packaging.

The maintenance of what is deemed 'essential' also became an explicit priority. The Coronavirus pandemic saw both supply chain failure and retail outlets being deliberately shut down to avoid people congregating and accelerating infection rates. This meant defining what is allowed to be supplied and what is not. For example, the UK government listed 'essential retailers' as including: supermarkets and other food shops, pharmacies, shops selling alcohol including those within breweries, petrol stations, newsagents, bicycle shops, home and hardware stores, launderettes and dry cleaners, garages, pet shops, post offices and banks. At the same time the UK's supermarkets were left to self-regulate how they would meet the essential needs of the public, as if the government should not intervene in the 'free market'. Cultural differences affect what is deemed necessary as a means to satisfy a need, but even more fundamentally the question arose as to what should be deemed essential? The British disputed whether chocolate Easter eggs should be sold (BBC News, 2020d), while Americans demanded gun shops be reopened after initial closure (Levin, 2020) and Florida deemed televised wrestling entertainment an essential service (BBC News, 2020e). Fundamental questions are evident here concerning how an economic system is structured to meet essential needs.

What should be supplied under what conditions and who should decide and on what basis? Why do some products appear and others get removed from the market place? The role of power and the influence of different actors (e.g. government, corporations, unions, civil society) is revealed through preferential treatment. Self regulation by corporations is the preferred neoliberal way and allows governments to shift responsibility, but policy response to address the Coronavirus stood in stark contrast to this. Ambivalence over the role of government could be seen in vacillation as to when to regulate, let alone what to regulate and how.

The potential for profiteering from supplying the 'non-essential' was quickly recognised by corporate online delivery services that went unregulated. Amazon provides an example of how such capitalist enterprises operate. They increased staff working hours and hired tens of thousands on temporary contracts and minimum wages, while providing no or inadequate virus protection and so partially countering the very reason their high-street competitors had been closed. When a New York worker led a strike, that demanded anti-Coronavirus measures and protective gear, he was fired (Evelyn, 2020). Meanwhile Amazon CEO, Jeff Bezos, the richest man in the world, asked for donations to his new Amazon Relief Fund promoted as necessary to aid his workers (Zoellner, 2020). Amazon pays a minimum wage of $15/hour, while Bezos earns $8,961,187/hour (Hoffower, 2019). The company pays no tax in the USA but is worth a trillion dollars (Zoellner, 2020). Protests by workers in France and small business concerns over unfair competition under Coronavirus regulations led Amazon to claim it would temporarily (for about two weeks) deliver only 'essentials', which it self-defined as those things in the highest demand (BBC News, 2020a; Guichard & Pailliez, 2020; Pailliez & Guichard, 2020). In April 2020 a French court in Nanterre ordered Amazon to limit its deliveries in France to essential goods only, amid claims of failing to protect its workers from Coronavirus, or suffer a penalty of one million euros per day (BBC News, 2020b). Shortly after Amazon shut down its six warehouses in France.

The allocation of essentials in price-making market economies works on the same basis as non-essentials. That is, self-interest and ability-to-pay determine who gets what, which means nations become unilateral and when panic buying hits there are empty supermarket shelves and some people go without. As work on famines shows (Sen, 1986), market capitalism diverts essentials away from those in most need to those with most money. There is a fundamental requirement for ethically guided government regulation in any market system, because there is no inherent capacity for social benefit or good in such a system. The inequity and inefficiency in meeting the needs of all are normally of no concern because the vast majority (at least in the global North) do not suffer enough to create political change.

As long as those at the bottom are a distant minority, and not simultaneously dying in embarrassingly large numbers, they can seemingly be ignored. However, in a major crisis the inequities become a matter of life and death even in the richest democratic nations. The homeless, who have been growing in numbers on the streets of the growth economies (700,000 in Europe and UK), appear as a group susceptibility to starvation (Boffey, 2020). The standard inadequacy of government policy is exposed leading to demands by concerned groups for emergency action to prioritise shelter and care (The Guardian, 2020). The Coronavirus outbreak revealed the speed with which a substantive policy change could be implemented given the political will to do so. Why is such funding, care and concern left to charities or absent in times of economic prosperity? Where are the claims of national unity and social inclusiveness then?

Prior to the Cornavirus pandemic, economies were regarded as booming with high growth rates while elected officials were pursuing austerity policies that cut down on public services and governments were busy removing support for those at the bottom. The gap was widening between the 'haves' and the 'have nots'. For those to whom it was previously of little concern, the crisis suddenly threw into stark relief the positon of being one of those without a job, ill, weak, old or homeless. Many realised their own precarious position in the system. Middle class, self-employed, small businesses owners became dependent on government handouts or faced bankruptcy with the prospect of joining the unemployed. There is nothing desirable about joining the groups marginalised by the productivist ideology of a competitive growth economy, where a good person is a good consumer with a salaried job.

The predicament of those at the bottom within the economies of the 'developed', industrialised, global North may be bad but it is much worse for those in the global South. Yet, economic growth has been promoted since the late 1940s as the only means for addressing poverty and sustaining 'development' (Sachs, 1999/2015). This persistent growth = development ideology has operated in denial of both social and ecological impacts. The pretence is that economic growth is, or could be, socially inclusive, environmentally benign and sustainable.

3. The lie of sustainable inclusive growth and a green economy

Within two weeks of lockdowns the lobbying was underway for more de-regulation and securing government as the ally of finance, business and corporate interests to fund bailouts and restart economic growth. In response to the economic impacts of Coronavirus policy, Mohamed El-Erian, chief economic adviser at Allianz (the world's largest financial services and insurance corporation) and former deputy director at the International Monetary Fund (IMF), recommended 'putting in place better foundations for structurally sound, sustainable and inclusive growth', because 'advanced economies are saddled with structural and institutional impediments that have stifled growth' (El-Erian, 2020). The rhetoric involves promoting the growth economy as the only option and as being totally compatible with delivering improvements in environmental quality and social equity with government intervention and regulations as impediments. The recommended policy response is the same as after the 2008 financial collapse. The positon was made quite explicit by World Bank President David Malpass at the (virtual) G20 meeting of Finance Ministers, 23rd March 2020:

> Countries will need to implement structural reforms to help shorten the time to recovery and create confidence that the recovery can be strong. For those countries that have excessive regulations, subsidies, licensing regimes, trade protection or litigiousness as obstacles, we will work with them to foster markets, choice and faster growth prospects during the recovery. (Malpass, 2020)

As with previous crises, Coronavirus quickly revealed that capitalist economies without growth are economies in total crisis, and that corporations are ultimately totally dependent on public funds and government intervention. After each crisis the public pays to protect billionaires and reformulate a new version of the same socially inequitable and environmentally destructive growth economy.

The claim that capitalist economies can be redesigned into some sort of inclusive and sustainable form has not been limited to corporations and financial vested interests. Some prominent authors, regarded as offering insights into future alternative economies to address the environmental crisis, have treated economic growth as if it were an optional extra for modem economies and capitalism in particular. The likes of Raworth (2017/2018), who defines herself as a 'radical economist', and van den Bergh (2011), an environmental economist, have advocated agnosticism about economic growth, while Jackson (2009, pp. 197–202), an ecological economist and post-growth advocate, regards economic growth as necessary for 'development' and dismisses any serious discussion of capitalism let alone taking issue with its structure (see Spash, 2020). That there is no capitalism without economic growth, and so no such thing as a Green capitalist economy, should by now be obvious. The only time greenhouse gases have fallen in the modern industrial period has been due to economic collapse typically during a recession/depression or due to total devastation by warfare.

The Coronavirus economic shutdown provided clear empirical evidence of the substantive impacts of economic activity on the environment (Edwards, 2020; Hauser & Jackson, 2020). The drop in material and energy throughput led to immediate reductions in noise pollution, improved water and air quality leading to better living conditions for humans and non-humans. The conflict between economic growth and the environment was made self-evident and visible. Fish returned to the canals of Venice, skies cleared over the industrial centres of China and smog disappeared from the world's capital cities. Environmentally destructive sectors, normally promoted as progressive leaders in the expansion of the growth economy, suddenly ceased operation, e.g. airlines. Up to 70,000 lives were estimated to have been saved (temporarily at least) by two months of clean air in China (McMahon, 2020), but somehow pollution, health impacts and lives lost to the growth economy just do not seem to count for much. For thirty years or more the oxymoron of sustainable inclusive growth has been advocated under a variety of titles from sustainable development (World Commission on Environment and Development, 1987) to the Green economy (UNEP, 2011) to the sustainable development goals (United Nations General Assembly, 2015).

4. Revisiting the defence of economic growth against limits

Since the rise of the environmental movement in the 1960s, the economic growth paradigm has been subject to social and ecological criticism, which bore fruit in numerous books in the 1970s (Daly,

1973; Easterlin, 1974; Hirsch, 1977; Meadows et al., 1972; Mishan, 1969; Schumacher, 1973; Scitovsky, 1976). A focal point for debate was the *Limits to Growth* (LTG) with its multiple scenario analysis (Meadows et al., 1972). The LTG modelled five factors: population growth, accelerating industrialisation, adequacy of agricultural production, depletion of natural resources and pollution. An economic system based on growth was revealed to be susceptible to collapse due to multiple potential interactions, making policy responses aimed at singular causes ineffective. The systemic problems indicated the need for changing the system.

However, most economists continued to unquestioningly promote capitalism due to their dogmatic and paradigmatic commitment to the growth imperative and price-making markets (Spash, 2020). This form of market has prices resulting from 'negotiations' between actors (e.g. firms-consumers; employer-employee) in contrast to being set by an administrative, or other, authority (Polanyi et al., 1957). Faith in price-making markets as resource allocators entails the belief that relative prices change to stimulate substitution and innovation, leading to technological fixes for any problems. Money as the measure of all values requires universal commensurability, so that everything appears substitutable for everything else. Treating the world as different forms of commensurable capital – human, natural, artefactual, social – makes none of any more importance than any other. So loss of natural capital is easily compensated by man-made (human, social, artefactual) capital. Armed with such 'logic', mainstream economists have denied the relevance of both the consequences of and limits to growth.

The LTG scenario analysis posed the challenge that no simple price adjustment, spread of private property rights or new technology could address the causal mechanisms that combine to create social-ecological crises. Relaxing various constraints would merely lead to a different ultimate cause of collapse due to exponential growth. Everybody today should be familiar with the implications of exponential growth (e.g. rates of virus infection and death) and the related impact or the speed of doubling times (e.g. total infections and deaths). It means that action waiting for empirical evidence comes too late, hence precaution is necessary to avoid catastrophe. The response of the Trump administration to the Coronavirus pandemic provides an outstanding example of failure in this regard, but one matched by others (e.g. France, Italy, Spain, Sweden, Netherlands, UK). The potential for exponential growth in harm due to the growth economy was similarly derided and dismissed.

Hostility towards the original LTG work by Meadows et al. (1972) was evident in a range of attacks on it by mainstream economists shortly after it was published. The same lines of reasoning in defence of economic growth and against environmentalism have persisted ever since. The claim is that there is only one relevant economic system (i.e. market capitalisms) and this reacts efficiently to shocks via unregulated price signals. The basic idea is that when supply is short relative to demand then prices will rise and supply will increase because higher prices stimulate production, exploitation of more costly resources and innovation. Typically defence of economic growth involves claiming the price mechanism has been ignored by critics, resources are abundant and human ingenuity can solve all problems sooner than changing the economic system.

Wilfred Beckerman (1974) wrote an entire book attacking the LTG thesis. Amongst other things he argues that there are no resource constraints because the planet can be mined throughout the continental crust to a depth of one mile, which he claims has a million times currently known reserves which will provide resources lasting a 100 million years. He then states: 'by the time we reach A.D 100,000,000 I am sure we will think up something' (1974, p. 219). Beckerman had clearly not consulted a geologist as to what constitutes the Earth's crust, and appears totally ignorant of the mineralogical barrier. Approximately 99.9% of the continental crust is composed of the oxides of just ten elements (Si, Ti, Al, Fe, Mn, Mg, Ca, Na, K and P) by weight. The remainder are defined as 'geo-chemically scarce elements' (Skinner, 1979). Their existence tells nothing of their quality, concentration or exploitability (technically, economically, politically or ethically). The 'mineralogical barrier' distinguishes the large amount of geochemically scarce elements from those available for mining – only 0.01% to 0.001%. Scarce elements are trapped in the atomic structure of common rock (silicate minerals), and Beckerman is wrong to suggest their availability. Besides the technological leap and environmental destruction, mining beyond the mineralogical barrier implies using massive energy inputs to extract small quantities of minerals from huge amounts of waste rock (Dieter, 2017).

Another line of criticism of LTG has been to note that predictions of resource depletion dates are repeatedly confounded by new sources being brought online as prices rise. This is then taken to constitute evidence that there are no imminent limits (e.g. Beckerman, 1993). However, Meadows et al. (1972) expected rising costs and political struggles over resources long before resource exhaustion. As they state:

> Given present resource consumption rates and the projected increase in these rates, the great majority of the currently important nonrenewable resources will be extremely costly 100 years from now. [...] Recent nationalisation of South African mines and successful Middle Eastern pressures to raise oil prices suggest that the political question may arise long before the ultimate economic one. (Meadows et al., 1972, pp. 66–67)

The 'political question' has indeed materialised in the form of supply-chain competition, militarisation, country destabilisation and resource wars (e.g. over Middle Eastern oil). The on-going geo-political struggles over controlling resources highlight the importance of maintaining access to scarce energy and material supplies for the growth economy. There is more to economics than prices!

The claim that the price mechanism is central to understanding of an economic system ignores variety in types of social provisioning systems and types of economies, and that not all aspects of an economy need include prices. Within the narrow theoretical confines of capitalist economies with idealised price-making markets, even mainstream economists create models without explicit prices (e.g. Leontief models, the Harrod-Domar model). Prices and their operation via supply and demand models are part of microeconomics and attempts to link macroeconomic models to these microeconomic foundations have failed. Thus, the Sveriges Riksbank ('Nobel') Economic Prize winner, Robert Solow has no explicit prices in his macroeconomic growth model, although this did not stop him criticising the LTG scenario analysis for not modelling prices (Georgescu-Roegen, 1975/2009, p. 348). Actually, the LTG simulations include the equivalent of price effects via relaxing model constraints, e.g. allowing increased resource supply. The explicit mechanisms (prices, technology, a miracle?), whereby supply increases, are irrelevant to the scenario analysis. As Meadows et al. (1977, p. 201) point out, relaxing the resource constraint means '[t]he ultimate regulating effect of the price system is thus included, but price does not explicitly appear in the model'. The point here is that economists erroneously and hypocritically promote the role of prices, but more than this fail to acknowledge that markets are politically constituted institutionalised processes.

Resource struggles highlight how prices are the outcome of a range of factors outside the orthodox economic model: collusion, power struggles, geo-politics, regulatory regimes, government bailouts, subsidies, funding of infrastructure and so on. For example, the price of oil does not consistently increase, despite its absolute physical decline and increasing absolute demand. Nation states seek to secure resources and may invest in stock-piling and over production relative to the requirement of production and consumption at a given time (e.g. North American investment in non-conventional fossil fuels, oil and gas). Cartels may restrict production to increase prices (e.g. OPEC). Countries may flood the market with oil to destroy the balance of payments of other countries (e.g. Russia vs. Saudi Arabia). Events and/or policies may restrict demand and cause it to collapse (e.g. recession, Coronavirus). By April 2020 oil producing nations had successfully colluded to cut production by 10% in their attempt to stabilise the price collapse due to the Coronavirus policy induced drop in demand (DW Akademie, 2020a). The basic point here is that markets do not operate in a political vacuum, as claimed by mainstream economists, and prices are not the outcome of some simple self-equilibrating, unregulated, contest between supply and demand, let alone stable.

4.1. Economic value and the consumer society

Measuring everything in money metrics helps maintain and spread such problematic theoretical abstractions as equilibrium prices and the idea that they represent some objective resource costs in a perfectly competitive world economy. In support of its demand theory, economics has adopted an individualist preference utilitarian philosophy of value with universal commensurability. Everything has an exchange value measurable by money, where harm is equated with good.

A paradigm case of such 'logic' in action is the work of 'climate economists' (e.g. William Nordhaus, Richard Tol, Lord Stern) on global cost–benefit analysis (for critical reviews see Spash, 2002a, 2007a, 2007b). For such economists, damages from human induced climate change can be cancelled out by increases in consumption goods measured by gross domestic product (GDP), Gross National Income (GNI) and/or money benefits. They measure the value of life itself by either lifetime earnings or an individual's willingness-to-pay to avoid risk of death. Lost lives (e.g. people drowning in Bangladesh due to flooding and sea level rise) can then be equated to more recreational opportunities (e.g. golfing days in the USA), while the rich are made more valuable than the poor. Indeed, representatives from industrially developing nations, led by India and China, refused to accept an Intergovernmental Panel on Climate Change report that included a willingness-to-pay based value of life attributing people in industrialised countries (e.g. Europe, USA) fifteen times the (monetary) value of those in less industrialised countries. The economic logic here justifies climate action as efficient if it saves one rich person rather than fourteen poor people. The economists involved asserted that the calculations merely reported the facts, revealing their empiricist naïve objectivism, and remained totally unrepentant, ignoring the ethical meaning and consequences of their valuations (Spash, 2002b).

The ethics of mainstream economics is about trade-offs in a fictional world where all values can be expressed in a single metric (i.e. money), all choices compared in terms of their costs and benefits and decisions made on the basis of optimising the net benefit. This is the same 'logic' used to argue that the costs to 'the economy' of implementing Coronavirus restrictions need to be weighed against the benefits in terms of lives saved and illness prevented. Similarly, maintaining restrictions (i.e. avoiding costs in terms of increased death and illness) competes with restoring economic growth always euphemistically referenced as creating 'jobs' (i.e. the benefit of increasing GDP). Thus, Austria's Chancellor, Sebastian Kurz, on announcing restriction relaxation emphasised that he wanted to 'come out of this crisis as quickly as possible and fight for every job in Austria' (BBC News, 2020c). This is the same conservative Chancellor that brought in legislation, in coalition with the far right, that increased the working day from 8 to 12 h, levels not seen for a century, against major labour union protests (DW Akademie, 2018), and so undermined the number of jobs and their quality.

That the leading measure of economic growth, GDP, is also highly problematic as an indicator of human well-being is commonly recognised (e.g. Stiglitz et al., 2009). Since the rise of sustainability, there have been numerous attempts to produce all sorts of adjustments and alternative indicators (Roman & Thiry, 2017). However, the general aim is not to overthrow the growth paradigm, but rather to reform evaluation of its operation, as if the issue were merely the wrong indicator, and not the wrong economics, economic system and way of living. Once the logic of economic value is unravelled the ethics of the society it aims to justify come into question, along with its practices.

Consumer society is built on promoting product disposal both physically and psychologically. For example, the life time of the average mobile phone is four years (UNEP, 2009), but they are discarded in North America in half that time, while the software on the devices changes in a six to twelve month cycle (Entner, 2011). Thus, the culture of a resource extracting, throwaway, fashion conscious society is backed by innovation and technical obsolescence. Claims for Green growth and circular economies do not even begin to address the structure of industrial economies and their linear systems of resource throughput and low entropy dependency (Giampietro, 2019).

The globalisation of this capitalist form of economic structure means domination of resource rich regions for extraction, control of ecosystems for productivist ends (goods and services) and social dependency on monetary flows. Within countries resource extraction wins over indigenous peoples' rights and Nature. This is the case in both the global South and North. German brown coal (lignite) extraction has destroyed much of the remnant of ancient Hambach forest while also evicting residents and destroying whole towns. Native Americans in Canada have suffered from tar sands extraction and in the USA lost against fossil fuels interests building oil and gas pipelines (e.g. Standing Rock protests against the Dakota Access Pipeline). Alternative economies and ways of social provisioning by indigenous communities are typically regarded as backward and unprogressive and their values derided. The economic rhetoric is about production, consumption, competition, innovation and government operating to support growth in corporate profits.

The consumerist tread mill involves 'keeping up with the Joneses', a syndrome activated and reinforced by corporate advertising promoting conspicuous consumption (a phenomenon recognised already by Veblen, 1899/1991). The impossibility of 'keeping-up' is explained as part of the social LTG by Hirsch (1977). Positional goods are limited by definition, so making them readily available destroys their positional value and motivates switching to alternatives. In a complementary critique, over several decades, Easterlin (1974, 1995, 2003) deconstructs the economic preoccupation with growth in income as a measure of happiness, and its failure to address what really counts in contributing to human well-being (i.e. non-positional 'goods' such as health, loving relationships, friends). Some have then moved to promoting subjective measures of well-being (Kahneman & Krueger, 2006), but these merely shift from one hedonic measure to another (O'Neill, 2006, 2008), in an attempt to avoid systemic change.

Attempts at reforming the economic system against its inherent failures are increasingly common in times of crisis. The modern calls for circular economies hark back to calls for recycling and reuse based on materials balance theory (Kneese et al., 1970). Ultimately, circular economies, recycling, increased product durability and technical efficiency are means of reducing or slowing material flows to the environment, but not of addressing the hedonistic consumer culture or overthrowing the basic laws of physics.

4.2. The biophysical basis of an economy

Georgescu-Roegen (1975/2009) analysed the frivolous use of resources in a consumer society, raising ethical issues about who gets to use which resources and for what. He based this analysis on the role of energy and materials in the reproduction of the economic system. The fiction of macroeconomic models is that goods and services can flow in a perpetual isolated cycle between households and firms without any relationship to either the necessary energy or material inputs, or the environment into which all energy and materials must ultimately go. Georgescu-Roegen (1971) related the economic process to physical laws and specifically the exploitation of low entropy resources. Entropy is a measure of the qualitative state of energy. Energy is conserved within an isolated system (where neither material nor energy enters or exits), but moves towards minimum usefulness (from low to high entropy). Earth has three main sources of low entropy (useful energy): (i) terrestrial stocks of concentrated minerals; (ii) solar flow of radiant energy; and (iii) the gravitational force of the moon, planets and sun. Industrialisation is built upon the exploitation of (i) and is totally dependent upon fossil fuel energy.

The energy transition from a solar economy (biomass and wood) to fossil fuel economy (coal, petroleum, natural gas, oil shale, fracking) is a standard aspect of industrialisation (Schandl & Schulz, 2002), and explains the social metabolism of the growth economy (Krausmann, 2017). The correlation of carbon dioxide (CO_2) emissions with economic growth is then a straight forward result of burning fossil fuels. As far as the physics is concerned, there should be no surprise that the outcome of economic growth is to enhance the greenhouse effect ultimately leading to global warming. Of course this is merely one amongst many environmental problems – soil erosion; deforestation; water salinisation; insecticides and pesticides; particulates in the air; tropospheric ozone pollution; stratospheric ozone loss; acidic deposition; toxic chemical waste; heavy metals; asbestos; nuclear waste; e-waste; biodiversity loss; acidification of the oceans; micro plastics; hormone discharges into the water supply and so on … The Laws of Conservation explain that energy and mass can neither be created nor destroyed. Economic growth via increased production and consumption must increase inputs of material and energy into the economy, and so increase waste loads into the environment. Pollution is an all pervasive problem for an industrialised growth economy.

What neoclassical economists regard as pollution 'externalities' are talked of as one-off minor aberrations in an otherwise perfectly functioning price-making market system. In reality they are a normal, indeed inevitable, part of economic processes and their significance increases as economic growth proceeds, while the ability of natural systems to assimilate them declines (Kneese et al., 1970). Negative externalities are not external to the economic system, but rather part of the established economic process of cost-shifting (Kapp, 1963/1978). Including the resulting social and environmental costs in markets, via internalising 'externalities', means changing all the prices in an economy, which means planned prices. If no existing prices are changed then the economy is merely 'planned' in a different way, by default (subject to institutional history and accident). Either way, prices reflect power relationships, not objective resource scarcity values. Yet, neoclassical economists ignore the implications of their own 'externality' theory and its implications that undermine their price theory of value (Spash, 2019).

Facing the inevitable evidence of increasing pollution, mainstream economists have produced a fall-back position that claims the environment is a luxury good. Once people are wealthy enough they can afford clean air, clear water and other environmental goods and services, but that requires they get rich first via economic growth. This ignores the essential role of ecological systems in social provisioning and waste assimilation for both rich and poor (e.g. see, Martinez-Alier, 2002). Belief in the possibility of environmental recovery after destruction by the growth economy is an artefact of mainstream economists' mechanistic models, and ahistorical concept of time, making all events reversible. That toxic waste has proven untreatable, extinct species do not return, ecosystems cannot be recreated and people who die from pollution are not brought back to life, seems to have no consequences for such 'economic logic'. Once again biophysical reality is simply ignored.

5. Concluding remarks

Whenever the capital accumulating economies of the world hit a crisis that threatens economic growth vested interests react by prioritising its re-establishment. Since the early 1990s the corporate business elite have successfully shifted attention from their being the cause of environmental destruction to increasingly claiming they must be seen as the champions of a Green new economy. That economic growth is more important than the environment or people's lives has often been apparent in the promotion of sustainable development and a Green economy. Prior to the Coronavirus crisis the climate crisis was high on the media agenda, but the difference in response is quite stark. The potential for exponential growth in virus infections and deaths led to direct regulation and restrictions on human behaviour (not nudging or market based instruments or price incentives). In contrast, for over thirty years no significant action has been taken to change the behaviour causing the exponential growth in greenhouse gas emissions.

Economic growth has always trumped environmental protection. Typically current jobs are prioritised over future human morbidity and mortality and any impacts on non-humans. The Global Commission on the Economy and Climate (GCEC) has promoted the slogan of 'Better Growth, Better Climate', and made very clear that its concern is that: 'In the long term, if climate change is not tackled, growth itself will be at risk' (GCEC, 2014, p. 9). Janez Potočnik, European Commissioner for Environment 2009–2014, concluded his opening address to the 2013 Green Growth conference hosted by the Organisation for Economic and Co-operation Development (OECD) by stating: 'basically, I do believe, I am not talking about environmental interests here, and that I am talking about new industrial policy needed, so its not actually about Green Growth, it's about growth, full stop. Thank you'.[4] Similarly, Ursula von der Leyen, European Commission President, has stated that 'Supported by investments in green technologies, sustainable solutions and new businesses […] The European Green Deal is our new growth strategy' (European Commission, 2019).

When the worlds leaders wrap themselves in national flags, and claim a concern for all their citizens, the structure of the system they promote and defend might easily be forgotten. In response to the Coronavirus pandemic the primary concern of international organisations and governments for economic growth was ever present, with even the potential death of millions seemingly relegated to a secondary concern until almost too late. While politicians were still debating what action should be taken to protect their populations' health they had already prioritised reducing interest rates, holding meetings with corporate bosses and promising billions in bailouts. Within a month of the first lockdown, outside China, the bailouts became unprecedented with the United States Senate approving a package of two trillion dollars stimulus plus four trillion dollars available for loans, the European Union half a trillion euros and Japan a trillion dollars. Political parties of the Left and Greens have typically been derided, under austerity politics, as irresponsible for advocating the ability of governments to spend in the public interest for such things as national health and preventing the environmental crisis. As under the 2008 collapse, there was no money until corporations, the stock market, financiers, billionaires and bankers were threatened.

Economic crises reveal the structure of the dominant political economy and offer an opportunity for rethinking and restructuring. Re-establishing the system will maintain humanity on its course towards increasing social division and ecological crisis. Prior to the Coronavirus pandemic the climate crisis had highlighted the need to move away from fossil-fuel intensive activities and sectors. Internationally hopes were placed on the Paris Agreement, but this was never based on a realistic assessment of policy to control greenhouse gases (Spash, 2016). Indeed, there has been no plan to dismantle the fossil-fuel sector, change infrastructure or economic activity, and no precaution in the face of increasing global temperatures. Since the signing of the Paris Agreement the world's largest investment banks have funnelled more than $2.66 trillion into fossil fuels (Greenfield & Makortoff, 2020). Oil markets collapsing, fossil-fuel investments being decimated, airlines cutting flying and going bankrupt and people stopping daily commuting should all have occurred when the Paris Agreement was signed, if it had any real teeth. Instead they occurred as a reaction to the Coronavirus pandemic and as things to be reversed as soon as possible.

The world's governments have failed to face up to the social-ecological challenges ahead and remain unprepared, having watched for forty years to 'see' evidence of climate change. What the Coronavirus pandemic indicates is that most elected politicians in capitalist economies will only act to counter corporate and financial interests, and the consumer throwaway society, under domestically actualised extreme circumstances. The evidence here is that action came once the body count started growing and threatened to explode exponentially in politicians own countries. Lessons should also be learnt from the differentiated responses and resulting impacts of Coronavirus. These include the necessity of precaution in the face of potentially catastrophic events and how neoliberal promotion of self-interest, individualism, consumerism and competition at the expense of community and solidarity create injustice and inequity, and stimulate panic and chaos in times of crisis. The scenario analysis of the LTG warned of what happens when harms grow exponentially: suddenly you run out of time to prevent catastrophe. Such warnings and even the very concept of limits have been repeatedly pushed aside by promises of more and better growth: sustainable development, Green growth, circular economy, sustainable inclusive growth, Green (new) deals. The harmful social and ecological implications of economic growth have been denied but never gone away.

The fear created by a crisis getting out of control raises the political danger of extreme right wing nationalism, authoritarianism, securitisation and militarisation. Nations turn inwards and act unilaterally. The hope is that the experience of a devastating global crisis will put the necessity of systems change high on the public agenda and create general awareness that 'the economy' cannot be allowed to go on as before, creating social division and gross inequalities while leaving humanity at the mercy of corporations, billionaires, speculators and profiteers. A global human health crisis has tested the system and shown its failings and should be taken as a warning in the face of the impending ecological crisis. As a fundamental starting point, economies are required that address those failings by providing robust democratic systems for basic social provisioning for all via socially and ecologically ethical means of production.

Notes

1. This is based on the success of initial responses evaluated up to mid-April 2020. Media coverage concentrated on total deaths and daily death rates, but per capita rates are more relevant in terms of assessing government policy. The top ten nations with the highest per capita death rates as of 14th April, in order, were: Spain, Italy, Belgium, France, UK, Netherlands, Switzerland, Sweden, Ireland, USA. This excludes countries with small populations (0.65 million or less). In terms of total deaths the top ten ranked nations, in order, were: USA, Italy, Spain, France, UK, Iran, Belgium, China, Germany, Netherlands; while Switzerland was 13th, Sweden 14th and Ireland 19th. Source: https://www.worldometers.info/coronavirus/#countries.

2. At this stage, the crisis had moved from China to Europe and then America and was just starting to grow exponentially in Brazil, Turkey, Iran, Indonesia, Mexico, India and Russia before even getting going in Africa.

3. WHO Director-General's opening remarks at the media briefing on COVID-19 https://www.who.int/dg/speeches/detail/who-director-general-s-opening-remarks-at-the-media-briefing-on-covid-19---3-march-2020. Accessed 14 April 2020.
4. The Annual Conference of the Green Growth Knowledge Platform (GGKP): Better Policies Better Lives, Paris, France, 4–5 April 2013. Speech transcribed from the film 'Banking Nature' (50.04–50.34 min).

Disclosure statement

No potential conflict of interest was reported by the author(s).

References

BBC News. (2020a). Coronavirus: Amazon blocks non-essential items from warehouses. *BBC News*. Retrieved March 27, 2020, from https://www.bbc.com/news/technology-51944759
BBC News. (2020b). Coronavirus: Amazon ordered to deliver only essential items in France. *BBC News*. Retrieved April 14, 2020, from https://www.bbc.com/news/world-europe-52285301
BBC News. (2020c). Coronavirus: Austria reopens some shops as lockdown eased. *BBC News*. Retrieved April 14, 2020, from https://www.bbc.com/news/world-europe-52275959
BBC News. (2020d). Coronavirus: Easter egg crackdown over essential status 'wrong'. *BBC News*. Retrieved March 27, 2020, from https://www.bbc.com/news/business-52090441
BBC News. (2020e). Coronavirus: WWE resumes live fights after being deemed 'essential'. *BBC News*. Retrieved April 14, 2020, from https://www.bbc.com/news/world-us-canada-52285742
Beckerman, W. (1974). *In defence of economic growth*. Jonathan Cape.
Beckerman, W. (1993). The environmental limits to growth: A fresh look. In H. Giersch (Ed.), *Economic progress and environmental concerns* (pp. 1–24). Springer-Verlag.
Boffey, D. (2020). Europe's homeless hit hard by coronavirus response. *The Guardian*. Retrieved April 4, 2020, from https://www.theguardian.com/world/2020/mar/31/europes-homeless-hit-hard-by-coronavirus-response
Brignall, M. (2020). Ryanair accused of ripping off passengers over rebooked flights. *The Guardian*. Retrieved March 27, 2020, from https://www.theguardian.com/business/2020/mar/26/ryanair-accused-of-ripping-off-passengers-over-rebooked-flights
Daly, H. E. (1973). *Towards a steady-state economy*. Freeman.
Dieter, A. (2017). Geophysical limits, raw materials use and their poicy implications. In C. L. Spash (Ed.), *Routledge handbook of ecological economics: Nature and society* (pp. 99–107). Routledge.
DW Akademie. (2018). Austria: Thousands protest against plans for 12-hour workday. *Made for Minds*. Retrieved April 14, 2020, from https://p.dw.com/p/30c1e
DW Akademie. (2020a). OPEC and allies agree to cut oil production to nearly 10 million barrels a day. *Made for Minds*. Retrieved April 13, 2020, from https://p.dw.com/p/3aoYw

DW Akademie. (2020b). US accused of seizing face mask shipments bound for Europe, Canada. *Made for Minds*. Retrieved April 8, 2020, from https://www.dw.com/en/us-accused-of-seizing-face-mask-shipments-bound-for-europe-canada/a-53010923

Easterlin, R. A. (1974). "Does economic growth improve the human lot?": Some empirical evidence. In P. A. David & M. W. Reder (Eds.), *Nations and households in economic growth: Essays in honor of moses abramovitz* (pp. 98–125). Academic Press.

Easterlin, R. A. (1995). Will raising the income for all increase the happiness for all? *Journal of Economic Behavior & Organization*, *27*(1), 35–47. https://doi.org/10.1016/0167-2681(95)00003-B

Easterlin, R. A. (2003). Explaining happiness. *PNAS*, *100*(19), 11176–11183. https://doi.org/10.1073/pnas.1633144100

Edwards, T. (2020). Coronavirus: Pollution levels fall 'dramatically'. *BBC News*. Retrieved April 1, 2020, from https://www.bbc.com/news/uk-england-london-52114306

El-Erian, M. (2020). Coronavirus forces economics profession to leave comfort zone. *The Guardian*. Retrieved March 27. 2020, from https://www.theguardian.com/business/2020/mar/30/coronavirus-forces-economics-profession-to-leave-comfort-zone

Entner, R. (2011). International comparisons: The handset replacement cycle. *Recon Analytics*.

European Commission. (2019). *What is the European green deal?*. https://ec.europa.eu/commission/presscorner/api/files/attachment/859152/What_is_the_European_Green_Deal_en.pdf.pdf

Evelyn, K. (2020). Amazon fires New York worker who led strike over coronavirus concerns. *The Guardian*. Retrieved April 1, 2020, from https://www.theguardian.com/us-news/2020/mar/31/amazon-strike-worker-fired-organizing-walkout-chris-smallls

GCEC. (2014). *Better growth better climate: The new climate economy report*. The synthesis report. The Global Commission on the Economy and Climate.

Georgescu-Roegen, N. (1971). *The entropy law and the economic process*. Harvard University Press.

Georgescu-Roegen, N. (2009). Energy and economic myths. In C. L. Spash (Ed.), *Ecological economics: Critical concepts in the environment* (4 Vols., pp. 328–373). Routledge. (Original work published 1975).

Giampietro, M. (2019). On the circular bioeconomy and decoupling: Implications for sustainable growth. *Ecological Economics*, *162*, 143–156. https://doi.org/10.1016/j.ecolecon.2019.05.001

Gills, B. (2020). Deep restoration: From the great implosion to the great awakening. *Globalizations*. https://doi.org/10.1080/14747731.2020.1748364

Gills, B., & Morgan, J. (2019). Global climate emergency: After COP24, climate science, urgency, and the threat to humanity. *Globalizations*. https://doi.org/10.1080/14747731.2019.1669915

Greenfield, P., & Makortoff, K. (2020). Study: Global banks 'failing miserably' on climate crisis by funneling trillions into fossil fuels. *The Guardian*. Retrieved April 1, 2020. https://www.theguardian.com/environment/2020/mar/18/global-banks-climate-crisis-finance-fossil-fuels

Greve, J. E., & McCarthy, T. (2020). Coronavirus US live: Cuomo says bidding war for ventilators is 'like being on eBay'. *The Guardian*. Retrieved March 31, 2020, from https://www.theguardian.com/us-news/live/2020/mar/31/coronavirus-us-live-new-york-governor-peak-cases-trump-america-outbreak-pandemic?

The Guardian. (2020). Coronavirus: Anger in Germany at report Trump seeking exclusive vaccine deal. Retrieved March 23, 2020, from https://theguardian.com/world/2020/mar/16/not-for-sale-anger-in-germany-at-report-trump-seeking-exclusivecoronavirus-vaccine-deal

Guichard, M., & Pailliez, C. (2020). French Amazon workers protest in coronavirus pushback. *Reuters*. Retrieved June 18, 2016, from http://reuters.com/article/us-health-coronavirus-france-amazon-idUSKBN2152MP

Hanieh, A. (2020, March 27). This is a global pandemic – let's treat it as such. https://www.versobooks.com/blogs/4623-this-is-a-global-pandemic-let-s-treat-it-as-such

Harper, J. (2020). Why orange juice prices are soaring on global markets. *BBC News*. Retrieved March 27, 2020, from https://www.bbc.com/news/technology-52030133

Hauser, J., & Jackson, A. (2020). NASA images show a decrease in China's pollution related to coronavirus shutdown. *Cable News Network*. https://edition.cnn.com/2020/03/01/world/nasa-china-pollution-coronavirus-trnd-scn/index.html

Hirsch, F. (1977). *Social limits to growth*. Routledge and Kegan Paul Ltd.

Hoffower, H. (2019). We did the math to calculate how much money Jeff Bezos makes in a year, month, week, day, hour, minute, and second. *Business Insider*. Retrieved April 1, 2020, from https://www.businessinsider.de/international/what-amazon-ceo-jeff-bezos-makes-every-day-hour-minute-2018-10/?r=US&IR=T

Jack, S. (2020). Coronavirus: Supermarkets 'drastically' cutting product ranges. *BBC News*. Retrieved March 19, 2020, from https://www.bbc.com/news/business-51961624

Jackson, T. (2009). *Prosperity without growth: Economics for a finite planet*. Earthscan.

Kahneman, D., & Krueger, A. B. (2006). Developments in the measurement of subjective well-being. *Journal of Economic Perspectives, 20*(1), 3–24. https://doi.org/10.1257/089533006776526030

Kapp, K. W. (1978). The nature and significance of social costs. In K. W. Kapp (Ed.), *The social costs of business enterprise* (2nd ed., pp. 13–27). Nottingham: Spokesman. (Original work published 1963).

Klein, N. (2007). *The shock doctrine: The rise of disaster capitalism*. Metropolitan Books; Henry Holt and Company, LLC.

Kneese, A. V., Ayres, R. U., & d'Arge, R. C. (1970). *Economics and the environment: A materials balance approach*. Resources for the Future.

Krausmann, F. (2017). 'Social metabolism'. In C. L. Spash (Ed.), *Routledge handbook of ecological economics: Nature and society* (pp. 108–118). Routledge.

Lawrence, F. (2020a). Millions to need food aid in days as virus exposes UK supply. *The Guardian*. Retrieved March 27, 2020, from https://www.theguardian.com/world/2020/mar/27/millions-to-need-food-aid-in-days-as-virus-exposes-uk-supply

Lawrence, F. (2020b). UK hunger crisis: 1.5 m people go whole day without food. *The Guardian*. Retrieved March 27, 2020, from https://www.theguardian.com/society/2020/apr/11/uk-hunger-crisis-15m-people-go-whole-day-without-food

Levin, D. (2020, March 25). Coronavirus and firearms: Are gun shops essential businesses? *New York Times*. Retrieved April 1, 2020, from https://nytimes.com/2020/03/25/us/coronavirus-guns-stores.html

Malpass, D. (2020). Remarks by World Bank Group President David Malpan on G20 Finance Ministers conference call on COVID-19. *G20 Finance Ministers conference call on COVID-19*, 1–3. Retrieved April 1, 2020, from https://www.worldbank.org/en/news/speech/2020/03/23/remarks-by-world-bank-group-president-david-malpass-on-g20-finance-ministers-conference-call-on-covid-19

Martinez-Alier, J. (2002). *The environmentalism of the poor: A study of ecological conflicts and valuation*. Edward Elgar.

McMahon, J. (2020). Study: Coronavirus lockdown likely saved 77,000 lives in China just by reducing pollution. *Forbes*. Retrieved April 1, 2020, from https://www.forbes.com/sites/jeffmcmahon/2020/03/16/coronavirus-lockdown-may-have-saved-77000-lives-in-china-just-from-pollution-reduction/

Meadows, D. H., Meadows, D. L. (1977). A summary of limits to growth: Its critics and its challenge. In H. J. Leonard (Ed.), *Business and environment: Toward common ground* (pp. 194–209). Conservation Foundation.

Meadows, D. H., Meadows, D. L., Randers, J., & Behrens III, W. W. (1972). *The limits to growth*. Universe Books.

Mirowski, P. (2013). *Never let a serious crisis go to waste: How neoliberalism survived the financial meltdown*. Verso.

Mishan, E. J. (1969). *Growth: The price we pay*. Staples Press.

O'Neill, J. F. (2006). Citizenship, well-being and sustainability: Epicurus or Aristotle? *Analyse & Kritik, 28*(2), 158–172. https://doi.org/10.1515/auk-2006-0203

O'Neill, J. F. (2008). Happiness and the good life. *Environmental Values, 17*(2), 125–144. https://doi.org/10.3197/096327108X303819

Pailliez, C., & Guichard, M. (2020). France says pressure on Amazon workers 'unacceptable' amid lockdown. *Reuters*. Retrieved June 18, 2016, from https://uk.reuters.com/article/uk-health-coronavirus-amazon-france/france-says-pressure-on-amazon-workers-unacceptable-amid-lockdown-idUKKBN21610B

Polanyi, K. (1957). The market as instituted process. In K. Polanyi (Ed.), *Trade and market in the early empires* (pp. 243–270). Henry Regnery Company.

Raworth, K. (2018). *Doughnut economics: Seven ways to think like a 21st-century economist*. Random House Business Books. (Original work published 2017).

Roman, P., & Thiry, G. (2017). Sustainability indicators. In C. L. Spash (Ed.), *Routledge handbook of ecological economics: Nature and society* (pp. 382–392). Routledge.

Sachs, W. (2015). *Planet dialectics: Explorations in environment and development*. Zed Books. (Original work published 1999).

Savage, M. (2020). Lockdown, what lockdown? Sweden's unusual response to coronavirus. *BBC News*. Retrieved March 29, 2020, from https://www.bbc.com/news/world-europe-52076293

Schandl, H., & Schulz, N. (2002). Changes in the United Kingdom's natural relations in terms of society's metabolism and land use from 1850 to the present day. *Ecological Economics*, *41*(2), 203–221. https://doi.org/10.1016/S0921-8009(02)00031-9

Schumacher, E. F. (1973). *Small is beautiful: A study of economics as if people mattered*. Sphere Books.

Scitovsky, T. (1976). *The joyless economy: An inquiry into human satisfaction and consuemr dissatisfaction*. University Press.

Sen, A. (1986). *Poverty and famines: An essay on entitlement and deprivation*. Clarendon Press.

Skinner, B. J. (1979). A second iron age ahead. In P. A. Trudinger & D. J. Swaine (Eds.), *Biogeochemical cycling of mineral-forming elements* (pp. 556–575). Elsevier Scientific Publishng Company.

Spash, C. L. (2002a). *Greenhouse economics: Value and ethics*. Routledge.

Spash, C. L. (2002b). Loading the dice?: Values, opinions and ethics. In C. L. Spash (Ed.), *Greenhouse economics: Value and ethics* (pp. 184–200). Routledge.

Spash, C. L. (2007a). The economics of climate change impacts à la Stern: Novel and nuanced or rhetorically restricted? *Ecological Economics*, *63*(4), 706–713. https://doi.org/10.1016/j.ecolecon.2007.05.017

Spash, C. L. (2007b). Problems in economic assessments of climate change with attention to the USA. In J. Erickson & J. Gowdy (Eds.), *Frontiers in ecological economic theory and application* (pp. 176–192). Edward Elgar Publishing Ltd.

Spash, C. L. (2016). This changes nothing: The Paris agreement to ignore reality. *Globalizations*, *13*(6), 928–933. https://doi.org/10.1080/14747731.2016.1161119

Spash, C. L. (2019). *Making pollution into a market failure rather than a cost-shifting success: The suppression of revolutionary change in economics*. Institute for Multilevel Governance and Development. https://ideas.repec.org/p/wiw/wiwsre/sre-disc-2019_06.html

Spash, C. L. (2020). A tale of three paradigms. *Ecological Economics*, *169*(March), 1–14. https://doi.org/10.1016/j.ecolecon.2019.106518

Stewart, H., & Busby, M. (2020). Coronavirus: Science chief defends UK plan from criticism. *The Guardian*. Retrieved April 14, 2020, from https://www.theguardian.com/world/2020/mar/13/coronavirus-science-chief-defends-uk-measures-criticism-herd-immunity

Stewart, H., Proctor, K., & Siddique, H. (2020). Johnson: Many more people will lose loved ones to coronavirus. *The Guardian*. Retrieved April 14, 2020, from https://www.theguardian.com/world/2020/mar/12/uk-moves-to-delay-phase-of-coronavirus-plan

Stiglitz, J. E., Sen, A., & Fitoussi, J.-P. (2009). Report by the commission on the measurement of economic performance and social progress. Retrieved October 22, 2009, from https://www.stiglitz-sen-fitoussi.fr/en/index.htm

Strassel, K. A. (2020). Coronavirus vindicates capitalism. *The Wall Street Journal*. Retrieved March 19, 2020, from https://www.wsj.com/articles/coronavirus-vindicates-capitalism-11584659306

Traill, K., & Schocher, S. (2020). Coronavirus coverup: Did Austrian politics and industry collude? Retrieved April 9, 2020, from https://www.dw.com/en/coronavirus-coverup-did-austrian-politics-and-industry-collude/a-53048958

UNEP. (2009). *Recycling: From e-waste to resources*. United Nations Environment Programme and University.

UNEP. (2011). *Towards a green economy: Pathways to sustainable development and poverty eradication*. United Nations Environment Programme.

United Nations General Assembly. (2015). *Resolution adopted by the general assembly on 25 September 2015: Transforming our world: The 2030 agenda for sustainable development*. United Nations.

van den Bergh, J. C. J. M. (2011). Environment versus growth: A criticism of "degrowth" and a plea for "a-growth". *Ecological Economics*, *70*(5), 881–890. https://doi.org/10.1016/j.ecolecon.2010.09.035

Veblen, T. (1991). *The theory of the leisure class*. Augustus M Kelley. (Original work published 1899).

World Commission on Environment and Development. (1987). *Report of the world commission on environment and development: Our common future*. United Nations. https://sustainabledevelopment.un.org/content/documents/5987our-common-future.pdf

Zoellner, D. (2020). Coronavirus: Jeff Bezos, world's richest man, asks public to donate to Amazon relief fund. *The Independent*. Retrieved April 1, 2020, from https://www.independent.co.uk/news/world/americas/coronavirus-amazon-jeff-bezos-relief-fund-covid-19-billionaire-net-worth-a9422236.html

What does degrowth mean? A few points of clarification

Jason Hickel

ABSTRACT
Degrowth is a planned reduction of energy and resource use designed to bring the economy back into balance with the living world in a way that reduces inequality and improves human well-being. Over the past few years, the idea has attracted significant attention among academics and social movements, but for people new to the idea it raises a number of questions. Here I set out to clarify three specific issues: (1) I specify what degrowth means, and argue that the framing of degrowth is an asset, not a liability; (2) I explain how degrowth differs fundamentally from a recession; and (3) I affirm that degrowth is primarily focused on high-income nations, and explore the implications of degrowth for the global South.

Introduction

Human civilization is presently overshooting a number of critical planetary boundaries and faces a multi-dimensional crisis of ecological breakdown, including dangerous climate change, ocean acidification, deforestation and biodiversity collapse (Lenton et al., 2020; Rockström et al., 2009; Steffen et al., 2015; Steffen et al., 2018). Contrary to the general narrative about the Anthropocene, this crisis is not being caused by human beings *as such*, but by a particular economic system: a system that is predicated on perpetual expansion, disproportionately to the benefit of a small minority of rich people (Moore, 2015).

The relationship between economic growth and ecological breakdown is now well demonstrated in the empirical record. In mainstream economics, the dominant claim is that we must continue to pursue perpetual growth (see Hickel, 2018a), and therefore must seek to decouple GDP from ecological impacts and make growth 'green'. Unfortunately, green growth hopes have little grounding. There is no historical evidence of long-term absolute decoupling of GDP from resource use (as measured by material footprint), and all extant models project that it cannot be achieved even under optimistic conditions (Hickel & Kallis, 2020; Vadén, Lähde, Majava, Järvensivu, Toivanen, & Eronen 2020; Vadén et al. 2020b). Absolute decoupling of GDP from emissions can be achieved simply by replacing fossil fuels with renewable energy; but this cannot be done quickly enough to respect carbon budgets for 1.5°C and 2°C if the economy continues to grow at usual rates. More growth means more energy demand, and more energy demand makes it all the more difficult to cover it with renewables in the short time we have left (Hickel & Kallis, 2020; Raftery et al., 2017; Schroder & Storm, 2020).

In light of this evidence, scientists and ecological economists are increasingly calling for a shift to 'post-growth' and 'degrowth' strategies. The 2018 special report of the IPCC indicates that, in the absence of speculative negative-emissions technologies, the only feasible way to remain within safe carbon budgets is for high-income nations to actively slow down the pace of material production and consumption (Grubler et al., 2018; IPCC, 2018). Reducing material throughput reduces energy demand, which makes it easier to accomplish a rapid transition to renewables. This approach is also ecologically coherent: reducing material throughput not only helps us to address climate change, but also removes pressure on other planetary boundaries.

This is known as 'degrowth'. Degrowth is a planned reduction of energy and resource throughput designed to bring the economy back into balance with the living world in a way that reduces inequality and improves human well-being (Kallis, 2018; Latouche, 2009). It is important to clarify that degrowth is *not* about reducing GDP, but rather about reducing throughput. From an ecological perspective, that is what matters. Of course, it is important to accept that reducing throughput is likely to lead to a reduction in the rate of GDP growth, or even a decline in GDP itself, and we have to be prepared to manage that outcome in a safe and just way. This is what degrowth sets out to do.

While degrowth theory is attracting increasing attention among academics and social movements, for people new to the idea it raises a number of questions. Here I address questions about language and terminology, questions about economic recession, and questions about international political economy and the North–South divide.

The language of degrowth

Many of the objections to degrowth have to do with the term itself. Some people worry that degrowth introduces confusion because it is not, in fact, the opposite of growth. When people say 'growth' they normally mean growth in GDP, so one might reasonably assume that degrowth is likewise focused on reducing GDP. Proponents of degrowth are therefore condemned to perpetually clarify that degrowth is not about reducing GDP, but rather about reducing material and energy throughput. It would seem that this creates unnecessary problems.

But, in fact, the problem here arises from the word growth, *not* degrowth. In reality, people pursue growth not in order to increase an abstract number (GDP), but because they want to consume or do more, which of course requires using more materials and energy. So when economists and politicians talk about growth they *really* mean an increase in materials and energy (and specifically an increase in *commodified* materials and energy), even though this is not stated outright. The preoccupation with GDP is a fetish that obscures this fact; it makes it seem as though growth is immaterial when in reality it is not. If GDP growth did not come along with an increase in material consumption, people would not pursue it (what's the point of having a higher income if it doesn't enable you to expand military spending, buy bigger houses and faster cars, or pay people to do things for you?). In this sense, degrowth, with its focus on reducing material and energy use (and reducing patterns of commodification), is in fact an appropriate opposite to growth, and indeed clarifies what growth itself is actually about.

Now, one might ask, why use the term degrowth at all, when you could just say 'we want to reduce energy and material throughput' and avoid the confusion? There are a few reasons for this. First, most economists would agree that reducing energy and material throughput is important, but they assume this can be accomplished while continuing to pursue economic growth at the same time (indeed, they may even believe that more growth will eventually lead to a reduction in throughput). We need some way of distinguishing the degrowth position from this standard 'green growth' assumption. If we accept the empirical evidence that green growth is unlikely to be achieved, then we have to accept that reducing throughput will impact on GDP itself, and we must focus on how to restructure the economy so that this can be managed in a safe and just way. For this, 'degrowth' is a simple, handy term that allows us to clarify what is at stake, and concentrates the mind on what is required.

Proponents of degrowth often argue that the word degrowth is useful as a 'missile' word. For an increasing number of people, it is obvious that perpetual growth is a problem; for them, degrowth seems intuitively correct as a response to ecological crisis, and they can get on board immediately. Other people have a negative initial reaction to the word, but it is nonetheless useful in such cases to the extent that it challenges and disrupts people's assumptions about how the economy should work, by questioning something that is generally taken for granted as natural and good. In many cases, negative initial reactions give way to contemplation (do high-income countries really need more growth?), and then curiosity (perhaps we can actually flourish with less throughput, and even less output?), and then investigation (what is the relevant empirical evidence?) that eventually leads people to change their views. This kind of intellectual transformation is enabled, not inhibited, by using a provocative term. Trying to avoid provocation, or trying to be agnostic about growth, creates a milieu where problematic assumptions remain unidentified and unexamined in favour of polite conversation and agreement. This is not an effective way to advance knowledge, especially when the stakes are so high.

Some people worry about using degrowth because it is a 'negative' term, rather than positive. But it is only negative if we start from the assumption that more growth is good and desirable. If we want to challenge that assumption, and argue the opposite (that more growth is unnecessary and damaging, and that it would be better if we slowed down), then degrowth is a positive term. Take the words colonization and decolonization, for example. We know that those who engaged in colonization felt it was a good thing. From their perspective – which was the dominant perspective in Europe for most of the past 500 years – decolonization would therefore seem negative. But the point is precisely to challenge the dominant perspective, because the dominant perspective is wrong. Indeed, today we can agree that this stance – a stance against colonization – is correct and valuable: we stand against colonization, and believe that the world would be better without it. That is not a negative vision, but positive; one that's worth rallying around. Similarly, we can and should aspire to an economy without growth just as we aspire to a world without colonization.

We can take this observation one step further. It is important to recognize that the word 'growth' has become a kind of propaganda term. In reality, what is going on is a process of elite accumulation, the commodification of commons, and the appropriation of human labour and natural resources – a process that is quite often colonial in character. This process, which is generally destructive to human communities and to ecology, is glossed as growth. Growth sounds natural and positive (who could possibly be against growth?) so people are easily persuaded to buy into it, and to back policies that will generate more of it, when otherwise they might not. Growth is the ideology of capitalism, in the Gramscian sense. It is the core tenet of capitalism's cultural hegemony. The word degrowth is powerful and effective because it identifies this trick, and rejects it. Degrowth calls for the reversal of the processes that lie behind growth: it calls for disaccumulation, decommodification, and decolonization.

Degrowth vs recession

Another common question about degrowth has to do with recessions. Indeed, when the COVID-19 recession hit, some detractors of degrowth pointed to it as an example of why degrowth would be a disaster. For the most part, this is not a good-faith argument but rather an intentional attempt to mislead, for it is impossible to make this mistake with even a cursory reading of the actual literature on degrowth. In fact, degrowth is in every way the opposite of a recession. We have different words for them because they are different things. Here are six key differences worth noting:

(1) Degrowth is a planned, coherent policy to reduce ecological impact, reduce inequality, and improve well-being. Recessions are not planned, and do not target any of these outcomes. They are not intended to reduce ecological impact (even though this might in some cases be an unintended outcome), and they are certainly not intended to reduce inequality and improve well-being – indeed, they do the opposite.

(2) Degrowth has a discriminating approach to reducing economic activity. It seeks to scale down ecologically destructive and socially less necessary production (i.e. the production of SUVs, arms, beef, private transportation, advertising and planned obsolescence), while expanding socially important sectors like healthcare, education, care and conviviality. Recessions, by contrast, do not discriminate so wisely. Indeed, they quite often destroy socially important sectors while empowering socially less necessary sectors. In the present COVID crisis, for instance, schools, recreational facilities and public transportation are negatively affected, while Amazon is expanding and stocks are rallying.

(3) Degrowth introduces policies to prevent unemployment, and indeed even to *improve* employment, such as by shortening the working week, introducing a job guarantee with a living wage, and rolling out retraining programmes to shift people out of sunset sectors. Degrowth is explicitly focused on maintaining and improving people's livelihoods despite a reduction in aggregate economic activity. Recessions, by contrast, result in mass unemployment and everyday people suffer loss of livelihood.

(4) Degrowth seeks to reduce inequality and share national and global income more fairly, such as with progressive taxation and living wage policies. Recessions, by contrast, tend to make inequality worse. Again, the COVID crisis presents an example of this, where the response packages (QE, corporate bailouts, etc.) have made the rich richer (specifically to the benefit of asset owners), and billionaires have added billions to their wealth, while virtually everybody else has lost, with the poorest 50% of humanity losing $4.4 billion per day (Sumner et al., 2020).

(5) Degrowth seeks to expand universal public goods and services, such as health, education, transportation and housing, in order to decommodify the foundational goods that people need in order to lead flourishing lives. Recessions, by contrast, generally entail austerity measures that cut spending on public services.

(6) Degrowth is part of a plan to achieve a rapid transition to renewable energy, restore soils and biodiversity, and reverse ecological breakdown. During recessions, by contrast, governments typically abandon such objectives in order to instead focus everything on getting growth going again, whatever the ecological cost might be.

We have different words for recession and degrowth because they are different things. Recessions happen when growth-dependent economies stop growing: it is a disaster that ruins people's lives and exacerbates injustices. Degrowth calls for a different kind of economy altogether: an economy that does not require growth in the first place, and which can deliver justice and well-being even while throughput declines.

Degrowth and the global South

Some people worry that proponents of degrowth want to see degrowth universally applied, in all countries. This would be problematic, because clearly many poor countries in fact need to increase resource and energy use in order to meet human needs. In reality, proponents of degrowth are clear that it is specifically high-income countries that need to degrow (or, more specifically, countries that exceed per capita fair-shares of planetary boundaries by a significant margin; see Hickel, 2019), not the rest of the world. Again, because degrowth is focused on reducing excess resource and energy use, it does not apply to economies that are not characterized by excess resource and energy use.

This brings us to an important implication of degrowth policy. The vast majority of ecological breakdown is being driven by excess consumption in the global North, and yet has consequences that disproportionately damage the South. We can see this in terms of both emissions and material extraction. (1) The North is responsible for 92% of global CO2 emissions in excess of the safe planetary boundary (Hickel, 2020a), and yet the South suffers the vast majority of climate change-related damages (in terms of both monetary costs as well as loss of life). (2) High-income countries rely on a large *net* appropriation of resources from the rest of the world (equivalent to 50% of their total consumption). In other words, resource consumption in the North has an ecological impact that registers largely in the South (Dorninger et al., 2020).

In terms of both emissions and resource use, then, excess consumption in the North relies on patterns of colonization: the appropriation of the South's fair share of atmospheric commons, and the plunder of Southern ecosystems. From this perspective, degrowth in the North represents a process of decolonization in the South, to the extent that it releases communities in the South from the pressures of atmospheric colonization and material extractivism.

Still, some worry that degrowth in the North might have a negative impact on economies in the South. After all, many global South economies rely heavily on exports of raw materials and light manufactures to the North. If Northern demand declines, where will they get their revenues? This might seem like a reasonable question on the face of it, but it rests on a problematic logic, namely, that excess consumption in the North must continue to rise, even if it causes ecological breakdown that disproportionately harms the South, because it is necessary for the South's development and *is ultimately for the South's own good*. This argument echoes arguments that were regularly made under colonialism, namely, that extraction and exploitation by the colonizer is ultimately good for the colonized. For instance, Nicholas Kristof, in a *New York Times* column titled 'Three cheers for sweatshops' has argued that sweatshops are the best way to get people out of poverty, so we need more of them: if we care about the poor, we should not boycott sweatshop products but rather consume more of them.

The fallacy in this argument shouldn't need to be pointed out. Obviously, the best way to reduce poverty isn't more exploitation, but more economic justice: the South should receive fair prices for the labour and resources they render to the global economy. No one would ever suggest that an American company paying American workers $2 a day is a good way to reduce poverty in America; we would insist that reducing poverty requires paying a living wage. But for some reason this logic is not applied to workers in the South, likely because it would reduce the rate of surplus accumulation among Northern companies and countries that rely on Southern labour and resources. In other words, justice for the South (fair wages for labour and fair prices for resources) would entail degrowth in the North. We should embrace this outcome. In fact, abandoning the pursuit of growth in the North would be salutary inasmuch as it would remove the constant pressure applied by Northern governments and companies to depress the costs of labour and resources in the South.

This brings us to another, related point. Degrowth in the North creates space for Southern economies to shift away from their enforced role as exporters of cheap labour and raw materials, and to focus instead on developmentalist reforms: building economies focused on sovereignty, self-sufficiency, and human well-being. This was the approach pursued by most global South governments in the immediate post-colonial decades, during the 1960s and 1970s, before the imposition of neoliberal structural adjustment from the 1980s onward (Hickel, 2018b). Structural adjustment sought to dismantle developmentalist reforms across the South in order to create new frontiers for Northern accumulation. In a degrowth scenario the pressure for this 'fix' would be ameliorated, and Southern governments would find themselves freer to pursue a more human-centered economics (Hickel, 2020b; Nirmal & Rocheleau, 2019). Here too, it becomes clear that degrowth in the North represents decolonization in the South.

Of course, the global South need not and should not wait for decolonization; they can cast off the chains themselves. Here I have in mind Samir Amin's notion of 'delinking': the refusal to submit national development policy to the imperatives of Northern capital. For instance, global South governments could organize collectively to increase the prices of their labour and resources, and could mobilize to demand fairer terms of trade and finance, and more democratic representation in global governance (as they did with the New International Economic Order in the early 1970s). These ideas are today represented in the discourse of post-development. In addition to rejecting the tenets of neoliberal globalization, post-development thought also rejects the notion (introduced by colonizers and international financial institutions) that GDP growth should be pursued for its own sake, preferring instead a focus on human well-being (Escobar, 2015; Kothari et al., 2019).

Either way, decolonization in the South along these lines would likely cause degrowth in the North. This is true in a very concrete sense. Right now, high-income nations maintain high levels of income and consumption through an ongoing process of net appropriation (of land, labour, resources and energy) from the South, through unequal exchange: in other words, they seek to depress the prices of labour and resources to below the global average price (Dorninger et al., 2020). This is a continuation of the basic tenets of the colonial relationship, although (in most cases) without the occupation. Ending this exploitative relationship would mean either ending the pattern of net appropriation *or* ending unequal exchange, both of which would likely result in a reduction in the rate of surplus accumulation by economic elites, and a reduction in the growth driven by this accumulation in the North, but to the benefit of communities and ecologies in the global South.

Disclosure statement

No potential conflict of interest was reported by the author(s).

References

Dorninger, C., Hornborg, A., Abson, D. J., von Wehrden, H., Schaffartzik, A., Giljum, S., Engler, J. O., Feller, R. L., Hubacek, K., & Wieland, H. (2020). Global patterns of ecologically unequal exchange: Implications for sustainability in the 21st century. *Ecological Economics*.
Escobar, A. (2015). Degrowth, postdevelopment, and transitions: A preliminary conversation. *Sustainability Science*, *10*(3), 451–462. https://doi.org/10.1007/s11625-015-0297-5

Grubler, A., Wilson, C., Bento, N., Boza-Kiss, B., Krey, V., McCollum, D. L., Rao, N. D., Riahi, K., Rogelj, J., De Stercke, S., Cullen, J., Frank, S., Fricko, O., Guo, F., Gidden, M., Havlík, P., Huppmann, D., Kiesewetter, G., Rafaj, P., … Valin, H. (2018). A low energy demand scenario for meeting the 1.5C target and sustainable development goals without negative emissions technologies. *Nature Energy*, *3*(6), 515–527. https://doi.org/10.1038/s41560-018-0172-6

Hickel, J. (2018a, December 6). The Nobel Prize for climate catastrophe. *Foreign Policy*.

Hickel, J. (2018b). *The divide: A brief guide to global inequality and its solutions*. Penguin Random House.

Hickel, J. (2019). Is it possible to achieve a good life for all within planetary boundaries? *Third World Quarterly*, *40*(1), 18–35. https://doi.org/10.1080/01436597.2018.1535895

Hickel, J. (2020a). Quantifying national responsibility for climate breakdown: An equality-based attribution approach to carbon dioxide emissions in excess of planetary boundaries. *Lancet Planetary Health*, Forthcoming.

Hickel, J. (2020b). *Less is more: How degrowth will save the world*. Penguin Random House.

Hickel, J., & Kallis, G. (2020). Is green growth possible? *New Political Economy*, *25*(4), 469–486. https://doi.org/10.1080/13563467.2019.1598964

IPCC. (2018). *Global warming of 1.5°c – summary for policymakers*.

Kallis, G. (2018). *Degrowth*. Agenda Publishing.

Kothari, A., Salleh, A., Escobar, A., Demaria, F., & Acosta, A. (Eds.). (2019). *Pluriverse: A post-development dictionary*. Tulika Books and Authorsupfront.

Latouche, S. (2009). *Farewell to growth*. Polity.

Lenton, T., Rockstrom, J., Gaffney, O., Rahmstorf, S., Richardson, K., Steffen, W., & Schellnuber, H. (2020). Climate tipping points too risky to bet against. *Nature*, *575*(7784), 592–595. https://doi.org/10.1038/d41586-019-03595-0

Moore, J. (2015). *Capitalism in the web of life*. Verso.

Nirmal, P., & Rocheleau, D. (2019). Decolonizing degrowth in the post-development convergence: Questions, experiences, and proposals from two indigenous territories. *Environment and Planning E: Nature and Space*, *2*(3), 465–492. https://doi.org/10.1177/2514848618819478

Raftery, A. E., Zimmer, A., Frierson, D. M. W., Startz, R., & Liu, P. (2017). Less than 2 °C warming by 2100 unlikely. *Nature Climate Change*, *7*(9), 637–641. https://doi.org/10.1038/nclimate3352

Rockström, J., Steffen, W., Noone, K., Persson, Å., Chapin, F. S. I., Lambin, E., Lenton, T. M., Scheffer, M., Folke, C., Schellnhuber, H. J., Nykvist, B., de Wit, C. A., Hughes, T., van der Leeuw, S., Rodhe, H., Sörlin, S., Snyder, P. K., Costanza, R., Svedin, U., … Foley, J. (2009). Planetary boundaries: Exploring the safe operating space for humanity. *Ecology and Society*, *14*(2), Article 32. https://doi.org/10.5751/ES-03180-140232

Schroder, E., & Storm, S. (2020). Economic growth and carbon emissions: The road to 'hothouse earth' is paved with good intentions. *International Journal of Political Economy*, *49*(2), 153–173. https://doi.org/10.1080/08911916.2020.1778866

Steffen, W., Richardson, K., Rockstrom, J., Cornell, S. E., Fetzer, I., Bennett, E. M., Biggs, R., Carpenter, S. R., de Vries, W., de Wit, C. A., Folke, C., Gerten, D., Heinke, J., Mace, G. M., Persson, L. M., Ramanathan, V., Reyers, B., & Sorlin, S. (2015). Planetary boundaries: Guiding human development on a changing planet. *Science*, *347*(6223), 736–46. https://doi.org/10.1126/science.1259855

Steffen, W., Rockström, J., Richardson, K., Lenton, T. M., Folke, C., Liverman, D., Summerhayes, C. P., Barnosky, A. D., Cornell, S. E., Crucifix, M., Donges, J. F., Fetzer, I., Lade, S. J., Scheffer, M., Winkelmann, R., & Schellnhuber, H. J. (2018). Trajectories of the earth system in the anthropocene. *Proceedings of the National Academy of Sciences*, *115*(33), 8252–8259. https://doi.org/10.1073/pnas.1810141115

Sumner, A., Ortiz-Juarez, E., & Hoy, C. (2020). *Precarity and the pandemic: COVID-19 and poverty incidence, intensity, and severity in developing countries* (WIDER Working Paper 2020/77).

Vadén, T., Lähde, V., Majava, A., Järvensivu, P., Toivanen, T., & Eronen, J. T. (2020). Raising the bar: On the type, size and timeline of a 'successful' decoupling. *Environmental Politics*, 1–15. Online. https://doi.org/10.1080/09644016.2020.1783951

Vadén, T., Lähde, V., Majava, A., Järvensivu, P., Toivanen, T., Hakala, E., & Eronen, J. T. (2020). Decoupling for ecological sustainability: A categorization and review of research literature. *Environmental Science and Policy*, *112*, 236–244. https://doi.org/10.1016/j.envsci.2020.06.016

What does Degrowth mean? Some comments on Jason Hickel's 'A few points of clarification'

Ted Trainer

ABSTRACT

In a recent edition of *Globalizations* Jason Hickel made three main points towards clarifying the discussion of Degrowth. His contribution reinforced some important elements in the Degrowth claim, especially the fact that it is in no way to be identified with recession, and that there is a vast amount of evidence against the belief that growth of GDP can be decoupled from growth in resource consumption. However, I want to argue against his perspective on distinguishing between Degrowth and reducing the GDP, his conception of Degrowth, and whether the Third World should be exempt from it.

Whilst it is important to acknowledge Jason has written many other works of greater detail and nuance (e.g. Hickel, 2020) some aspects of his recent essay in *Globalizations* are challengeable. It conveys the impression that reduced GDP might not be necessary, it implicitly defines Degrowth in terms of a particular pattern of elements when others are conceivable, and it reinforces the impression that the global South can persist with the conventional basic development paradigm geared to prospering within the global economy. The main point is I want to emphasize that Degrowth is a broad and diverse movement, including The Simpler Way perspective which is significantly different in its goals and means from the conception of Degrowth indicated in Jason's essay.

Degrowth and GDP

I think Jason's discussion of the relation between Degrowth and GDP is not satisfactory. He says

> Degrowth is a planned reduction of energy and resource throughput designed to bring the economy back into balance with the living world in a way that reduces inequality and improves human well-being … It is important to clarify that degrowth is not about reducing GDP, but rather about reducing throughput.

In my view, it is unnecessary and unwise to mention this distinction. It leaves open the door to belief that growth of GDP is conceivable or possible while resource and ecological impact is reduced. This impression is also given soon after when Jason says ' … reducing throughput is likely to lead to a reduction in the rate of GDP growth, or even a decline in GDP itself'. The word 'likely' is quite inappropriate because many detailed studies, one of the most impressive being by Hickel and

Kallis (2019), rule out any realistic possibility that there can be growth in GDP without growth in resource consumption.

The limits to growth literature has long since made it clear that the extent to which we have exceeded the limits means that enormous reductions in GDP must be made if sustainability is to be achieved. Simple arithmetic applied to a few basic factors, such as rich world per capita consumption rates, global population expectation, and economic growth assumptions leaves no doubt about this (TSW, 2018a). If all the world's expected 2050 population were to have the 'living standards' rich countries would have then given 2–3% economic growth, total global economic output would be 10–20 times the present volume. Yet the WWF (2018) estimates that right now we would need 1.7 planet earths to derive present consumption rates sustainably. Given the situation re the 'decoupling' faith noted above, this means that the top priority of Degrowth advocates should be to emphasize that we have to face up to something like 90% reductions in rich world per capita GDP. It is therefore not appropriate to say that ' … degrowth is not about reducing GDP'.

The Degrowth literature has not sufficiently emphasized this magnitude point. When it is focused on it leads to dramatically radical shifts in thinking about solutions. If only relatively minor reductions are thought to be required then only relatively minor adjustments in the present industrial-affluent-consumer-capitalist society might suffice. But when it is realized that the reductions must be very great it becomes evident that they cannot be achieved unless there is transition to very different systems and to a very different culture.

A particular version of Degrowth is being selected; it is not a discussion of the general or generic Degrowth position

My second concern is that Jason is assuming a particular conception of Degrowth, one among other possibilities, and thus is not discussing Degrowth-in-general. For instance, he says,

> Degrowth introduces policies to prevent unemployment, and indeed even to improve employment, such as by shortening the working week, introducing a job guarantee with a living wage, and rolling out retraining programmes to shift people out of sunset sectors. … Degrowth seeks … to share national and global income more fairly, such as with progressive taxation and living wage policies. (… and …) to expand universal public goods and services, such as … transportation … .

Many discussions of Degrowth take it to involve these kinds of policies. The issue is not their desirability; it is that there are members of the Degrowth camp who do not advocate them and who conceive Degrowth quite differently. Some regard these kinds of goals as taking for granted a basic conception of society which they do not hold. The Campesinos and Zapatistas for instance are for a kind of society to which some of these concepts are not relevant, such as equalizing national income, implementing progressive taxation and expanding public transport. Advocates of The Simpler Way (Alexander & Rutherford, 2020) argue that the foregoing analysis of the magnitude of the limits to growth means that there must be Degrowth to a form of society in which there is no such thing as unemployment, many goods and services are 'free', 'work' might be said not to exist, taxes are in general not paid in money, the term 'working week' is rather meaningless and the national income is irrelevant and ignored rather than shared more equitably. Thus Jason's account in this essay of what Degrowth is for specifies a form of society (or elements within one) that various Degrowth theorists and practitioners do not endorse. (In other works he regards the Zapatistas as being within the Degrowth camp.)

In other words, the kinds of elements Jason, and many within the movement, list define specific/particular/selected/preferred Degrowth paths or systems or visions which some but not all members of the Degrowth movement are for. It is not appropriate for any one of these visions to be stated or treated as if it is what the Degrowth movement is for. It is not desirable for the movement to become identified with a particular form of society, other than in the general sense of a society with a reduced GDP. This leaves open the possibility of debating which forms are to be preferred. The significance of this mistake becomes even clearer when the concept of 'development' is considered.

The conception of third world 'development' assumed

That Jason is arguing from a particular version among many possibilities within the Degrowth category is most evident in his comments on 'development'. In addition, it is a seriously mistaken prescription. He says,

> Some people worry that proponents of degrowth want to see degrowth universally applied, in all countries. This would be problematic, because clearly many poor countries in fact need to increase resource and energy use in order to meet human needs. In reality, proponents of degrowth are clear that it is specifically high-income countries that need to degrow … not the rest of the world. Again, because degrowth is focused on reducing excess resource and energy use, it does not apply to economies that are not characterized by excess resource and energy use.

This statement implies that Third World countries do not need to depart from the basic development path they are on. That path is the resource squandering road to affluent lifestyles and complex energy-intensive debt-fuelled systems, by prospering through trading within a globalized trade-intensive economy. Normal, conventional development goals and mechanisms are not questioned. (… although in other places Jason's writings rightly reject them.) From the perspective of The Simpler Way (Alexander & Rutherford, 2020) and others that path is at the heart of the planetary catastrophe and sensible, appropriate, sustainable and just development contradicts all its elements (TSW: http://thesimplerway.info/THIRDWORLDDEVLong.html).

It is necessary to briefly indicate how different this version is from others under the general Degrowth umbrella. The Simpler Way case is that appropriate development for rich and poor countries must involve embracing as its goal lifestyles and systems that are very frugal and materially simple and which reverse many now dominant assumptions and practices. Poor countries as well as rich countries must abandon affluence, centralization, urbanization, large scale and globalization, and must adopt as the basic social form the small scale highly self-sufficient, self-governing and cooperative community. Economies must be needs-driven not profit-driven but most production could be via privately owned small firms and farms. Much production and community maintenance would be via cooperatives, commons, gift economies and spontaneous citizen action, thereby greatly reducing the need for money. Few functions would need to be left for central organization, and these would be under the control of the local communities via classical anarchist processes (e.g. federations, delegates and participatory democracy). The argument is that these elements are in general not negotiable; a sustainable and just society in a world of intense resource scarcity cannot be attained without them. Only arrangements of this kind can get the per capita consumption rates of resources right down (Trainer, Malik and Lenzen, 2019).

Because such structures and practices enable extremely low resource demand it is not the case that as Jason says ' … many poor countries in fact need to increase resource and energy use in order to meet human needs'. Most if not all of the poorest countries are presently using far more resources, capital and human energy to do far more producing and to generate far higher GDP than would be necessary to give all their people a high quality of life. The trouble is that the conventional development path gears most of these to the enrichment of foreign corporations and rich world shoppers. At Dancing Rabbit ecovillage in Missouri (Lockyer, 2017) resource consumption per capita is 5–10% of various US national averages, and the quality of life is higher. At Pigface point (TSW, 2018b) the power consumption is 0.6% of the Australian household average. Such figures are due to the adoption of goals and systems which totally reject the conventional development path.

The Zapatistas and Campesinos and many alternative initiatives around the world, such as the building of Eco-villages in Senegal (St Onge, 2015), provide other examples of development which contradicts the conventional vision and which do not require increased consumption of energy, resources, loans, or consumer goods. Simpler Way development theory elaborates on the practices which might enable the poorest countries to achieve quite satisfactory conditions with negligible dollar, ecological and non-renewable resource costs, by turning away from conventional theory and practice (Alexander & Rutherford, 2020, pp. 128–156).

Jason goes on to deal with the argument that if the rich ceased its colonial extraction of wealth from the Third World, living conditions there would crash. He says, 'Obviously, the best way to reduce poverty isn't more exploitation, but more economic justice: the South should receive fair prices for the labour and resources they render to the global economy.' ' … justice for the South … ' means … ' fair wages for labour and fair prices for resources'. This reveals a merely redistributivist conception of justice, i.e. more even sharing of the benefits of extractivism. The same assumption is implicit in the statement, ' … global South governments could organize collectively to increase the prices of their labour and resources, and could mobilize to demand fairer terms of trade and finance, and more democratic representation in global governance'. This is basically only tweeking the existing system.

The Simpler Way alternative assumes a radically different system, centred on enabling poor people to control the land, water, forests, and fisheries around them to collectively provide for themselves the basic goods and services they need and giving little or no attention to banks, foreign investment, corporations, exporting or the GDP.

The point is again that Jason's statements represent a particular view of an alternative development path, and there are others and some of them strongly reject the view he has put. Again, care should be taken to make clear that such proposals are from one of the many possible perspectives to be found within the Degrowth camp, and should not be taken to be what Degrowth in general stands for.

Concluding note

These comments are intended to be constructive in clarifying and strengthening the Degrowth notion, hopefully towards a theoretically unified critique of the dominant assumption that some form of 'business as usual' is viable (e.g. a 'Green New Deal'.) They attempt to head off potentially divisive disputes over whether various positions are really instances of Degrowth, by arguing for a generic conception focused on GNP and inclusive of a wide variety of approaches.

Disclosure statement

No potential conflict of interest was reported by the author(s).

References

Alexander, S., & Rutherford, J. (Eds.). (2020). *The simpler way: The collected writings of Ted Trainer.* Simplicity Institute.

Hickel, J. (2020). *Less is more: How degrowth will save the world.* Penguin Random House.

Hickel, J., & Kallis, G. (2019). Is green growth possible? *New Political Economy.* https://doi.org/10.1080/13563467.2019.1598964

Lockyer, J. (2017). Community, commons, and de-growth at dancing rabbit eco-village. *Political Ecology,* 24, 519–542.

St Onge, E. (2015, June 17). Senegal transforming 14,000 villages into ecovillages! https://www.collective-evolution.com/2015/06/17/senegal-transforming-14000-villages-into-ecovillages/

Trainer, T., Malik, A., & Lenzen, M. (2019). A comparison between the monetary, resource and energy costs of the conventional industrial supply path and the "simpler way" path for the supply of eggs. *BioPhysical Economics and Resource Quality,* September.

TSW. (2018a). *The limits to growth case.* http://thesimplerway.info/LIMITS.htm

TSW. (2018b). *Pigface point: An alternative lifestyle educational site.* http://thesimplerway.info/PigfacePointOutline.html

World Wildlife Fund. (2018). *Living planet report: Aiming higher.* World Wildlife Fund and London Zoological Society. https://wwf.panda.org/knowledge_hub/all_publications/living_planet_report_2018/

Economics and the climate catastrophe

James K. Galbraith

ABSTRACT

The acute awareness of scarcity, land rent, fixed costs and environmental limits that characterized the classical period was largely forgotten during the hey-day of neoclassical growth economics. Awareness has now returned, and many scientists and engineers are devoting themselves to these issues. But a revolution in economic thought, bringing economics into line with biophysical principles and the challenges of climate change, consistent with the laws of thermodynamics, has not occurred. The paper closes with examples of the application of basic principles to the policy choices that lie ahead, and some suggestions for the future of economics.

In the conditions of 18th and 19th century Britain that gave rise to classical political economy, land was the portmanteau concept standing in for resources of all kinds, in fixed supply and giving rise to scarcity, to wealth, and therefore to power. The productivity of the soil was limited, hence also the food supply, the real wage and ultimately the working population. This was the Malthusian demon. To it David Ricardo (1952) added a clear understanding that as the productivity of the soil was variable, rent could be charged on the differential between the parcel in question and the least productive land in use. In this way, by controlling the fixed, scarce and immutable factor, landlords would appropriate the totality of the surplus, beyond a subsistence wage and a competitive rate of profit.

New and productive lands, acquired by conquest, settlement and displacement, often stocked with slaves, could and did banish the Malthusian demon and break the Ricardian spell. In northern North America, farming began on bad land – for example on New England hilltops where trees were relatively sparse and could be cleared in a season. The farms then moved downhill and later on westward, to better, flatter, richer land. As Henry Carey (1852) recognized, farming had increasing returns, contrary to the Malthusian view. This fostered rising real wages, faster population growth and immigration, limiting the land monopoly in an emergent culture of limitless bounty, which made possible the rapid growth of industry behind walls of protection and with the support of public works, underpinned by the surplus of the farms. In the twentieth century the mechanization of farming, the advent of oil and of nitrogen-based fertilizers extended and multiplied the bounty. Landlordism in America became – predominantly – an urban and peri-urban phenomenon, a cause of unjust enrichment and equally unjust poverty. But it was not a serious constraint on food, real wages or population growth.

In this 'happy' setting but evidently unaware of it, neoclassical economics was born and flourished from the late nineteenth century onward. Curiously, and perhaps not by accident, its sponsors were anxious to banish the land question in all of its forms, and so the classical triad of land, labour and capital was reduced to labour and capital alone. Contrary to Karl Marx, labour and capital were supposed to exist in cooperation, not conflict, each rewarded in line with its contribution, as determined in a competitive market. The facts of increasing returns in both agriculture and industry and the experience of protection were ignored. The issue of resources, not being urgent, simply disappeared. That of the disposal of waste, in the seemingly vast expanses of the Americas, did not arise as an issue until the 1960s, when it was forced into economics by outsiders. That this way of thinking would suit an age of rapacity and pollution is no accident and no surprise.

Neoclassical economics also neglected another major feature of its time. It was the age of empires. The empire was internal in the case of America, but for Britain, France, Holland, Belgium and Germany the empires were all over Africa and Asia. Resources could be extracted from distant and subjugated peoples, excluded from the calculus of pleasures and pain and generally ignored (Carter, 2020) unless they made trouble, as they sometimes did . But then in the twentieth century, wars bankrupted the empires, changing technology made them militarily untenable, changing ideology made them unattractive, and the potential for revolution necessitated an adjustment if not a full-scale change of ideas. The adjustment took the form of development economics, a fraught postwar endeavour which, casting for expedients, advanced the idea that all countries could follow the developmental path of the original – imperial – powers, especially the UK and the US (Rostow, 1960). Where the resources would come from, the development economists did not say. The Green Revolution came along shortly after, apparently promising abundant nourishment to the rapidly growing populations of the Third World.

The Club of Rome (Meadows et al., 1972) attempted to resurrect the Malthus-Ricardo (and, to give fair credit, William Stanley Jevons) tradition, by pointing out the incompatibility of exponential growth and finite resources. Theirs was a simple argument bolstered by what was, for the time, an elaborate computer simulation. Essentially, the Club held that when a force, however strong, hits an immovable object, something must give way. The simulation projected a crisis in the supply of critical resources from the end of the century onward, with a resulting sharp reduction in global population.

Neoclassical economists reacted with peremptory derision, brushing the limits aside on two grounds. The first was that *known* resource reserves are always limited by the resources invested in exploration; thus when more is searched for, more is found. The second was that substitution and technical change had always yielded a steady progression of superior, cheaper resources, from wood to coal to oil to gas, and on (it was then thought) to nuclear power, and there was no reason to suppose that this pattern would be broken. Both of these were perfectly valid statements about the past and perfectly worthless guides to the indefinite future.

Through all of this, the assumption of free disposal – that the physical environment was a free good with unlimited capacity – remained. It remained until the blight and poison of the high industrial manifested in London and Los Angeles smogs, disappearing birds, flaming rivers and blight became intolerable as a political matter. The economists then modified free disposal by introducing the concepts of externalities and social costs, and thus made pollution manageable, within the neoclassical framework, through taxes and regulation. This continues to be their go-to illusion. Mainstream economists appear to believe that price changes can induce substitution away from carbon-based energy, the motor of the industrial revolution for two centuries, more or less as easily as such a shift can increase the consumption of chicken, relative to beef, in the household diet. Moreover, they appear to believe that any welfare losses from the switch can be compensated by an infusion of cash.

Thus when climate change emerged as an inescapable global challenge, the economic mainstream fell into line behind two proposals. The first was cap-and-trade, a system for marketizing greenhouse gases by assigning a price to their release into the atmosphere, along lines pioneered by congestion-pricing on highways and in the release of certain pollutants into particular air and water basins. The difficulty is that these markets could be, and were, undermined by evasion, poor accounting and the effective impossibility of indirect control over the decisions of profit-seeking enterprises to release greenhouse gases. Eventually those efforts collapsed, to be replaced by the simpler mechanism of a 'carbon tax', in some formulations compensated by cash compensation.

The fallacy is transparent. As a political matter it was exposed by the Yellow Vests (*Gilets Jaunes*) in France, whose fixed investments in diesel cars and farm equipment were abruptly devalued, along with their real incomes, by a supposedly conservationist tax on diesel fuel. One cannot easily acquire the alternative machinery, which is not in perfectly elastic supply, and in any event not at the price that the taxed machinery will fetch on the second-hand lot. Moreover, people care about wealth. The discovery that their accumulations, carefully invested in productive assets, have become worthless is a deeply unpleasant experience, and is not readily compensated by a small boost to current income.

Then there is a deeper problem. There are substitutes for specific grains, for lentils of one colour or another, for the protein of different animals and seafood. But in reality there is no substitute for energy. Energy is the resource required to make everything work. And while carbon-based energy is a subset of all types of energy, the substitutes for carbon-based energy are few, and expensive. Basically there is hydro-electric, wind and tidal power, limited by nature, and nuclear power, limited by safety concerns, as well as solar collection, limited by scale and cost. And all of them, using cement and metals, require energy to produce – energy that comes, mainly, from carbon-based fuels.

To introduce any new technology for the form of energy, even where they are available and in principle viable, is costly. It involves making fixed investments in advance, initially in research and development, later in engineering, and finally in physical equipment for production and distribution. Economists suppose that this can be induced by changing relative prices. But in the real world, price signals are weak, income effects from price changes are strong, and the wealth effects that follow when prices change are political dynamite. Compensated price signals applied to climate change – shift the prices and then send a check to cover the income loss, are a particular economist's fantasy. They suppose that myriad decentralized personal incentives can achieve what is actually only possible – if at all – by concentrated planned action and social mobilization – or in the alternative, by civilizational collapse.

While it obliterated land, neoclassical economics also largely erased the concept of fixed cost, treating as the 'ideal case' the model of perfect competition in the long run. In that ideal case, fixed costs do not figure, revenues just cover variable costs, and economic profits are therefore zero. But this is not compatible with actual life in the real world. All economic activity – indeed all activity – aims to generate a surplus, and for this some form of fixed investment, made in advance, is a prerequisite and a necessity. Even wild beasts, who build nests, or dig burrows, invest in order to live, grow and reproduce. Even the cave man, who raised his family in a natural shelter, had to find the shelter, and had to be prepared to defend it.

It is a further fact of nature that larger investments, more costly, extract resources more efficiently. That is why they are worth making. They also emit more waste heat and (if getting heat from combustion) more carbon dioxide. Hence they do more damage to the biosphere, and are more fragile, more ultimately doomed to failure and extinction. Hunter-gatherers and cave-dwellers lasted for hundreds of thousands of years. Major civilizations, from Rome and before to the Maya and Triple Alliance, rise and fall and rarely last more than a millennium.

Coming-to-grips with the role of resources and with the trade-off between efficiency and resilience is a task beyond the reach of neoclassical economics. This is so, notwithstanding the occasional persistence of cost curves, imperfect competition and models of natural monopoly in mainstream texts. Those are drawn from pre-neoclassical, Keynesian or institutionalist thinking, and are included in the texts for practical reasons, not because they flow from the first principles that dominate the syllabus and frame the ideal types.

What is necessary instead is an approach explicitly consistent with the biophysical realities (Galbraith & Chen, 2012a, 2012b). These are specified under the second law of thermodynamics, the entropy law from which there is no escape and to which everything must conform (Georgescu-Roegen, 1971). And further, economics must be adjusted to the peculiar circumstances of the planet Earth, surrounded as it is by a fragile sheath of light gases, one of which has the annoying habit of trapping heat. The ability to withstand the heating of the atmosphere imposes a global limit, against which there is no appeal. An economics oriented toward the long term survival of human society in tolerable form must be adjusted to the reality of that limit, in which the terminal constraint is not the availability of carbon in the ground, but the necessity to restrict the concentrations in the air.

What do the basic principles of thermodynamics tell us about resource use under the constraint of a global carbon budget?

First, thermodynamics tells us that to decarbonize energy production *at present levels of energy use* will require massive *further* investments and a consequent *increase* in the consumption of carbon reserves and emission of greenhouse gases. The infrastructure to replace carbon-based energy must be built – if it can be built – which is another physical and engineering question. A significant share of the remaining accessible carbon reserves on the planet will be burned, up front, to produce the non-carbon means of production for energy. The problem cannot be bootstrapped away. There is no way to produce renewable energy without first building the equipment from existing, mostly non-renewable resources. This means that major additional human effort must go into the production of the means of clean energy production, which is itself an activity with no early pay-off in terms of private consumption or environmental quality. So to get from here to there requires *either* major increases in greenhouse gas emissions in the near term, or major reductions in other uses.

The only other way to decarbonize is to effect a major reduction in emissions-generating activity. That is, to reduce the production and consumption of energy-using goods and services. There are three ways to do this: to reduce investment, to reduce consumption, and to reduce energy waste. Investment is the production of goods to expand future production and consumption; consumption is of course production for current use, from the existing capital stock. Waste is superfluous activity, that can in the limit be foregone.

Reducing investment is ongoing in the wake of the covid-19 pandemic. Many things, such as offices and shops and aircraft, previously planned-for or anticipated, will not be produced in the future because there is no demand for them. However, to reduce current investment generally means to have less future consumption. If consumption is to be maintained without significant impairment, then the existing capital assets must be maintained, their lives prolonged, so that they can be replaced at a slower pace than would otherwise be the case. Indeed the existing capital goods become more valuable as the prospects for replacing them diminish. So the gain is not entirely on a net basis.

Reducing current consumption is an unpleasant prospect, sure to provoke two questions: How much? And whose? Moreover consumption by one person or group is income and employment to another. It is possible – as the pandemic is also teaching – to reduce consumption in wealthy societies and to do so with relatively small loss of psychic well-being, so long as basic needs are met. A great many leisure-time activities that are energy-intensive – recreational travel is a major one – are simply superfluous in the pandemic and will go away on their own. But the problem of ensuring that basic needs are met is one that cannot be solved at the same time through reliance on the market.

Reducing waste is another area of promise, and perhaps the most important to target for early gains. Much energy use is incidental to functions that were never designed with an energy budget in mind, and simply evolved in an age of cheap suburban land and cheap oil. Commuting by car is a major example. Though done in private cars, at private expense, it is an adjunct to work, and one that goes away as white-collar work relocates to the home. Similarly the heating, cooling and upkeep of commercial office space becomes less necessary as fewer people use the space. Shopping has been energy-intensive, but becomes less so as physical locations are replaced by centralized warehouses and deliveries. A reduction of daily commuting through work-at-home policies, strategic abandonment of unneeded office space, reorganization of supply chains, and above all a reduction in superfluous activities are all part of a path toward sustainable greenhouse gas emissions.

Thus there are two paths: a massive expansion in new energy, and a massive conservation of existing reserves, designed to be as tolerable as possible. Those are the only two potentially feasible paths. The first may or may not be operable within a tolerable greenhouse gas and climate budget. If the carbon needed to produce a green transition is more than the planet and the biosphere can withstand, that game is lost from the beginning. The second route is more promising, especially in those societies, especially the United States, whose economies are built on flamboyant activities and the superfluous use of energy, as well as gross inefficiencies built into the system at a time when resources were cheap and the disposal of waste was not a concern. The Covid-19 pandemic has made it clear that there is scope for progress along these lines.

Whether there is *enough* scope, is a matter for physicists, chemists, geoscientists and engineers. But the economists? It is difficult to see how a discipline whose ideal types are perfect competition, full efficiency and high levels of substitutability can deal with a problem whose chief features are large scale, wastage, and technological lock-in. Indeed, mainstream economics is, and always has been, an active obstacle to clear thought and effective action on resources, the environment, and climate change. Since reform of an ideological project is an effective impossibility, perhaps the best thing is for university administrators and foundations to move the resources that presently sustain economics departments, over time, into alternative organizational forms, such as departments of resource and environmental science. In this way they may once again create the intellectual climate necessary for ideas to become, once again, relevant to effective action.

Disclosure statement

No potential conflict of interest was reported by the author(s).

References

Carey, H. (1852). *The harmony of interests: Agricultural, manufacturing, and commercial.* M. Finch.

Carter, Z. D. (2020). *The price of peace: Money, democracy and the life of John Maynard Keynes*. Random House.

Galbraith, J., & Chen, J. (2012a). A common framework for evolutionary and institutional economics. *Journal of Economic Issues*, 46(2), 419–428. https://doi.org/10.2753/JEI0021-3624460217

Galbraith, J., & Chen, J. (2012b). Austerity and fraud under different structures of technology and resource abundance. *Cambridge Journal of Economics*, 36(1), 335–343. https://doi.org/10.1093/cje/ber027

Georgescu-Roegen, N. (1971). *The entropy law and economic process*. Harvard University Press.

Meadows, D. H., Meadows, D. L., Randers, J., & Behrens III, W. W. (1972). *Limits to growth*. Club of Rome.

Ricardo, D. (1952). *Principles of political economy and taxation*. P. Sraffa (Ed.). Cambridge University Press.

Rostow, W. W. (1960). *The stages of economic growth: A non-communist manifesto*. Cambridge University Press.

Apologists for growth: passive revolutionaries in a passive revolution

Clive L. Spash

ABSTRACT

Popular authors and international organizations recommend transformation to a 'new economy'. However, this is misleadingly interpreted as radical or revolutionary. Two problematic positions are revealed: being pro-growth while seeking to change the current form of capitalism (e.g. Ha-Joon Chang), and being anti-growth on environmental grounds but promoting growth for poverty alleviation and due to agnosticism about growth (e.g. Tim Jackson and Kate Raworth). Both positions involve contradictions and an evident failure to address, or perhaps even a denial of, the actual operations of capital accumulating economies. Thus, economists ostensibly critical of capitalism turn out to be apologists for growth who conform to the requirements of a top-down passive revolution, that leaves power relations undisturbed and the economic structure fundamentally unchanged. The growth economy is shown to include technocracy, productivism associated with eugenics, inequity disguised as meritocracy, competition concealing militarism and imperialism, imposition of development as progress, and financialization and commodification of Nature.

1. Introduction

A range of arguments have long been made about the problems with the growth economy. Since the rise of the environmental movement in the 1960s, the economic growth paradigm has been subject to social and ecological criticism which bore fruit in numerous books in the 1970s (Daly, 1973; Easterlin, 1974; Hirsch, 1977; Meadows et al., 1972; Mishan, 1969; Schumacher, 1973; Scitovsky, 1976). A key theoretician of how the ecological economic system operates was Georgescu-Roegen (1975/2009). His work highlighted the role of energy and materials in the reproduction of industrial economies and how economic theory failed to take into account ecological, source and sink dependencies. He noted the frivolous use of scarce resources in a consumer society, raising ethical issues about who gets what and for what ends. The problems are social (ethical, political), ecological and economic. I will not rehearse the long standing arguments here, but note that they are the theoretical core of ecological economics (Martinez-Alier, 2013; Røpke, 2004; Spash, 1999), which has informed steady-state, degrowth and post-growth ideas. Over the last thirty years the social aspects of this theory have been increasingly recognized as in need of explicit attention with corresponding links to critical institutionalism, political ecology and political economy (see Koch & Buch-Hansen, 2020;

Spash, 2020b). The theoretical foundations of this paper are those of the emerging social-ecological economic paradigm that calls for radical transformation (Spash, 2017, 2011, 2020d).

A contrast is then to be drawn between reform and revolution, transition and transformation, lifestyle choice and systems change. Mild reformists regard revelation of the failures of the dominant economic system of capital accumulation (whether by USA 'private' or Chinese 'public' corporations, or some hybrid of public-private partnership) as suggesting the need for new organizational approaches and adjustments to institutional arrangements that maintain the basic system intact and reinforce it. The neoliberal and financialized form of corporate capitalism, that became dominant from the early 1980s, excluded the idea of alternative types of economies for social provisioning. Questioning capitalism was no longer legitimate, as exemplified by Margret Thatcher's phrase 'there is no alternative' (TINA). However, the 2008 financial crash stimulated the return of popular criticism of capitalism (especially neoliberalism), corporations, the financial system and the super rich 1%. Economic theories were also targeted as requiring pluralist rethinking (Fischer et al., 2018). A range of populist works, 'best sellers' and articles made their authors highly cited under the guise of being outside the orthodoxy, radical and alternative. For example, Cambridge University's Ha-Joon Chang, an author now cited 30,000 times (Google Scholar), first came to popular attention with his book *23 Things They Don't Tell You About Capitalism* (Chang, 2011). The reorganization of capitalism he advocates is a neo-Keynesian society with strong central government to ameliorate the socially divisive excesses of the economic system. Yet, all Keynesian approaches, in all their various forms, have failed to address the biophysical basis of the economy and so chosen to unscientifically ignore reality. Even less recognized is the type of society such pro-growth economists typically advocate, both in terms of the treatment of Nature (reduced to a resource for human ends), role of humans in society (reduced to labourer, consumer), human motivation (selfish interest, materialism), politics (nationalism, liberalism) and ethics (preference utilitarianism, hedonism).

Yet, Ha-Joon Chang is just one of many claiming capitalism can be reformed and growth maintained for 'the common good' (e.g. GCEC, 2014, 2018; Jacobs & Mazzucato, 2016; OECD, 2020; Stern et al., 2006; von der Leyen, 2019). At the World Economic Forum (WEF) in Davos 2020 the talk was of inclusive 'stakeholder capitalism', resurrecting an idea from when capitalism was in crisis during the 1930s (Denning, 2020). This is offered as the 'new' hope to counter a range of criticisms that capitalism is socially unjust, rewards an elite, dispossess the poor, supports psychopathic corporations and self-serving financiers, as well as causing ecological destruction (Bakan 2004; Bienkowski, 2013; Leonard, 1988; van Huijstee et al., 2011). Amongst the invited guest speakers at Davos 2019 and 2020 was Greta Thunberg whose emotive calls to address the 'climate emergency' have added urgency to the latest reformist 'solutions'. Her speeches have been direct and included strong anti-corporate elements (Aronoff, 2019), but remain unfocussed in terms of political content and unspecific on necessary action or what to do about the powerful organizations she is criticizing. Thus, her and others' strong direct language of a climate catastrophe/emergency/crisis can be and has been adopted and redirected by fossil fuel and corporate interests for their own purposes (Spash, 2020c, 2020a).

While only one of many environmental problems, human induced climate change has come to represent the failings of the current economic system. It is ever more present in the mind of humanity as extreme weather events become more frequent, temperature records are consistently broken year on year, ice sheets and glaciers melt, wild fires spread, and the threat of unknown catastrophic events looms larger. The 'climate emergency' has pushed transformation to the top of the political agenda, where it contests with other threats to the financial markets and stability of the world economic order, such as the Coronavirus pandemic (Spash, 2020b). The importance allocated to addressing human induced climate change has led to two reactions: denialism and reframing policy within terms that protect and enhance capitalism. The latter is the concern here. Direct attempts to supress problems of fossil fuel industrialism under a capital accumulating growth economy have come from members of the Davos elite in the guise of the Global Commission on the Economy and Climate (GCEC, 2014, 2018) and billionaire Richard Branson's B-Team and Carbon War Room that attempt to justify his Virgin corporation's aerospace and airline industrial expansion with carbon offsetting and trading. Financiers, bankers and super-rich entrepreneurs are rebranded as planetary saviours in our time of crisis.

Corporations, pro-growth governments and bureaucrats, have already adopted FridaysForFuture (FFF) and Extinction Rebellion (XR) calls for urgent action to advocate a range of environmental 'deals', such as the European Commission (EC) 'Green Deal' (European Commission, 2019), the United Nations (UN) Conference on Trade and Development (UNCTAD) 'Global Green New Deal' (UNCTAD, 2019), and the UN Environment Programme (UNEP) 'New Deal for Nature' (UNEP, 2019). Continuation of the capital accumulating economic structure remains key to these initiatives, and their aim is to organize society to fit. At the UN Framework Convention on Climate Change (UNFCCC) Conference of the Parties (COP) meeting in Madrid, EC President, Ursula von der Leyen (2019) announced the European Green Deal as

> Europe's new growth strategy. It will cut emissions while also creating jobs and improving our quality of life. For that we need investment! Investment in research, in innovation, in green technologies. [...] EUR 1 trillion of investment over the next decade. [...] This will include extending emission trading to all relevant sectors. CO_2 has to have a price.

The role of price-making markets, corporations and capitalism are not in question. Typical of all these 'deals' are claims of coordinating and organizing stakeholders, having civil society and government work with, or more accurately for, 'industry', with promises of economic growth, jobs and climate stability.

The top-down approach to diverting attention from the need for systems change is something Gramsci (1971, pp. 106–114) referred to as a 'passive revolution'. This relates to the passive integration of subordinate segments of society while keeping them powerless. The potential revolutionary or oppositional intellectuals and leaders are absorbed into the system (see also Candeias, 2011). If successful those in power remain, the basic structure of the system is unchanged, and radical and revolutionary thinkers are co-opted into powerless positions and/or support roles. What I will argue is that just such a passive revolution is evident in populist books by self proclaimed radical economists. For example, Kate Raworth's *Doughnut Economics*, shortlisted for *The Financial Times* best economics book of 2017, is entirely oriented around economic growth and criticisms of mainstream economics, but fails to take any stand against economic growth, let alone capitalism. Tim Jackson with over 22,000 (Google Scholar) citations produced *Prosperity Without Growth*, a book that has over 7,000 cites. Yet, as I will show, he also adopts a position that advocates growth as essential for 'development'.

In covering and explaining these positions I address some of the silences and absences in theorizing about economic growth in terms of its implications for social organization, how growth impacts on poverty and social inequality, what are the institutional foundations of growth ideology, how alternatives to growth are delegitimized, and in so doing specify a range of organizations attempting to prevent transformation away from growth and the capital accumulating economy. Geo-political and macro-economic structures and mechanisms maintaining the economic growth imperative are identified along the way. The paper is distinct from, but complementary to, my other article in this forum issue of *Globalizations* (Spash, 2020b). There I focus on drawing out lessons from the Coronavirus pandemic about concrete structural aspects of the operation of actual economies, which are then placed in the context of long running systems critiques from ecological economics and fallacious arguments by mainstream economists denying limits to growth. Both papers complement others in this special issue that expose the failures of economics as a discipline (Galbraith, 2020; Keen, 2020) and the related necessity of and potential for alternative approaches that connect economics to social, political and ecological reality (Gills & Morgan, 2020; Koch & Buch-Hansen, 2020).

In order to understand why systems change is necessary, and how it might be achieved, the structural aspects of that system must be understood, including the mechanisms by which it operates and reproduces itself. In Section 2, the organization of society to maintain a productive growth economy is shown to have multiple unsavoury implications some of which are acknowledge while others are rarely mentioned, such as links to eugenicist positons held by several famous economists (e.g. Keynes, Edgeworth and Meade). The claims made for capitalism, being inclusive and providing freedom from coercion, contrast with the advocacy of a smart, competitive meritocracy and an actualized world order built on the militarized and securitized nation State. In Section 3, the claims for economic growth being the means to development are shown to have been part of a foreign policy agenda of the United States of America (USA) that was adopted, maintained and promoted via international organizations such as the UN, World Bank and International Monetary Fund (IMF). Bodies of the UN have supported the continual rebirth of economic growth – as development, progress, sustainable development, Green growth, Green New Deal. In Section 4, I then turn to explicit coverage of how the ecological crisis, and specifically human induced climate change, is employed to support a new era of growth. In both Sections 3 and 4 I make explicit reference to some populist authors whose work has appeared growth critical and anti-capitalist but has in fact been neither.

This paper reveals how various attempts by different individuals and organizations to claim that growth is good, justifiable or even neutral, form part of a passive revolution that fails to address some basic social and ecological realities. Economic works publicized as critical and progressive prove to be otherwise. One set of ostensibly critical approaches to capitalism claim the right form is all that is required to avoid problems but fail to properly consider climate and ecological crises (e.g. Ha-Joon Chang and post-Keynesians). They also ignore the growth economy's negative psychological and ethical implications (that Keynes explicitly recognized), undesirable productivist aspects, and tendency in times of crisis to foster extreme right wing political groups. Another set of ostensibly growth critical approaches is explicitly environmentally concerned, but still advocate policies promoting growth (e.g. Jackson, Raworth). These regard growth as necessary for 'development' but pay no attention to the competitive asymmetry it entails and lack analysis of the structure of capitalism. Their pragmatic commitment to economic growth results in maintaining capitalism by default and contradicts concern for the evidence of material impacts and social inequities of the system, its tendencies to exploit and create crises.

2. The social organization of humanity for growth

Since the end of World War II, the governments of all major nation States have been committed to a macroeconomic model termed by its advocates the 'growth economy', and by its critics growth-mania (Daly, 1992; Georgescu-Roegen, 1975/2009, p. 349). Built on a fossil fuel industrial economic structure, such growth has long been confronting environmental limits, and even longer the social inequities created by worldwide resource extraction and the profit motive (Brand & Wissen, 2017). Yet, it has repeatedly been adjusted and saved from ultimate collapse as explained by the French Regulation School building from the 1976 book 'Régulation et crises du capitalism' (Aglietta, 1979/2015). In this section I illustrate how apparently radical heterodox economic critique of capitalism plays its role in a passive revolution supporting economic growth. That the recommended economic system requires social adjustment and normalization of humans to the system and the type of adjustments required are concealed, denied or simply ignored. Here some of these basic social implications and potentialities are specified.

2.1. The Keynesian productivist society

The work of Ha-Joon Chang has been marketed as a critique exposing many fallacies of capitalism commonly held and perpetuated by economists, the media and politicians. His work has been well received in heterodox economic circles as providing a critique of mainstream economics and austerity politics. However, Chang is no radical anti-capitalist seeking an alternative system and restricts his critique to 'free-market' neoliberalism. He quotes Winston Churchill, who quipped that capitalism is the best economic system because all the others are worse (Chang, 2011, p. 253); the same position as Thatcher's TINA.

Chang (2011) offers a mixture of post-Keynesian and neo-Austrian economics that recommends a (collective) entrepreneurial capitalist economy operating within a welfare State. This is something reminiscent of the post-war compromise in the West between labour and capital, and a form of Polanyian double-movement (Polanyi, 1944). Consistent with the rejection of alternatives, this approach promises to use economic growth to benefit a wider public. Full employment and more growth is then associated with more social benefit. According to Chang (2011, p. 253), one of the problems with 'free-market' capitalism is that it 'slows down the economy', i.e. economic growth. A core idea amongst his conclusions, for tweaking the system to make it less socially divisive and objectionable, is that: 'Industrial policy needs to be redesigned to promote key manufacturing sectors with high scope for productivity growth' (Chang, 2011, p. 259). An approach otherwise commonly known as productivism and associated with expansion of economic output via ever increasing inputs.

Among the things Ha-Joon Chang (2011) 'does not tell us' about his advocated productivist industrial growth economy is where the inputs come from, or how it will avoid resource wars, prevent the ecological crises and protect the non-human world. Typical of most non-ecological economists, his worldview excludes Nature, and has no conception of the necessary ecosystems that sustain economies (Spash & Smith, 2019). Keynesian economics is at core based on the idea of boosting aggregate demand (i.e. consumerism) through government expenditures to fully employ resources (including humans and non-humans) and maximize growth, i.e. throughput of energy, materials and so waste. The ecological consequences are far reaching but so also are the social ones.

Keynes (1930) regarded the growth economy as a temporary phenomena lasting 100 years. He believed that growth would solve the economic problem, specified as meeting people's absolute needs. In the process, unethical values and undesirable behaviour would be promoted and institutionalized: greed, usury and the desire for ever more money. Abolishing such practices would only be possible on reaching the end goal. At that time:

> We shall be able to rid ourselves of many of the pseudo-moral principles which have hag-ridden us for two hundred years, by which we have exalted some of the most distasteful of human qualities into the

position of the highest virtues. We shall be able to afford to dare to assess the money-motive at its true value. The love of money as a possession—as distinguished from the love of money as a means to the enjoyments and realities of life—will be recognised for what it is, a somewhat disgusting morbidity, one of those semi-criminal, semi-pathological propensities which one hands over with a shudder to the specialists of mental disease. All kinds of social customs and economic practices, affecting the distribution of wealth and of economic rewards and penalties, which we now maintain at all costs, however distasteful and unjust they may be in themselves, because they are tremendously useful in promoting the accumulation of capital, we shall then be free, at last, to discard. [...] But beware! The time for all this is not yet. For at least another hundred years we must pretend to ourselves and to everyone that fair is foul and foul is fair; for foul is useful and fair is not. (Keynes, 1930, p. 97)

This prescription requires that we value the useful over the good in the blind pursuit of future wealth, ignoring our actions' 'own quality or their immediate effects on our own environment' (Keynes, 1930, p. 97). In two generations transformation to a more ethical society would be permissible, but here Keynes appears politically and institutionally naïve, ignoring psychological, social and political lock-in and the creation of powerful interests vested in maintenance of the growth economy. A problematic organizational aspect is the creation of a professional managerial class rotating jobs between business and government enabling regulatory capture. This controlling corporate elite is what Galbraith (1967/2007) termed the technostructure.

There is another, potentially more sinister, side to the social organization of a Keynesian productivist economy that 'they don't tell you', but in this case neither did Keynes. A growth economy requires certain types of people and is not designed to cater for existing diversity (e.g. indigenous cultures), but on this topic modern economists and growth advocates appear silent. Yet, this easily becomes 'economics because the economy matters' in contrast to Schumacher's (1973) 'economics as if people mattered'. Most obviously, the productivist economy discriminates against the 'unproductive' and ascetic. More bleakly, in connecting ideas of efficient, productivity and competitiveness, with an idealized workforce that is fit to the tasks of production and consumption, there is a potentially short step from economics to eugenics. This worrisome association deserves more attention because in times of economic and political crisis the extreme right once again offers to become the saviour of capitalism.

The connections of productivist economics to eugenics go back to the origins of modern economics both in the USA (Leonard, 2005) and the UK (Aldrich, 2019). The rise of neoclassical economics from the late 1800s created a focus on utilitarian ethics and the pain/pleasure principle that became individualized (i.e. as preference utilitarianism). Utilitarianism was combined with growth and consumerism to promote hedonism as the ultimate, individual and (under methodological individualism) societal, goal. Oxford Professor, Francis Edgeworth (1845–1926) connected this to eugenics using his 'Hedonic Calculus', which recommends replacing those less able to enjoy hedonic pleasure by individuals with a superior capacity for doing so, in order to increase societal happiness. He was inspired by the idea of social sanctions to discourage the multiplication of the inefficient and encourage reproduction of the most efficient (Aldrich, 2019).

Eugenics was a popular movement and Keynes joined the Cambridge Eugenic Society, as its Treasurer, on its foundation in 1911. From 1937–1944 he held offices in the (British) Eugenics Society – Fellow, Director, Vice-President. At the end of his life in 1946, when eugenics had fallen from grace due to the Nazi extermination camps, he praised Galton (its founder) and claimed eugenics was 'the most important, significant and, I would add, genuine branch of sociology which exists' (Aldrich, 2019). There is some speculation that his eugenic references to the quality of the population meant increasing the 'best and noblest intelligences' relative to others (Aldrich,

2019), and offered him an ultimate means of transformation for his unethical growth society (Sing-erman, 2016). This would match the technocracy – breeding an elite to run society – also advocated amongst his contemporaries in the Oxbridge elite. For example, Julian Huxley promoted technoc-racy and eugenics, in association with H.G. Wells, and this inspired his brother Aldous to write the dystopian novel *Brave New World* (Huxley, 1932). However, there appears to be no explicit eugenics policy in Keynes economic writings (Aldrich, 2019). The same is not true of other econ-omists. Even into the 1970s, Cambridge Professor, James Meade (1907–1995) was arguing for 'the reduction of the relative fertility of those with low earning capacity' (Aldrich, 2019, p. 50).

A strong State promoting a productivist fully employed economy then appears potentially oppressive with a dark side that Chang and others (e.g. Jacobs & Mazzucato, 2016) fail to register. A national growth economy aimed at creating a productive population is totally consistent with the politics of having 'the right people' populate society. From Nazi propaganda of the 1930s through to campaigns of modern right-wing parties and fascists in Europe today, the association of the deser-ving, fit, hard working, nationalist is set against the undeserving, unfit, lazy, immigrant 'other'. Nationalism is easily connected to such political rhetoric, and both derive support from the more common and accepted discourse promoting the competitive race for growth and leadership.

2.2. The smart competitive meritocracy

Economic growth is marketed as if a harmonious new world order were on offer, where the poorest will join the richest. Some, like Ha-Joon Chang (2011, p. 263), advocate changing the rules to allow poor countries 'breaks to have a hope of catching up'. This ignores how competitive growth institu-tionalizes and rationalizes the fight over energy, materials and ecological space. Competition is then a good and efficient means of determining winners, whose gains are justified as being won on the basis of their own merit. A large question mark hangs over how a stable and just world is meant to be achieved by increasing national and corporate competition for technology, resources and markets!

The contradictions are evident in the 2020 policy agenda set by the European Commission's (2010) *Strategy for Smart, Sustainable and Inclusive Growth*. They define 'sustainable growth' in tra-ditional economic terms as promoting a more resource efficient, greener and more competitive economy.

> An industrial policy for the globalisation era to improve the business environment, notably for SMEs, and to support the development of a strong and sustainable industrial base able to compete globally. (European Commission, 2010, p. 4)

However, the report notes the intensifying competitive pressure coming from both developed (i.e. North American) and emerging (i.e. Chinese) economies, affecting exports and resource avail-ability. The sustainable growth strategy requires exploiting Europe's leadership in the race to develop new processes and technologies before others. The European Union is noted as 'largely a first mover in green solutions, but its advantage is being challenged by key competitors', and it should maintain its lead in the market for green technologies; in fact 'we must improve our com-petitiveness vis-à-vis our main trading partners through higher productivity' (European Commis-sion, 2010, p. 12). Boosting market consumerism is central and the internet a key part of the strategy with the vision of 'a Digital Single Market based on fast and ultra fast internet and inter-operable applications, with broadband access for all' (European Commission, 2010, p. 12). The idea of a responsible citizen, contributing to society, is defined in terms of being a good consumer buy-ing and consuming as much and as fast as possible.

> To gear the single market to serve the Europe 2020 goals requires well functioning and well-connected markets where competition and consumer access stimulate growth and innovation. […] Citizens must be empowered to play a full part in the single market. This requires strengthening their ability and confidence to buy goods and services cross-border, in particular on-line. (European Commission, 2010, p. 19)

The priorities are clear, in 30 pages, there are 84 references to markets, 83 to growth, 45 to innovation, 38 to competition, 29 to technology, 17 to consuming/consumers and 14 to greening.

Sustainable growth will make 'us' winners in the global competition, if 'we' can stay ahead of everybody else, i.e. be more productive and grow faster. Allowing poor countries to catch-up defies the specific economic logic of competition – efficiency, innovation, copyright, private ownership, cost-shifting, entrepreneurship and growth as progress – with the most economically advanced being the winners in a meritocracy. This is not, and cannot be, an inclusive project where rich and poor all obtain global-North modes of living. Indeed, as Josef Ackermann, the CEO of Deutsche Bank has made very clear, this is a race for leadership:

> Make no mistake: a new world order is emerging. The race for leadership has already begun. For the winners, the rewards are clear: Innovation and investment in clean energy technology will stimulate green growth; it will create jobs; it will bring greater energy independence and national security. (Statement made December 2010; cited by Jaeger et al., 2011)

Make no mistake, where there are winners there will be losers, as there always have been in the geopolitics of the competitive industrial growth economy, 'sustainable' or otherwise. Germany wins Spain, Portugal, Italy, Greece lose; China wins USA loses; USA wins Europe loses; and so on.

2.3. A secure militarized system

Another ignored aspect of the competitive growth economy is how it is backed by military force, as and when necessary, to secure supply chains, resources and markets for trading. The current political economy is built on fossil fuel expansion. Government plans are to pour trillions of dollars in that direction (International Energy Agency, 2014) to secure a traditional leadership position in the growth race; a strategy backed by military concerns over security and demands from the fossil fuel and associated industries (e.g. aerospace, automobiles). Fossil fuels must be secured, requiring military investment.

Modern growth economies are heavily militarized. Twenty eight governments spend 10% or more of their budgets on the military. Table 1 shows the top ten nations by military expenditure. The dominant imperialist status of the USA is quite self-evident, with a military budget larger than the next seven highest military spenders combined. If Western Europe is taken as a whole then it ranks second both on military spending and Gross Domestic Product (GDP). The strong connections between ranking of military expenditure and GDP continues as one moves through such data. That is, extending beyond Table 1, the next three countries (Brazil, Italy, Canada) rank 8th, 9th and 10th by GDP and 11th, 12th and 14th in terms of military expenditure, and so on.

The strong association of corporate industrialism with a productivist technologically driven militarized nation State, and a permanent armament industry, was an outcome of World War II. In 1961, former Supreme Allied Commander in Europe and five star General, Dwight D. Eisenhower, made his final televised speech as President of the USA. He felt the need to warn the nation that: 'In the councils of government, we must guard against the acquisition of unwarranted influence, whether sought or unsought, by the military-industrial complex'. The modern industrial nation State was established as combining military supremacy with advanced

Table 1. Top ten military nations (expenditure by country 2018).

		GDP world rank	Military expenditure			
			Amount (millions US$)	GDP (% of)	Per capita (US$)	Government expenditure (% of)
1	USA	1	648798	3.2%	1986	9.0%
2	China*	2	249997	1.9%	177	5.5%
3	Saudi Arabia*	19	67555	8.8%	2013	24.6%
4	India	5	66510	2.4%	49	8.7%
5	France	7	63800	2.3%	978	4.1%
6	Russia	11	61388	3.9%	426	11.4%
7	UK	6	49997	1.8%	751	4.6%
8	Germany	4	49471	1.2%	601	2.8%
9	Japan	3	46618	0.9%	367	2.5%
10	Korea, South	12	43070	2.6%	842	12.4%

Notes: Data on GDP from The World Bank, latest figures for 2017.
Data source on military expenditure Stockholm International Peace Research Institute (SIPRI).
Figures are in US $ in current prices, converted at the exchange rate for the given year.
*Figures are SIPRI estimates.

technology in a race for material growth and capital accumulation. The apologists for growth broker no discussion of the military-industrial complex, how supply chains and resources are secured or society is oppressively structured. Yet the evidence is in the news everyday: military power displays, political and military intervention, surveillance, militarized police, violent suppression of dissent, secret service supported terror, militias and coups, and ultimately war.

3. Poverty and progress: old bad, new good

Alternative ways of living are either co-opted into the economic growth paradigm or condemned as backward or primitive. Alternative approaches to development are removed from the policy agenda (Gudynas, 2016). A society condemned as backward and primitive is then prey to those of the more 'advanced' world who claim moral authority to impose 'development'. Peoples that oppose this 'development logic' are deposed and dispossessed, indigenous cultures are denigrated and destroyed and their autonomy removed. Indeed, the term primitive economies is used in an inherently derogatory way associated with undesirable living conditions caricatured as 'mud huts' and 'hair shirts'. This is where the next class of passive revolutionary, apologists for growth, enter. Here we find those who appear critical of economic growth on ecological and social grounds, but contradictorily leave economic growth, as development, firmly in place. The 'hair shirt' is a repeated, societal level, metaphor employed rhetorically to deride alternative economies and to equate them with an undesirable past. In particular, Kallis et al. (2012) cite the phrase as regularly employed to deride others in talks by Tim Jackson, and similar occurrence in the work of Juliet Schor against advocates of 'simplicity' and materially minimalist living (e.g. degrowth). Authors, such as Jackson and Schor, promote the idea of a 'new economy of prosperity' (Kallis et al.. 2012), so that apparent criticism of capitalist growth is combined with retention of some of its core structural elements and claims. The idea of a 'new economy' that is supposed to solve problems without changing the fundamental structure of capitalism is prevalent amongst apologists for growth.

3.1. Growth as development: the passive revolution

As a former World Bank chief economist and corporate executive, Lord Stern has heavily promoted the growth = development synonym, which he associates with poverty alleviation. In a press interview he stated:

> To those who want to knock out growth from objectives, I find they're close to reprehensible ... I think to say that we should just switch off growth is to miss big aspects of what matters about poverty. And so it worries me. It's also politically very naive. If you turn it into a pissing contest between growth on the one hand and climate and environment on the other and say you've got to choose, you're setting your-self up for failure. (Confino, 2014)

This kind of rhetorical bullying ignores the history and geo-politics of economic growth as devel-opment as well as the actual impacts it has on 'poor people'.

The post-development school documents how equating development with growth has been an imperialist policy, initiated by the USA for its own benefit (Sachs, 1999/2015). President Truman's 20 January 1949 inaugural address set out the agenda for a technical and scientific programme to assist 'backward' areas of the world in the context of the Cold War. The fourth objective of this foreign policy speech set-out an agenda for promoting growth, scientific advance and industrial progress of underdeveloped areas where 'economic life is primitive and stagnant' and poverty is 'a threat both to them and to more prosperous areas'. The threat being that of becoming anti-USA, anti-capitalist and aligned to the USSR. This became a government funded project called the 'Point Four Program'. Contrary to the political rhetoric of helping poor people, the actual pro-gramme was for extraction of other countries' minerals to avoid resource shortages in the USA and to secure the supply chains of their corporations.

Black (2016) documents how public–private collusion in the USA operated to reorder political and legal institutions and their operation in foreign countries to favour the global spread of capitalism.

> U.S. decision-makers grasped for a way to extract foreign minerals without triggering anti-imperialist alarms, and Point Four—a systematic effort to improve conditions in the developing world—became a chosen vehicle toward that material end. (Black, 2016)

The USA's government field agents advanced national interests by using a time-tested procedure to achieve resource extraction: (i) conduct geological surveys, (ii) perform laboratory tests, (iii) implement mining operations, (iv) revise local mining laws, and (v) bring-in interested corpor-ations from the USA (Black, 2016).

Rather than simply empowering and enriching lives, development policy has also denigrated and destroyed the cultures of non-industrialized countries, livelihoods of the rural and materially poor, and removed their autonomy. Sachs (1999/2015) differentiates the materially poor into what can be described as living frugally, suffering deprivation and living under systems of economic scarcity. The implications are summarized by Spash and Smith (2019) as follows. Traditional societies have economic systems of social provisioning that are structured on frugality and sufficiency. Interventions to 'develop' their economic circumstances have typically resulted in expropriation and forms of primitive accumulation. Culture is destroyed along with sustainable livelihoods. Land is grabbed, resources exploited, agriculture is industrialized and the environ-ment is polluted. The result is exponential growth in urban slum dwellers, more than a billion on conservative UN estimates more than a decade ago (Davis, 2006, p. 23). A class of people ready for exploitation as commodified labour due to their newly-created wage dependency and their new lives as those saved from 'poverty' to live in the economy of material scarcity measured by money. As discussed below, the World Bank has focussed on increasing money income as an improvement that removes people from poverty, but ignores the structural and social changes that typically transform self-sufficiency in rural communities within social networks into indus-trial dependency in urban slums as isolated individuals living in polluted environments, working under dehumanizing productivist conditions.

Sachs (1999/2015) explains how the growth = development agenda has been repeatedly adjusted and revised in response to problems becoming overwhelmingly obvious. Sustainable development then appears as a response to the environmental criticism of the 1970s and specifically the limits to growth literature (Meadows et al., 1972). The World Commission on Environment and Development, established in 1983 by the UN, under chairwoman Gro Brundtland, produced the widely employed definition of sustainable development, but this is normally quoted without the follow-on sentence. The two together read as follows:

> Sustainable development seeks to meet the needs and aspirations of the present without compromising the ability to meet those of the future. Far from requiring the cessation of economic growth it recognises that the problems of poverty and underdevelopment cannot be solved unless we have a new era of growth in which developing countries play a large role and reap large benefits. (World Commission on Environment and Development 1987, Chapter 1, para. 49)

The Commission recognized no insurmountable conflict with the environment and they looked forward to a five to ten fold increase in economic growth. Neither would growth in the global economy exclude expansion of the industrially developed countries' economies.

> The medium-term prospects for industrial countries are for growth of 3–4 per cent, the minimum that international financial institutions consider necessary if these countries are going to play a part in expanding the world economy. Such growth rates could be environmentally sustainable if industrialised nations can continue the recent shifts in the context of their growth towards less material—and energy—intensive activities and the improvement of their efficiency in using materials and energy. (World Commission on Environment and Development 1987, Chapter 2 para. 32)

This claimed 'solution' to social-ecological crises, that 'decoupling' economic growth from environmental destruction is feasible, has become increasingly common in recent times, because otherwise the contradictions become overwhelmingly obvious. It provides the magic bullet solution (for criticisms of decoupling see Fletcher & Rammelt, 2017; Giampietro, 2019; Parrique et al., 2019).

Over the history of engagement by the UN on environment and development, going back to the 1972 conference, the discourse has been pacified and alternatives to capitalism, and more generally economic growth, delegitimized. Early principles claimed concern over futurity, equity, public participation, and environmental integrity. Some affirmation of intrinsic values in Nature was also recurrent (e.g. as in IUCN, UNEP, and WWF, 1980 Sec.9 ft.nt.3, Sec.10 figure; United Nations General Assembly, 2012, p. 38). However, circa 1980, the emphasis became utilitarian use, economic market instruments, natural capital maintenance, production and economic efficiency. Thus, the support is for neoliberal Green Growth not post-growth, degrowth or post-development. This then relates to a conflict and divorce between what may be believed by individuals and what is regarded as acceptable to express in international political and administrative circles, such as those of the UN (Craig et al., 1993). To be accepted, play a role and have a seat at the table requires conforming to the system and its discourse. The result being a new environmental pragmatism matching the rise of neoliberalism (Spash, 2009; Spash & Aslaksen, 2015). Hence, there should be little surprise that the 2015 UN Resolution on sustainable development goals promotes the oxymoron of 'sustainable economic growth', uses the rhetoric of decoupling to dismiss environmental concerns and seeks 7% growth rates.

The underlying claim that growth is the 'solution' to poverty has two false but common subsidiary claims. First, the argument is that the more the economy grows the more happiness will increase. This has been effectively deconstructed by Easterlin (1974, 1995, 2003) and Hirsch (1977). The basic point being that hedonic pleasures are limited in their relationship to well-being. Happiness via income has relative meaning of worth in relation to the status of others so that more income for all does not mean more happiness for all (Easterlin, 1995). In addition, status free, or non-positional, contributions to well-being are undervalued by the materialist and money oriented growth society. People then invest in gaining things that do not make them happier (material stuff, bigger objects, the latest things) while side-lining substantive non-material contributors (e.g. friends, family, relationships, health).

> Once it is recognised that individuals are unaware of some of the forces shaping their choices, it can be no longer argued that they will successfully maximize their well-being. (Easterlin, 2003, p. 11181)

Such a conclusion runs counter to the claims of those supporting liberal and neoliberal political ideologies as well as economists supporting consumer sovereignty and minimalist government.

Second, is the myth that income inequity is addressed by economic growth because of trickle down. This is the myth that rich people allow the crumbs to fall from the table that enrich the poor. The persistence of poverty and increasing inequity in the richest nations offers the counter experience, as does the dependency of the wealthy and wealthy nations on exploitation of the poor and poorer nations for their labour and resources. Moreover, there is nothing in economic theory to support trickle down. Even Stiglitz, part of the establishment who firmly believes growth = development, had to admit that, after thirty years of the World Bank trying:

> The evidence was overwhelming that growth did not *necessarily* reduce poverty. Trickle-down economics did not *necessarily* work. If growth was accompanied by increasing inequality, poverty could actually increase. The problem was that many of the Washington Consensus policies that the Bank and the IMF had argued for in the past had contributed to—or had at least been associated with—increasing inequality. (Stiglitz, 2009, p. 144)

3.2. Prosperity after growth: the passive revolutionary

A widely cited and apparently growth critical work is, ecological economist, Tim Jackson's book *Prosperity Without Growth*. Jackson's arguments appear to be anti-growth with strong critiques of the prospects for decoupling the economy from environmental damages. He adopts a post-growth position with the recommendation of a 'new economy' based on services. Unfortunately, this might not actually address the problem because, in practice, the move to such economies has been 'systematically linked to an increase in per capita energy and material consumption' (Krausmann et al., 2008, p. 197). So the form of alternative economy is in question, but the implication is that some serious restructuring is necessary, and, with growth gone, apparently this means the abolition of capitalism. However, Jackson (2009, pp. 197–202) fudges the issue, weakly joking that he is actually advocating 'capitalism, but not as we know it', and asking rhetorically 'Does it really matter?' Capital accumulation appears as an optional extra for capitalism, while capitalism itself remains basically unaddressed and undefined.

Jackson advocates contract and convergence, stating that, 'A key motivation for rethinking prosperity in the advanced economies is to make room for much-needed growth in poorer nations' (Jackson, 2009, p. 175). He equates economic growth with development. In particular, he notes how self-reported happiness studies show increases in happiness before it declines as growth continues.

> These [life satisfaction] data underline one of the key messages of this book. There is no case to abandon growth universally. But there is a strong case for the developed nations to make room for growth in poorer countries. It is in these poorer countries that growth really does make a difference. (Jackson, 2009, p. 41)

Now, this position is no different from that of Keynes, Stern or the international pro-growth lobbies. Yet the practical implications are left out. What does it mean in practice to advocate growth as the means of poverty alleviation?

According to the UN there are 1.34 billion people (19% of humanity) across 105 countries living in multidimensional poverty – reflecting acute deprivation in health, education and standard of living.[1] The World Bank's preferred measure of extreme poverty is the US dollar. The threshold set in 1990 at $1/day, increased to $1.25 in 2005, adjusted in 2011 to $1.90 purely for inflation and exchange rate changes, i.e. they claim $1.90 (2011) buys the same as $1.25 (2005) in poor countries. The World Bank (2018) then triumphantly proclaims growth policies have halved extreme poverty since 1990. Others disagree with their approach and claims, while pointing out the increasing inequities are actually created by growth.

That the cost of living varies by country is recognized by the 2018 World Bank report including higher thresholds – $3.20 per day and $5.50 per day – to represent extreme poverty in lower-income and upper-middle-income countries. As shown in Table 2, 46% of humanity live below $5.50 per day. If the requirement is moved higher to $10/day then 71%. Such figures hide distributional inequity, regional and national differences. Table 2 shows greater income poverty amongst rural populations, while some countries may have much higher than 10% in extreme poverty. India, for example, has over 30% below the $1.25/day threshold, while growth there between 1980 and 2016 increased the income share of the richest 10% by more than 20%, giving them 55% of all income (Nilsen, 2018).

What all this means for Jackson's call to address poverty by economic growth is mass expansion of the industrial economy for the vast majority of humanity. In order to reach the basic poverty threshold of the USA would require growth for almost the entire world's population on an ongoing basis. Even a level 60% below that threshold (i.e. $10/day) would mean imposing the growth economy on 71% of the world's population. He is certainly not then calling for *Prosperity Without Growth*! However, the issue here is not only the hidden advocacy of such a massive global expansion of economic production, but also that growth itself has been highly problematic as a means for addressing poverty. As Nilsen (2018) notes the majority of the world's poor live in countries that have experienced strong economic growth and the growth strategies these countries have practised

Table 2. Population in poverty.

	Population (%)	Income/yr (US $)	Source
Population below US$1.90 per day according to World Bank	10.0	694	http://www.worldbank.org/en/topic/poverty/overview
Indian population below international poverty line of US$1.25 per day 2007–2011	32.7	456	http://www.unicef.org/infobycountry/india_statistics.html
Population below US$2 per day in rural areas	60.0	730	http://www.un.org/en/globalissues/briefingpapers/ruralpov/vitalstats.shtml
Population below US$3.20 per day according to World Bank	26.3	1168	World Bank (2018, p. 8)
Population below US$5.50 per day according to World Bank	46.0	2007	World Bank (2018, p. 8)
Population on US$10 per day or less	71.0	3650	https://www.pewresearch.org/fact-tank/2015/09/23/seven-in-ten-people-globally-live-on-10-or-less-per-day/
USA 2016 Federal Poverty Guidelines income threshold below		11880	http://familiesusa.org/product/federal-poverty-guidelines#2015
USA 2017 Official Poverty rate	12.3		https://www.census.gov/library/publications/2018/demo/p60-263.html

create and reproduce poverty. In addition, as shown in Table 2, poverty has not been removed even from the richest nations in the world and in some it is institutionalized and increasing (e.g. Jacksons' own country, the UK, the sixth richest nation in the world by GDP, has been criticized for increases in extreme poverty, while, as shown in Table 2 the USA, the richest country in the world, has over 12% officially living in poverty).[2]

4. Organizing a green and growing 'new' economy

That environmental problems are an all pervasive part of modern economic systems is a core lesson of ecological economics based on the laws of thermodynamics and conservation of matter. Energy and materials that go into the economic system are not destroyed but transformed, degraded in terms of human usefulness, and returned to the environment in equal mass. The correlation between GDP and greenhouse gas (GHG) emissions directly results from this basic biophysical reality. Such natural scientific understanding is ignored by economists' externality theory which treats pollution as a minor aberration in an otherwise perfectly functioning market system (Spash, 2021). As one-off correctible market failures pollutants are treated as singular policy problems not systemic failures.

The resulting policy reductionism has facilitated exclusion of all other environmental problems by climate change, and then reducing GHG mitigation policy to focus on CO_2 (typically termed 'carbon') as the principle concern. That even this singular gas is a systemic problem related to the growth economy, rather than a one-off aberration, seems rather self-evident. The majority of world CO_2 emissions comes from the same handful of high GDP nations as shown in Table 1. These are China (30%), USA (15%), India (7%), Russia (5%), Japan (4%) and Germany (2%). As a collective the EU28 would rank 3rd (10%) with highest polluters Germany followed by the UK, Italy and France (around 1% each). The nine highest CO_2 emitting countries rank in the top eleven countries with the highest GDP.[3] Yet the institutionalization of a passive revolution has sought to effectively turn reality on its head to claim economic growth as the solution to not the cause of, human induced climate change.

4.1. Better growth, better climate: the green passive revolution part I

The Paris Agreement (Article 2) has a stated aim of holding global average temperature increases to well below 2°C, and an aspiration of pursuing 'efforts to limit this to 1.5°C, in order to reduce the risk and impacts from climate change'. Article 2 is qualified by the phrase: 'in the context of sustainable development and efforts to eradicate poverty'. Indeed the whole Paris Agreement is set within the context of the Sustainable Development Goals (SDGs), which promote economic growth, technology, industrialization and energy use (Spash, 2016b, 2016a). SDG Goal 8 is to sustain per capita economic growth at a rate of at least 7% GDP per annum in the least developed countries. The expected environmental destruction is to be addressed by the 'endeavour to decouple economic growth from environmental degradation'. This would require absolute decoupling which is simply impossible for the SDG envisioned industrial economy promoted in Goal 9. The Paris Agreement follows suit with techno-optimism and growth; Article 10 states that: 'Accelerating, encouraging and enabling innovation is critical for an effective, long-term global response to climate change and promoting economic growth and sustainable development'.

The resource extracting, fossil-fuel driven economies of the world are claiming they can stop the exponential growth path of GHG emissions, while making no substantive change in the structure of the growth economy or society, and indeed by promoting capitalist financial markets as 'the solution' (Spash, 2016b). At the UNFCCC COP25 conference in Madrid 2019 the major contention and dispute concerned what the doublespeak of Paris called 'internationally transferred mitigation outcomes' (clause 108 and Article 6). This was the term that appeared in the Paris Agreement instead of emissions trading, carbon markets, cap and trade or offsets. In short the Paris Agreement is being directed towards establishing financial markets based on carbon trading because this offers a business as usual approach.

For example, if aviation were a nation State it would be the seventh largest CO_2 emitter.[4] Yet increasing flying is at the leading edge of growth. Manufacturers expect to double the passenger aircraft fleet, with 'emerging' economies, and especially China, tripling those flying. The cost, $5.3 trillion by 2036 for the new commercial fleet, and more for training over half a million new pilots.[5] Already 550 new airports are planned or under construction, combined with new runways and airport expansion there are an estimated 1200 new airport infrastructure projects (Smith, 2019, p. 18). Christiana Figueres – former Executive Secretary of the UNFCCC and now member of Richard Branson's B-Team – justifies this massive expansion as 'carbon neutral growth' (Figueres & Tubiana, 2016). The means on offer for claiming the possibility of such neutrality are the notoriously problematic market-mechanisms of carbon trading and offsetting (Spash, 2010, 2015; Spash & Theine, 2018).

Similarly, the highly publicized report by Stern et al. (2006) advocated emissions trading while pronouncing that: 'Tackling climate change is the pro-growth strategy for the longer term, and it can be done in a way that does not cap the aspirations for growth of rich or poor countries' (Stern et al., 2006, p. viii). In 2014, the self-aggrandizing Global Commission on the Economy and Climate (GCEC) published *Better Growth Better Climate: The New Climate Economy Report* with Stern as lead economist. Apparently ' … set up to examine whether it is possible to achieve lasting economic growth while also tackling the risks of climate change' (GCEC, 2014, p. 8). Actually, a purely rhetorical question because the answer was already given by Stern in 2006. Unsurprisingly then, 'The report's conclusion is that countries at all levels of income now have the opportunity to build lasting economic growth at the same time as reducing the immense risks of climate change' (GCEC, 2014). Their 2018 report headlines 'the inclusive growth story', but the real concern seems to be capturing government investment for corporate business interests by diverting 'US $90 trillion to build the right infrastructure now' in order to 'deliver a new era of economic growth' (GCEC, 2018, p. 10). The 'new' growth seems very much like business-as-usual: rapid technological innovation, infrastructure investment, increased resource productivity, jobs, economic savings, competitiveness and market opportunities (GCEC, 2018, p. 8). The inclusiveness also seems illusionary because, once again, the competitive race is on: 'Leaders are already seizing the exciting economic and market opportunities of the new growth approach' and 'laggards' are losing out (GCEC, 2018, p. 9).

Stern and others have been keen to promote climatic disaster prevention as bringing economic prosperity. Similarly, Jaeger et al. (2011) describe GHG emissions reduction as a new opportunity to increase growth rates. A key part of such stories is that pricing and marketing non-market goods, internalizing externalities via full cost accounting, and pricing 'carbon', will correct market failures, increase efficiency and provide a Green and growing economy. In the process there is money to be made from GHG commodification and for bankers and financiers.

Capital markets, banks and other financial institutions will have a vital role in raising and allocating the trillions of dollars needed to finance investment in low-carbon technology and the companies producing the new technologies. [...] Trading on global carbon markets is now worth over $10bn annually. (Stern et al., 2006, p. 270)

As Hirsch (1977) pointed-out long ago, there is no economic welfare gain from such 'defensive expenditures'. More resources for environmental protection (like those on the military or police) are not signs of increasing human well-being but societal failure. The more pollution created, the more clean-up activities required and the higher is GDP, because it merely measures activity, not why activity is required. Stern and colleagues make a most basic economic error in claiming GDP growth due to attempting to prevent a human induced climatic disaster is a good thing.

There is also a strong underlying claim that price-making markets can reflect 'true costs'. This form of market has prices resulting from 'negotiations' between actors (e.g. firms-consumers; employer-employee) in contrast to being set by an administrative, or other, authority (Polanyi, 1957). The GCEC (2014, p. 42) state that 'Competitive markets in which prices properly reflect the full costs of production are vital to enable resources to flow to where they are most productive'. In order for prices to 'properly reflect the full costs' would require knowing all the damages related to all the GHG pollutants in the world across time and space for every level of production in order to create a marginal shadow price. As discussed in the next section, this engages in universal commensurability and converting everything (e.g. loss of life) into money values, and means planning all prices via explicit cost calculations (Spash, 2002). Regardless of ethical concerns, the technical problems are totally insurmountable and the idea absolutely impracticable, but calls for 'full cost accounting of externalities' keep appearing (e.g. GCEC, 2018). The only way to interpret such claims is as a rhetorical power play, aimed at convincing non-economists that markets are efficient resource allocators, and where markets fail they can be corrected by expert informed price adjustments.

The GCEC (2014) State 'we can create lasting economic growth', but who are we? In this case those speaking for the 'global we' are a political elite (two majors, five ex-heads of State, two associated with the UN), thirteen financers and bankers and four leaders of international organizations (World Bank, IEA, OECD, ITUC), plus Lord Stern. They are backed-up by 'The Economic Advisory Panel' comprising nine economics professors/Nobel winners and six other experts in economics/finance (in total two women, thirteen men). GCEC is a mainstream economics lobby group for international financers and businessmen. Ultimately their concern is the threat to and protection of the capital accumulating growth economy, above all else.

In the long term, if climate change is not tackled, growth itself will be at risk. (GCEC, 2014, p. 9).

The rhetoric of environmental and social concern thinly veils the aim of getting government funds for the transition to a 'new economy' that will be socially and economically unchanged, and merely produce different products, while trillions of dollars are poured into corporate pockets.

4.2. Nature as a financial capital asset: the green passive revolution part II

In 2011, the UNEP initiated a campaign for the 'Green Economy', with a report over 600 pages long (UNEP, 2011b), aimed at influencing the 2012 Rio Plus 20 meeting. This includes expressions of concern for the poor, the seriousness of environmental problems and the need for change. For the UN the Green Economy 'is a new development path that is based on sustainability principles and ecological economics' (UNEP, 2011a, p. 1). However, the approach is built around market mechanisms and economists' (or rather accountants') ability to conduct shadow pricing to value the environment – 'a common language of comprehensive ecosystem valuation' – and to institutionalize those values via private property rights for private gain.

> In the transition to a Green Economy, policymakers should ensure that the full range of goods and services provided by ecosystems, including those which are currently non-monetised, are fully integrated in decision making and public policy. [...] Placing a value on ecosystem services through mechanisms that facilitate investment in ecosystems will at the same time benefit local people and the private sector who are rewarded for good environmental stewardship. (UNEP, 2011a, p. 3)

The mythical full cost accounting is central. The UNEP (2011a, p. 7) makes clear that they want to use 'economic models for wealth creation, to focus increasingly on the value of ecosystem goods and services and natural capital'. They believe that, 'Compared with previous development paths, the uniqueness of a Green Economy is that it can directly turn natural capital into economic value whilst maintaining it, and conduct total cost accounting' (UNEP, 2011a, p. 8). Ecologists can be replaced by accountants as the environment neatly slips off the agenda and is replaced by growth, jobs, capital investment and wealth accumulation.

Neither is the growth model new. Growth is designated Green because it will promote specific types of productivism (e.g. solar and wind electricity generation, electric cars, digital economies) assumed, but not shown, to have lower environmental impacts (e.g. on cars see Morgan, 2020). This does nothing to address the scale of energy and material throughput, social impacts of accelerating the mode of living and continually introducing new technologies. Nor does it address how advancing new interventions into the environment destroys natural systems' structure and functioning, and partially substitutes for this with technology dependent upon low entropy concentrated minerals (e.g. fossil fuels), while causing an increase in unwanted surprise events. Thus, arguments for decoupling and circular economies fail to address the relationships between human systems and ecosystems (Giampietro, 2019). The concern here is not really maintaining ecological or environmental systems, but once again a financially driven growth economy.

The UNEP's association of their Green Economy with ecological economics relates to researchers who have promoted the adoption of natural capital as a means of reflecting ecological value (Jansson et al., 1994) and claim to have valued the worlds ecosystems (Costanza et al., 1997). Criticism of such work has extended from the actual studies (e.g. Norgaard & Bode, 1998; Toman, 1998) to the more general unscientific form of new environmental pragmatism that this entails (Spash, 2013). Natural capital is also a long contested concept (Spash & Clayton, 1997), and the adoption of the capital approach from mainstream economics highly problematic.

The mainstream economic argument is that, even in the absence of any technological progress, exhaustible resources do not pose a fundamental problem if reproducible man-made capital is sufficiently substitutable for natural capital (Dasgupta & Heal, 1979; Hartwick, 1977; Solow, 1974). In terms of sustainability criterion, the concern is to achieve a non-declining income flow from capital which maintains or increases utility. If natural capital is reduced then man-made capital will need to compensate for the yield lost. Thus, the Hartwick (1977) rule suggests achieving intertemporal efficiency in resource allocation by investing depletable-resource rents in man-made capital, and so maintaining a constant consumption stream. However, the simple Hartwick rule depends upon man-made capital: (i) failing to depreciate, (ii) being a substitute for, rather than a complement to, natural capital, and (iii) being unrelated to rather than produced from natural capital (Victor, 1991). The self-evident lack of realism is ignored. Instead an extreme position on substitution is adopted by the capital approach, namely that:

> We can pass on less environment so long as we offset this loss by increasing the stock of roads and machinery, or other man-made (physical) capital. Alternatively, we can have fewer roads and factories so long as we compensate by having more wetlands or mixed wood lands or more education. (Turner et al., 1994, p. 56)

As Munda (1997, p. 217) has stated this weak sustainability approach requires a very strong assumption, namely perfect substitutability between the different forms of capital. All values are equated and everything is made commensurate and can be substituted.

4.3. Do nought economics: the passive revolutionary

Kate Raworth's book, *Doughnut Economics*, is entirely oriented around economic growth and criticisms of mainstream economics. She associates economic growth with social and environmental problems, and planetary boundaries (Rockström et al., 2009). Various links, loosely drawn and briefly made, connect to an ecological economics perspective, but primarily the anti-growth work of Herman Daly. However, when recounting having to choose between Green growth and degrowth (mentioned once), Raworth (2017/2018, p. 244) goes on to sympathetically, if critically, discuss the former, while totally dismissing the latter. In the penultimate chapter her position is made explicit 'Be Agnostic About Growth' she proclaims. Her attempt to distinguish this from apathy leads to a definition that claims she wants to be 'agnostic in the sense of designing an economy that promotes human prosperity whether GDP is going up, down, or holding steady' (Raworth, 2017/2018, p. 245). Her final recommendations for a future economy provide a mix of ecological modernization, Green Economy and techno-optimism.

On her website, Raworth claims the mantel of being a 'renegade economist', but her apologetics for growth are clear in the linked blogs: 'GDP could grow, so long as it remained compatible with staying within social and planetary boundaries'.[6] This fundamentally misunderstands the role of capital accumulation, corporations, profit seeking, competition and consumerism in the structure of the modern economy. Despite passing references to Karl Marx (Raworth, 2017/2018, p. 88,142, 165, 272), her book makes no connection between systemic issues and the structure of capitalism. Capitalism is mentioned in passing a dozen times, but it is never defined in the book nor regarded as a serious concern; indeed for Raworth, like other apologists for growth, it can be redesigned to a new updated version. All the criticisms of growth that she references appear irrelevant because Raworth's position is basically that there are no *a priori* problems with economic growth itself, this is something that does or does not result from economic practice, a side issue to the practical problem of designing the right (capitalist) economy. She asserts, with no evidence at all, that: 'No country has ever ended human deprivation without a growing economy' (Raworth, 2017/2018, p. 245); which is an amazingly ahistorical and ill-informed statement, and if she believed this to be true it would seem to commit her to growth not agnosticism. Indeed, the evidence shows that no growth economy has ever ended human deprivation. What totally passes-by Raworth in making this claim is the role that economic growth has played in causing inequality and deprivation.

Raworth also exemplifies how apologists for growth argue around issues, rather than directly addressing them. For example, Meadows et al.'s (1972) limits to growth thesis is mentioned (Raworth, 2017/2018, pp. 154–155), but emphasis is placed on pollution not resources. The idea of a 'circular economy' is later promoted with rhetorical claims of potential 98% efficiency (Raworth, 2017/2018, pp. 220–222), which merely reproduces the fallacies of closed systems thinking inherent in the macroeconomic circular flow diagram of GDP, criticized earlier in her book. The text then evidences repeated failures to understand the logic of the critical literature cited.[7] In order to counter material reality, 'knowledge' is introduced as if it could avoid the laws of physics. Despite Georgescu-Roegen (1971) receiving passing acclamation (Raworth, 2017/2018, p. 252), the implications of economic growth for materials and energy throughput, and the role of entropy in the economic process, are basically absent or bypassed with another bout of rhetorical flourish. The fact that Georgescu-Roegen (1979/1995) concluded in favour of degrowth is also totally ignored.

Faith in economic prosperity through capitalism is an underlying theme. Despite critical reflections on neoliberalism, and linking it to the neo-Austrian economists of the Mont Pèlerin Society (for more depth see Mirowski & Plehwe, 2009), she supports the core Austrian economic and neoliberal belief in entrepreneurs as central economic actors, business as the source of innovation and technology as progress. Thus, digital futures, robots and knowledge economies are combined, to suggest a decoupled economy that saves the basic capitalist structure, as new corporate forms enable the Davos elite to become socially and environmentally responsible in the belief that they will happily reform themselves and stop shifting-costs on to others.

As a senior associate at the Cambridge Institute for Sustainability Leadership, Raworth unsurprisingly leaves a large role for business and corporate entrepreneurs as the future leaders. That Institute's website states their commitment to working with multinational businesses.[8] Their clients include major corporations and financial interests (e.g. Shell, Coca-Cola, Unilever, Deloitte, General Electric and Nestle). Connecting to the Davos elite, Raworth has contributed to the World Economic Forum, where her 'renegade' claims are dropped, and mild reform appears in an ecological modernist mode of Green corporate capitalism.

George Monbiot has claimed Raworth to be the Keynes of this century.[9] Her book bears no comparison to his work at all. It is a popularly written collection of anecdotally and metaphorically structured arguments, presented as a series of stories, lacking depth of attention to cited sources and offering no coherent economic theory. Typical of apologists for growth it offers comforting pictures of positive futures that will build upon the basic structures of Western capitalism and sustain it. Therein lies the contradiction, the arguments for alternatives stand in opposition to the arguments for keeping business-as-usual. The only proximity to Keynes is in an attempt to save the capitalist system from itself by *a posteriori* corrections to its inherent tendency for exploitation of, and cost-shifting onto, 'others'. Of course, as discussed above, Keynes himself was the ultimate apologist for growth.

5. Concluding discussion

Economic growth is synonymous with progress and development, yet the phenomena is a relatively new one. The modern economic growth paradigm was popularized after World War II both academically and politically. Academically, Keynes (1936/1978) invented macroeconomics and formalized the operations of modern capitalism, including the role of money as already recognized by Marx (1867). Keynesian economics justified government intervention to stimulate growth. Politically, the foreign policy of the USA adopted economic growth as synonymous with development, and development with progress, as a means of international intervention (Black, 2016). Organizations such as the IMF and the World Bank helped push the imperialist agenda (Sachs, 1999/ 2015). The Cold War added an arms race. As a geo-political tool, the capital accumulating growth economy had soon spread globally from market capitalism to centrally planned productivism.

Capitalist price-making markets contribute their own dynamics of commodification, competition over market share, power over suppliers and consumers, cost-shifting and profit seeking.

Structured to maximize 'exchange values', such markets must grow because the reasons for capital investment is to increase returns through the exchange process. Thus, the on-going promotion of economic growth as development by Western governments has promoted materialism, consumerism, trade, commodification of Nature, reduction of values to monetary metrics, corporate profiteering, the military-industrial complex and cultural imperialism.

The growth economy is a hegemonic power structure. Hegemony is a political concept describing an ideological position that comes to dominate,

> to prevail, to gain the upper hand, to propagate itself throughout society – bringing about not only a unison of economic and political aims, but also intellectual and moral unity, [...] thus creating the hegemony of a fundamental social group over a series of subordinate groups. (Gramsci, 1971, pp. 181–182)

The consensus across political systems and parties is that economic growth forms the unquestionable goal of modern society to which all should aspire. More than this, the expressed belief is that imposing economic growth on all others is a moral duty to help them 'develop', and not to do so is reprehensible (as noted by Lord Stern).

The basic physical, social, economic and psychological criticisms of the resulting economic system, as raised in the 1970s, have never been addressed. As social-ecological economists have repeatedly noted, most economists have wilfully ignored the biophysical reality of economic processes and the social structure of actual economies (Spash, 2017). As social, ecological and economic crises increasingly become actualized so do the pundits with their old growth wine in new economy bottles – neo-Keynesian productivism, climate economy, Green growth, Green economy, Green new deal, new deal for nature, sustainable development, sustainable economic growth, bio-economy, circular economy, digital economy, knowledge economy. Whatever the title the contradiction remains between sustaining capital accumulating industrial growth and reducing the social-ecological impacts of its material and energy throughput.

For the top few per cent of the worlds' population who own the vast majority of its wealth, and run its corporate businesses's, ecological and economic crises are just another opportunity to make money. One person's loss is another's gain. Disasters are potential trade openings for the businessmen and women with the right goods and services in the right place at the right time (Spash, 2012). That is the whole thrust the EC's 2020 vision, GCEC and Stern's new climate economy and the UN's Green Economy. Trillions of dollars are just waiting to be grabbed in the transition to the next form of capitalism. One may speculate as to their motives but they presumably believe in either short termism or that they can survive regardless of general and widespread catastrophes and suffering of others; in both cases there appear to be psychopathic and sociopathic traits in the corporate world (Bakan, 2004; Black, 2001).

The elite of financiers, bankers, billionaires and corporate managers appear less concerned about social-ecological crises than that the disenfranchised majority might get rebellious and demand a reorganization of the economic and political system. Rather than circuitous economic growth and promises of trickle down they might demand redistribution, social justice, goods and services in-kind, public ownership and social provisioning to meet social needs. The hard-line response is alliance with the right-wing, shutting borders to immigrants, designating critics as terrorists and threats to national security, authoritarian control using securitization via police and military power. This is an on-going process across nations, including Western democracies. The soft-option is a continuing series of passive revolutions to appease subordinate segments of society with mild reformist agendas from the top that keep the elite in power. What the review and critical reflection presented here shows is the prevalence of such conformity across a range of societal actors and how this involves the absorption of potential revolutionary or oppositional intellectuals and leaders.

The resulting policy recommendations represent superficial change that does nothing to address the fundamental social-ecological crises created by the structure of modern economies and their problematic systems of social provisioning (see my other article in this special forum: Spash, 2020b). That systemic change is necessary is well founded on basic biophysical principles whose importance for sustained social provisioning is core to ecological economics. Recognizing how systemic change is being prevented is necessary to activate counter mechanism to achieve social-ecological transformation. What has been shown here is that any serious transformation away from growthmania will need to address a set of international organizations ideologically committed to economic growth that is integrally linked to corporate interests and the militarized nation State. In addition, a range of supposedly radical and critical thinkers can be identified as compromised partners in maintaining the system. The apologists for growth help secure the passive revolution.

Notes

1. http://hdr.undp.org/en//2018-MPI
2. The UK's failures were cited by the UN Special Rapporteur on extreme poverty and human rights 16 November, 2018 https://www.ohchr.org/en/NewsEvents/Pages/DisplayNews.aspx?NewsID= 23884&LangID=E
3. Switching to total GHGs, from just CO2, and including emissions from land use change and forestry pushes Indonesia and Brazil up the league table into fifth and sixth positions, but the list of countries accounting for about 70% of GHG emission, and those at the top, remains the same.
4. https://www.fern.org/climate/aviation/ [Accessed 20/07/2019]
5. http://news.airwise.com/story/airbus-says-world-jet-fleet-to-double [Accessed 02/09/2017].
6. Accessed 3rd February 2018, https://www.humansandnature.org/economy.
7. The problems with the circular economy and its failure to understand biophysical reality are explained by Giampietro (2019) with reference to the work of Georgescu-Roegen.
8. Accessed 3rd February 2018, https://www.cisl.cam.ac.uk/about/who-we-work-with/clients.
9. Accessed 14th May 2019, https://www.theguardian.com/commentisfree/2017/apr/12/doughnut-growth-economics-book-economic-model.

Disclosure statement

No potential conflict of interest was reported by the author(s).

References

Aglietta, M. (2015). *A theory of capitalist regulation: The US experience*. Translated by D. Fernbach. London: Verso. (Original work published 1979)

Aldrich, J. (2019). *Eugenics in British economics from Marshall to Meade*. Southampton University.

Aronoff, K. (2019). Don't be fooled by fossil fuel companies' green exterior. *Rolling Stone*. Retrieved January 22, 2020, from https://www.rollingstone.com/politics/politics-features/dont-be-fooled-by-fossil-fuel-companies-green-exterior-850285/

Bakan, J. (2004). *The corporation: The pathological pursuit of profit and power*. Free Press, Simon & Schuster Inc.

Bienkowski, B. (2013, February 12). Corporations grabbing land and water overseas. *Scientific American*.

Black, E. (2001). *IBM and the Holocaust: The strategic alliance between Nazi Germany and America's most powerful corporation*. Crown Publishers.

Black, M. (2016). Interior's exterior: The state, mining companies, and resource ideologies in the point four program. *Diplomatic History*, 40(1), 81–110. https://doi.org/10.1093/dh/dhu055

Brand, U., & Wissen, M. (2017). 'The Imperial mode of living'. In C. L. Spash (Ed.), *Routledge handbook of ecological economics: Nature and society* (pp. 152–161). Routledge.

Candeias, M. (2011). *'Passive revolution vs. Socialist transformation'*. Rosa Luxemburg Foundation.

Chang, H.-J. (2011). *23 things they don't tell you about capitalism*. Penguin.

Confino, J. (2014, September 22). Lord Stern: Global warming may create billions of climate refugees. *Guardian*, Guardian Sustainable Business.

Costanza, R., d'Arge, R., deGroot, R., Farber, S., Grasso, M., Hannon, B., Limburg, K., Naeem, S., ONeill, R. V., Paruelo, J., Raskin, R. G., Sutton, P., & van den Belt, M. (1997). The value of the world's ecosystem services and natural capital. *Nature*, 387(6630), 253–260. https://doi.org/10.1038/387253a0

Craig, P. P., Glasser, H., & Kempton, W. (1993). Ethics and values in environmental policy: The said and the UNCED. *Environmental Values*, 2(2), 137–157. https://doi.org/10.3197/096327193776679945

Daly, H. E. (1973). *Towards a steady-state economy*. Freeman.

Daly, H. E. (1992). 'The steady-state economy: Alternative to growthmania'. In H. E. Daly (Ed.), *Steady-state economics: Second edition with new essays* (pp. 180–194). Earthscan.

Dasgupta, P. S., & Heal, G. M. (1979). *Economic theory and exhaustible resources, Cambridge economic handbooks*. Cambridge University Press.

Davis, M. (2006). *Planet of slums*. Verso.

Denning, S. (2020). Why stakeholder capitalism will fail. *Forbes*.

Easterlin, R. A. (1974). Does economic growth improve the human lot?: Some empirical evidence. In P. A. David, & M. W. Reder (Eds.), *Nations and households in economic growth: Essays in honor of Moses Abramovitz* (pp. 98–125). Academic Press.

Easterlin, R. A. (1995). Will raising the income for all increase the happiness for all? *Journal of Economic Behavior & Organization*, 27(1), 35–47. https://doi.org/10.1016/0167-2681(95)00003-B

Easterlin, R. A. (2003). Explaining happiness. *Proceedings of the National Academy of Sciences*, 100(19), 11176–11183. https://doi.org/10.1073/pnas.1633144100

European Commission. (2010). Europe 2020: A European strategy for smart, sustainable and inclusive growth. In *Communication from the European Commission*. Brussels.

European Commission. (2019). What is the European Green Deal?. Brussle: European Commission,. https://ec.europa.eu/commission/presscorner/api/files/attachment/859152/What_is_the_European_Green_Deal_en.pdf.pdf

Figueres, C., & Tubiana, L. (2016). The dawn of climate-friendly air travel. *Project Syndicate*. Retrieved February 7, 2017, from https://www.project-syndicate.org/commentary/airline-carbon-emissions-agreement-by-christiana-figueres-and-laurence-tubiana-2016-10

Fischer, L., Hasell, J., Proctor, J. C., Uwakwe, D., Ward-Perkins, Z., & Watson, C. (Eds.). (2018). *Rethinking economics: An introduction to pluralist economics*. Routledge, Taylor & Francis.

Fletcher, R., & Rammelt, C. (2017). Decoupling: A key fantasy of the post-2015 sustainable development agenda. *Globalizations*, 14(3), 450–467. https://doi.org/10.1080/14747731.2016.1263077

Galbraith, J. K. (2007). *The new industrial State*. Princeton University Press. (Original work published 1967)

Galbraith, J. K. (2020). Economics and the climate catastrophe. *Globalizations*. https://doi.org/10.1080/14747731.2020.1807858

GCEC. (2014). Better growth better climate: The new climate economy report; The synthesis report. F. Calderon et al. Washington, D.C.: The Global Commission on the Economy and Climate.

GCEC. (2018). Unlocking the inclusive growth story of the 21st century: Accelerating climate action in urgent times. F. Calderon et al. Washington, D.C.: World Resources Institute.

Georgescu-Roegen, N. (1971). *The entropy law and the economic process*. Harvard University Press.

Georgescu-Roegen, N. (1995). *La décroissance. Entropie-Écologie-Économie*. Translated by J. Grinevald and I. Rens. Paris: Sang de la terre. (Original work published 1979)

Georgescu-Roegen, N. (2009). Energy and economic myths. In C. L. Spash (ed), *Ecological economics: Critical concepts in the environment, 4 Volumes*, pp.328-373. London: Routledge. (Original work written 1975)

Giampietro, M. (2019). On the circular bioeconomy and decoupling: Implications for sustainable growth. *Ecological Economics, 162*, 143–156. https://doi.org/10.1016/j.ecolecon.2019.05.001

Gills, B., & Morgan, J. (2020). Teaching climate complacency: Mainstream economics textbooks and the need for transformation in economics education. *Globalizations*. https://doi.org/10.1080/14747731.2020.1808413

Gramsci, A. (1971). *Selections from the prison notebooks of Antonio Gramsci*. Translated by Q. Hoare and G. N. Smith. International Publishers (Original work written 1929–1935).

Gudynas, E. (2016). Beyond varieties of development: Disputes and alternatives. *Third World Quarterly, 37*(4), 721–732. https://doi.org/10.1080/01436597.2015.1126504

Hartwick, J. M. (1977). Intergenerational equity and the investing of rents from exhaustible resources. *American Economic Review, 67*(5), 972–974.

Hirsch, F. (1977). *Social limits to growth*. Routledge and Kegan Paul Ltd.

Huxley, A. (1932). *Brave new world*. Catto & Windus.

International Energy Agency. (2014). *World energy investment outlook: Special report*. IEA/OECD.

IUCN, UNEP and WWF. (1980). *World conservation strategy: Living resource conservation for sustainable development*. IUCN. https://portals.iucn.org/library/efiles/documents/WCS-004.pdf

Jackson, T. (2009). *Prosperity without growth: Economics for a finite planet*. Earthscan.

Jacobs, M., & Mazzucato, M. (2016). *Rethinking capitalism: Economics and policy for sustainable and inclusive growth*. Wiley-Blackwell.

Jaeger, C. C., Paroussos, L., Mangalagiu, D., Kupers, R., Mandel, A., & Tàbara, J. D. (2011). A new growth path for Europe: Generating prosperity and jobs in the low-carbon economy: Synthesis report. Potsdam: European Climate Forum.

Jansson, A., Hammer, M., Folke, C., & Costanza, R. (Eds.). (1994). *Investing in natural capital: The ecological economics approach to sustainability*. Island Press.

Kallis, G., Kerschner, C., & Martinez-Alier, J. (2012). The economics of degrowth. *Ecological Economics, 84*, 172–180. https://doi.org/10.1016/j.ecolecon.2012.08.017

Keen, S. (2020). The appallingly bad neoclassical economics of climate change. *Globalizations*. https://doi.org/10.1080/14747731.2020.1807856

Keynes, J. M. (1930). Economic possibilities for our grandchildren. *Nation and Athenaeum* 48(11 and 18), 36–37, 96–98.

Keynes, J. M. (1978). *The general theory of employment, interest and money*. Macmillan. (Original work published 1936)

Koch, M., & Buch-Hansen, H. (2020). In search of a political economy of the postgrowth era. *Globalizations*. https://doi.org/10.1080/14747731.2020.1807837

Krausmann, F., Schandl, H., & Sieferle, R. P. (2008). Socio-ecological regime transitions in Austria and the United Kingdom. *Ecological Economics, 65*(1), 187–201. https://doi.org/10.1016/j.ecolecon.2007.06.009

Leonard, H. J. (1988). *Pollution and the struggle for the world product: Multinational corporations, environment, and international comparative advantage*. Cambridge University Press.

Leonard, T. C. (2005). Retrospectives: Eugenics and economics in the progressive era. *Journal of Economic Perspectives, 19*(4), 207–224. https://doi.org/10.1257/089533005775196642

Martinez-Alier, J. (2013). 'Ecological economics'. In *international encyclopedia of the social and behavioural sciences, J. D. Wright*. Elsevier.

Marx, K. (1867). *Das Kapital. Krtiik der Polotischen Oekonomie. Buch I: Dar Producktionsprocess des Kapitals* (1st ed.). Hamburg.

Meadows, D. H., Meadows, D. L., Randers, J., & Behrens III, W. W. (1972). *The limits to growth.* Universe Books.

Mirowski, P., & Plehwe, D. (Eds.). (2009). *The road to Mont pèlerin: Making of the neoliberal thought collective.* Harvard University Press.

Mishan, E. J. (1969). *Growth: The price we pay.* Staples Press.

Morgan, J. (2020). Electric vehicles: The future we made and the problem of unmaking it. *Cambridge Journal of Economics, 44*(4), 953–977. https://doi.org/10.1093/cje/beaa022

Munda, G. (1997). Environmental economics, ecological economics, and the concept of sustainable development. *Environmental Values, 6*(2), 213–233. https://doi.org/10.3197/096327197776679158

Nilsen, A. G. (2018). Why the World Bank's optimism about global poverty misses the point. *The Conversation.* Retrieved May 19, 2019, from https://theconversation.com/why-the-world-banks-optimism-about-global-poverty-misses-the-point-104963

Norgaard, R. B., & Bode, C. (1998). Next, the value of God, and other reactions. *Ecological Economics, 25*(1), 37–39. https://doi.org/10.1016/S0921-8009(98)00012-3 doi:10.1016/S0921-8009(98)00012-3

OECD. (2020). *Beyond growth: Towards a new economic approach, new approaches to economic challenges.* Organisation for Economic Cooperation and Development. https://doi.org/10.1787/33a25ba3-en

Parrique, T., Barth, B. F., Kerschner, C., Kraus-Polk, A., Kuokkanen, A., & Spangenberg, J. H. (2019). *Decoupling debunked: Evidence and arguments against green growth as a sole strategy for sustainability.* European Environmental Bureau.

Polanyi, K. (1944). *The great transformation* (1st ed.). Rinehart & Company.

Polanyi, K. (1957). The market as instituted process. In K. Polanyi, C. M. Arensberg, & H. W. Pearson (Eds.), *Trade and market in the early empires* (pp. 243–270). Henry Regnery Company.

Raworth, K. (2018). *Doughnut economics: Seven ways to think like a 21st-century economist.* Random House Business Books. (Original work published 2017)

Rockström, J., Steffen, W., Noone, K., Persson, Å, Chapin, F. S., Lambin, E., Lenton, T. M., Scheffer, M., Folke, C., Schellnhuber, H., Nykvist, B., De Wit, C. A., Hughes, T., van der Leeuw, S., Rodhe, H., Sörlin, S., Snyder, P. K., Costanza, R., Svedin, U., … Foley, J. (2009). Planetary boundaries: Exploring the safe operating space for humanity. *Ecology and Society, 14*(2), 1–32. https://doi.org/10.5751/ES-03180-140232

Røpke, I. (2004). The early history of modern ecological economics. *Ecological Economics, 50*(3-4), 293–314. https://doi.org/10.1016/j.ecolecon.2004.02.012

Sachs, W. (2015). *Planet dialectics: Explorations in environment and development.* Zed Books. (Original work published 1999)

Schumacher, E. F. (1973). *Small is beautiful: A study of economics as if people mattered.* Sphere Books.

Scitovsky, T. (1976). *The joyless economy: An inquiry into human satisfaction and consumer dissatisfaction.* University Press.

Singerman, D. R. (2016). Keynesian eugenics and the goodness of the world. *Journal of British Studies, 55* (July), 538–565. https://doi.org/10.1017/jbr.2016.56

Smith, T. (Ed.). (2019). *Degrowth of aviation: Reducing air travel in a just way.* Stay Grounded / Kollektiv Periskop.

Solow, R. (1974). Intergenerational equity and exhaustible resources. *The Review of Economic Studies, 41,* 29–45. https://doi.org/10.2307/2296370

Spash, C. L. (1999). The development of environmental thinking in economics. *Environmental Values, 8*(4), 413–435. https://doi.org/10.3197/096327199129341897

Spash, C. L. (2002). *Greenhouse economics: Value and ethics.* Routledge.

Spash, C. L. (2009). The new environmental pragmatists, pluralism and sustainability. *Environmental Values, 18*(3), 253–256. https://doi.org/10.3197/096327109 (1247473937637 0

Spash, C. L. (2010). The brave new world of carbon trading. *New Political Economy, 15*(2), 169–195. https://doi.org/10.1080/13563460903556049

Spash, C. L. (2011). Social ecological economics: Understanding the past to see the future. In F. S. Lee (Ed.), *Social, methods, and microeconomics: Contributions to doing economics better* (pp. 39–74). Wiley-Blackwell.

Spash, C. L. (2012). Editorial: Response and responsibility. *Environmental Values, 21*(4), 391–396. https://doi.org/10.3197/096327112X13466893627941

Spash, C. L. (2013). The shallow or the deep ecological economics movement? *Ecological Economics, 93* (September), 351–362. https://doi.org/10.1016/j.ecolecon.2013.05.016

Spash, C. L. (2015). Bulldozing biodiversity: The economics of offsets and trading-in nature. *Biological Conservation, 192*(December), 541–551. https://doi.org/10.1016/j.biocon.2015.07.037

Spash, C. L. (2016a). The political economy of the Paris agreement on human induced climate change: A brief guide. *Real World Economics Review, 75*(June), 67–75. http://www.paecon.net/PAEReview/issue75/Spash75.pdf

Spash, C. L. (2016b). This changes nothing: The Paris agreement to ignore reality. *Globalizations, 13*(6), 928–933. https://doi.org/10.1080/14747731.2016.1161119

Spash, C. L. (2017). Social ecological economics. In C. L. Spash (Ed.), *Routledge handbook of ecological economics: Nature and society* (pp. 3–16). Routledge.

Spash, C. L. (2020a). The capitalist passive environmental revolution. *Ecological Citizen, 4*(1), forthcoming.

Spash, C. L. (2020b). 'The economy' as if people mattered: Revisiting critiques of economic growth in a time of crisis. *Globalizations.* https://doi.org/10.1080/14747731.2020.1761612

Spash, C. L. (2020c). The revolution will not be corporatised!. *Environmental Values, 29*(2), 121–130. https://doi.org/10.3197/096327120X15752810323968

Spash, C. L. (2020d). A tale of three paradigms: Realising the revolutionary potential of ecological economics. *Ecological Economics, 169*(March), 1–14. https://doi.org/10.1016/j.ecolecon.2019.106518

Spash, C. L. (2021). The contested conceptualisation of pollution in economics: Market failure or cost shifting success? *Cahiers D'Économie Politique,* forthcoming.

Spash, C. L., & Aslaksen, I. (2015). Re-establishing an ecological discourse in the policy debate over how to value ecosystems and biodiversity. *Journal of Environmental Management, 159*(August), 245–253. https://doi.org/10.1016/j.jenvman.2015.04.049

Spash, C. L., & Clayton, A. M. H. (1997). The maintenance of natural capital: Motivations and methods. In A. Light, & J. M. Smith (Eds.), *Space, place and environmental ethics* (pp. 143–173). Rowman & Littlefield Publishers.

Spash, C. L., & Smith, T. (2019). Of ecosystems and economies: Re-connecting economics with reality. *Real-World Economics Review, 87*(March), 212–229. Retrieved March 19. http://www.paecon.net/PAEReview/issue87/SpashSmith87.pdf

Spash, C. L., & Theine, H. (2018). Voluntary individual carbon trading: Friend or foe?. In A. Lewis (Ed.), *Handbook of psychology and economic behaviour* (pp. 595–624). Cambridge University Press.

Stern, N. H., Peters, S., Bakhshi, V., Bowen, A., Cameron, C., Catovsky, S., Crane, D., Cruickshank, S., Dietz, S., Edmondson, N., Garbett, S.-L., Hamid, L., Hoffman, G., Ingram, D., Jones, B., Patmore, N., Radcliffe, H., Sathiyarajah, R., Stock, M., … Zenghelis, D. (2006). *Stern review on the economics of climate change.* UK Government Economic Service. www.sternreview.org.uk

Stiglitz, J. E. (2009). The world development report: Development theory and policy. In S. Yusuf (Ed.), *Development economics through the decades: A critical look at 30 years of the world development report* (pp. 139–151). World Bank.

Toman, M. (1998). Why not to calculate the value of the world's ecosystem services and natural capital. *Ecological Economics, 25*(1), 57–60. https://doi.org/10.1016/S0921-8009(98)00017-2

Turner, R. K., Pearce, D. W., & Bateman, I. (1994). *Environmental economics.* Harvester Wheatsheaf.

UNCTAD. (2019). *Trade and development report 2019: Financing a global green new deal.* Geneva: United Nations Conference on Trade and Development. https://unctad.org/en/PublicationsLibrary/tdr2019_en.pdf

UNEP. (2011a). Restoring the natural foundation to sustain a green economy: A century-long journey for ecosystem management. *International ecosystem management partnership (IEMP) policy brief.*

UNEP. (2011b). *Towards a green economy: Pathways to sustainable development and poverty eradication.* United Nations Environment Programme.

UNEP. (2019). *A new deal for nature: Account for the true value of nature.* United Nations. https://www.unenvironment.org/resources/policy-and-strategy/new-deal-nature

United Nations General Assembly. (2012). *The future we want: Resolution adopted by the general assembly on 27 July 2012* New York: United Nations. https://www.un.org/ga/search/view_doc.asp?symbol=A/RES/66/288&Lang=E

van Huijstee, M., Pollock, L., Glasbergen, P., & Leroy, P. (2011). Challenges for NGOs partnering with cor-
    porations: WWF Netherlands and the environmental defense fund. *Environmental Values, 20*(1), 43–74
    https://doi.org/10.3197/096327111 (12922350166030

Victor, P. A. (1991). Indicators of sustainable development: Some lessons from capital theory. *Ecologica
    Economics, 4*(3), 191–213. https://doi.org/10.1016/0921-8009(91)90051-F

von der Leyen, U. (2019). Speech by President von der Leyen on the occasion of the COP25 [as delivered]
    Brussels: European Commission. https://ec.europa.eu/commission/presscorner/api/files/attachment
    859088/Speech%20by%20President%20von%20der%20Leyen%20at%20the%20COP25%20-%20Madrid%
    202%20December%202019%20-%20as%20delivered_EN.pdf

World Bank. (2018). Piecing together the poverty puzzle: Poverty and shared prosperity 2018. Washington
    DC: International Bank for Reconstruction and Development / The World Bank.

World Commission on Environment and Development. (1987). Report of the world commission on environ-
    ment and development: Our common future. United Nations. https://sustainabledevelopment.un.org
    content/documents/5987our-common-future.pdf

The appallingly bad neoclassical economics of climate change

Steve Keen (iD)

ABSTRACT
Forecasts by economists of the economic damage from climate change have been notably sanguine, compared to warnings by scientists about damage to the biosphere. This is because economists made their own predictions of damages, using three spurious methods: assuming that about 90% of GDP will be unaffected by climate change, because it happens indoors; using the relationship between temperature and GDP today as a proxy for the impact of global warming over time; and using surveys that diluted extreme warnings from scientists with optimistic expectations from economists. Nordhaus has misrepresented the scientific literature to justify the using a smooth function to describe the damage to GDP from climate change. Correcting for these errors makes it feasible that the economic damages from climate change are at least an order of magnitude worse than forecast by economists, and may be so great as to threaten the survival of human civilization.

Introduction

William Nordhaus was awarded the *Sveriges Riksbank Prize in Economic Sciences in Memory of Alfred Nobel* (Mirowski, 2020) in 2018 for his work on climate change. His first major paper in this area was 'World Dynamics: Measurement Without Data' (Nordhaus, 1973), which attacked the pessimistic predictions in Jay Forrester's *World Dynamics* (Forrester, 1971, 1973) on the grounds, amongst others, that his predictions were not firmly grounded in empirical research:

> The treatment of empirical relations in World Dynamics can be summarised as *measurement without data* ... Not a single relationship or variable is drawn from actual data or empirical studies. (Nordhaus, 1973, p. 1157; italics in original, subsequent emphases added)

> *There is no explicit or apparent reference to data or existing empirical studies.* (Nordhaus, 1973, p. 1182)

> *Whereas most scientists would require empirical validation of either the assumptions or the predictions of the model* before declaring its truth content, Forrester is apparently content with subjective plausibility. (Nordhaus, 1973, p. 1183)

> Sixth, there is some lack of humility toward predicting the future. Can we treat seriously Forrester's (or anybody's) predictions in economics and social science for the next 130 years? Long-run economic forecasts have generally fared quite poorly ... And now, *without the scantest reference to economic theory or empirical data*, Forrester predicts that the world's material standard of living will peak in 1990 and then decline. (Nordhaus, 1973, p. 1183)

After this paper, Nordhaus's own research focused upon the economics of climate change. One could rightly expect, from his critique of Forrester, that Nordhaus was scrupulous about basing his modelling upon sound empirical data.

One's expectations would be dashed. Whereas Nordhaus characterized Forrester's work as 'measurement without data', Nordhaus's can be characterized as 'making up numbers to support a pre-existing belief': specifically, that climate change could have only a trivial impact upon the economy. This practice was replicated, rather than challenged, by subsequent Neoclassical economists – with some honourable exceptions, notably Pindyck (2017), Weitzman (2011a, 2011b), DeCanio (2003), Cline (1996), Darwin (1999), Kaufmann (1997, 1998), and Quiggin and Horowitz (1999).

The end product is a set of purported empirical estimates of the impact of climate change upon the economy that are utterly spurious, and yet which have been used to calibrate the 'Integrated Assessment Models' (IAMs) that have largely guided the political responses to climate change. DeCanio expressed both the significance and the danger of this work very well in his book *Economic Models of Climate Change: A Critique*:

> Perhaps the greatest threat from climate change is the *risk* it poses for large-scale catastrophic disruptions of Earth systems …
>
> Business as usual amounts to conducting a one-time, irreversible experiment of unknown outcome with the habitability of the entire planet.
>
> Given the magnitude of the stakes, it is perhaps surprising that much of the debate about the climate has been cast in terms of *economics* …
>
> Nevertheless, it is undeniably the case that economic arguments, claims, and calculations have been the dominant influence on the public political debate on climate policy in the United States and around the world … It is an open question whether the economic arguments were the cause or only an *ex post* justification of the decisions made by both administrations, but there is no doubt that economists have claimed that their calculations should dictate the proper course of action. (DeCanio, 2003, pp. 2–4)

The impact of these economists goes beyond merely advising governments, to actually writing the economic components of the formal reports by the *IPCC* ('Intergovernmental Panel On Climate Change'), the main authority coordinating humanity's response, such as it is, to climate change. The blasé conclusions they reach – such as the following from the *2014 IPCC Report* (Field et al., 2014) – carry far more weight with politicians, obsessed as they are with their countries' GDP growth rates, than the much more alarming ecological warnings in the sections of the Report written by actual scientists:

> Global economic impacts from climate change are difficult to estimate. Economic impact estimates completed over the past 20 years vary in their coverage of subsets of economic sectors and depend on a large number of assumptions, many of which are disputable, and many estimates do not account for catastrophic changes, tipping points, and many other factors. With these recognized limitations, *the incomplete estimates of global annual economic losses for additional temperature increases of ~2°C are between 0.2 and 2.0% of income.* (Arent, Tol, et al., 2014, p. 663; emphasis added)

This is a prediction, not of a drop in the *annual rate* of economic growth – which would be significant even, at the lower bound of 0.2% – but a prediction that the *level* of GDP will be between 0.2% and 2% lower, when global temperatures are 2°C higher than pre-industrial levels, compared to what they would have been in the complete absence of global warming. This involves a trivial decline in the predicted rate of economic growth between 2014 and whenever the 2°C increase occurs, even at the upper bound of 2%.

Given the impact that economists have had on public policy towards climate change, and the immediacy of the threat we now face from climate change (Amen et al., 2008; Gills, 2020; Gills & Morgan, 2019), this work could soon be exposed as the most significant and dangerous hoax in the history of science.

Fictional empirics

The numerical relationships that economists assert exist between global temperature change and GDP change were summarized in Figure 1 of the chapter 'Key Economic Sectors and Services' (Arent et al., 2014b) in the 2014 IPCC Report Climate *Change 2014: Impacts, Adaptation, and Vulnerability* (Field et al., 2014). It is reproduced below as Figure 1.

The sources of these numbers – as I explain below, they cannot be called 'data points' – are given in Table SM10-1 from the supplement to this report (Arent et al., 2014a, p. SM10-4).[1] Four classifications of the approaches used were listed by the IPCC: 'Enumeration' (ten studies); 'Statistical' (5 studies); 'CGE' ('Computable General Equilibrium': 2 studies – one with 2 results); and 'Expert Elicitation' (1 study).

Enumeration: it's what you don't count that counts

The bland description of what the 'Enumeration' approach entails given by Tol makes it seem unobjectionable:

In this approach, estimates of the "physical effects" of climate change are obtained one by one from natural science papers, which in turn may be based on some combination of climate models, impact models, and laboratory experiments. The physical impacts must then each be given a price and added up. For

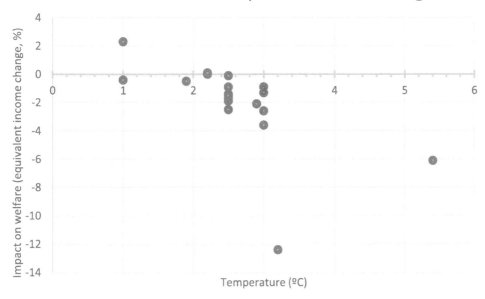

Figure 1. Figure 10.1 from Chapter 10 'Key Economic Sectors and Services' of the IPCC report climate change 2014 impacts, adaptation, and vulnerability.

agricultural products, an example of a traded good or service, agronomy papers are used to predict the effect of climate on crop yield, and then market prices or economic models are used to value the change in output. (Tol, 2009, pp. 31–32)

However, this analysis commenced from the perspective, stated in the very first reference in this tradition (Nordhaus, 1991), that climate change is a relatively trivial issue:

> First, it must be recognised that human societies thrive in a wide variety of climatic zones. *For the bulk of economic activity, non-climate variables like labour skills, access to markets, or technology swamp climatic considerations in determining economic efficiency.* (Nordhaus, 1991, p. 930; emphasis added)

If there had been a decent evaluation process in place at this time for research into the economic impact of climate change, this paragraph alone should have raised alarm bells: yes, it is quite likely that climate *today* is a less important determinant of 'economic efficiency' *today* than 'labour skills, access to markets, or technology', when one is comparing one region or country with another *today*. *But what is the relevance of this cross-sectional comparison to assessing the impact of drastically altering the entire planet's climate over time, via the retention of additional solar energy from additional greenhouse gases?*

One sentence further on, Nordhaus excludes 87% of US industry from consideration, on the basis that it takes place 'in carefully controlled environments that will not be directly affected by climate change':

> Table 5 shows a sectoral breakdown of United States national income, where the economy is subdivided by the sectoral sensitivity to greenhouse warming. The most sensitive sectors are likely to be those, such as agriculture and forestry, in which output depends in a significant way upon climatic variables. *At the other extreme are activities, such as cardiovascular surgery or microprocessor fabrication in 'clean rooms', which are undertaken in carefully controlled environments that will not be directly affected by climate change.* Our estimate is that approximately 3% of United States national output is produced in highly sensitive sectors, another 10% in moderately sensitive sectors, and *about 87% in sectors that are negligibly affected by climate change.* (Nordhaus, 1991, p. 930; emphasis added)

The examples of 'cardiovascular surgery or microprocessor fabrication in 'clean rooms'' might seem reasonable activities to describe as taking place in 'carefully controlled environments'. However, Nordhaus's list of industries *that he simply assumed* would be negligibly impacted by climate change is so broad, and so large, that it is obvious that what he meant by 'not be directly affected by climate change' is anything that takes place indoors – or, indeed, underground, since he includes mining as one of the unaffected sectors. Table 1, which is an extract from Nordhaus's breakdown of economic activity by vulnerability to climatic change in US 1991 $ terms (Nordhaus, 1991, Table 5 p. 931).

Since this was the first paper in a research tradition, one might hope that subsequent researchers challenged this assumption. However, instead of challenging it, they replicated it. The *2014 IPCC*

Table 1. Extract from Nordhaus's breakdown of economic activity by vulnerability to climatic change in US 1991 $ terms (Nordhaus, 1991, p. 931).

Sector	Value (billions)	Percentage of total
Negligible effect		
Manufacturing and mining	627.4	26.0
Other transportation and communication	132.6	5.5
Finance, insurance, and balance real estate	274.8	11.4
Trade and other services	674.6	27.9
Government services	337.0	14.0
Rest of world	50.3	2.1
Total 'negligible effect'	**2096.7**	**86.9**

Report repeats the assertion that climate change will be a trivial determinant of future economic performance:

> For most economic sectors, the impact of climate change will be small relative to the impacts of other drivers (*medium evidence, high agreement*). Changes in population, age, income, technology, relative prices, lifestyle, regulation, governance, and many other aspects of socioeconomic development will have an impact on the supply and demand of economic goods and services that is large relative to the impact of climate change. (Arent et al., 2014b, p. 662)

It also repeats the assertion that indoor activities will be unaffected. The one change between Nordhaus in 1991 and the IPCC Report 23 years later is that it no longer lumps mining in the 'not really exposed to climate change' bracket (Nordhaus, 1993).[2] Otherwise it repeats Nordhaus's assumption that anything done indoors will be unaffected by climate change:

FAQ 10.3 Are other economic sectors vulnerable to climate change too?

> Economic activities such as agriculture, forestry, fisheries, and mining are exposed to the weather and thus vulnerable to climate change. *Other economic activities, such as manufacturing and services, largely take place in controlled environments and are not really exposed to climate change.* (Arent et al., 2014b, p. 688; emphasis added)

All the intervening papers between Nordhaus in 1991 and the IPCC in 2014 maintain this assumption: neither manufacturing, nor mining, transportation, communication, finance, insurance and non-coastal real estate, retail and wholesale trade, nor government services, appear in the 'enumerated' industries in the 'Coverage' column in Table A1. *All these studies have simply assumed that these industries, which account for of the order of 90% of GDP, will be unaffected by climate change.*

There is a 'poker player's tell' in the FAQ quoted above which implies that these Neoclassical economists are on a par with United States President, Donald Trump, in their appreciation of what climate change entails. This is the statement that 'Economic activities such as agriculture, forestry, fisheries, and mining *are exposed to the weather and thus vulnerable to climate change'. Explicitly,* they are saying that if an activity is exposed to the weather, it is vulnerable to climate change, but if it is not, it is 'not really exposed to climate change'. *They are equating the climate to the weather.*

While this is a harsh judgment to pass on fellow academics, there is simply no other way to make sense of their collective decision to exclude, by assumption, almost 90% of GDP from their enumeration of damages from climate change. Nor is there any other way to interpret the core assumption of their other dominant method of making up numbers for their models, the so-called 'statistical' or 'cross-sectional' method.

The 'Statistical approach'

While locating the fundamental flaw in the 'enumeration' approach took some additional research, the flaw in the statistical approach was obvious in the first reference I read on it, Richard Tol's much-corrected (Tol, 2014) and much-criticised paper (Gelman, 2014, 2015, 2019; Nordhaus & Moffat, 2017, p. 10), 'The Economic Effects of Climate Change':

> An alternative approach, exemplified in Mendelsohn's work (Mendelsohn, Morrison, et al., 2000; Mendelsohn, Schlesinger, et al., 2000) can be called the statistical approach. It is based on direct estimates of the welfare impacts, *using observed variations (across space within a single country) in prices and expenditures to discern the effect of climate.* **Mendelsohn assumes that the observed variation of economic**

activity with climate over space holds over time as well; and uses climate models to estimate the future effect of climate change. (Tol, 2009, p. 32)

If the methodological fallacy in this reasoning is not immediately apparent – bearing in mind that numerous academic referees have let pass papers making this assumption – think what it would mean if this assumption were correct.

Within the United States, it is generally true that very hot and very cold regions have a lower level of per capita income than median temperature regions. Using the States of the contiguous continental USA for those regions, Florida (average temperature 22.5°C) and North Dakota (average temperature 4.7°C), for example, have lower per capita incomes than New York (average temperature 7.4° C). But the difference in average temperatures is far from the only reason for differences in income, and in the greater scheme of things, the differences are trivial anyway: as American States, at the global level they are all in the high per capita income range (respectively $26,000, $26,700 and $43,300 per annum in 2000 US dollars). A statistical study of the relationship between 'Gross State Product (GSP) per capita and temperature will therefore find a weak, nonlinear relationship, with GSP per capita rising from low temperatures, peaking at medium ones, and falling at higher temperatures.

If you then assume that this same relationship between GDP and temperature will apply as global temperatures rise with Global Warming, you will conclude that Global Warming will have a trivial impact on global GDP. *Your assumption is your conclusion.*

This is illustrated by Figure 2, which shows a scatter plot of deviations from the national average temperature by State in °C, against the deviations from the national average (GDP per capita) of Gross State Product per capita in percent of GDP (the source data is in Table A2), and a quadratic fit to this data, which has a coefficient of -0.00318,[3] and, as expected, a weak correlation coefficient of 0.31.[4]

This regression thus yields a very poor, but not entirely useless, 'in-sample' model of how temperature deviations from the USA average today slightly influence deviations from average US GDP per capita today. In words, Equation (1) asserts that Gross State Product per capita falls by 0.318% (of the national average GDP per capita) for every 1°C difference in temperature (from the national average temperature) squared:

$$GSP_{PC}(\Delta T) = -0.318\% \times \Delta T^2 \tag{1}$$

An absurd 'out of sample' policy recommendation from this model would be that the US's GDP would increase if hotter and colder States could move towards the average temperature for the USA. This absurd recommendation could be 'refined' by using this same data to calculate the optimum temperature for the USA's GDP, and then proposing that all States move to that temperature. Of course, these 'policies' are clearly impossible, because the States can't change their location on the planet.

However, the economists doing these studies reasoned that Global Warming would achieve the same result over time (with the drawback that it would be applied equally to all regions). So they did indeed calculate optimum temperatures for each of the sectors they expected to be affected by climate change – *with their calculations excluding the same list of sectors that the 'enumeration' approach assumed would be unaffected (manufacturing, mining, services, etc.):*

> Both the reduced-form and cross-sectional response functions imply that the net productivity of sensitive economic sectors is a hill-shaped function of temperature (Mendelsohn, Schlesinger, et al., 2000). Warming creates benefits for countries that are currently on the cool side of the hill and damages for countries on the warm side of the hill. The exact optimum temperature varies by sector. For example,

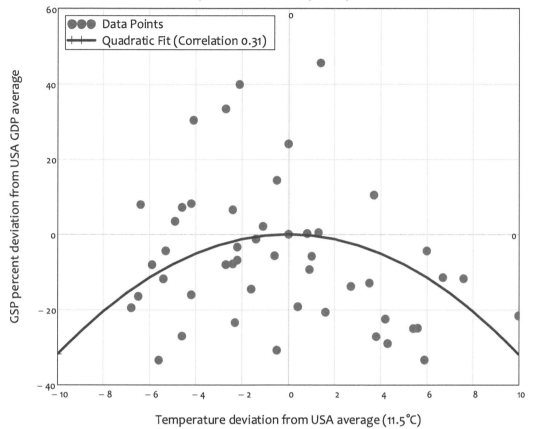

Figure 2. Correlation of temperature and USA Gross State Product per capita.

according to the Ricardian model, the optimum temperatures for agriculture, forestry, and energy are 14.2, 14.8 and 8.6°C, respectively. With the reduced form model, the optimum temperatures for agriculture and energy are 11.7 and 10.0. (Mendelsohn, Morrison, et al., 2000, p. 558)

They then estimated the impact on GDP of increasing global temperatures, *assuming that the same coefficients they found for the relationships between temperature and output today* (using what Tol called 'the statistical' and Mendelsohn more accurately labels the 'cross-sectional' approach) *could be used to estimate the impact of global warming*. This resulted in more than one study which concluded that increasing global temperatures via global warming would be *beneficial* to the economy. Here, for example, is Mendelsohn, Schlesinger, et al. (2000) on the impact of a 2.5°C increase in global temperatures:

> Compared to the size of the economy in 2100 ($217 trillion), the market effects are small ... The Cross-sectional climate-response functions imply a narrower range of impacts across GCMs: from $97 to $185 billion of *benefits* with an average of $145 billion of *benefits* a year. (Mendelsohn, Schlesinger, et al., 2000, p. 41; emphasis added)

The, once more, *explicit* assumption these economists are making is that it doesn't matter how you alter temperature. Whether this is hypothetically done by altering a region's location on the planet –

which is impossible – or by altering the temperature of the entire planet – which is what Climate Change is doing – they assumed that the impact on GDP would be the same.

Expert opinions – real and imagined

Nordhaus conducted the only two surveys of 'expert opinions' to estimate the impact of global warming on GDP, in 1994 (Nordhaus, 1994a), and 2017 (Nordhaus & Moffat, 2017). The former asked people from various academic backgrounds to give their estimates of the impact on GDP of three global warming scenarios: (A) a 3°C rise by 2090; (B) a 6°C rise by 2175; and (C) a 6°C rise by 2090. The numbers used by the IPCC from this study in Figure 1 were a 3°C temperature rise for a 3.6% fall in GDP.

Expert opinions are a valid procedure to aggregate knowledge in areas that require a large number of disparate fields to be aggregated, as the climate scientist Tim Lenton and co-authors explained in their paper 'Tipping elements in the Earth's climate system' (Lenton et al., 2008):

> formal elicitations of expert beliefs have frequently been used to bring current understanding of model studies, empirical evidence, and theoretical considerations to bear on policy-relevant variables. From a natural science perspective, a general criticism is that expert beliefs carry subjective biases and, moreover, do not add to the body of scientific knowledge unless verified by data or theory. Nonetheless, expert elicitations, based on rigorous protocols from statistics and risk analysis, have proved to be a very valuable source of information in public policymaking. It is increasingly recognized that they can also play a valuable role for informing climate policy decisions. (Lenton et al., 2008, p. 1791)

I cite this paper in contrast to Nordhaus's here for two reasons: (1) it shows how expert opinion surveys should be conducted; (2) Nordhaus later cites this survey in support of his use of a 'damage function' for climate change which lacks tipping points, when this survey explicitly rejects such functions.

Lenton et al.'s survey was sent to 193 scientists, of whom 52 responded. Respondents were specifically instructed to stick to their area of knowledge, rather than to speculate more broadly: 'Participants were encouraged to remain in their area of expertise' (Lenton et al., 2008, p. 10). These are listed in Table 2.

Nordhaus's survey began with a letter requesting 22 people to participate, 18 of whom fully complied, and one partially. Nordhaus describes them as including 10 economists, 4 'other social scientists', and 5 'natural scientists and engineers', but also notes that eight of the economists come from 'other subdisciplines of economics (those whose principal concerns lie outside environmental economics)' (Nordhaus, 1994a, p. 48). This, *ipso facto*, should rule them out from taking part in this expert survey in the first place.

Table 2. Fields of expertise for experts surveyed in (Lenton et al., 2008); abridged from Table 1 in (Lenton et al., 2008, p. 10).

Field	Number
Glaciology	10
Ice sheet modelling	3
Ecology	4
Ecosystem modelling	7
Marine biosphere modelling	4
Oceanography	9
Climate Modelling	15

One of them was Larry Summers, who is probably the source of the choicest quotes in the paper, such as 'For my answer, the existence value [of species] is irrelevant – I don't care about ants except for drugs' (Nordhaus, 1994a, p. 50).

Lenton's survey combined the expertise of its interviewees in specific fields of climate change to compile a list of large elements of the planet's climatic system (>1000 km in extent) which could be triggered into a qualitative change of state by increases in global temperature of between 0.5°C (disappearance of Arctic summer sea ice) and 6°C (amplified En Nino causing drought in Southeast Asia and elsewhere), on timescales varying from 10 years (Arctic summer sea ice) to 300 years (West Antarctic Ice Shelf disintegration) (Lenton et al., 2008, p. 1788).

Nordhaus's survey was summarized by a superficially bland pair of numbers – 3°C temperature rise and a 3.6% fall in GDP – but that summary hides far more than it reveals. There was extensive disagreement, well documented by Nordhaus, between the relatively tiny cohort of actual scientists surveyed, and, in particular, the economists 'whose principal concerns lie outside environmental economics'. The quotes from the economists surveyed also reveal the source of the predisposition by economists in general to dismiss the significance of climate change.

As Nordhaus noted, 'Natural scientists' estimates [of the damages from climate change] were 20–30 times higher than mainstream economists'' (Nordhaus, 1994a, p. 49). The average estimate by 'Non-environmental economists' (Nordhaus, 1994a, Figure 4, p. 49) of the damages to GDP a 3°C rise by 2090 was 0.4% of GDP; the average for natural scientists was 12.3%, and *this was with one of them refusing to answer Nordhaus's key questions*:

> Also, although the willingness of the respondents to hazard estimates of subjective probabilities was encouraging, it should be emphasized that most respondents proffered these estimates with reservations and a recognition of the inherent difficulty of the task. One respondent (19), however, was a holdout from such guesswork, writing:

> I must tell you that I marvel that economists are willing to make quantitative estimates of economic consequences of climate change where the only measures available are estimates of global surface average increases in temperature. As [one] who has spent his career worrying about the vagaries of the dynamics of the atmosphere, I marvel that they can translate a single global number, an extremely poor surrogate for a description of the climatic conditions, into quantitative estimates of impacts of global economic conditions. (Nordhaus, 1994a, pp. 50–51)

Comments from economists lay at the other end of the spectrum from this self-absented scientist. Because they had a strong belief in the ability of 'human societies' to adapt – born of their acceptance of the Neoclassical model of capitalism, in which 'the economy' always returns to equilibrium after a 'exogenous shock' – they could not imagine that climate change could do significant damage to the economy, whatever it might do to the biosphere itself:

> One respondent suggested whimsically that it was hardly surprising, given that the economists know little about the intricate web of natural ecosystems, whereas *natural scientists know equally little about the incredible adaptability of human societies …*

> There is a clear difference in outlook among the respondents, depending on their assumptions about the ability of society to adapt to climatic changes. One was concerned that society's response to the approaching millennium would be akin to that prevalent during the Dark Ages, whereas *another respondent held that the degree of adaptability of human economies is so high that for most of the scenarios the impact of global warming would be "essentially zero".*

An economist explains that in his view energy and brain power are the only limits to growth in the long run, and with sufficient quantities of these it is possible to adapt or develop new technologies *so as to prevent any significant economic costs.* (Nordhaus, 1994a, pp. 48–49; all emphases added)

Given this extreme divergence of opinion between economists and scientists, one might imagine that Nordhaus's next survey would examine the reasons for it. In fact, the opposite applied: his methodology excluded non-economists entirely.

Rather than a survey of experts, this was a literature survey (Nordhaus & Moffat, 2017), which *ipso facto* is another legitimate method to provide data for a topic subject that is difficult to measure, and subject to high uncertainty. He and his co-author searched for relevant articles using the string '(damage OR impact) AND climate AND cost' (Nordhaus & Moffat, 2017, p. 7), which is reasonable, if too broad (as they admit in the paper).

The key flaw in this research was where they looked: they executed their search string in *Google*, which returned 64 million results, *Google Scholar*, which returned 2.8 million, and the economics-specific database *Econlit*, which returned just 1700 studies. On the grounds that there were too many results in Google and Google Scholar, they ignored those results, and simply surveyed the 1700 articles in *Econlit* (Nordhaus & Moffat, 2017, p. 7). *These are, almost exclusively, articles written by economists.*

Nordhaus and Moffat read the abstracts of these 1700 to rule out all but 24 papers from consideration. Reading these papers led to just 11 they included in their survey results. The supplemented this 'systematic research synthesis (SRS)' with:

a second approach, known as a "non-systematic research summary." In this approach, the universe of studies was selected by a combination of formal and informal methods, such as the SRS above, the results of the Tol survey, and other studies that were known to the researchers. (Nordhaus & Moffat, 2017, p. 8)

Their labours resulted in the addition of just five studies which had not been used either by the IPCC or by Tol in his aggregation papers (Tol, 2009, 2018), with an additional 6 results, and 4 additional authors – Cline, Dellink, Kemfert and Hambel – who had not already cited in the empirical estimates literature (though Cline was one of Nordhaus's interviewees in his 1994 survey).

Remarkably, given that Nordhaus was the lead author of this study, one of the previously unused studies was by Nordhaus himself in 2010 (Nordhaus, 2010). Nordhaus and Moffat (2017) does not provide details of this paper, or any other paper they uncovered, but I presume it is (Nordhaus, 2010), given the date, and the fact that the temperature and damages estimates given in it – a 3.4°C increase in temperature causing a 2.8% fall in GDP – are identical to those given in this paper's Table 2.

It may seem strange that Nordhaus did not notice that his own paper was not included in previous studies. But in fact, there is a good reason for this omission: (Nordhaus, 2010) was not an enumerative study, nor a statistical one, let alone the results of an 'expert elicitation', *but the output of a run of Nordhaus's own 'Integrated Assessment Model' (IAM), DICE!* Treating this as a 'data point' is using an output of a model to calibrate the model itself.[5] Nonetheless, these numbers – and the five additional pairs from the four additional studies uncovered by their survey – were added to the list of numbers from which economists like Nordhaus could calibrate what they call their 'damage functions'.

Damage functions

'Damage functions' are the way in which Nordhaus and many other Neoclassical economists connect estimates from scientists of the change in global temperature to their own, as shown in previous sections, utterly unsound estimates of future GDP, given this change in temperature. They reduce GDP from what they claim it would have been in the total absence of climate change, to what they claim it will be, given different levels of temperature rise. The form these damage functions take is often simply a quadratic:

$$GDP(T) = a + b \times T + c \times T^2 \qquad (2)$$

Nordhaus justifies using a quadratic to describe such an inherently discontinuous process as climate change *by misrepresenting the scientific literature* – specifically, the careful survey of expert opinions carried out by Lenton et al. (2008) and contrasted earlier to Nordhaus's survey of largely non-experts (Nordhaus, 1994a). Nordhaus makes the following statement in his DICE manual, and repeats it in (Nordhaus & Moffat, 2017, p. 35):

> The current version assumes that damages are a quadratic function of temperature change and does not include sharp thresholds or tipping points, but *this is consistent with the survey by* Lenton et al. (2008) (Nordhaus & Sztorc, 2013, p. 11. Emphasis added)

In *The Climate Casino* (Nordhaus, 2013), Nordhaus states that:

> There have been a few systematic surveys of tipping points in earth systems. A particularly interesting one by Lenton and colleagues examined the important tipping elements and assessed their timing … *Their review finds no critical tipping elements with a time horizon less than 300 years until global temperatures have increased by at least 3°C.* (Nordhaus, 2013, p. 60; emphasis added)

These claims can only be described as blatant misrepresentations of 'Tipping elements in the Earth's climate system' (Lenton et al., 2008). The very first element in Lenton et al.'s table of findings meets the two numerical criteria that Nordhaus gave: Arctic summer sea-ice could be triggered by global warming of between 0.5°C and 2°C, and in a time span measured in decades – see Figure 3.

Nordhaus justifies his omission via a third criterion of 'level of concern' in his table N1 (see Figure 4), where Arctic summer sea ice receives the lowest ranking (*). This apparently justifies his statement that there was 'no *critical* tipping point' in less than 300 years, and with less than a 3°C temperature increase.

However, *no such column exists in Table 1 of* Lenton et al. (2008),[6] while their discussion of the ranking of threats puts Arctic summer sea ice first, not last:

> We conclude that *the greatest (and clearest) threat is to the Arctic* with summer sea-ice loss likely to occur long before (and potentially contribute to) GIS melt. (Lenton et al., 2008, pp. 1791–92; emphasis added)

Their treatment of time also differs substantially from that implied by Nordhaus, which is that decisions about tipping elements with time horizons of several centuries can be left for decision

Table 1. Policy-relevant potential future tipping elements in the climate system and (below the empty line) candidates that we considered but failed to make the short list*

Tipping element	Feature of system, F (direction of change)	Control parameter(s), p	Critical value(s),[†] p_{crit}	Global warming[†‡]	Transition timescale,[†] T	Key impacts
Arctic summer sea-ice	Areal extent (−)	Local ΔT_{air}, ocean heat transport	Unidentified[§]	+0.5–2°C	~10 yr (rapid)	Amplified warming, ecosystem change

Figure 3. An extract from Table 1 of 'Tipping elements in the Earth's climate system' (Lenton et al., 2008, p. 1788).

Table N-1.

Tipping element	Time scale (years)	Threshold warming value	Level of concern (most concern = ***)	Concern
Arctic summer sea ice	10	+0.5–2°C	*	Amplified warming, ecosystems
Sahara/Sahel and West African monsoon	10	+3–5°C	**	Wet period

Figure 4. Nordhaus's table purporting to summarize Lenton's findings.

makers several centuries hence. While Lenton et al. do give a timeframe of more than 300 years for the complete melting of the Greenland Ice Sheet (GIS), for example, they note that they considered only tipping elements *whose fate would be decided this century*:

> Thus, we focus on the consequences of decisions enacted within this century that trigger a qualitative change within this millennium, and we exclude tipping elements whose fate is decided after 2100. (Lenton et al., 2008, p. 1787)

Thus, while the GIS might not melt completely for several centuries, the human actions that will decide whether that happens or not will be taken in this century, not in several hundred years from now.

Finally, the paper's conclusion began with the warning that smooth functions should not be used, noted that discontinuous climate tipping points were likely to be triggered this century, and reiterated that the greatest threats were Arctic summer sea ice and Greenland:

Conclusion
> *Society may be lulled into a false sense of security by smooth projections of global change.* Our synthesis of present knowledge suggests that a variety of tipping elements could reach their critical point within this century under anthropogenic climate change. *The greatest threats are tipping the Arctic sea-ice and the Greenland ice sheet,* and at least five other elements could surprise us by exhibiting a nearby tipping point. (Lenton et al., 2008, p. 1792; emphasis added)

I consulted Lenton on whether there were any grounds for Nordhaus's interpretation of his paper that I might have missed (Keen & Lenton, 2020). He replied that there were not, that my interpretation of the paper was correct, and that there were several other papers which also strongly reject the proposition that a smooth function is appropriate for assessing the dangers from climate change (Cai et al., 2016; Kriegler et al., 2009; Lenton et al., 2019; Lenton & Ciscar, 2013).

There is thus no empirical or scientific justification for choosing a quadratic to represent damages from climate change – the opposite in fact applies. Regardless, this is the function that Nordhaus ultimately adopted. Given this assumed functional form, the only unknowns are the values of the coefficients a, b and c in Equation (2).

How low can you go?

Ever since Nordhaus started using a quadratic, he has consistently reduced the value of its parameters, from an initial 0.0035 for the quadratic term – which means that global warming is assumed to reduce GDP by 0.35% times the temperature (change over pre-industrial levels) squared – to a final value of 0.00227 (see Equation (3)). Source documents here are (Nordhaus & Sztorc, 2013, p. 83, 86, 91 & 97 for the 1992, 1999, 2008 and 2013 versions of DICE.; Nordhaus, 2017, p. 1 for 2017; Nordhaus 2018b, p. 345 for 2018):

$$
\begin{array}{ccc}
\text{Year} & \text{Damage Function} & \text{Parameters} \\[4pt]
1992 & \dfrac{1}{1 + \dfrac{a}{9} \times \sqrt{T}} & a = 0.0133 \\[12pt]
1999 & \dfrac{1}{1 + b \times T + c \times T^2} & \begin{array}{l} b = 0.0045 \\ c = 0.0035000 \end{array} \\[12pt]
2008 & \dfrac{1}{1 + c \times T^2} & c = 0.0028388 \\[12pt]
2013 & \dfrac{1}{1 + c \times T^2} & c = 0.0026700 \\[8pt]
2017 & 1 - c \times T^2 & c = 0.0023600 \\[4pt]
2018 & 1 - c \times T^2 & c = 0.0022700
\end{array}
\tag{3}
$$

This reduction progressively reduced his already trivial predictions of damage to GDP from global warming. For example, his prediction for the impact on GDP of a 4°C increase in temperature – the level he describes as optimal in his 'Nobel Prize' lecture, since according to his model, it minimises the joint costs of damage and abatement (Nordhaus, 2018a, Slides 6 & 7) – was reduced from a 7% fall in 1992 to a 3.6% fall in 2018 (see Figure 5).

I now turn to doing what Nordhaus himself said a scientist should do, when deriding Forrester's model – 'require empirical validation of either the assumptions or the predictions of the model before declaring its truth content' (Nordhaus, 1973, p. 1183). This is clearly something neither Nordhaus nor any other Neoclassical climate change economist did – apart from the honourable mentions noted earlier.

Deconstructing neoclassical delusions: GDP and energy

Nordhaus justified the assumption that 87% of GDP will be unaffected by climate change on the basis that:

> for the bulk of the economy—manufacturing, mining, utilities, finance, trade, and most service industries—it is difficult to find major direct impacts of the projected climate changes over the next 50–75 years. (Nordhaus, 1991, p. 932)

In fact, a direct effect can easily be identified by surmounting the failure of economists in general – not just Neoclassicals – to appreciate the role of energy in production. Almost all economic models use production functions that assume that 'Labour' and 'Capital' are all that are needed to produce 'Output'. However, neither Labour nor Capital can function without energy inputs: 'to coin a phrase, labour without energy is a corpse, while capital without energy is a sculpture' (Keen et al., 2019, p. 41). Energy is directly needed to produce GDP, and therefore if energy production has to fall because of global warming, then so will GDP.

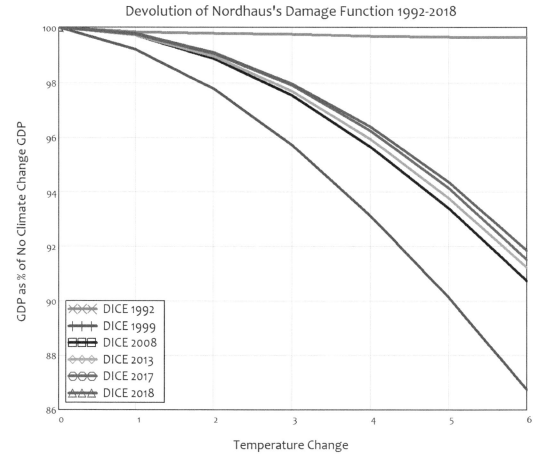

Figure 5. How low can you go? Nordhaus's downward revisions to his damage function.

The only question is how much, and the answer, given our dependence on fossil fuels, is a lot. Unlike the trivial correlation between local temperature and local GDP used by Nordhaus and colleagues in the 'statistical' method, the correlation between global energy production and global GDP is overwhelmingly strong. A simple linear regression between energy production and GDP has a correlation coefficient of 0.997 – see Figure 6.[7]

GDP in turn determines excess CO2 in the atmosphere. A linear regression between GDP and CO2 has a correlation coefficient of 0.998 – see Figure 7.

Lastly, CO2 very tightly determines the temperature excess over pre-industrial levels. A linear regression between CO2 and the Global Temperature Anomaly has a correlation of 0.992 using smoothed data (which excludes the effect of non-CO2 fluctuations such as the El Nino effect) (Figure 8).[8]

Working in reverse, if climatic changes caused by the increase in global temperature persuade the public and policymakers that we must stop adding CO2 to the atmosphere 'now', whenever 'now' may be, then global GDP will fall roughly proportionately to the ratio of fossil-fuel energy production to total energy production at that time.

As of 2020, fossil fuels provided roughly 85% of energy production. So, if 2020 were the year humanity decided that the growth in CO2 had to stop, GDP would fall by of the order of 85%. Even if the very high rate of growth of renewables in 2015 were maintained – when the *ratio* of

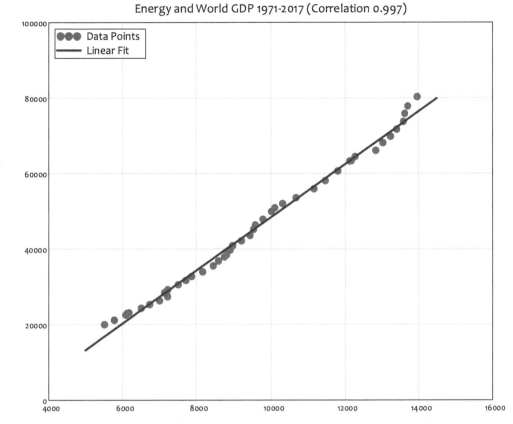

Figure 6. Energy determines GDP.

renewables to total energy production was growing at about 3% per annum – renewables would still yield less than 40% of total energy production in 2050 – see Figure 9. This implies a drop in GDP of about 60% at that time. On this basis alone, the decision by Neoclassical climate change economists to exclude 'manufacturing, mining, utilities, finance, trade, and most service industries' from any consequences from climate change is thus utterly unjustified.

Deconstructing neoclassical delusions: statistics

The 'cross-sectional approach' of using the coefficients from the geographic temperature to GDP relationship as a proxy for the global temperature to GDP relationship is similarly unjustified. It assumes that it doesn't matter how one alters temperature: the effect on GDP will be the same. This belief was defended by Tol in an exchange on Twitter between myself, the Climate scientist Daniel Swain (Swain et al., 2020), and the Professor of Computational Astrophysics Ken Rice (Köhler et al., 2018) on June 17–18 2019:[9]

> Richard Tol: 10 K is less than the temperature distance between Alaska and Maryland (about equally rich), or between Iowa and Florida (about equally rich). Climate is not a primary driver of income. https://twitter.com/RichardTol/status/1140591420144869381?s=20

Daniel Swain: A global climate 10 degrees warmer than present is not remotely the same thing as taking the current climate and simply adding 10 degrees everywhere. This is an admittedly widespread misconception, but arguably quite a dangerous one. https://twitter.com/Weather_West/status/11406706473 13584129?s=20

Richard Tol: That's not the point, Daniel. We observe that people thrive in very different climates, and that some thrive and others do not in the same climate. Climate determinism therefore has no empirical support. https://twitter.com/RichardTol/status/1140928458853421057?s=20

Richard Tol: And if a relationship does not hold for climate variations over space, you cannot confidently assert that it holds over time. https://twitter.com/RichardTol/status/1140928893878263808?s=20

Steve Keen: The cause of variations over space is utterly different to that over time. That they are comparable is the most ridiculous and dangerous "simplifying assumption" in the history of economics. https://twitter.com/ProfSteveKeen/status/1140941982082244608?s=20

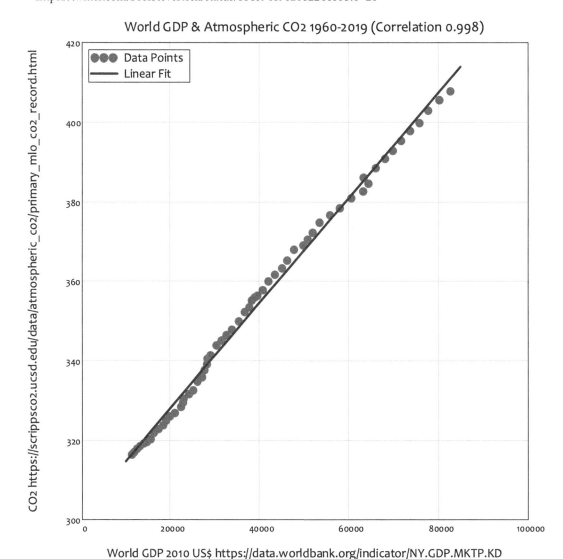

Figure 7. Without significant de-carbonization, GDP determines CO2.

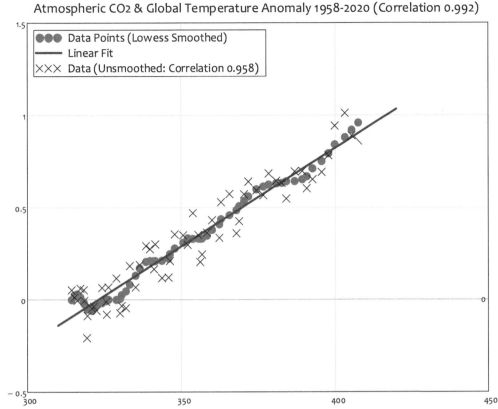

Figure 8. CO2 determines global warming.

Ken Rice: Can I just clarify. Are you actually suggesting that a 10 K rise in global average surface temperature would be manageable? https://twitter.com/theresphysics/status/1140661721633308673?s=20

Richard Tol: We'd move indoors, much like the Saudis have. https://twitter.com/RichardTol/status/1140669525081415680?s=20

As with the decision to exclude ~90% of GDP from damages from climate change, Tol's assumed equivalence of weather changes across space with climate change over time ignores the role of energy in causing climate change. This can be illustrated by annotating his third tweet above with respect to the amount of energy needed to bring about a 10°C temperature increase for the atmosphere:

And if a relationship does not hold for climate variations over space [without changing the energy level of the atmosphere], you cannot confidently assert that it holds over time [as the Solar energy retained in the atmosphere rises by more than 50,000 million Terajoules]. (Trenberth, 1981)

To put this level of energy in more comprehensible terms, this is the equivalent of 860 million Hiroshima atomic bombs, or 1.6 bombs per square kilometre of the planet's surface.[10]

A 10°C average temperature increase would also lead to sustained 'wet bulb' temperatures that would be fatal for humans in the Tropics and much of the sub-tropics (Raymond et al., 2020; Xu, et al., 2020). It is of the order of the increase which caused the end-Permian extinction event, the

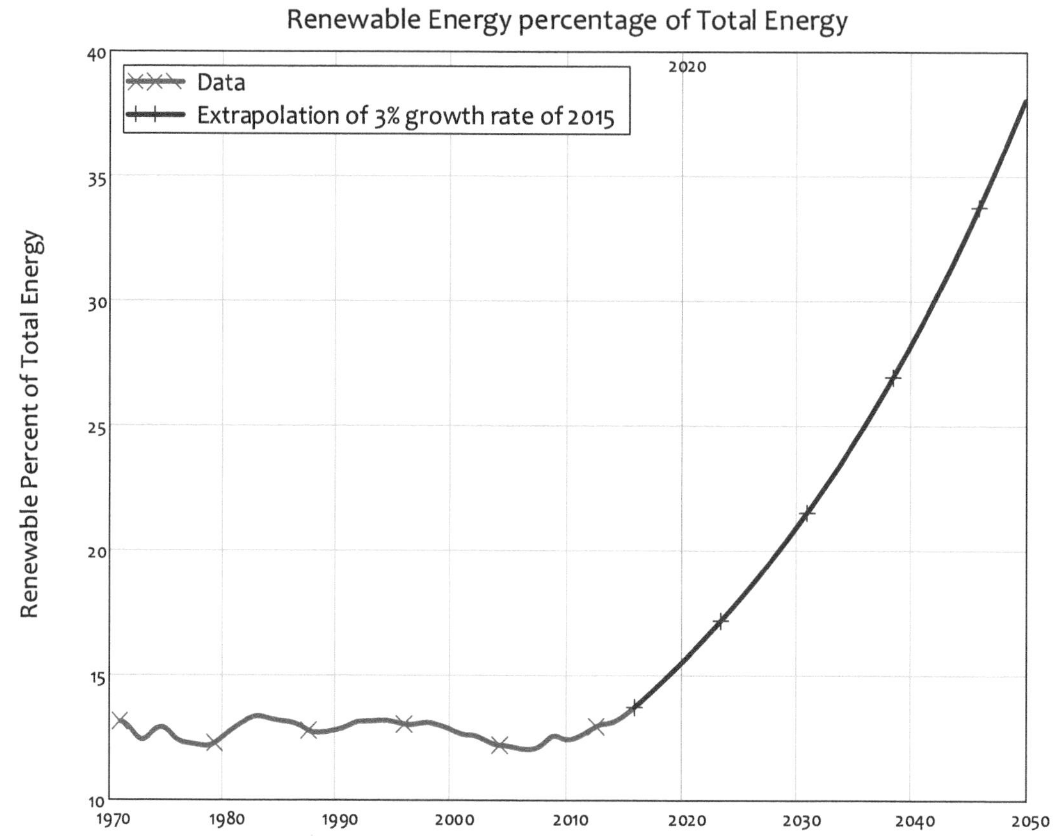

Renewable Energy percentage of Total Energy

Figure 9. Renewable energy as a percentage of total energy production.

most extreme mass-extinction in Earth's history (Penn et al., 2018). It is five times the level of globa‸ temperature increase (2°C) that climate scientists fear could trigger 'tripping cascades' which coulᴅ transform the planet into a 'Hothouse Earth' (Lenton et al., 2019; Steffen et al., 2018) that is poten‸ tially incompatible with human existence:

> Hothouse Earth is likely to be uncontrollable and dangerous to many, particularly if we transition into it in only a century or two, and it poses severe risks for health, economies, political stability (especially for the most climate vulnerable), and ultimately, the habitability of the planet for humans. (Steffen et al., 2018, p. 8256)

It therefore very much does matter how one alters the temperature. At the planetary level, there are ‸ main determinants of the average yearly temperature at any point on the globe:

1. Variations in the solar energy reaching the Earth;
2. Variations in the amount of this energy retained by greenhouse gases; and
3. Differences in location on the planet – primarily differences in distance from the Equator

What the 'cross-sectional method' did was derive parameters for the third factor, *and then simpl‸ assume that the same parameters applied to the second.* This is comparable to carefully measuring th‸ terrain of a mountain in the North–South direction, and then using that information to advise on th‸ safety of an expedition to traverse it from East to West, in the dark.

Econometrics before ecology

This weakness of the 'cross-sectional approach' has been admitted in a more recent paper in this tradition:

> Firstly, the literature relies primarily on the cross-sectional approach, and as such *does not take into account the time dimension of the data (i.e., assumes that the observed relationship across countries holds over time as well)*. (Kahn et al., 2019, p. 2; emphasis added)

This promising start was unfortunately neutered by their eventual simple linear extrapolation of the change in the relationship temperature to GDP relationship between 1960 and 2014 forward to 2100:

> We start by documenting that the global average temperature has risen by 0:0181 degrees Celsius per year over the last half century … We show that an increase in average global temperature of 0:04°C per year— corresponding to the Representative Concentration Pathway (RCP) 8.5 scenario (see Figure 1), which assumes higher greenhouse gas emissions in the absence of mitigation policies— reduces world's real GDP per capita by 7.22 percent by 2100. (Kahn et al., 2019, p. 4)

Their predictions for GDP change, as a function of temperature change, is the shaded region in Figure 10 (which reproduces their Figure 2). The linearity of their projection is evident: it presumes no structural change in the relationship between global temperature and GDP, even as temperature rises by 3.2°C, over their time horizon of 80 years (0.04°C per year from 2020 till 2100).

The failure of this paper to account for the obvious discontinuities such a temperature increase will wreak on the planet's climate was acknowledged by one of the authors on Twitter on October 31st 2019:

> Kamiar Mohaddes: I also want to be clear that we cannot, and do not, claim that our empirical analysis allows for rare disaster events, whether technological or climatic, which is likely to be an important consideration. From this perspective, the counterfactual outcomes that we discuss … in Section 4 of the paper (see: https://ideas.repec.org/p/cam/camdae/1965.html) should be regarded as conservative because they only consider scenarios where the climate shocks are Gaussian, without allowing for rare disasters. https://twitter.com/KamiarMohaddes/status/1189846383307694084?s=20; https://twitter.com/KamiarMohaddes/status/1189846648366796800?s=20

> Steve Keen: Kamiar, the whole point of #GlobalWarming is that it shifts the entire distribution. What is "rare" in our current climate—like for example the melting of Greenland—becomes a certainty at higher temperatures. https://twitter.com/ProfSteveKeen/status/1189849936290029569?s=20

What Mohaddes called 'rare disaster events' – such as, for example, the complete disappearance of the Arctic Ice sheet during summer – would indeed be rare at our current global temperature. But they become certainties as the temperature rises another 3°C (Steffen et al., 2018, Figure 3, p. 8255). This forecast is as useful as a study of the relationship between temperature and speed skating, which concludes that it would be advantageous to increase the temperature of the ice from −2°C to +2°C.

This recent paper alerted me to one potentially promising study I had previously missed: the significant outlier in Figure 10 by Burke et al. (2015). This was at least outside the economic ballpark, if not in that of scientists like Steffen, who expect a 4°C increase in temperature to lead to the collapse of civilization (Moses, 2020).

As its title 'Global non-linear effect of temperature on economic production' implies, it did at least consider nonlinearities in the Earth's climate. But once again, this was restricted to nonlinearities in the relationship between 1960 and 2010, which were then extrapolated to a future planet with a vastly different climate:

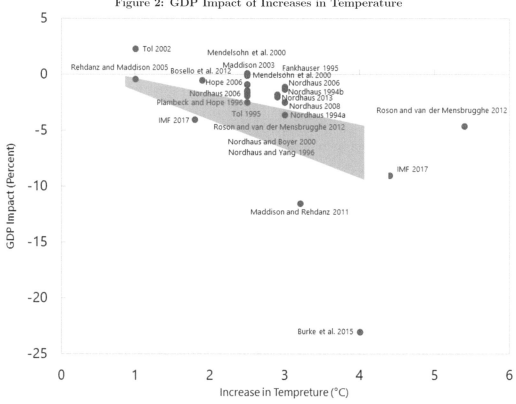

Figure 10. Kahn and Mohaddes's linear extrapolation of the temperature: GDP relationship from 1960–2014 out till 2100 (Kahn et al., 2019, p. 6).

> We quantify the potential impact of warming on national and global incomes by combining our estimated non-linear response function with 'business as usual' scenarios of future warming and different assumptions regarding future baseline economic and population growth. *This approach assumes future economies respond to temperature changes similarly to today's economies*—perhaps a reasonable assumption given the observed lack of adaptation during our 50-year sample … climate change reduces projected global output by 23% in 2100 relative to a world without climate change, although statistical uncertainty allows for positive impacts with probability 0.29 (Burke et al., 2015, pp. 237–38; emphasis added)

As applies to so much of this research, these two recent papers show the authors delighting in the ecstasy of econometrics, while failing to appreciate the irrelevance of their framework to the question at hand.

GIGO: Garbage in, garbage out

When I began this research, I expected that the main cause of Nordhaus's extremely low predictions of damages from climate change would be the application of a very high discount rate (Nordhaus, 2007)[11] to climate damages estimated by scientists (Hickel, 2018), and that a full critique of his work would require explaining why an equilibrium-based Neoclassical model like DICE[12] was the wrong tool to analyse something as uncertain, dynamic and far-from-equilibrium as climate change (Blatt, 1979; DeCanio, 2003).[13] Instead, I found that the computing adage 'Garbage In, Garbage Out'

(GIGO) applied: it does not matter how good or how bad the actual model is, when it is fed 'data' like that concocted by Nordhaus and the like-minded Neoclassical economists who followed him. The numerical estimates to which they fitted their inappropriate models are, as shown here, utterly unrelated to the phenomenon of global warming. Even an appropriate model of the relationship between climate change and GDP would return garbage predictions if it were calibrated on 'data' like this.

This raises a key question: how did such transparently inadequate work get past academic referees?

Simplifying assumptions and the refereeing process: the poachers becomes the gatekeepers

One reason why this research agenda was not drowned at birth was the proclivity for Neoclassical economists to make assumptions *on which their conclusions depend*, and then dismiss any objections to them on the grounds that they are merely 'simplifying assumptions'.

As Paul Romer observed, the standard justification for this is 'Milton Friedman's (1953) methodological assertion from unnamed authority that 'the more significant the theory, the more unrealistic the assumptions' (Romer, 2016, p. 5). Those who make this defence do not seem to have noted Friedman's footnote that 'The converse of the proposition does not of course hold: assumptions that are unrealistic (in this sense) do not guarantee a significant theory' (Friedman, 1953, p. 14).

A simplifying assumption is something which, if it is violated, makes only a small difference to your analysis. Musgrave points out that 'Galileo's assumption that air-resistance was negligible for the phenomena he investigated was a true statement about reality, and an important part of the explanation Galileo gave of those phenomena' (Musgrave, 1990, p. 380). However, the kind of assumptions that Neoclassical economists frequently make, are ones where if the assumption is false, then the theory itself is invalidated (Keen, 2011, pp. 158–174).

This is clearly the case here with the core assumptions of Nordhaus and his Neoclassical colleagues. If activities that occur indoors are, in fact, subject to climate change; if the temperature to GDP relationships across space cannot be used as proxies for the impact of global warming on GDP, then their conclusions are completely false. Climate change will be at least one order of magnitude more damaging to the economy than their numbers imply – working solely from rejecting their spurious assumption that about 90% of the economy will be unaffected by it. It could be far, far worse.

Unfortunately, referees who accept Friedman's dictum that 'a theory cannot be tested by the 'realism' of its 'assumptions'' (Friedman, 1953, p. 23) were unlikely to reject a paper because of its assumptions, especially if it otherwise made assumptions that Neoclassical economists accept. Thus, Nordhaus's initial sorties in this area received a free pass.

After this, a weakness of the refereeing process took over. As any published academic knows, once you are published in an area, journal editors will nominate you as a referee for that area. Thus, rather than peer review providing an independent check on the veracity of research, it can allow the enforcement of a hegemony. As one of the first of the very few Neoclassical economists to work on climate change, and the first to proffer empirical estimates of the damages to the economy from climate change, this put Nordhaus in the position to both frame the debate, and to play the role of gatekeeper. One can surmise that he relished this role, given not only his attacks on Forrester and the *Limits to Growth* (Meadows, Randers, et al., 1972; Nordhaus, 1973; Nordhaus et al., 1992), but also his attack on his fellow Neoclassical economist Nicholas Stern for using a low discount rate in *The Stern Review* (Nordhaus, 2007; Stern, 2007).

The product has been an undue degree of conformity in this community that even Tol acknowledged:

> it is quite possible that the estimates are not independent, as there are only a relatively small number of studies, based on similar data, by authors who know each other well … although the number of researchers who published marginal damage cost estimates is larger than the number of researchers who published total impact estimates, it is still a reasonably small and close-knit community who may be subject to group-think, peer pressure, and self-censoring. (Tol, 2009, p. 37, 42–43)

Indeed.

Conclusion: drastically underestimating economic damages from global warming

Were climate change an effectively trivial area of public policy, then the appallingly bad work done by Neoclassical economists on climate change would not matter greatly. It could be treated, like the intentional Sokal hoax (Sokal, 2008), as merely a salutary tale about the foibles of the Academy.

But the impact of climate change upon the economy, human society, and the viability of the Earth's biosphere in general, are matters of the greatest importance. That work this bad has been done, and been taken seriously, is therefore not merely an intellectual travesty like the Sokal hoax. If climate change does lead to the catastrophic outcomes that some scientists now openly contemplate (Kulp & Strauss, 2019; Lenton et al., 2019; Lynas, 2020; Moses, 2020; Raymond et al., 2020; Wang et al., 2019; Xu et al., 2020; Yumashev et al., 2019), then these Neoclassical economists will be complicit in causing the greatest crisis, not merely in the history of capitalism, but potentially in the history of life on Earth.

Notes

1. It is reproduced below as Table A1 in the Appendix, with the addition of Nordhaus (1991), additional empirical studies located by Nordhaus and Moffat (2017), and one additional methodology.
2. Perhaps this was a concession to the fact that many mines today are open cut. In 1993, Nordhaus specifically noted that 'underground mining' was safe from climate change: 'In reality, most of the U.S. economy has little direct interaction with climate … More generally, *underground mining*, most services, communications, and manufacturing are sectors likely to be largely unaffected by climate change—sectors that comprise around 85 percent of GDP' (Nordhaus, 1993, p. 15). That said, none of the 'enumeration' studies actually considered the impact of climate change on mining—see Table A1.
3. This is in fact very close to the coefficient Nordhaus used in his damage function in 1999, and higher than he has used since 2008, as discussed on page 14.
4. This data is an amalgam of average temperature by State from 1971 to 2000, real GDP in 2000, and population in 2010. However, similar results would apply with a more coherent set of data, and the regression result derived from it is for illustration purposes only.
5. For this same reason, I do not consider the use of Computable General Equilibrium models to generate numbers for calibrating IAMs, the fourth technique listed by the IPCC in (Arent et al., 2014a, p. SM10-4).
6. The column 'Critical values' in Lenton, Held et al.'s Table 1 relates to whether there is a known empirical magnitude that will trigger the tipping point, not whether the tipping point itself is of critical significance. The symbol next to the word 'Unidentified', which is used to describe Arctic summer sea ice, states that 'Meaning theory, model results, or paleo-data suggest the existence of a critical threshold but a numerical value is lacking in the literature' (Lenton et al., 2008, p. 1788).
7. I use a raw linear regression here just to emphasisz how incorrect it is for Neoclassicals to neglect the impact of energy when discussing climate change. A log-log regression, which is more suitable for

forward or backward extrapolation of this relationship, has an even higher correlation coefficient of 0.998. An appropriate nonlinear relation should be used in any realistic model of long term change.

8. The correlation with non-smoothed data is still extremely high at 0.958.

9. This and a later Twitter exchange cited in this paper have been slightly edited for tone and to correct spelling mistakes.

10. Trenberth estimates the mass of the atmosphere at 513.7×10^{18} kilograms (Trenberth, 1981, p. 5238). Raising the temperature of one kilogram of air by 1°C requires 1004 joules of energy: the product is 5.158×10^{22} joules, or 51,575 million Terajoules. 1 Hiroshima bomb is equivalent to 60 Terajoules (https://www.justintools.com/unit-conversion/energy.php?k1=hiroshima-bomb-explosion&k2= terajoules). The planet's area is 510 million square kilometres. These calculations do not factor in the energy needed to raise average temperature of the oceans as well, which global warming is also doing, though more slowly. Their mass is about 250 times that of the atmosphere.

11. Nordhaus does use a high discount rate, and criticized Stern for using a much lower one. However, the primary reason Nordhaus uses a high rate is that, in his words, 'with the low interest rate, *the relatively small damages in the next two centuries* get overwhelmed by the high damages over the centuries and millennia that follow 2200.' (Nordhaus, 2007, p. 202. Emphasis added). As I show here, the key weakness of his work is not the discount rate, but the conclusion that there will be 'relatively small damages in the next two centuries'.

12. DICE stands for 'Dynamic, Integrated Climate & Economics'. It is dynamic and integrated in name only.

13. DeCanio does a very good job on this topic, though his critique applies equally well to applying Neo-classical 'representative agent' models to any macroeconomic issue, let alone to climate change. Other endemic weaknesses of this analysis include the application of cost-benefit analysis rather than the 'Precautionary Principle' to such an uncertain topic as climate change, and the poor handling of uncertainty by Neoclassical economics in general.

Disclosure statement

No potential conflict of interest was reported by the author(s).

ORCID

Steve Keen ⓘ http://orcid.org/0000-0002-0439-1809

References

Amen, M., Bosman, M. M., & Gills, B. K. (2008). Editorial: The urgent need for global action to combat climate change. *Globalizations, 5*(1), 49–52. https://doi.org/10.1080/14747730701850886

Arent, D. J., Tol, R. S. J., Faust, E., Hella, J. P., Kumar, S., Strzepek, K. M., Tóth, F. L., & Yan, D. (2014a). Key economic sectors and services – supplementary material. In C. B. Field, V. R. Barros, D. J. Dokken et al. (Eds.), *Climate change 2014: Impacts, adaptation, and vulnerability. Part A: Global and sectoral aspects. Contribution of working Group II to the fifth assessment report of the intergovernmental panel on climate change.*

Arent, D. J., Tol, R. S. J., Faust, E., Hella, J. P., Kumar, S., Strzepek, K. M., Tóth, F. L., & Yan, D. (2014b). Key economic sectors and services. In C. B. Field, V. R. Barros, D. J. Dokken et al. (Eds.), *Climate change 2014: Impacts, adaptation, and vulnerability. Part A: Global and sectoral aspects. Contribution of working Group II to the fifth assessment report of the intergovernmental panel on climate change.* (pp. 659–708). Cambridge University Press.

Blatt, J. M. (1979). Investment evaluation under uncertainty. *Financial Management, 8,* 66–81. https://doi.org/ 10.2307/3665352

Bosello, F., Eboli, F., & Pierfederici, R. (2012). Assessing the economic impacts of climate change. An updated CGE point of view. https://doi.org/10.22004/ag.econ.121700

Burke, M., Hsiang, S. M., & Miguel, E. (2015). Global non-linear effect of temperature on economic production Supplementary information. *Nature, 527*(7577), 235–239. https://doi.org/10.1038/nature15725

Cai, Y., Lenton, T. M., & Lontzek, T. S. (2016). Risk of multiple interacting tipping points should encourage rapid CO2 emission reduction. *Nature Climate Change, 6*(5), 520–525. https://doi.org/10.1038/ nclimate2964

Cline, W. (1996). The impact of global warming on agriculture: Comment. *The American Economic Review, 86* (5), 1309–1311. https://doi.org/10.2307/2118295

Darwin, R. (1999). The impact of global warming on agriculture: A Ricardian analysis: Comment. *American Economic Review, 89*(4), 1049–1052. https://doi.org/10.1257/aer.89.4.1049

DeCanio, S. J. (2003). *Economic models of climate change: A critique.* Palgrave Macmillan.

Fankhauser, S. (1995). *Valuing climate change: The economics of the greenhouse.* Earthscan.

Field, C. B., Barros, V. R., Mach, K. J., Mastrandrea, M. D., Bilir, T. E., Chatterjee, M., Ebi, K. L., Estrada, Y. O. Genova, R. C., Girma, B., Kissel, E. S., Levy, N., MacCracken, S., Mastrandrea, P. R., & White, L. L. (2014) IPCC, 2014: Climate change 2014: Impacts, adaptation, and vulnerability. Part A: Global and sectoral aspects. Contribution of working Group II to the fifth assessment report of the intergovernmental panel on climate change. Cambridge University Press.

Forrester, J. W. (1971). *World dynamics.* Wright-Allen Press.

Forrester, J. W. (1973). *World dynamics.* Wright-Allen Press.

Friedman, M. (1953). The methodology of positive economics. In M. Friedman (Eds.), *Essays in positive economics* (pp. 3–43). University of Chicago Press.

Gelman, A. (2014). A whole fleet of gremlins: Looking more carefully at Richard Tol's twice-corrected paper "The Economic Effects of Climate Change". *Statistical modeling, causal inference, and social science.* https:// statmodeling.stat.columbia.edu/2014/05/27/whole-fleet-gremlins-looking-carefully-richard-tols-twice-corrected-paper-economic-effects-climate-change/

Gelman, A. (2015). More gremlins: "Instead, he simply pretended the other two estimates did not exist. That is inexcusable". *Statistical Modeling, Causal Inference, and Social Science.* https://statmodeling.stat.columbia edu/2015/07/23/instead-he-simply-pretended-the-other-two-estimates-did-not-exist-that-is-inexcusable/

Gelman, A. (2019). The climate economics echo chamber: Gremlins and the people (including a Nobel prize winner) who support them. https://statmodeling.stat.columbia.edu/2019/11/01/the-environmental-economics-echo-chamber-gremlins-and-the-people-including-a-nobel-prize-winner-who-support-them/

Gills, B., & Morgan, J. (2019). Global climate emergency: After COP24, climate science, urgency, and the threat to humanity. *Globalizations.* https://doi.org/10.1080/14747731.2019.1669915

Gills, B. K. (2020). Deep restoration: From the great implosion to the great awakening. *Globalizations, 17*(4) 577–579. https://doi.org/10.1080/14747731.2020.1748364

Hickel, J. (2018). The Nobel prize for climate catastrophe. *Foreign Policy.* https://foreignpolicy.com/2018/12 06/the-nobel-prize-for-climate-catastrophe/

Hope, C. (2006). The marginal impact of CO2 from PAGE2002: An integrated assessment model incorporating the IPCC's five reasons for concern. *Integrated Assessment, 6*(1), 19–56. https://journals.sfu.ca/int_assess index.php/iaj/article/viewFile/227/190

Kahn, M. E., K. Mohaddes, Ng, R. N. C., Pesaran, H., Raissi, M., & Yang, J.-C. (2019). Long-term macroeco nomic effects of climate change: A cross-country analysis. https://doi.org/10.24149/gwp365

Kaufmann, R. K. (1997). Assessing the dice model: Uncertainty associated with the emission and retention of greenhouse gases. *Climatic Change, 35*(4), 435–448. https://doi.org/10.1023/A:1005372513452

Kaufmann, R. K. (1998). The impact of climate change on US agriculture: A response to Mendelssohn et al (1994). *Ecological Economics, 26*(2), 113–119. https://doi.org/10.1016/S0921-8009(97)00058-X

Keen, S. (1995). Finance and economic breakdown: Modeling Minsky's 'financial instability hypothesis' *Journal of Post Keynesian Economics, 17*(4), 607–635. https://doi.org/10.1080/01603477.1995.11490053

Keen, S. (2011). *Debunking economics: The naked emperor dethroned?* Zed Books.

Keen, S. (2017). *Can we avoid another financial crisis? (The future of capitalism)*. Polity Press.

Keen, S., Ayres, R. U., & Standish, R. (2019). A note on the role of energy in production. *Ecological Economics*, *157*, 40–46. https://doi.org/10.1016/j.ecolecon.2018.11.002

Keen, S., & Lenton, T. (2020). Draft paper on Nordhaus et al which cites you. T. Lenton. Trang, Keen, Steve.

Köhler, P., Hauck, J., Völker, C., Wolf-Gladrow, D. A., Butzin, M., Halpern, J. B., Rice, K., & Zeebe, R. E. (2018). Comment on "Scrutinizing the carbon cycle and CO2 residence time in the atmosphere" by H. Harde. *Global and Planetary Change*, *164*, 67–71. https://doi.org/10.1016/j.gloplacha.2017.09.015

Kriegler, E., Hall, J. W., Held, H., Dawson, R., & Schellnhuber, H. J. (2009). Imprecise probability assessment of tipping points in the climate system. *Proceedings of the National Academy of Sciences*, *106*(13), 5041–5046. https://doi.org/10.1073/pnas.0809117106

Kulp, S. A., & Strauss, B. H. (2019). New elevation data triple estimates of global vulnerability to sea-level rise and coastal flooding. *Nature Communications*, *10*(1), 4844. https://doi.org/10.1038/s41467-019-12808-z

Lenton, T., & Ciscar, J.-C. (2013). Integrating tipping points into climate impact assessments. *Climatic Change*, *117*(3), 585–597. https://doi.org/10.1007/s10584-012-0572-8

Lenton, T. M., Held, H., Kriegler, E., Hall, J. W., Lucht, W., Rahmstorf, S., & Schellnhuber, H. J. (2008). Supplement to tipping elements in the earth's climate system. *Proceedings of the National Academy of Sciences*, *105*(6), 1786–1793. https://doi.org/10.1073/pnas.0705414105

Lenton, T. M., Rockström, J., Gaffney, O., Rahmstorf, S., Richardson, K., Steffen, W., & Schellnhuber, H. J. (2019). Climate tipping points — too risky to bet against. *Nature*, *575*(7784), 592–595. https://doi.org/10.1038/d41586-019-03595-0

Lynas, M. (2020). *Our final warning: Six degrees of climate emergency*. HarperCollins Publishers.

Maddison, D. (2003). The amenity value of the climate: The household production function approach. *Resource and Energy Economics*, *25*(2), 155–175. https://doi.org/10.1016/S0928-7655(02)00024-6

Maddison, D., & Rehdanz, K. (2011). The impact of climate on life satisfaction. *Ecological Economics*, *70*(12), 2437–2445. https://doi.org/10.1016/j.ecolecon.2011.07.027

Meadows, D. H., Randers, J., & Meadows, D. (1972). *The limits to growth*. Signet.

Mendelsohn, R., Morrison, W., Schlesinger, M. E., & Andronova, N. G. (2000). Country-specific market impacts of climate change. *Climatic Change*, *45*(3), 553–569. https://doi.org/10.1023/A:1005598717174

Mendelsohn, R., Schlesinger, M., & Williams, L. (2000). Comparing impacts across climate models. *Integrated Assessment*, *1*(1), 37–48. https://doi.org/10.1023/A:1019111327619

Mirowski, P. (2020). The neoliberal Ersatz Nobel Prize. In D. Plehwe, Q. Slobodian, & P. Mirowski (Eds.), *Nine lives of neoliberalism* (pp. 219–254). Verso.

Moses, A. (2020). 'Collapse of civilisation is the most likely outcome': top climate scientists. Voice of Action. Melbourne, Australia.

Musgrave, A. (1990). Unreal assumptions. In J. C. Wood & R. N. Woods (Eds.), *Economic theory: The F-twist untwisted. Milton Friedman: Critical assessments* (Vol. 3, pp. 333–342). Routledge.

Nordhaus, W. (2007). Economics: Critical assumptions in the Stern review on climate change. *Science*, *317* (5835), 201–202. https://doi.org/10.1126/science.1137316

Nordhaus, W. (2008). *A question of balance*. Yale University Press.

Nordhaus, W. (2013). *The climate Casino: Risk, uncertainty, and economics for a warming world*. Yale University Press.

Nordhaus, W. (2018a). Nobel lecture in economic sciences. Climate change: The ultimate challenge for economics. https://www.nobelprize.org/uploads/2018/10/nordhaus-slides.pdf

Nordhaus, W. (2018b). Projections and uncertainties about climate change in an era of minimal climate policies. *American Economic Journal: Economic Policy*, *10*(3), 333–360. https://doi.org/10.1257/pol.20170046

Nordhaus, W., & Boyer, J. G. (2000). *Warming the world: Economic models of global warming*. MIT Press.

Nordhaus, W., & Sztorc, P. (2013). DICE 2013R: Introduction and user's manual.

Nordhaus, W. D. (1973). World dynamics: Measurement without data. *The Economic Journal*, *83*(332), 1156–1183. https://doi.org/10.2307/2230846

Nordhaus, W. D. (1991). To slow or not to slow: The economics of the greenhouse effect. *The Economic Journal*, *101*(407), 920–937. https://doi.org/10.2307/2233864

Nordhaus, W. D. (1993). Reflections on the economics of climate change. *The Journal of Economic Perspectives*, *7*(4), 11–25. https://doi.org/10.1257/jep.7.4.11

Nordhaus, W. D. (1994a). Expert opinion on climatic change. *American Scientist*, *82*(1), 45–51. https://www.jstor.org/stable/29775100

Nordhaus, W. D. (1994b). *Managing the global commons: The economics of climate change*. MIT Press.

Nordhaus, W. D. (2006). Geography and macroeconomics: New data and new findings. *Proceedings of the National Academy of Sciences of the United States of America*, *103*(10), 3510–3517. https://doi.org/10.1073/pnas.0509842103

Nordhaus, W. D. (2010). Economic aspects of global warming in a post-Copenhagen environment. *Proceedings of the National Academy of Sciences of the United States of America*, *107*(26), 11721–11726. https://doi.org/10.1073/pnas.1005985107

Nordhaus, W. D. (2017). Revisiting the social cost of carbon Supporting information. *Proceedings of the National Academy of Sciences*, *114*(7), 1518–1523. https://doi.org/10.1073/pnas.1609244114

Nordhaus, W. D., & Moffat, A. (2017). *A survey of global impacts of climate change: Replication, survey methods, and a statistical analysis* (Discussion Paper No. 2096). Cowles Foundation.

Nordhaus, W. D., Stavins, R. N., & Weitzman, M. L. (1992). Lethal Model 2: The limits to growth revisited. *Brookings Papers on Economic Activity*, *1992*(2), 1–43. https://doi.org/10.2307/2534581

Nordhaus, W. D., & Yang, Z. (1996). A regional dynamic general-equilibrium model of alternative climate-change strategies. *The American Economic Review*, *86*(4), 741–765. https://doi.org/2118303

Penn, J. L., Deutsch, C., Payne, J. L., & Sperling, E. A. (2018). Temperature-dependent hypoxia explains biogeography and severity of end-Permian marine mass extinction. *Science*, *362*(6419). Article eaat1327. https://doi.org/10.1126/science.aat1327

Pindyck, R. S. (2017). The use and misuse of models for climate policy. *Review of Environmental Economics and Policy*, *11*(1), 100–114. https://doi.org/10.1093/reep/rew012

Plambeck, E. L., & Hope, C. (1996). PAGE95: An updated valuation of the impacts of global warming. *Energy Policy*, *24*(9), 783–793. https://doi.org/10.1016/0301-4215(96)00064-X

Quiggin, J., & Horowitz, J. K. (1999). The impact of global warming on agriculture: A Ricardian analysis: Comment. *The American Economic Review*, *89*(4), 1044–1045. https://doi.org/10.1257/aer.89.4.1044

Raymond, C., Matthews, T., & Horton, R. M. (2020). The emergence of heat and humidity too severe for human tolerance. *Science Advances*, *6*(19). Article eaaw1838. https://doi.org/10.1126/sciadv.aaw1838

Rehdanz, K., & Maddison, D. (2005). Climate and happiness. *Ecological Economics*, *52*(1), 111–125. https://doi.org/10.1016/j.ecolecon.2004.06.015

Romer, P. (2016). *The trouble with macroeconomics*. https://paulromer.net/trouble-with-macroeconomics-update/WP-Trouble.pdf

Roson, R., & Mensbrugghe, D. v. d. (2012). Climate change and economic growth: Impacts and interactions. *International Journal of Sustainable Economy*, *4*(3), 270–285. https://doi.org/10.1504/IJSE.2012.047933

Sokal, A. D. (2008). *Beyond the hoax: Science, philosophy and culture*. Oxford University Press.

Steffen, W., Rockström, J., Richardson, K., Lenton, T. M., Folke, C., Liverman, D., Summerhayes, C. P., Barnosky, A. D., Cornell, S. E., Crucifix, M., Donges, J. F., Fetzer, I., Lade, S. J., Scheffer, M., Winkelmann, R., & Schellnhuber, H. J. (2018). Trajectories of the earth system in the anthropocene. *Proceedings of the National Academy of Sciences*, *115*(33), 8252–8259. https://doi.org/10.1073/pnas.1810141115

Stern, N. (2007). *The economics of climate change: The Stern review*. Cambridge University Press.

Swain, D. L., Singh, D., Touma, D., & Diffenbaugh, N. S. (2020). Attributing extreme events to climate change: A new frontier in a warming world. *One Earth*, *2*(6), 522–527. https://doi.org/10.1016/j.oneear.2020.05.011

Tol, R. S. J. (1995). The damage costs of climate change toward more comprehensive calculations. *Environmental and Resource Economics*, *5*(4), 353–374. https://doi.org/10.1007/BF00691574

Tol, R. S. J. (2002). Estimates of the damage costs of climate change. Part 1: Benchmark estimates. *Environmental and Resource Economics*, *21*(1), 47–73. https://doi.org/10.1023/A:1014500930521

Tol, R. S. J. (2009). The economic effects of climate change. *The Journal of Economic Perspectives*, *23*(2), 29–51. https://doi.org/10.1257/jep.23.2.29

Tol, R. S. J. (2014). Correction and update: The economic effects of climate change. *The Journal of Economic Perspectives*, *28*(2), 221–226. https://doi.org/10.1257/jep.28.2.221

Tol, R. S. J. (2018). The economic impacts of climate change. *Review of Environmental Economics and Policy*, *12*(1), 4–25. https://doi.org/10.1093/reep/rex027

Trenberth, K. E. (1981). Seasonal variations in global sea level pressure and the total mass of the atmosphere. *Journal of Geophysical Research*, 86(C6), 5238–5246. https://doi.org/10.1029/JC086iC06p05238

Wang, X. X., Jiang, D., & Lang, X. (2019). Extreme temperature and precipitation changes associated with four degree of global warming above pre-industrial levels. *International Journal Of Climatology*, 39(4), 1822–1838. https://doi.org/10.1002/joc.5918

Weitzman, M. L. (2011a). Fat-tailed uncertainty in the economics of catastrophic climate change. *Review of Environmental Economics and Policy*, 5(2), 275–292. https://doi.org/10.1093/reep/rer006

Weitzman, M. L. (2011b). Revisiting Fat-tailed uncertainty in the economics of climate change. *REEP Symposium on Fat Tails*, 5(2), 275–292. https://doi.org/10.1093/reep/rer006.

Xu, C., Kohler, T. A., Lenton, T. M., Svenning, J.-C., & Scheffer, M. (2020). Future of the human climate niche. *Proceedings of the National Academy of Sciences*, 117(21), 11350–11355. https://doi.org/10.1073/pnas.1910114117.

Yumashev, D., Hope, C., Schaefer, K., Riemann-Campe, K., Iglesias-Suarez, F., Jafarov, E., Burke, E. J., Young, P. J., Elshorbany, Y., & Whiteman, G. (2019). Climate policy implications of nonlinear decline of Arctic land permafrost and other cryosphere elements. *Nature Communications*, 10(1), 1900. https://doi.org/10.1038/s41467-019-09863-x

Appendix

Table A1. Table SM10-1, p. SM10-4 of IPCC 2014 Chapter 'Key Economic Sectors', plus other studies by economists

Authors (with citations where available)	Year	Warming (°C)	Impact (% GDP)	Method	In IPCC 2014?	Coverage
Nordhaus (1991)	1991	3	−0.25	Enumeration	No	Agriculture, forestry, electricity demand, space heating, Sea level rise
Cline	1992	2.50	−1.1		No	
Cline	1992	10	−6.0		No	
Nordhaus (1994b)	1994	3	−1.3	Enumeration	Yes	Agriculture, energy demand, sea level rise
Nordhaus (1994a)	1994	3	−3.6	Expert elicitation	Yes	Total welfare
Fankhauser (1995)	1995	2.5	−1.4	Enumeration	Yes	Sea level rise, biodiversity, agriculture, forestry, fisheries, electricity demand, water resources, amenity, human health, air pollution, natural disasters
Tol (1995)	1995	2.5	−1.9	Enumeration	Yes	Agriculture, biodiversity, sea level rise, human health, energy demand, water resources, natural disasters, amenity
Nordhaus and Yang (1996)	1996	2.5	−1.7	Enumeration	Yes	Agriculture, energy demand, sea level rise
Plambeck and Hope (1996)	1996	2.5	−2.5	Enumeration	Yes	Sea level rise, biodiversity, agriculture, forestry, fisheries, electricity demand, water resources, amenity, human health, air pollution, natural disasters
Mendelsohn, Morrison, et al. (2000)	2000	2.2	0	Enumeration	Yes	Agriculture, forestry, sea level rise, energy demand, water resources
Nordhaus and Boyer (2000)	2000	2.5	−1.5	Enumeration	Yes	Agriculture, sea level rise, other market impacts, human health, amenity, biodiversity, catastrophic impacts
Mendelsohn, Morrison, et al. (2000)	2000	2.2	0.1	Statistical	Yes	Agriculture, forestry, energy demand
Tol (2002)	2002	1	2.3	Enumeration	Yes	Agriculture, forestry, biodiversity, sea level rise, human health, energy demand, water resources
Maddison (2003)	2003	2.5	−0.1	Statistical	Yes	Household consumption

(Continued)

Table A1. Continued.

Authors (with citations where available)	Year	Warming (°C)	Impact (% GDP)	Method	In IPCC 2014?	Coverage
Rehdanz and Maddison (2005)	2005	1	−0.4	Statistical	Yes	Self-reported happiness
Hope (2006)	2006	2.5	−0.9	Enumeration	Yes	Sea level rise, biodiversity, agriculture, forestry, fisheries, energy demand, water, resources, amenity, human health, air pollution, natural disasters
Nordhaus (2006)	2006	3	−0.9	Statistical	Yes	Economic output
Nordhaus (2008)	2008	3	−2.6	Enumeration	Yes	Agriculture, sea level rise, other market impacts, human health, amenity, biodiversity, catastrophic impacts
Maddison and Rehdanz (2011)	2011	3.2	−12.4	Statistical	Yes	Self-reported happiness
Bosello et al. (2012)	2012	1.9	−0.5	CGE	Yes	Energy demand; tourism; sea level rise; river floods; agriculture; forestry; human health
Roson and Mensbrugghe (2012)	2012	2.9	−2.1	CGE	Yes	Agriculture, sea level rise, water resources, tourism, energy demand, human health, labour productivity
Roson and Mensbrugghe (2012)	2012	5.4	−6.1	CGE	Yes	Agriculture, sea level rise, water resources, tourism, energy demand, human health, labour productivity
Dellink	*2012*	*2.50*	*−1.1*		*No*	
Kemfert	*2012*	*0.25*	*−0.17*		*No*	
Hambel	*2012*	*1*	*0.3*		*No*	
Burke et al. (2015)	*2015*	*4*	*−23*	*Linear extrapolation*	*No*	
Kahn et al. (2019)	*2019*	*3.2*	*−7.22*	*Linear extrapolation*	*No*	

Table A2. USA average temperature, GDP/GSP and Population data.

State	Avg °C 1971–2000	GDP 2000	Population 2010	GDP per capita	°C Deviation	GDP per capita Deviation
Alabama	17.1	119242.4	4779736	$24,947	5.6	−$8,259
Arizona	15.7	164611.6	6392017	$25,753	4.2	−$7,454
Arkansas	15.8	68770	2915918	$23,584	4.3	−$9,622
California	15.2	1366561	37253956	$36,682	3.7	$3,476
Colorado	7.3	180605.5	5029196	$35,911	−4.2	$2,705
Connecticut	9.4	165898.7	3574097	$46,417	−2.1	$13,210
Delaware	12.9	43389.4	897934	$48,321	1.4	$15,115
Florida	21.5	489488.1	18801310	$26,035	10	−$7,172
Georgia	17.5	307611.6	9687653	$31,753	6	−$1,454
Idaho	6.9	37992.8	1567582	$24,237	−4.6	−$8,970
Illinois	11	487212.7	12830632	$37,973	−0.5	$4,766
Indiana	10.9	203052.9	6483802	$31,317	−0.6	−$1,890
Iowa	8.8	93028.6	3046355	$30,538	−2.7	−$2,669
Kansas	12.4	85853.2	2853118	$30,091	0.9	−$3,115
Kentucky	13.1	114293.2	4339367	$26,339	1.6	−$6,868
Louisiana	19.1	132809.9	4533372	$29,296	7.6	−$3,910
Maine	5	36841	1328361	$27,734	−6.5	−$5,472
Maryland	12.3	192106.3	5773552	$33,274	0.8	$67
Massachusetts	8.8	289926.5	6547629	$44,280	−2.7	$11,073
Michigan	6.9	351572.7	9883640	$35,571	−4.6	$2,365
Minnesota	5.1	189964.8	5303925	$35,816	−6.4	$2,609
Mississippi	17.4	65645.9	2967297	$22,123	5.9	−$11,083
Missouri	12.5	187296.8	5988927	$31,274	1	−$1,933
Montana	5.9	21885.2	989415	$22,119	−5.6	−$11,087
Nebraska	9.3	56503.7	1826341	$30,938	−2.2	−$2,268
Nevada	9.9	76627.1	2700551	$28,375	−1.6	−$4,832
New Hampshire	6.6	45225.5	1316470	$34,354	−4.9	$1,147

(Continued)

Table A2. Continued.

State	Avg °C 1971–2000	GDP 2000	Population 2010	GDP per capita	°C Deviation	GDP per capita Deviation
New Jersey	11.5	362006.9	8791894	$41,175	0	$7,969
New Mexico	11.9	55232.9	2059179	$26,823	0.4	−$6,384
New York	7.4	838660.3	19378102	$43,279	−4.1	$10,072
North Carolina	15	275694.2	9535483	$28,912	3.5	−$4,294
North Dakota	4.7	17976.1	672591	$26,727	−6.8	−$6,480
Ohio	10.4	391137.8	11536504	$33,904	−1.1	$698
Oklahoma	15.3	90792.7	3751351	$24,203	3.8	−$9,004
Oregon	9.1	117258.3	3831074	$30,607	−2.4	−$2,599
Pennsylvania	9.3	407652.8	12702379	$32,093	−2.2	−$1,114
Rhode Island	10.1	34516.4	1052567	$32,793	−1.4	−$414
South Carolina	16.9	115246.8	4625364	$24,916	5.4	−$8,290
South Dakota	7.3	22690.7	814180	$27,869	−4.2	−$5,337
Tennessee	14.2	181629.5	6346105	$28,621	2.7	−$4,586
Texas	18.2	738871	25145561	$29,384	6.7	−$3,823
Utah	9.2	70291.8	2763885	$25,432	−2.3	−$7,774
Vermont	6.1	18311.9	625741	$29,264	−5.4	−$3,942
Virginia	12.8	266886.4	8001024	$33,357	1.3	$150
Washington	9.1	237831.8	6724540	$35,368	−2.4	$2,161
West Virginia	11	42606.9	1852994	$22,994	−0.5	−$10,213
Wisconsin	6.2	180539	5686986	$31,746	−5.3	−$1,460
Wyoming	5.6	17205.4	563626	$30,526	−5.9	−$2,680
USA	11.5	10252347	3.09E+08	$33,206	0	$0

The failure of Integrated Assessment Models as a response to 'climate emergency' and ecological breakdown: the Emperor has no clothes

Salvi Asefi-Najafabady, Laura Villegas-Ortiz and Jamie Morgan

ABSTRACT

In this brief commentary we provide some parallel points to complement Steve Keen's paper in the recent *Globalization's* special forum on 'Economics and Climate Emergency'. Keen's critique of climate and economy Integrated Assessment Models (IAMs) is wide-ranging, but there is still scope to bring to the fore the general issues that help to make sense of the critique. Accordingly, we set out six key inadequacies of IAMs and argue towards the need for a different approach that is more realistic regarding the limits to growth.

In this brief commentary we provide some parallel points to complement Steve Keen's paper in the recent *Globalization's* special forum on 'Economics and Climate Emergency' (Gills & Morgan 2020; Keen, 2020). There are now many critiques of Integrated Assessment Models (IAM) and these range from technical disputes regarding appropriate quantities for variables to more fundamental critiques of the assumptions, concepts and purposes of IAMs (for the latter see also Dale 2018; Hickel, 2018; Murphy, 2018). Keen's critique encompasses much of this range, but there is still scope to bring to the fore the general issues that help to make sense of the critique. As Keen's paper suggests, IAMs give the impression of being rooted in data, which tends to give them status as science as well as policy influence in key decision making and advisory circles (governments, the IPCC, etc.). Climate and economy focused IAMs are, however, deeply unrealistic in how they represent Earth and Human systems and the relation between the two. This applies to what are termed 'simple' IAMs, such as 'DICE', but also 'complex' IAMs (see later).[1] By underestimating the real consequences of human activity – built into economic structure – IAMs convey the impression that planetary wide economic growth and thus continued expansion of material and energy use is feasible (on growth see e.g. Smil, 2019). This distracts from development of alternatives better able to assess the potential future risks of climate change, which would in turn lead to more appropriate policy responses at a basic societal level. In so far as IAMs promote complacency they undermine attempts to inform the public and induce appropriate concern, despite that there clearly is increasing disquiet being expressed in many quarters regarding Climate Emergency and ecological breakdown (for context of arguments for delay see Galbraith, 2020; Lamb et al., 2020). Moreover, in promoting complacency IAMs disguise what George Monbiot refers to as a 'grim truth' i.e. 'that the rich are able to live as they do only because others are poor: there is neither the physical nor the ecological space for everyone to pursue private luxury'. As such, IAMs serve to reproduce inequality whilst facilitating the reproduction of types of economy that are simply not sustainable. This must change and making ad-hoc tweaks to standard models to fix some superficial aspects of shortcomings will not be enough to drive that change.

The need for proper context

For the majority of human history, the long term rate of economic growth per capita was close to zero. Societies were mostly agricultural and the production processes they sustained depended partly on rudimentary technologies, such as plows and domesticated animals, but mostly on access to sunlight, water, and soil nutrients – all factors that are made available through natural cycles in the Earth's System. Prosperity has varied as civilizations have risen and fallen, but it wasn't until very recently, when humans found a way to harness new forms of energy (i.e. energy that was buried in the form of fossil fuels) that societies' populations and economies began to grow continuously and significantly. Since 1800, the world population has grown from one billion to 7.76 billion in 2018 and some projections anticipate 10 billion by the end of the century. The story of economic growth follows a similar path. It was not until the invention of the steam engine and the discovery of coal as a source of energy that societies began experiencing rates of economic growth larger than 0.14%. Between 1500 and 1820, the growth rate of per capita income in Western Europe was 0.14% – not too different from the growth rate between 1000 and 1500, which was 0.12% (see Chang, 2014).[2] And a policy focus on GDP metrics really only came to the fore with the development of national income accounting and then the dissemination of this after World War II (Masood, 2016; Spash, 2020). According to the World Bank, global GDP was US$ 1.4 trillion in 1960 and it was US$ 87.6 trillion in 2019. Of course, reference to just the numbers tells us nothing about distribution and responsibility for associated climate effects, it just tells us that there are more of us affecting more of the planet (modifying land, sea and air). However, if we focus on consumption of resources and carbon emissions, it remains the case that the vast majority of *impact* is created by relatively few countries, corporations and people (see Gore, 2020; Heede, 2014).[3]

In any case, for the last 200 years, the unlocking of energy from fossils has allowed humans to grow in population and measured 'wealth' at a rate beyond that which an 'unperturbed' biogeochemical cycle is capable of maintaining (see e.g. Motesharrei et al., 2016). Fossil fuels are reservoirs of energy and historically have enabled humans to use more energy than is made available to them in the form of wind, sunlight, fire, and running water. It is by using additional fossil fuel energy sources that humans have been able to develop economic systems of resource use that have sustained growth at levels well beyond that of previous societies. However, there is no evidence that they are able to avoid or manage the consequences of doing this. There is no evidence that contemporary economies have or are able to in the near future decisively 'dematerialise' or transition from some degree of 'relative decoupling' to 'absolute decoupling' of economic activity and growth in material and energy use and associated issues like carbon emissions (see e.g. Fletcher & Rammelt, 2017; Parrique et al., 2019). And it is now widely acknowledged that we have surpassed the Earth's capacity to restore and repair the damage imposed by this kind of increasing human activity (e.g. Ripple et al., 2020). Current trends in extinction rates, coral reef decay, ocean pollution and acidification, overfishing, deforestation, air pollution and climate change point towards critical tensions, if not collapse (e.g. Ceballos et al., 2017; Lenton et al., 2020). Increased social strife around the world can be considered another sign of unsustainable growth pathways (e.g. Abel et al., 2019; Gleick, 2014). Ultimately ecological damage and accelerated climate change and its consequences are a signal that economic growth and likely population growth are not realistic options if we are to avoid dangerous Earth System transitions.

The recent IPCC *Global Warming of 1.5°C* report (IPCC, 2018) and the deficits published in the annual UNEP *Emissions Gap* reports (see Christensen & Olhoff, 2019) have placed greater pressure on governments across the world to immediately increase investment in mitigation and adaptation and take more urgent action to reduce emissions – and this has resulted in further negotiations via the COP process and the UNFCCC and different countries are now beginning to announce they will aim for 'net zero' emissions by mid-century (though currently statutory commitments, detailed plans and implementation are mainly lacking and there is considerable scepticism regarding what 'net' might mean). Still, it is increasingly clear that more delay and gradual incremental change will be insufficient. Moreover, it remains the case that the IPCC approach to change is itself not sufficiently ambitious. This brings us to the subject of Integrated Assessment Models and what follows is best read in the context of Keen's paper (Keen, 2020). IPCC reports include various 'simulated scenarios' generated from IAMs.[4] Whilst there are many uses for IAMs we are mainly interested in those used to estimate the 'social cost of carbon' and to evaluate alternative abatement policies. As Keen makes abundantly clear, although these seem rigorous and are technically impressive in their apparent complexity, they are fundamentally flawed. In principle IAMs explore how the 'Human System' (essentially economic activity) affects and interacts with the Earth System, but the assumptions used to construct IAMs are unrealistic and the relation between Human Systems and the Earth System is unrepresentative. Ultimately IAMs are a symptom, a reflection of an even more profound problem with how social planners, policymakers, and global political and economic powers are dictating the way in which natural and human resources are managed (or mismanaged).

In the following section, we identify several major flaws in IAMs. Conclusions from IAMs about the impact of a warming scenario are unreliable, misleading, and founded on oversimplifying assumptions. Although much of the discussion will only focus on 'simple' IAMs, the main criticism applies also to what are termed 'complex' IAMs (see below).

Key inadequacies of IAMs

1. The rational expectations assumption

IAMs incorporate mainstream macroeconomic models and these are typically constructed using an assumption of 'rational expectations'. In general, this means models represent individual components of the system as optimizing agents with full information of the system and with a clear 'decision rule'. This facilitates tractability, ensuring definite outcomes. Real behaviour in human societies is different, participants have limited knowledge, diverse information, interests and motivations and systems are emergent, organic and evolving. These restrictions have important implications for the economic outcomes of the models.[5] Ultimately, IAMs impose unrealistic assumptions about behaviour and therefore represent the *wrong* system. Put another way, they model human systems inadequately but do so because this leads to equilibrium solutions and optimality when equations are solved. This leads to further practical problems of expression built into the mathematics and coding.

2. Lack of real complexity

IAMs are limited in their capacity to incorporate complexities, nonlinearities, non-convexities, tipping points, and uncertainties: all typical features of climate change. Often, IAMs are formulated in an optimization language such as GAMS (General Algebraic Modelling System) or AMPL (A Mathematical Programming Language). At the same time, IAMs leave many 'degrees of freedom' for the modeller. This means the modeller has great leeway in choosing the functional forms and parameter values used in the model. Clearly, this can (and has in many high profile cases) led to radically varying conclusions regarding the implied 'social cost of carbon' (SCC) and 'optimal' abatement policy. For example, Nordhaus (2008) finds that optimal abatement should initially be very limited, consistent with a SCC of around $20 or less, while Stern (2008) concludes that an immediate and drastic cut in emissions is necessary, consistent with a SCC above $200. Whilst survey research indicates that many modellers prefer higher values for costs (and lower discount rates) than Nordhaus (Drupp et al., 2020), his work as Nobel prizewinner is extremely influential and the more important point is that there is *no decisive* (objective) determinant of the values used in these models.

In general, modelling offers an overly optimistic future, predicting the impact of climate change to be only a few points decrease in otherwise expanding world GDP per capita by the end of the century – even for high levels of warming. In some models, even a global temperature increase above +5 degrees Celsius would cost less than 7% of the world's future GDP (see Nordhaus, 1994; Roson & Van der Mensbrugghe, 2012). This leads to complacency – statements such as 'a century of climate change is about as good/bad for welfare as a year of economic growth' (see Tol, 2018). Moreover, there is a major disjuncture here with the consensus amongst Climate Scientists and Earth System scientists regarding the nature and significance of changes in climate and ecosystems (Lenton et al., 2020). This raises deep questions regarding the integration of climate science into IAMs.

3. 'Integrated' does not mean what you think it means

'Simple' IAMs, such as 'DICE', are narrowly focused, they set up some way to measure cost and benefits of climate change – typically the relationship between some measure of economic activity and emissions i.e. the 'social cost of carbon'. As such, they do not model more complex economic and climate processes. 'Complex' IAMs use additional linked modules representing the global economy, as well as its energy, land, and climate systems to look at energy technologies, energy use choices, land-use changes, and the societal trends behind emissions of greenhouse gases (GHG). There are numerous identified conceptual or technical problems with these. For example, the use of a climate sensitivity parameter, dubious presuppositions such as a continual optimal rate of fossil fuel *extraction*, and dubious assumptions such as infinite potential sinks for carbon and instantaneous effects of emissions reduction policy. Perhaps the most fundamental problem is that in IAMs Earth and Human Systems do not feedback on each other. The use of terms such as 'coupling' (focused on 'uni-coupling') tends to obscure this deep lack of realism.

For example, in reality, changes in climate hazards can trigger human migration across different regions of the world, which in turn will have effects on land use, water availability, deforestation, desertification, and so on. Also, climate change may eventually make certain areas of the world hostile living places based on temperature rises leading to falling economic output, population decline, social inequality and political crises. However, these complex feedbacks are not adequately expressed in IAMs. Instead they depend on exogenous projections fed into the models. This lack of realistic feedback means IAMs are unable to accurately estimate the economic cost of environmental degradation (including climate change). They are unable to adequately represent human responses to changing climate and ecological processes. This also affects complementary scenario analyses, and these too are unable to represent realistic human responses to environmental impacts, including in regional economic activity. These may take forms in reality that are assumed away in the majority of simulated exercises, notably responses leading to real collapses in economic activity and thus measured GDP. The general problem is revealed by the form that Representative Concentration Pathways, or RCPs, and Shared Socioeconomic Pathways, or SSPs take. These are set out in IPCC reports and population distribution and population density projections from current IAMs are *exactly the same* for a scenario with sustainable development (SSP1) and a scenario with fossil-fuel intensive development (SSP5) (see Asefi-Najafabady et al., 2018).[6] This is obviously implausible, revealing a lack of sensitivity to the specifics of possible processes (the real evolution of a mutually dependent system). Clearly, current analytical approaches are unfit for impact evaluation or adaptation and mitigation planning – at the local and global level (given the obvious scalability problem). To reiterate a point made earlier, the apparent rigor and technical complexity of IAMs convey a sense of authority that is unfounded.

4. The use of a 'representative agent' in the economic model

We have already suggested that IAMs model human systems inadequately, but there is more to this. The economy that IAMs model is built from a kind of economic agent whose behaviour bears no resemblance to real people, real people whose actual activity would (will) in reality play a key role in how an economy and society evolve in the context of a changing climate. In a simple IAM, much like in any other mainstream macroeconomic model, there is, for the purpose of simplicity, only *one* agent, the 'representative agent'. This agent is supposed to represent the economic decisions of all actors in the global economy. Since this economic agent makes all decisions in the economy, she effectively determines who gets what (the distribution and, since she is 'representative', all wealth is effectively equally distributed in the model – between herself). By implication, institutional contexts and thus variation in and significance of government and governance decisions are rendered irrelevant by this simplification. As a representative agent she stands in for both a simplified *consumer* and *producer*.

   In reality, of course, consumers have *different* traditions and habits, religions, income levels, access to resources, and risk preferences. Producers also vary in size from sole traders to global corporations, and so vary in market sector, use of technologies and a whole host of other issues expressive of power and influence both economic and political. Moreover, real people are *not* narrowly focused optimizing calculative economically 'rational' entities. They are not 'consumers' or 'producers' in this reductive sense and yet a simplified economic agent is basic to the agent as both consumer and producer in the form of a mathematical 'function'.

5. The economic agent as consumer: discounts that shouldn't count

Real people bear no resemblance to the consumer as decisionmaker in a discounted utility or preference function for the kind of agent found in the models. For the agent in the function 'satisfaction' is derived from only two activities: consumption and leisure. Effectively, the agent maximizes her 'welfare' through the value placed on *current* consumption (or leisure). She rationally prefers more to less and, rather than delay, she derives *more* satisfaction from *instantaneous* rather than future consumption ('discounting' the future merely determines the relative *weight* placed on the present compared to the future and this agent is incapable of attaching meaning to projects or goals as 'dreams'). Here, experience of the world is as a pure processor of all available 'information', but as a fully equipped optimizer she cannot be persuaded in or more importantly *against* her own best interest, she cannot be misinformed through ideology or manipulated through marketing. In this model world, there is implied foresight regarding a known future and no true or fundamental 'uncertainty', and she is always in or tending to an 'equilibrium' position (a curious term in so far as a representative agent applies).

Moreover, in 'assessing' consumption no attention is paid by the agent to the type of good or service produced, where it is produced and how it is produced – whether it involves practices that are environmentally and socially harmful, whether the supply chain operates via adverse incorporation, modern slavery, human rights abuse and/or in undemocratic places. This agent does not hold moral views that prevent her *over*-consuming. Nor is this agent capable of kindness, generosity, or compassion towards others – not only because there are no others, but also because even if there were others, she would not derive any 'satisfaction' from any of these activities. She is, however, capable of 'risk aversion', but in the models this is a constant, which means it does not change based on level of wealth.

Clearly, all this is deeply problematic in so far as the agent is an amoral unit making brute calculations in an amoral economy, which itself lacks adequate mutual relation to the environment on which she depends. Learning and evolution play no real role here despite that models run as simulations. Nowhere is this more obvious than when making decisions with inter-generational consequences. A discount rate in an IAM is a way to 'distribute' the generational wealth gap (and we will return later to this idea of 'wealth'). Having a positive discount rate means a combination of three things: (1) the agent values her own well-being over the well-being of descendants, (2) She discounts the wealth of future generations because she expects them to be wealthier, and (3) there is some reason why it is not 'optimal' in the model to transfer some well-being onto future generations. Point one introduces a tacit utilitarian and potentially selfish variant of individualism into the agent despite the amorality of agents in other respects, whilst points two and three are inconsistent and likely unfounded *if* our economies continue to operate along the grounds presupposed by the models, since those models legitimate destructive expansionary economies by misrepresenting their real consequences. It is not a given that future generations will be better off in a climate and ecologically damaged future and so there are in fact *many* morally rational reasons to engage in 'transfer' (whilst again acknowledging that even the language of this seems odd to anyone less transactional than a mainstream economist). It may be the case that discounting makes some sense for some purposes and especially over short time horizons, but *not* when considering the fate of the species.

Discount rates have been a major source of distraction and delay over the decades, but in so far as they have influence it is important to consider their implications – the higher they are then the more the present is valued over the future.[7] A recent essay in *Time Magazine* attempts to express the weirdness of the calculation by drawing on the work of the Oxford moral philosopher Derek Parfit (Walsh, 2019). At a discount rate of 5% annually, one death next year is more important than a billion deaths in 500 years. Or in monetary terms, with a 5% discount rate, it would be worth spending *no more than* $2200 today in order to try to prevent US$ 87 trillion in damages in 500 years. This US$ 87 trillion is equivalent to global GDP in 2019. The numbers matter less here than the absurdity of, in effect, thinking about what the future is 'worth' in this way (for Parfit it led to unpleasant consequentialist conclusions about the value of a human). According to this logic we would be prepared to spend *less* than what a couple of expensive computers might cost in order to secure economic activity on a scale currently seen for the whole planet. A typical IAM uses a 3% discount rate. For reference, the climate-change denying Trump administration has used an annual discount rate of 7% for its analysis of the social cost of carbon.

6. The economic agent as producer: the damage done by damage functions

The economic agent as producer is equally problematic. In a simple model, the agent produces only one aggregate or composite good that represents all possible goods and services in the global economy. There is only one way to produce this good and it is to use Capital and Labor drawing on available technology. This single composite good/sector typically takes a neoclassical 'Constant Elasticity of Substitution' functional form, though this can be relaxed and more sectors can be added to the model.[8] Perhaps more important is the role of technology in the model and how environmental degradation affects production. Besides the production function, there are two factors that enter the production decision: technology and a penalty term that represents 'lost production' due to environmental degradation. In the models, technological advancement is exogenous and there are no delays in its impact on production.[9] Exogeneity essentially means that technology is *not* an induced or learned response to cumulative environmental consequences – deliberate investment in R&D to invent more fuel-efficient machines, or new methods to drill non-conventional sources of oil and gas, carbon capture, development of renewables, etc.

New technologies in IAMs simply appear (at a given rate) and impact the entire production composite instantly and uniquely. Moreover, it is only through technology that the system moves forward. Production does not involve 'learning' to use capital and labour differently, decisions cannot involve consequences of education or law – doing more with less, doing less with less or any other range of changes to the social arrangement of production. There is no presumption of response in these terms, but production is the major way in which IAMs give the impression (not the reality) of responsiveness to ecological and climate effects via the penalty term for environmental degradation's effect on production – the so-called damage function. As with discount rates, the construction of the function is conceptually dubious and the values used are highly disputable. The damage function reduces the output level by some fraction that supposedly reflects how natural conditions reduce productive capacity. Damage functions have been heavily criticized for their lack of empirical or theoretical foundations.

The typical damage function only takes mean global temperature into account. As Keen shows and others have before him, the values and calibrations used in the models are easily manipulated (and even some of those who construct IAMs acknowledge this, see Keen, 2020; Pindyck, 2013, 2017; Pottier, 2016; Weitzman, 2011). Formally, the penalty term only affects the output level and not output growth. This means that 'damage' amounts to some reduction in that output level as an economy *expands*. This is quite different than allowing global temperature increases to have permanent impacts through time. And more fundamentally it is quite different than the more comprehensive approach to a system of *embedded* measurement of throughput pioneered by ecological economists (see Spash, 2017). Furthermore, the probability distributions that stand behind damage functions do not allow for 'fat tails' or high impact climate events. More fundamentally, the whole approach does not allow for the basic uncertainty inherent to complex evolutionary processes – a situation where it makes less sense to rely on probability distributions for degrees of precision and more on commonsense prudential conduct, based on a deeper understanding of systems, sub-systems, structures and tendencies (IAM use is thus typically quite different in context than the approach pioneered in early works, like the *Limits to Growth*, Meadows et al., 1972). Overall, the use of a damage function is profoundly misleading if policymakers take the output from popular IAMs as guidance for policy action. Costs from climate change and ecological breakdown tend to be radically underestimated and benefits from investment in mitigation and adaptation (as well as social redesign to just stop doing things that have clear adverse cumulative consequences tend to be woefully underappreciated.

Conclusion

It should be clear that the IAM Emperor has 'no clothes' and that we need different attire. In addition to Keen's essay, these are issues explored across the various other essays in the special forum on Climate Emergency, and of course, in many other places (e.g. Hickel & Kallis, 2019). It should also be clear that IAMs play a key role in distracting attention from the feasibility of societies and economies built around the assumption of limitless economic growth. Historical trends of natural resource depletion show that economic growth is no longer sustainable. Yet, the mainstream narrative, even among some scientists (climate, and environmental scientists included), is failing to embrace the idea that the core force driving our current environmental problems is limitless economic growth. When leaders and experts claim the global economy is growing, what they call growth does not really account for the depletion of natural resources or the environmental damage that industrialization and superfluous consumption tied to obsolescence and 'lifestyles' (which are available to relatively few but offered as an aspiration for all) are causing to the entire planet. In any case, the purpose of societies should not be just to grow in the sense of becoming materially richer based on some reductive concept of GDP (and there are of course many alternatives to this measurement). And whilst reducing carbon emissions is merely one step that must be taken to address climate change, it is far from sufficient to resolve catastrophic planet-wide ecological consequences. It is a disturbing idea that getting our economic accounting systems to recognize environmental costs and benefits is not primarily an issue of data quality: measurement systems tell as much about the motives of their designers as they do about what is being measured (Masood, 2016). Failing to account for environmental damages only means increased economic growth is convenient for those designing the accounting system.

Countries in the global North are not genuinely more sustainable in ecological or climatological terms in so far as they have transferred polluting industries to 'developing' countries such as China and India. This transfer of low-tech and polluting industries has now made China the world's biggest polluter (see Smith, 2016).[10] Overwhelmed with pollution, China is now transferring some of its own industrial pollution to other countries.[11] The level of irony in this story is epic and the message is clear, transfers and technological change alone cannot solve planetary-scale problems if undifferentiated and continuous economic growth remains the basic premise of our economic system, since this has inevitable consequences for continued material and energy *overuse*. This must change and it seems this is something that civil society around the world increasingly recognizes, despite the policy drag created by IAMs. For example, and as the Covid-19 pandemic also illustrates, the USA has had to contend with the weaponization of science for ideological ends and this is very evident in the case of partisan divides on climate change. But partisanship only goes so far and in a recent Pew Research Center survey, over 74% of American adults agreed that 'the country should do whatever it takes to protect the environment', compared with 23% who said 'the country has gone too far in its efforts to protect the environment'.[12] Forest fires, droughts, floods and hurricanes, it seems, are becoming more persuasive than complacent political rhetoric, but more needs to be done to develop and propagate real solutions and 'just transitions' (Newell & Simms, 2020).

Notes

1. 'DICE' stands for 'Dynamic Integrated model of Climate and the Economy. The regional version is referred to as 'RICE'.
2. Note Chang's work has become a subject of critique by Clive Spash because of his lack of attention to limits to growth.

3. The richest 26 people in the world possess the same wealth as the poorest half of humanity, and they are also disproportionate emitters of GHG (the top 10% of the world's top earners produce almost half of the world's carbon emissions).
4. To be clear, the IPCC and various modelers recognize that IAMs can be problematic but still continue to use them. See, https://www.carbonbrief.org/qa-how-integrated-assessment-models-are-used-to-study-climate-change
5. For example, a standard result of mainstream models is the full employment of labor in the economy: meaning that anyone who is willing and able to work can find a job and unemployment is zero.
6. And see also Asefi-Najafabady et al. (2014).
7. For classic argument see Nordhaus (1991).
8. And of course, mirroring the utility function, work is a disutility rather than a complex phenomenon constituted through social relations and providing a source of meaning and status.
9. Although some IAMs try to model these delays by imposing a logistic function on how new technologies are adopted.
10. However, Smith argues that whilst it is true China produces emissions on behalf of other countries, China also has its own internal dynamics of ecological and climate effects (the role of the CCP), see also Smith (2020).
11. See: https://www.npr.org/2019/04/29/716347646/why-is-china-placing-a-global-bet-on-coal
12. A support rate of 74% is far greater than the support received by the Civil Rights movement in America in the 1960s. A nationwide Gallup poll in February 1965 found 26% of Americans citing civil rights as a problem facing the nation, second only to the expanding war in Vietnam, cited by 29%. See: https://www.pewresearch.org/fact-tank/2015/03/05/50-years-ago-mixed-views-about-civil-rights-but-support-for-selma-demonstrators/

Disclosure statement

No potential conflict of interest was reported by the author(s).

References

Abel, G. J., Brottrager, M., Cuaresma, J. C., & Muttarak, R. (2019). Climate, conflict and forced migration. *Global Environmental Change, 54*, 239–249. https://doi.org/10.1016/j.gloenvcha.2018.12.003

Asefi-Najafabady, S., Rayner, P. J., Gurney, K. R., McRobert, A., Song, Y., Coltin, K., & Baugh, K. (2014). A multiyear, global gridded fossil fuel CO2 emission data product: Evaluation and analysis of results. *Journal of Geophysical Research: Atmospheres, 119*(17), 10–213. https://doi.org/10.1002/2013JD021296

Asefi-Najafabady, S., Vandecar, K. L., Seimon, A., Lawrence, P., & Lawrence, D. (2018). Climate change, population, and poverty: Vulnerability and exposure to heat stress in countries bordering the Great Lakes of Africa. *Climatic Change, 148*(4), 561–573. https://doi.org/10.1007/s10584-018-2211-5

Ceballos, G., Ehrlich, P. R., & Dirzo, R. (2017). Biological annihilation via the ongoing sixth mass extinction signaled by vertebrate population losses and declines. *Proceedings of the National Academy of Sciences, 114*(30), E6089–E6096. https://doi.org/10.1073/pnas.1704949114

Chang, H. J. (2014). *Economics: The user's guide.* Bloomsbury.

Christensen, J., & Olhoff, A. (2019). *Lessons from a decade of emissions gap assessments*. UNEP.

Dale, G. (2018, October 12). The Nobel Prize in climate chaos. *The Ecologist*. https://theecologist.org/2018/oct/12/nobel-prize-climate-chaos-romer-nordhaus-and-ipcc

Drupp, M. A., Freeman, M., Groom, B., & Nesje, F. (2020). Discounting disentangled. *American Economic Journal: Economic Policy*, *10*(4), 109–134. https://doi.org/10.1257/pol.20160240

Fletcher, R., & Rammelt, C. (2017). Decoupling: A key fantasy of the post-2015 sustainable development agenda. *Globalizations*, *14*(3), 450–467. https://doi.org/10.1080/14747731.2016.1263077

Galbraith, J. K. (2020). Economics and the climate catastrophe. *Globalizations*. https://doi.org/10.1080/14747731.2020.1807858

Gills, B. K., & Morgan, J. (2020). Economics and climate emergency. *Globalizations*, online, latest articles. https://doi.org/10.1080/14747731.2020.1841527

Gleick, P. H. (2014). Water, drought, climate change, and conflict in Syria. *Weather, Climate, and Society*, *6*(3), 331–340. https://doi.org/10.1175/WCAS-D-13-00059.1

Gore, T. (2020, September 21). *Confronting carbon inequality*. Oxfam.

Heede, R. (2014). Tracing anthropogenic carbon dioxide and methane emissions to fossil fuel and cement producers, 1854–2010. *Climatic Change*, *122*(1-2), 229–241. https://doi.org/10.1007/s10584-013-0986-y

Hickel, J. (2018, December 6). The Nobel Prize for climate catastrophe. *Foreign Policy*.

Hickel, J., & Kallis, G. (2019). Is green growth possible? *New Political Economy*, *25*(4), 469–486. https://doi.org/10.1080/13563467.2019.1598964

IPCC. (2018, October). *Global warming of 1.50C: Summary for policymakers*.

Keen, S. (2020). The appallingly bad neoclassical economics of climate change. *Globalizations*. https://doi.org/10.1080/14747731.2020.1807856

Lamb, F. W., Mattioli, G., Levi, S., Roberts, J. T., Capstick, S., Creutzig, F., Minx, J. C., Muller-Hansen, F., Culhane, T., & Steinberger, J. K. (2020). Discourses of climate delay. *Global Sustainability*, *3*(e17), 1–5. https://doi.org/10.1017/sus.2020.13

Lenton, T. M., Rockstrom, J., Gaffney, O., Rahmstorf, S., Richardson, K., Steffen, W., & Schellnuber, H. J. (2020, November 28). Climate tipping points too risky to bet against. *Nature*, *575*(7784), 592–595. https://doi.org/10.1038/d41586-019-03595-0

Masood, E. (2016). *The great invention: The story of GDP and the making and unmaking of the modern world*. Pegasus Books.

Meadows, D., Meadows, D., Randers, J., & Behrens, W. (1972). *The limits to growth*. American Library [Club of Rome].

Motesharrei, S., Rivas, J., Kalnay, E., Asrar, G. R., Busalacchi, A. J., Cahalan, R. F., & Hubacek, K. (2016). Modeling sustainability: Population, inequality, consumption, and bidirectional coupling of the earth and human systems. *National Science Review*, *3*(4), 470–494. https://doi.org/10.1093/nsr/nww081

Murphy, R. (2018, October). William Nordhaus versus the United Nations on climate change economics. The Library of Economics and Liberty. https://www.econlib.org/library/Columns/y2018/MurphyNordhaus.html

Newell, P., & Simms, A. (2020). How did we do that? Histories and political economies of rapid and just transitions. *New Political Economy*. https://doi.org/10.1080/13563467.2020.1810216

Nordhaus, W. (1991). To slow or not to slow: The economics of the greenhouse effect. *The Economic Journal*, *101*(407), 920–937. https://doi.org/10.2307/2233864

Nordhaus, W. (1994). Expert opinion on climatic change. *American Scientist*, *82*(1), 4551.

Nordhaus, W. (2008). *The challenge of global warming: Economic models and environmental policy*. Yale University.

Parrique T., Barth J., Briens F., Kerschner, C., Kraus-Polk A., Kuokkanen A., & Spangenberg J. H. (2019, July). Decoupling debunked. *European Environmental Bureau*. eeb.org/library/decoupling-debunked.

Pindyck, R. (2013). Climate change policy: What do the models tell us? *Journal of Economic Literature*, *51*(3), 86072. https://doi.org/10.1257/jel.51.3.860

Pindyck, R. (2017). The use and misuse of models for climate policy. *Review of Environmental Economics and Policy*, *11*(1), 100114. https://doi.org/10.1093/reep/rew012

Pottier, A. (2016). *Comment les économistes réchauffent la planète*. Le Seuil.

Ripple, W. J., Wolf, C., Newsome, T. M., Barnbard, P., Moomaw, W. R., & 11,258 signatories. (2020). World scientists' warning of a climate emergency. *BioScience*, *70*(1), 8–12. https://doi.org/10.1093/biosci/biz152

Roson, R., & Van der Mensbrugghe, D. (2012). Climate change and economic growth: Impacts and inter-actions. *International Journal of Sustainable Economy*, 4(3), 270285. https://doi.org/10.1504/IJSE.2012.047933

Smil, V. (2019). *Growth: From microorganisms to megacities.* MIT.

Smith, R. (2016). *Green capitalism: The God that failed.* College Publications.

Smith, R. (2020). *China's engine of environmental collapse.* Pluto Press.

Spash, C. (2017). *Routledge handbook of ecological economics: Nature and society.* Routledge.

Spash, C. (2020). Apologists for growth: Passive revolutionaries in a passive revolution. *Globalizations.* https://doi.org/10.1080/14747731.2020.1824864

Stern, Nicholas. 2008. The economics of climate change. *American Economic Review*, 98, 1–37.

Tol, R. (2018). The economic impacts of climate change. *Review of Environmental Economics and Policy, 12* (1), 401–425. https://doi.org/10.1093/reep/rex027

Walsh, B. (2019, August 14). Why your brain can't process climate change. *Time Magazine.*

Weitzman, M. L. (2011). Fat-tailed uncertainty in the economics of catastrophic climate change. *Review of Environmental Economics and Policy*, 5(2), 275–292. https://doi.org/10.1093/reep/rer006

Teaching climate complacency: mainstream economics textbooks and the need for transformation in economics education

Barry Gills and Jamie Morgan

ABSTRACT

In this paper we ask, what is mainstream economics education conveying to its students? Standard mainstream economics textbooks treat the environment as a specialist issue in addition to standard concerns and based on solutions that conform to those standard concerns. When viewed as socialisation for students this is a major problem. To illustrate the problems we set out key aspects of the standard format, and draw attention to the structure and contents from two well-known textbooks. Standard textbooks convey the impression that the 'environmental issue' is appropriately incorporated and exhibit two complacency-creating features. First, fundamental problems (acute global ecological breakdown, biodiversity loss, climate change crisis etc), issues and urgency cannot be adequately conveyed to students within this way of framing economics. Second, specific theory and policy solutions suggest that the problem is well in hand. We illustrate using the theory of negative externalities.

Introduction

As we suggested in the Editorial Introduction to this special forum, delay in responding to the global ecological and climate emergency has been endemic (see also Amen et al., 2008; Gills & Morgan, 2020; Newell & Taylor, 2020). A key question is how did we get here, and an important frame of reference, as ecological economists and critical social scientists have argued for years, is that mainstream economic theory of the environment is falsely posed and fosters dangerous complacency (e.g. Daly, 1974, 1997, 2015, Hickel, 2018; Keen, 2020). It is important to note that economics is not just a theory that directly shapes policy. It is also socially significant on a broader scale through its contribution to educational curricula. Economics is 'socialisation via education' (Daly & Morgan, 2019). It has what the cognitive linguist George Lakoff terms 'framing' effects (e.g. Lakoff, 2010).[1]

In this paper we want to draw attention to the systematic failure of mainstream economics to adequately incorporate the real consequences of economic activity. Economic activity involves material processes that affect the world on which our existence depends, and yet mainstream economics does not take this reality as its fundamental point of departure. For students, mainstream foundational focus, concepts, and policy arguments form the basis of an economics education, and key to this is the role of the mainstream economics textbook. Mainstream economics, and by extension environmental economics, (in contrast to ecological economics), are deeply problematic and as things stand a mainstream economics education is a significant impediment to grasping the reality and urgency of our present situation. This must change radically and quickly if economics is to play a future positive role in the needed transformation of the human relationship with the web of life (Gills, 2008, 2020).

Where did this delay and complacency come from?

Though there are alternative sources (Bacevic, 2020; Oreskes and Conway, 2010; Stevenson, 2020 and, for degrowth, Hickel & Kallis, 2020; Kallis et al., 2020; Koch & Buch-Hansen, 2020; Morgan 2017; Spash, 2018), mainstream economic theory has been one of the main sources of authority responsible for climate action delay and environmental complacency, and this has been the case across the whole array of possible environmental problems, not just on emissions and climate change. Whilst acknowledging that there are different positions within ecological economics (e.g Spash, 2020b), to an ecological economist an economy is a set of material processes, it involves thermodynamic consequences, entropy, waste creation, and basic bio-physical modification of the world around us (see Spash, 2017).[2] Climate and ecosystems are highly complex, and change can be irreversible, for example, inducing system state transitions and positive feedback loops (Steffen et al. 2018). Fundamentally, to an ecological economist, the economy is embedded (as is society more broadly) in the material world, and the economy evolves as a sub-system in mutual relation with the material world on which it (and thus we) *depend.*

In mainstream economics, by contrast, the focus is determination of *exchange values* in an economic system of measured wealth creation (O'Neill, 2007). In mainstream economics, organizations provide goods and services according to production costs of labour and capital and in relation to the subjective preferences of customers or consumers. Supply and demand are expressed in marginal relations and the two are resolved through convergence on prices some will pay and profits others will earn, based on what some will pay. This occurs in one market and generalizes to all markets According to such theory, when left to run unimpeded, the result is a system where 'price signals' and profit motives provide an engine of economic development and economic growth (presumably to the benefit of all. This is the foundational premise, or ideological framing, by mainstream economics of the 'system'. The 'system' is focused on meeting subjective preferences and earning further profits in a competitive process that induces organizations to innovate, reduce costs, struggle for market share, and to identify new unexploited or currently non-existent markets, leading to technological progress and 'dynamic efficiency' (doing more in aggregate, but more with 'less' and meeting more needs or wants: in a utilitarian virtuous circle). At a macro-level this 'system' is represented through a 'circular flow of income' with a focus on national income accounts and a set of standard metrics that measure how well a (national) economy is doing in terms of economic growth, according to the dictates of exchange values.

The important point, however, is that the 'environment' in this schema is reduced to resources used in solving problems of *relative scarcity* and allocation as an economy evolves (and this is mainly about valuations, costs, and 'substitution' choices between resources).[3] The significance of material processes in general is tacitly assumed to be adequately accounted for through the exchange valuation system (essentially what we will pay). For this reason, 'environmental issues' as such are not fundamental to the theorization of an economy, but are rather merely an additional specialist sub-discipline for self-designated 'environmental economists'. Their job has been to theorize 'the environment', but crucially by adapting their concepts from *within* the framework of mainstream economics. So the context in which problems are recognized and policy solutions are formulated flow *from* this mainstream framework, focusing on resource choice, substitution decisions, distortions to and failures in otherwise (presumably) 'efficient' processes of exchange valuation. We provided a long list in the forum Editorial Introduction of different forms this has taken, whilst acknowledging there has been some development of more sophisticated forms over the years. The issue remains, however, that ecological science is marginal to the foundations of mainstream economics, whereas it could and should constitute an indispensable basis upon which economic theory is constructed.

The key point to take from the above is that despite an economy being fundamentally a *material process*, material processes and consequences are *not* what mainstream economics directly orients on. Moreover, there is no acknowledgement that economic expansion has *inherent* material limits dictated by the material world or actual existing planetary system. Instead, because there is no measured foundation for material processes within the way the economic system is theorized, and because the engine of this theorized system is inherently expansionary, there is a tacit assumption that the economic system is *without* absolute limits.[4] That is, there are no biophysical boundary states in mainstream economics, only price signals that tell us whether we want to do things in relation to pecuniary choices.[5] As ecological economists argue, the lack of real biophysical planetary limits might have seemed like less of an omission when the world's population was small and there were only a few industrialized countries, and relatively few people living high consumption lives (though classical political economy did speculate on limits to growth (e.g. J. S. Mill), and Marxists' critique of 'vulgar political economy' has always had a strand questioning the ideology of capitalist expansion, see: Dale, 2020 for both sides of this). Today, however, when pointed out to them, it seems genuinely weird to non-economists that economics lacks *primary and universal* attention to the materiality of the economy and the actual material consequences of growth. This is the equivalent of finding out that cosmologists are not interested in gravity! (Daly & Morgan, 2019). In any case, material consequences and limits are conceptually problematic in mainstream economics, and this transfers to environmental economics. As we shall see, this has basic consequences for the teaching of economics.

Many standard mainstream economics textbooks include little or no recognition of 'environmental' issues (let alone ecological science, or earth system dynamics) and those that do tend to treat the environment as a specialist issue *in addition* to standard concerns and based on solutions that conform to those standard concerns. When viewed as socialization for students this is a major problem. In effect, mainstream economics conveys a worldview, a profound and lasting 'framing' of the world, one conditioning thought and behaviour in the future (for some well-known work on issues of context see, Callon, 2007; Çalişkan & Callon, 2009; Frank et al., 1993).

Mainstream economics, however, self-identifies as a social *science* with the accent on the latter. It places great emphasis on its quantifications and its status as a science, so to an external observer it must surely seem odd that *thinking like a* mainstream economist creates a blind spot regarding the basic material consequences of something as fundamentally material as an economy. Given that it is mainstream economists and a subset of the mainstream (environmental economists for our purposes) who then write the textbooks and teach most of the courses on how an economy operates and with what consequences, this is a significant issue of education as socialization. What is mainstream economics education conveying to its students (who then as citizens affect policy …)?

An economics education and the textbook format

Until relatively recently many standard introductory mainstream economics textbooks (and bear in mind these are supposed to articulate what is *fundamental* to economics) have included little or no recognition of 'environmental' issues. And as we have suggested, those that have incorporated them have tended to treat the environment as merely a specialist issue *in addition* to standard concerns, and based on solutions that conform to those standard concerns. To illustrate how this has evolved and what it has meant, we first set out key aspects of the standard format, and then in the next section we briefly draw attention to the structure and contents from two well-known textbooks.

Standard introductory undergraduate economics textbooks tend to conform to the template pioneered and popularized by Paul Samuelson in his 1948 book *Economics* (see Samuelson, 1998). As critics and authors of heterodox alternatives often note, mainstream economics textbooks are unusual in the social sciences (e.g. Birks, 2016; Earle et al., 2017; Komlos, 2019; Madi & Reardon, 2014; Reardon et al., 2018; Söderbaum, 2018; Zuidhof, 2014).[6] Most social science textbooks set out a series of issue areas and emphasize that there are enduring disputes and competing theories and perspectives. In other words, they recognize an open field of studies, characterized by contestation and debate, rather than a received framework presumably representing a scientific consensus regarding underlying law-like conditions. The impression conveyed is of legitimate diversity and pluralism in the pursuit of knowledge (though we by no means wish to suggest this is unproblematic, merely subtly different than a mainstream economics textbook format). Though most mainstream economists would probably dispute this (see Morgan, 2015), economics textbooks, by contrast, are set out more as 'training manuals' to learn a set of designated key concepts. There is typically an initial chapter entitled something along the lines of 'the economic problem' or 'thinking like an economist'. Here, the distinction between positive and normative economics is introduced, though in recent years the terminology for this has sometimes been modified (substituting the term 'quantified science' for 'positive science', but without significant change in claims and implications). The claim is made that economics deals predominantly with payments and prices and rewards, and other transactional behaviours with observable quantity components or consequences. Moreover, attention is often drawn to the abundance of publicly recorded economic 'data' from which to study patterns, and the further claim is made (or implication given) that this allows the economist to infer and test (presumably) law-like regularities. As such, mainstream economists claim their discipline can be an applied science of economic behaviour, one that bears greater similarity to the natural sciences than to the other social sciences – hence 'quantified' carries a host of legitimation claims. Indeed, some critics note that the aspiration and self-representation to reproduce the 'rigour' of the natural sciences is one of the defining characteristics as well as fundamental flaws characterizing mainstream economics.[7] As regards normativity, at this point in the initial chapter(s), some recognition is usually given to the general notion that economists often disagree over policy because of their different values, but this is overridden by the claim that they share an analytical framework or key concepts and first principles, and these ground the collective capacity to 'think like an economist'. There is generally a silence over the question of the 'instrumentality' of the economics discipline in relation to reproduction of the capitalist economy, reigning business practices, and the pursuit of capital accumulation, that may however be the hidden driving force behind this particular approach to understanding economics.

In the standard textbook format the process then begins of introducing students to first principles and fundamental concepts. These include scarcity, rationally preferring more to less, (profit or growth) maximization, (investment and consumer) choice and allocation, marginal analysis, preferences and factor costs, equilibrium, efficiency and optimization, opportunity cost, cost-benefits, economic surplus, elasticity, and so forth. These form a conceptual 'toolkit' and this is typically first introduced to demonstrate the mechanics of demand and supply in a single 'market'. *Demonstration*, moreover, also involves a standardized format: a statement of founding assumptions (i.e. foundational axioms), which in combination lead to definite consequences (such as convergence on equilibrium). As such, students are taught both a mode of thought and a basic idea of what constitutes theory and proof (a deductive logical form, where consequences *must* follow). This readily translates into graphs (geometric illustrations) and simple sets of formal mathematical proofs (typically using calculus). Once the student has been introduced to the founding principles and some initial concepts and a way of demonstrating the adequacy of a theory, this way of 'thinking' is then successively developed and extended to different subject areas and scales (e.g. microeconomics and market structures, macroeconomics and the state, fiscal policy and the scale and scope of the public sector, international trade, balance of payments and exchange rates, monetary policy, banking and finance and so forth). These elements are normally presented as if they are transhistorically and universally valid (and ultimately based upon assumptions about natural or universal propensities in 'human nature'). Indeed, it appears to now be the norm that teaching long term and global economic history, as well as teaching the history of economic thought itself and all its principal schools of thought, is regarded as either supplementary or even unnecessary. Critical and radical accounts of both economic history and economic thought have been eschewed in favour of an acceptable conservative canon of classics. For example, Samuelson dismissively referred to Karl Marx as 'a minor neo-Ricardian'.

The point we want to emphasize here is what the textbook format conveys to a student: there is a fundamental analytical framework, or way of thinking like an economist, this can be applied successively to different subjects or issue areas. The world may change but economics is *comprehensive*. And not only this, it is a consistent, coherent and unified body of applied knowledge, providing the social science equivalent of an engineering manual. Economic theory may involve some policy disagreement, but this is mainly restricted to values, built into different choices or assumptions in the 'normative' part of economics. Mainstream Economics is overwhelmingly presented to the student as a 'positive' science through its quantifications.[8]

Moreover, as anyone who has been taught mainstream economics will also realize, there is a subtle socialization of perspective built into both the deductive method used for theory demonstration and the specific assumptions and axioms that tend to dominate. Students are invited to think that people are (and so it is natural and morally appropriate to be) individualistic, self-interested, calculative instrumental optimizers. This will later influence how economists view the natural world (as objectified instrumentally positioned exploitable resources). Moreover, since the general mode of demonstration is overwhelmingly of one kind (and this is heavily emphasized as what it means to *think* like an economist), students are invited to think that reasoning in general reduces to deductive method and calculative rationality, i.e. this is what 'good argument' looks like (i.e. it is clear, logical, precise and rigorous – even if this is more assertion than reality, since it is often premised on spurious precision and can include numerous axiomatic sleights of hand).[9] Since textbooks typically start by establishing a market situation of equilibrium, the idea of what good argument looks like is also subliminally being associated with market logics – this is not just where rigour and clarity (*sic*) are demonstrated, the very idea of a 'market' is positioned as, implicitly or explicitly, a morally desirable construct, even in positive economics (for context, see Amadae, 2005; Fourcade & Healy, 2007). Case studies or examples may be used, but the concept of 'the market' is still overwhelmingly presented as apolitical and ahistorical; an impersonal domain of 'free' conduct and choice, in which multiple self-interests converge, leading to benefits (of different types and degree) to all. This, of course, is a distorted version of Adam Smith's argument in *The Wealth of Nations*. The important point, however, is that the association of 'the market' with good reasoning and mutual benefit means students are being pre-persuaded that 'markets' are foundational to policy prescription. This provides another way in which economic thinking influences an economists view of the natural world: if a problem exists but no market exists, solve the problem by creating a market. Recognition of the multiplicity of possible forms of 'market' and knowledge about the immense variety of historical forms of markets is normally excluded from the curriculum, rendering the concept of 'the market' not only ahistorical but also ideological (in sharp contrast to, say, Karl Polanyi's work).

Concomitantly, even when it is not formally stated, a series of associations for the student are being set in motion by the standard textbook format: market competition is primary in the logic of economics, *every* social context is presented as if it involves something like market competitive behaviour (we are universally rational, calculative, instrumental, acquisitive and self-interested *individuals*), markets are basic to growth, growth means progress, progress means growth through markets.[10] Moreover, the very idea of 'progress', developed primarily in Western thought over the past two centuries or more, is foundational to the worldview underlying mainstream economics, and a subtle source of its social legitimation and acceptance. Clearly, none of these points follow *necessarily* in mainstream economics and none of what we have just suggested is about the specifics or technicalities of theory, but rather the associations created by the characteristics of theory and how it is presented. One might be sceptical that any of this is the case. But we would suggest the whole will be familiar to anyone who has taken some equivalent to 'Econ 101' and been taught using a standard introductory economics textbook.

It is in the context of the associations set out, that the general point we began with has its greatest force. We began by noting that mainstream economics does not take as its point of departure the materiality of an economy and its embedded consequences. So, if students are told that there is a unified analytical framework and toolkit, and that they are being taught how to think like economists, and that this is successively applicable to *all* aspects of an economy and possibly to all aspects of society, then the overwhelming effect is to suggest *nothing is missing* and all possible questions or doubts will be subsequently answered as and when the analytical framework is applied to those problems – whatever they are.[11] In broader social science contexts, this type of idea would be called a 'totalizing concept'. For example, 'Globalization' was presented as such a totalizing concept early in its intellectual 'career'; and moreover as a received theory based on some type of presumed social scientific 'consensus', which however did *not* exist (see Amoore et al., 1997). In any case, the mainstream economics textbook combination of associations has socializing effects that work like misdirection in a magic trick: the glaring omission of materiality is masked. Hence, mainstream economics is an impediment (to alternatives) through its socializing effects.

Not only is the crucial omission masked, the capacity to fundamentally question what is being learned (including exposing the omission) is masked by the kind of institutionalized teaching practices that tend to go hand in hand with the mainstream economics textbook format. To be clear, this does not require mainstream economists to be uncaring or idiotic, it does not require them to be climate change deniers, and the point is not personal (ad hominem). A singular analytical framework, deductive method, the use of mathematical proofs etc. tend to invite a didactic teaching style where lecturers exhort students to simply accept the logic ('*get it* and all will become clear'). Ironically, but revealing a profound historical amnesia in the mainstream circles of economics, it was an early progenitor of the modern mainstream, Alfred Marshall, who suggested economists ought to 'use the mathematics … then burn it': i.e. he was keen to highlight mathematization as both path and obstacle to adequate understanding of economics.

So, we contend that there is a basic pedagogy that is typical in mainstream economics, and it too seems more like an engineering manual approach than that which is typical in other social sciences: teaching tends to focus on setting out the mechanics of a concept or theory and providing worked examples, and students are often invited to go through the steps and *confirm* their understanding by emulation. Even if lecturers want to do something different (and sometimes they do) they find themselves working *against* the evolved characteristics of the economics textbook format and expectations in the profession. In any case, the overwhelming focus is on demonstrating a facility with the technical aspects of theory and applications. There are 'problems' to solve, but 'problem solving' is about demonstrating capability with what is taught. Any critique students are invited to make – for which they will be credited rather than treated as 'difficult' students – tends also to be limited to discussion of the relative merits of a range of basically similar technical alternatives. As such, pedagogically the economic textbook format and typical practice subtly suppresses critical thinking, even though academic economists are just as likely as any other group who work in education to formally recognize that critical thinking is of value (it is after all a basic academic norm in many countries and, somewhat contradictorily, is increasingly likely to be formally stated as a desirable curriculum component – because of a general instrumental turn in education systems – since critical thinking enhances 'employability'). In any case, for both students and lecturers the focus on technical demonstration and confirmation, leading to active suppression of critical thinking, has self-reproducing effects: successive generations of economists are selected and socialized through this form of education, and so these students thus trained go on to contribute to perpetuating its form and the reproduction of mainstream economics.[12]

Two textbooks

Gregory Mankiw is one of the most prominent mainstream economists of the twenty-first century and his and Mark Taylor's *Economics* is one of the more popular introductory textbooks in the UK.[13] It is currently (Mankiw & Taylor, 2020) in its fifth edition and all five editions closely follow the format we have set out: a Part 1, what is economics, thinking like an economist, how economists disagree; a Part 2 consisting of several chapters setting out the theory of competitive markets, demand, supply, equilibrium and efficiency; a Part 3 introducing the scope of the state and policy intervention into a market economy, and then a series of other parts introducing additional subjects and issues. Notably, it is not until Chapter 9 that environmental issues start to be *substantively* introduced, but in the form of 'externalities'. In the third edition this occurs in Chapter 11. Interestingly, the fifth edition includes a later section Part 8 (with fewest chapters in the book) introducing 'heterodox economics' and this is a notable change. It is also notable that the authors overtly think of their textbook as encouraging critical thinking and as facilitating open minds. Students are, for example, reminded 'not to forget the real world', and each chapter has case studies and a set of follow up self-study questions (though most of these involve a calculation and/or reiteration of a concept or theory and thus confirmation of a concept or theory). What has not changed, however, is that reference to the environment is scattered through the text rather than being primary to the construction of economics. Production and growth appear as Chapter 21. The question, of course, is whether a critical 'real world' thinker can have an adequate sense of an economy if the economy is theorized as an exchange value process of mutual benefit, subject to failures and with some specific issue areas that require more or less state intervention as it grows and as industrial-consumption economies spread.

Gregory Mankiw is part of the New-Keynesian-New-Classical Economics synthesis movement of the economics mainstream and is a well-known and controversial conservative voice in economics in the USA, so selecting a textbook he has authored may seem self-serving. And it is worth acknowledging that Mankiw's textbook's worldview is quite US-centric, but it is also worth noting an American view of economics is global in reach via the influence of its main academic institutions and journals and via the American Economic Association (see Fourcade, 2006). Whilst cases and some issues included in textbooks may be local, the economics textbook format is framed as being universal. Still, it is worth making some brief reference to another textbook to highlight their family resemblance. (The role of US 'hegemony' in the world economy and world order more generally, and its influence on shaping mainstream economics is another subject worthy of discussion, but is outside the scope of the present article).

John Sloman's *Economics* is also amongst the more popular standard introductory undergraduate textbooks in the UK. It was first published in 1991 and (with contributions from various subsequent collaborators) is now in its tenth edition and has over the years been substantially revised to reflect changes in the kinds of problems recognized in the world. For example, the tenth edition begins by bulleting a whole series of 'challenges', including Brexit, populism, financialization, rapid development of some countries – e.g. China, and critique of market liberalism. As the list indicates, *Economics* is amongst the more 'progressive' mainstream textbooks, but framing is still a significant issue. To a non-economist Sloman et al.'s list would suggest the rest of the book will introduce economics as a multi-disciplinary, complex account of the world that recognizes how deeply integrated real economies are with politics at every scale. This, however, is not what follows. The first part of the book parallels Mankiw, the student is reminded that 'critical thinking' will render them highly employable and that it is analysis and problem solving that form the basis of critical thinking. However, the authors then state that the textbook will introduce them to how to analyse by 'thinking like an economist' and it is that which will be basic to critical thinking. By way of adding some humour the authors then suggest that a 'word of warning' is required: 'Once you are thinking like an economist there's no turning back. It's a skill that will be with you for your life. Just bear in mind that the non-economists around you may need convincing of the beauty of the subject' (Sloman et al., 2018, p. 5).[14]

For critics of the mainstream approach, Sloman et al.'s humorous 'warning' is very necessary, but carries opposite connotations to those intended by the authors: intentions notwithstanding, the educational effect is more in the form of indoctrination than 'critical thinking' and that is why non-economists are so hard to convince. In any case, the authors then set out the structure and purpose of the textbook, highlighting that to develop the skillset of 'thinking like an economist' students will be introduced to 15 key concepts and 40 ideas that comprise a 'toolkit' that can be applied to ANY situation. The book then proceeds much like Mankiw and Taylor by first setting out demand and supply moves on to microeconomic market constructions, and then starts to open out to various issue areas. It is not until Chapter 13 that we are introduced to a substantive 'environmental policy' chapter. Here, students are introduced to market failure, and how to solve a problem of 'externalities' through such means as taxes, before moving onward to address the problem of how to respond when no market exists (which is how the problem of carbon emissions is typically posed: i.e. create a market, with property rights, to 'trade' the problem away). Chapter 13 is just 27 pages out of more than 800 pages which comprise the whole textbook. Growth theory, meanwhile, is introduced as Chapter 23 and focuses on factors, productivity and technology, and unemployment in the context of supply-side policy. Chapter 26 brings the textbook to a close with a focus on an 'interdependent world'. The subject matter of Chapter 26 is globalization, instability, debt, trade and issues of inequality – important issues, clearly, but not in isolation from the basic relationship between economies, scale and intensity and the material world. The basic problem here is clear as early as the third edition.

In the third edition, in introducing theories of growth, Sloman poses the core question of 'the costs of economic growth, is more necessarily better?' but suggests this as an issue of 'opportunity cost' and thus choice and preferences within the context of cost-benefits, and this is a 'constrained optimisation' problem. He concludes: 'the question of the desirability of economic growth is a normative one. It involves judgement about what a desirable society should look like' (Sloman, 1997, p. 410). This makes our point eloquently, i.e. that it is only by being educated to think like an economist that one would be persuaded that we can simply choose more or less 'environment' and that the problem reduces to whether we have more or less of a rate of growth. The third edition was 1997, the year of Kyoto, and after decades of *learned* complacency we are finally approaching a situation where we will not be asking is more 'desirable' but rather 'is more going to be suicidal?'[15]

To be clear, the point of these textbook illustrations is not to single out the authors. The purpose has been to focus on sociology of knowledge effects. Sloman and his colleagues did not invent mainstream economics. Our underlying point is that textbook socialization works against fundamentally questioning a mainstream economics framework from *within* and that framework has a glaring *foundational absence*. As we suggested in the Editorial Introduction, this way of thinking has been basic to 'business as usual' perspectives, and though it is increasingly coming under pressure, remains problematic. Environmental issues are not entirely omitted from textbooks and it is notable that environmental 'challenges' are being increasingly recognized, but the subject is still treated as an additional specialist sub-disciplinary issue in one or two specific chapters that apply the analytical framework, its toolkit and concepts. As such, the context in which the 'environmental problem' is recognized and policy solutions are formulated flow *from* the mainstream framework and again this is important from a socialization point of view. (In other words, the only 'critical thinking' encouraged in this perspective is a type that functions to reproduce the very framework that critical thinking might purport to criticize: thus obstructing the possibility of any real critical thinking much less introduction of any radical alternative paradigm).

Significantly, the socializing effect of the economic textbook is to convey the impression that the 'environmental issue' is already appropriately incorporated into mainstream economics. This has two complacency-creating features worth highlighting. First, the generalized effect invites complacency, since the actually existing fundamental problems (including an acute global ecological breakdown, biodiversity loss, and climate change crisis), issues and urgency cannot be adequately conveyed to students within this way of framing economics. Second, the specific forms of theory and policy solutions also invite complacency, since they seem to suggest that the problem is well in hand (or will ultimately be solved in the future). The consequences of this can be multiple for students, extending to a kind of cognitive dissonance, based on a split between the complacency or confidence induced by economics and the concern and fear induced by attention to other sources of knowledge and information. At worst mainstream economics socialization militates against taking urgent action to address present day fundamental issues: immediate social redesign, a halt and reversal to expansion in scale and intensity of economies, etc. (Galbraith, 2020; Kallis et al., 2020).

Of course, one might respond that it is unfair to highlight introductory economics rather than focus on 'state of the art' sophistication at the forefront of mainstream economics. But both share the fundamental absence highlighted by ecological economics and arguably it is introductory economics textbooks that have the most significant educational influence. Whilst environmental economics now includes many different kinds of theory and policy foci, few economics students will come across these unless they take an elective in environmental economics. Most students will, therefore, only be familiar with what is conveyed in introductory textbooks, and this is also true for the many social science students required to take some version of 'Econ 101'. As the above also indicates, it is two policies in particular regarding the present climate change and ecological breakdown crisis that economics students are likely to be familiar with: taxing negative externalities, and creating property rights through issuing permits for carbon trading. That is, fixing a market failure and creating a market where none previously existed in order to trade a problem of externalities away. In order to underscore the problem of socialized complacency we now briefly establish that these kinds of policy ideas are entirely inadequate, and we will use the externality argument to demonstrate this.

Market failure and negative externalities

We set out right at the beginning that the focus of mainstream economics is determination of *exchange values* in an economic system of measured wealth creation. Moreover, the significance of material processes in general is tacitly assumed to be adequately accounted for through the exchange valuation system (essentially what we will pay). As such, one of the main ways material processes become an issue is when this exchange valuation system is deemed to not be working adequately, and this is one of the chief ways in which 'environmental issues' arise in mainstream economics. This is where sub-disciplinary expertise is called upon. A 'negative externality' occurs when the full (including environmental) 'social' costs of the production of a product or provision of a service are *not* included in the pricing. This means that there are some costs that are not paid by either the producer or consumer, but instead those costs fall on others in society. The archetypal environmental example is the social costs of vehicle emissions, i.e. the costs of acid rain and environmental damage, pollution and healthcare provision and so on. Since 'social' costs are higher than 'private' costs, the costs currently incorporated into the supply schedule are lower at every possible output level than would otherwise be the case. In marginal analysis this means that supply is currently higher than it would otherwise be at every price level. As such, for any given standard demand curve the 'equilibrium' will be at a lower price and greater output than would otherwise be the case, i.e. the good or service is systematically oversupplied and over-consumed. 'Price signaling' is not working 'properly' and hence a 'market failure'.

According to mainstream theory, since the problem is a pricing 'error' in the exchange valuation system, the solution to this failure is to 'fix' the pricing error, i.e. 'internalize' the external cost by applying a tax or some other strategy that makes the social cost part of the pricing decision. In theory this reduces supply at every price level and leads to a new equilibrium between demand and supply at a higher market price and lower output, i.e. the good or service is no longer systematically over-supplied and over-consumed and *market allocation* is now 'efficient'. When first presented, the negative externality argument seems reasonable and elegant, a clear development from the general framework of price signaling. But what has this achieved in practice and in what context? In textbooks the focus via case studies is how to calculate and price a tax, who to levy it on, and with what differential effects on market equilibrium. For example, environmental harm in the form of acid rain flows over national borders, so those causing specific harms may be outside of the legal jurisdiction of the taxing authority. One may also face decisions regarding how to calculate costs in any given jurisdiction (what are the *sources* of a measurable cost-based harm, such as an increase in the national incidence of asthma?) and how to apportion taxes across a supply chain (oil producers, petrol refiners, car drivers etc.). Furthermore, since different market participants may have different price and income 'elasticities' there is also a further problem of how to distribute the internalization of external costs in any given equilibrium situation.

The focus then is typically technical and quasi-practical. But significantly the whole works with and assumes the general efficacy and adequacy of the price signaling approach. But consider the whole again. The intent of internalizing a negative externality is to moderate behaviour, not to prevent it. This is an indirect way of enabling the continuation of an activity. The initial implication is that the harmful activity is *reduced*. But this is a sleight of hand. At best the theory indicates the activity is reduced per person per unit of income they have that can be used to afford the activity, and even this does not follow. Consider driving a car, for example. A larger population with higher incomes or more access to affordable financing (debt) in a transport system which invests in road infrastructure (making cars convenient or necessary) and a corporate system that invests in marketing cars to make them desirable status goods, is one where numbers of cars and miles driven can increase even as the negative externality is successively 'internalized'. And this has been our observed experience all around the world (see Morgan, 2020). From a mainstream economic theory point of view this still looks like more 'efficient allocation' because in theory it incorporates 'costs' and represents production decisions and preference choices (what we will pay).[16]

It is also worth noting that even when an action such as buying an internal combustion engine car has characteristics that may be 'individually rational' as a choice within conventional parameters of economic understanding, such behaviour may be 'collectively irrational' when practised on societal scale by large numbers of individuals. Here, the standard methodological individualism of mainstream economics supports a 'fallacy of composition' by producing climate change consequences after purchase of millions of privately owned cars. This may also be termed a 'rationality paradox' embedded in the mainstream economics approach to understanding 'negative externalities'. That is, the very form of presumably normal and rational behaviour advocated by the perspective itself produces collective problems which were unintended by individuals, but for which they will be forced to bear significant social consequences and costs.

Moreover, recall that the point of internalizing the externality is to solve a problem. The underlying problem created by our industrialized and consumer-based economies is, in combination, environmental destruction and dangerous climate change. These are consequences of the scale and intensity of material processes and they are exacerbated as economies grow (so the problem to solve is constantly expanding). Moreover, many of the consequences are ingrained based on what we do now that affects natural systems later, and they are cumulative, complexly emergent, and subject to tipping points and fundamental uncertainty. An externalities solution is supposed to make prices reflect *all* costs to shift a market in the direction of efficient allocation. This, of course, is never in practice really achieved, but this is not just a practical issue, it is a theoretical incoherence. Why would uncoordinated 'blind' human inventions (conventions) such as pricing signaling be able to adequately reflect our cumulative ingrained and baked-in *future* impacts on the material world, based on what we are prepared to 'pay' now and in relation to what we can try to calculate as 'the cost' on a market by market basis? Clearly, a moment's reflection indicates that this is impossible.

Many ecological economists have pointed out the theoretical impossibility of mainstream negative externality approaches: no truly representative price can be calculated for any given market and so no 'true price' from an ecological point of view exists in any market – as such there is no genuinely 'efficient' allocation possible in this *theoretical* system. The very existence of a policy stance that claims to fix the failure in the theoretical system serves the ideological purpose of marginalizing the otherwise obvious case to simply STOP or prohibit doing harmful things based on what the bio-physical sciences are telling us NOW will be the eventual consequences. Concomitantly, ecological economists also highlight from a political economy perspective that an approach that claims to 'fix' market failures inadvertently misrepresents the activity of firms and depoliticizes the political. For example, deliberate 'cost shifting' by firms easily become constituents in 'external social costs', but only because firms have influenced the legal and institutional context and lobbied to shift responsibility in the first place. Yet for a student engaging with a textbook, the theory of negative externalities seems very much an empirically grounded solution to a recognized problem, subject mainly to technical problems of measurement. And fundamentally, from the point of view of socialization of students, given the lack of due attention to a material growth system, the textbook conveys the impression that we can continue to do what we are already doing.

To be clear, our intent here is not to denigrate any and all attempts to intervene in and address problems of our economies. The point is to highlight the issue of proper context, points of departure, sufficiency and adequacy. Taxes on environmentally harmful activity, for example, are not pointless. But we must start to take seriously the real nature and consequences of our economies and the absolute limits the material world imposes. Mainstream economics is problematic in general and problematic as a mode of socialization for students via what textbooks convey to students. We could go on, and there are other debates that could be had (e.g. the status and significance of the 'circular economy' concept, the scope for 'green growth', new innovations and movements in the economics curriculum such as the 'CORE' project, and whether it is better or merely different – arguably merely different etc.), but the arguments set out should be sufficient to establish that there is a major issue to address in terms of the role of mainstream economics as a source of (mis)education, complacency and continuing dangerous delay.

Conclusion: transforming economics education

Economics is a field of knowledge with immense social power and influence. We are living in an era of intense systemic crises and system failure, of which the ongoing global climate change crisis and ecological breakdown are central aspects (e.g. Morgan, 2016). The study of the 'failure of civilizations' has become widespread recently, and this is symptomatic of a growing awareness that our current form of civilization is in deep historical crisis and cannot continue (Gills, 2020). Civilization itself must be radically transformed in the future. Given the power and influence of mainstream economics, in order to transform society in response to these deep crises, the field of economics must also be radically transformed and Covid-19 has only served to reinforce this point (Alves & Kvangraven, 2020). We need a revolution in economics education, placing biophysical processes at the heart of the study of economy (e.g. Røpke, 2020; Spash, 2017). The analysis of Earth System dynamics; planetary boundaries, feedback loops, thresholds and tipping points in the planetary biophysical system(s) should be core and compulsory knowledge in the field of economics. But given the nature of the influence mainstream economics has already wielded and the delay and complacency it has fostered, an economics education also needs to involve *unlearning* what it has previously enabled.

Economics as a mainstream discipline is characterized by three 'separations': the separation of economics from politics; the separation of economic theory from socio-economic reality; and the separation of economics from ecology. Each of these three separations and their consequences can usefully be critiqued as part of a new economics education and then ought to be profoundly resolved into a new form of unity where 'the economy':

- is no longer presented (explicitly or implicitly) as a sphere unto itself separated from the state, society and nature.
- is no longer understood on the analogy of a machine, operating on objective 'laws' where abstract economic models are presented as reality.

Instead economics ought to be taught in an integrated way that includes economic history and the history of economic thought, as well as bio-physical science. And real historical processes should be studied and understood, including global environmental history. There are several aspects to this: the pursuit of growth has been intrinsic to capitalism and this has had some obviously beneficial features in terms of science, medicine, technology, and (if we recognize that surplus and division of labour create scope) arts and so forth, but it has not been an anodyne tale of 'progress'. Rather real history has been a complex process of struggle, difference and exploitation of peoples, places and species that has also produced specific harms and ills and more fundamentally has come at a cost to the planet we live on. An economics education ought to convey that crises are intrinsic to rather than accidents of the kind of economies we have created, beginning in the Global North, but it ought also to convey that a basic crisis is built into our economies as growth systems that push against planetary boundaries. The danger here, however, is that education becomes an exercise in fear-inducing apocalypse-aversion, as though we were being asked to simply sacrifice and suffer in a new era of unavoidable austerity (Kallis, 2019). This is not necessarily our future and this too should be made part of economics textbooks.

The overwhelming evidence suggests that we need to reduce the scale and intensity of our economies and live differently. We need to be realistic about this and choose our futures rather than resist the obvious, since it is by resisting the obvious that worst-case scenarios may become our future. The future will have to be radically different, but this can be achieved by constructive design rather than through civilizational collapse. This is the domain of degrowth, and this too ought to become a component of future economics textbooks (Kallis et al., 2020; Spash, 2020a; Fullbrook & Morgan, 2019).[17] Whilst by no means ignoring the huge challenge that such transformation represents (and the problems we are already increasingly starting to experience in terms of ecological damage and climate change), advocates of degrowth make the case that alternative ways of living do not imply second best societies, but ones in which we stop doing superfluous things, shift resources to socially constructive activities, and focus on what matters to well-being (in societies that can still be technologically and socially progressive based on different criteria than those that currently determine the system we live in). If this suggestion seems absurd to you then chances are you have already been influenced by the dominant economic worldview. We humbly suggest that you should consider whether your 'hard-headed realism' is simply a form of cynicism, built on fantasy, or more disturbingly perhaps, your surrender to the 'logic' of mainstream economics?

Notes

1. Lakoff is not a material reductionist or behavioral determinist regarding the brain-mind, but he does argue that we develop a set of neural circuitry that is triggered by situations and language use and which shapes how we think about given subjects:

   we think in terms of typically unconscious structures called 'frames' [which] include semantic roles, relations between roles and relations to other frames ... All our knowledge makes use of frames, and every word is defined through the frames it neurally activates. All thinking and talking involves 'framing'. (Lakoff, 2010, pp. 71–72)

Lakoff's work has been influential across the social sciences (notably his *Philosophy in the Flesh*). Our focus here is economics education, and Lakoff's work (2010) on environmental issues is not specifically about this, though it is relevant in so far as education is part of socialization. Lakoff's subject was public understanding of environmental issues and his point was that activists need more than facts (based on the implicit Enlightenment assumption that people will simply respond positively to the evidence, once conveyed to them). According to Lakoff activists need a more effective communication strategy leading to an alternative framing, which can compete with a conservative 'let the market' decide framing. That strategy needs to form institutions, highlight spokespeople and develop characteristic modes of unifying argument and language use that each specific issue and event can trigger in the public. For a different perspective on new materialist framing, see Fox and Alldred (2020).

2. Increasing frustration with mainstream economics during the 1980s led to formation in 1989 of the International Society for Ecological Economics and the journal *Ecological Economics* (and there have been many notable figures besides Daly, for example, Robert Costanza). Over the years, ecological economics has become a parallel discipline to mainstream economics and environmental economics. Like many movements that find themselves seeking to influence or displace a dominant approach, it has faced challenges regarding the concessions and compromises that might be involved (and criticisms range from the claim that some working on 'ecological economics' are methodologically little different than mainstream economists, to the claim that there needs to be a more urgent focus on policy activism that squarely confronts the need for both degrowth and a transition away from capitalism). Since the purpose of this paper is to highlight the socializing effects of mainstream economics rather than the relative merits of different strands of ecological theory and activism, we merely acknowledge that there are important differences (and that Clive Spash provides extensive discussion of the issues in his various writings e.g. Spash, 2018). Julie Nelson, for example, looks at the issues differently than Spash (Nelson & Morgan, 2020).

3. There are many critiques of the ideological role of scarcity in economics in systems of abundance predicated on the creation of superfluous need (perhaps the best known in the mainstream is Galbraith 1958, but there are numerous works with more ecological focus, e.g. Schumacher, 1993).

4. To be clear, data exist on 'material flows', the point is that this is *not* what economics is founded on (see Wiedmann et al., 2015).

5. To be clear, one can distinguish between *material* growth and *valuation* growth; GDP measures valuation growth, but the basis of an economy remains material process.

6. To be clear, however, this is not to suggest alternatives are necessarily ecological in focus (this varies) merely that they note a set of standard characteristics in mainstream economic textbooks (most commonly a monistic unified and analytical framework, heavy initial focus on market competition and general absence of real pluralism and encouragement of critical thinking – despite that mainstream economists think that their work is diverse, plural and critical).

7. The best known 'ontological' version of this critique derives from the work of Tony Lawson (e.g. Lawson 2015).

8. This remains the case even when mainstream economists are more reticent regarding use of the term 'positive', since they simply substitute the phrase quantified science and make equivalent claims.

9. Note, the point is that deduction is basic to demonstration of mainstream theory via axiomatic constructs and mathematical proofs; the mainstream also recognizes induction, but has problems with abduction and other approaches.

10. Our purpose here is to emphasize that mainstream economics focuses on the individual; it is also the case that mainstream economic theory presupposes structural conditions (even though it usually adopt methodological individualism) and one should note that the focus on the individual is itself a consequence of structured social relations. One might also note that it is increasingly common in economic to recognize limits to the rationality of economic agents; however, this still takes as its point of departure or benchmark the ideal rational calculative type. Referring to more realistic behavior as irrational speaks volumes.

11. There is, as readers may be aware, a longstanding project in economics of 'imperialism' set in motion by the Chicago School economists George Stigler and Gary Becker in the last century.

12. So, the textbook format is just one component of a complex process of socialization that has made mainstream economics quite different than other social sciences. Besides heterodox critics, the sociologists

Marion Fourcade is perhaps best known for exploring this subject (Fourcade et al., 2015; Fourcade, 2009).

13. Mankiw's textbooks, like those of many prominent mainstream economists, have a global reach and extend beyond the English speaking world.

14. The reader may see that the subtext here is that 'beauty' is a much valued virtue in mathematics. At the time of the early phase of the Global Financial Crisis, Paul Krugman wrote an open letter to his fellow economists (though we note that Krugman is also a mainstream New Keynesian economist who has continued to support axiomatic theory forms) and in that letter (which eventually over a thousand others signed, including one of the authors of this article) he made the argument that Economics as a discipline should not be criticized for not predicting the great financial crisis of 2008 (though some economists, notably Steve Keen, had in fact anticipated the crisis), but rather for having taken 'the beauty of their equations' to represent 'truth' about the Real Economy.

15. And to illustrate how pervasive this reasoning has been, (noting again the list we made in the Editorial Introduction) William Nordhaus calculated an 'optimum' increase in global temperature of plus 4 degrees centigrade, based on a similar perspective, while however ignoring the mounting scientific consensus that such a level of global temperature increase over pre-industrial levels would at the very least cause vast ecological and social damage and perhaps produce runaway and irreversible warming, leading to the extinction of the human species.

16. In a price signaling market system, 'sustainable' means no more than 'is profitable'. A production process or the use of a resource can remain 'sustainable' in this sense for a lot longer than 'sustainable' might mean in terms of the effects of the market process on the environment. Cars may be market 'sustainable' as long as we can afford petrol – but the effects may not be objectively sustainable long before we run out of oil and long before we are individually prepared to give cars up or society has provided us with alternatives. In any case, what people want doesn't necessarily equal what is sustainable or socially desirable from a price signaling point of view (bottled water and chewing gum?).

17. To be clear, degrowth is being used loosely here to refer to advocacy of reduced scale, rather than to refer only to the social movement, which is just one project among many with this goal.

Disclosure statement

No potential conflict of interest was reported by the author(s).

References

Alves, C., & Kvangraven, I. (2020). Changing the narrative: Economics after Covid-19. *Review of Agrarian Studies*, *10*(1). http://ras.org.in/77067f7af922c604062edadadc5b3bd8

Amadae, S. (2005). *Prisoners of reason*. Cambridge University Press.

Amen, M., Bosman, M. M., & Gills, B. K. (2008). Editorial: The urgent need for global action to combat climate change. *Globalizations*, 5(1), 49–52. https://doi.org/10.1080/14747730701850886

Amoore, L., Dodgson, R., Gills, B., Langley, P., Marshall, D., & Watson, I. (1997). Overturning 'globalization': Resisting teleology, reclaiming politics. *New Political Economy*, 2(1), 179–195. https://doi.org/10.1080/13563469708406294

Bacevic, J. (2020). Unthinking knowledge production: From post-Covid to post-carbon futures. *Globalizations*. https://doi.org/10.1080/14747731.2020.1807855

Birks, S. (2016). *40 critical pointers for students of economics*. WEA Books.

Callon, M. (2007). What does it mean to say that economics is performative? In D. MacKenzie, F. Muniesa, & L. Siu (Eds.), *Do economists make markets?* (pp. 311–357). Princeton University Press.

Çalişkan, K., & Callon, M. (2009). Economization, part 1: Shifting attention from the economy towards processes of economization. *Economy and Society*, 38 (3), 369–398. https://doi.org/10.1080/03085140903020580

Dale, G. (2020). Rule of nature or rule of capital? Physiocracy, ecological economics, and ideology. *Globalizations*. https://doi.org/10.1080/14747731.2020.1807838

Daly, H. (2015). *Essays against growthism*. WEA/College Books.

Daly, H. (1997). Forum, Georgescu–Roegen vs. Solow/Stiglitz. *Ecological Economics*, 22, 261–266.

Daly, H. (1974). The economics of the steady–state. *American Economic Review*, 64(2), 15–20.

Daly, H., & Morgan, J. (2019). The importance of ecological economics: An interview with Herman Daly. *Real-World Economics Review*, 90, 137–154.

Earle, J., Moran, C., & Ward-Perkins, Z. (2017). *The econocracy*. Penguin.

Fourcade, M. (2006). The construction of a global profession: The transnationalization of economics. *American Journal of Sociology*, 112(1), 145–194. https://doi.org/10.1086/502693

Fourcade, M. (2009). *Economists and societies*. Princeton University Press.

Fourcade, M., & Healy, K. (2007). Moral views of market society. *Annual Review of Sociology*, 33(1), 285–311. https://doi.org/10.1146/annurev.soc.33.040406.131642

Fourcade, M., Ollion, E., & Algan, Y. (2015). The superiority of economists. *Journal of Economic Perspectives*, 29(1), 89–114. https://doi.org/10.1257/jep.29.1.89

Fox, N., & Alldred, P. (2020). Economics, the climate change policy-assemblage and the new materialisms: Towards a comprehensive policy. *Globalizations*. https://doi.org/10.1080/14747731.2020.1807857

Frank, R., Gilovich, T., & Regan, D. (1993). Does studying economics inhibit cooperation? *Journal of Economic Perspectives*, 7(2), 159–171. https://doi.org/10.1257/jep.7.2.159

Fullbrook, E., & Morgan, J. (eds.) (2019). *Economics and the ecosystem*. World Economic Association Books.

Galbraith, J. K. (1958). *The affluent society*. Hamish Hamilton.

Galbraith, J. K. (2020). Economics and the climate catastrophe. *Globalizations*. https://doi.org/10.1080/14747731.2020.1807858

Gills, B. K. (2008). Climate change: A global call to action. *Globalizations*, 5(1), 83–87. https://doi.org/10.1080/14747730701587371

Gills, B. K. (2020). Deep Restoration: From the great implosion to the great awakening. *Globalizations*, 17(4), 577–579. https://doi.org/10.1080/14747731.2020.1748364

Gills, B. K., & Morgan, J. (2020). Global climate emergency: After COP24, climate science, urgency, and the threat to humanity. *Globalizations*, 17(6), 885–902. https://doi.org/10.1080/14747731.2019.1669915

Hickel, J. (2018). The Nobel prize for climate catastrophe. *Foreign Policy*. 6 December.

Hickel, J., & Kallis, G. (2020). Is green growth possible? *New Political Economy*, 25(4), 469–486. https://doi.org/10.1080/13563467.2019.1598964

Kallis, G. (2019). *Limits: Why Malthus was wrong and why environmentalists should care*. Standford University Press.

Kallis, G., Paulson, S., D'Alisa, G., & Demaria, F. (2020). *The case for degrowth*. Polity Press.

Keen, S. (2020). The appallingly bad neoclassical economics of climate change. *Globalizations*. https://doi.org/10.1080/14747731.2020.1807856

Koch, M., & Buch-Hansen, H. (2020). In search of a political economy of the postgrowth era. *Globalizations*. https://doi.org/10.1080/14747731.2020.1807837

Komlos, J. (2019). *Foundations of real-world economics*. Routledge.

Lakoff, G. (2010). Why it matters how we frame the environment. *Environmental Communication*, 4(1), 70–81. https://doi.org/10.1080/17524030903529749

Lawson, T. (2015). *Essays on The nature and state of modern economics*. Routledge.

Madi, M., & Reardon, J. (eds.) (2014). *The economics curriculum*. WEA Books.

Mankiw, G., & Taylor, M. (2020). *Economics*. Cemgage Learning EMEA.

Morgan, J. (2015). Is economics responding to critique? What do the UK QAA 2015 subject benchmarks for economics indicate? *Review of Political Economy*, *27*(4), 518–538. https://doi.org/10.1080/09538259.2015.1084774

Morgan, J. (2016). Paris COP21: Power that speaks the truth? *Globalizations*, *13*(6), 943–951. https://doi.org/10.1080/14747731.2016.1163863

Morgan, J. (2017). Piketty and the growth dilemma revisited in the context of ecological economics. *Ecological Economics*, *136*, 169–177. https://doi.org/10.1016/j.ecolecon.2017.02.024

Morgan, J. (2020). Electric Vehicles: The future we made and the problem of unmaking it. *Cambridge Journal of Economics*, *44*(4), 953–977. https://doi.org/10.1093/cje/beaa022

Nelson, J. A., & Morgan, J. (2020). Ecological and feminist economics: An interview with Julie A. Nelson. *Real-World Economics Review*, *91*, 146–153.

Newell, P., & Taylor, O. (2020). Fiddling while the planet burns? COP 25 in perspective. *Globalizations*, *17*(4), 580–592. https://doi.org/10.1080/14747731.2020.1726127

O'Neill, J. (2007). *Markets, deliberation and environment*. Routledge.

Oreskes and Conway. (2010). *Merchants of doubt*. Bloomsbury.

Reardon, J., Madi, M., & Scot-Cato, M. (2018). *Introducing a new economics*. Pluto Press.

Røpke, I. (2020). Econ 101—In need of a sustainability transition. *Ecological Economics*, *169*), article 106515. https://doi.org/10.1016/j.ecolecon.2019.106515

Samuelson, P. (1998). How foundations came to be. *Journal of Economic Literature*, *36*(3), 1375–1386. https://www.jstor.org/stable/2564803

Schumacher, E. (1993). *Small is Beautiful: A study of economics as if people Mattered*. Vintage. (Original work published 1973)

Sloman, J. (1997). *Economics* (3rd ed.). Prentice Hall.

Sloman, J., Guest, J., & Garratt, D. (2018). *Economics* (10th ed.). Pearson.

Söderbaum, P. (2018). *Economics, ideological orientation and democracy for sustainable development*. WEA Books.

Spash, C. (ed.) (2017). *Routledge handbook of ecological economics: Nature and society*. Routledge.

Spash, C. (2018). Facing the truth or living a lie: Conformity, radicalism and activism. *Environmental Values*, *27*(3), 215–222. https://doi.org/10.3197/096327118X15217309300804

Spash, C. (2020a). The economy as if people mattered: Revisiting critiques of economic growth in a time of crisis. *Globalizations*. https://doi.org/10.1080/14747731.2020.1761612

Spash, C. (2020b). A tale of three paradigms: Realising the revolutionary potential of ecological economics. *Ecological Economics*, *169*. https://doi.org/10.1016/j.ecolecon.2019.106518

Steffen, W., Rockström, J., Richardson, K., Lenton, T. M., Folke, C., Liverman, D., … Schellnhuber, H. J. (2018). Trajectories of the earth system in the anthropocene. *Proceedings of the national academy of sciences of the USA*, 115, 8252–8259.

Stevenson, H. (2020). Reforming global climate governance in an age of bullshit. *Globalizations*. https://doi.org/10.1080/14747731.2020.1774315

Wiedmann, T., Schandl, H., Lenzen, M., Moran, D., Suh, D., West, J., & Kanemoto, K. (2015). The material footprint of nations. *Proceedings of the National Academy of Sciences*, *112*(20), 6271–6276. https://doi.org/10.1073/pnas.1220362110

Zuidhof, P. (2014). Thinking like an economist: The neoliberal politics of the economics textbook. *Review of Social Economy*, *72*(2), 157–185. https://doi.org/10.1080/00346764.2013.872952

Unthinking knowledge production: from post-Covid to post-carbon futures

Jana Bacevic

ABSTRACT

The past years have witnessed a growing awareness of the role of institutions of knowledge production in reproducing the global climate crisis, from research funded by fossil fuel companies to the role of mainstream economics in fuelling the idea of growth. This essay argues that rethinking knowledge production for post-carbon futures requires engaging with the co-determination of modes of knowing and modes of governing. The ways in which knowledge production is embedded in networks of global capitalism shapes how we (can) think about the future. The essay argues for an attentivity to the material and infrastructural sides of knowledge production, which will enable us to re-think transition to post-carbon futures in ways that recognize the deep structural, spatial and social inequalities underpinning knowledge production.

Introduction

The Covid-19 pandemic has posed an unprecedented challenge to institutions of knowledge production. As campuses shut down, universities sent – sometimes almost forcibly – students back to their 'homes', and research facilities limited their activities to essential maintenance, shock and confusion were replaced by a sense of foreboding: what kind of future awaits higher education and research in a world in which these disruptions – caused not only by pandemics but also by the worsening climate crisis – are becoming more common?

For many scholars, the Covid-induced shutdown also presented an opportunity to think about alternatives to capitalist modes of production (e.g. Alves & Kvangraven, 2020; Mair, 2020; Spash, 2020). Over the past years, a consensus has emerged about the links between the current configurations of global capitalism and the climate crisis. The tendency of capitalist modes of production to extract, use, and dispose of natural resources in ways that systematically harm both the people and the environment has reached the point of emergency (e.g. Gills & Morgan, 2019). The role of economics, and in particular the specific kind of economics defined by mathematical modelling, has often been identified as one of the main 'epistemic handmaidens' to extractive capitalism (e.g. Callon, 2007; Çalışkan & Callon, 2009; Lawson, 2016). This means thinking about post-carbon futures needs to account for the role of disciplinary knowledge(s) in creating the conditions for the current crisis – and, presumably, their role in overcoming it.

The argument of this essay is that this project is complicated by two factors. One is the history of Western knowledge production, and the way in which institutions such as universities carry the legacies not only of colonialism and slavery – something that they have reluctantly begun to address – but also of extractive logic of global capitalism. The other is the degree to which our own thinking – including thinking about alternatives to capitalist modes of knowledge production – continues to rely on an extractivist logic that remains conveniently blind to infrastructural and material affordances. As a consequence, any attempt to think about the future that is *not* capitalist or extractive-colonial faces the seemingly impossible task of undoing its own conditions of possibility (Arendt, 1961; Mignolo, 2011). This requires us to connect our own projects of critique and reform to material and infrastructural affordances of contemporary capitalism, and their role in climate crisis.

The essay begins to trace these relations by highlighting the co-determination of modes of knowing and modes of governing – including capitalism – and their role in climate futures. This foregrounds the question of the relationship between knowledge and political order (cf. Shapin & Schaffer, 1985/2011). While critical and heterodox economists have recently started paying more attention to the role of (mainstream) economics discipline and economics teaching in reproducing conditions of capitalist exploitation (e.g. Mearman et al., 2018; Spash ed., 2017; Çalışkan & Callon, 2009; Callon, 2007), the organization of knowledge production *in relation to* broader socio-political context has remained somewhat underexplored. This essay contributes to the focus of this special issue – the role of economics in post-Covid, post-carbon futures – by offering a conceptualization of knowledge production that emphasizes its relationship to the legacies of capitalist extraction, in order to highlight how we might begin to overcome them in the future.

Fear of the future

Future-oriented research, having all but disappeared from the agenda after the dissolution of the Soviet Union and the pronouncement of the end of history, has received a renewed impetus in the past ten years (Amsler & Facer, 2017; Andersson, 2018). While we should not underestimate the relevance of changing funding conditions on shaping institutional isomorphism or 'branding', at least a part of this impetus comes from the perception of the risk that processes such as climate change and the development of autonomous technologies pose to the future of humankind.[1] As other scholars have argued, the implicit universalism of 'humanity' can exclude different populations and political subjects that have been historically marked as 'Other' – indigenous peoples, ethnic minorities, refugees and migrants, and the poor (Clark, 2011; Yusoff, 2018). Less well documented, however, is how thinking about the future impacts of climate change can simultaneously exclude the consideration of the impact of climate change on one's own practices, including knowledge production itself.

There is an extensive literature on knowledge production that is critical of capitalism, and, in particular, of neoliberalism as its most recent manifestation (e.g. Bok, 2003; Giroux, 2014; Newfield, 2003). While this kind of writing has tended to foreground the questions of justice and/or the exploitation of academic labour, it rarely engages directly with *climate* justice or the value or the exploitation of *non-humans*. In this sense, academic critique of neoliberalism tends to exhibit a particular kind of anthropic bias, in the sense of inability to imagine a world that doesn't involve the standpoint of an (at least implicitly human) observer (Bostrom, 2010). Of course, 'non-humans' have been a trendy topic in social theory for a number of years, in part because of a growing realization of the relevance of non-human 'Others' to human survival on the planet (e.g. Blok & Jensen, 2019; Danowski & Viveiros de Castro, 2017; Haraway, 2016; Latour, 2017; Tsing, 2015). Yet, with very few exceptions (e.g. Wark, 2015; Yusoff, 2018), these treatises have seen the production of theory as distinct from the question of knowledge production and its role in climate change.

This isn't to engage in performative moralization of academic behaviour akin to 'shaming' climate researchers for taking long-haul flights. It is, rather, to draw attention to the fact that all forms of knowledge always include ignorance (e.g. McGoey, 2019, 2012). Ignorance occurs not only as 'lack' or 'absence', but also as blind spots systematically produced by focusing on specific research objects (Bacevic, 2020). This assumption – that better critique leads to better practice – is the contemporary version of scholastic fallacy, something I have dubbed 'gnossification' (Bacevic, 2019). Of course, there is nothing particularly original in noting that knowledge production relies on other forms of reproduction (cf. Bourdieu, 1997; Woolf, 1929/1992). Challenging – and changing – academic practices is necessary. Yet, while 'green' values, curricula, syllabi, and practices are relevant they are not sufficient for a transition to a low-carbon economy. Students may adopt sustainable values, beliefs and practices, but these would not help if the only jobs available in 20 years are provided by fossil fuel companies (Su & Su, 2019; van Dijk, 2019). We may reform the curriculum (and other academic practices) so as to reflect a commitment to decarbonization, but this does not mean that academic knowledge production becomes detached from the commitment to profit that ensures carbon emissions continue to rise.

In the context of this essay, I draw attention to the fact that systematic 'forgetting' of the infrastructural and material affordances of knowledge production means that most initiatives for low-carbon, 'sustainable' academic knowledge production do not disrupt the broader capitalist logic of extraction.[2] In other words, they produce increasingly nuanced analyses, but not necessarily better ways of changing the status quo. Disentangling these habits requires not only acknowledging how the infrastructures of knowledge production are rooted in capitalist pasts, but also how they shape how we think about the future.

Capitalist pasts

The emergence of global networks of knowledge production is deeply intertwined with the history of global capitalism (see e.g. Connell, 2007; Kamola, 2019; Santos, 2014). Collaboration and exchange between scholars, of course, pre-dated both the emergence of capitalism and the emergence of nation-states (Perraton, 2014; Pietsch, 2016, 2013). Yet, the organized production and exchange of knowledge cannot be separated from systems of global trade and colonial extraction (Bhambra 2014; Moore, 2015; Stein & Andreotti, 2016). While institutions of knowledge production have belatedly started acknowledging the role of colonialism and slavery (Wilder, 2013), they are still far away from recognizing the degree to which they not only contribute to, but benefit from, modes of production that both created and sustain the global climate crisis.

This may sound counterintuitive, as many institutions of knowledge production in the past years have been quite vocal about taking steps to combat climate change (Rickards & Pietsch, 2020). In some cases, this has included decisions to divest, which usually means withdraw their funding and/or assets (proprietary technologies, research facilities, staff) from activities that directly contribute to the climate crisis (for instance, fossil fuel extraction). Some institutions have refused to perform research for or accept funding from companies that pollute the environment or engage in environmentally harmful practices. Many more have adopted various packages of so-called 'green' policies: from incentivizing commuting by bike or public transport, installing systems that conserve energy, to recycling on campus, and, in some cases, mandating the use of biodegradable or carbon neutral materials and technologies in catering, cleaning, and other maintenance services.

As commendable as these initiatives are, a deeper look at the political economy of knowledge production suggests they are minor in comparison with the broader 'footprint' of relations and practices that underpin them. The expansion of higher education in the second half of the twentieth century was primarily driven by the perceived link between knowledge and economic growth (Newfield, 2003; Wilder, 2013; World Bank, 2000). Scientific research was similarly stimulated by the assumption that knowledge provides economic and political advantage, both in 'peacetime' – through innovative technologies designed to boost production – and in situations of possible conflict (e.g. Chomsky et al., 1997). After the Cold War, the technoscientific race became transposed on to the global knowledge market, with countries – and, increasingly, supranational entities – competing for ideas, innovations, and technologies that could be sold at the highest price. This shift from the idea that knowledge afforded advantage in trading, to the idea that knowledge itself can be traded, gave rise to the concept of 'knowledge economies'.

The concept of knowledge economies effectively involved outsourcing production (especially 'dirty', polluting forms of industry) to China and other Asian countries, while retaining the development of 'software' – innovation and technologies – in countries of the Global North, primarily US and Western Europe. This amplified regional inequalities: despite improving the living conditions of *some* people everywhere, it increased the gap between the wealthy and the poor (see Hickel, 2017 for a comprehensive treatment of the idea that the world is becoming more equal). Equally importantly, it amplified global CO_2 emissions (Jiang et al., 2019), both through the intensification of global trade, with emissions related to both production and transport across increasing distances, and through increased mobility of people. Both were connected to global business and, increasingly, to education and research, as countries struggled to attract the 'brains' – that is, people – who could drive innovation (Wildavsky, 2010; Zemach-Bersin, 2009).

What is usually called the neoliberalisation of higher education, therefore, needs to be seen as only the most recent phase in the co-evolution of knowledge and global socio-political order (see e.g. Hartmann, 2019). The growth of higher education was primarily driven by private investment, either through inter-generational transfer (i.e. parents financing their children's education) or through graduate debt (Bok, 2003; McGettigan, 2013). For global centres of knowledge production – primarily Europe and North America, closely followed by Australia and New Zealand – substantial portion of investment came from tuition fees charged to international (non-domiciled) students. In most cases, this effectively means cross-border transfer of private funds, where students rely on personal or family income, or take out private loans in countries of origin. While some EU member states allow for (intra-union) portability of grants and loans, and generations of students have benefited from grants provided by governments (e.g. European Commission's Erasmus scheme) or private foundations (e.g. Gates), these forms of investment are usually seen as contributions to the development of 'human capital' and/or instruments of 'soft diplomacy' (Perraton, 2014).

Global flows of capital and global networks of knowledge production, in this sense, reflect and reproduce colonial relationships between 'centres' and 'peripheries', but they also create new ones. In the recent few years, China's Belt and Road initiative has intensified the competition between European, North American, Australian and New Zealand institutions, for whom Chinese students constitute a significant portion of income (Robertson, 2017). In this sense, the Covid-19 crisis only rendered visible – or more visible – the degree to which contemporary networks of knowledge production were deeply rooted in the global economic and political order. This, importantly, is the case regardless of the degree to which specific institutions or systems are 'internationalized'. Even seemingly protectionist policies, such as educating students for the (national) labour market, are oriented towards economic growth, which takes place in the context of global competition (Bacevic,

2014). This means that thinking about knowledge production beyond 'growth' requires thinking about the future of capitalism and the global configurations of power that might arise from it.

Climate futures

In *Climate Leviathan: A political theory of our planetary future*, Geoff Mann and Joel Wainwright (2018) theorize forms of governance that might arise in response to the reframing of the living conditions in a changing climate. They identify two main axes along which these configurations of the political might assemble: from capitalist to anti-capitalist; and from global, or planetary, to smaller-scale, from national to local. This produces a grid of four ideal-typical regimes, which they dub Climate Leviathan, Climate Behemoth, Climate Mao, and Climate X. While there are obvious limits to grid/group scenarios, this framing provides a good starting point for thinking about the relationship between knowledge production and geopolitical governance of climate futures.

Climate Leviathan and Climate Behemoth both assume the continuation of capitalism as the dominant mode of production. However, whereas Climate Leviathan assumes the continuation of some form of global governance – akin to the current role of the United Nations Intergovernmental Panel on Climate Change (UN IPCC) and the Conference of Parties (COP) – Climate Behemoth does not. In Climate Behemoth, states – or, possibly, smaller, warring entities – are left to address the consequences of climate change for themselves. Regardless of whether political units choose to focus on mitigation, adaptation, or some mixture of both, this approach retains capitalist accumulation as the primary goal of economy, but with possible protectionism applied to national markets. This, for instance, could be seen as Donald Trump's strategy since the withdrawal of the US from the Paris Agreement in 2017.

The two remaining regimes, Climate Mao and Climate X, are characterized by departure from the capitalist mode of production. As can probably be discerned from the name, Climate Mao assumes the emergence of China (or a similar world power) as the planetary sovereign, steering away from the capitalist logic of accumulation and profit. Yet even if China could be reliably identified as anti-capitalist[3] (cf. Szelényi & Mihályi, 2019; Zhang & Peck, 2016) at the present moment it is not entirely clear how the entirety of global production could be organized from one world-state. What is pretty certain, however, is that this level of global governance would need to depart significantly from the (at least in principle) voluntary participation that currently characterizes international cooperation, towards a more centralized and possibly authoritarian forms of governance. Of course, given so far extremely limited capacity of capitalist or market incentives (carbon trading and 'offsetting' schemes) to address climate change (Wright & Nyberg, 2014; Grumbach, 2015; Gunderson et al., 2018) this kind of solution might prove necessary to prevent the worst-case scenarios of warming of 5 degrees Celsius and above – providing, of course, there is a political actor capable of implementing it.

Last, but not least, 'Climate X' stands for the little-explored space of possibility that departs from both capitalism as the dominant mode of production and global governance as its mode of coordination. While there is a longer tradition of research and writing on utopian collectives, this kind of political organization has so far remained confined to small, self-sufficient communes or movements, like the Zapatistas. As Mann and Wainwright acknowledge, we needn't paint too rosy a picture of what the future in which these forms of self-organization would become more numerous would look like. After all, most present-day self-sustaining communities exist at the 'edges' of capitalism, rather than completely outside of it (Grubacic & O'Hearn, 2016; see also Kallis et al., 2020). In this sense, we do not really know in what form they would continue to exist if it ended – and how, of course.[4] This presents a particular problem for thinking about knowledge production in post-carbon futures.

Post-Covid disaster capitalism?

Reactions of institutions of knowledge production to the Covid-19 pandemic so far have overwhelmingly followed the approach best described as 'disaster capitalism' (Klein, 2007, 2014). After initial expressions of care and gestures of solidarity, most institutions have resorted to cutting down staff and/or wages, either through flat-rate deductions or promotion and pay freezes. Networks of circulation and exchange of data (pre-print-servers such as ArXiv as well as social media) were quickly matched by private sector investments or takeovers, compounding the tendency for seemingly 'free' knowledge to become enrolled in the logic of capitalism (Bacevic & Muellerleile, 2018; Kelty, 2014).

Fears of declining numbers of international students and the possibility of 'domestic' or home students deciding to defer have led universities in the US and the UK to push for the resumption of in-person teaching. Similarly, the possibility that the US Government may revoke visas to international students whose courses have shifted online suggests an intensification of the relationship between universities, immigration regimes, and border control (Giroux, 2007). Stronger integration between state-governed mechanisms of surveillance and forms of international mobility – along the lines already present in the UK, where universities and research institutes are required to report on their international staff and students – could eventually give rise to a 'Knowledge Leviathan', with internationally-coordinated mobility of the highly skilled, and stronger, if not impermeable, borders for everyone else. On the other hand, it is also possible that the tendency towards centralization and agglomeration of teaching and research would compound the nationalization or protectionism of certain regimes.

Under conditions of capitalist competition – those that would, presumably, characterize both 'Climate Leviathan' and 'Climate Behemoth' regimes – it makes sense to assume that the pressure on institutions will be to return to 'business as usual' as quickly as possible. This, so far, has mostly taken the form of prioritizing the kind of education and research that can generate profit – from programmes highlighting 'employability' (like business and marketing) to commercial research that offers the possibility of developing and patenting technologies that provide a competitive advantage in the new climate – the Coronavirus vaccine being the most proximate, and urgent, one. Another strategy has been to tie education and research more closely to the state, with subsidized programmes that are projected to directly contribute to economic competitiveness, and others – most likely arts and humanities – left to 'the market'.

Of course, not all institutions can return to business as usual. In the first period following the pandemic, we may see a wave of closures, either through bankruptcies, or through mergers and takeovers, with smaller institutions being 'swallowed' by larger, more resilient ones. This might introduce a distinction between institutions that continue to operate on a 'global' scale, attracting international students (and fee income), and those that focus on more 'localized' provision. Some universities would probably continue to attract students (and, to a smaller degree, staff) from across the globe, retaining the majority of education and research operations in existing (or new) buildings on campus. This kind of knowledge production tends to be most carbon intensive, as it requires both travel – both in terms of students relocating from other countries, and in terms of staff commuting to work – and campus-based resource use.

The other distinction will probably be between institutions that shift to decentralized, online delivery, and those that prioritize in-situ training. While the former is the model most universities have been forced to temporarily transition to during the Covid-19 pandemic, there are reasons to believe that the predominantly online or 'blended' offline/online learning model would become more prominent in the future. It would be a mistake, however, to assume online learning would necessarily be more climate-friendly. Digital technology comes with its own, rapidly growing, footprint. A study in 2015 estimated cloud computing is responsible for 2% of global emissions, on par with emissions from global aviation (Greenpeace, 2015); a more recent report puts it at 3.7%, predicted to grow by 8% annually (The Shift Project, 2019) – and this was all prior to the big 'online transition' stimulated by the pandemic.

These statistics, however, cover only a fraction of digital technologies' impact. Emissions are also produced by the manufacture, shipping, and disposal of digital technologies, including their energy consumption when 'offline'. Furthermore, access to 'high-speed' internet is both carbon intensive and distributed in ways that are socially unjust (Allman & Hazas, 2019). In a rapidly destabilizing world, institutions of knowledge production that are most likely to survive will be those that have access to technologies and data that will allow them to adapt to a shifting climate. This includes not only data (weather satellites, meteorological observations) but also the ways in which people, communities and societies are responding to, adapting, or suffering in the climate crisis. The impact of climate change on grid stability and energy provision is likely to exacerbate these inequalities.

Of course, there are many ways in which institutions can be made 'greener' or more resilient in terms of energy use. Universities that have access to land could develop, or, where existing, extend sustainable food production in order to become both self-sufficient and to contribute to local food resilience.[5] They could also provide shelter during extreme weather events, generate energy (wind, water, solar) that could be shared the local population, and provide services such as hospitals, nurseries and schools for local residents. This might compound the existing trend of 'science parks' or 'innovation campuses', with spatial integration of research, innovation, and production. Universities and research institutes would thus increasingly become 'total institutions' (Goffman, 1961), morphing the public and private (or economically and socially reproductive) sides of life.

However, there is also a possibility that these institutions will become increasingly insulated – both spatially and conceptually – from the 'outside world', especially under conditions of political instability. In the future, institutions of knowledge production may come to resemble the scientific compounds described in Margaret Atwood's MaddAddam trilogy (2009, 2010, 2014) – self-enclosed communities mutually connected by high-speed trains, and protected from the poverty, chaos, and (climate) instability on the outside by walls and security guards. This model converges with the scenario in which political futures entail disintegration into smaller, conflicting city-states or statelets, along the lines of 'Climate Behemoth'.

Innovation and science campuses are, of course, not limited to capitalist modes of production. In this sense, it is quite possible that the knowledge production complexes could be enrolled to support centrally planned economies of the sort Mann and Wainwright depict in 'Climate Mao'. While there are reasons to believe this kind of massive coordination is already underway in China, it is difficult to see how the centralization of knowledge production would, in itself, lead to the reduction of carbon emissions unless accompanied by an overall reduction in resource use. One of the paradoxes of central planning is that it can ensure the most rational and resource-efficient distribution of resources, but only under the assumption that systems are relatively stable. In this sense, forms of disruption or instability that will become more frequent – extreme weather events, grid and infrastructure failures, and public health problems (see Hartmann, 2019) – would all limit the capacity of this kind of system to adjust to rapid changes.

This leaves the kind of knowledge production that might arise in small, decentralized communities based on mutual aid and similar principles of cooperation – the kind of political future Mann and Wainwright label 'Climate X' (see also Hamed Hoseini et al., 2020). This mode of knowledge production calls for the longest stretch of imagination, in part because, as this essay argued, thinking about knowledge production is itself rooted in the history of capitalism. This means we need to be careful about the romance of localism (Patomäki, 2019), without a clear plan on how to 'divest' not only from visible ties with the fossil fuel industry, but also from our own dependence on networks of global capital.

The Covid-19 pandemic allowed a 'pre-view' of the degree to which knowledge production draws on the extractive and connectionist logic that fuelled the climate crisis. The grounding of international flights demonstrated, for those who may have remained blind to this previously, how dependent institutions in the 'Global North' are on fees from international students. Closure of campuses, schools, and offices made obvious the degree to which academic knowledge production – and that includes our own – relies on multiple forms of labour, including childcare, care for the elderly, and the provision of food and other necessities. An overwhelming portion of this labour is performed by women, reflected in stark gender inequalities in data reported on rates of submission to peer-reviewed journals since the start of the pandemic (Minello, 2020). Yet an equally significant, but even less visible portion is performed by underpaid precarious labourers of all genders, many of them migrants with few rights or protections, like the agricultural workers flown in to harvest asparagus in Germany.

This 'selective ignorance' of the material and infrastructural affordances of knowledge production creates not only a lack of resilience – including in situations like disruptions of food supply chains, likely to become more frequent in the future – but also enables the continuation of exploitative labour relations that underpin modes of capitalist production. This demonstrates that environmental justice and labour justice cannot be separated (Hampton, 2018), despite organized labour's somewhat ambiguous relationship to the climate crisis (see Stevis et al., 2018).

In their masterful argument for rethinking the main paradigm of economics in the aftermath of the Covid-19 crisis, Carolina Alves and Ingrid Kvangraven write:

> Situating the economy in society enables exploration of the intricacies between the economy and nature, for example, by food systems researchers or ecological economists … to scholars with a broader understanding of how production affects food and ecological systems, the rise and spread of Covid-19 was less of a surprise. Such a perspective starkly contrasts to viewing the pandemic as an exogenous shock. Therefore, it is now time to emphasise that capitalist production is intertwined with nature and cannot be seen as separate – an important lesson for many heterodox economists as well. (Alves & Kvangraven, 2020, p. 4)

And go on to argue:

> The inherent instability of capitalism and the need to put distributional conflicts at the centre of any economic analysis is also a recurring characteristic of heterodox approaches … the low wages among essential workers are determined by policy, rather than being a reflection of a market-determined price. Some of these weaknesses bluntly exposed by the pandemic include the high degrees of homelessness, precarious workforces, and poverty.

In this sense, drawing attention to infrastructure (Easterling, 2016; Edwards et al., 2009) serves to underline the way in which our own projects, including projects of reform, rely on modes and relations of production that are part and parcel of the climate crisis. Similar to how 'soup, salmon and ducklings' in Virginia Woolf's *A room of one's own* (1929/1992) reveal the gender inequality fuelling Oxbridge scholarship, thinking about how thinking about post-carbon futures itself relies on capitalist forms of production gives us a good starting point from which to apprehend the scale of change necessary. From this perspective, we can ask any number of questions – who gets an internet connection? Who maintains our libraries? Who harvests the vegetables for our casseroles or mills and packs ingredients for our sourdough? – to start thinking seriously about what disruptions in food supply, grid failures, and, not least, social inequalities, mean for the future of knowledge production.

Conclusions

This essay argued that thinking about the futures of knowledge production in climate emergency requires us to engage seriously with the degree to which the history of contemporary knowledge production is rooted in the history of global capitalism, including colonialism and extractivism. This requires undoing not only of modes of production (capitalism) *or* habits of thought (Occidentalism, Eurocentrism) that have arisen as a consequence of this history, but the modes of production *of* thought that are, themselves, its product.

Recognizing that our knowledge practices do not only reflect the legacy of these modes of exploitation, but directly benefit from them, requires us to think carefully about projects of reform. This highlights the ownership and management of infrastructure (Easterling, 2016) as one of the key questions for the future of knowledge production. Arguing for a decolonized curriculum or an ecological economics remains little more than perfunctory if we are not prepared to rethink our own reliance on modes of socioeconomic reproduction that sustain – and amplify – the climate crisis (cf. Spash, 2017; see also EXALT project at the University of Helsinki[6]). In this sense, online learning, working from home, and bread-baking should not be seen as 'minor disruptions' to business-as-usual: instead, we they should force us to acknowledge the material and immaterial affordances of our own knowledge production.

To foreground knowledge infrastructures, then, is to foreground not only the future of the world, but our own role in it. Without paying attention to these elements, we are left to the project akin to building electric cars without roads or ways of life that support them (Mattioli et al., 2020; Morgan, 2020), or advocating Open Access without acknowledging how status inequalities intersect with the valuation of academic labour (Bacevic & Muellerleile, 2018). In other words, not only do we fail to engage with the material 'base' of knowledge production, we fail to acknowledge the ways *not* thinking about certain forms of material and immaterial labour precludes certain kinds of political futures.

To think about knowledge production in post-carbon futures requires us to engage with these forms of exploitation at the same time as we argue for transition to clean energy, better working environment, and anti-neoliberal curricula. This, in turn, is to foreground issues of justice and distribution. After all, surviving in a changing climate will require an extensive sharing of knowledge. Whether this knowledge will be used to create competitive advantage for individuals, countries and other political units, or whether it can be used for the benefit of all, is the key political question for climate futures.

Notes

1. For instance, the University of Cambridge recently saw the establishment of the Centre for the Study of Existential Risk (CSER) and the Centre for the Future of Intelligence (CFI); the University of Oxford hosts the Future of Humanity Institute; Digital Futures Institute is a new major investment at the University of Bristol; and Lancaster University's Institute for Social Futures was founded in 2015.
2. There is an extensive literature dealing with the relationship between capitalism and academic labour, in particular precarity and casualization. The constraints of space in this article made it impossible to engage with in detail, but (see e.g. Gill, 2014 as well as Bacevic & Muellerleile, 2018).
3. This, of course, would be an entirely separate discussion, but my view is that it cannot.
4. David Harvey recently provoked an outcry on the Left by suggesting that capitalism was 'too big to fail' in the sense of awareness that there are currently no guarantees any political movement or societal formation could survive broad-range destruction of current (capitalist) modes of existence. As unpalatable as it may seem, this analysis represents an accurate assessment of the current state of anti-capitalist movements (see e.g. Seymour, 2020).

5. Issues related to land use are of particular significance for universities with endowments in the UK (like Oxford and Cambridge) or land-grant universities in the US; of course, ownership or use of land does not in and of itself prevent extractive and exploitative practices – (see e.g. Christophers, 2019).
6. https://www.helsinki.fi/en/conferences/exalt-2020/about-the-initiative.

Disclosure statement

No potential conflict of interest was reported by the author(s).

References

Allman, K., & Hazas, M. (2019, October). *The impact of new and emerging internet technologies on climate change and human rights.* Submission to the Advisory Committee to the UN Human Rights Council. Online: https://ohrh.law.ox.ac.uk/publications/the-impact-of-new-and-emerging-internet-technologies-on-climate-change-and-human-rights-submission-to-the-advisory-committee-to-the-un-human-rights-council/

Alves, C., & Kvangraven, I. (2020). Changing the narrative: Economics after Covid-19. *Review of Agrarian Studies, 10*(1), http://ras.org.in/77067f7af922c604062edadadc5b3bd8

Amsler, S., & Facer, K. (2017). Contesting anticipatory regimes in education: Exploring alternative educational orientations to the future. *Futures, 94*, 6–14. https://doi.org/10.1016/j.futures.2017.01.001

Andersson, J. (2018). *Future of the world: Futurology, futurists, and the struggle for the post-Cold War imagination.* Oxford University Press.

Arendt, H. (1961). *Between past and future: Six essays in political thought.* The Viking Press.

Atwood, M. (2009). *Oryx and crake.* Anchor.

Atwood, M. (2010). *The year of the flood.* Anchor.

Atwood, M. (2014). *Maddaddam.* Anchor.

Bacevic, J. (2014). (Education for) work sets you free: 'Employability' and higher education in former Yugoslavia and its successor states. *European Journal of Higher Education, 4*(3), 281–296. https://doi.org/10.1080/21568235.2014.916534

Bacevic, J. (2019). Knowing neoliberalism. *Social Epistemology, 33*(4), 380–392. https://doi.org/10.1080/02691728.2019.1638990

Bacevic, J. (2020). *On (not) knowing the future: prediction, legitimation, and the Yugoslav crisis.* https://thedisorderofthings.com/2020/07/03/on-not-knowing-the-future-prediction-legitimation-and-the-yugoslav-crisis/

Bacevic, J., & Muellerleile, C. (2018). The moral economy of open access. *European Journal of Social Theory, 21*(2), 169–188. https://doi.org/10.1177/1368431017717368

Bhambra, G. K. (2014). *Connected sociologies.* Bloomsbury Academic.

Blok, A., & Jensen, C. B. (2019). The anthropocene event in social theory: On ways of problematizing nonhuman materiality differently. *The Sociological Review, 67*(6), 1195–1211. https://doi.org/10.1177/0038026119845551

Bok, D. (2003). *Universities in the marketplace: The commercialization of higher education.* Princeton University Press.

Bostrom, N. (2010). *Anthropic bias: Observation selection effects in science and philosophy.* Routledge.

Bourdieu, P. (1997). *Pascalian meditations.* Polity.

Callon, M. (2007). What does it mean to say that economics is performative? In D. MacKenzie, F. Muniesa, & L. Siu (Eds.), *Do economists make markets?* (pp. 311–357). Princeton University Press.

Chomsky, N., Katznelson, I., Lewontin, R. C., Montgomery, D., Nader, L., Ohmann, R., Siever, R., Wallerstein, I., & Zinn, H. (1997). *The Cold War and the university: Toward an Intellectual history of the postwar years.* New Press.

Christophers, B. (2019). *New enclosure: Appropriation of public land in neoliberal Britain.* Verso.

Clark, N. (2011). *Inhuman nature: Sociable life on a dynamic planet.* Sage.

Connell, R. (2007). *Southern theory: The global dynamics of knowledge in social science.* Polity Press.

Çalışkan, K., & Callon, M. (2009). Economization, part 1: Shifting attention from the economy towards processes of economization. *Economy and Society, 38*(3), 369–398. https://doi.org/10.1080/03085140903020580

Danowski, D., & Viveiros de Castro, E. (2017). *The ends of the world.* Polity Press.

Easterling, K. (2016). *Extrastatecraft: The power of infrastructure space.* Verso.

Edwards, P., Bowker, G. C., & Jackson, S. J. (2009). Introduction: An agenda for infrastructure studies. *Journal of the Association for Information Systems, 10*(5), 364–374. https://doi.org/10.17705/1jais.00200

Gill, R. (2014). Academics, cultural workers and critical labour studies. *Journal of Cultural Economy, 7*(1), 12–30. https://doi.org/10.1080/17530350.2013.861763

Gills, B. K., & Morgan, J. (2019). Global climate emergency: After COP24, climate science, urgency, and the threat to humanity. *Globalizations,* https://doi.org/10.1080/14747731.2019.1669915

Giroux, H. A. (2007). *The university in chains: Confronting the military-industrial-academic complex.* Paradigm.

Giroux, H. A. (2014). *Neoliberalism's war on higher education.* Haymarket.

Goffman, E. (1961). *Asylums: Essays on the social situation of mental patients and other inmates.* Anchor Books.

Greenpeace International. (2015). *How dirty is your data? A look at energy choices that power cloud computing.* Greenpeace.

Grubacic, A., & O'Hearn, D. (2016). *Living at the edges of capitalism: Adventures in exile and mutual aid.* University of California Press.

Grumbach, J. M. (2015). Polluting industries as climate protagonists: Cap and trade and the problem of business preferences. *Business and Politics, 17*(4), 633–659. https://doi.org/10.1515/bap-2015-0012

Gunderson, R., Stuart, D., & Petersen, B. (2018). Ideological obstacles to effective climate policy: The greening of markets, technology, and growth. *Capital & Class, 42*(1), 133–160. https://doi.org/10.1177/0309816817692127

Hamed Hoseini, S. A., Goodman, J., Motta, S., & Gills, B. (Eds.). (2020). *The Routledge handbook of transformative global studies.* Routledge.

Hampton, P. (2018). Trade unions and climate politics: Prisoners of neoliberalism or swords of climate justice? *Globalizations, 15*(4), 470–486. https://doi.org/10.1080/14747731.2018.1454673

Haraway, D. (2016). *Staying with the trouble: Making kin in the chthulucene.* Duke University Press.

Hartmann, E. (2019). The future of universities in a global risk society. *Globalizations, 16*(5), 717–736. https://doi.org/10.1080/14747731.2019.1583412

Hickel, J. (2017). Is global inequality getting better or worse? A critique of the World Bank's convergence narrative. *Third World Quarterly, 38*(10), 2208–2222. https://doi.org/10.1080/01436597.2017.1333414

Jiang, L., He, S., Zhong, Z., Zhou, H., & He, L. (2019). Revisiting environmental kuznets curve for carbon dioxide emissions: The role of trade. *Structural Change and Economic Dynamics, 50*, 245–257. https://doi.org/10.1016/j.strueco.2019.07.004

Kallis, G., Paulson, S., D'Alisa, G., & Demaria, F. (2020). *The case for degrowth.* Polity Press.

Kamola, I. (2019). *Making the world global: U.S. universities and the production of the global imaginary.* Duke University Press.

Kelty, C. (2014). Beyond copyright and technology: What open access can tell us about precarity, authority, innovation, and automation in the university today. *Cultural Anthropology, 29*(2), 20–34. https://doi.org/10.14506/ca29.2.02

Klein, N. (2007). *The shock doctrine: The rise of disaster capitalism.* Metropolitan Books; Henry Holt and Company, LLC.

Klein, N. (2014). *This changes everything: Capitalism vs. the climate.* Simon & Schuster.

Latour, B. (2017). *Facing Gaia: Eight lectures on the new climatic regime.* Polity.

Lawson, T. (2016). What is this 'school' called neoclassical economics? *Cambridge Journal of Economics, 37*(5), 947–983. https://doi.org/10.1093/cje/bet027

Mair, S. (2020, March 30). What will the world be like after coronavirus? Four possible futures. *The Conversation*. https://theconversation.com/what-will-the-world-be-like-after-coronavirus-four-possible-futures-134085

Mann, G., & Wainwright, J. (2018). *Climate leviathan: A political theory of our planetary future*. Verso.

Mattioli, G., Roberts, C., Steinberger, J., & Brown, A. (2020). The political economy of car dependence: A systems of provision approach. *Energy Research & Social Science, 66*, 1–18. https://doi.org/10.1016/j.erss.2020.101486

McGettigan, A. (2013). *The great university gamble: Money, market and the future of higher education*. Pluto Press.

McGoey, L. (2012). Strategic unknowns: Towards a sociology of ignorance. *Economy and Society, 41*(1), 1–16. https://doi.org/10.1080/03085147.2011.637330

McGoey, L. (2019). *The unknowers*. Zed.

Mearman, A., Guizzo, D., & Berger, S. (2018). Whither political economy? Evaluating the CORE project as a response to calls for change in economics teaching. *Review of Political Economy, 30*(2), 241–259. https://doi.org/10.1080/09538259.2018.1426682

Mignolo, W. D. (2011). *The darker side of western modernity: Global futures, decolonial options*. Duke University Press.

Minello, A. (2020, April 17). The pandemic and the female academic. *Nature*, https://www.nature.com/articles/d41586-020-01135-9

Moore, J. (2015). *Capitalism in the web of life: Ecology and the accumulation of capital*. Verso.

Morgan, J. (2020). Electric vehicles: The future we made and the problem of unmaking it. *Cambridge Journal of Economics, 44*(4), 953–977. https://doi.org/10.1093/cje/beaa022

Newfield, C. (2003). *Ivy and industry: Business and the making of the American University, 1880–1980*. Duke University Press.

Patomäki, H. (2019). Repurposing the university in the 21st century: Toward a progressive global vision. *Globalizations, 16*(5), 751–762. https://doi.org/10.1080/14747731.2019.1578533

Perraton, H. (2014). *A history of foreign students in Britain*. Palgrave.

Pietsch, T. (2013). *Empire of scholars: Universities, networks and the British academic world 1850–1939*. Manchester University Press.

Pietsch, T. (2016). Between the local and the university: Academic worlds and the long history of the university. In M.-H. Chou, I. Kamola, & T. Pietsch (Eds.), *The transnational politics of higher education: contesting the global/transforming the local* (pp. 21–41). Routledge.

Rickards, L., & Pietsch, T. (2020, June 3). Climate change is the most important mission for universities of the 21st century. *The Conversation*, https://theconversation.com/climate-change-is-the-most-important-mission-for-universities-of-the-21st-century-139214

Robertson, S. R. (2017). Colonising the future: Mega-trade deals, education services and global higher education markets. *Futures, 94*, 24–33. https://doi.org/10.1016/j.futures.2017.03.008

Santos, B. d. S. (2014). *Epistemologies of the South: Justice against epistemicide*. Paradigm Publishers.

Seymour, R. (2020, June 25). Is capitalism too big to fail? https://www.patreon.com/posts/is-capitalism-to-38532977

Shapin, S., & Schaffer, S. (2011). *Leviathan and the air-pump: Hobbes, boyle, and the experimental life (with a new introduction by the authors)*. Princeton University Press. (Original work published 1985).

The Shift Project. (2019). *Lean ICT: Towards digital sobriety*.

Spash, C. (ed.). (2017). *Routledge handbook of ecological economics: Nature and society*. Routledge.

Spash, C. L. (2020). 'The economy' as if people mattered: Revisiting critiques of economic growth in a time of crisis. *Globalizations*, https://doi.org/10.1080/14747731.2020.1761612

Stein, S., & Andreotti, V. O. (2016). Higher education and the modern/colonial global imaginary. *Cultural Studies ↔ Critical Methodologies, 17*(3), 1–9. https://doi.org/10.1177/1532708616672673

Stevis, D., Uzzell, D., & Räthzel, N. (2018). The labour–nature relationship: Varieties of labour environmentalism. *Globalizations, 15*(4), 439–453. https://doi.org/10.1080/14747731.2018.1454675

Su, H., & Su, S. (2019). Why solving intergenerational injustice through education does not work. *On Education: Journal for Research and Debate, 2*(4).

Szelényi, I., & Mihályi, P. (2019). *Varieties of post-communist capitalism: A comparative analysis of Russia, Eastern Europe and China*. Brill.

Tsing, A. L. (2015). *The mushroom at the end of the world: On the possibility of life in capitalist ruins*. Princeton University Press.

van Dijk, N. (2019). Playing the long game: Rethinking education for sustainability; A reply to Su and Su and Niebert. *On Education: Journal for Research and Debate, 2*(4), https://doi.org/10.17899/on_ed.2019.4.9

Wark, M. (2015). *Molecular red: Theory for the anthropocene*. Verso.

Wildavsky, B. (2010). *The great brain race: How global universities are reshaping the world*. Princeton University Press.

Wilder, C. S. (2013). *Ebony and Ivy: Race, slavery, and the troubled history of America's universities*. Bloomsbury.

Woolf, V. (1992). A room of one's own. In *A room of one's own & three guineas*, edited with an introduction by Morag Shiach. Oxford University Press. (Original work published 1929).

World Bank. (2000). *Higher education in developing countries: Peril and promise. Task force on higher education and society*.

Wright, C., & Nyberg, D. (2014). Creative self-destruction: Corporate responses to climate change as political myths. *Environmental Politics, 23*(2), 205–223. https://doi.org/10.1080/09644016.2013.867175

Yusoff, K. (2018). *A billion black anthropocenes or none*. University of Minnesota Press.

Zemach-Bersin, T. (2009). Selling the world: Study abroad marketing and the privatization of global citizenship. In R. Lewin (Ed.), *The handbook of practice and research in study abroad: Higher education and the quest for global citizenship* (pp. 303–320). Routledge.

Zhang, J., & Peck, J. (2016). Variegated capitalism, Chinese style: Regional models, multi-scalar constructions. *Regional Studies, 50*(1), 52–78. https://doi.org/10.1080/00343404.2013.856514

In search of a political economy of the postgrowth era

Max Koch and Hubert Buch-Hansen

ABSTRACT

Against the backdrop of the ecological and climate emergencies and several other deep crises, advocates of degrowth call for democratic transitions towards societies that can thrive beyond economic growth within ecological boundaries while being socially equitable. In recent years, scholarship has emerged that brings together the emerging degrowth paradigm with insights from political economy. Yet much contemporary political economy continues to ignore the environment and, by implication, the ecological downsides of economic growth. The present contribution criticizes this state of affairs and highlights the promises of a synthesis of contemporary critical political economy and the growth-critical tradition in ecological economics. It hints at how concepts of one particular strand of critical political economy, namely regulation theory, may be of use in analyses of (trajectories to) the postgrowth era.

Introduction

Our societies are in danger of collapsing under the combined weight of several deep and interrelated crises. In addition to a social crisis, which for instance manifests itself in massive inequality, and a political crisis, which takes the form of a march towards post-democracy (Crouch, 2016), we also face catastrophic global ecological and climate breakdowns and an economic downturn caused by the covid-19 pandemic. The ecological and climate emergencies above all result from the functioning of the growth-addicted capitalist system and have both accelerated under its prevailing form in recent decades, namely that of global neoliberal capitalism. The pandemic lockdowns serve to underscore once again that when economic growth comes to a halt, this economic system immediately enters a state of crisis. The predicament is that the available evidence provides little reason to think that it will be possible to halt the ecological and climate emergencies while the global economy grows. For instance, for all the optimism of advocates of 'green growth', the strong long-term correlation between global GDP growth and global GHG emissions continues to exist (Steffen et al., 2015).

As the planet burns, and world leaders continue to distractive fiddling (Newell & Taylor, 2020), there is a growing realization in academia and beyond that the ecological and climate emergencies demand a profound transformation of our civilization (e.g. Gills & Morgan, 2019, p. 2; Ripple et al.,

2019; Spash, 2020a). An increasing number of scholars and activists call for 'degrowth' or 'post-growth'. In their view, continued global economic growth cannot be reconciled with environmental sustainability, as a result of which we cannot afford to go back to business as usual in the wake of the covid-19 pandemic. Instead, they call for democratic transitions towards post-capitalist societies that can function within ecological boundaries while being socially equitable. Premised on sufficiency, deceleration, care, sharing, participation and conviviality such societies are envisioned to come about through transformations at different scales, ranging from deep lifestyle changes at the micro-level to top-down policies implemented by states and international organizations at the macro-level (Cosme et al., 2017; Demaria et al., 2013; Rutt, 2020).

Rooted in ecological economics, the emerging degrowth paradigm has connected to various disciplines and perspectives. One promising encounter is that with political economy scholarship (Chertkovskaya et al., 2019a). Political economy with its focus on the social, political, ideational and institutional contexts into which capitalism is embedded, and its emphasis on power relations, interests and struggles, has crucial insights to bring to degrowth scholarship. Conversely, political economy has much to gain from a synthesis with growth-critical scholarship if it is to produce knowledge contributing towards the ecological and social transformations required to re-embed production and consumption patterns in environmental limits.

What could such a combined analysis involve? What traditions in political economy could be a natural part of it? In the present contribution, we start out by reviewing and criticizing how contemporary mainstream political economy relates to the environment. We then highlight the promises of fusing contemporary critical political economy in the Marxian tradition and the growth-critical tradition in ecological economics and discuss some of the emerging and diverse critical political economy analyses relating to the postgrowth era. Finally, we illustrate how concepts of one particular strand of critical political economy, namely regulation theory, may be of use in analyses of (trajectories to) this era, focusing specifically on the example of the potential role of the state in supporting and perhaps initiating degrowth transitions.

The environment and (the poverty of) mainstream political economy

How does mainstream (constructivist and rationalist) international and comparative political economy (IPE/CPE) research relate to the environment? For the most part, it does not relate to it at all. For decades, while it became increasingly apparent that an ecological collapse was imminent, most mainstream political economists remained silent on the issue and the ecological dimension was absent in the main debates defining the field (Buch-Hansen, 2019). Certainly, many of the major IPE textbooks had and have a chapter or section on the environment and mainstream political economy theories have been applied in studies of various cases relating to environmental sustainability for instance renewable energy transitions (e.g. Wood et al., 2020). Yet because the environment is absent in the leading theories of the field, such applications tend to miss out on critical issues.

An example of a mainstream CPE theory neglecting the environment is that of Hall and Soskice's Varieties of Capitalism (VoC) perspective, which introduced the famous distinction between coordinated and liberal market economies. In the seminal text outlining this perspective (Hall & Soskice, 2001), the only environment considered worthy of attention is the business environment. Some of the scholars applying the perspective in sustainability-related cases propose that coordinated market economies may be in a better position to introduce green technologies than are liberal market economies (e.g. Ćetković & Buzogány, 2016; Mikler & Harrison, 2012). Other studies find that the VoC perspective is of little use when making sense of the clean energy global division of labour (Lachapelle et al., 2017). Overall, it is safe to say that this theory will not have much explanatory power in ana-lyses of most environmental aspects of the political economy. Due to its neglect of the environment its concepts will for instance typically not be useful for explaining why some countries emit more CO_2 per capita or perform better on other ecological parameters than do other countries. The same applies more generally to political economy perspectives neglecting the environment, ranging from work on growth models (Baccaro & Pontusson, 2016) over constructivist political economy (Abdelal et al., 2011) to the welfare regime typology of Esping-Andersen (1990). The latter typology was nevertheless applied in the 'synergy' hypothesis (Gough et al., 2008), according to which countries with a social-democratic welfare regimes, which perform best in relation to inequality, would also do so in ecological and climate terms and gradually turn into 'eco-social states'. However, this hypothesis could not be verified in comparative empirical research (Koch & Fritz, 2014).

The absence of the environment in mainstream political economy theory means that critical issues become none-issues. Most importantly, this is seen in how economic growth is viewed, namely in an altogether one-sided (positive) manner. GDP growth is regarded as *the* most important measure of economic performance (Hall & Gingerich, 2009) and is thus widely used as the key par-ameter for comparing how successful specific countries are. With inspiration from mainstream econ-omics, 'good' institutions are seen as those capable of delivering high GDP and productivity growth rates, while 'bad' institutions are those delivering the opposite (Amable & Palombarini, 2009, pp. 123–124). A blind eye is turned to the fact that economic growth has massive ecological downsides – as reflected in the abovementioned correlation between global GDP growth and global CO_2 emis-sions. That the ecological downsides of economic growth become a none-issue shows in research applying mainstream political economy theories to sustainability-related issues. Such research is typically tacitly premised on an acceptance of the green growth notion that the solution to the cli-mate crisis is to be found in investments in technological fixes and market based solutions. It ignores that this notion has by now been largely debunked in several recent studies (e.g. Haberl et al., 2020; Hickel & Kallis, 2020; Parrique et al., 2019).

A major reason why the ecological dimension is widely overlooked in mainstream political econ-omy is that it is rooted in a flat, anthropocentric ontology. That is, a worldview placing human beings and their constructs at the centre of the universe while disregarding the impacts of biophysical reality on social systems and vice versa. As Morgan (2016, p. 15) notes in a different context, the nature of reality ought to make a difference to how it is studied by a social science. His focus is mainstream economics, which has been demonstrated by Lawson (1997, 2019) to study the economy with methods that do not match the nature of social and economic reality, the result being widespread explanatory failure. Mainstream political economy has not lost touch with social and economic rea-lity to the same extend as neoclassical economics. Still, that social reality is embedded in nature ought to make a much bigger difference to how political economic-matters are generally studied.

New beginnings

If empirical proof for sufficient absolute decoupling of matter and energy use and carbon emissions in production and consumption patterns, on the one hand, and GDP growth, on the other hand, to remain within planetary limits and reach the Paris climate goals cannot be provided, economic growth should be deprioritized as policy goal, while scholarly efforts should be directed towards a political economy of the postgrowth era. Such an approach cannot afford the luxury of assuming away the environment. Consequently, it needs to abandon the anthropocentric ontology and leave behind mainstream political-economic theory. Moreover, it cannot look to neoclassical economics – including its subfield of environmental economics – for inspiration (it would indeed do well to break with it completely). Fortunately, there are other rich traditions it can build on and synthesize with. We see great potential in a fusion of the growth-critical tradition in ecological economics, particularly post- and degrowth scholarship, and contemporary critical political economy in the Marxian tradition.[2]

Ecological economics, specifically what Spash (2020b) refers to as 'social ecological economics', is premised on an ontology according to which reality is hierarchically ordered into a number of strata and higher strata presuppose lower and less complex ones. Consistently with critical realist philosophy of science (Bhaskar, 2015), the mechanisms of higher strata (say, the social stratum) are held to possess emergent properties as a result of which they are irreducible to, and qualitatively different from, their lower stratum foundations (say, the physical stratum). While the laws of physics never cause social outcomes, the social is nonetheless subject to biophysical structures (Spash, 2020b). Reversely, social activities can impact biophysical structures. Unlike the anthropocentric ontologies underpinning mainstream economics/political economy, then, this deep ontology – which also in critical respects resonates with Marxist political economy (Buch-Hansen & Nielsen, 2020) – constitutes a worldview that has the potential to fruitfully underpin a postgrowth political economy.

As regards the Marxian tradition in political economy, we will relate specifically to some recent interpretations of regulation theory as they constitute the perhaps most promising political economy attempts to systematically link analyses of production and consumption patterns with the environment. In contrast to neoclassical economics, the regulation approach does not view consumption as an isolated or behavioural phenomenon – the result of autonomous individual choices – but within its social genesis and context (Boyer & Saillard, 2002). Purchase decisions or the 'demand side' of economics are neither 'formally rational' nor 'autonomous', but instead are greatly influenced by structural factors such as income inequality and corporate sales strategies. A 'mode of regulation' comprises an ensemble of social networks as well as rules, norms, and conventions, which together facilitate the seamless reproduction of an 'accumulation regime'. This is further conceptualized in terms of 'institutional forms', which comprise the wage-labour nexus, the enterprise form, the nature of money, the state, as well as international and energy regimes (Cahen-Fourot & Durand, 2016). The analysis of the latter focuses on, among other things, the environmental impacts of historical periods of capitalist growth such as Fordism or finance-driven capitalism (Koch, 2012).

Before hinting at how the concept of 'institutional forms' can enter analyses of (trajectories to) the postgrowth era, we turn to recent encounters between postgrowth scholarship and various strands of critical political economy. Indeed, not only have critical political economy scholars begun to consider the environment systematically (for overviews see Buch-Hansen, 2014, 2019; Cahen-Fourot, 2020) but degrowth theorists have started to envision a 'political economy of degrowth' (Chertkovskaya et al., 2019a; Parrique, 2019). These new beginnings have in common a reconceptualization of the welfare-work nexus and relate to two kinds of 'liberations': 'from work' and 'of work'. Parrique (2019) and Chertkovskaya et al. (2019b) plead to understand 'work' and 'the economy' in wider terms than currently and to reach out to alternative political economy approaches such as that of 'diverse' and/or 'local' economies by Gibson-Graham (2006, 2008) and ecofeminism (Mies, 1998; Salleh, 2017; Wichterich, 2015). A 'political economy of degrowth' would then be oriented at the totality of the 'various forms of economic activity' (Chertkovskaya et al., 2019b, p. 4), that is, including those that are currently not or only marginally tied to the production of monetary value and economic growth, and promote values like 'care, cooperation, mutual aid, solidarity, conviviality, autonomy' (Chertkovskaya et al., 2019b, p. 4).

One of the greatest contributions of Chertkovskaya et al.'s book lies in relating the degrowth debate to more traditional forms of working class interest representation (Barca, 2019). This has the potential of not only strengthening growth-critical thought and activism but also other heterodox schools of political economy. Leonardi (2019), especially, shows that André Gorz was a pioneer of both degrowth and ecosocialism, and he convincingly argues that an important precondition for building an alternative hegemony within and beyond the reign of work would be a reunification of both schools. We agree that an intensified dialogue with the Marxian tradition could facilitate the formulation of a political economy of degrowth that is not limited to normative postulations and (nomadic) utopian sketches of a different economy. Though this is doubtless significant, a political economy in keeping with the times should also entail and start from an analysis of how various economic categories and forms of work became structurally valued, undervalued combined in the present economic outlook (Castree, 1999; Schmid & Smith, 2020; Stevis et al., 2018). Studies into how different principles of domination – particularly those of class, gender and ethnicity – intersect in particular conjunctures and social positions could also facilitate the identification of openings for alternative economies to be upscaled from niches to centres, and hence, for transformational social change.

For any study of the currently predominating division of labour we regard Marx's original discussion of the key problem of allocation of societal work relative to human needs and wants as fundamental. While all societies (including degrowth societies) must organize the division of labour in particular ways to satisfy their needs, it is particular to capitalism that this 'proportionalization' is carried out via the 'exchange value' or 'commodity' character of work products or 'behind the backs' (Marx, 1990) of the producers. The fact that work takes the form of exchange value (on top of use value) leads to a simultaneous generalization and diminishing of the concept of work in that everything that produces (surplus) value (or contributes towards it) counts as productive work, while many functions that are doubtless useful from a wider societal viewpoint do not count as having value. This includes a range of the work functions listed by Gibson-Graham (2006; see Gregoratti & Raphael, 2019) that are today not recognized as 'gainful employment'. Hence, a Marxian perspective may help understand the structural – capitalist – background and the corresponding power relations within which these forms of work became under-appreciated. However, Marx was well aware of the fact that his capitalist 'mode of production' was an abstraction from much more complex economies and societies in the real world. Poulantzas (1975), for example, built on this in arguing that actual capitalist economies and societies – he called these 'social formations' – are dominated by the capitalist mode of production but nevertheless also feature elements of non-capitalist economies, corresponding forms of domination and a range of real-type combinations of productive and unproductive as well as paid and unpaid work.[3]

The basic contradiction between use value and exchange value of the commodity and work, which Marx uses as point of departure in *Capital*, expresses at the most abstract level the social and ecological tensions to be found in further economic categories such as money, capital, interest and rent (Foster, 2000; Koch, 2012; Saito, 2017).[4] Hence, in contrast to the negligence or ignorance of the matter and energy aspect of production and consumption relations in neoclassical approaches, Marx builds on the difference of value and money, on the on hand, and matter and energy, on the other, from the beginning. Yet he also points out that under the imperative of valorization, the concrete, material and energetic aspects of labour, which is reflected in the use value of work, is subordinated to abstract labour and abstract value. Marx goes on to trace the origin of the growth imperative in his discussion of relative surplus production, and addresses the ways in which the historically and specific principles of capitalist production – including the systematic under-appreciation of work carried out at the margins of the capitalist work-valorization nexus – are reflected in the actors' minds. *Capital* in fact entails an analysis of an entire 'stepladder of mystifications' starting from the commodity and money fetish with the wage form as its basis, where all difference of necessary and surplus work has disappeared. The result is that the capitalist growth economy appears to be the natural and eternal way of running 'the' economy – an enormous structural and ideological obstacle that oppositional forces should reckon with (Koch, 2018).

With respect to the naturalization of consumption relations, Bourdieu (1984) argues that people, whether they are aware of this or not, are part of a general competition for legitimate tastes, to which he refers as 'distinction' – a structurally determined imperative to search and compete for ever-new lifestyles and use values with severe ecological effects. Social differences, especially those of class, tend to be reproduced in the sphere of lifestyles, the social genesis of which is hidden from view. Yet the agents' consciousness is never completely ideological and always entails elements of a practical knowledge that points beyond the status quo. The capability of becoming tastemakers and influencing power relations more generally differs with position in social space, that is, according to the distribution of economic, cultural and social 'capital'. Future empirical studies could raise issues such as whether or not mindsets that point beyond the growth imperative are more often represented in particular socio-demographic groups than others.[5] Such research could help building political alliances and seems to be of special relevance during crises such as in the current covid-19 context, when the customary correspondence of 'habitus', practice and social structures breaks and alternative discourses gain ground (Koch, 2020a).

The state as an institutional form in the postgrowth context

At a more concrete level of abstraction, degrowthers and ecosocialists aspiring to formulate a political economy of the postgrowth era could build on the regulation theoretical notion of 'institutional forms' (see above). Critical issues to be studied include the conjunctural features of the wage-labour nexus (including patterns of marginalization, precarization and devaluation of certain work functions), enterprise forms, the kinds and functions of money and of the international political regime in a (transition to a) postgrowth economy as well as an operational division of labour of scales in a corresponding mode of regulation. And it would need to be discussed how the single institutional forms could evolve in parallel and at roughly the same speed, so that experiences of exclusion and anomie are avoided during the downscaling process of matter and energy throughputs in production and consumption.[6] An early example for a reinterpretation of institutional forms in this light is the role of the state. There is a recent rereading of some classics of state theory from a degrowth and transformational change perspective (D'Alisa & Kallis, 2020; Koch, 2020b).[7]

Materialist state theory – especially Gramsci (1971), Poulantzas (1978) and Bourdieu (2015) – constructs the state as a relatively autonomous sphere, where dominating and dominated groups represent and struggle for their interests. State policies cannot be reduced to the strategic interests of single actors, but rather develop as a result of the heterogeneity, compromises and changing dynamic of social forces within and beyond the state apparatus. The more socially coherent the coalition of forces that influences the state, the lesser the contradictions across its policies. Hence, according to the mentioned state theorists – and provided the necessary civil society mobilization (Buch-Hansen, 2018) – the existing state apparatus could be used to challenge the growth imperative. This would, however, presuppose a simultaneous change of the internal structure of the state, as Poulantzas already highlighted. Similarly, Max-Neef (1991, p. 62) argued that, in an ecological and social transition, the state apparatus would need to open up for state-civil society relations, in which the 'political autonomy that arises from civil society' serves as counterbalance to the 'state's logic of power'. The main challenge for activists continues to be the avoidance of 'cooptation strategies of the state' as a result of which 'micro-organizations' may 'lose control … ' (Guillén-Royo, 2015, p. 112; Max-Neef, 1991, p. 75).[8]

Conclusion

In times where planetary boundaries are reached or crossed, mainstream political economy choses to either completely ignore the environment or reproduce the myth of green growth. If political economy intends to contribute towards re-embedding production and consumption patterns in environmental limits and indeed a corresponding ecological and social transformation, we have here argued that it needs to abandon its anthropocentric ontology and reposition itself in the postgrowth context. This presupposes a break with mainstream economics and an amalgamation with heterodox approaches such as ecological economics, ecofeminism and degrowth. Within the emerging and diverse political economy of and for the postgrowth era, the Marxian tradition, with its simultaneous focus on historically specific economic categories, social relations and modes of consciousness, is capable of playing a constructive part. And some of the concepts of contemporary critical political economy approaches such as regulation theory may give a hint into the further particulars of an analysis of this new epoch. Like growth economies, postgrowth economies will have institutions that may be understood in terms of 'institutional forms'.

We discussed this further at the example of the state. In our reading, a societal mobilization beyond, through and by the state would be necessary to push through an eco-social agenda with the potential of initiating degrowth. A range of corresponding policies and policy instruments have been identified including proposals for work sharing, minimum income schemes, caps on wealth and income, time-banks or job guarantees. Indeed, overall, there is no lack of more or less developed policy suggestions to which activists may turn. The problem continues to be that these are often fragmented and in need of being unified in a coherent strategy for the social and ecological transformation of the rich countries. It is encouraging that this issue is increasingly reflected in recent contributions that explore the synergy potential of single policies in terms of 'recipes' for a degrowth transition (Parrique, 2019) or 'virtuous circles of sustainable welfare' (Hirvilammi, 2020). Contributing to advance this agenda could be an entry point for political economists wishing to move beyond narrow anthropocentric perspectives to generate knowledge relevant for the postgrowth era. Whereas mainstream economics by means of its theory form and policy recommendations actively contributes to obstruct the economic and social transformations urgently needed to halt the climate and ecological crises, much political economy scholarship inadvertently plays a negative role by reproducing key ideas of mainstream economics – such as the notion that endless economic growth is unproblematic and desirable. If the discipline of political economy is to retain its relevance in the years to come, it needs to free and distance itself from this delusion.

Notes

1. We consider some Marxian and ecofeminist exceptions to this rule below.
2. See Pirgmaier and Steinberger (2019) for a similar ambition.
3. On 'peripheral social formations' within the international division of labour see Amin (1974).
4. Altvater (1993) and Moore (2015) tabled Marx-inspired analyses of contemporary capitalism that consider the environment systematically.

5. See Fritz and Koch (2019) and Eversberg (2020) for preliminary analyses.
6. On complexity issues associated with a degrowth transition see Büchs and Koch (2017, 2019).
7. See also Görg et al. (2017) and Buch-Hansen and Koch (2019).
8. See Gudynas (2013) for a discussion of the potential role of the state in a 'post extractivist' political economy and Eskelinen et al. (2020) on cooptation practices in the context of a Nordic welfare state.

Acknowledgements

Max Koch's contribution benefited from funding from the Swedish Energy Agency (*Energimyndigheten*) project 'Sustainable Welfare for a New Generation of Social Policy' [project no. 48510-1].

Disclosure statement

No potential conflict of interest was reported by the author(s).

Funding

This work was supported by the Swedish Energy Agency (Energymyndigheten) [grant number 48510-1].

References

Abdelal, R., Blyth, M., & Parsons, C. (Eds.). (2011). *Constructing the international economy*. Cornell University Press.
Altvater, E. (1993). *The future of the market. An essay on the regulation of money and nature after the collapse of 'actually existing socialism'*. Verso.
Amable, B., & Palombarini, S. (2009). A neorealist approach to institutional change and the diversity of capitalism. *Socio-economic Review*, 7(1), 123–143. https://doi.org/10.1093/ser/mwn018
Amin, S. (1974). *Accumulation on a world scale: A critique of the theory of underdevelopment*. Monthly Review Press.
Baccaro, L., & Pontusson, J. (2016). Rethinking comparative political economy: The growth model perspective. *Politics & Society*, 44(2), 175–207. https://doi.org/10.1177/0032329216638053
Barca, S. (2019). An alternative worth fighting for: Degrowth and the liberation of work. In E. Chertkovskaya, A. Paulsson, & S. Barca (Eds.), *Towards a political economy of degrowth* (pp. 175–192). Rowman & Littlefield.
Bhaskar, R. (2015). *The possibility of naturalism. A philosophical critique of the contemporary human sciences fourth edition with a new introduction*. Routledge.
Bourdieu, P. (1984). *Distinction: A social critique of judgement and taste*. Harvard University Press.
Bourdieu, P. (2015). *On the state. Lectures at the Collège de France 1989–1992*. Polity.
Boyer, R., & Saillard, Y. (Eds.). (2002). *Regulation theory: The state of the art*. Routledge.
Buch-Hansen, H. (2014). Capitalist diversity and de-growth trajectories to steady-state economies. *Ecological Economics*, 106, 173–179. https://doi.org/10.1016/j.ecoleng.2014.07.028
Buch-Hansen, H. (2018). The prerequisites for a degrowth paradigm shift: Insights from critical political economy. *Ecological Economics*, 146, 157–163. https://doi.org/10.1016/j.ecolecon.2017.10.021

Buch-Hansen, H. (2019). Reorienting comparative political economy: From economic growth to sustainable alternatives. In E. Chertkovskaya, A. Paulsson, & S. Barca (Eds.), *Towards a political economy of degrowth* (pp. 39–54). Rowman & Littlefield.

Buch-Hansen, H., & Koch, M. (2019). Degrowth through income and wealth caps? *Ecological Economics, 160*, 264–271. https://doi.org/10.1016/j.ecolecon.2019.03.001

Buch-Hansen, H., & Nielsen, P. (2020). *Critical realism: Basics and beyond.* Macmillan/Red Globe Press.

Büchs, M., & Koch, M. (2017). *Postgrowth and wellbeing: Challenges to sustainable welfare.* Palgrave Macmillan.

Büchs, M., & Koch, M. (2019). Challenges to the degrowth transition: The debate about wellbeing. *Futures, 105*, 155–165. https://doi.org/10.1016/j.futures.2018.09.002

Cahen-Fourot, L. (2020). Contemporary capitalisms and their social relation to the environment. *Ecological Economics, 172*, 106634. https://doi.org/10.1016/j.ecolecon.2020.106634

Cahen-Fourot, L., & Durand, C. (2016). La transformation de la relation sociale à l'énergie du Fordisme au capitalisme néolibéral: Une exploration empirique et macro-économique comparée dans les pays riches (1950–2010). *Revue de la Régulation: Capitalisme, Institutions, Pouvoirs, 20*(2), Online: https://doi.org/10.4000/regulation.12015

Castree, N. (1999). Envisioning capitalism: Geography and the renewal of Marxian political economy. *Transactions of the Institute of British Geographers, 24*(2), 137–158. https://doi.org/10.1111/j.0020-2754.1999.00137.x

Chertkovskaya, E., Barca, S., & Paulsson, A. (Eds.). (2019a). *Towards a political economy of degrowth.* Rowman & Littlefield.

Chertkovskaya, E., Barca, S., & Paulsson, A. (2019b). Introduction: The end of political economy as we knew it? From growth realism to nomadic utopianism. In E. Chertkovskaya, A. Paulsson, & S. Barca (Eds.), *Towards a political economy of degrowth* (pp. 1–18). Rowman & Littlefield.

Cosme, I., Santos, R., & O'Neill, D. W. (2017). Assessing the degrowth discourse: A review and analysis of academic degrowth policy proposals. *Journal of Cleaner Production, 149*, 321–334. https://doi.org/10.1016/j.jclepro.2017.02.016

Crouch, C. (2016). The march towards post-democracy, ten years on. *The Political Quarterly, 87*(1), 71–75. https://doi.org/10.1111/1467-923X.12210

Ćetković, S., & Buzogány, A. (2016). Varieties of capitalism and clean energy transitions in the European Union: When renewable energy hits different economic logics. *Climate Policy, 16*(5), 642–657. https://doi.org/10.1080/14693062.2015.1135778

D'Alisa, G., & Kallis, G. (2020). Degrowth and the state. *Ecological Economics, 169*, 106486. https://doi.org/10.1016/j.ecolecon.2019.106486

Demaria, F., Schneider, F., Sekulova, F., & Martinez-Alier, J. (2013). What is degrowth? From an activist slogan to a social movement. *Environmental Values, 22*(2), 191–215. https://doi.org/10.3197/096327113X13581561725194

Eskelinen, T., Hirvilammi, T., & Venäläinen, J. (Eds.). (2020). *Enacting community economies within a welfare state.* Mayfly Books.

Esping-Andersen, G. (1990). *The three worlds of welfare capitalism.* Princeton University Press.

Eversberg, D. (2020). Who can challenge the imperial mode of living? The terrain of struggles for social-ecological transformation in the German population. *Innovation: The European Journal of Social Science Research, 33*(2), 233–256. https://doi.org/10.1080/13511610.2019.1674129

Foster, J. B. (2000). *Marx's ecology. Materialism and nature.* Monthly Review Press.

Fritz, M., & Koch, M. (2019). Public support for sustainable welfare compared: Links between attitudes towards climate and welfare policies. *Sustainability, 11*(15), 4146. https://doi.org/10.3390/su11154146

Gibson-Graham, J. K. (2006). *Postcapitalist politics.* University of Minnesota Press.

Gibson-Graham, J. K. (2008). Diverse economies: Performative practices for 'other worlds'. *Progress in Human Geography, 3*(2), 613–632. https://doi.org/10.1177/0309132508090821

Gills, B., & Morgan, J. (2019). Global climate emergency: After COP24, climate science, urgency, and the threat to humanity. *Globalizations*, https://doi.org/10.1080/14747731.2019.1669915

Gough, I., Meadowcroft, J., Dryzek, J., Gerhards, J., Lengefeld, H., Markandya, A., & Ortiz, R. (2008). JESP symposium: Climate change and social policy. *Journal of European Social Policy, 18*(4), 25–44. https://doi.org/10.1177/0958928708094890

Görg, C., Brand, U., Haberl, H., Hummel, D., Jahn, T., & Liehr, S. (2017). Challenges for social-ecological trans-formations: Contributions from social and political ecology. *Sustainability*, *9*(7), 1045. https://doi.org/10.3390/su9071045

Gramsci, A. (1971). *Selections from the prison notebooks*. Lawrence and Wishart.

Gregoratti, C., & Raphael, R. (2019). The historical roots of a feminist 'degrowth': Maria Mies's and Marilyn Waring's critiques of growth. In E. Chertkovskaya, A. Paulsson, & S. Barca (Eds.), *Towards a political economy of degrowth* (pp. 83–98). Rowman & Littlefield.

Gudynas, E. (2013). Transitions to post-extractivism: Directions, options, areas of action. In M. Lang & D. Mukrani (Eds.), *Beyond development – alternative visions from Latin America* (pp. 165–188). Rosa Luxemburg Foundation.

Guillén-Royo, M. (2015). *Sustainability and wellbeing: Human scale development in practice*. Routledge.

Haberl, H., Wiedenhofer, D., Virág, D., Kalt, D., Plank, B., Brockway, P., Fishman, T., Hausknost, D., Krausmann, F., Leon-Gruchalski, B., Mayer, A., Pichler, M., Schaffartzik, A., Sousa, T., Streeck, J., & Creutzig, F. (2020). A systematic review of the evidence on decoupling of GDP, resource use and GHG emissions, part II: Synthesizing the insights. *Environmental Research Letters*, *15*(6), 065003. https://doi.org/10.1088/1748-9326/ab842a

Hall, P. A., & Gingerich, D. W. (2009). Varieties of capitalism and institutional complementarities in the political economy: An empirical analysis. *British Journal of Political Science*, *39*(3), 449–482. https://doi.org/10.1017/S0007123409000672

Hall, P. A., & Soskice, D. (2001). *Varieties of capitalism: The institutional foundations of comparative advantage*. Oxford University Press.

Hickel, J., & Kallis, G. (2020). Is green growth possible? *New Political Economy*, *25*(4), 469–486.

Hirvilammi, T. (2020). The virtuous circle of sustainable welfare as a transformative policy idea. *Sustainability*, *12*(1), 391. https://doi.org/10.3390/su12010391

Koch, M. (2012). *Capitalism and climate change. Theoretical discussion, historical development and policy responses*. Palgrave Macmillan.

Koch, M. (2018). The naturalisation of growth: Marx, the regulation approach and Bourdieu. *Environmental Values*, *27*(1), 9–27. https://doi.org/10.3197/096327118X15144698637504

Koch, M. (2020a). Structure, action and change: A Bourdieusian perspective on the preconditions for a degrowth transition. *Sustainability: Science, Practice and Policy*, *16*(1), 4–14. https://doi.org/10.1080/15487733.2020.1754693

Koch, M. (2020b). The state in the transformation to a sustainable postgrowth economy. *Environmental Politics*, *29*(1), 115–133. https://doi.org/10.1080/09644016.2019.1684738

Koch, M., & Fritz, M. (2014). Building the eco-social state: Do welfare regimes matter? *Journal of Social Policy*, *43*(4), 679–703. https://doi.org/10.1017/S004727941400035X

Lachapelle, E., MacNeil, R., & Paterson, M. (2017). The political economy of decarbonisation: From green energy 'race' to green 'division of labour'. *New Political Economy*, *22*(3), 311–327. https://doi.org/10.1080/13563467.2017.1240669

Lawson, T. (1997). *Economics & reality*. Routledge.

Lawson, T. (2019). *The nature of social reality: Issues in social ontology*. Routledge.

Leonardi, E. (2019). The topicality of André Gorz's political ecology: Rethinking *Écologie et liberté* (1977) to (re-)connect Marxism and degrowth. In E. Chertkovskaya, A. Paulsson, & S. Barca (Eds.), *Towards a political economy of degrowth* (pp. 69–82). Rowman & Littlefield.

Marx, K. (1990). *Capital: A critique of political economy*, Vol. 1. Penguin Classics.

Max-Neef, M. (1991). *Human scale development. Conception, application and further reflections*. The Apex Press.

Mies, M. (1998). *Patriarchy and accumulation on a world scale: Women in the international division of labour*. Zed Books.

Mikler, J., & Harrison, N. E. (2012). Varieties of capitalism and technological innovation for climate change mitigation. *New Political Economy*, *17*(2), 179–208. https://doi.org/10.1080/13563467.2011.552106

Moore, J. W. (2015). *Capitalism in the web of life: Ecology and the accumulation of capital*. Verso.

Morgan, J. (2016). Critical realism as a social ontology for economics. In F. Lee & B. Cronin (Eds.), *Handbook of research methods and applications in heterodox economics* (pp. 15–34). Edward Elgar.

Newell, P., & Taylor, O. (2020). Fiddling while the planet burns? COP25 in perspective. *Globalizations, 17*(4), 580–592. https://doi.org/10.1080/14747731.2020.1726127

Parrique, T. (2019). *The political economy of degrowth* [PhD thesis]. Economics and Finance at University Clermont Auvergne and Stockholm University. Online: https://tel.archives-ouvertes.fr/tel-02499463/document

Parrique, T., Barth, J., Briens, F., Kerschner, C., Kraus-Polk, A., Kuokkanen, A., & Spangenberg, J. H. (2019). Decoupling debunked. *Evidence and arguments against green growth as a sole strategy for sustainability. A study edited by the European Environment Bureau EEB.*

Pirgmaier, E., & Steinberger, J. (2019). Roots, riots, and radical change – a road less travelled for ecological economics. *Sustainability, 11*(7), 2001. https://doi.org/10.3390/su11072001

Poulantzas, N. (1975). *Classes in contemporary capitalism.* NLB.

Poulantzas, N. (1978). *State, power and socialism.* NLB.

Ripple, W. J., Wolf, C., Newsome, T. M., Barnard, P., & Moomaw, W. R. (2019). World scientists' warning of a climate emergency. *BioScience, 70*(1), 8–12. https://doi.org/10.1093/biosci/biz088

Rutt, R. L. (2020). Cultivating urban conviviality: Urban farming in the shadows of Copenhagen's neoliberalisms. *Journal of Political Ecology, 27*(1), 612–634.

Saito, K. (2017). *Karl Marx's ecosocialism: Capital, nature and the unfinished critique of political economy.* Monthly Review Press.

Salleh, A. (2017). *Ecofeminism as politics: Nature, Marx and the postmodern.* ZED Publishings.

Schmid, B., & Smith, T. (2020). Social transformation and postcapitalist possibility: Emerging dialogues between practice theory and diverse economies. *Progress in Human Geography,* https://doi.org/10.1177/0309132520905642

Spash, C. L. (2020a). A tale of three paradigms: Realising the revolutionary potential of ecological economics. *Ecological Economics, 169.* https://doi.org/10.1016/j.ecolecon.2019.106518

Spash, C. L. (2020b). 'The economy' as if people mattered: Revisiting critiques of economic growth in a time of crisis. *Globalizations.* https://doi.org/10.1080/14747731.2020.1761612

Steffen, W., Broadgate, W., Deutsch, L., Gaffney, O., & Ludwig, C. (2015). The trajectory of the anthropocene: The great acceleration. *The Anthropocene Review, 2*(1), 81–98. https://doi.org/10.1177/2053019614564785

Stevis, D., Uzzell, D., & Räthzel, N. (2018). The labour-nature relationship: Varieties of labour environmentalism. *Globalizations, 15*(4), 439–453. https://doi.org/10.1080/14747731.2018.1454675

Wichterich, C. (2015). Contesting green growth, connecting care, commons and enough. In W. Harcourt & I. L. Nelson (Eds.), *Practicing feminist political ecologies: Moving beyond the green economy* (pp. 67–100). ZED Books.

Wood, G., Finnegan, J., Allen, M. L., Allen, M. M. C., Douglas Cumming, S. J., Nicklich, M., Endo, T., Lim, S., & Tanaka, S. (2020). The comparative institutional analysis of energy transitions. *Socio-Economic Review, 18*(1), 257–294. https://doi.org/10.1093/ser/mwz026

Rule of nature or rule of capital? Physiocracy, ecological economics, and ideology

Gareth Dale ⓘ

ABSTRACT

This century has not been kind to mainstream economics. It has failed to notice the planet is afire. Anti-ecological, it ignores natural limits. Its 'peak prometheanism' arrived in the 1980s, but how far back does the rot go? Some ecological economists locate the wrong turn in the nineteenth century. Before that was physiocracy (meaning 'rule of nature'). The physiocrats were the first to call themselves 'economists,' and to formalise political economy as an objective science tasked to anatomise general economic laws. Were they the pioneers of a genuinely 'ecological' tradition of economics? In this essay I subject physiocracy to critical analysis, focussing on agrarian capitalism and laissez-faire economics, as well as class, colonialism, environmentalism and the growth paradigm. I ask whether physiocracy was science masquerading as mysticism or the reverse. Finally, I reflect on the ideology of economics and the limits of 'image-focused' alternatives such as Kate Raworth's 'doughnut economics.'

Introduction: a tale of two doughnuts

This century has not been kind to economics. In 2008, its foremost practitioners failed to predict the crash. Famously, in deferential Britain, economists sent a letter of apology to Queen Elizabeth II. And now it is coming under fire for its failure to notice the world is burning. Economists, in their neglect of climate breakdown, 'are failing the world, including their own grandchildren and great-grandchildren', blaze Andrew Oswald and Nicholas Stern (2019) in the newsletter of the Royal Economic Society. 'Humans of the future' are likely to 'judge our profession harshly'. They evidence their disciplinary auto-critique with surveys of journal content. *The Quarterly Journal of Economics*, for example, has been edited from Harvard since the late 1800s and is the top-ranked journal in the field (according to the 2019 Web of Science impact-factor ranking). On climate change the number of articles it has published is – don't hold your breath – precisely zero. In indignation, Oswald and Stern seek to rally their colleagues: economics 'must be at the heart of' discussion of climate change. In my view, their diagnosis of the ecological illiteracy of economics is essentially correct, but a different conclusion should be drawn.

As a way into the subject, let us ask: has mainstream economic theory *ever* been ecologically minded? Clearly, in the neoclassical system, material constraints are brushed aside. It obscures from view the dependence of economic action on energy and natural resources, treating them as free gifts. In the judgement of ecological economist Paul Christensen (1992, p. 76), it 'lacks any representation of the materials, energy sources, physical structures, and time-dependent processes that are basic to an ecological approach'. Joan Martinez-Alier (1997) agrees. It discards completely 'the biophysical framework within which the human economy [is] necessarily inscribed'. Arguably, peak Prometheanism was reached in 1981 when the Chicago School economist Julian Simon (1981) declared that 'no meaningful physical limit' exists to the world economy's propensity 'to keep growing forever'. Or perhaps it arrived a little later, in 1987, when the so-called Nobel Prize for Economics was awarded to Robert Solow 'for his theory of economic growth based on the dispensability of nature', as Jay Griffiths (2000, p. 192) sardonically described it.

Solow's notoriety among ecological economists stems from his paper on 'The Economics of Resources' (2018 [original in 1974]). He begins with a supercilious kvetch: he had been 'suckered' into reading *The Limits to Growth*. The essay then proceeds to knock down 'limits' arguments. 'Given that the exhaustion of this or that resource leads us to switch to others, there is in principle 'no problem. The world can, in effect, get along without natural resources'. The latter phrase is an 'if … then' conjecture, but it's of a piece with Solow's general approach: on natural resource availability (not a major problem), the substitutability of resources (invariably sufficient), economic production (a function only of capital and labour), and broader ecological problems (sit back and be optimistic), not to mention North-South inequality (convergence is inevitable).

Solow was, however, a 'new Keynesian', aware that the market as imagined in economics classes can never exist in reality and that the inevitable imperfections necessitate state intervention. In The Economics of Resources (2018, p. 177) he puts it like this:

> Many discussions of economic policy boil down to a tension between market allocation and public intervention. Marketeers keep thinking about the doughnut of allocative efficiency … and *dirigistes* are impressed with the size of the hole containing externalities, imperfections, and distributional issues.

When applied to non-renewable resources, the doughnut is the wonders that can be accomplished by markets ('including futures markets'), while the hole is 'our actual oligopolistic, politically involved, pollution-producing industry' – which is hardly 'what the textbook ordered'.

In the work of Simon and Solow we see clearly the elision of nature in economic theory – and they are representative of mainstream economics in general. But how far back does the rot go? To approach an answer, one could do worse than bite into another doughnut, Kate Raworth's *Doughnut Economics*. Raworth (2017) is dismissive of mainstream economics, not least for its neglect of the economy's embeddedness in the biosphere. She draws a new image of the economy, one that is embedded 'within society and within nature, and powered by the sun'. To 'the early economists', she goes on,

> Earth's importance for the economy was self-evident. … In the eighteenth century, François Quesnay and his fellow physiocrats took their name from their belief that agrarian land was the key to understanding economic value. Yes, these early economists based their ecological thinking narrowly on agricultural land alone, but at least the living world got a mention. From there, however, things began to go awry.

The physiocrats' successors, Smith and Ricardo, recognized land, alongside labour and capital, as factors of production, but they prepared the way for further degeneration (Dale, 2012). By the late twentieth-century mainstream economics included only labour and capital as factors, 'and if ever land did get a mention, it was as just another form of capital'. As a result, Raworth concludes,

> mainstream economics is still taught today with scant attention paid to the living planet that supports us and the blazing star whose energy we depend upon. It relegates ecological stresses such as climate

change ... to the periphery of economic thought, until they become so severe that their damaging economic impacts demand attention.

Were the physiocrats the ancestors of today's ecological economists? Christensen (1992), answering the question 'where economics went wrong', draws the line in the mid-nineteenth century. The classicals – Petty, Cantillon and the physiocrats, Smith and Malthus – adopted a 'physical approach to production' and recognized that economies run on matter and energy, but this recognition was obliterated by the neoclassical revolution. Kenneth Stokes (1992) describes ecological economics as neophysiocratic, and Cutler Cleveland (1999) and Ole Bjerg (2016) follow suit, pointing to the physiocrats' 'steadfast belief that Nature was the source of wealth' and their 'emphasis on the real dimension of the eco'. Peter Bartelmus (2012) sees Quesnay as the first ecological economist, while for Steve Keen (2016), "the Physiocrats were the only School of economics to properly consider the role of energy in production. They ascribed it solely to agriculture exploiting the free energy of the Sun and specifically to land, which absorbed this free energy and stored it in agricultural products.' Alf Hornborg (2013, p. 52) draws a line connecting the physiocrats to ecological economist Nicholas Georgescu-Roegen (for, in energy terms, he viewed industry as "completely tributary" to agriculture and mining) and another line that divides modern mainstream economics, on one hand, and Marxist and ecological economics on the other. The latter currents retain "the concern of Physiocracy and classical economics with the physical, material aspects of economic activity" (Hornborg, 2014, p. 86).

Physiocratic thought was influential not only in France but also overseas. Richard Grove has documented the labours of physiocratic reformers in Mauritius, notably Pierre Poivre. They marshalled climatic arguments against deforestation and persuaded the colonial authorities of their importance. They turned the island into a site for innovative experiments in 'systematic forest conservation, water-pollution control and fisheries protection' (Grove, 1995, p. 9). One physiocrat-authored ordinance in 1769, for example (Grove, 1995, p. 220), 'attempted to redress the complex impact of destructive artificially induced environmental change, including processes, such as soil erosion, which were little known in Europe but highly characteristic of denuded tropical lands' Grove (1995, p. 223) goes so far as to propose that:

> environmentalism was, to a great extent, born out of a marriage between Physiocracy and the mid-eighteenth-century French obsession with the island as the speculative and Utopian location for the atavistic 'discovery' of idyllic societies or the construction of new European societies.

What did the physiocrats themselves say? Keen (2016) quotes the proto-physiocrat Richard Cantillon who in 1730 stated that 'The Land is the Source or Matter from whence all Wealth is produced'. Turgot spoke of the land as offering 'a pure gift to him who cultivates it', of 'profits [which] always come from the earth', and of the 'revenue of the soil, a gift of nature' (Turgot, 2011, p. 30, 65; and in Gudeman & Rivera, 1990, p. 32). For Mirabeau (in Gudeman, 1980, p. 247), 'the land is the mother of all goods', and, with Quesnay, he wrote of 'the spontaneous gifts of nature'. In nature, Quesnay remarked (1962, p. 204), 'everything is intertwined, everything runs through circular courses which are interlaced with one another'.

In their holism and in their reverence for nature as all-generative and regenerative, anthropologist Stephen Gudeman supposes (1980, p. 247), the physiocrats may seem more closely aligned with 'exotic tribal groups such as the Bemba or the Bisa' than with our world today. However, he adds, there was another side. They 'also maintained that nature is the *source of a surplus*, ... as not only returning costs but yielding something more'. In this essay I suggest that this second facet, nature as the wellspring of profit and rent, was the physiocrats' *only* concern. Their identification of land as the source of value was the cornerstone of their manifesto for agrarian capitalism – a system geared to the accumulation of capital by farmers and landowners. I submit that the physiocrats are more properly seen as the *font* of the tradition that issues in Simon and Solow, and not its prelapsarian antithesis. Economics didn't simply 'go wrong' in the 1870s (although it did that too); it had been 'wrong' all along.

Providential positivism: economics as science as ideology

Economic theory is normally thought of as a discipline geared to the (more or less accurate) description of economic processes and to the scientific elaboration of concepts, models, and modes of reasoning that facilitate our understanding of economic behaviour. It also, however, contains ontological, epistemological, and metaphysical claims. These concern what 'the economy' is, its 'construction', its claims to scientific status, and its position within a broader field of social (including symbolic) relations. They pertain to what economics 'does', its effects on the world, and what interests it serves and how it serves them – in short, its performative and ideological functions. The physiocrats were the first to be labelled economists and are commonly credited as the founders of the discipline. Certainly they were the first to formalize political economy as an objective science, tasked to anatomize general economic laws (Røge, 2013). They originated the concept of the 'national economy', which they theorized as a system, comprehensible because subject to laws (Fourcade, 2009). It was their great merit, as Marx puts it in *Theories of Surplus Value* (1861–1863), to have conceived of the system of production as a 'physiological' form of society, 'arising from the natural necessity of production itself' and 'independent of anyone's will or of politics, etc.' They aspired to map out 'the whole production process of capital as a process of reproduction' – indeed, according to Rosa Luxemburg (2003, p. 3), they were the last to attempt this before Marx himself. They, moreover, developed the concepts of capital and profit, and Quesnay's *Tableau Economique* has been hailed as a forerunner of 'modern numerical techniques, capital theory and general equilibrium theory' (Gudeman, 1980). On all these achievements a voluminous literature exists. I wish instead to look at the ideological assumptions that are stated explicitly in, or smuggled into, their works. Was physiocracy 'science masquerading as mysticism', as Peter Gay suggests (1996, p. 349)? Or the reverse?

The physiocrats' most obviously mystical commitments were spiritual and religious. They were restoring 'oeconomia' from a submerged 'oikonomia', to use Giorgio Agamben's terms (2011, p. xi, 277; see also Holmes, 2018, p. 47). *Oikonomia* identifies God's revelation in the ordering of the material world and human populations. *Oeconomia* refers to the management of people and things – in accordance, of course, with divine disposition. Apropos physiocracy, Agamben (2011, p. 278) remarks on 'the curious circumstance that the modern science of economics and government has been constituted on the basis of a paradigm that had been developed within the horizon of the theological *oikonomia*'. Or as Istvan Hont has put it (2005, p. 104), the basis of Quesnay's economics, in his faith that God's purposes on earth could be discerned in the laws of nature, was 'an elaborate theodicy'. Theology played midwife at the birth of scientific economics.

As deistic materialists, the physiocrats conceived of the cosmos as a 'great machine' in 'perpetual movement', in Mirabeau's words (in McNally, 1988, pp. 122–123), one that God had set in motion but which is then 'animated and directed by its own springs' without the need for outside direction. Quesnay (1962, p. 53) divides natural law into physical and moral categories, each of which is decreed by the Supreme Being. Physical law refers to 'the regular course of all physical events in the natural order', moral law to social behaviour insofar as it conforms to the physical laws. These laws, 'instituted by the Supreme Being', are 'self-evidently the most advantageous to the human race'. The economy, likewise, is understood as an intricately constructed machine – 'la machine économique' in Mirabeau's phrase (in McNally, 1988, p. 111). It, and other social subsystems such as the state, function properly only if they adhere to the 'supreme laws' (McNally, 1988, p. 122).

In its method and metaphysics we can call this 'providential positivism', for it holds the study of social order to be a science in the manner of astronomy or mechanics, with a comparable inherent orderliness. As Louis Dumont once observed (1977, p. 41), Quesnay's holistic and equilibrium-oriented conception of political economy resulted 'from the projection on the economic plane of the general conception of the universe as an ordered whole'.

It may sound paradoxical, but the physiocrats viewed the existing order in France as artificial, such that their task was to urge its reconstruction along natural lines. Searching for 'the natural laws which form the basis of the best government possible' (Quesnay, 1962, p. 53), they found them in monarchy, enlightened despotism, a centralized state, colonialism, class domination, private property, and the market economy – institutions that, coincidentally or not, all existed in late eighteenth-century France and were compatible with, and in most cases essential to, the expansion of capitalism on the British model that the physiocrats happened to favour. In essence, they urged the state to undertake a passive revolution, one that would abolish feudal privileges and establish the framework for 'an English-style transformation of agrarian economy' (McNally, 1988, p. 89). To have openly advocated the anglicization of French political economy would have raised eyebrows, against the backdrop of Britain's defeat of France in the world war of 1756–1763. Divinely ordained natural law offered a suitably non-treacherous euphemism.

Cultivating social hierarchy

In what did the physiocrats' bourgeois horizon consist? Above all, their concepts of property, class, and wealth. Natural law decrees that those who have property can lawfully dispose over it. Property ownership, in Quesnay's deafening words (1962, p. 232), should be guaranteed to its lawful possessors, 'for SECURITY OF OWNERSHIP IS THE ESSENTIAL FOUNDATION OF THE ECONOMIC ORDER'. Property, for the physiocrats, is the single inviolable right. Its assured possession, uninhibited by customary claims, is the bedrock of the prosperity and endeavour of all social classes (Saisselin, 1992, p. 76).[1] It is what connects private interests together within an overarching order, enabling individuals to interact economically in a way that marries their own interest to the needs of public virtue and happiness. Their notion of class, Rémy Saisselin (1992, p. 72) points out, superseded feudal and Christian traditions, not to mention myths of the nobility's superior race. That is, it abstracts from 'rank, privileges, precedence, prestige, and tradition', emphasizing instead productive property and the economic actor's role within the purportedly natural order. Their model contrasted with the focus on the economy as the extension of the royal household that one finds in the traditional monarchical states of Europe (and beyond).[2] Instead they construe the economic space as that of the nation, with free individuals engaging in material activity, overseen by the state.

On wealth, likewise, the physiocrats' conception is impeccably agrarian-bourgeois. They helped to shift definitions of wealth away from the extent of land held (the feudal yardstick) and away from commodities and bullion (the mercantilist focus) and towards land *insofar as it is productive*. The true wealth of the nation is not the stock of land or accumulated goods but the flow of *revenues*; its source is not foreign trade but *production*, above all the consumable produce of agriculture, forestry, and mining (Quesnay, 1972; see also Huberman, 1937; Rubin, 1979). The power of the state, as

Quesnay put it (1972), is based not on the possession of land but on its flourishing, for on this depends 'the permanent well-being of the tax-paying section of a nation'.

None of this has anything in common with Gudeman's 'Bemba and Bisa'. Quesnay (1962, p. 257) made this crisply clear in his description of 'the savages of Louisiana'. Although they enjoyed 'many goods, such as water, wood, game, and the fruits of the earth', these 'did *not* constitute wealth because they had no market value'. Only after they had begun to trade with European settlers did some of their goods 'acquire market value and become wealth'. The products of land, he wrote elsewhere (*pace* Cutler Cleveland), 'do not by any means constitute wealth in themselves. They constitute wealth only in so far as they are necessary to man *and in so far as they are exchangeable*' (Quesnay, 1962, p. 83, emphasis added). The land, in short, may be the ultimate source of wealth, but it is agriculture that causes wealth to increase. And not agriculture in the abstract, but particular agents. It is

> the wealth of the farmers which renders the land fertile; the cultivation of the land entails considerable expenses, and the more these expenses are increased, the more fruitful the land is, and the greater are the gains for the country workers, the profits for the farmers and the revenue for the proprietors. (Quesnay, 1962, p. 106)

This last comment makes it seem that although the agent of increase is agrarian capital, the resulting revenues will be distributed among the various classes. But that is not the point at all. The physiocrats' case unmistakeably promoted class polarization in the interests of 'primitive accumulation'. It may be an exaggeration to say that they openly advocated this. Cantillon, for example (in Grove, 1995, p. 191), harboured misgivings over inequality, famously likening the very rich to 'pikes in a pond' who devour their smaller neighbours. That said, the *Tableau* and most other physiocratic texts are paeans to wealthy capitalist farmers. Only the farmer, and *not* his hirelings 'produces more than the wages of his labor', indeed he 'is the unique source of all wealth' (Turgot, 2011, p. 9). Turgot made abundantly clear that the physiocratic goal of surplus-producing agriculture presupposed 'primitive accumulation', the diremption of the peasantry from the land and their transformation into 'wage-labourers' (Turgot, in McNally, 1988, p. 142). For Quesnay, likewise (1962, p. 205, 212), the 'most honourable, praiseworthy, and important' citizens of the realm are the aristocrats and the landowners, followed by the 'wealthy husbandmen [farmers] and wealthy merchants'. 'The rich', and the landowners who inject capital into agriculture, are the esteemed classes, for they maintain the land 'in a cultivable state', they 'cause the soil' to produce, and they distribute the net product to the artisans and farm workers, providing them with jobs and subsistence, as well as taxes for the sovereign and tithes for the clergy (Quesnay, 1962; Turgot, 2011, p. 96). It is wealthy farmers and merchants who 'stimulate agriculture, conduct its operations [and] safeguard the nation's revenue' (Quesnay, 1962, p. 247). It is their demands that the government should meet before all others, for they invest the capital that leavens the bread for all, as contrasted with 'the small-scale cultivation carried on by poor métayers [sharecroppers]' (Quesnay, 1962, p. 234). The latter work largely to feed themselves, so the land should not be 'entrusted' to them. It should go to the wealthy and their animals. Not peasants but 'animals should plough and fertilize your fields' – and, as a bonus, they fertilize the fields with their dung, generating richer harvests (Quesnay, 1962, p. 260; 1976, p. 301). Cultivation by wealthy landowners reaps scale economies, and this justifies the expediting of enclosures and the replacement of people by cattle. Mirabeau, for example (in McNally, 1988, p. 120), criticized those 'barbarous' laws which impede 'the proprietor from enclosing his field, his pastureland, his woods'. They 'violate the laws of property'. Quesnay concurred (1962, p. 213, pp. 234–235). Proprietors should lease their lands 'only to rich farmers', and lands 'should be brought together into large farms worked by rich husbandmen'. Poor peasants should be thrown off their plots, to become wage labourers. And competition among labourers should be encouraged, 'in order to save as much expense as possible'.

In these respects the physiocrats' goals were perfectly plain: to press government to remove obstructions to the flow of capital into agriculture and to put its weight behind wealthy 'improving' farmers (or agricultural 'entrepreneurs'), the vanguard agents of the shift to capitalist agriculture on English lines (Meek, 1962a, p. 24). Less visible but no less ideological was the appearance of these same commitments in 'scientific' guise, as assumptions nested within physiocratic value theory and their models of economic reproduction. 'In depicting the economy as a self-regulating mechanism', David McNally argues (1988, p. 111, 118), Quesnay 'deemphasized the social and political assumptions of his model'. Crucially, he places the landed proprietors and their revenue at the centre of his zigzag in the *Tableau*, such that without their revenues the entire economy would collapse. As to value theory, what appears to some as a progressive recognition of our reliance on nature is more accurately seen as a rationalization of the enrichment of big landowners and the exploitation of the workforce. The physiocrats' *produit net* arises from a peculiarity of nature, 'the earth's bounty' (Quesnay, 1962, p. 115). Because nature yields more than the expenses of the landowning noble and capitalist farmer, their receipt of rent and profit, their entitlement to the bulk of the surplus, is fully justified. The thesis that the land produces value, which appears earthily materialist, is a mystification that serves particular social ends: enclosures, capital accumulation, and aristocratic power.

And God said, *Laissez faire*

'The whole magic of well-ordered society', as Mirabeau and Quesnay saw it, 'is that each man works for others, while believing that he is working for himself' (Quesnay, 1962, p. 70). Agriculture, industry, commerce, prices, and so on, Guillaume Le Trosne insisted (in McNally, 1988, p. 123), 'must not be objects of administration and should be left to the free interaction of particular interests'. Turgot (in McNally, 1988, p. 134) reasoned that 'in all respects in which commerce may interest the State, unrestrained individual interest will always produce the public welfare more surely than the operations of the government'. The state, Quesnay and company are saying, provides the legal and institutional integument that allows the economic machine to reproduce itself, driven and regulated by the principle of individual self-interest. Evidently, physiocracy anticipated the idea of the 'invisible hand'. Yet on this question some uncertainty exists, due not least to Michel Foucault's claim (2008, pp. 285–286) that physiocratic laissez faire represented the *antithesis* of Smith's invisible hand. Smithian theory, he says, represented a liberal critique of the physiocrats' despotism – their urge to vest all power over the nation's business in an economically omniscient state, one that knows no external 'limitation' or 'counterbalance' and which 'completely controls' economic life.

Now, it is well known that Smith raised criticisms of aspects of physiocratic thought, from a liberal-democratic position, and his confidence that individuals' efforts will 'naturally' lead to prosperity and progress was greater than theirs (Rubin, 1979). But to present this as an opposition is misleading. It flies in the face of the physiocrats' concern to stake out *liberal limits* to state intervention. Foucault (2008, p. 285) partially acknowledges this when presenting the physiocrats as having argued for the limitation of government power 'by the evidence of economic analysis which it knows has to be respected'. But even if this took form as a call for governmental omniscience, 'economic analysis', here, is at bottom a reference to the independent power of bourgeois property. They justified the separation of the political and economic spheres, and presented the laws of the market as natural laws anterior to social order. In Turgot's vision (2011, p. 256), the 'course of commerce is no less necessary and no less irresistible than the course of nature', and government should surrender itself to both, and not seek to regulate. Quesnay campaigned tirelessly for free trade: for 'no barriers at all [on] external trade in raw produce', and for 'FULL FREEDOM OF COMPETITION' as the policy that is 'THE MOST CORRECT, AND THE MOST PROFITABLE FOR THE NATION AND THE STATE' (Nisbet, 1975; Quesnay, 1962, pp. 235–237). The most salient practical example of this was the physiocrats' vocal and influential advocacy for the 1760s reforms, under Louis XV, which sought to completely and rapidly liberalize the grain trade. These reforms, historian Steven Kaplan describes (1976, p. xxvi and *passim*), marked an attempted shift from 'intervention' to laissez faire. They required the government to break its 'unwritten covenant with consumers' by declaring subsistence as no longer its paramount responsibility. Instead, subsistence was 'for the individual to work out on his own'. Thus the reforms, being 'an experiment in (a theoretically) free market economy', were also a milestone in the transformation of relations between state and society, between political power and economic power, and the public and private sectors.

If we step back and survey the broader historical context and its intellectual trends, the physiocrats and Smith appear alike as critics of mercantilism and progenitors of economic liberalism. The context was the rise of mercantile and then agrarian capitalism in Italy, the Netherlands, England, France, and their colonies. It underlay, and was reinforced by, transformations in the sciences (Galileo and the Newtonian model of a physical order regulated by its own laws), philosophy (Descartes, utilitarianism), and intellectual culture (the Enlightenment). The increasing connectedness of economic activities through market transactions enabled 'the economy' to be conceived of as law-governed, analogously to natural processes and amenable to analysis with similar scientific methods (Meek, 1962b).

Out of these ingredients a vision began to be constructed of the market economy as an autonomous system, one that is by nature self-regulating, is best left to find its own equilibrium, and tends to harmonize individual and social interests. This proto-liberal vision was given shape by English, Dutch, and French economic theorists such as Hugo Grotius, John Locke, Pierre le Pesant (alias Boisguilbert), Bernard Mandeville, and Cantillon. In contrast to traditional, theocratic, and autocratic justifications of social order, they laid the foundations for a model of social order as arising unintentionally and automatically from the aggregate actions of myriad individuals seeking to improve their lives, processes that manifest in the forces of supply and demand, and with the tendency of some to gain at the expense of others being checked not by sovereign power but by market competition (Tieben, 2012). In France, the evolution of this idea ran through Boisguilbert and Cantillon.

The seminal concept of Boisguilbert was the 'natural' economic order, one that arises from the aggregate acts of individual self-interest (Heilbron, 1998). He portrayed the economy as akin to the physical systems studied by Descartes and Newton, a system in ceaseless motion (or circulation), with wealth unfolding in 'a continual exchange of what one has in excess with another, taking in return that which the person one is dealing with has in plenty' (Faccarello, 1999). Just as physical processes regulate themselves to restore nature's balance when disturbed, in the economic sphere the market tends to equilibrium, distributing justice to all through the mechanism of proportional prices (Tieben, 2012). Thanks to the 'spirit of all markets' as they manifest in the 'desire for profit', an 'equilibrium' or 'balance' is created between supply and demand (Boisguilbert, in Boltanski & Thévenot, 2006). To achieve this, one must 'laisser faire la nature' (Boisguilbert, in Christensen, 2003). Accordingly, the state's principal task is to construct a framework to enable the workings of natural law to play out, through the self-regulating market mechanism (McNally, 1988). Working by analogy with Newtonian physics, which modelled the cosmos as a harmonious mechanism operating through divinely established laws, Boisguilbert *et al.* deduced the socio-political complement. A harmonious society depends on the continuous reproduction of wealth, and government, in their model, should allow the natural laws of the economy to run their course without let or hindrance. Quesnay was later to develop this line of thinking, to infuse it with a Taoist philosophy of 'wu-wei' (achieving goals through non-action (Hobson, 2004)), and to coin the phrase 'laissez faire, laissez passer'.

Cantillon's framework built on Boisguilbert's (Benitez-Rochel & Robles, 2003). His writings, too, prefigure the invisible hand, with the economy presented as 'as an interconnected whole made up of rationally functioning parts' that tends to equilibrium. The engine and guarantor of equilibrium is the 'free play of self-interested entrepreneurs' (I'm borrowing Robert Ekelund and Robert Hébert's paraphrase: 2013, p. 79). It 'keeps the system in adjustment by their conduct of "all the exchange and circulation of the State"'. The adjustment process is driven by the self-interested pursuit of profit, a motive of such universal ubiquity that it takes the position in Cantillon's inquiry which 'Newton's "universal principle of attraction" (i.e. gravity) took in his' (Ekelund & Hébert, 2013, p. 78). Therefore, economies function perfectly well without intervention in their internal mechanisms; indeed government interference tends to breed perverse effects. Crucial actors in the equilibrating process are 'entrepreneurs' – a term which, in its modern usage, Cantillon coined. But in his economic hierarchy they occupy a middling rank, subordinate to the gentry, the landowners, on whom the entire population depends (Cantillon, 2001, p. 92). An arresting thesis of Cantillon (and altogether neglected, except by Michael Perelman) concerns the free play of market competition as the mechanism by which the social hierarchy is fixed into place. He was one of the first, perhaps the first, to recognize that a system of prices could produce and reproduce essentially the same social hierarchy as does a feudal system based on the direct command over labour. Market forces are not simply a mechanism of value circulation but a force of social control (Perelman, 1983, p. 71). In the *Essay on the Nature of Commerce*, for example, he spells out how the market-mediated polarization of property generates harmonious hierarchy. From a condition of hypothetical equality, those petty proprietors who are relatively 'lazy, prodigal, or sickly' will have no option but to sell their land to the one who is 'frugal and industrious'. The latter 'will continually add to his Estate by new purchases and will employ upon it the Labour of those who having no Land of their own are compelled to offer him their Labour in order to live'.[3] In Cantillon we see the stirrings of a secular concept of liberal governmentality, in which political economy sets the frame for social order, with class division determined and justified by economic competition rather than divine decree.

The natural law of inexhaustible wealth

The conception of 'the economy' as a distinct entity that comprises phenomena (prices, money, trade, etc.) that move in orderly ways and are subject to the operation of laws is a fundamental element of the growth paradigm – the ideology of economic growth. By this I mean the idea that growth is good, imperative, essentially limitless, and the principal remedy for a litany of social problems. In physiocratic times, the growth paradigm was still embryonic. Growth was not assumed to be naturally rapid, continuous, or infinite. To them, all wealth stemmed from a sector, agriculture, which was, as Turgot noted, subject to diminishing returns. For Quesnay (1759), too, growth was a fragile sprout. It could be easily thrown into reverse, for example, by onerous taxation, the 'personal vexations' of rural folk, or the excessive diversion of income to luxury expenditure.

These caveats notwithstanding, Quesnay and friends made a seminal contribution to growth ideology, in several ways.[4] Their contribution to the 'market paradigm' and their agrarian-capitalist redefinition of wealth are discussed above. As has widely been noted they also originated the idea of production as a surplus producing activity (although this idea, in a vaguer form, had been adumbrated by William Petty (Pearson, 1957)). They posited wealth expansion as the defining measure of whether or not natural law, and thereby the Supreme Being's will, is being followed. The entire 'moral and physical advantage' of a society, for Mirabeau (in Cleveland, 1999, p. 126), is summed up in its capacity to increase the surplus product. For Quesnay, similarly (1962, p. 55, emphasis added), following natural law means observing whichever 'sovereign laws would *abundantly increase the wealth* necessary for men's subsistence and for the maintenance of the tutelary authority'. He equates socio-economic improvement with capital accumulation, and he comes close to identifying virtue with growth and profits. 'The administration of a kingdom', he counsels (1962, p. 257), must aim to procure for the nation 'the greatest possible abundance of products and the greatest possible market value'. What economists can do is supply policymakers with 'knowledge of the true sources of wealth, and of the means of increasing and perpetuating them'; this will spur virtuous circles, for 'wealth attracts men; men and wealth make agriculture prosper, expand trade, give new life to industry, and increase and perpetuate wealth' (Quesnay, 1972, p. 22). Again and again he enjoins the state to take measures to expand the nation's revenue. And what measures should they be? Among others, to put 'wealthy men' in charge of rural trade and 'agricultural enterprises' (farms), 'in order to enrich yourselves, to enrich the state, and to enable inexhaustible wealth to be generated' (Quesnay, 1962, p. 88, 260). And of course, as discussed above, to deregulate the grain trade, allowing market forces to strengthen – including enclosures and proletarianization (McNally, 1988). This will raise profits, investment, productivity, revenues, and so on in a virtuous circle. Above all, the physiocrats were the first to argue that wealth expansion depends on increasing valuable output and that this requires economic reorganization on market lines. They were pioneering theorists of, and propagandists for, capital accumulation, and, as such, they were the fathers of 'growth economics' (Brewer, 2010). Turgot, in particular, has a claim to be the first to posit capital accumulation as the primary source of growth and to see continual growth over indefinite time periods as a normal state of affairs. According to McNally, he went so far as to analyse capital accumulation as 'the decisive process within all sectors of the economy', with its driving force seen as saving: 'The spirit of economy in a nation continually tends to increase the sum of its capitals' (in McNally, 1988, p. 82).

A further fundamental element of the growth paradigm is the links it establishes between economic growth and historical progress, national prowess, and global leadership (aka imperialism). The crucible in which it took shape was the transition from feudalism to capitalism, which was a global process involving conquest and interstate rivalry, colonialism and slavery, and commercial expansion. Here too, the physiocrats were early adopters of the creed. Quesnay liked to remind readers and policymakers that growth is conducive not only to welfare but also to warfare. The aim for each state, he writes (1962, p. 81), is to rapidly 'progress to a high degree of power and prosperity'. He criticizes feudal attitudes to land, for they emphasize land ownership *per se*, forgetting 'that the true foundation of the military strength of a kingdom is the nation's prosperity itself' (Quesnay, 1976, pp. 94–95; 1962, p. 160). As McNally (1988) has pointed out, drawing on Trotsky's theory of uneven and combined development, the physiocratic impulse to emulate Britain was motivated by geopolitical rivalry. Britain's military machine had become 'inexhaustible', in Quesnay's words (in McNally, 1988, p. 146), 'by reason of its ever-renascent wealth' perpetually replenishing the Treasury. To compete, the French state must revolutionize the economy as a whole – and if no gradual path towards the English model could be discerned through empirical study, rationalism offered the physiocrats an alternative approach.

The agrarian-capitalist trajectory that England undertook in the seventeenth century was adopted in the eighteenth century across northern France (Normandy, Picardy, Île-de-France (Engels, 1877)), but also in other French territories, including the plantation slave economies of Saint Domingue and the Iles du Vent (Pierre Pluchon, in Blackburn, 1997, p. 439). The physiocrats were ambivalent towards slavery – Quesnay and Mirabeau opposed it, others did not – and toward colonialism (Dobie, 2010; Røge, 2013). Quesnay favoured a liberal reform of the empire, with slaves bought, freed, and settled in colonies where they would work the fields with 'military-like organization'. Damien Tricoire (2017, p. 33) describes the strategy as 'tutelary colonisation', the aim being to 'civilise the Negroes', above all through instructing them – still an underclass – on how to produce cane sugar. In Mauritius meanwhile, Poivre, who we encountered above, aspired to build the island into a 'powerful colony' and a centre of spice cultivation (Grove, 1995). This should prompt us to briefly revisit physiocratic environmentalism. The unprecedented degree of environmental damage that Poivre *et al.* were addressing through environmental science and innovative reform was occasioned by the worldwide drive to enclosure, a process that was justified and applauded by the physiocratic programme. In a sense, Poivre's stance was 'we broke it, therefore we own the problem, and the solution'. The title of Grove's book, 'Green Imperialism', captures this neatly.

A final element of the growth paradigm to which the physiocrats made a seminal contribution is the yoking of economic growth together with the Enlightenment schema of historical progress. The immediate spur to the development of the latter, Ronald Meek suggests (1976), was the European encounter with the 'primitive' peoples of the New World. From this, some began to spin a new narrative of the human story as a history of social progress. If 'they' are at the primitive stage, had 'we' once occupied it too? If so, how had 'we' got from there to here? In *The Origin of Fables* (in Meek, 1976, p. 27), Bernard de Fontenelle – who was, incidentally, Boisguilbert's cousin – sketched the rudiments of a stadial progress theory. In the first ages of the world, human beings were mired in the same depths of ignorance and barbarism as 'the Kaffirs, the Lapps, or the Iroquois today'. But just as the Greeks long ago evolved into rational beings, so too, given time and tutelage, will the Native Americans. With the original stage of humanity imagined as savage and contemptible, the conceptual space was created for a liberal-imperialist 'stages' model of progress to emerge, one that alloyed rhetorical universalism to the presumption of European command and control. Jesuit missionaries were innovators here, but Turgot, writing in 1750, is generally acknowledged as the first to have proposed that historical progress is, at bottom, an economically driven stadial process. In the 'discourses on universal history' he maps out a stadial history of the human race, depicting progress as a process of civilization, one that is defined by increasingly advanced socioeconomic formations (from hunting to pastoral to agricultural and – implicitly – commercial), with the expansion of the economic surplus as the basic motor of change, and commerce and colonization as vital accelerators (Nisbet, 1975; Tricoire, 2017). In identifying a historical ladder stretching from barbarism to civilization, Turgot's progress concept hammered the diversity of human populations into a distinctive temporal-economic chain, with the richer nations (and 'races') indexed as history's vanguard. As Uday Mehta observes (1999, p. 84), because Turgot 'mapped the idea of historical progress onto the notion of the stages of human development', the theory was perfectly suited to legitimate liberal colonialism. The nations that were adopting this notion of progress were simultaneously institutionalizing capitalist economic forms and cultivating the ideology of growth. The narratives of progress, growth, and marketization coalesced together in the liberal mind. The assumption – for Turgot and the liberal rhetoric that he helped inspire – was that growth benefits all. Turgot (2011, p. 256) cites the iron industry as an example: as it declines in prosperous Britain so will it flourish in France, Germany, and thence to Siberia and the American colonies and beyond, until a global 'balance' is achieved. But, in fact, the favoured few enjoyed quicker growth and used this platform to dominate the rest.

Value, alienation, and enterprise

Were the physiocrats propounding science in the form of mystification, or the reverse? The answer is 'both'. They contributed to the knowledge of the inner workings of capitalist economy, but each step in their argument, each concept they used, was suffused with ideological preconceptions, and contributed to the constitution of economics as an apparatus of bourgeois power. Most immediately, this was in the sense that they voiced and gave shape to the interests of a hegemonic class project: to convert France's political economy to the English model, with agrarian capitalists as vanguard force and principal beneficiaries. To this end, they presented capital accumulation as the general interest, justified capitalist exploitation and appropriation – including its egregiously 'primitive' moments (enclosures, colonialism) – in the language of welfare, growth, and national power, and promulgated idealized models of economic behaviour that function only if the mass of the population accept their position in the social hierarchy. The social hierarchy in the physiocratic model is essentially modern, in that it marries entrenched hierarchy to incessant fluidity. The 'bourgeois class', Gramsci once wrote (1971, p. 260), portrays itself 'as an organism in continuous movement', one that absorbs 'the entire society'. Let us adapt this thought by substituting 'the economy' for bourgeois class. As we've seen, the physiocrats contributed as much as any group of thinkers to conceptualizing the economy as an organism in continuous movement, one that absorbs the entire society into the circuits of capital.

Economics, then, did not 'take a wrong turn'; it began life as the intellectual avatar of commodity fetishism. Nor should the physiocratic approach to nature be taken as a model for ecological economics. They wrought the concept in several ways, all of them deeply problematic. First, they constructed economics and nature as 'non-interactionist'; that is, economics does not theorize nature in its interrelations with human society but takes it as a given (Gudeman, 1980). Secondly and relatedly, they saw in nature simply natural resources, 'free gifts' for exploitation (just as Smith, Malthus, Ricardo, and John Stuart Mill after them; (Foster et al., 2010)). Thirdly, they theorized market economy as ordained by natural law, with the corollary that economic science should emulate the natural sciences. With this, capitalism is *naturalized* – literally, with capitalist social relations posited as natural and eternal, alongside limestone and onions – and sanctified, for nature's laws are God's laws. Rather marvellously, Mother Nature had given birth to eighteenth-century capitalism which had always existed. Thus, the tendencies the physiocrats championed – to enclose and encroach on land, to deregulate markets – were not processes of class domination but individuals following nature's course. They were, moreover, pioneers of the line of argument that contravening the market is contravening the laws of nature. It was only a short step to the likes of Joseph Townsend and Edmund Burke, who inveighed against market-inhibiting welfare legislation on the grounds that it interferes with the laws of nature (Holmes, 2018).

In short, the physiocrats were propagandists for liberal capitalism, and helped construct a discipline, political economy, to defend and naturalize it. It's little wonder that paeans to physiocracy are nowadays published by the Heartland Institute (Ebeling, 2016), the Future of Freedom Foundation (McElroy, 2010), and other think-tanks belonging to the Koch-funded climate denial apparatus (Greenpeace, 2017). But did the physiocrats also contribute to *critical* political economy? Notwithstanding the caveats discussed above, in a backhanded way indeed they did, through their theorization of the systemic character of capitalism, and in particular the concept of value. Marx (1861–1863) credited them with a 'great' contribution, namely that 'they derive value and surplus-value not from circulation but from production'. For him (1863–1878), physiocratic analysis was the first attempt 'to analyse the nature of surplus-value in general', and 'the first systematic conception of capitalist production'. These two insights cohere together, for conceiving of economic affairs as a system requires attention to what connects its parts (market transactions) and, in turn, what enables commensuration (value). The recognition of value as a homogenous, circulating economic element was conjoined to the understanding of the economy as a dynamic totality. As long as the market was a subsidiary crutch to the organization of livelihoods, qualitative connotations of value prevailed (Mirowski, 1989, p. 146), but with the emergence of market society as an integrated system – clearly visible in Britain and in patches on physiocracy's home turf – the universal operation of prices drew attention to the commensurability of commodities and the question of what renders them commensurable.

Marx, as is well known, reworked these concepts for critical analysis. By value he understood the mechanism of compulsive commensuration that comes into being in a society of generalized commodity relations – a historically specific society divided on class lines between owners of capital and propertyless workers. Value, for him, is the representation of wealth under capitalist conditions and the engine of alienation. It *governs* capitalist economy, and is the secret of its organization of people and nature. The heartbeat of the system is accumulation: the expansion of value. Far from being anti-ecological, Marx's rejection of physiocratic value theory in favour of his labour theory of value opens the door to an ecologically oriented critique of political economy.[5] His labour theory of value, one should note, has little in common with the value theory of Locke or Smith,[6] and it does not treat value as a material ether but as a social relation abstracted of all materiality. In his words (1867, 1861–1863), his concept of value is 'a definite social mode of existence of human activity', in contrast to the physiocrats for whom it 'consists of material things – land, nature, and the various modifications of these material things'. Nor is Marx's value theory a normative quest to affirm labour's social worth over and above nature. Rather, it is the core element of a multifaceted critique, one that integrates the theory of capital accumulation (self-expanding value that accumulates through the exploitation of wage labour) with a critique of classical political economy for its neglect of the specific social form of capitalist production. It understands alienation and exploitation in capitalist conditions as a conceptual dyad: labour produces the value that capital uses to dominate the world, establishing structures that alienate the worker from herself, from other workers, their products, and nature. Capitalist reproduction thus appears as a systemic totality: geared to compulsive accumulation, resting on the exploitation of labour, and treating the realms of nature and social reproduction as 'external' and thus as the source of 'free gifts'. A system based on value cannot genuinely 'value' the natural and social-reproductive processes on which human life depends.

This approach may be contrasted with that which prevails among ecological economists today. Take for example Raworth. Her book is helping to enlighten the discipline of economics in respect of its ecological and ethical shortcomings, and she is certainly right to propose that a new way of thinking about the economy is urgently needed. However, as Gills and Morgan point out (2019), in neglecting to consider the 'system of capital accumulation with its commitment to material growth of economies', she leaves unexplored the fundamental dynamic of the system. She does not apprehend the world economy as a system based on compulsive relations of class and competition, indeed she barely mentions capitalism and has little conception of social class (and certainly not as a dynamic category). For her, the goals of the economy are not determined principally by social structures but by a 'paradigm' – in essence, the framework of mainstream economics. For radical change, it follows, we need to find the flaws and fix the frame, appeal to the ethics of business leaders and introduce tougher regulation of business, with altered tax regimes and incentives for improved product and process design. The market system should remain, but its power should be 'wisely embedded within public regulations, and within the wider economy' (Raworth, 2017, p. 70). The heroes in her new image of economics are not wholly different from Quesnay's, for they are chiefly entrepreneurs (the designers of new business models, the inventors of digital currencies, etc.) and consumers (investing their savings 'ethically,' using complementary currencies). The capitalist ownership model which has dominated the nineteenth and twentieth centuries, she argues (2017), is not determined by social relations of production, entrenched relations of power, or the compulsion of the market, but is merely 'one among many possible enterprise designs'. A different enterprise design is the non-profit, and the decision to produce this way, rather than for profit, is ultimately a question of will and ethics. We can, for example, set up 'no-growth enterprises' which pay 'resilient financial returns' to investors. If such steps are taken many-fold, they would dethrone the growth drive from its place at the heart of the financial system (Raworth, 2017, p. 232). As regards the environment, Raworth (e.g. in Mobertz, 2017) advocates the greening of business. Firms should make profits, but ecologically. Anita Roddick, founder of Body Shop, is a trailblazer. In contrast to CEOs who believe their firm's mission 'is to increase its profits, … she set out to create a business that was socially and environmentally regenerative by design' (Raworth, 2017, p. 197).

Conclusion

Political economy, and value theory in particular, took a turn towards mystification with the marginalist revolution of the 1870s. Re-theorized as a subjective category, value found itself removed from labour and from nature. Surplus value disappeared from sight, erasing exploitation. Social class vanished, and nature too. 'Environment' eventually found its way back into economics, not as its radical basis but as an issue area, with its proper little sub-discipline (see, e.g. Dale, 2017b). All of these belong to the story of the unfolding social and environmental catastrophes today. But the 1870s turn was not from useful to useless. It was from bad to worse. In this paper I have, following convention, taken the physiocrats as the first economists. I argued that the tribute they paid the role of land was largely insofar as it served rapacious ends. In their view, those who possess nature and put fences around it are entitled to its surplus value. Their positivist misreading of value as a natural substance underlay their justification of the systemic value transfer from labour to capital. Some physiocrats were pioneers in environmentalism, yet the inherent logic of their system necessitated ongoing enclosures and the despoliation of natural habitat. And although some physiocrats advocated the abolition of slavery, they were defenders of colonialism, and their ideology of progress became a powerfully influential buttress of it. Their major economic policy proposal, the removal of political restrictions and moral restraints on grain markets, was designed above all to enable the bourgeoisie and landowning nobility to accumulate capital (Goldman, 1973). The political economy they crafted while making this case was an avowedly objective, value-free science, even as it relied on a positivist metaphysics which packaged market relations as the natural outcome of humanity's need for subsistence and capitalism as the natural telos of human progress. In a sense they espoused materialism, in that their economic laws supposedly derive from man's 'three original needs': subsistence, preservation, and 'the perpetuation of his species' (Quesnay, 1962, p. 59). But their materialism was vulgar and ahistorical, it did not lend itself to critical analysis of capitalism's specific forms of wealth appropriation (Burkett, 2009). Instead, the economic logics that they championed gained a grip on the world and are now imperilling subsistence, the preservation of human life, and the perpetuation of homo sapiens and other species.

In its essentials, physiocracy set the tone for economics to come. That is to say, economics became in a sense a science, but of the idealized workings of capitalist markets. A strange science, then, in that its basis is commodity fetishism. This is why Oswald and Stern are mistaken to suggest that economics should be at the heart of any serious analysis of climate breakdown, and why Raworth's doughnut does not go far enough. The obliteration of ecology by economics is not an aberration, or a myopia that can be overcome with a corrective lens or different 'image'. Rather, it expresses a truth, the fidelity of the discipline to the economic order that begat it. Any serious addressing of the economic causes of climate breakdown will indeed entail a transformation of economics, but in the form of negation, through the overcoming of the system that it represents, justifies, and naturalizes.

Notes

1. The physiocrats found inspiration in John Locke's views on liberty and on private property, and in Calvinist perspectives on the link between the saving of money and the saving of souls. I am grateful to the peer reviewers for this and several other observations.
2. For example, Mauryan India, discussed in Dale (2017a).
3. Cantillon (2001, p. 6). Some political theorists suppose the market-driven harmonization of private interests to be a trope unique to British political economy of the era, but one finds it in Cantillon too. E.g. Wood (2012, pp. 24–25, p. 168).
4. We may note, obliquely, a certain etymological fit between physiocracy and the growth paradigm, in that φύσις originally derives from φύω: 'to grow' (Schliephake, 2016).
5. From a burgeoning literature, see e.g. John Bellamy Foster, *Marx's Ecology*, Andreas Malm, *The Progress of this Storm*, and Kohei Saito, *Karl Marx's Ecosocialism*.
6. For discussion and references, see Dale (2016, Chapter 2).

Disclosure statement

No potential conflict of interest was reported by the author(s).

ORCID

Gareth Dale ⓘD http://orcid.org/0000-0003-4991-6063

References

Agamben, G. (2011). *The kingdom and the glory: For a theological genealogy of economy and government*. Stanford University Press.
Bartelmus, P. (2012). *Sustainability economics: An introduction*. Routledge.
Benitez-Rochel, J., & Robles, L. (2003). The foundations of the Tableau Economique in Boisguilbert and Cantillon. *The European Journal of the History of Economic Thought*, 10(2), 231–248. https://doi.org/10.1080/0967256032000066882
Bjerg, O. (2016). *Parallax of growth: The philosophy of ecology and economy*. Polity Press.
Blackburn, R. (1997). *The making of new world slavery: From the Baroque to the modern, 1492–1800*. Verso.
Boltanski, L., & Thévenot, L. (2006). *On justification: Economies of worth*. Princeton University Press.
Brewer, A. (2010). *The making of the classical theory of economic growth*. Routledge.
Burkett, P. (2009). *Marxism and ecological economics: Toward a red and green political economy*. Haymarket.
Cantillon, R. (2001). *Essay on the nature of commerce in general*. Transaction. (Original work published 1755

Christensen, P. (1992). Driving forces, increasing returns and economic sustainability. In R. Costanza (Ed.), *Ecological economics: The science and management of sustainability* (pp. 101–128). Columbia University Press.

Christensen, P. (2003). Epicurean and Stoic sources for Boisguilbert's physiological and hippocratic vision of nature and economics. *History of Political Economy, 35*(5), 101–128. https://doi.org/10.1215/00182702-35-Suppl_1-101

Cleveland, C. (1999). Biophysical economics: From physiocracy to ecological economics and industrial ecology. In J. Gowdy & K. Mayumi (Eds.), *Bioeconomics and sustainability: Essays in Honor of Nicholas Georgescu-Roegen* (pp. 125–154). Edward Elgar.

Dale, G. (2012). Adam Smith's green thumb and Malthus's three horsemen: Cautionary tales from classical political economy. *Journal of Economic Issues, 46*(4), 859–880. https://doi.org/10.2753/JEI0021-3624460402

Dale, G. (2016). *Reconstructing Karl Polanyi: Excavation and critique*. Pluto Press.

Dale, G. (2017a). Seventeenth century origins of the growth paradigm. In I. Borowy & M. Schmelzer (Eds.), *History of the future of economic growth: Historical roots of current debates on sustainable degrowth* (pp. 71–95). Routledge.

Dale, G. (2017b). Sustaining what? Scarcity, growth and the natural order in the discourse on sustainability. In J. Caradonna (Ed.), *Routledge handbook of the history of sustainability* (pp. 27–51). Routledge.

Dobie, M. (2010). *Trading places: Colonization and slavery in eighteenth-century French culture*. Cornell University Press.

Dumont, L. (1977). *From Mandeville to Marx: Genesis and triumph of economic ideology*. University of Chicago Press.

Ebeling, R. (2016). *Economic Ideas: The French physiocrats and the case for laissez-faire*. www.heartland.org/news-opinion/news/economic-ideas-the-french-physiocrats-and-the-case-for-laissez-faire

Ekelund, R., & Hébert, R. (2013). *A history of economic theory and method* (6th ed.). Waveland Press.

Engels, F. (1877). *Anti-Dühring*. www.marxists.org/archive/marx/works/1877/anti-duhring/

Faccarello, G. (1999). *The foundations of laissez-faire: The economics of Pierre de Boisguilbert*. Routledge.

Foster, J. B., Clark, B., & York, R. (2010). *The ecological rift: Capitalism's war on the earth*. Monthly Review Press.

Foucault, M. (2008). *The birth of biopolitics: Lectures at the Collège de France, 1978–79*. Palgrave.

Fourcade, M. (2009). *Economists and societies*. Princeton University Press.

Gay, P. (1996). *The Enlightenment: An interpretation. The science of freedom*. W.W. Norton.

Gills, B. K., & Morgan, J. (2019). Global climate emergency: After COP24, climate science, urgency, and the threat to humanity. *Globalizations*. https://doi.org/10.1080/14747731.2019.1669915

Goldman, L. (1973). *The philosophy of the Enlightenment: The Christian Burgess and the Enlightenment*. Routledge & Kegan Paul.

Gramsci, A. (1971). *Selections from the prison notebooks*. Lawrence & Wishart.

Greenpeace. (2017). *State Policy Network: Koch industries climate denial front group*. www.greenpeace.org/usa/global-warming/climate-deniers/front-groups/state-policy-network-spn/

Griffiths, J. (2000). *Pip pip. A sideways look at time*. Flamingo.

Grove, R. (1995). *Green imperialism: Colonial expansion, tropical island Edens and the origins of environmentalism, 1600–1860*. Cambridge University Press.

Gudeman, S. (1980). Physiocracy: A natural economics. *American Ethnologist, 7*(2), 240–258. https://doi.org/10.1525/ae.1980.7.2.02a00020

Gudeman, S., & Rivera, A. (1990). *Conversations in Colombia: The domestic economy in life and text*. Cambridge University Press.

Heilbron, J. (1998). French moralists and the anthropology of the modern era: On the genesis of the notions of "interest" and "commercial society". In J. Heilbron, L. Magnusson, & B. Wittrock (Eds.), *The rise of the social sciences and the formation of modernity: Conceptual change in context, 1750–1850* (pp. 77–106). Springer.

Hobson, J. (2004). *The Eastern origins of Western civilisation*. Cambridge University Press.

Holmes, C. (2018). *Polanyi in times of populism: Vision and contradiction in the history of economic ideas*. Routledge.

Hont, I. (2005). *Jealousy of trade: International competition and the nation-state in historical perspective*. Harvard University Press.

Hornborg, A. (2013). The Fossil Interlude: Euro-American power and the return of the physiocrats. In S. Strauss, S. Rupp, & T. Love (Eds.), *Cultures of energy: Power, practices, technologies* (pp. 41–59). Left Coast Press.

Hornborg, A. (2014). Why solar panels don't grow on trees: Technological utopianism and the uneasy relation between ecomarxism and ecological economics. In K. Bradley & J. Hedrén (Eds.), *Green utopianism: Perspectives, politics and micro-practices* (pp. 76–97). Routledge.

Huberman, L. (1937). *Man's worldly goods: The story of the wealth of nations.* Gollancz.

Kaplan, S. (1976). *Bread, politics and political economy in the reign of Louis XV.* Martinus Nijhoff.

Keen, S. (2016). *Incorporating energy into production functions.* https://rwer.wordpress.com/2016/09/05/incorporating-energy-into-production-functions/#more-25623

Luxemburg, R. (2003). *The accumulation of capital.* Routledge. (Original work published 1913)

Martinez-Alier, J. (1997). Some issues in agrarian and ecological economics, in memory of Georgescu-Roegen. *Ecological Economics, 22*(3), 225–238. https://doi.org/10.1016/S0921-8009(97)00076-1

Marx, K. (1861–1863). *Theories of surplus value.* www.marxists.org/archive/marx/works/1863/theories-surplus-value/ch02.htm

Marx, K. (1863–1878). *Capital, Volume II.* www.marxists.org/archive/marx/works/1885-c2/ch19.htm#1

Marx, K. (1867). *Capital, Volume I.* www.marxists.org/archive/marx/works/1867-c1/

McElroy, W. (2010). *The physiocrats.* www.fff.org/explore-freedom/article/physiocrats/

McNally, D. (1988). *Political economy and the rise of capitalism: A reinterpretation.* University of California Press.

Meek, R. (1962a). Introduction to physiocracy. In R. Meek (Ed.), *The economics of physiocracy: Essays and translations* (pp. 15–36). Routledge.

Meek, R. (1962b). The interpretation of physiocracy. In R. Meek (Ed.), *The economics of physiocracy: Essays and translations* (pp. 368–398). Routledge.

Meek, R. (1976). *Social science and the ignoble savage.* Cambridge University Press.

Mehta, U. (1999). *Liberalism and empire: A study in nineteenth-century British liberal thought.* University of Chicago Press.

Mirowski, P. (1989). *More heat than light. Economics as social physics: Physics as nature's economics.* Cambridge University Press.

Mobertz, L. (2017). Interview: "renegade" economist Kate Raworth on future-proofing business. *Conscious Company.* https://consciouscompanymedia.com/the-new-economy/interview-renegade-economist-kate-raworth-future-proofing-business/

Nisbet, R. (1975). Turgot and the contexts of progress. *Proceedings of the American Philosophical Society, 119*(3), 214–222.

Oswald, A., & Stern, N. (2019). Why does the economics of climate change matter so much—and why has the engagement of economists been so weak? *Royal Economic Society, October 2019 newsletter.*

Pearson, H. (1957). The economy has no surplus: Critique of a theory of development. In K. Polanyi (Ed.), *Trade and market in the early empires: Economies in history and theory* (pp. 63–97). Beacon Press.

Perelman, M. (1983). *Classical political economy, primitive accumulation and the social division of labor.* Rowman & Allanheld.

Quesnay, F. (1759). *Tableau Economique.* www.marxists.org/reference/subject/economics/quesnay/1759/tableau.htm

Quesnay, F. (1962). Essays. In R. Meek (Ed.), *The economics of physiocracy: Essays and translations* (pp. 43–264). Routledge.

Quesnay, F. (1972). *Tableau Économique.* M. Kuczynski and R. Meek (Eds.). Macmillan.

Quesnay, F. (1976). *Ökonomische Schriften, Band II, Erster Halbband.* Akademie-Verlag.

Raworth, K. (2017). *Doughnut economics: Seven ways to think like a 21st-century economist.* Random House.

Røge, P. (2013). A natural order of empire: The physiocratic vision of colonial France after the Seven Years' war. In S. Reinert & P. Røge (Eds.), *The political economy of empire in the early modern world* (pp. 263–285). Palgrave.

Rubin, I. (1979). *A history of economic thought.* Ink Links. (Original work published 1929)

Saisselin, R. (1992). *The Enlightenment against the Baroque: Economics and aesthetics in the eighteenth century.* University of California Press.

Schliephake, C. (Ed.). (2016). *Ecocriticism, ecology, and the cultures of Antiquity.* Lexington.

Simon, J. (1981). *The ultimate resource.* www.juliansimon.com/writings/Ultimate_Resource/TCONCLUS.txt

Solow, R. (2018). The economics of resources or the resources of economics. In J. Scheraga (Ed.), *Discounting and environmental policy* (pp. 163–177). Routledge. (Original work published 1974)

Stokes, K. (1992). *Man and the biosphere: Toward a coevolutionary political economy.* M.E. Sharpe.

Tieben, B. (2012). *The concept of equilibrium in different economic traditions: An historical investigation.* Edward Elgar.

Tricoire, D. (2017). *Enlightened colonialism: Civilization narratives and imperial politics in the age of reason.* Springer.

Turgot, A. (2011). *The Turgot collection: Writings, speeches, and letters of Anne Robert Jacques Turgot.* D. Gordon (Ed.). Mises Institute.

Wood, E. (2012). *Liberty and property: A social history of Western political thought from renaissance to Enlightenment.* Verso.

Economics, the climate change policy-assemblage and the new materialisms: towards a comprehensive policy

Nick J. Fox ⓘ and Pam Alldred ⓘ

ABSTRACT

Climate change policy is a contested field, with rival perspectives underpinning radically different policy propositions: from encouraging the market to innovate technical solutions to climate change through to the replacement of a market economy with an eco-socialist model. These differing policy options draw upon a variety of economic concepts and approaches, with significant consequent divergences in their policy recommendations. In this paper, we consider policy as assembled from a wide range of sociomaterial components – some human, others non-human. Using a 'new materialist' toolkit, we explore four contemporary climate change policies to unpack these policy-assemblages, and assess the different uses made of economics in each assemblage. We conclude that none of these contemporary policies is adequate to address climate change. Yet despite the incommensurability between how these disparate policies use economic concepts and theories, we suggest a materialist synthesis based on a comprehensive climate change policy-assemblage.

Introduction

This paper focuses on the sociomaterial production of climate change policy, and the part that economics and economic theory plays – sometimes explicitly, but on other occasions implicitly and uncritically – within the climate change 'policy-assemblage'.

With escalating global concern about environmental degradation and the effects of humanity on the planet's climate, policy discussions around sustainable development have been of growing importance over the past 30 years. A series of high-level international treaties have been signed to limit greenhouse gas emissions, while activism to pressure governments to implement these treaties have become part of the twenty-first century policy landscape. Despite these initiatives, there remains a lack of consensus over how precisely to achieve the objectives set out in documents such as the United Nations (2016) *Sustainable Development Goals*. Policy approaches vary across the political landscape, from marketised solutions entailing the innovation of green technologies (so-called 'green capitalism') (Zysman & Huberty, 2014) to radical alterations to the economic system, replacing a market economy with a socialist alternative (Baer, 2012). Most policy perspectives incorporate some aspects of economic theory, though focusing on different concepts or models. As a consequence, the actions proposed in differing policy approaches may conflict, or even be diametrically opposed.

This incommensurability increases the likelihood that climate change policy will be decided on the basis of economic or political preferences, rather than on the validity of the underlying science. Furthermore, the differing economic theory underpinnings prevent productive engagements between advocates of disparate policy perspectives.

In this paper we employ an innovative 'new materialist' approach to policy assessment, which explores policy-making as an assemblage of multiple human and non-human components. This enables us to assess which components are missing from a policy; explore the interactions between a policy and the event is seeks to address; and ask of the policy, what does it actually do? In turn, this allows us to evaluate the adequacy and appropriateness of different policy options, but also enables us to postulate a comprehensive climate change policy that can cut across differing policy positions founded within contradictory economic and political preferences. We begin by setting out this perspective on policy-as-assemblage. We then review four major climate change policy perspectives, revealing both their strengths and their limitations (which derive in part from their differing economic underpinnings). To overcome the shortcomings of these differing policies, we conclude by offering a materialist synthesis of approaches, offering the foundations for a comprehensive climate change policy.

Policy, policy-making and the 'policy-assemblage'

Policy may be defined as an engagement or intervention that addresses an issue, event or interaction, with the aim of improving or reforming the social or natural world (Shore & Wright, 1997, pp. 30–31; Taylor Webb & Gulson, 2012, pp. 87–88). Conventionally, discourse analytic approaches have been applied to assess policies (Gasper & Apthorpe, 1996), while policy development and implementation have been explored by analysing the influence of interest groups (Burstein & Linton, 2002) and/or institutional structures (Wiktorowicz, 2003, p. 618).

Our work has been based upon a different – materialist – ontology of policy (Fox & Alldred, 2020). This approach draws upon a cultural geography literature that explores policy-making and implementation in terms of a 'policy-assemblage' (McCann, 2011; McCann & Ward, 2012; Prince, 2010; Ureta, 2014). 'An implemented policy', Prince (2010:, p. 173) suggests 'is an assemblage of texts, actors, agencies, institutions and networks [that] come together at particular *policy-making locales*' (emphasis in original). Policy-assemblages are dynamic and unstable (Ureta, 2014, p. 305): a feature that has made this approach conceptually attractive when studying policy implementations on complex and contested topics (McCann, 2011, p. 145).

However, these authors have freely admitted that their conceptualization of the policy-assemblage has remained largely descriptive (McCann & Ward, 2012, p. 43). We have sought to remedy this (Fox & Alldred, 2020) by situating the policy-assemblage firmly within a 'new materialist' (Coole & Frost, 2010) conceptual framework,[1] in order to establish an approach to policy-as-assemblage for analytical ends. This enabled us to consider what policies do and the extent to which they are adequate to meet their stated objectives. Our framing entails two distinct assessments: of the issue (Ureta, 2014, p. 306) or 'event' (the topic of a particular policy) and of the policy that aims to engage and influence this issue.

In terms of the former: the 'event' of anthropogenic climate change may be analysed as an assemblage of multiple human and non-human elements. Later in the paper we offer our assessment of a comprehensive climate change event-assemblage. For now – to illustrate the approach – we may consider a much-simplified assemblage, comprising – at least – the following components (in no particular order):

oceans; atmosphere; greenhouse gases; the Sun; humans; human activities; industry

Natural and social science evidence suggests this climate change event-assemblage (EA) works as a consequence of the following 'affect-economy'[2]: greenhouse gases prevent the Sun's heat from escaping from the atmosphere; this increases the Sun's capacity to heat the Earth's oceans; humans use fossil fuels as an energy source; industrialization and a market economy massively increased fossil fuel use; consequent rising ocean temperatures is now producing global climate changes.

Policy-making to address climate change can be considered, within this ontology, as an event in its own right, and consequently may also be analysed as a material-semiotic assemblage. A climate change policy-assemblage (PA) comprises a multiplicity of elements and actors from scientific evidence to a range of stakeholders (Baer, 2012, p. 267; Dror, 2017; Yearley, 2014):

> evidence of climate changes; relevant natural and social science theories; experts; policy-makers; stakeholders; energy producers; money; economic theory; social and political processes and perspectives; policy documents; audience

Within this PA, policy makers will be affected by the evidence of climate changes from scientific studies or from expert witnesses, and by theories explaining climate change. They will also be affected by economic and political considerations and theories, as well as particular perspectives or orientations (for instance, a commitment to protecting wildlife or an emphasis on achieving North/South global equity).

There is a dialectical relationship between an event-assemblage and the policy-assemblage that addresses it. This is summarised in Figure 1. In this dialectic, policy works as a consequence of two interactions. First, the PA must be capable of identifying the components and interactions within the EA (for instance, the interactions between humans, fossil fuels, the economic system, the atmosphere and the Sun). This will depend in part on the adequacy of evidence available. It follows that if evidence is not considered or economic or political factors not acknowledged during this policy-formulation activity, the PA may fail to identify potentially crucial aspects of the climate change EA.

Second, when implemented, a policy-assemblage must be capable of *adequately* and *appropriately* affecting the event it is targeting (as opposed to having little or no effect, or affecting other irrelevant

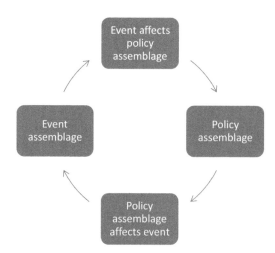

Figure 1. Interactions between event-assemblage and policy assemblage.

processes) (Dror, 2017, pp. 34–35). For instance, a global policy to replace fossil fuels with renewable energy sources will – according to the theory of anthropogenic climate change – have a beneficial impact by limiting greenhouse gas emissions. But this capacity to affect the event will depend upon many aspects of what a PA can actually do. If, for instance, a PA does not include adequate and appropriate resources or involve dominant economic or political actors, it may have little influence on events.

In the following section, we will use this dialectical interaction between EA and PA as the means by which to analyse four contemporary climate change PAs, and evaluate the likely success or failure of each policy. For each, we will pull apart the PA, to identify which components of the underlying EA it addresses. This will enable us to evaluate both its adequacy to analyse comprehensively the social and physical complexities of climate change, and its consequent capacity to achieve the changes that are needed to limit or reverse global climate change (for instance, by substantial reductions in greenhouse gases).

Climate change: four policy-assemblages

In our research, we analysed four broad policy perspectives on anthropocentric climate change: 'liberal environmentalism', the United Nations policy approach, 'green capitalism' and a 'no-growth' policy. For each of these policies, we were able to 'reverse engineer' its policy-assemblage, in order to identify which elements of the climate change it addressed and which it ignored. For this special issue, we identify in particular the economic elements within the associated policy-assemblage, and assess how these contribute to the policy. This enables us to evaluate the adequacy of the each policy to fulfil an action plan that can address the current crisis of anthropocentric climate change.

Liberal environmentalism

The liberal environmentalism (LE) perspective formulates policies and actions to ameliorate the environmental impact of human practices, principally by efforts to alter individual or collective behaviour (Yearley, 2014, p. 98). It is well-represented in the focus of charities that aim to conserve an endangered species and in popular TV documentaries on 'the natural world'. In relation to climate change, LE encourages the public to buy low energy household appliances, switch to electric vehicles or use public transport or bikes, or eat less meat.

Some such 'green' behaviour-modifications have been informed by behavioural economic theories ('nudging'), which acknowledge that human actions rarely conform to the 'rational actor' model of *homo economicus* (Schubert, 2017, p. 331). Significantly, however, LE formulates its policies and actions without critical assessment of the interactions between a market economy and environmental degradation (Bernstein, 2001, p. 3; Talshir, 2012, p. 18; Whitehead, 2014); nor does it challenge a liberal model of the environment as a resource to be exploited for human gain and well-being.

A policy to reduce meat consumption supplies an example of how these priorities and lacunae within the LE approach affect the interactions *between* policy and event assemblages outlined in Figure 1. The EA with which this policy perspective interacts includes the following elements (in no particular order):

animals; land; famers; feed; diesel; consumers; greenhouse gas emissions; atmosphere, the Sun

Behind this EA is an expectation that a shift in consumer demand away from meat will lead to changes that will reduce greenhouse gas emissions. However, the broader socioeconomic forces driving the production of meat protein (such as agribusiness interests, poverty, a shortage of grazing pastures, the low value of forested land, farming subsidies, population growth and the marketing of fast meat-based foods) are not considered. Excluding these powerful forces (most of which derive ultimately from a globalized capitalist economy) raises questions over the capacities of an LE policy to adequately reduce meat consumption globally. At best, consumers' choices will have a marginal effect on reducing meat production and halting rainforest clearance if action to address the broader socioeconomic processes fuelling meat production and consumption are ignored.

These limitations of the LE approach undermine its adequacy and appropriateness as a policy intervention to limit anthropogenic climate change. By sidelining the needs of a market economy for sustained growth, it is incapable of addressing the complex social processes that are the drivers of anthropogenic environmental impacts.

The United Nations and sustainable development

The United Nations (UN) has offered a consistent policy perspective on climate change and sustainable development, dating from the 1987 *Report of the World Commission on Environment and Development* (World Commission on Environment and Development, 1987) to its *Agenda for Sustainable Development* (UN, 2015). This approach sets out twin objectives of environmental sustainability and human socioeconomic development (Whitehead, 2014, p. 259), and argues that these are inextricably linked (Fleurbaey et al., 2014, p. 322). In its 2016 document *Sustainable Development Goals*, 13 of its 17 objectives focus upon the quality of human life (for example, ending poverty, achieving gender equality, access to clean water and affordable energy), with only three on the rest of the environment.

Unlike the LE policy perspective discussed previously, in the UN position, the role of economic growth in human development is made explicit. Hence, the climate change event assemblage (EA) that this policy position conceptualizes comprises at least the following relations (in no particular order):

> Earth; material resources; biosphere (animals and plants); humans; the global economy; poverty and wealth inequalities; economic development; social and political development; nations and governments; global North; global South; pollution; energy; greenhouse gases; future human generations

However, the insistence that environmental sustainability can only be achieved through economic growth (UN, 2015: 4) excludes any acknowledgement that it is indeed economic growth and the increase in human economic prosperity that has led to environmental degradation and climate change since the industrial revolution (Stern, 2007, p. xi; Wallis, 2010; Yearley, 2014, p. 104). This foundational economic blind-spot – driven by the UN's political imperatives to reduce North/South economic inequality (Whitehead, 2014) – consequently limits the capacity of this policy-assemblage adequately and appropriately to address environmental challenges.

Green capitalism

The liberal environmentalist (LE) position considered earlier gains a couple of additional twists in positions that have been called 'green capitalism': perspectives often promoted by right-leaning politicians and some business leaders. While LE was generally silent on the negative effects on the environment of a market economy, green capitalism regards the market as the means whereby the environment will be protected from human depredations, or even as its saviour.

Green capitalism is founded in one of two alternative propositions. The first argues that climate change represents a catastrophic failure of market mechanisms (Stern, 2007, p. i), but that with some revisions – top-down management, international trading of carbon, and innovative technology – a market economy can be made environment-friendly (see also Pearce et al., 1989, pp. 153–171). For Stern, capitalist markets failed because the producers of greenhouse gases (primarily nations in the North) can avoid the full global consequences of resultant climate change, while affecting parts of the world not responsible for their production (negative externality). His recommendations were for intervention in market economies through regulation, taxation and international collaboration (Stern, 2007, pp. xviii–xxi).

A second perspective transforms LE into a 'neoliberal environmentalism', in which entrepreneurialism and capitalism's never-ending quest for profit will save Earth from climate change and other environmental degradations through environment-friendly technological innovation (Prudham, 2009, p. 1596). Proponents argue that a market economy is the best means to reverse these impacts through human ingenuity and entrepreneurialism, while ensuring the continuity of the economic growth that they argue has been the engine of both national and individual prosperity since the industrial revolution. Others, such as Zysman and Huberty (2014) regard such environmental innovations as a new strategy for capital accumulation, with both a free market economy and the environment benefiting.

In both these manifestations, climate change policy is tied to market economics, though unlike the UN policy position, they de-couple climate sustainability from the social and political development of the global South. Green capitalist policies are founded on an event-assemblage (EA) comprising at least:

> material resources ('the environment'); consumers; capital; industry; entrepreneurs; production; profit; growth; developing and developed nations and governments; energy; greenhouse gases; the Sun; climate; technologies

This EA is 'capitalocentric', with an overarching focus on the operation of the capitalist market and the accumulation of wealth: any benefits for the natural world are entirely incidental (see Moore, 2018). The inherent wastefulness of competitive capitalist markets (Yearley, 2014, p. 106) and the endless drive for growth (Bosquet, 1977, p. 166) are ignored as sources of environmental degradation. Furthermore, the differential impact of climate change upon rich and poor, global North and South remain unacknowledged: inequalities largely produced by capitalist accumulation and globalization. These economic lacunae again force us to conclude that a green capitalist policy-assemblage is inadequate and inappropriate to address climate change.

No growth policies

Activists within the global Green movement and political Left have advocated a zero-growth economic system as a climate change policy position,[3] and have been critical of liberal environmentalist approaches and the 'green capitalist' approaches just considered (Baer, 2012; Bernstein, 2001; Brand, 2012). These, they argue, simply sustain a market economy whose quest for continual economic growth has led to ever-increasing inputs of environmental resources (including fossil fuels), while concomitant growth in outputs contributes to inexorable rises in waste and pollutants (Daly & Cobb, 1994, p. 4; Fournier, 2008). This has not only led to environmental crises but also ensures social and economic inequalities between poor and wealthy, and an economic divide between global North and South. Advocates for zero -growth economics also require shifts in social relations to achieve an equitable global re-distribution of resources (Randers, 2012, p. 105), or a 'sharing economy'

(Heinrichs, 2013). For Baer (2012:, p. 208), however, the adoption of a sustainable no-growth economics is predicated on the wholesale move from capitalist production to 'democratic eco-socialism'.

The no growth event-assemblage differs markedly from those previously analysed, but once again is selective over which elements of the climate change EA are included. This climate change event-assemblage comprises (in no particular order):

> human consumers; finite non-human environment; market economy; industrialisation; production; profit; energy; waste; greenhouse gases; Sun; climate

This event-assemblage casts the capitalist economic system and environmental sustainability as fundamentally opposed, with the former wastefully plundering the Earth's finite resources. However, this event-assemblage understates the inertia associated with the wider political contexts of market economies (for instance, the vested interests within capitalist economies, the military-industrial complex that ties production directly to national or regional ideologies, the dependency of democratic societies upon taxation to fund welfare and a public sector) and the global character of growth-oriented market economics (Elbe & Long, 2020; Sell & Williams, 2020; Wright & Nyberg, 2015). This political edifice limits the potential for a swift shift from a capitalist to a no-growth economic model. Such a shift shows no sign of emerging among such political stakeholders, and is unlikely to be readily embraced by politicians or public any time soon in the world's major climate change polluter: the US. Once again, we are forced to conclude that this PA is inadequate to address the pressing issue of climate change.

Discussion: terminal incommensurability or synthetic opportunity?

The policy-assemblage analysis that we have conducted on four differing policy positions on climate change has revealed the differing engagements each has with the material elements within the climate change event-assemblage, including economic concepts and approaches. More significantly, the analysis also reveals that all these policies are based on partial acknowledgement of the complexities of the climate change assemblage. As a consequence, we conclude that none is adequate or appropriate to address these environmental challenges.

However, a policy assemblage analysis, unlike approaches such as policy discourse analysis (Gasper & Apthorpe, 1996), also supplies an ontological foundation upon which to design a critical policy assemblage that *is* adequate and appropriate. Key to this endeavour is a reversal of the conventional policy-development process. Rather than being driven by the political, economic or other ideological commitments of stakeholders, the first step must be to establish a comprehensive understanding of the climate change event-assemblage itself, based on a broad understanding of the relevant natural and social science (see for example, IPCC, 2013, 2014).[4] In place of the partial engagements that each of the four earlier policy positions reflects, this suggests a climate change assemblage comprising:

> Earth; Sun; atmosphere; oceans; land and other physical resources; animals; plants; soil; humans; industry; consumption; greenhouse gases; market; capitalist economic model; profit; growth; nations; governments; global North; global South; ideologies; wealth and health inequalities

This event-assemblage is drawn together by a complex affect-economy comprising physical, chemical, social, economic and political interactions between assembled components, and acknowledges the interdependence of social and material worlds and how these interact in the era of anthropogenic climate change. As such, it can supply an adequate basis for a policy assemblage that has the capacity to capture the complexities of the affective movements in this event assemblage, and to formulate actions that will engage adequately and appropriately with these affects.

When analysing the four policies on climate change we reviewed earlier, we noted their very different emphases (for instance, upon economic development in the UN approach, market-driven technological innovation in the green capitalist perspective, and rolling-back the capitalist economic system in the no-growth model). But a policy-assemblage analysis reveals that this apparent incommensurability (particularly in relation to economic commitments) derives from the partiality of the event-assemblages upon which the different policies have been founded. Each of these four event-assemblages incorporate parts of the comprehensive event-assemblage we have just set out. Consequently, a policy-assemblage based on this comprehensive analysis can be synthetic: drawing upon features of the different policies we have reviewed, while acknowledging the foundational differences and consequent contradictory recommendations that also flow from these policies.

Elsewhere (Fox & Alldred, 2020) we have set out some of the elements that can be incorporated into a comprehensive climate change policy. From the *liberal environmentalist* policy, a focus on environmental protection and efforts to change individual and collective human behaviour to lower energy and fossil fuel use, reduce consumption of other resources and the production of waste. From the *United Nations* policy assemblage, action to redistribute income locally and globally, recognising that poverty is one of the drivers of environmental destruction. From the *green capitalism* assemblage: support for technological innovation to limit and remove greenhouse gases from the environment. From the *no-growth* policy, action to limit economic growth and wasteful competition. These provide the foundation for incremental actions locally, nationally and globally to address the physical, biological, social, economic and political affects within the climate change event-assemblage. Some of the practical actions that flow from these are set out in Table 1.

What this analysis also reveals is that despite the potential to synthesise some aspects of existing climate change policies, some incommensurability between policy objectives remains. This principally derives from the disparate use of economic theory and concepts underpinning different climate change policy-assemblages. As sociologists we shall make no attempt here to address the complexities of economic theory or transcend the irresolvable divergences between neoliberal and eco-socialist economics. Our proposition is a modest first step: a pragmatic (with a small 'p') response to climate change policy, based on a comprehensive and non-ideological analysis of climate change itself, and a focus on what a policy actually needs to *do* to be successful.

Clearly, the challenge of such a programme is immense, and to be effective will require new social, economic and political collaborations and alliances, both within countries and internationally. As far as possible, climate change policy needs to be removed from ideology and party politics, though we

Table 1. A synthesis of climate change policy initiatives.

Environment Protection	***Human economic and social security***
Enhanced environmental protection of biological and natural resources.	Increase economic aid to assist global South.
Use 'nudges', legislative and fiscal measures to encourage climate-friendly behaviour by individual, groups, businesses, and nations.	Reduce inequalities via universal basic income or tax credit schemes, funded by higher rates of taxation of personal income, corporation tax on profits and penalties for environmental pollution.
Fiscal measures to capture the true environmental costs of goods and services	
Penalise use of non-reusable or polluting resources.	Education and training to lift people out of poverty, encourage smaller families.
Technological solutions	***Restrict economic growth***
Support development of technological fixes that replace polluting and wasteful production.	Incentivise future proofing, longevity and quality of goods.
Nationalise industrial infrastructure (energy, transport, services) and increase spending on research and development.	Replace global free trade with regional economic trade zones.

see progressive governments and organisations such as the United Nations and Intergovernmental Panel on Climate Change (IPCC) as key future players, along with social and natural scientists who are refining our understanding of the Earth's environment and climate.[55] For all these actions, economic and governance support will also be required by countries in the global South to move towards these challenging policies. Working through the economic implications of the policy initiatives that our synthesis implies, we respectfully leave to those better qualified for the task.

Notes

1. The 'new materialisms' encompass a range of perspectives including actor-network theory, assemblage theories, biophilosophy/biocentrism, feminist materialism, onto-epistemology, non-representational theory, posthumanism, Spinozist ethology and some non-Western and indigenous ontologies (Fox & Alldred, 2017, p. 14; Rosiek et al., 2020). Our work draws principally on the Deleuzian tradition within new materialism, and is predicated on two moves. First, it replaces notions of pre-existent, fixed entities such as bodies, animals, fossil fuels, atmospheric conditions and governments with *relational* materialities that gain form and continuity when disposed alongside other materialities within *assemblages* (Bennett, 2005, p. 445; Deleuze, 1988, p. 125; DeLanda, 2016, p. 10). Second, new materialisms consider that all the disparate materialities within an assemblage have capacities to affect, or to be affected by, other assembled relations (Deleuze, 1988, p. 101): humans are no longer the prime movers in this ontology. The collective 'economy' (Clough, 2004, p. 15) of *affects* within such an assemblage determines what it (and its constituent human and non-human relations) can do. The breadth of any relation's *capacities* – be it human or non-human, biological or inorganic – will depend entirely upon the richness of its affective interactions.
2. See Note 1 for an explanation of 'affect-economy'.
3. Alongside 'no-growth' or 'zero-growth' positions, this policy orientation may be taken to include 'degrowth' – a downward re-sizing of the economy to within the support capacity of the biosphere that addresses human well-being rather than wealth accumulation (Whitehead, 2013, p. 142), and efforts by Herman Daly and others to theorise a 'steady-state' economics that does not regard economic growth as an essential feature of a market economy (Kerschner, 2010, p. 545).
4. We acknowledge that the science rallied behind a policy can never be considered complete: our knowledge of climate change is continually being refined. Nor is it the case that scientific knowledge is independent of social processes: a comprehensive event-assemblage must include a reflexive social scientific component capable of recognising how knowledge is produced and used socially, politically and economically.
5. See, for example, the work of the Stockholm Resilience Centre and others on planetary boundaries (Rockström et al., 2009).

Disclosure statement

No potential conflict of interest was reported by the author(s).

ORCID

Nick J. Fox ⓘ http://orcid.org/0000-0003-2037-2664
Pam Alldred ⓘ http://orcid.org/0000-0002-5077-7286

References

Baer, H. (2012). *Global capitalism and climate change*. AltaMira Press.

Bennett, J. (2005). The agency of assemblages and the North American blackout. *Public Culture, 17*(3), 445–465. https://doi.org/10.1215/08992363-17-3-445

Bernstein, S. (2001). *The compromise of liberal environmentalism*. Columbia University Press.

Bosquet, M. (1977). *Capitalism in crisis and everyday life*. Harvester Press.

Brand, U. (2012). Green economy – the next oxymoron? No lessons learned from failures of implementing sustainable development. *GAIA – Ecological Perspectives for Science and Society, 21*(1), 28–32. https://doi.org/10.14512/gaia.21.1.9

Burstein, P. and Linton, A. (2002). The impact of political parties, interest groups, and social movement organizations on public policy: some recent evidence and theoretical concerns. *Social Forces, 81*(2), 380–408.

Clough, P. T. (2004). Future matters: Technoscience, global politics, and cultural criticism. *Social Text, 22*(3), 1–23. https://doi.org/10.1215/01642472-22-3_80-1

Coole, D. H., & Frost, S. (2010). Introducing the new materialisms. In D. H. Coole & S. Frost (Eds.), *New materialisms. Ontology, agency, and politics* (pp. 1–43). Duke University Press.

Daly, H. E., & Cobb, J. B. (1994). *For the common good* (2nd ed.). Beacon Press.

DeLanda, M. (2016). *Assemblage theory*. Edinburgh University Press.

Deleuze, G. (1988). *Spinoza: Practical philosophy*. City Lights.

Dror, Y. (2017). *Public policymaking reexamined*. Routledge.

Elbe, S., & Long, C. (2020). The political economy of molecules: Vital epistemics, desiring machines and assemblage thinking. *Review of International Political Economy, 27*(1), 125–145. https://doi.org/10.1080/09692290.2019.1625560

Fleurbaey, M., Kartha, S., Bolwig, S., et al. (2014). Sustainable development and equity. In O. Edenhofer, R. Pichs-Madruga, & Y. Sokona et al. (Eds.), *Climate change 2014: Mitigation of climate change. Contribution of working Group III to the fifth assessment report of the intergovernmental panel on climate change* (pp. 283–350). Cambridge University Press.

Fournier, V. (2008). Escaping from the economy: The politics of degrowth. *International Journal of Sociology and Social Policy, 28*(11/12), 528–545. https://doi.org/10.1108/01443330810915233

Fox, N. J., & Alldred, P. (2017). *Sociology and the new materialism*. Sage.

Fox, N. J., & Alldred, P. (2020). Re-assembling climate change policy: Materialism, posthumanism and the policy assemblage. *The British Journal of Sociology, 71*(2), 269–283. https://doi.org/10.1111/1468-4446.12734

Gasper, D., & Apthorpe, R. (1996). Introduction: Discourse analysis and policy discourse. *The European Journal of Development Research, 8*(1), 1–15. https://doi.org/10.1080/09578819608426650

Heinrichs, H. (2013). Sharing economy: A potential new pathway to sustainability. *GAIA – Ecological Perspectives for Science and Society, 22*(4), 228–231. https://doi.org/10.14512/gaia.22.4.5

IPCC. (2013). *Climate change 2013: The physical science basis. Contribution of working Group I to the fifth assessment report of the intergovernmental panel on climate change*. Cambridge University Press.

IPCC. (2014). *Climate change 2014: Mitigation of climate change. Contribution of working Group III to the fifth assessment report of the intergovernmental panel on climate change*. Cambridge University Press.

Kerschner, C. (2010). Economic de-growth vs. steady-state economy. *Journal of Cleaner Production,* 18(6), 544–551.

McCann, E. (2011). Veritable inventions: Cities, policies and assemblage. *Area, 43*(2), 143–147. https://doi.org/10.1111/j.1475-4762.2011.01011.x

McCann, E., & Ward, K. (2012). Assembling urbanism: Following policies and 'studying through' the sites and situations of policy making. *Environment and Planning A: Economy and Space, 44*(1), 42–51. https://doi.org/10.1068/a44178

Moore, J. W. (2018). The Capitalocene Part II: Accumulation by appropriation and the centrality of unpaid work/energy. *The Journal of Peasant Studies, 45*(2), 237–279. https://doi.org/10.1080/03066150.2016.1272587

Pearce, D., Markandya, A., & Barbier, E. B. (1989). *Blueprint for a green economy.* Earthscan.

Prince, R. (2010). Policy transfer as policy assemblage: Making policy for the creative industries in New Zealand. *Environment and Planning A: Economy and Space, 42*(1), 169–186. https://doi.org/10.1068/a4224

Prudham, S. (2009). Pimping climate change: Richard Branson, global warming, and the performance of green capitalism. *Environment and Planning A: Economy and Space, 41*(7), 1594–1613. https://doi.org/10.1068/a4071

Randers, J. (2012). The real message of *The Limits to Growth.* A plea for forward-looking global policy. *GAIA – Ecological Perspectives for Science and Society, 21*(2), 102–105. https://doi.org/10.14512/gaia.21.2.7

Rockström, J., Steffen, W., Noone, K., Persson, Å, Chapin, F. S., Lambin, E., Lenton, T. M., Scheffer, M., Folke, C., Schellnhuber, H. J., Nykvist, B., de Wit, C. A., Hughes, T., van der Leeuw, S., Rodhe, H., Sörlin, S., Snyder, P. K., Costanza, R., Svedin, U., … Foley, J. (2009). Planetary boundaries: Exploring the safe operating space for humanity. *Ecology and Society, 14*(2), 32. https://doi.org/10.5751/ES-03180-140232

Rosiek, J. L., Snyder, J., & Pratt, S. L. (2020). The new materialisms and indigenous theories of non-human agency: Making the case for respectful anti-colonial engagement. *Qualitative Inquiry, 26*(3-4), 331–346. https://doi.org/10.1177/1077800419830135

Schubert, C. (2017). Green nudges: Do they work? Are they ethical? *Ecological Economics, 132,* 329–342. https://doi.org/10.1016/j.ecolecon.2016.11.009

Sell, S. K., & Williams, O. D. (2020). Health under capitalism: A global political economy of structural pathogenesis. *Review of International Political Economy, 27*(1), 1–25. https://doi.org/10.1080/09692290.2019.1659842

Shore, C., & Wright, S. (1997). Policy: A new field of anthropology. In C. Shore & S. Wright (Eds.), *Anthropology of policy* (pp. 3–36). Routledge.

Stern, N. (2007). *The economics of climate change: The stern report.* Cambridge University Press.

Talshir, G. (2012). The role of environmentalism. In Y. Levy & M. Wissenburg (Eds.), *Liberal democracy and environmentalism. The end of environmentalism?* (pp. 22–43). Routledge.

Taylor Webb, P., & Gulson, K. N. (2012). Policy prolepsis in education: Encounters, becomings, and phantasms. *Discourse: Studies in the Cultural Politics of Education, 33*(1), 87–99. https://doi.org/10.1080/01596306.2012.632169

United Nations (UN) 2015. *Transforming our World: The 2030 Agenda for Sustainable Development.* UN General Assembly Resolution 70/1. Geneva: United Nations. https://sustainabledevelopment.un.org/post2015/transformingourworld/publication.

United Nations. (2016). *Sustainable development goals.* http://www.un.org/sustainabledevelopment/

Ureta, S. (2014). Policy assemblages: Proposing an alternative conceptual framework to study public action. *Policy Studies, 35*(3), 303–318. https://doi.org/10.1080/01442872.2013.875150

Wallis, V. (2010). Beyond 'green capitalism'. *Monthly Review, 61*(9), 32. https://doi.org/10.14452/MR-061-09-2010-02_3

Whitehead, M. (2013). Degrowth or regrowth? *Environmental Values, 22*(2), 141–145.

Whitehead, M. (2014). Sustainability. In C. Death (Ed.), *Critical environmental politics* (pp. 257–266). Routledge.

Wiktorowicz, M. (2003). Emergent patterns in the regulation of pharmaceuticals: Institutions and interests in the United States, Canada, Britain, and France. *Journal of Health Politics, Policy and Law, 28*(4), 615–658. https://doi.org/10.1215/03616878-28-4-615

World Commission on Environment and Development. (1987). *Our common future (The Brundtland Report).* Oxford University Press.

Wright, C., & Nyberg, D. (2015). *Climate change, capitalism and corporations.* Cambridge University Press.

Yearley, S. (2014). *The green case: A sociology of environmental issues, arguments and politics.* Routledge.

Zysman, J., & Huberty, M. (2014). *Can green sustain growth? From the religion to the reality of sustainable prosperity.* Stanford University Press.

From climate change to economic change? Reflections on 'feedback'

James Goodman [ID] and James Anderson

ABSTRACT
'Feedback' from climate change into the economy is critical. But what kind of 'feedback'? Given capitalist structures and inter-state rivalry in the global economy, there is little in the way of overall planning, and certainly no effective power to act for capitalism 'in general'. The fossil fuel bloc is deeply embedded in the economy, and is not afraid to press its advantage; the emerging renewable economy is gaining strength, but remains subordinate. Yet intensifying climate change and failing climate policy are creating new political pressures. This article addresses efforts to target fossil fuel corporates through divestment campaigns and argues the main 'feedback' to date is socio-political. It tracks how the threat of climate policy translates into 'transition risk' for investment strategy, and produces a growing loss of confidence in fossil capital. In this, we argue the climate contradictions of capitalist society have destructive effects but offer transformative potential.

With decades of climate science we are fully aware of the impact of the global economy on climate change. There is, as we know, a direct correlation between global economic growth on the current carbon-intensive model, and rising global temperatures and associated climate disruption. But what is the impact of climate change on the economy, and what prospect is there for feedback to force economic decarbonization? On the face of it, with greenhouse gas emissions growing unabated and only limited decoupling of economic growth from emissions (Cohen et al., 2018; Global Carbon Project, 2019), the answer to that question has to be 'very little'. Persistent failure points to a deep-seated contradiction between the current logic of economic development and socio-ecological stability. The structures of capitalist society are riven with internal contradiction, and these have both destructive effects and transformative potential. There is no significant self-adjustment underway; instead, socio-political feedback is forcing new forms of 'transition risk' into the fossil fuel economy, disrupting it in new and potentially transformative ways.

The growing politicization of carbon-intensive development has indeed generated new economic antagonisms and transformations. A widening gulf has emerged between the fossil fuel economy and emerging renewable economies, sparking conflicts that reach from the streets and social media, to state structures, and to the centre of finance capital. Thirty-five of the world's largest banks have together invested US$2.7 trillion into fossil fuels since the Paris Agreement (Banktrack, 2020). Yet even J.P. Morgan, by far the largest investor in fossil fuels at about $70 billion annually has privately acknowledged that the globe is set on a 3.5°C trajectory of warming with no solution in sight and no ability to understand the economic impacts (Mackie & Murray, 2020, p. 13). Climate antagonism is now inside the logic of capital, on the corporate agenda even for J.P. Morgan, dubbed the 'doomsday' bank (Banktrack, 2020).

These conflicts are here interpreted as part of a society-wide 'climatisation' dynamic (Aykut et al., 2017). The article offers an assessment of the feedbacks at work, from climate to economy, analysing divestment campaigns and official policy designed to accommodate global finance to 'climate risks'. It finds political and social drivers are uppermost – that 'feedback' is principally a product of socio-political pressure on the economy and an outcome of strategy and mobilization. The article addresses systemic forces against effective climate action but at the same time identifies fissures in the edifice, to draw-out dynamics to force a reckoning.

Climate change is a product of the socio-ecological dynamics of capitalist development over the very recent two hundred years, labelled the 'capitalocene' (Moore, 2016). At its centre is the uniquely forceful drive for accumulation and economic advantage, founded on ecological appropriation (Anderson & Goodman, 2020). In combination these aspects help explain the persistence of green-house gas emissions, and demonstrate the kinds of transformations necessary to overcome it.

With capitalism ecology is appropriated, transformed and degraded. But the internalization of ecology is never complete – biophysical forces retain their autonomy, producing crisis. So for climate change the biophysical process of burning fossil fuels releases both energy and carbon dioxide (and particulate pollution). As such, climate change is an aspect of the socio-ecological dynamic where biophysical relations are combined with and collide with capitalist social relations (Moore, 2015). In that process, best understood dialectically, climate climate has become a product of society; but equally, society has become climatised and reshaped by climate disruption.

In this nexus socio-political agency is re-engaged with the wider ecological crisis, to become the central means of 'feedback' to transform the economy. As Hulme points out, we have lived with many years of inadvertent climate agency; the challenge of the last thirty years or so, dating perhaps from the formation of the Inter-Governmental Panel on Climate Change (IPCC) in 1988, has been to exercise deliberate or 'purposeful' climate agency (Hulme, 2010). Such socio-political agency requires a new form of historical consciousness, across geological time, and a global capacity to act, on an unprecedented scale. The depth of the required transformation is truly awe-inspiring: as the Governor of the Bank of England put it in 2015, the fossil fuel-intensive sector accounts for 'one third of global equity and fixed income assets' (Carney, 2015, p. 11). The urgent challenge for climate agency today is to overcome the resulting deeply-entrenched political power of fossil fuel interests (see Goodman et al., 2020).

Climate-economy feedback?

Overcoming the power of the fossil fuel bloc requires socio-political feedback from climate crisis into the economy. In different ways direct climate disruption and associated climate policy create a block-age in the circuit of capital (Harvey, 2015). Disruption destroys capital and breaks the process of accumulation; climate policy requires the destruction of fossil fuel assets and the creation of new dec-arbonized relations. In pre-capitalist societies underproduction due to poor harvests was the typical cause of economic crisis, but now we find climate disruption having a similar impact. A useful con-trast is the recent socio-ecological threat posed by Covid 19, which has forced a dramatic global pro-cess of underproduction: as most people stayed away from work as officially advised, global production and profits fell sharply and (to date) have kept falling.

Unlike Covid 19, the climate threat is long-term and mostly still in the future, and for capitalists concerned with immediate profits, remedial action can be delayed. The climate crisis has been building for decades but so far its direct economic impact has generally been patchy and fragmented, both across space and time. While global warming is clearly causing an increase in extreme weather events they are separate episodes and still relatively regionalized. Heat waves and resulting wildfires are becoming more extreme but are far from global. Droughts can be more widely disruptive, though again, to date, these have been contained both spatially and over time, as rains allow a return to business as usual. Even the threat of something as uniformly global as the rising sea-level is still mainly perceived as a threat confined to low-lying coastal areas (see Anderson & Shuttleworth, 2020).

The much more serious threats from irreversible changes to the world's climatic zones, such as alterations to ocean currents, and the loss of continental sea-ice in the Antarctic, lie in the future (Steffen et al., 2018). Hence, despite the 'feedback' warnings, official action on climate falls victim to capitalism's built-in tendency to favour short-term considerations. The anticipation of crisis can even intensify the short-term profit imperative: the expectation of climate crisis can create a strong incentive for fossil fuel corporates to exploit reserves now, while they can.

In policy terms the solution only compounds this effect. Decarbonization requires a limit on the accumulation of fossil fuels, for 'unburnable fuels' to be left in the ground, unexploited and 'locked up'. Constraining supply and pricing-out fossil fuels on the existing model of accumulation can simply cut jobs and livelihood. A changed economic strategy is required – based on state action for just transitions and a more socialized renewable economy, for instance in the form of a 'Green New Deal'. Here the imperative for emissions reduction drives a wide-scale transformation in both the economy and the state, and in relations between them (see Aranof et al., 2019). The political prospects for the Green New Deal remain weak but the agenda is moving fast. As Foster points out, the widespread experience of changing climate, and the failure to act on it, has in recent years sparked a renewed political and social upsurge (Foster, 2019). As argued here, the new politics of urgency is forcing a new set of social and political feedback pressures on fossil fuel capital.

Feedback and 'socialisation'

Our economy remains in large part ruled by the anarchy of the market with no overall control, democratic or otherwise: capitalism is uniquely good at producing ecological problems, but it also appears to be uniquely incapable of dealing with them. That incapacity points to new social models, what O'Connor characterized as a 'socialisation' process, of addressing the nature-capital contradiction through more effective social ownership and state action (O'Connor, 1998).

Certainly climate policy is delivering energy transition in some parts of the world as innovation substantially reduces the cost of renewable technology, but fossil fuels remain the default power source globally. At present there is no global agent capable of producing the system-wide change that is required (see Mann & Wainwright, 2018). The narrative of climate negotiations under the United Nations demonstrates the difficulties at play, where concerns intensify, but agreements remain inadequate (see Cabello & Gilbertson, 2015). There may be plenty of feedback across society but the key problems of growth, rivalry and appropriation combine to prevent effective action by world powers.

Despite the weak systemic drivers for climate action, there are political imperatives that arise from policy failure and climate disruption. Productive forces can be transformed with a new renewable economy, but only if the consequences of inaction in terms of the destructive impact of climate disruption are politicized and mobilized to transform the economic calculus. From this perspective the political realm, and the issue of social agency, comes to the fore, with the key issue being whether there is enough social and political pressure to overcome the power of fossil capital.

The problem is not a lack lack of feedback but an incapacity to respond to it: this is important as the failure to act only sharpens the contradiction and fuels political instability. States and corporations are forced to acknowledge anthropogenic climate change, but are demonstrably incapable of acting on it. The result is a widening legitimacy problem, offering scope for transformative political strategy. Indeed, the gap between necessity and reality is now directly measurable: the 2019 Emissions Gap report for instance highlighted the need to triple global emissions reductions commitments to meet the target of no more than 2°C of warming above preindustrial levels (UNEP, 2019).

Arguably it matters little whether global elites are aware of the climate crisis when the imperative for action falls on deaf ears. However, we would counter, to the contrary, that it is critical that feedback is widely understood yet is unheeded by those claiming the authority to act. The capacity to chart the bio-physical impacts in terms of policy failure, has become a vital strategic resource. A cascading process of deepened politicization and socialization opens up as a result, driven by the ongoing failure to reduce emissions and prevent climate disruption. In this context the solutions advanced yesterday quickly become today's failures, pointing to the necessity for further-reaching action.

The widening legitimacy gap places great premium on strategy and policy formation. Strategic responses embrace effective state action and a process of 'socializing' the climate crisis as a public priority, requiring a new model for democratized state authority. As noted, a radical and systemic agenda for climate policy along these lines had begun to emerge in 2019, especially in the form of the proposed 'Green New Deal'. A key aspect of this is the deepening contradiction in the economy between fossil fuels and the renewable economy, and growing divisions in finance capital as the political contradiction feeds into the logic of capital. We now turn to these themes, focusing especially on divisions centred on divestment, risk and disclosure.

Socializing climate risk?

Climate change and failing climate policy produces a process of political risk-making against fossil fuels, and for renewables (Gills & Morgan, 2020). Where once fossil fuels were understood to be an unquestioned economic asset, under climate change they are now increasingly being recast as a liability, as a 'stranded asset'. The shift from asset to liability is mainly driven by socio-political feedback from climate disruption into economic activity. The political feedback prefigures new governance arrangements, in terms of limiting fossil fuels, extending possibilities for renewables.

From 2009, with the failure of the UN Copenhagen summit, climate activists had become increasingly disenchanted with state-led global climate policy. Instead they sought to address the problem 'at source' and to target the global fossil fuel industry: instead of 'parts per million' the new focus was on 'unburnable carbon', a term coined by the NGO Carbon Tracker in 2011 (Carbon Tracker, 2011. Edwards, 2019).

Two key insights helped precipitate and focus this strategic shift. The first was the vitally important research published first in 2009 in *Nature*, that measured the emissions potential of existing fossil fuel reserves against the remaining global carbon budget for limiting global warming to 2°C above preindustrial levels (Meinshausen et al., 2009). This was then amplified and elaborated by Carbon Tracker (2011) and by the climate campaigner Bill McKibbon, who charted a new pathway for climate activism of targeting the fossil fuel sector as 'Public Enemy Number One' (2012). The data was elaborated still further in 2015 with detailed country-level obligations to ensure that a third of oil reserves, half of gas reserves and over 80 per cent of current coal reserves could be written-off (McGlade & Ekins, 2015). Related, and equally important, was the research from Heede in 2014, that focused on the sources of global emissions and found that sixty-five per cent of world emissions 1751–2010 had been produced by just ninety entities, two-thirds of which were corporations (Heede, 2014). This was elaborated in 2017 with the 'Carbon Majors Report' that found just 100 corporate and state entities were responsible for 71 per cent of emissions from 1988 when the IPCC was established, to 2015 (Griffin, 2017).

The new focus on the material process of emissions production drew the climate conflict into direct 'close combat' with some of the world's largest corporations and their economic allies (Foran, 2017; Princen et al., 2015). Halting fossil fuels and advancing renewables also opened the movement to new alliances, from communities affected by fossil fuels to renewable energy corporates, and gave it a new political impetus as an explicitly justice-centred movement (Jafry, 2019; Rosewarne et al., 2013). The key focus was on the fossil fuel corporation as the new global pariah.

Corporates were becoming increasingly sensitive to threat of climate regulation, and of investor or consumer strikes. Responses took the form of standard-setting 'benchmarks', climate pledges, or some form of voluntary code of conduct at corporate or sectoral level. A 2013 report from the US Congress noted the growing prevalence of these codes (Jackson, 2013), and a more recent survey tracked their emergence on climate and emissions reduction issues (Vandenbergh & Gilligan, 2017). This inter-corporate 'private' regulation is aimed at preventing state intervention and reflects the neoliberal doctrine of market rule-making (Cutler, 2003; Goodman, 2014; Soederberg, 2010). Yet with climate change intensifying these containment efforts can spill-over, in a dynamic that politicizes corporate decision-making and legitimizes state intervention.

Codes themselves are responses to regulatory failure and paradoxically demonstrate their own inadequacy. As Diller found in relation to labour codes, the principal benefit of corporate codes is in offering a 'means of leveraging public efforts' (Diller, 1999, p. 122). A similar lesson has emerged on climate issues, where corporates face a new vulnerability to climate reputation, which can translate into climate litigation (Ganguly et al., 2018; Setzer & Vanala, 2018). Strategic legal action is increasingly targeted at the more visible 'fossil fuel majors', and those that invest in them, for failure to adequately disclose and act on climate risks (Setzer & Brynes, 2019). We can observe the resulting socio-political pressure on corporate climate decision-making. The two aspects discussed here – divestment pressures and disclosure frameworks – are centred on generating precisely this kind of socio-political feedback.

Divestment campaigns

Corporate divestment campaigning has generally focused on particular corporates, rather than on a sector, and has not generally been used as a means of leveraging global governance. With fossil fuel divestment the approach has been adapted into a deliberate political strategy to enhance economic feedback from climate crisis into the corporate sector. Born in part of frustration with directly political mechanisms, divestment campaigning sought to build pressure for decarbonization within the wider economic system. At one level it promoted the naïve (and dangerous) assumption that ethical climate investment would reorient the economy. But strategically it has had a different purpose, of delegitimising the fossil fuel sector, delinking it from wider economic interests and enabling a more forceful policy response.

For its advocates fossil fuel divestment is conceived as a complement rather than an alternative to global climate policy. In 2013 an assessment of the climate divestment campaigns published by the

Oxford-based Stranded Assets Program concluded unequivocally that indirect impacts on the reputation of the fossil fuel sector, a 'stigmatisation process', were far more important than any direct impacts on investment flows: 'The process by which uncertainty surrounding the future of fossil fuel industry will increase is through stigmatisation. In particular, the fossil fuel divestment campaign will increase legislative uncertainty … '; this translated into a clear recommendation for campaigners, that 'direct impacts are likely to be minimal' and 'the campaign might be most effective in stigmatising the fossil fuel industry' (Ansar et al., 2013, pp. 71–73).

Reflecting its political strategy, the campaign targets institutions that have high public reputation, arguing their values prevent them from continuing to invest in fossil fuels. Religious and educational institutions, for instance, may have very little capital to withdraw from fossil fuel companies but, as they mobilize ethical claims, they can have a major public impact when they do so. Universities were an early focus, with student-led campaigns making gains on campuses beginning with Stanford in May 2014, extending to a lawsuit against Harvard, the world's richest university. The same pressures were then put on charitable bodies, local councils, and other public authorities, all seen as expressing public values and interests.

Reflecting its ideological impact the divestment campaign produced a political counter-response from fossil fuel corporates and allied governments. In Australia for instance Prime Minister Tony Abbott's defence of the coal industry as 'good for humanity' came in the wake of a decision at the Australian National University to divest (Cox, 2014). Revealingly, fossil fuel advocates have focused on the economic arguments, stating that fossil fuels will never become stranded as climate policy will never force a phase-out. The Independent Petroleum Association of America for instance has had a 'Divestment Facts' website highlighting 'the real cost of fossil fuel divestments', in terms of lost revenue to endowments (IPAA, 2020). The emphasis is on the strong economic returns to fossil fuel investments, predicted to continue with the ongoing failure of climate policy. Other defences include the claim that the fossil fuel export trade increases energy access and reduces energy poverty, along with accusations that divestment constitutes 'green imperialism' (Saunders, 2014). A further argument suggested that coal divestment activism deliberately distorts financial decision-making, offering the claim that 'stigmatisation is an assault on property rights' (Davidson, 2014).

The counter-arguments provide opportunities for intensified and more polarized debate between protagonists, forcing sharper public deliberation. Divestment, in this way, provokes a wider 'contest for legitimacy' (Ayling, 2017; Edwards, 2019). As the debate ranges further across institutions we can see a process of climate politicization extending across society. The material effects of divestment may be minor, but the ideological impacts, as recognized by the corporates themselves, can be extensive. As noted, this reflects movement aims, which are 'far more concerned with engaging in symbolic political action, raising consciousness, and shifting public opinion about climate change than they are with more pragmatic economic ends' (Ayling & Gunningham, 2017, p. 143). Here it is 'the political' sphere that drives the economic feedback, a process replicated in climate risk debates.

Risk and disclosure models

There has certainly been growing political feedback from climate into the economy – or at least the appearance of it – following the 2015 Paris Agreement. The creation of a global target of net zero emissions by 2050 rather than a temperature target, has created a timeline for a phase-out of the fossil fuel sector. The policy horizon has generated social and political risks in the present-day, and has led to the construction of various quasi-legal regulatory frameworks designed to help re-stabilise the legitimacy of the corporate sector in the face of pressures for divestment and decarbonization.

The sector most exposed to direct climate risks is arguably the insurance industry, yet even here the estimates are relatively low. Reinsurer Swiss RE for instance has stated climate disruption poses a serious threat: 'increased frequency and intensity of weather-related events, and also unforeseen changes in climate conditions and socio-economic developments, could bring the insurability of assets' (Swiss RE 2020, p. 26). It estimated economic losses from weather-related events had risen from an average of $90 billion in the 1980s to $270 billion in the 2010s. Yet this remains a small price to pay: Aramco had revenue of USD414 billion in 2018 and global fossil fuel revenue is estimated at USD3.7 trillion (Leitch, 2019). Political 'transition risk' appears to be much more substantial and pervasive.

In 2015, in anticipation of the Paris Agreement, a model for managing the growing climate policy risk was developed by the Mercer Group, a large US-based asset manager (not linked to the US conservative financier Robert Mercer) (Mercer Group, 2015). Mercer's model identified four risk factors: technology change; resource shortages; the impact of climate events; and policy risk in terms of climate policy (dubbed 'TRIP'). Their analysis of the four risks positioned policy as having the greatest impact across all sectors: climate policy, or in other words socio-political feedback, posed the greatest risk to rates of return and especially in the fossil fuel sector.

Equally significant, the Mercer report found that under the UN's minimum-necessary scenario of no more than 2°C warming, emissions reduction hinged on policy becoming the 'dominant climate change risk factor' (not technology, resources or impact) (Mercer, 2015, p. 95). On their schematic model, policy risk for the 2°C outcome was ten times more important than resource scarcity or direct climate impacts (with technology eight times more important). The 2019 'sequel' report made similar observations, creating a new set of risk factors: spending on transition, transition policy, climate change impacts and resource availability (Mercer, 2019). The 2015 study was funded by the World Bank with the UK and German Governments and, as noted in the 2019 sequel, was highly influential.

Also hard on the heels of the Paris Agreement, and on the initiative of the Bank of England, in 2015 the Financial Security Board of the Bank for International Settlements established a 'Task Force on Climate-related Financial Disclosures' (TCFD). This broadly reflected the Mercer report. The intent was to prevent a financial-climate meltdown though a pre-emptive 'repricing' of risk: the TCFD goal is that 'risks and opportunities will be more accurately priced, allowing for the more efficient allocation of capital and contributing to a more orderly transition to a low-carbon economy' (TCFD, 2019, p. v). The solution reflects recommendations following the financial crisis of 2008–2009, where the British Academy (in response to a query from the monarch) put faith in assessing 'risk to the system' with 'a new, shared horizon-scanning capability' (Besley & Hennessy, 2009, p. 10). Risk-scanning was deemed the cure-all once again.

Yet, climate risk assessment is by necessity highly contingent – as mainly an assessment of social and political 'transition risk'. Under the TCFD's final recommendations, 'climate-related risks and financial impacts' are categorized into 'transition risk' and 'physical risk', with transition risks encompassing a wide range of aspects, including policy and litigation, emerging climate technologies and resulting substitution, market risks and consumer behaviour, and reputational risks. Physical risks are much more restricted, in terms of weather variability, changed rainfall patterns and the rising sea level. The TCFD judged the physical risks as currently 'acute' but 'event-driven'; only in the longer-term would physical risks become 'chronic' (TCFD, 2017a).

Equally significant, the TCFD recommended the adoption of climate targets, stating that these should be 'in line with anticipated regulatory requirements or market constraints or other goals'; they required details on whether the target is absolute or intensity-based, time frames and base year, with performance indicators and how they are calculated (TCFD, 2017b, p. 19). In 2019 the

TCFD reported that 40 per cent of the world's largest companies by sector had adopted such targets for emissions reduction, mainly based on anticipated policy regulation (TCFD, 2019). The TCFD initiative appears to have spilled-over into various contexts, with numerous international finance services sector organizations developing their own mechanisms, including reserve banks, stock exchange bodies, prudential insurance, accounting and auditing standards bodies (as outlined in TCFD, 2019).

The five leading private investors in fossil fuels, J.P. Morgan, Wells Fargo, Citi, Bank of America and the Royal Bank of Canada, had all signed up to the TCFD, yet together had together invested $960 billion in fossil fuels in the three years after the Paris agreement (2016–2019) (Banktrack, 2020). Several participated in the UNEP Finance Initiative and had issued statements in support of the Paris Agreement. Disclosure remained opaque, though in March 2020 several of leading banks – Wells Fargo, Goldman Sachs, Morgan Stanley and Bank of America – announced they would undertake carbon footprint analysis for their investments. National reserve banks, such as the Bank of England, had begun assessing national economic exposure to fossil fuels, in terms extraction or power generation, estimating the extent of change required (Bank of England, 2020, p. 21). In early 2020 some less-exposed banks made commitments to halve fossil fuel investments by 2030 (Lloyds and Royal Bank of Scotland) (Banktrack, 2020).

None of these measures are in any way adequate to the challenge posed by climate change – or even to meet the requirements of the Paris Agreement. The 2020 Banktrack report stipulated that financiers had to 'Prohibit all financing for all fossil fuel expansion projects' and 'commit to phase out all financing for fossil fuel extraction and infrastructure, on an explicit timeline that is aligned with limiting global warming to 1.5°C' (Banktrack, 2020, p. 84). None of the large players have signed up to this. Despite the lauded disclosure initiatives there is zero evidence that fossil fuel investment has slowed since the Paris Agreement. Further, it is important to be alive to the perverse effects of a change of rhetoric, in terms of managing corporate legitimacy, and further legitimizing and entrenching fossil fuels. That said, these developments certainly demonstrate 'feedback' and the centrality of political and social risks in driving it.

Conclusions

In 2019 the Queensland State Government approved a new coalmine, opening up a new mining region in the Galilee Basin in Northern Australia. Several mining companies were queued-up to exploit the region's 7750 million tonnes of coal, which if approved would extract 300 million tonnes each year, equivalent to about 700 million tonnes of Greenhouse gas emissions annually (Steffen, 2015). The initial mine was relatively small, to be run by the Adani India-based conglomerate, and had been strongly opposed by a national 'Stop Adani' campaign.

The company may have assumed that the State approval would settle the matter. A direct action movement aiming to physically prevent the mine going ahead would have been expected – but not the high-profile corporate campaign that unfolded, which sought to target every company that sought to work with Adani, calling on them to sever ties with the mine. The fossil fuel campaign group 'Market Forces' ran a campaign that persuaded sixteen insurance companies, thirty-seven international banks, twelve construction firms and two out of three coal haulage firms to boycott the project (Market Forces, 2020). When the Australian arm of the German engineering firm Siemens signed a contract with the Adani mine a wave of action erupted in Germany, and is on-going.

The Adani case demonstrates a wider dynamic as global investment funds have come under pressure to disinvest from fossil fuel projects (see Global Witness, 2019; Influence Map, 2019).

Black Rock, for instance, the worlds largest asset manager with USD7 trillion invested, was a target for several years. In January 2020 the Black Rock CEO Larry Fink announced in a letter to companies that Black Rock believed climate risks had become investor risks (Fink, 2020). In response, Black Rock would itself divest from coal-fired power and would require companies to plan for emissions reduction 'for operating under a scenario where the Paris Agreement's goal of limiting global warming to less than two degrees is fully realized'.

The letter is remarkable in its certainty that a dramatic global exit from fossil fuels, a 'fundamental reshaping of finance', was imminent. Black Rock had revealed that climate change was 'almost invariably the top issue' for investors, who were concerned at 'both the physical risks associated with climate change as well as the ways that climate policy will impact prices, costs, and demand across the entire economy' (Fink, 2020). Bill McKibbon called it a 'watershed moment in climate history' (McKibbon, 2020). Observers noted the decision was a long time coming: fossil fuel energy stocks had been depressed for a decade (NY Times, 2020); campaigners intensified efforts, highlighting how climate was still not being addressed by the company, despite its rhetoric (Black Rock's Big Problem, 2020).

From the Galilee basin in central Queensland to the hallowed halls of global finance these developments demonstrate just how far the process of delegitimising fossil fuels has come. In the decade since the 'Carbon Bubble' data was first released and popularized by Carbon Tracker, the global fossil fuel industry has been forced into pariah status. The shift, as outlined here, is multi-level and multi-faceted, reflecting the ubiquity of fossil capital in the history and development of capitalist societies (Malm, 2016).

The process of politicizing fossil fuels, and socializing the process of establishing a renewable economy, is certainly hard-fought and on-going. It is an existential battle – for fossil fuel corporates, but also for the wider society, and one that has unfolded against all the systemic pressures to maintain 'business as usual'. As is clear from this article, and in the context of the other contributions to the special forum, addressing the challenges of the climate and ecological emergency must overcome the limits and barriers of mainstream economics. As we have argued, it is the process of political and social mobilization and the associated strategy and action that has forced something of a reckoning for fossil fuels. To date there is still no meaningful corporate shift to decarbonization; the resulting spill-over into concerted state action, for a fossil fuel phase-out and for a Green New Deal, is already underway, pointing not just to decarbonization but also to a much wider socialization process, beyond capitalism 'as we know it'.

Disclosure statement

No potential conflict of interest was reported by the author(s).

ORCID

James Goodman ⓘ http://orcid.org/0000-0003-3211-3416

References

Anderson, J., & Goodman, J. (2020). Crises of capital and climate: Three contradictions and prospects for contestation. In S. A. Hamed Hosseini, J. Goodman, S. C. Motta, & B. K. Gills (Eds.), *Routledge handbook of transformative global studies* (pp. 58–68). Routledge.

Anderson, J., & Shuttleworth, I. (2020, July 8). Fiction and political ecology in a time of crisis. *The Ecologist*

Ansar, A., Caldecott, B., & Tilbury, J. (2013). *Stranded assets and the fossil fuel divestment campaign: What does divestment mean for the valuation of fossil fuel assets?* Stranded Assets Program, Smith School of Enterprise and the Environment.

Aranof, K., Ballasoni, A., Cohen, D., & Riofrancos, T. (2019). *A planet to win: Why we need a green new deal*. Verso.

Aykut, S., Foyer, J., & Morena, E. (Eds.). (2017). *Globalising the climate. COP21 and the climatisation of global debates*. Routledge.

Ayling, J. (2017). A contest for legitimacy: The divestment movement and the fossil fuel industry. *Law and Policy, 39*(4), 349–371. https://doi.org/10.1111/lapo.12087

Ayling, J., & Gunningham, N. (2017). Non-state governance and climate policy: The fossil fuel divestment movement. *Climate Policy, 17*(2), 131–149. https://doi.org/10.1080/14693062.2015.1094729

Bank of England. (2020). *The Bank of England's climate-related financial disclosure 2020.*

Banktrack. (2020). *Banking on climate change: Fossil fuel finance report 2020.*

Besley, B., & Hennessy, T. (2009). The global financial crisis – why didn't anybody notice? *British Academy Review, 14*, 9–10.

Black Rock's Big Problem. (2020, July 15). *Black rock falls short on 2020 climate votes*. Retrieved August 5, 2020 from www.blackrocksbigproblem.com

Cabello, J., & Gilbertson, T. (Eds.). (2015). *Paths beyond Paris: Movements, action and solidarity towards climate justice*. Corner House.

Carbon Tracker. (2011). *Unburnable carbon: Are the world's financial markets carrying a carbon bubble?.*

Carney, M. (2015). *Breaking the tragedy of the horizon: Climate change and financial stability*. Governor of the Bank of England.

Cohen, G., Jalles, J., Loungani, P., & Marto, R. (2018). *The long-run decoupling of emissions and output Evidence from the largest emitters*. IMF Working Paper, Washington.

Cox, L. (2014, October 15). Tony Abbott attacks ANU's "stupid decision" to dump fossil fuel investments. *Sydney Morning Herald.*

Cutler, C. (2003). *Private power and global authority: Transnational merchant law in the global political economy*. Cambridge University Press.

Davidson, S. (2014). *A critique of the coal divestment campaign*. Minerals Council of Australia.

Diller, J. (1999). A social conscience in the global marketplace? Labour dimensions of codes of conduct, social labelling and investor initiatives. *International Labour Review, 138*(2), 99–102. https://doi.org/10.1111/j.1564-913X.1999.tb00062.x

Edwards, G. (2019). Coal and climate change. *WIRES Climate, 10*(5), 1–10. https://doi.org/10.1002/wcc.607

Fink, L. (2020, January 14). A fundamental reshaping of finance. *Letter to CEOs*. Retrieved August 5, 2020 from www.blackrock.com

Foran, J. (2017). Reimagining radical climate justice. In P. Wapner & H. Elbver (Eds.), *Reimagining climate change* (pp. 150–170). Routledge.

Foster, J. (2019). On fire this time. *Monthly Review, 71*(6), 1–17. https://doi.org/10.14452/MR-071-06-2019-10_1

Ganguly, G., Setzer, J., & Heyvaert, V. (2018). If at first you don't succeed: Suing corporations for climate change. *Oxford Journal of Legal Studies, 38*(4), 841–868. https://doi.org/10.1093/ojls/gqy029

Gills, B., & Morgan, J. (2020). Global climate emergency: After COP24, climate science, urgency, and the threat to humanity. *Globalizations, 17*(6), 885–902. https://doi.org/10.1080/14747731.2019.1669915

Global Carbon Project. (2019). *Global energy growth is outpacing decarbonisation.*

Global Witness. (2019). *Overexposed: How the IPCC's 1.5°C report demonstrates the risks of overinvestment in oil and gas.*

Goodman, J. (2014). New spheres of global authority: Non-state actors and private international law. In M. Steger, P. Battersby, & J. Siracusa (Eds.), *Sage handbook of globalisation* (pp. 560–578). Sage.

Goodman, J., Connor, L., & Ghosh, D. (2020). *Beyond the coal rush: A turning point for global energy and climate policy?* Cambridge University Press.

Griffin, M. (2017). *Carbon majors report.* CDP and Climate Accountability Institute.

Harvey, D. (2015). *Seventeen contradictions and the end of capitalism.* Oxford University Press.

Heede, R. (2014). Tracing anthropogenic carbon dioxide and methane emissions to fossil fuel and cement producers, 1854–2010. *Climatic Change, 122*(1–2), 229–241. https://doi.org/10.1007/s10584-013-0986-y

Hulme, M. (2010). Mapping climate knowledge: An editorial essay. *Wiley Interdisciplinary Reviews of Climate Change, 1*(1), 1–8. https://doi.org/10.1002/wcc.3

Independent Petroleum Association of America (IPAA). (2020). *Divestment facts.* Retrieved July 27, from https://divestmentfacts.com/about/

Influence Map. (2019). *Asset managers and climate change.*

Jackson, J. (2013). *Codes of conduct for multinational corporations: An overview.* Report for Congress, Congressional Research Service.

Jafry, T. (Ed.). (2019). *Routledge handbook of climate justice.* Routledge.

Leitch, D. (2019, April 24). Globe watch: $US3.7 trillion a year of fossil fuel revenue has to go away. *Renew Economy.* Retrieved August 5, 2020, from www.reneweconomy.com.au

Mackie, D., & Murray, J. (2020). *Risky business: The climate and the macroeconomy* (Special Report). J.P. Morgan. Retrieved July 27, 2020, from www.rebellion.earth

Malm, A. (2016). *Fossil capital.* Verso.

Mann, G., & Wainwright, J. (2018). *Climate leviathan: A political theory of our planetary future.* Verso.

Market Forces. (2020). *The adani list.* Retrieved July 27, from www.marketforces.org.au

McGlade, C., & Ekins, P. (2015). The geographical distribution of fossil fuels unused when limiting global warming to 2°C. *Nature, 517*(7533), 187–190. https://doi.org/10.1038/nature14016

McKibben, B. (2012, August 2). Global warming's terrifying new math. *Rolling Stone,* pp. 1–11.

McKibbon, B. (2020, January 16). Citing climate change Black Rock will move away from fossil fuels. *New Yorker.*

Meinshausen, M., Meinshausen, N., Hare, W., Raper, S. C. B., Frieler, K., Knutti, R., Frame, D. J., & Allen, M. R. (2009). Greenhouse-gas emission targets for limiting global warming to 2°C. *Nature, 458*(7242), 1158–1163. https://doi.org/10.1038/nature08017

Mercer Group. (2015). *Investing in a time of climate change.*

Mercer Group. (2019). *Investing in a time of climate change: The sequel.*

Moore, J. (2015). *Capitalism in the web of life.* Verso.

Moore, J. (Ed.). (2016). *Anthropocene or capitalocene?* PM Press.

NY Times. (2020, January 14). Black Rock C.E.O. Larry Fink: Climate crisis will reshape finance. *New York Times,* Dealmaker Blog. Retrieved August 6, 2020, from www.nytimes.com

O'Connor, J. (1998). *Natural causes: Essays in ecological Marxism.* Guilford Press.

Princen, T., Manno, J., & Martin, P. (Eds.). (2015). *Ending the fossil fuel era.* MIT Press.

Rosewarne, S., Goodman, J., & Pearse, R. (2013). *Climate upsurge: The ethnography of climate movement politics.* Routledge.

Saunders, A. (2014, August 28). Whitehaven coal boss lashes "green imperialism". *Sydney Morning Herald.*

Setzer, J., & Brynes, R. (2019). *Global trends in climate change litigation: 2019 snapshot* (Policy Report). Grantham Research Institute.

Setzer, J., & Vanala, L. (2018). Climate change litigation: A review of research on courts and litigants in climate governance. *WIRES Climate Change*, 22, 1–19. https://doi.org/10.1002/wcc.580

Soederberg, S. (2010). *Corporate power and ownership in contemporary capitalism.* Routledge.

Steffen, W. (2015). *Galilee basin: Unburnable coal.* Climate Council.

Steffen, W., Rockström, J., Richardson, K., Lenton, T. M., Folke, C., Liverman, D., Summerhayes, C. P., Barnosky, A. D., Cornell, S. E., Crucifix, M., Donges, J. F., Fetzer, I., Lade, S. J., Scheffer, M., Winkelmann, R., & Schellnhuber, H. J. (2018). Trajectories of the earth system in the anthropocene. *Proceedings of the National Acdemy of Sciences*, *115*(33), 8252–8259. https://doi.org/10.1073/pnas.1810141115

Swiss RE. (2020). *Natural catastrophes in times of economic accumulation and climate change, sigma 2.*.

TCFD. (2017a). *Recommendations of the task force on climate-related financial disclosures.*

TCFD. (2017b). *Implementing the recommendations of the task force on climate-related financial disclosures.*

TCFD. (2019). *Task force on climate-related financial disclosures: Status report.*

United Nations Environment Program (UNEP). (2019). *Emissions gap report.*

Vandenbergh, M., & Gilligan, J. (Eds.). (2017). *Beyond politics: The private governance response to climate.* Cambridge University Press.

The regenerative turn: on the re-emergence of reciprocity embedded in living ecologies

Jonas Egmose ⓘ, Stefan Gaarsmand Jacobsen, Henrik Hauggaard-Nielsen ⓘ and Lars Hulgård

As the introduction to this collection suggests, many of the collected essays identify problems and challenges rooted in orthodoxies (see Gills & Morgan, 2020). Concomitantly, what is yet to be learned in the context of globalized extractivism, and teetering on the edge of the abyss of biodiversity loss and climate change, is that crisis cannot be met by adapting to its consequences whilst replicating its root causes. While discourses of transformational change reflect an awakening to this challenge, we still seem blind to the fact that what we are facing is a truly plural and interconnected crisis, named by its multiple symptoms: the climate – (IPCC, 2019); ecological – (IPBES, 2019); economic – (Piketty, 2013); and even – and perhaps most essentially – epistemological crisis (Santos, 2008).

These interconnected indicators cannot be separated from the results of historical and structural ecological impoverishment (Bonneuil & Fressoz, 2017; IPBES, 2019). At the core of the plural crisis, we see not only the destruction of human and ecological livelihoods but also the erosion (Negt, 1984) of our human and societal sense of being members of societies and embedded in ecologies. The crisis (or convergent crises) does not merely concern an outer environment (Sachs, 2010). Essentially, it is of relations between humans and their wider ecologies: in human, social and ecological relations constituting those living livelihoods we are inherently part of; the way we understand and conceptualize these relations; and in the way, we organize ourselves embedded in these. More than anything the plural crisis calls for cultural renewal in terms of understanding how we are related; attentiveness towards the ecologies in which we are embedded; and the very nature of human engagement.

It is in this particular context we draw attention towards what we currently see as a 'regenerative turn' re-emerging in the margins of industrialized farming and consumption, which might imply shifts from historical notions of mastery and extraction towards renewed attentiveness and human engagement. Fuelled by the technological development within mechanization, fertilizer and pesticide use, industrialized food production has grown bigger than ever. Concurrently a self-reinforcing decline in soil organic matter, through the interplay of human and natural processes (Rockström et al., 2009), has reduced natural capital at a speed never seen before (Steffen et al., 2018). This development, we argue, can be understood as somatic extractivism exploiting natural resources in close conjuncture with modern industrialism (Fraser & Jaeggi, 2018) and with increasing global inequality (Piketty, 2013). In contrast, and for centuries, traditional farmers have managed diverse self-sufficient and self-regulating locally adapted agriculture with ingenious practices that often result in both community food security and the conservation of agrobiodiversity (Altieri, 2004). It is such practices often associated with the so-called global South, which we now see as a regenerative turn in the so-called global North. This is the case in the field of agriculture where practices of agroecology, permaculture and regenerative farming emerges (Ferguson & Lovell, 2014; Soto et al., 2020; Wezel et al., 2015). These pay greater attention to the inherent capacity of living ecologies to regenerate through diversity and reciprocity in human-nature relations. This renewal is the case in democratic urban and rural counter-movements challenging the way we inhabit the ecologies in which we are embedded (Fadaee, 2017; Martinez-Alier et al., 2016). It is the case in new cooperative forms of organization challenging existing value chains through solidarity economy and food sovereignty, with the transformative potential to reconnect, what has being disconnected: the relation between rural and urban, food production and consumption, through mutual and direct principles of organization (Gliessman et al., 2019).

Reconnection, however, equally implies altering practices and epistemological transformations. While Western science has provided the foundation for industrialized practices, Northern epistemology has equally served as the knowledge part of global colonization (Santos, 2008). Distinctions regarding what counts as valid knowledge follow the hegemony of deeming certain practices, types of production and entire cultures irrelevant, including how they interact with soil and land. Since the seventeenth century scientific revolution, major sciences have built on dualistic Cartesian division between humans and nature. Fuelled by the aspiration of freeing humans from nature, the division has encouraged ideas of complete mastery over nature. With the increasing specialization of scientific disciplines, the ambition of steering, controlling and manipulating physical processes has intensified despite intermittent reactions (Bonneuil & Fressoz, 2017). The Cartesian *cogito ergo sum* remains emblematic for the extractivist position in the sense that the monopoly of thought provides human beings with the right and the means to control and master. Early critical theory's critique of the dialectics of enlightenment (Adorno & Horkheimer, 1944) establishes that the human aspiration of enlightenment through rational thinking inherently implies barbarous potential in the context of mastery of human, cultural and ecological relations. Monopolizing thought in enlightenment thinking implies the power to define who and what should count. For Locke the human ability to change nature through labour served to signify what should count as property and what should count as waste, implying that nature without alteration through human labour was wasteful (Wenzel, 2016). Hence, the foundation of mastery and extractivism is truly epistemological, neglecting that we are embedded in living ecologies, which humans have the capacity to destroy and to let live (Elhacham et al., 2020; IPBES, 2019). Thus, we stand at a crossroad and need to re-negotiate the way in which we live in the world. To engage in a process of re-negotiating, epistemological foundations may cause much anxiety among scholars, since many concepts, theories and even entire philosophy of sciences, which we have taken for granted, cannot be exempted from this process of re-negotiation. We need to re-address what has become absent and suppressed by hegemonic forms of 'development' and re-approach practices that may appear to be new, but are, in fact, drawing upon practices and knowledges that could re-emerge when interacting with the movement of counter-hegemonic globalization (Santos, 2008).

As stated by ecofeminist academics (Plumwood, 1993) we will argue that what has effectively become invisibilized is the basic regenerative capacity of the living, and the ways we are embedded in living ecologies through multiple entanglements. Through the combination of scientific reductionism and systemic thinking, mastery of nature was brought into modern environmentalism, being able to monitor but struggling to safeguard the emergent capacities of the living to be sustained. Thus, modernist environmentalism has been left in a paradox. The ever-advancing strategies of monitoring, modelling and protecting Earth's environments always seem one step behind the continual and cumulative forces leading to ecological destruction. The epistemological challenge is firstly to renegotiate understandings of the inherent regenerative capacity of the living, and secondly to redefine our human relational engagement with the living in ways, which might enable living ecologies to sustain.

How can we understand the inherent capacity of the living to regenerate? Over the last decade, the notion of resilience has attracted increasing attention amongst scholars. This spans the political, social and environmental sciences and conceptualizes an adaptive capacity to resist outer pressure for everything from the atmosphere, organizations, to cities and agriculture as eco-systems (Folke, 2006). Not surprisingly, this 'resilience' concept has gained popularity in the context of the climate crisis, given its promise to withstand environmental disasters. For example, in the context of farming, shifting from sole cropping to crop-diversification, which counters the current commercial cultivars that narrow the genetic base, is a well-known strategy. It offers productive, diversified and resilient agroecological cropping systems less dependent on external inputs than current systems (Brooker et al., 2015). However, while the concept of resilience importantly draws attention to the inherent capacity to regenerate, its epistemological foundation in system thinking risks neglecting the ontological relatedness of embedded living ecologies. Where this is so, demands to master, cope and securitize are reproduced for everything from high-carbon urban lifestyles to unsustainable agriculture (Blythe et al., 2018; Dalby, 2013). What we can learn from resilience thinking is that an essential feature of the living is the inherent regenerative capacity to sustain. But we need to transcend the epistemological boundaries of systems thinking in order to acknowledge the ways in which we are not only detached from but also truly *embedded in* living ecologies. This requires relational epistemologies, which acknowledge the indefinite entanglements of the living.

Understanding everything as related is obviously not an easy task for evermore specialized scientific disciplines. These acquire analytical strength and political power by setting up self-evident ontological boundaries, which serve also to constitute themselves. In a broader historical perspective, therefore, it should be of great interest, how plural attempts are currently emerging to re-invent our very thinking, language and methods. This plurality searches beyond contemporary epistemologies for qualitatively different ways of understanding ourselves and our entanglements with the world.

Within academia, the search is not least the case in recent ecofeminist and ecological thinking. This thinking transcends traditional scientific disciplines across ecology and humanities, re-negotiating possible ways in which humans are interweaved in the 'more-than human' (Haraway, 2016). New flat ontologies, however, will not do the job if they overlook that everything is not only related, but also structured (Bonneuil & Fressoz, 2017). Humans can act and exert changes on nature, ecosystems and communities both in regenerative and extractivist ways (Hornborg, 2017; Malm, 2020). The challenge is not to find renewed strategies for mastery and extraction in a post-apocalyptic world. The task is to find ways in which we can actually practise living in ways that make other worlds possible for the living to sustain (Gibson-Graham et al., 2013; Roelvink et al., 2015). This task is not to be confused with the abstract language of securing eco-system services or a safe operating space for humanity (Rockström et al., 2009). Rather it implies not only finding new languages, but also enabling, reinventing and learning from real practices, demonstrating that relations beyond mastery and extractivism *are possible in practice* and in very concrete ways.

This is where we want to draw attention to the regenerative turn currently taking place in the organization of agriculture and food sovereignty. This, in turn, implies new cropping practices that, rather than constituting themselves primarily by principles of industrialized production systems, become more attentive to the living soil, and to experimentation with agricultural, cooperative and economic structures beyond extractivism. Clearly, potential pitfalls for regenerative thinking exist, but so do links between new ways of thinking across initiatives in the global South and (the global South in) the global North. Much might still to be learned for instance from indigenous philosophy and practices such as buen vivir, living well in harmony between nature and community (Morales et al., 2019) and how such thinking and practice can guide and transform current practices from the inside across the world.

A guiding principle must be to work *with people* in transitions and with democratic openness towards other ways of thinking. In very concrete ways transitions from extractivism and mastery have to be meaningful to people in their lives - citizens, practitioners, policy makers – for concrete, political and societal change to happen (Altieri & Rosset, 1996; Toffolini et al., 2017). In this context, a return to the meaning in, of, and attentiveness to the living soil, can serve as guide facilitating transition to new ways of organizing human practice. While the regenerative turn is a movement of practice, research can play important roles in enabling infrastructures for exchange of marginalized experience and consolidation of emerging knowledges.

This challenge readdresses the question of the character of humans engagement in living ecologies. As humans we are not only in the world, but always also in-relation with the world, hence our human freedom and responsibility. Such relationship, however, does not per se mean mastery. What we need, is to re-negotiate what reciprocity means. And ask: what human qualities characterize responsibility; carefulness; attentiveness? How can we translate such qualities across multiple practices, knowledges and contexts grasping entanglements of the living? Perhaps now is not the time for final answers, but rather to initiate and search for qualitatively new kinds of questions for the re-emergence of an embedded reciprocity in living ecologies.

Disclosure statement

No potential conflict of interest was reported by the author(s).

ORCID

Jonas Egmose ⓘ http://orcid.org/0000-0002-1090-253X
Henrik Hauggaard-Nielsen ⓘ http://orcid.org/0000-0001-8929-9691

References

Adorno, T., & Horkheimer, M. (1944). *Dialectic of enlightenment*. University of California Press.

Altieri, M. (2004). Linking ecologists and traditional farmers in the search for sustainable agriculture. *Frontiers in Ecology and the Environment*, *2*(1), 35–42. https://doi.org/10.1890/1540-9295(2004)002 [0035:LEATFI]2.0.CO;2

Altieri, M. A., & Rosset, P. (1996). Agroecology and the conversion of large-scale conventional systems to sustainable management. *International Journal of Environmental Studies*, *50*(3–4), 165–185. https://doi.org/10.1080/00207239608711055

Blythe, J., Silver, J., Evans, L., Armitage, D., Bennett, N. J., Moore, M.-L., Morrison, T. H., & Brown, K. (2018). The dark side of transformation: Latent risks in contemporary sustainability discourse. *Antipode*, *50*(5), 1206–1223. https://doi.org/10.1111/anti.12405

Bonneuil, C., & Fressoz, J. B. (2017). *The shock of the anthropocene: The earth, history and us*. Verso.

Brooker, R. W., Bennett, A. E., Cong, W.-F., Daniell, T. J., George, T.S., , Hallett, P. D., Hawes, C., Iannetta, P. P. M., Jones, H. G., Karley, A. J., Li, L., McKenzie, B. M., Pakeman, R. J., Paterson, E., Schöb., C., Shen., J., Squire, G., Watson, C. A., Zhang, C., ... White, P. J. (2015). Improving intercropping: A synthesis of research in Agronomy, Plant Physiology and Ecology. *New Phytologist 206*(1): 107–17. https://doi.org/10.1111/nph.13132.

Dalby, S. (2013). Biopolitics and climate security in the anthropocene. *Geoforum*, *49*, 184–192. https://doi.org/10.1016/j.geoforum.2013.06.013

Elhacham, E., Ben-uri, L., Grozovski, J., Bar-on, Y. M., & Milo, R. (2020). Global human-made mass exceeds all living biomass. *Nature*, *2019*. https://doi.org/10.1038/s41586-020-3010-5

Fadaee, S. (2017). Bringing in the south: Towards a global paradigm for social movement studies. *Interface: A Journal for and About Social Movements*, *9*(2), 45–60.

Ferguson, R. S., & Lovell, S. T. (2014). Permaculture for agroecology: Design, movement, practice, and worldview. A review. *Agronomy for Sustainable Development*, *34*(2), 251–274. https://doi.org/10.1007/s13593-013-0181-6

Folke, C. (2006). Resilience: The emergence of a perspective for social-ecological systems analyses. *Global Environmental Change*, *16*(3), 253–267. https://doi.org/10.1016/j.gloenvcha.2006.04.002

Fraser, N., & Jaeggi, R. (2018). *Capitalism. A conversation in critical theory*. Polity Press.

Gibson-Graham, J. K., Camaron, J., & Healy, S. (2013). *Take back the economy*. University of Minnesota Press.

Gills, B., & Morgan, J. (2020). Economics and climate emergency. *Globalizations*. https://doi.org/10.1080/14747731.2020.1841527.

Gliessman, S., Friedmann, H., & Howard, P. H. (2019). Agroecology and food sovereignty. *IDS Bulletin 50*(2): 91–110. https://doi.org/10.19088/1968-2019.120.

Haraway, D. (2016). *Staying with the trouble: Making Kin in the Chthulucene*. Duke University Press.

Hornborg, A. (2017). Artifacts have consequences, not agency: Toward a critical theory of global environmental history. *European Journal of Social Theory*, *20*(1), 95–110. https://doi.org/10.1177/1368431016640536

IPBES. (2019). *Global assessment report on biodiversity and ecosystem services of the intergovernmental science-policy platform on biodiversity and ecosystem services*.

IPCC. (2019). *Climate Change and Land: An IPCC special report on climate change, desertification, land degradation, sustainable land management, food security, and greenhouse gas fluxes in terrestrial ecosystems*.

Malm, A. (2020). *The progress of this storm nature and society in a warming world.* Verso Books.

Martinez-Alier, J., Temper, L., Del Bene, D., & Scheidel, A. (2016). Is there a global environmental justice movement? *The Journal of Peasant Studies, 43*(3), 731–755. https://doi.org/10.1080/03066150.2016.1141198

Morales, A., Spear, R., Ngoasong, M., & Sacchetti, S. (2019). Buen Vivir as an innovative development model. In S. Banerjee, S. Carney, & L. Hulgard (Eds.), *People-centered social innovation. Global perspectives on an emerging paradigm,* (pp. 128–55). Routledge.

Negt, O. (1984). *Lebendige Arbeit, Enteignete Zeit. Politiche Und Kulturelle Dimensinen Des Kampfes Um Die Arbeitszeit.* Campus.

Piketty, T. (2013). *Capital in the twenty-first century.* Haward University Press.

Plumwood, V. (1993). *Feminism and the mastery of nature.* Routledge.

Rockström, J., Steffen, W., Noone, K., Persson, Å, Chapin, F. S., Lambin, E. F., Lenton, T. M., Scheffer, M., Folke, C., Schellnhuber, H. J., Nykvist, B., de Wit, C. A., Hughes, T., van der Leeuw, S., Rodhe, H., Sörlin, S., Snyder, P. K., Costanza, R., Svedin, U., ... Foley, J. A. (2009). A safe operation space for humanity. *Nature, 461*(7263), 472–475. https://doi.org/10.1038/461472a

Roelvink, G., St. Martin, K., & Gibson-Graham, J. K. (2015). *Making other worlds possible. Performing diverse economies.* University of Minnesota Press.

Sachs, W. (2010). Environment. In W. Sachs (Ed.), *Development dictionary. A guide to knowledge as power* (2nd ed., pp. 24–37). Zed Books.

Santos, B. D. S. (2008). *Another knowledge is possible: Beyond northern epistemologies.*

Soto, L., Padilla, R. C., & de Vente, J. (2020). Participatory selection of soil quality indicators for monitoring the impacts of regenerative agriculture on ecosystem services. *Ecosystem Services, 45*, Article 101157. https://doi.org/10.1016/j.ecoser.2020.101157

Steffen, W., Rockström, J., Richardson, K., Lenton, T. M., Folke, C., Liverman, D., Summerhayes, C. P., Barnosky, A. D., Cornell, S. E., Crucifix, M., Donges, J. F., Fetzer, I., Lade, S J., Scheffer, M., Winkelmann, R., & Schnellhuber, H. J. (2018). Trajectories of the earth system in the anthropocene. *Proceedings of the National Academy of Sciences of the United States of America, 115*(33), 8252–8259. https://doi.org/10.1073/pnas.1810141115

Toffolini, Q., Jeuffroy, M.-H., Mischler, P., Pernel, J., & Prost, L. (2017). Farmers' use of fundamental knowledge to re-design their cropping systems: Situated contextualisation processes. *NJAS – Wageningen Journal of Life Sciences, 80*, 37–47. https://doi.org/10.1016/j.njas.2016.11.004

Wenzel, J. (2016). Afterword: Improvement and overburden. *Postmodern Culture, 26*(2), 1–7. https://doi.org/10.1353/pmc.2016.0003

Wezel, A., Soboksa, G., McClelland, S., Delespesse, F., & Boissau, A. (2015). The blurred boundaries of ecological, sustainable, and agroecological intensification: A review. *Agronomy for Sustainable Development, 35*(4), 1283–1295. https://doi.org/10.1007/s13593-015-0333-y

The global climate of land politics

Jennifer C. Franco and Saturnino M. Borras, Jr

ABSTRACT
Land is a key input in economic production and production-waste sink. This links land to the causes of and responses to climate change. The dominant climate action ideas are based on the concept of 'land tenure security' which, in a global context marked by land-based inequities, means ratifying what already exists. This reinforces undemocratic social structures and institutions that themselves contribute to climate change. A restructuring of global land politics is called for, without which any analyses of and responses to climate change are at best superficial, and at worst, flawed and self-defeating. What is needed is to acknowledge the pervasive land-based social inequities in the world, and to end such inequities by pursuing a redistribution of a range of access to a range of land and resources in ways that categorically benefit the working people.

1. Introduction

Land is a key input in economic production and a dump or sink for the waste generated by production. It is directly associated with the causes of and responses to climate change, a substantial part of which is linked to agriculture and food, thereby implicating rural land politics. But the nature of the link between climate change and land is not uncontested. For example, a neoliberal notion of land as input in production and a sink for waste (World Bank, 2007) is fundamentally different from agroecology's perspective (Rosset & Altieri, 2017). Past reports by the Intergovernmental Panel on Climate Change (IPCC) touched on this issue, but generally focused on the biophysical aspect of the relationship. However, the 2019 IPCC special report, *Climate Change and Land*, broke new ground (IPCC, 2019). This report covers a wide range of themes, from biophysical to land tenure issues, and has bravely flagged the subject of global land grabs. This in itself is a huge accomplishment. But with this achievement come pitfalls. The report embraces 'land tenure security' as its principal framework for land-based climate change mitigation and adaptation, but it remains silent on what this actually means for land-based social relations in today's socially differentiated societies. This is a major Achilles' heel inasmuch as 'securing' land tenure in the context of high inequality is likely to become an exercise in ratifying what already exists, that is, interpreting and implementing the framework in a way that reinforces undemocratic social structures and institutions that also happen to significantly contribute to climate change.

Building consensus at the centre may be worthwhile under certain conditions. But a major problem today lies in the tendency of such a strategy to incorporate contested concepts by emptying them of class analysis and definition (Arsel, 2019). Class – along with co-constitutive social identities, especially gender, race/ethnicity, generation and religion – intersect and influence the causes, conditions and consequences of climate change and political responses to the climate crisis we are now facing. Without class analysis, how can one understand how climate change shapes – and is shaped by – decisions about who should control land, how much, where and for what purposes, and who must lose, or be denied, access? If our assumption is that land-based inequalities must be addressed, then it is 'redistributive land policy' – *not* 'land tenure security' – that becomes urgent and necessary. In societies marked by land-based inequities, land tenure security in the form of formalization of land claims *without* redistributive and restitutive content is likely to legitimize and reinforce inequities. Land tenure security through formalization of land claims per se is not problematical because it can result to real benefits for working poor people, but where this occurred in the absence of accompanying redistributive and restitutive policies the outcomes tend to be ad hoc and limited, and sometimes essentially a counter-reform. Inherently a class-relational approach, social justice-oriented redistributive land policy requires an understanding of the underlying class character and direction of the flow of change in social relations. Gaining land access or suffering land dispossession are not random or neutral social processes, unmarked by purposive political action and theories of social change. *In short, redistributive land policies necessarily include a component of land tenure security in the form of formalization of land claims and land titling, but stand-alone 'land tenure security' through formalization of land claim or land titling on its own does not necessarily and always have redistributive and restitutive substance.*

In the current context, the 'land tenure security' framing in the IPCC report is likely to be interpreted and implemented in a way that reinforces the very structures and institutions in land politics that contribute to climate change, such as capitalist intrusion into land frontiers resulting in forest clearing, and capitalist industrial and fossil energy-based monocrop plantations (Liao et al., 2021; Peluso & Lund, 2011; Rasmussen & Lund, 2018). Generalized conditions of precarious or non-existent land access, caused by capitalist market relations or extra-economic coercion, wars or disasters, make social justice-oriented redistributive land policies difficult yet unavoidable requirements for addressing climate change.

In the course of the twentieth century, far-reaching redistributive land policies were carried out across the world based on specific economic imperatives (Akram-Lodhi et al., 2007; de Janvry, 1981; Griffin et al., 2002; Kay, 2002a; Thiesenhusen, 1989), on political arguments such as ending violence (Fajardo, 2014; Kay, 2001), or to further democratization (Fox, 1990). These arguments remain urgent and relevant today, but have less political force despite the pressing need for such policies. A social justice-oriented strategy for combating climate change could be a powerful argument in support of redistributive land policies, but the current dominant narrative points in the opposite direction, undermining broad-based, genuinely democratic land policies.

This paper takes a critical look at the relationship between land and climate change politics partly by examining the 2019 IPCC land report. A basic assumption we have is that whether or not some rural people become vulnerable to climate change depends in part on their location in the spheres of production and social reproduction; and in the rural areas, access to land can be a decisive factor, where some may prosper while most others suffer pauperization amid severe climatic disruptions (see, e.g. Watts, 1983/2013). *Access* to land – that is, social relations and politics of land – is thus key in thinking about how to address climate change from a social justice perspective especially because a significant part of climate mitigation and adaptation ideas and actions require maintaining or reordering access to natural resources (land, forest, water). We argue that problems in access to land (lack of, diminished, or precarious access) are the dominant defining feature of contemporary rural land politics in the world, and this problem is exacerbated by climate actions that do not address the land question from a redistributive justice perspective. Prior and/or accompanying democratization of access to land are key to climate justice, but the current global climate in land policy is overwhelmingly against redistributive approaches. Policy perspectives that do not specify what they mean by 'land tenure security' are likely to be interpreted within the dominant non-redistributive framework, and are thus dangerous for rural working people. We construct our argument by mapping, historicizing and typologizing key currents in mainstream political stance on land policies, and what these imply for climate actions.

2. Land and climate change politics

There are three conceptual building blocks that, together, serve as the spine of our argument. First, the term 'land politics' is used here to refer to the land-based social relations between social classes and groups within society, and between the state and society, that are structured by formal and informal, state and non-state rules, procedures or norms, and the degrees of autonomy and capacity of actors to understand their situation and take actions to maintain or change it. State land policies are thus a small fraction of land politics; institutions through which working people access land are diverse: state and non-state, formal and informal, and the degree of autonomy and capacity of access land and derive benefit from it varies based on class, ethnicity, gender and generation (Ribot & Peluso, 2003). In land politics the concept of 'land tenure security' is highly contested: whose tenure and whose security, tenure security for what end? For example, the Vacant, Fallow and Virgin (VFV) Land Management Law of Myanmar calls for ordinary villagers to formally register their land claims purportedly to provide land tenure security. There are two less publicly spoken about implications of this process: (a) villagers who engage in shifting agriculture are unlikely to get registration for his/her full range of land, and at best, may get a small parcel suitable only for sedentary farming; (b) all lands that are not or cannot be claimed by the villagers are then claimed by the state, deemed as virgin, fallow and vacant land, and are then reallocated to corporate investors; or that, only the remaining lands after corporate investors took over vast tracts of lands were then opened up to land registration for ordinary villagers. So, the question is: whose tenure is it that was secured in this process? Land grabbing in Myanmar has been carried out through this legal mechanism loosely billed as a 'land tenure security' instrument by the government, and in constrast, labelled by autonomous civil society groups as the 'land grabbing law' (Franco & Borras, 2019; Ra et al., 2021).

Second, our paper is not about climate change per se; rather, it is about the politics of climate change. Building on earlier work (Borras et al., 2020, p. 2), we define climate change *politics* as:

> the dynamics operating in the spheres of social structures, institutions and political agency – namely, social relations; policies, treaties, laws, procedures, norms; projects, programs, narratives, ideas, advocacies, mobilizations and social movements, memories, rumors, or gossip – separately and collectively, among and between different social classes and groups within the state and in society that set and shape the meanings of climate change, its causes and consequences, how it can be addressed, by whom, where and when.

The definition separates, but at the same time binds together, politics and policies or projects – categories that are often muddled in the literature. Formally constituted and recognized climate change policies or projects are one of the components of climate change politics – the same relationship that land policies have to land politics. Labelled as climate change mitigation or adaptation measures, such policies and projects include 'Bio-energy with Carbon Capture and Storage'

(BECCS) as well as officially recognized big forest conservation projects and REDD+ (Corbera, 2012). But as many scholars working from political economy and political ecology perspectives (e.g. Paprocki, 2019) remind us these are not the only things that matter. Social relations of production and ecological and political conditions of nature (land, water, forest) could be significantly altered not only by climate change (e.g. droughts, floods) or formal climate change policies or projects, but also by wild speculations, rumours, gossip, spectacle or frenzy inspired or triggered by measures purported to address climate change. For example, many land brokers and speculators who have orchestrated the grabbing of land from ordinary villagers in diverse societies during the past decade have carried out their schemes by invoking the urgent need to address climate change through large-scale investments such as opening a plantation to cultivate feedstock for biofuel production – whether biofuel production actually takes place, is seriously planned, or is only wildly speculated (Fairhead et al., 2012; Franco & Borras, 2019; Hunsberger et al., 2017).

Looking at climate change politics means subjecting climate change mitigation and adaptation narratives and practices to a reality check. It allows for a politicized and historicized analysis of social processes, the evolution of climate change mitigation and adaptation, and social class relations, and a scrutiny of terminologies such as 'vulnerability' and 'scarcity' (following Ribot 2014; Scoones et al., 2019). In our definition, climate change politics can be crudely categorized as progressive or regressive. By progressive climate change politics we mean 'those social dynamics that shape the meanings of climate change, its causes and consequences, how it can be addressed, by whom, where and when in ways that advance "agrarian justice" and "climate justice", separately and together' (Borras et al., 2020, p. 2).[1] By regressive climate change politics we refer to 'social and political processes that block, undermine or reverse advocacy for or gains in progressive climate change politics' (Borras et al., 2020, p. 2).

Third, the principal accomplishment of the 2019 IPCC land report lies in putting together ground-breaking knowledge on the biophysical, agroecological, technical and management dimensions of the link between climate change and land. But the link between climate change and land is also inherently political, a reality that does not come out sufficiently clear enough in IPCC reports. For example, reduced annual rainfall in a microregion is likely to have a differential impact upon socially differentiated communities engaged in the spheres of agriculture and food production, circulation, exchange and consumption, where some are likely to lose out and become impoverished while a handful of others may accelerate and expand capital accumulation (see e.g. Watts, 1983, 2013, Ch. 7). An extreme weather disturbance might expel fisher-farmers from their land near the seashore, while a real estate and hotel conglomerate grabs their land (Uson, 2017). It is not uncommon for ordinary poor people to lose their productive assets (access to land, forest, herd, house) not because of the extreme weather disturbance itself, but because of coercion deployed by the state and powerful elites who take advantage of the disaster – what Klein (2007) calls 'disaster capitalism'.

3. Land tenure in the IPCC land report: one step forward?

The extent to which the 2019 IPCC *Climate Change and Land* report addresses the *political dimension* of land and its link to climate change is encouraging albeit limited. The concentrated discussion on 'land tenure' is to be found in one section of Chapter 7, or six pages of this nearly 900-page report, with the bulk of the discussion in a tabulated format (Table 7.7). We present its highlights not randomly, but selecting what we feel to be relevant to our discussion.

For a report of IPCC to claim that there is global 'land grabbing' – using this politically loaded term – demonstrates courage, and is laudable. It is probably one of the most significant elements of the report because it brings the conversation right into the very heart of global land politics. The IPCC report states:

> Understanding of land tenure under climate change also has to take account of the growth in large-scale land acquisitions (LSLAs), also referred to as land-grabbing, in developing countries ... Land grabs ... are often driven by direct collaboration of politicians, government officials and land agencies ... involving corruption of governmental land agencies, failure to register community land claims and illegal land uses and lack of the rule of law and enforcement in resource extraction frontiers ... The literature expresses different views on whether these acquisitions concern marginal lands or lands already in use ... Land-grabbing is associated with and may be motivated by the acquisition of rights to water, and erosion of those rights for other users .... (IPCC, 2019, p. 750)

In response to the requirements of climate change mitigation and adaptation that have relevance to land, and partly in recognition of global land grabs as a key context, the IPCC report summarizes its essential points on land tenure, pointing out the way forward, as follows:

> Land tenure systems have implications for both adaptation and mitigation, which need to be understood within specific socio-economic and legal contexts, and may themselves be impacted by climate change and climate action (*limited evidence, high agreement*). Land policy (in a diversity of forms beyond focus on freehold title) can provide routes to land security and facilitate or constrain climate action, across cropping, rangeland, forest, fresh-water ecosystems and other systems. Large-scale land acquisitions are an important context for the relations between tenure security and climate change, but their scale, nature and implications are imperfectly understood. (IPCC, 2019, p. 677)

> Insecure land tenure affects the ability of people, communities and organisations to make changes to land that can advance adaptation and mitigation (*medium confidence*). Limited recognition of customary access to land and ownership of land can result in increased vulnerability and decreased adaptive capacity (*medium confidence*). Land policies (including recognition of customary tenure, community mapping, redistribution, decentralisation, co-management, regulation of rental markets) can provide both security and flexibility response [*sic*] to climate change (*medium confidence*). (IPCC, 2019, p. 29)

The report also emphasizes the issue of indigenous peoples and customary land tenure, and the lack of formal registration of these lands, stating that, 'Agricultural practices that include indigenous and local knowledge can contribute to overcoming the combined challenges of climate change, food security, biodiversity conservation, and combating desertification and land degradation (*high confidence*)' (IPCC, 2019, p. 31). Furthermore: 'around 521 million ha of forest land is estimated to be legally owned, recognised, or designated for use by indigenous and local communities as of 2017 ... In 2005 only 1% of land in Africa was legally registered' (IPCC, 2019, p. 749). It goes on:

> Much of the world's carbon is stored in the biomass and soil on the territories of customary landowners, including indigenous people ... making securing of these land tenure regimes vital in land and climate protection. These lands are estimated to hold at least 293 GtC of carbon, of which around one-third (72 GtC) is located in areas where indigenous peoples and local communities lack formal recognition of their tenure rights. (IPCC, 2019, p. 749)

These policy assumptions and implications are broad; they are made somewhat more specific in the tabulated format (IPCC, 2019, pp. 751–752: Table 7.7), the highlights of which are as follows:

> *Assumption:* Insecure land rights are one factor deterring adaptation and accentuating vulnerability. Specific dimensions of inequity in customary systems may act as constraints on adaptation in different

contexts. LSLAs may be associated with monoculture and other unsustainable land use practices, have negative consequences for soil degradation and disincentivize more sustainable forms of agriculture.

Implications: Secure land rights, including through customary systems, can incentivize farmers to adopt long-term climate-smart practices, e.g. planting trees in mixed cropland/forest systems. Landscape governance and resource tenure reforms at farm and community levels can facilitate and incentivize planning for landscape management and enable the integration of adaptation and mitigation strategies.

Assumption: Land tenure security can lead to improved adaptation outcomes, but land tenure policy for forests that focuses narrowly on cultivation has limited ability to reduce ecological vulnerability or enhance adaptation. Secure rights to land and forest resources can facilitate efforts to stabilize shifting cultivation and promote more sustainable resource use if appropriate technical and market support are available.

Implications: Land tenure insecurity has been identified as a key driver of deforestation and land degradation leading to loss of sinks and creating sources of greenhouse gases. While land tenure systems interact with land-based mitigation actions in complex ways, forest decentralization and community co-management have shown considerable success in slowing forest loss and contributing to carbon mitigation. Communal tenure systems may lower transaction costs for REDD+ schemes, though with risk of elite capture of payments.

Assumption: Many pastoralists in lands at risk from desertification do not have secure land tenure, and erosion of traditional communal rangeland tenure has been identified as a determinant of increasing vulnerability to drought and climate change and as a driver of dryland degradation.

Implications: Where pastoralists' traditional land use does not have legal recognition, or where pastoralists are unable to exclude others from land use, this presents significant challenges for carbon sequestration initiatives. Carbon sequestration initiatives on rangelands may require clarification and maintenance of land rights.

4. Two steps backwards: a critical analysis of the IPCC report's land tenure content

Without dismissing the significance of the IPCC report's brave treatment of land tenure issues, we offer some critical observations. First, while the report claims that land grabbing is 'imperfectly' understood (we agree), it does not offer a way to understand it better. The report simply repeats the well-known drivers of land grabs, namely, the 2007–2008 food price spike and the rush for biofuel production. During the last decade, there has been a 'literature rush' on land grabs (Oya, 2013) resulting in the currently huge body of work on the topic.[2] There is a significant cluster within this literature dedicated to 'green grabbing', i.e. land grabbing in the name of the environment (Benjaminsen & Bryceson, 2012; Fairhead et al., 2012; Ojeda, 2012). Yet, the report's engagement with the scientific literature on land grabs is thin, and there is no engagement with the cluster on 'green grabbling', even though this is the form of land grabbing which is most directly related to the relationship between climate change and land. The report's treatment of the land grabbing issue falls far short of the state of the art. How do climate change mitigation and adaptation measures result in land grabbing, and how do land grabs result in deepening the climate crisis? These questions are at the heart of the relationship between climate change and land, with emerging evidence suggesting that recent land grabs are contributing significantly to greenhouse gas emissions. For instance, Liao et al. (2021, p. 15) studied 36.7 million hectares of large-scale land deals and found that, 'clearing lands transacted between 2000 and 2016 (36.7 Mha) could have emitted ~2.26 GtC, but constraining land clearing to historical deforestation rates would reduce emissions related to large-scale land transactions to ~0.81 GtC'. But these questions are not addressed in the

IPCC report. But even the so-called 'green solutions' – even if these help save or reduce emissions – can lead to deeply unjust social outcomes. For example, the shift to renewable energy may, under certain conditions, entail committing larger areas of land to produce energy (at best at the same given level now), given the lower power density of renewables, such that energy production becomes a key driver of land use change under a low-carbon scenario (see Scheidel & Sorman, 2012, p. 588).[3] Recent corporate plans to pursue carbon offsetting based on trees and lands are likely to combine the two dimensions of green grabbing just cited. In its estimates, Oxfam reported that: 'Shell would need about 28.6 mmillion hectares by 2050 … while TotalEnergies plans to offset about 7% of its emissions, needing about 2.6 million hectares by 2050' (Harvey, 2021, n.p.). Moreover, the report claims that 'BP has not set out its plans in detail, but is likely to require as much as 22.5 million hectares for offsetting as much as 15% of its emissions' (Harvey, 2021, n.p.). These all sound like Tsing's notion of 'economy of appearances' (Tsing, 2000), and so, whether or not these plans materialize, their implications for recasting access to land can be palpable in the real world.

Second, the report is overly focused on the partial, fragile, or non-existent formal recognition of existing access to land as the main problem that purportedly causes land tenure insecurity, and thus can undermine climate change mitigation and adaptation, or can result in mitigation and adaptation measures having adverse impacts on local communities. For the dominant narrative, the solution is to push for the formal recognition of existing land tenure, where land tenure security is essentially taken to mean the formal recognition of pre-existing access to land. There are two problems with this. On the one hand, not all compelling issues involving land are related to lack of recognition of existing tenure. For example, there are many who are landless or land-poor who need access to land, but for whom that land access is absent, or diminished, or degraded. Their status compels them to largely rely on selling their labour power, often cheaply, in order to survive. These are the world's 'precariat' (Standing, 2014), 'working people' (Shivji, 2017), or 'classes of labour' (Bernstein, 2006), who number at least a billion (Davis, 2006). Moreover, by 2020 there were 50.8 million reported internally displaced peoples (IDPs), of which 45.7 million were displaced due to conflict and violence, and 5.1 million due to disasters (NRC, 2020). Formal recognition of existing land tenure is not relevant to these landless and land-poor working people, but land redistribution and restitution are urgent priorities.

On the other hand, there are working people who need land and who still have a degree of access to a range of land and resources, but whose access is under constant threat from the social forces driving global land grabs. Land tenure security through formal recognition may be relevant to them, but there are four problematical aspects of formal recognition as a strategy which need to be considered. (1) In societies marked by pre-existing land-based inequalities, formalizing land tenure *without* prior or accompanying redistributive or restitutive reforms is likely to result in the formalization of inequalities. Those who were previously differentiated out or expelled from their lands are excluded from even making claims for tenure security, because they do not have existing land tenure to secure, as in the cases of the related land policies carried out in Myanmar from 2012 to 2020 (Ra et al., 2021; Ra & Ju, 2021). (2) Formalization in the context of relatively mobile systems of production almost always means sedentarization: from shifting cultivation to sedentary farming, from mobile pastoralism to ranching, from artisanal fishing to industrial fishpond production. It is a shift from an extensive land/nature-based system to an intensive capitalized system in which very few will socio-economically survive, let alone flourish (Woods, 2020). And once mobile producers are sedentarized, what happens to the land resources freed up by the formalization process? These are almost always converted into exclusionary capital-intensive, industrial-production systems of farming, ranching or aquaculture. (3) Land claims, like laws and policies, do not self-interpret nor self-implement (Franco, 2008). Claims are interpreted and implemented in messy political struggles within and between social classes and groups within the state and society. There is nothing inherently pro-poor in land registration and formal recognition of land tenure. The actual balance of social forces that act for or against working people's interests ultimately shapes the character and trajectory of public action on tenure recognition, and in virtually all cases, the political power of working people tends to be weaker. (4) The assumption that formal land titles shield land-dependent working people from the differentiating currents of commoditization or expulsion through extra-economic coercion is questionable. The differentiating effects of capitalist market relations or the expelling power of extra-economic coercion cut across institutional status of land claims – with or without land titles, as many previous land reform beneficiaries in different countries who later gave up their lands show (Adam, 2013; Moyo, 2011). In many settings, powerful economic forces even prefer lands with formal land titles because land deals look more legitimate; in such cases, deals are more secure, not for working people, but for corporations – as Deininger explicitly suggested (noted elsewhere in this paper).

Our third critical observation is that the IPCC report tends to idealize indigenous peoples' production systems and customary land tenure. In other words, these societies and their lands – accounting for around half a billion hectares of land globally – are assumed not only to be intact, but to be inherently democratic in political character (that is, not socially differentiated), and ecologically sustainable as sources of production inputs and as waste sinks. Yet, there is ample evidence to show that the territories claimed by indigenous peoples have been significantly transformed over time and across space, marked by social differentiation, commodification and agroecological diminution and degradation. It is not uncommon to find indigenous communities that managed to get formal certification of their land rights, only to lease these out to agribusiness corporations or mining companies. In many other cases, while indigenous peoples continue to claim a territory and the central state formally classifies it as indigenous peoples' territory, in reality it could have already been transformed, in its entirety or in part, into a plantation or commercial real estate hub. The case of Davao's Unified Bagobo-Tagabawa Tribe (UBTT) in the Philippines that got ancestral land title to their 38,000 hectares land is relevant: AgriNurture Inc. (ANI), a big agribusiness, signed a long-term lease contract a huge portion of this land for 25 years, renewable for another 25 years, to develop agricultural plantations.[4] This is not the first time that ANI engaged in such an activity in southern Philippines. There are several mining operations in the Philippines that operate in similar ancestral lands. The study by Vidal (2004) shows how a mining company deployed the classic divide-and-conquer tactic to secure free, prior and informed consent from the indigenous community that holds an ancestral land title in order to carry out extensive mining operations inside the indigenous territory. Contemporary communities under customary land tenure are also known to be subject to dynamic social differentiation and class conflict (Peters, 2004). We are not being dismissive of the importance of indigenous peoples' production systems and customary land tenure. We believe that whatever their state of being at the current conjuncture, they must be taken seriously because indeed they have important contributions to make to a positive alternative future. What we are less convinced about is by an idealized view of these communities and spaces.

Finally, and equally important, are the deafening silences in the IPCC report. A great number of working people in the world today need a range of access to a range of land and nature. The report is silent as to whether climate change mitigation and adaptation measures require prior or accompanying equitable distribution of control over land and other resources. Moreover, the report says nothing about how to equitably *redistribute or restitute* land to working people, and how to protect the threatened land access of working people. The term 'redistribution' (of land) is mentioned occasionally in the report, but with no explanation or definition. The report also mentions 'land-scape' and 'landscape governance', which is a promising lead (Hunsberger et al., 2017), but again says nothing of what these might mean. The concept of 'landscape' is highly contested in the litera-ture (see Mitchell, 1996), and without clarifying what it means in the IPCC report, it is likely to be subsumed by the neoliberal 'land tenure security' framework. We do not suggest that IPCC reports should get into prescriptive operational matters; but specifying fundamental principles that define categories and concepts could clarify perspectives and positions, especially amid competing narra-tives not only on land politics but on climate change (Borras et al., 2021). While it is laudable that the report notes, albeit rather weakly, the issue of emissions by monoculture plantations, it is gen-erally silent about what kind of agriculture contributes to and aggravates climate change, and – beyond enumeration of some technical and management-related issues in farming and soil man-agement – on what type of agriculture can help mitigate climate change. This lacuna gives the impression that agriculture as a whole is the culprit. Our starting point in this paper is that it is capitalist industrial agriculture – which is not just an agroecological and technical farming system, but a socioeconomic and political system – that contributes significantly to climate change.

5. Four political acts: roll back, contain, block, promote

The global climate of land politics is currently defined by a strong aversion to any state-driven, class-based redistributive land policies, and an ideological obsession with privatization of land rights as the main thrust, and land sales and rental markets as the main mechanism for reallocating access to and use of land. Four mutually reinforcing political acts emanating from a single social force and ideology have converged to construct and maintain the current structure of the global land politics architecture: *roll back, contain, block, promote*. These are wilful, orchestrated actions by social groups within the state and in society in pursuit of particular socioeconomic and political interests.

In places where there have been gains in redistributive land policies under varying regimes, either socialist or capitalist, the thrust has been to *roll back* those gains. The rollback campaign started at the onset of global neoliberalism, beginning with the partial rollback of land reforms initiated by Frei and Allende in Chile, immediately after General Pinochet seized state power through a military coup (Kay, 2002b, pp. 470–471). This rollback campaign has gained momentum since then. The dismantling of regulatory institutions in land, such as state cooperatives and col-lective farms, spread rapidly – if unevenly – in the 1990s (Ho & Spoor, 2006; Lahiff et al., 2007; Spoor, 2008). Institutions in land access that regulate land sales and rental markets such as land size ceiling laws, or those that actively promote community or collective arrangements, such as the *ejido* system in Mexico to prevent land concentration, have increasingly been deregulated (Akram-Lodhi et al., 2007; Zoomers & van der Haar, 2000). State support to beneficiaries of land redistribution has been withdrawn.

In addition, in situations where there were ongoing redistributive land policies, the overall main-stream strategy has been to *contain* the scope, pace and momentum of such policies. Only a handful of countries have been able to pursue progressive redistributive land policies during neoliberalism, namely, Brazil and the Philippines since 1988 (Franco, 2011; Wolford, 2010); South Africa, with different variants of a hybrid market-led/state-driven land redistribution (Cousins, 2009; Ntsebeza & Hall, 2007); Colombia (Grajales, 2015); Zimbabwe since 2000 (Moyo, 2011; Scoones et al., 2010); Mozambique's 1997 Land Law (Negrão, 1999) and the retention of Indonesia's Basic Agrarian Law of 1960 through the neoliberal era. In each of these cases, the strategy deployed by mainstream political forces was to limit and contain the scope and pace of policy implementation. Outright abandonment of existing redistributive land policies may prove to be too politically risky because of possible popular protest. The strategy for containing such policies involves slowing down the speed of implementation, delimiting the scope, defunding the land agency or ministry, or rendering altogether dormant a potentially redistributive land policy – as seen, in varying contexts and extents, in the countries referenced in this paragraph.

Meanwhile, in settings with significant numbers of landless or land-poor, and thus in need of land redistribution and restitution but there are no existing appropriate policies or laws, the mainstream strategy deployed has been to *block* any land policy that is redistributive or restitutive in character. A classic example is Myanmar where the World Bank, USAID and other international agencies that were advising the government (before the February 2021 military coup) pushed for market-oriented land policies, essentially blocking the possibility of system-wide redistributive and restitutive land policies (Ra et al., 2021; Ra & Ju, 2021). The cases of Brazil, Philippines South Africa, Mozambique, Zimbabwe and Colombia, already mentioned, are among the few exceptions: no other national redistributive land policy has been passed or implemented during the neoliberal period, despite the unprecedented levels of land concentration established or maintained by neoliberalism. The Indonesian BAL of 1960 has been retained but kept dormant. Even those laws and policies that have sought to regulate the frenzied land rush of the past decade have been applied only peripherally; regulation has been used in order to facilitate large-scale land deals by minimizing collateral damage such as expulsions of affected villagers without monetary compensation. Arguably, the most pervasive form of the blocking strategy is having a 'no policy' policy. This refers to societies where there is a compelling case for redistributive land policies but where governments choose not to adopt any policies to achieve this end.

These three political acts, separately and together, ultimately seek to *promote* market-friendly land policies. While neoliberal land policies are constituted, interpreted and implemented in a highly uneven manner, idealized versions take the defining features of privatized, deregulated and demand-driven land policies aimed at stimulating land sales and rental markets, joint ventures and credit markets. This can be facilitated by ensuring the availability of transparent data and information about private property in land that can in turn allow for informed transactions – by willing sellers and willing buyers – which require minimum bureaucracy and are enforceable with minimal transaction costs. The objective is to use land and nature in the most economically efficient manner (Pereira, 2021). The notions of appropriate land use and appropriate land users are defined by a mainstream concept of economic efficiency, centred around the maximization of use of scarce land resources for a free market-driven economic growth that could satisfy the profit- and utility-maximizing impulses of individuals (Deininger & Byerlee, 2011). Formal private land titles can ensure the 'security' necessary to facilitate dynamic land and rental markets, joint venture and credit markets. In this context, security means, primarily, security for owners of capital – from corporate agribusiness to finance capital, from traders to rich farmers (Deininger, 2011). It is less about the security for working poor people from being discriminated against, or from being coerced to give up control of land. This is part of the dominant neoliberal narrative where 'investment' becomes synonymous to 'corporate investments', consciously or unconsciously dismissing the two other equally important (if not more important) investments, namely, public investments and investments of working poor people themselves (Kay, 2014). The guiding principle is to ensure that the most economically efficient users (in neoclassical economics/new institutional economics terms) are able to access and use land in the most economically efficient manner

– that is, the greatest profit that can be derived from economic undertaking. This might entail individual or group rights, freehold title or formalizing customary land tenure, or a combination of these; the bottom line is whether it will allow for land sales and rental markets, joint ventures and credit markets, to emerge and flourish, thereby assuring would-be capitalist investors of the security of their investments.

This is captured in the views of Klaus Deininger, author of the 2003 World Bank land policy framework (Deininger, 2003), and co-author of the World Bank's 2011 report on the global land grabs (Deininger & Byerlee, 2011). Deininger stressed the importance of enabling relevant actors to 'register group rights in a way that allows for community management of basic land administration processes (such as allocation of individual rights ...); boundaries are recorded and a clear internal governance structure ... is established to allow interaction with outsiders'. He explained that this is important 'to allow land users to enter into joint ventures with investors, or to allow groups to gradually individualize land rights if desired' (Deininger, 2011, p. 237). A key neoliberal framework on agriculture and development that is fundamentally anchored on the 2003 World Bank land policy document (see also De Soto, 2000) is the *World Development Report (WDR) 2008* (World Bank, 2007). Like its 2003 forerunner, the *WDR 2008* strategy framework synthesizes the past and frames the future in relation to what role agriculture, land and nature will have to play in economic activity. It states: 'Land markets ... can raise productivity, help households diversify their incomes, and facilitate exit from agriculture', and continues: 'land markets are needed to transfer land to the most productive users and to facilitate participation in the rural nonfarm sector and migration out of agriculture', before concluding: 'insecure property rights, poor contract enforcement, and stringent legal restrictions limit the performance of land markets, creating large inefficiencies in both land and labor reallocation' (World Bank, 2007, p. 9).[5] The key documents referenced here all point to the question of reallocating land use to more economically efficient users (again, in the definition by neoclassical and new institutional economics) through free market-based mechanisms. The non-efficient and non-viable users have to be assisted in their exit options out of agriculture through a variety of safety net programmes, including cash transfer programmes.

The political acts of *rollback*, *containment*, *blocking* and *promoting* have resulted in the current global land politics architecture. As such, the land policy structure is an inherent component of global neoliberal capitalism where it serves at least two major roles: as a strategy to address the capitalist crisis of over-accumulation (Harvey, 2003) by using land/nature for cheap inputs in production; and, at the same time, as a strategy to address the ecological crisis of capitalist production by expanding the role of land/nature as sink for production waste (Fraser, 2021; Martinez-Alier, 2021; O'Connor, 1998). This is not an original political strategy. The *roll back*, *contain* and *block* strategies against redistributive land policies emerging out of socialist or anti-colonial revolutions or electoral victories of left-wing political parties were deployed by conservative political forces worldwide during the Cold War, from the 1950s to the beginning of neoliberalism in the early 1980s. These forces included political coalitions like the 1960s' US-driven Alliance for Progress, as well as key individuals such as Roy Prosterman and Wolf Ladejinski (Putzel, 1992). During the Cold War, the roll back–contain–block strategy fed into the strategy to promote counter and/or pre-emptive land policy reforms. These took the form of formal land titling, land resettlement or internal colonization, limited liberal redistributive land reforms, or a combination of these. This type of intervention was described by Diskin (1989), in the context of El Salvador, as reforms that prevent change. The nature of the contemporary roll back–contain–block–promote political acts is the same as that observed by Diskin decades ago.

6. The global climate of land politics

Land tenure security is central to the dominant development policy narrative and practice. Front and centre in 'land tenure security' frameworks is the security of capitalist investors – not that of working poor people. Yet this concept and practice are contested. How to make it socially legitimate is a challenge. Deininger is keen on striking a balance between capital accumulation and political legitimacy imperatives by way of formalizing land rights, but again, centrally in order to protect the interest of capitalist investments:

> Understanding and respecting these rights is important if investments are to be socially legitimate and legally secure. Failure to do so can lead to conflict and strife that will negatively affect the economic viability of land-related investments. Failure to map and record land rights ... makes it difficult to identify boundaries and legitimate owners as a basis for engaging in mutually agreed-to land transfers. Recording rights provides outside investors with somebody to talk to, a legitimate and authorized partner to negotiate the nature of investments and compensation. (Deininger, 2011, p. 236)[6]

The principal narrative animating the global political acts of roll back, contain, block and promote is the notion that the key to addressing the economic and climate crises is to take land and nature from their current *economically inefficient* use by their economically inefficient users. The assumption is that land, when used efficiently by efficient users, can function maximally as production input and as waste sink. The push for the twin policies of deregulated markets and private property in land has been uneven across societies and over time, in part because of varying degrees of resistance to it (Deininger, 2003; World Bank, 2007). Despite such political contestations, neoliberal forces have managed to bring the world to its current state of land politics.

In addition, and especially during the past decade, an old narrative that disparages agrarian societies has been revived and given a new impetus. According to this narrative, some agrarian systems – such as shifting agriculture and forest foraging, mobile pastoralism and artisanal fishing – are *ecologically destructive*, and thus are causing or aggravating the climate crisis.[7] But this narrative can be politically complicated in many societies. For example, while a government may release public statements saying it respects customary land tenure arrangements, it may in practice refuse to register land claims by those practising shifting cultivation, or only register a plot that is a small fraction of the total cultivated land area, and excludes fallow land. The only way for such a small plot to be productively viable is to shift the farming system to a sedentary method. The net effect of this is the cessation of customary production systems and the abrupt shift to sedentary cultivation (in the cases of pastoralism and artisanal fishing, a shift to ranching or aquaculture), which is capital-intensive and dependent on fossil-based inputs. Another implication of this policy action is the freeing up of a large portion of land originally used in mobile production systems. This is immediately captured by the state for reallocation to more socioeconomically and politically powerful capitalist investors. This is what has been unfolding in many borderland ethnic communities in Myanmar during the past decade, for example (Ra et al., 2021; Springate-Baginski & Kamoon, 2021) Acknowledging that this process and outcome have been common practice for a long time, Deininger states: 'many countries have considered land and associated natural resources not formally registered as property of the state, which governments could dispose of at will, often without considering the actual status of occupation' (Deininger, 2011, pp. 236–237). He explains that this widespread practice 'presumes any unclaimed or unregistered land to be "empty" and thus available for transfer with few safeguards. This bias can take many forms, including the recognition of rights only to land currently cultivated (i.e. excluding fallow land)' (Deininger, 2011, p. 237).

Climate change is used by dominant actors – state and non-state, corporate and non-corporate – to revive the old claims that some agrarian systems are ecologically destructive, in order to justify the use of extra-economic coercion and radically shift the land use to capitalist production systems that they deem offer a greater degree of economic efficiency in allocative, distributive and technical terms. This is a concrete manifestation of the vital importance of understanding climate change *not only* in terms of biophysical links and in terms of projects and policies, *but equally importantly*, in terms of politics. The dominant understanding of climate change mitigation and adaptation is framed within the capitalist economic development framework of endless capital accumulation, which sees land and nature as a productive input and a waste sink. Even before Climate Smart Agriculture was popularized in the UNFCC Conference of the Parties (COP) events, the *WDR 2008*, released in the same year as the COP Bali in 2007, had already established the framework for the relationship between land/nature and climate change mitigation and adaptation, and how the free market should govern such a relationship. The *WDR 2008* states:

> Based on the polluter-pays principle, it is the responsibility of the richer countries to compensate the poor for costs of adaptation ... . Developing country agriculture and deforestation are also major sources of greenhouse gas emissions: they contribute ... up to 30 percent of total emissions, more than half of which is from deforestation ... caused by agricultural encroachment (13 million hectares of annual deforestation globally). (World Bank, 2007, p. 17)

It concludes by emphasizing market-based solutions: 'Carbon-trading schemes – especially if their coverage is extended to provide financing for avoided deforestation ... offer significant untapped potential to reduce emissions from land-use change in agriculture' (World Bank, 2007, p. 17). It has to be pointed out, however, that in the era of financialization, corporate investments are far more transnational. It is thus problematical to talk about 'developing country agriculture and deforestation' as if *global* capital, that is, especially North-based capital, is not deeply involved in such transformation (Clapp & Isakson, 2018; Fairbairn, 2020; Visser et al., 2015).

The foundational position advanced by the *WDR 2008* also underpins the construction of Climate Smart Agriculture (CSA), which has been promoted as a framework for climate change mitigation and adaptation in the context of the world's agriculture (FAO, 2013; World Bank, 2016). The World Bank defines CSA as, 'an integrated approach to managing landscapes – cropland, livestock, forests and fisheries – that address [*sic*] the interlinked challenges of food security and climate change'.[8] It is a three-pronged strategy aimed at achieving: increased *productivity* (to produce more food), enhanced *resilience* (to reduce vulnerability to climate change-related shocks and long-term climatic stresses), and *reduced emissions* (to lower emissions for each calorie of food produced, avoiding deforestation from agriculture and capturing carbon out of the atmosphere).[9] There is minimal mention of land tenure in CSA. In the few places where land is mentioned, the policy strategy builds on the notion of 'land tenure security'.

Viewed from this perspective, we see 'land tenure security' as essentially a formal land registration campaign that targets lands of shifting cultivators, forest foragers, pastoralists and artisanal fishers. The goal seems to be to seize the greater portion of land, water, grazing land and forests, freeing them from so-called inefficient land users and land uses, and reallocating them to efficient users and uses. Meanwhile, for the working poor people who depend on land for a livelihood, fully or partially, or for those who would choose such a livelihood but are currently outside the agrarian system, the only way to secure access to land and resources is through the market. This means in practice that their chances are almost zero, because they are the least able to participate in any land sales and rental market.

This strategic shift towards neoliberal global land politics has been facilitated by a hegemonic narrative with two interlinked aspects: the purported political *impossibility and undesirability* of state-driven, system-wide, class-based redistributive land policies, on the one hand, and the practical political feasibility and desirability of market-based, privatized, so-called demand-driven and 'multistakeholder' approaches, on the other hand (Herring, 2003). This narrative has led to a recasting of the unit of analysis and public action: from transforming inequitable land-based social relations into more egalitarian relations based on social justice, to formalizing institutions of private property to invigorate land markets. Some critical questions are provoked by this conservative shift: can the capitalist market relations that caused landlessness self-correct towards egalitarian land-based social relations? Will the institutions and actors that deployed extra-economic coercion that caused widespread expulsions from the land turn back and self-correct via self-imposed reparation? Not impossible but unlikely in the current conjuncture. The 'land tenure security' strategy seems to suggest that we just forget, forgive and formalize land dispossession caused by extra-economic coercion. In short, and to put it in polemical terms, the implication of the above is to shift public action from dismantling land-based inequality to formalizing inequality.

The hegemonic narrative of land tenure security has been operationalized in part through the mantra of 'what is do-able' – that is, do-able within a given balance of social forces within the state and in society for or against redistributive land policy – and no longer daring to think about 'what is possible', which necessarily includes the need to disrupt the balance of social forces. This means that redistributive land policy has been eschewed, while what is perceived to be politically harmless and economically desirable 'land tenure security' is celebrated and pursued. It also means the diminution of land politics: from redistributive land policies for class-based reforms for system change, to land tenure security for project-based social entrepreneurship for economic growth. The shift has stripped transformative land policy of its inherently irreverent and subversive political character, and has reduced policy to a tamed multistakeholder process aimed at finding a consensus at the centre (Li, 2021; McKeon, 2017). It is a shift from the class-relational zero-sum political process, into a positive-sum idea – firmly within the questionable win-win formula of *WDR 2008* (Oya, 2009), and the problematical win-win formula of the concept of 'responsible agriculture investment' in response to land grabs (De Schutter, 2011).

Governmental funds have been raised and channelled by, through and for inter-governmental development organizations, bilateral and multilateral agencies, big philanthropic organizations, academic research institutions, and thousands of NGOs worldwide that in turn generated further narratives supporting, directly and indirectly, consciously or unconsciously, this policy shift.[10] It is part of a broader politics of knowledge around climate change that has been shaped over time. Nightingale et al. (2020, p. 347) emphasize 'how the current framing of global climate change and the scientific-policy apparatus built to tackle it limit our imagination and narrow the range of potential responses'. They elaborate:

> Together, they have influenced the expertise that is brought to bear, the questions that can be asked, the people assumed to need assistance, versus those with important knowledge to govern change, and the scales at which responses should be organized. (Nightingale et al. 2020, p. 347)

The fixation on what is 'do-able' has led to petty reforms in land politics. The rise of a global complex of state and non-state actors that have inserted themselves into the political acts of rollback, containment, blocking and promoting of land politics, and the apparent consensus among the dominant socioeconomic classes, together form a historic bloc, the main political force that has transformed what might 40 years ago have been a laughable definition of land tenure security into the current hegemonic narrative that is made authoritative in society by consent and coercion. Thus, petty reforms eventually attain an ideological structure and become 'petty reformism': small reforms that are purposively not meant to be ratcheted up into higher and more radical transformation.[11] It is within this tradition that the concept and practice of 'land tenure security' have emerged, been sustained, and received a boost from the mainstream idea and practice of climate change mitigation and adaptation.

7. Conclusion and implications: changing the global climate of land politics

The scholarly literature on the politics of land (access and control, distribution, redistribution, restitution, recognition) is extensive, rich and diverse, historically and at present. Yet, we seldom see any serious and significant engagement with this set of literature in the rapidly expanding research on the politics of climate change, even those subsets of the latter that directly relate to the issue of land. One outcome of this is that the climate change scholarship misses some of the enduring puzzles and questions in relation to the politics of land control that should be made front and centre of any land-based mitigation and adaptation actions. In this regard, we pointed out some of the contentious issues in the relationship between climate change and land.

One assumption we have in our paper is that the location of rural working people in the spheres of production and social reproduction shapes one's position in relation to climate change (that is, whether one becomes vulnerable or not, and if so, to what extent is their vulnerability, and so on) amid climate change. In the rural areas, access to land can be a decisive factor in this context where, as Watts (1983/2013) demonstrated in the case of Northern Nigeria, some prosper while others are differentiated out in times of severe climatic disruptions largely due to pre-existing structural condition and land access is key to this. The problem today is that current state of global land access is marked by widespread landlessness and near-landlessness of many rural working people, and precarious access by those who still have some land access. It is a highly uneven, inegalitarian distribution of land access, and many of the mainstream climate actions exacerbate this further. In turn, policies that promote land tenure security can only have democratic content if and when it has the fundamental elements of redistribution, recognition and restitution (Franco & Borras, 2021), as we have demonstrated historically and through several illustrative country cases. This is key to a just transition, but the difficult challenge is that the contemporary global climate in land policy is too market-oriented, eschewing social justice-oriented redistributive approaches in land policies. This has to change.

There have been increasing calls to change the intellectual climate in scientific research and policy circles in order to reset our perspective on the causes, conditions and consequences of climate change, and the requirements and possibilities of addressing it effectively (Castree et al., 2014; Gills & Morgan, 2020; Nightingale et al., 2020). We locate our argument within these emerging critical voices. While 'land politics' is a narrow theme, it nevertheless acts as a lynchpin in the actual world of agriculture and food, so that the essence of our argument has broader resonance. On the one hand, agriculture contributes *at least* 30% of the world's total greenhouse gas emissions. On the other hand, significant elements within mitigation and adaptation ideas and practice are related to land and nature – as productive inputs for carbon-saving or carbon-neutral commodity production systems and as a sink for waste (Fraser, 2016, 2021; Martinez-Alier, 2021; O'Connor, 1998). Ultimately, a huge part of the global complex of responses to climate change is linked to agriculture and food (Borras et al., 2021), and thus inherently to land.

Changing the global climate of land politics is key, and it is urgent. Without it, any analyses of and responses to climate change are at best superficial, and at worst, flawed and self-defeating – and are likely to only add to the growing list of what Gills and Morgan (2020) call 'successful failures'. But this does not imply changing the global climate of land politics in a random way. Rather, it calls for a very specific character and direction of change: to acknowledge the pervasive land-based social inequities in the world today, and to take a position to end such inequalities by pursuing an egalitarian distribution of a range of access to a range of land and resources that explicitly benefits the working people that, in turn and ultimately, can only be made possible through structural transformation.

Notes

1. A broad definition of agrarian justice is used in this paper, that is, 'the agenda of carrying out a sense of fairness for historically oppressed social classes and groups in agrarian societies' (Franco & Borras 2019, p. 197; also Borras & Franco, 2018). For a conceptual discussion of climate justice, see Harris (2016, pp. 35–36).
2. There is a wide-ranging scope in the global land grabs literature. A selection of studies includes: Alonso-Fradejas (2012), Dell'Angelo et al. (2017), Edelman et al. (2013), Hall (2011), Moreda (2017), Müller et al. (2021), Rahmato (2011), Rulli et al. (2013), White et al. (2012), Wolford et al. (2013), Xu (2019), Zoomers (2010).
3. We thank one of the peer reviewers for this important point.
4. See: https://business.inquirer.net/316863/ancestral-lands-in-davao-to-be-planted-with-rice-corn; downloaded 23 February 2021.
5. For critiques, see Akram-Lodhi (2008), Li (2009) and Oya (2009).
6. See O'Connor (1973) and Fox (1993, especially Ch. 2) for discussions about the two permanent but contradictory tasks of the state, namely, facilitating capital accumulation while maintaining political legitimacy.
7. This claim is contested in the scientific community. For critiques, see among others, Dressler et al. (2017), Scheidel (2019) and van Vliet et al. (2012).
8. https://www.worldbank.org/en/topic/climate-smart-agriculture. Downloaded 28 March 2020.
9. For critical reflections, see Clapp et al. (2018), Newell and Taylor (2018) and Taylor (2018).
10. See, for example, discussion in Chapter 7 of Edelman and Borras (2016).
11. See Wright (2019) for an elaborated discussion on various strands of anti-capitalist struggles in the twenty-first century. See also Borras (2020) on petty reformism, especially on land issues.

Acknowledgements

We are grateful to the anonymous reviewers for their critical, constructive and helpful comments and suggestions that helped improve the clarity of our argument. Finally, we thank Paula Bownas for her excellent copy editing assistance.

Disclosure statement

No potential conflict of interest was reported by the author(s).

Funding

This study has received funding from the European Research Council (ERC) under the European Union's Horizon 2020 research and innovation programme [grant number 834006], under the ERC Advanced Grant project RRUSHES-5, as well as from the Transnational Institute (TNI).

References

Adam, J. (2013). Land reform, dispossession and new elites: A case study on coconut plantations in Davao Oriental, Philippines. *Asia Pacific Viewpoint, 54*(2), 232–245. https://doi.org/10.1111/apv.12011

Akram-Lodhi, A. H. (2008). (Re)imagining agrarian relations? The world development report 2008: Agriculture for development. *Development and Change, 39*(6), 1145–1161. https://doi.org/10.1111/j.1467-7660.2008.00511.x

Akram-Lodhi, A. H., Borras, S. M., Jr., & Kay, C. (2007). *Land, poverty and livelihoods in an era of globalization: Perspectives from developing and transition countries.* Routledge.

Alonso-Fradejas, A. (2012). Land control-grabbing in Guatemala: The political economy of contemporary agrarian change. *Canadian Journal of Development Studies/Revue canadienne d'études du développement, 33*(4), 509–528. https://doi.org/10.1080/02255189.2012.743455

Arsel, M. (2019, May). *Climate change and class conflict in the Anthropocene.* Inaugural lecture. International Institute of Social Studies (ISS).

Benjaminsen, T. A., & Bryceson, I. (2012). Conservation, green/blue grabbing and accumulation by dispossession in Tanzania. *Journal of Peasant Studies, 39*(2), 335–355. https://doi.org/10.1080/03066150.2012.667405

Bernstein, H. (2006). Is there an agrarian question in the 21st century? *Canadian Journal of Development Studies/Revue canadienne d'études du développement, 27*(4), 449–460. https://doi.org/10.1080/02255189.2006.9669166

Borras, S. M. (2020). Agrarian social movements: The absurdly difficult but not impossible agenda of defeating right-wing populism and exploring a socialist future. *Journal of Agrarian Change, 20*(1), 3–36. https://doi.org/10.1111/joac.12311

Borras, S. M., Jr., & Franco, J. C. (2018). The challenge of locating land-based climate change mitigation and adaptation politics within a social justice perspective: Towards an idea of agrarian climate justice. *Third World Quarterly, 39*(7), 1308–1325. https://doi.org/10.1080/01436597.2018.1460592

Borras, S. M., Franco, J. C., & Nam, Z. (2020). Climate change and land: Insights from Myanmar. *World Development, 129*, 104864. https://doi.org/10.1016/j.worlddev.2019.104864

Borras, S. M., Scoones, I., Baviskar, A., Edelman, M., Peluso, N. L., & Wolford, W. (2021). Climate change and agrarian struggles. *Journal of Peasant Studies.* Advance online publication. https://doi.org/10.1080/03066150.2021.1956473

Castree, N., Adams, W. M., Barry, J., Brockington, D., Büscher, B., Corbera, E., Demeritt, D., Duffy, R., Felt, U., Neves, K., Newell, P., Pellizzoni, L., Rigby, K., Robbins, P., Robin, L., Rose, D. B., Ross, A., Schlosberg, D., Sörlin, S., … Wynne, B. (2014). Changing the intellectual climate. *Nature Climate Change, 4*(9), 763–768. https://doi.org/10.1038/nclimate2339

Clapp, J., & Isakson, S. R. (2018). *Speculative harvests: Financialization, food, and agriculture.* Practical Action, Rugby UK.

Clapp, J., Newell, P., & Brent, Z. W. (2018). The global political economy of climate change, agriculture and food systems. *Journal of Peasant Studies, 45*(1), 80–88. https://doi.org/10.1080/03066150.2017.1381602

Corbera, E. (2012). Problematizing REDD+ as an experiment in payments for ecosystem services. *Current Opinion in Environmental Sustainability, 4*(6), 612–619. https://doi.org/10.1016/j.cosust.2012.09.010

Cousins, B. (2009). Land reform in South Africa. *Journal of Agrarian Change*, 9(3), 421–431. https://doi.org/10.1111/j.1471-0366.2009.00218.x

Davis, M. (2006). *Planet of slums*. Verso.

de Janvry, A. (1981). *The agrarian question and reformism in Latin America*. Johns Hopkins University Press.

De Schutter, O. (2011). How not to think of land-grabbing: Three critiques of large-scale investments in farmland. *Journal of Peasant Studies*, 38(2), 249–279. https://doi.org/10.1080/03066150.2011.559008

De Soto, H. (2000). *The mystery of capital: Why capitalism triumphs in the west and fails everywhere else*. Civitas Books.

Deininger, K. (2003). *Land policies for growth and poverty reduction*. World Bank.

Deininger, K. (2011). Challenges posed by the new wave of farmland investment. *Journal of Peasant Studies*, 38(2), 217–247. https://doi.org/10.1080/03066150.2011.559007

Deininger, K., & Byerlee, D. (2011). *Rising global interest in farmland: Can it yield sustainable and equitable benefits?* World Bank.

Dell'Angelo, J., D'odorico, P., Rulli, M. C., & Marchand, P. (2017). The tragedy of the grabbed commons: Coercion and dispossession in the global land rush. *World Development*, 92, 1–12. https://doi.org/10.1016/j.worlddev.2016.11.005

Diskin, M. (1989). El Salvador: Reform prevents change. In W. Thiesenhusen (Ed.), *Searching for agrarian reform in Latin America* (pp. 429–450). Allen and Unwin.

Dressler, W. H., Wilson, D., Clendenning, J., Cramb, R., Keenan, R., Mahanty, S., Bruun, T. B., Mertz, O., & Lasco, R. D. (2017). The impact of swidden decline on livelihoods and ecosystem services in Southeast Asia: A review of the evidence from 1990 to 2015. *Ambio*, 46(3), 291–310. https://doi.org/10.1007/s13280-016-0836-z

Edelman, M., & Borras, S. M., Jr. (2016). *Political dynamics of transnational agrarian movements*. Practical Action.

Edelman, M., Oya, C., & Borras, S. M., Jr. (2013). Global land grabs: Historical processes, theoretical and methodological implications and current trajectories. *Third World Quarterly*, 34(9), 1517–1531. https://doi.org/10.1080/01436597.2013.850190

Fairbairn, M. (2020). *Fields of gold: Financing the global land rush*. Cornell University Press.

Fairhead, J., Leach, M., & Scoones, I. (2012). Green grabbing: A new appropriation of nature? *Journal of Peasant Studies*, 39(2), 237–261. https://doi.org/10.1080/03066150.2012.671770

Fajardo, D. (2014). *Estudio sobre los orígenes del conflicto social armado, razones de su persistencia y sus efectos más profundos en la sociedad colombiana*. Comisión Histórica del Conflicto y sus Víctimas. https://www.centrodememoriahistorica.gov.co/descargas/comisionPaz2015/FajardoDario.pdf

FAO. (2013). *Climate-smart agriculture sourcebook*.

Fox, J. (1993). *The politics of food in Mexico: State power and social mobilization*. Cornell University Press.

Fox, J. A. (1990). The challenge of rural democratization: Perspectives from Latin America and the Philippines. *Journal of Development Studies*, 26(4), 1–18. https://doi.org/10.1080/00220389008422171

Franco, J. C. (2008). Making land rights accessible: Social movements and political-legal innovation in the rural Philippines. *Journal of Development Studies*, 44(7), 991–1022. https://doi.org/10.1080/00220380802150763

Franco, J. C. (2011). *Bound by law: Filipino rural poor and the search for justice in a plural-legal landscape*. Ateneo de Manila University Press.

Franco, J. C., & Borras, S. M., Jr. (2019). Grey areas in green grabbing: Subtle and indirect interconnections between climate change politics and land grabs and their implications for research. *Land Use Policy*, 84, 192–199. https://doi.org/10.1016/j.landusepol.2019.03.013

Franco, J. C., & Borras, S. M. (2021). *The 5Rs in Myanmar: Five principles for a future federal democratic system where rural working people can flourish*. Transnational Institute. https://www.tni.org/en/publication/the-5rs-in-myanmar

Fraser, N. (2016). Contradictions of capital and care. *New Left Review*, 100(July/Aug), 99–117. https://newleftreview.org/issues/ii100/articles/nancy-fraser-contradictions-of-capital-and-care

Fraser, N. (2021). Climates of capital. *New Left Review*, 127(Jan/Feb), 94–127. https://newleftreview.org/issues/ii127/articles/nancy-fraser-climates-of-capital

Gills, B., & Morgan, J. (2020). Global climate emergency: After COP24, climate science, urgency, and the threat to humanity. *Globalizations*, 17(6), 885–902. https://doi.org/10.1080/14747731.2019.1669915

Grajales, J. (2015). Land grabbing, legal contention and institutional change in Colombia. *Journal of Peasant Studies*, *42*(3-4), 541–560. https://doi.org/10.1080/03066150.2014.992883

Griffin, K., Khan, A. R., & Ickowitz, A. (2002). Poverty and the distribution of land. *Journal of Agrarian Change*, *2*(3), 279–330. https://doi.org/10.1111/1471-0366.00036

Hall, R. (2011). Land grabbing in Southern Africa: The many faces of the investor rush. *Review of African Political Economy*, *38*(128), 193–214. https://doi.org/10.1080/03056244.2011.582753

Harris, P. G. (2016). *Global ethics and climate change*. Edinburgh University Press.

Harvey, D. (2003). *The new imperialism*. Oxford University Press.

Harvey, F. (2021, August 3). Reforestation hopes threaten global food security, Oxfam warns. *The Guardian*, no pagination. Retrieved August 5, 2021, from https://www.theguardian.com/environment/2021/aug/03/reforestation-hopes-threaten-global-food-security-oxfam-warns

Herring, R. (2003). Beyond the political impossibility theorem of agrarian reform. In P. Houtzager & M. Moore (Eds.), *Changing paths: International development and the new politics of inclusion* (pp. 58–87). University of Michigan Press.

Ho, P., & Spoor, M. (2006). Whose land? The political economy of land titling in transitional economies. *Land Use Policy*, *23*(4), 580–587. https://doi.org/10.1016/j.landusepol.2005.05.007

Hunsberger, C., Corbera, E., Borras, S. M., Franco, J. C., Woods, K., Work, C., de la Rosa, R., Eang, V., Herre, R., Kham, S. S., Park, C., Sokheng, S., Spoor, M., Thein, S., Aung, K. T., Thuon, R., & Vaddhanaphuti, C. (2017). Climate change mitigation, land grabbing and conflict: Towards a landscape-based and collaborative action research agenda. *Canadian Journal of Development Studies/Revue canadienne d'études du développement*, *38*(3), 305–324. https://doi.org/10.1080/02255189.2016.1250617

IPCC. (2019). *Climate change and land. An IPCC special report on climate change, desertification, land degradation, sustainable land management, food security, and greenhouse gas fluxes in terrestrial ecosystems.* Retrieved May 17, 2020, from https://www.ipcc.ch/srccl/

Kay, C. (2001). Reflections on rural violence in Latin America. *Third World Quarterly*, *22*(5), 741–775. https://doi.org/10.1080/01436590120084584

Kay, C. (2002a). Chile's neoliberal agrarian transformation and the peasantry. *Journal of Agrarian Change, 2* (4), 464–501. https://doi.org/10.1111/1471-0366.00043

Kay, C. (2002b). Why East Asia overtook Latin America: Agrarian reform, industrialisation and development. *Third World Quarterly*, *23*(6), 1073–1102. https://doi.org/10.1080/0143659022000036649

Kay, S. (2014). *Reclaiming agricultural investment: Towards public-peasant investment synergies* (TNI agrarian justice programme policy paper). Transnational Institute. http://www.tni.org/sites/www.tni.org/files/download/reclaiming_agricultural_investment.pdf

Klein, N. (2007). *The shock doctrine: The rise of disaster capitalism*. Macmillan.

Lahiff, E., Borras, S. M., Jr., & Kay, C. (2007). Market-led agrarian reform: Policies, performance and prospects. *Third World Quarterly*, *28*(8), 1417–1436. https://doi.org/10.1080/01436590701637318

Li, T. (2009). Exit from agriculture: A step forward or a step backward for the rural poor? *Journal of Peasant Studies*, *36*(3), 629–636. https://doi.org/10.1080/03066150903142998

Li, T. M. (2021). Commons, co-ops, and corporations: Assembling Indonesia's twenty-first century land reform. *Journal of Peasant Studies*, *48*(3), 613–639. https://doi.org/10.1080/03066150.2021.1890718

Liao, C., Nolte, K., Sullivan, J. A., Brown, D. G., Lay, J., Althoff, C., & Agrawal, A. (2021). Carbon emissions from the global land rush and potential mitigation. *Nature Food*, *2*(1), 15–18. https://doi.org/10.1038/s43016-020-00215-3

Martinez-Alier, J. (2021). *Mapping ecological distribution conflicts: The EJ atlas*. Extractive Industries and Society. https://doi.org/10.1016/j.exis.2021.02.003

McKeon, N. (2017). Are equity and sustainability a likely outcome when foxes and chickens share the same coop? Critiquing the concept of multistakeholder governance of food security. *Globalizations*, *14*(3), 379–398. https://doi.org/10.1080/14747731.2017.1286168

Mitchell, D. (1996). *The lie of the land: Migrant workers and the California landscape*. University of Minnesota Press.

Moreda, T. (2017). Large-scale land acquisitions, state authority and indigenous local communities: Insights from Ethiopia. *Third World Quarterly*, *38*(3), 698–716. https://doi.org/10.1080/01436597.2016.1191941

Moyo, S. (2011). Three decades of agrarian reform in Zimbabwe. *Journal of Peasant Studies*, *38*(3), 493–531. https://doi.org/10.1080/03066150.2011.583642

Müller, M. F., Penny, G., Niles, M. T., Ricciardi, V., Chiarelli, D. D., Davis, K. F., Dell'Angelo, J., D'Odorico, P., Rosa, L., Rulli, M. C., & Mueller, N. D. (2021). Impact of transnational land acquisitions on local food security and dietary diversity. *Proceedings of the National Academy of Sciences*, *118*(4), e2020535118. https://doi.org/10.1073/pnas.2020535118

Negrão, J. (1999). *The land campaign in Mozambique*. Oxfam.

Newell, P., & Taylor, O. (2018). Contested landscapes: The global political economy of climate-smart agriculture. *Journal of Peasant Studies*, *45*(1), 108–129. https://doi.org/10.1080/03066150.2017.1324426

Nightingale, A. J., Eriksen, S., Taylor, M., Forsyth, T., Pelling, M., Newsham, A., Boyd, E., Brown, K., Harvey, B., Jones, L., Kerr, R. B., Mehta, L., Naess, L. O., Ockwell, D., Scoones, I., Tanner, T., & Whitfield, S. (2020). Beyond technical fixes: Climate solutions and the great derangement. *Climate and Development*, *12*(4), 343–352. https://doi.org/10.1080/17565529.2019.1624495

Norwegian Refugee Council (NRC). (2020). *Global report on internal displacement*. NRC.

Ntsebeza, L., & Hall, R. (Eds.). (2007). *The land question in South Africa: The challenge of transformation and redistribution*. HSRC Press.

O'Connor, J. (1973). *The fiscal crisis of the state*. Routledge.

O'Connor, J. (1998). *Natural causes: Essays in ecological Marxism*. Guilford Press.

Ojeda, D. (2012). Green pretexts: Ecotourism, neoliberal conservation and land grabbing in Tayrona National Natural Park, Colombia. *Journal of Peasant Studies*, *39*(2), 357–375. https://doi.org/10.1080/03066150.2012.658777

Oya, C. (2009). The world development report 2008: Inconsistencies, silences, and the myth of 'win-win' scenarios. *Journal of Peasant Studies*, *36*(3), 593–601. https://doi.org/10.1080/03066150903142949

Oya, C. (2013). Methodological reflections on 'land grab' databases and the 'land grab' literature 'rush'. *Journal of Peasant Studies*, *40*(3), 503–520. https://doi.org/10.1080/03066150.2013.799465

Paprocki, K. (2019). All that is solid melts into the bay: Anticipatory ruination and climate change adaptation. *Antipode*, *51*(1), 295–315. https://doi.org/10.1111/anti.12421

Peluso, N. L., & Lund, C. (2011). New frontiers of land control: Introduction. *Journal of Peasant Studies*, *38*(4), 667–681. https://doi.org/10.1080/03066150.2011.607692

Pereira, J. M. M. (2021). The World Bank and market-assisted land reform in Colombia, Brazil, and Guatemala. *Land Use Policy*, *100*, 104909. https://doi.org/10.1016/j.landusepol.2020.104909

Peters, P. E. (2004). Inequality and social conflict over land in Africa. *Journal of Agrarian Change*, *4*(3), 269–314. https://doi.org/10.1111/j.1471-0366.2004.00080.x

Putzel, J. (1992). *A captive land: The politics of agrarian reform in the Philippines*. Monthly Review Press.

Ra, D., & Ju, K. K. (2021). 'Nothing about us, without us': Reflections on the challenges of building land in our hands, a national land network in Myanmar/Burma. *Journal of Peasant Studies*, *48*(3), 497–516. https://doi.org/10.1080/03066150.2020.1867847

Ra, D., Kham, S. S., Barbesgaard, M., Franco, J. C., & Vervest, P. (2021). The politics of Myanmar's agrarian transformation. *Journal of Peasant Studies*, *48*(3), 463–475. https://doi.org/10.1080/03066150.2021.1901689

Rahmato, D. (2011). *Land to investors: Large-scale land transfers in Ethiopia*. African Books Collective.

Rasmussen, M. B., & Lund, C. (2018). Reconfiguring frontier spaces: The territorialization of resource control. *World Development*, *101*, 388–399. https://doi.org/10.1016/j.worlddev.2017.01.018

Ribot, J. (2014). Cause and response: Vulnerability and climate in the anthropocene. *Journal of Peasant Studies*, *41*(5), 667–705. https://doi.org/10.1080/03066150.2014.894911

Ribot, J. C., & Peluso, N. L. (2003). A theory of access. *Rural Sociology*, *68*(2), 153–181. https://doi.org/10.1111/j.1549-0831.2003.tb00133.x

Rosset, P. M., & Altieri, M. A. (2017). *Agroecology: Science and politics*. Practical Action.

Rulli, M. C., Saviori, A., & D'Odorico, P. (2013). Global land and water grabbing. *Proceedings of the National Academy of Sciences*, *110*(3), 892–897. https://doi.org/10.1073/pnas.1213163110

Scheidel, A. (2019). Carbon stock indicators: Reductionist assessments and contentious policies on land use. *Journal of Peasant Studies*, *46*(5), 913–934. https://doi.org/10.1080/03066150.2018.1428952

Scheidel, A., & Sorman, A. H. (2012). Energy transitions and the global land rush: Ultimate drivers and persistent consequences. *Global Environmental Change*, *22*(3), 588–595. https://doi.org/10.1016/j.gloenvcha.2011.12.005

Scoones, I., Marongwe, N., Mavedzenge, B., Mahenehene, J., Murimbarimba, F., & Sukume, C. (2010). *Zimbabwe's land reform: Myths & realities.* James Currey.

Scoones, I., Smalley, R., Hall, R., & Tsikata, D. (2019). Narratives of scarcity: Framing the global land rush. *Geoforum; Journal of Physical, Human, and Regional Geosciences, 101,* 231–241. https://doi.org/10.1016/j.geoforum.2018.06.006

Shivji, I. G. (2017). The concept of 'working people'. *Agrarian South: Journal of Political Economy, 6*(1), 1–13. https://doi.org/10.1177/2277976017721318

Spoor, M. (Ed.). (2008). *The political economy of rural livelihoods in transition economies: Land, peasants and rural poverty in transition.* Routledge.

Springate-Baginski, O., & Kamoon, M. (2021). Defending Shan state's customary tenure systems from below through collective action research. *Journal of Peasant Studies, 48*(3), 541–559. https://doi.org/10.1080/03066150.2021.1887145

Standing, G. (2014). The precariat. *Contexts, 13*(4), 10–12. https://doi.org/10.1177/1536504214558209

Taylor, M. (2018). Climate-smart agriculture: What is it good for? *Journal of Peasant Studies, 45*(1), 89–107. https://doi.org/10.1080/03066150.2017.1312355

Thiesenhusen, W. C. (1989). *Searching for agrarian reform in Latin America.* Allen and Unwin.

Tsing, A. L. (2000). Inside the economy of appearances. *Public Culture, 12*(1), 115–144. https://doi.org/10.1215/08992363-12-1-115

Uson, M. A. M. (2017). Natural disasters and land grabs: The politics of their intersection in the Philippines following super typhoon Haiyan. *Canadian Journal of Development Studies/Revue canadienne d'études du développement, 38*(3), 414–430. https://doi.org/10.1080/02255189.2017.1308316

van Vliet, N., Mertz, O., Heinimann, A., Langanke, T., Pascual, U., Schmook, B., Adams, C., Schmidt-Vogt, D., Messerli, P., Leisz, S., Castella, J.-C., Jørgensen, L., Birch-Thomsen, T., Hett, C., Bech-Bruun, T., Ickowitz, A., Vu, K. C., Yasuyuki, K., Fox, J., … Zeigler, A. D. (2012). Trends, drivers and impacts of changes in swidden cultivation in tropical forest-agriculture frontiers: A global assessment. *Global Environmental Change, 22*(2), 418–429. https://doi.org/10.1016/j.gloenvcha.2011.10.009

Vidal, A. T. (2004). *Conflicting laws, overlapping claims: The politics of indigenous peoples' land rights in Mindanao.* Alternate Forum for Research in Mindanao.

Visser, O., Clapp, J., & Isakson, S. R. (2015). Introduction to a symposium on global finance and the agri-food sector: Risk and regulation. *Journal of Agrarian Change, 15*(4), 541–548. https://doi.org/10.1111/joac.12123

Watts, M. J. (1983/2013). *Silent violence: Food, famine, and peasantry in Northern Nigeria.* University of Georgia Press.

White, B., Borras, S. M., Jr., Hall, R., Scoones, I., & Wolford, W. (2012). The new enclosures: Critical perspectives on corporate land deals. *Journal of Peasant Studies, 39*(3-4), 619–647. https://doi.org/10.1080/03066150.2012.691879

Wolford, W. (2010). *This land is ours now: Social mobilization and the meanings of land in Brazil.* Duke University Press.

Wolford, W., Borras, S. M., Jr., Hall, R., Scoones, I., & White, B. (2013). Governing global land deals: The role of the state in the rush for land. *Development and Change, 44*(2), 189–210. https://doi.org/10.1111/dech.12017

Woods, K. M. (2020). Smaller-scale land grabs and accumulation from below: Violence, coercion and consent in spatially uneven agrarian change in Shan State, Myanmar. *World Development, 127,* 104780. https://doi.org/10.1016/j.worlddev.2019.104780

World Bank. (2007). *World development report 2008: Agriculture for development.*

World Bank. (2016, April 7). *World Bank group climate change action plan.*

Wright, E. O. (2019). *How to be an anticapitalist in the twenty-first century.* Verso.

Xu, Y. (2019). Rethinking the politics of land-use change: Insights from the rise of the industrial tree plantation sector in Southern China. *Land Use Policy, 87,* 104025. https://doi.org/10.1016/j.landusepol.2019.104025

Zoomers, A. (2010). Globalisation and the foreignisation of space: Seven processes driving the current global land grab. *Journal of Peasant Studies, 37*(2), 429–447. https://doi.org/10.1080/03066151003595325

Zoomers, A., & van der Haar, G. (2000). *Current land policy in Latin America: Regulating land tenure under neo-liberalism.* Royal Tropical Institute, KIT.

From the Paris Agreement to the Anthropocene and Planetary Boundaries Framework: an interview with Will Steffen

Will Steffen and Jamie Morgan

ABSTRACT

In this wide-ranging interview, the well-known Earth System scientist Professor Will Steffen introduces and discusses the influential planetary boundaries (PB) framework, the potential for a Hothouse Earth pathway and the relevance of the Anthropocene concept. He elaborates on the role of emergence, complexity, feedback and irreversibility and draws attention to updates for the nine PBs.

Will Steffen is Emeritus Professor at the Fenner School of Environment and Society, the Australian National University (ANU), Canberra. Professor Steffen is an Earth System scientist, known for his advocacy, with Paul Crutzen, of the concept of the Anthropocene and for his collaborative work with Johan Rockström, Tim Lenton, Katherine Richardson and many others, which explores the complex interrelations and dependencies of humans with their environment. In 2009 Steffen, Rockström and a team of researchers published a 'planetary boundaries' framework in *Nature* and their work has been widely cited and used (informing, for example, the Rio+20 summits' work on sustainable development). In addition, Steffen has published numerous other papers over the years and was a contributing author or reviewer of five IPCC reports. He has held a series of significant academic and policy advice positions and been the recipient of numerous honours. He is currently honorary professor at Copenhagen University, a senior fellow at the Stockholm Resilience Centre, a Fellow at the Beijer Institute of Ecological Economics, also in Stockholm, former chair of the Australian Government's Antarctic Science Advisory Committee and sits on the advisory committee of the APEC Climate Centre. Following the dissolution of the Australian Climate Commission in 2013 by then Prime Minister Tony Abbott, Steffen and several of his fellow commissioners crowdfunded an independent Climate Council and he remains a Councillor. He is currently working on the ERC 'Earth Resilience in the Anthropocene' project, jointly coordinated at the Stockholm Resilience Centre and the Potsdam Institute for Climate Impact Research. He holds a BSc from the University of Missouri (1970), and an MSc (1972) and PhD (1975) in chemistry, both from the University of Florida, as well as honorary doctorate degrees from Stockholm University and the University of Canberra.[1]

The following interview with Professor Steffen was conducted by Professor Jamie Morgan for *Globalizations*.

Jamie Morgan (JM): After years of increasingly urgent warnings from natural scientists, ecological economists and activists, it is now widely acknowledged that we have entered a period of 'climate emergency' and cumulative ecological breakdown. The Alliance of World Scientists is now actively promoting the concepts and raising awareness and academics, politicians and the public are increasingly familiar with related language and issues, but many are likely less familiar with Earth System science and the role it plays.[2] So, it might be useful to start with a brief explanation of what an Earth System approach is, what you and your colleagues work focusses on and what a 'planetary boundaries' framework entails.

Will Steffen (WS): Basically, the 'Earth System' refers to the interacting physical, chemical and biological processes that operate across, and link, the atmosphere, cryosphere (ice), land, ocean and lithosphere. These processes create 'emergent properties' – that is, properties and features of the Earth System as a whole which arise from the interaction amongst these spheres. Global average surface temperature is a good example – it is a property of the Earth System as a whole.

JM: Emergence is a concept that is probably most familiar to philosophically inclined readers (via the work of John Stuart Mill, Jaegwon Kim, etc. and most especially issues in philosophy of mind and the nature of consciousness; see O'Conner, 2020). But, clearly, it refers to any type of system in so far as its properties do not reduce to those of its parts in isolation.

WS: The human body is a good analogy for the Earth System. Although we are all made of individual parts – bones, skin, muscle, etc. and contain organs that carry out specific functions – heart, lungs, liver, brain, etc. – we are one single, integrated organism with properties at the level of the entire human. Also, we have intangible features like feelings and emotions which arise from complex interactions within our bodies and between our bodies and the external world. So, in that analogy, the Earth System, too, has intangible, emergent properties that characterize the system as a whole.

In fact, the Earth System exists in well-defined states, the most recent of which is the Holocene, an 11,700-year epoch in the Geologic Time Scale. In terms of an Earth System framework, the Holocene refers to a well-defined, stable state of the system, with a stable climate system, well-defined patterns of atmospheric and ocean circulation, and stable distribution of biomes around the planet. It is in this stable Holocene state that humanity has been able to expand and thrive.

JM: And the planetary boundaries (PB) framework?

WS: The planetary boundaries is a framework designed to assess what is required to maintain the Earth System in a stable Holocene-like state. We defined the state of the Earth System based on nine processes or features – such as climate stability, biosphere integrity, the water cycle, land-cover change and so on.[3] For each process, we have a control variable which measures the level of human perturbation and a response variable that measures the changes in the Earth System as a result of this pressure. Our present estimate is that four of the nine boundaries have been transgressed, including the two key ones of climate stability and biosphere integrity. This assessment is consistent with the scientific evidence showing that the Earth System has already left the Holocene and has entered the Anthropocene, a proposed new epoch in Earth history.[4]

At present, my work is focussed on the development of scenarios of potential future trajectories of the Earth System, based on a synthesis of modelling studies, observations, process studies and palaeo records. The ultimate question is when could the Earth System be pushed onto an irreversible trajectory towards a much hotter state – Hothouse Earth – and how close are we to pushing it onto that trajectory.[5]

JM: And as I understand it you have built into your boundary framework a degree of prudential leeway to ensure that the system stays some ('safe') distance from any given tipping point? For example, for the category of 'Climate Change' in terms of Earth System processes, you use 350 parts per million (ppm) by volume atmospheric carbon dioxide concentration as a proposed boundary. In the 2009 *Nature* paper (Rockström et al., 2009) you noted the current level was 387 ppm and the pre-industrial level 280 ppm. The UK Met Office is forecasting a level varying around 417 ppm for 2021–2.29 ppm higher than 2020, 30 ppm higher than your 2009 figure and around 50% higher than the pre-industrial level.[6] Moreover, according to the UK Met Office, the measurements indicate it took around 200 years for the ppm to increase by 25% but just the last 30 for it to approach 50%. So, the direction of travel does not seem to have changed in this case, quite the reverse. Is the same true of all the 'parameters' you use? In the 2009 paper, three of the planetary boundaries had been 'overstepped' …

WS: When we first developed the planetary boundaries framework, we agreed that we should apply the precautionary principle. This meant that when we proposed where a boundary might lie, we wanted to make sure that the 'safe operating space', that is, the 'planetary space' where the control variables for all of the boundary processes are indeed below the boundary itself is indeed safe. By 'safe' here, we mean that there is very little risk that the Earth System will move towards less-stable conditions driven by its own internal feedbacks. That is, the Earth System will be stable and remain in Holocene-like conditions.

In the 2015 update of the planetary boundaries framework, we introduced the idea of a 'zone of uncertainty' to account that there are indeed large uncertainties about where the boundary should be placed, given gaps in scientific understanding as well as intrinsic variability in Earth System dynamics. The boundary itself was placed at the lower end of the zone of uncertainty, based on our assessment that we would be safe if the control variable was placed below that level. However, as the name indicates, the zone of uncertainty is an area within which we don't know whether the Earth System will be safe or stable, or whether we may have triggered a tipping point or driven an unacceptable level of change to the particular Earth System process. Beyond the zone of uncertainty, there is a very high risk of large, potentially irreversible and often abrupt changes to Earth System process. That would indeed be dangerous planetary territory. So staying within the boundary itself, and not entering the zone of uncertainty, is what is required to remain within the Earth System's 'safe operating space'.

The climate planetary boundary is a good example of how this system works. We set the boundary at an atmospheric CO_2 concentration of 350 ppm. Both observations and model simulations show that such a boundary would cap temperature rise at much less than 1°C, and the Earth System would remain stable at that level. We set the zone of uncertainty at 350–450 ppm CO_2. The idea is that the risks of climate impacts and of triggering a trajectory of the Earth System away from Holocene conditions increases as the CO_2 concentration rises. Observations bear this out. At over 410 ppm, we are already experiencing increases in the frequency and severity of several damaging extreme weather events – extreme heat, drought, intense rainfall, wildfires, tropical cyclones. In addition, several tipping points in the Earth System that could drive it towards hotter conditions, even without any further human forcing, are becoming active. These include loss of Arctic sea ice, melting of Greenland and West Antarctic ice sheets, drought and fires in the Amazon forest, melting of Siberian permafrost, and slowdown of the Atlantic Ocean circulation.

In general, most of the control variables for the boundaries are moving away from the safe operating space, or, if they were within, are moving closer to the boundary itself. An exception to this trend is atmospheric ozone depletion, where the banning of CFCs had led to a stabilization of ozone levels with a good prospect of increasing ozone concentration over the southern hemisphere polar regions over the coming decades. For all of the other boundaries, however, the control variable is moving in the wrong direction. When the next major update of the PB framework is published, hopefully later in 2021, it is likely that at least six of the nine boundaries will be transgressed.

JM: Interesting, reference to the precautionary principle raises a whole set of issues regarding the nature of objectivity and how others interpret and use evidence, including that drawn from your own work. As I am sure you are aware, Article 3 (3) of the 1992 United Nations Framework Convention on Climate Change (UNFCCC) is:

> The Parties should take precautionary measures to anticipate, prevent or minimize the causes of climate change and mitigate its adverse effects. Where there are threats of serious or irreversible damage, lack of full scientific certainty should not be used as a reason for postponing such measures, taking into account that policies and measures to deal with climate change should be ***cost-effective*** so as to ensure ***global benefits at the lowest possible cost***. To achieve this, such policies and measures should take into account different socio-economic contexts, be comprehensive, cover all relevant sources, sinks and reservoirs of greenhouse gases and adaptation, and comprise all economic sectors. Efforts to address climate change may be carried out cooperatively by interested Parties. (UNFCCC, 1992, p. 4 [emphasis added])

Though well-intentioned perhaps, this places prudential action in the context of economic systems and thus opens up policy choices and timing to a whole set of additional considerations that have seemingly affected if and when to address changes to the different control variables your work uses – cost effectiveness, benefits (to who and where?), etc. Do you worry about the misuse and misinterpretation of your work and your colleagues work?

WS: Yes, misrepresentation is indeed a problem. But I think we need to differentiate misrepresentation by those who are using the science and some misrepresentation within the scientific community itself. As an example, there has certainly been misrepresentation of the planetary boundaries framework, and also some possible misuse, at both levels.

The most prominent case of misinterpretation – an apparently deliberate misinterpretation – is the claim by some critics within the scientific community that not all boundary processes have well-defined thresholds or tipping points. That is, there has been a conflation of a boundary with a tipping point. We were very clear that not all boundary processes had tipping points, and even if a boundary process had a tipping point, the boundary itself would be set well upstream of the tipping point. Some critics attempted to discredit the framework by arguing that not all boundary processes had tipping points, despite the fact that we explicitly pointed out that some processes were more gradual, with no discernible tipping point, but nevertheless pushing the process too far would move the Earth System out of Holocene conditions.

Potential misuse, in my view, can occur when the planetary boundary framework is applied to uses or situations for which it was not designed. This type of misuse occurs in the user community, rather than in the scientific community itself. The primary issue here is the framework is explicitly designed to operate at the global level. This has not stopped the 'down-scaling' of the framework to be applied at the level of individual countries or corporations or other economic entities. The problem here is that not all boundary processes scale linearly as one goes down from the global to smaller scales, so setting the portion of the safe operating space that country X, for example, can 'use' is fraught with many difficulties. In terms of corporations, trying to match supply chains with the planetary boundary framework can quickly become extremely difficult to implement.

JM: There is an important issue here that a great deal of business school work on 'sustainable development' tends to neglect. While it is potentially constructive for each and every significant entity to have 'sustainable development' policies, whether in fact an activity is 'sustainable' is not set at the level of that entity, but of the totality of them in so far as the level of activity and its consequences are within the tolerance of systems. Of course, one might think that enough entities undertaking change might mean that change is sufficient to place the aggregate within that tolerance and this seems, for example, to be basic to the 'bottom up' approach adopted for the nationally determined contributions (NDCs) of the Paris Agreement. Your planetary boundaries framework is more broadly based than the main focus on emissions and temperature in Paris Article 2 (1a) (UN, 2015). What scope do you see for that broader based approach to inform the implementation of the Paris Agreement, given that, as you say, the situation seems to have moved from 3 to 4 and perhaps 6 Earth System processes exceeding boundaries – and perhaps you might mention which these others are and what their significance might be?

WS: The two additional boundaries that probably have been transgressed are ocean acidification and freshwater use. In the 2015 assessment of the PBs, ocean acidification was virtually on the boundary itself. Since then, emissions of CO_2 have continued to increase, with the oceans absorbing about 25% of these emissions, thus causing ocean acidification to increase, most likely beyond its boundary value. The other PB that is likely to have been transgressed now is freshwater use. It continues to increase and, along with that issue, we are re-examining where that boundary should be set based on new analyses in the peer-reviewed literature. That is a work-in-progress and we hope to have an update later in the year.

The issue of novel entities will also be updated in our 2021 analysis. At present, there is no suggested boundary. This is an extremely complex process to deal with, starting with the definition of novel entities themselves. Much of the focus so far has been on chemical pollutants, and we are using that as a model for how one sets boundaries for such substances. Late in 2020, we ran a workshop bringing together experts on chemical pollutants and their impact on the environment. An interesting suggestion, which is getting quite a bit of support, is that the boundary for chemical pollution should be set at zero. As the name indicates, a 'novel entity' is something entirely new to the Earth System so the system has no experience in dealing with or metabolizing such materials. This makes sense from a scientific perspective, but it would be very confronting for the chemicals industry. In essence, a PB set at zero for chemical pollution would mean that we would have to develop circular economies and industrial systems, where there are no pollutants or effluents released to the environment. They are all captured and re-used.

JM: Yes, this seems likely to be controversial – not because it is unreasonable, but because of the ingrained problems of industrial processes and uses.[7] Over the last thirty years, plastics producers, for example, have placed considerable resources into convincing the public that recycling has been relatively effective in addressing some of the problems of plastics production and use – yet, as I am sure you know, only a small fraction of plastics are recyclable and are recycled and of these a great proportion are 'down-cycled' rather than 'closed-loop' (a bottle becomes something else rather than a bottle stays a bottle). The level of plastics in our environment, especially micro-plastics, is, of course, now a matter of growing concern and awareness. But, given this is something readers probably already know something about it might be worth illustrating a slightly different issue here in order to reinforce understanding of some of the key issues your PB approach highlights. The idea of feedback seems extremely important, would it be possible to provide an example of a feedback process? Moreover, complexity seems to be an important facet of the Earth System and uncertainty seems to be a key issue arising from interactions which influence feedbacks, so perhaps you might comment on this too. Clearly, uncertainty should not be taken as grounds for complacency, as though it amounted to 'we don't know, so there is no need for concern' – this is intrinsic to the adequacy of a precautionary principle isn't it?

WS: You've certainly raised some important issues here. First, the fact that the Earth System is a complex system is very important but also widely misunderstood. Here, the term 'complex system' is used in a technical sense and not simply to mean a system that is highly complicated with many 'moving parts'. Rather, complex systems are systems that typically exist in well-defined states that are stable and resilient to external forcing agents or internal dynamics. Their resilience is often built around 'negative', or dampening, feedback processes that act to maintain the system in its existing stable state. For example, over half of the human emissions of carbon dioxide to the atmosphere are absorbed by the ocean and land, thus reducing the amount that remains in the atmosphere and acting to maintain the climate in a stable state. In general, the Holocene – the most recent 11,700-year epoch in Earth history – was a stable, resilient state of the Earth System because of these intrinsic negative feedbacks.

However, once complex systems are forced too far away from their stability domains and their dampening feedback mechanisms are overwhelmed, they can move rapidly and irreversibly towards a new state as 'positive' (reinforcing) feedback mechanisms take over. This is the risk that we currently face with the accelerating trajectory of the Earth System away from the Holocene. At present, dampening feedbacks still dominate the overall behaviour of the system, but positive feedbacks are being activated. These include melting permafrost, increasing drought and fire in the Amazon rainforest, and a slowing of the Atlantic Ocean circulation.

The second important issue you've raised above is how to deal with uncertainty. We know, with a high degree of certainty, that many positive feedback processes exist, but we don't know – with a high degree of certainty – where the tipping points for these processes might lie. That is, where is the level of forcing (e.g. temperature rise) beyond which permafrost melt becomes self-reinforcing and thus unstoppable? Even more uncertainty surrounds the interactions among these feedback processes, interactions that could lead to a global tipping cascade. In effect, this is the process that would drive the Earth System from one stable state – the Holocene – into another stable, but much hotter, state, sometimes called 'Hothouse Earth'. Large uncertainties remain regarding the point at which such a global tipping cascade, if it exists, could be initiated. So this is the ultimate challenge for humanity in terms of dealing with the uncertainty-complacency issue, and in applying the precautionary principle. And, of course, the planetary boundary framework is designed to err on the side of safety. That is, if the boundaries are respected, we argue that there is only a very low probability of initiating a tipping cascade.

JM: Coming back to the core focus of Paris via Article 2 (1a), all of this seems to suggest that climate and ecological breakdown is a more complex set of issues than Paris alone can and does address.

WS: Yes, it certainly is. We use the term 'biosphere degradation' for ecological breakdown, and give it core boundary status along with climate change. Core PBs, according to our definition, can change the state of the Earth System on their own. This is clear for climate change. But in the past, major changes to the biosphere have also marked different states of the Earth System as a whole, and many of them have acted as feedback processes that have pushed the Earth System from one state to another. Examples include mass extinction events and the evolution of new life forms. Today there are multiple threats to the biosphere, including the potential for the sixth mass extinction event in Earth's history.

There have been several assessments of how humanity is changing the biosphere now, irrespective of climate change. For example, the big international assessment effort called IPBES (Intergovernmental Science-Policy Platform on Biodiversity and Ecosystem Services) in 2019 came up with a number of overarching conclusions on human-driven degradation of the biosphere. Three of the most prominent ones are: (i) Nature is declining globally at rates unprecedented in human history; (ii) around one million animal and plant species are now threatened with extinction, many within decades, (iii) the web of life on Earth is getting smaller and increasingly frayed.[8]

Palaeo-botanist Mark Williams and his collaborators have examined human degradation of the biosphere in a very long-term perspective and suggest that our impact on the biosphere could represent the third major stage in the evolution of the biosphere in Earth history. They suggest four criteria: (i) global homogenization of flora and fauna; (ii) humans commandeering 25%–40% of the net primary productivity (NPP) of the biosphere and the mining of fossil NPP (fossil fuels); (iii) human-directed evolution of other species; and (iv) increasing interaction of the biosphere and the technosphere (e.g. chemical pollutants).

Although there are certainly some connections between these changes to the biosphere and climate change, often through the carbon cycle, it is absolutely clear that dealing with these profound changes to the biosphere are well beyond the remit of the Paris Accord.

JM: Your comments on degradation, mass extinctions, etc. all speak to issues of conditions and cause and thus evoke the concept of an 'Anthropocene', in so far as our species is not a mere bystander or observer in events but is, rather, the prime mover in them. But before we come to that, given we have raised the issue of Paris, and you had some role in the 2018 IPCC *Global Warming of 1.5°C* report (IPCC, 2018), I am curious as to your opinion on its subsequent reception. On the one hand it has precipitated a significant increase in awareness of the need to urgently tackle climate change and GHG emissions (targets for 2030, net-zero by mid-century, the UN 'Race to Zero campaign etc.).[9] On the other hand, there was considerable wrangling regarding what status to give to the report (bearing in mind it had been invited/commissioned) within the COP process – at COP 24 in Katowice the US, Saudi Arabia, Russia and Kuwait objected to the phrase 'welcomes the report' and preferred 'noted'. Did you find this 'disappointing'?

WS: The reception to the IPCC SR1.5 report was generally very good, despite a few countries apparently not wanting to 'welcome' it. The report has indeed supported the growing calls for much more urgent action on climate change and has also focussed on near-term action with interim emission reduction targets for 2030 becoming much more prominent. The report also provides a stark assessment of the large increase in risks and impacts that will occur at 2°C of warming compared to 1.5°C. A decade or so ago, a 2°C target was thought to be adequate or even 'safe', but the IPCC SR1.5 report seriously challenged that assumption.[10] In addition to the urgency message the SR1.5 report also hammered home the message that the more we learn about climate change the riskier it looks.

JM: This brings us to the Anthropocene. When did you and others start thinking about using this term and what exactly do you mean by it?

WS: The term 'Anthropocene' was introduced by Paul Crutzen in February 2000 at a meeting of the IGBP (International Geosphere-Biosphere Programme) Scientific Committee in Cuernavaca, Mexico. Paul was becoming agitated at continuing references to the Holocene in our discussions of impacts on the Earth System, and he finally interrupted the discussion and forcefully said that we are no longer in the Holocene; we are in the … Anthropocene. He coined the term at just that moment.

The term 'Anthropocene' had two distinct meanings from the beginning. One was clearly based on the Geologic Time Scale, in which the geological history of Earth is divided into time units – eras, periods, epochs and so on. The Anthropocene was suggested as a new epoch to terminate the Holocene, based on the mass of evidence that was being gathered by the IGBP and other research efforts. The second – closely related – meaning was that the Earth System has left the

11,700-year relatively stable Holocene state and was now in a rapid trajectory away from the Holo-cene into significantly new and different conditions. The term Anthropocene also implied that this trajectory away from the Holocene was not being driven by natural forces within or external to the Earth System (e.g. volcanic eruptions, changes in solar intensity, meteorite strikes) but rather by the activities of *Homo sapiens*. As the Anthropocene concept became more broadly known, its interpretations multiplied, primarily in terms of unpacking what aspects of the 'human enterprise' and what segments of the global human population were primarily responsible for the Anthropo-cene. The start date for the Anthropocene is also an interesting topic for discussion, with the geo-logic and Earth System science communities agreeing that the most appropriate start for the Anthropocene is the mid-twentieth century.

JM: This raises a whole set of important issues for how one develops and applies the concept of an Anthropocene and perhaps we could start to draw the interview to a close by inviting you to comment on this? Early on you referred to measures of 'human perturbation' for each of the 9 pro-cesses in the PB framework in relation to response variables. And as you say, there is a great deal of unpacking to do in terms of the nature of human enterprise that underpins the concept of an Anthropocene. Insofar as humans have become a primary influence on the Earth System this evokes the subsequent questions, what human systems, what places, practices, organizations, and policies are producing 'human perturbation'? Some combination of answers to these questions lead to the kinds of consequences the PB identifies. Clearly, the nature of explanations of human systems bears on the adequacy of explanation of how our species has found itself in a period of climate emergency and ecological breakdown, and as a corollary, this must have some bearing on how we view the scope and adequacy of solutions, and conversely, it bears on where we might expect to find impediments to adequate solutions – a subject that ranges across knowledge/theory and its framing effects as well as its influence on research applications, politics and policy.[11]

Ecological economists, of course, are distinguished from other economists by their focus on an economy as a set of material processes, involving thermodynamic consequences, entropy, waste creation, and basic bio-physical modification of the world. This approach brings into ques-tion standard economics, which focuses primarily on the exchange value of goods and services, that, in turn, supports an idea of an economy as a circular flow of income, targeting *continual* economic growth. The standard economic approach disembeds an economy and then, 'environ-mental economics' tries to adapt standard economics to the real-world problems this has pro-duced, by adding on environmental concerns as modifications to the core of the economics. For an ecological economist, this is insufficient to address the generalized problem that human systems are dependent on and consequential for a material world i.e. that there are limits to what can be safely done.[12] However, once this distinction has been made ecological economics starts to divide as the political economy of causation comes to the fore and the problem of 'what is to be done?' is evoked. There is, for example, work that modifies the concept of an Anthro-pocene as a 'Capitalocene', there is renewed debate over limits to growth, but now in the context of 'green new deals', there is scepticism regarding the kinds of integrated assessment models that have dominated debate in environmental economics (the social cost of carbon approach), there is scepticism regarding the influence that faith in solutions stemming from future technology, etc. might have on the 'net' in net-zero (what it will mean in practice), there is a host of work on 'social ecological economics', 'postgrowth' and 'degrowth', which argues that fundamen-tal changes are required in the way society and economies are organized and motivated (and this is different than just massive investment in infrastructure organized around a transition, since it begs the question of, 'from what and to what?'), etc.[13]

I am not sure how familiar you are with this kind of work, so perhaps you might comment on that. Clearly, the importance of your work is not reduced by any of these issues noted above, but they do seem to have some bearing on the timing of an Anthropocene (the subjective aspects perhaps), but more importantly on how we might move towards the 'Alternative Stabilized Earth Pathway' your work draws attention to – one that avoids crossing thresholds that lock us into a 'Hothouse Earth pathway'. And this seems especially so once one starts to think of the focus of Paris as vital yet partial from a more holistic PB perspective ...

WS: You've raised a number of very important issues above, and I'll start with the last one first – the timing of the Anthropocene. If we go back to the original sources of the Anthropocene concept – basically Earth System science and geology/stratigraphy, we have two different criteria for determining the start of the Anthropocene epoch. The Earth System science definition is based on the time at which the trajectory of the Earth System clearly left the 11,700-year stable Holocene epoch, and there is a mass of evidence that points to the mid-twentieth century for that start date. Stratigraphers examine changes in the Earth's stratigraphic record – e.g. ice cores, tree rings, lake and coastal sediments and so on. Can they see a clear line of demarcation where the indicator in the core – isotopic signature, pollen record, nitrate concentration, etc. – clearly changes from one level to another? Again, there is a mass of stratigraphic evidence that shows a break in the stratigraphic record around the mid-twentieth century. Consistent with this bio-physical evidence, historian John McNeill, in his landmark book *Something New Under the Sun*, has described the changes in the human component of the Earth System – governance, technology, economies, international relations – that led to the explosion of human activity from the mid-twentieth century onwards, a phenomenon he labelled the 'Great Acceleration'.[14]

A very interesting point of discussion and debate is just which humans have been most responsible for the Great Acceleration, and hence for driving the Earth System out of the Holocene. And this question has led to some variants on the Anthropocene, such as the 'Capitalocene' and the 'Manthropocene'. The basic point here is that not all humans have been equally responsible for the Anthropocene. In our original analysis of the Anthropocene data, we had lumped all of humanity together as one whole. But in an update of the data to 2010, we divided humanity into three groups – the OECD (wealthy) countries, the so-called BRICS emerging countries (Brazil, Russia, India, China, South Africa) and all the others – the poorer countries. The outcome of this analysis was striking. From 1950 to 2010, nearly all of the population growth was in the BRICS and developing countries, who accounted for about 80% of the global population, yet 74% of the world GDP, and hence consumption, occurred in the OECD countries. That is, the data showed huge inequalities within the human component of the Earth System. These data are from 2010, so the rapid rise of China, for example, would probably change this analysis somewhat if it was taken to 2020. Nevertheless, the analysis of the rapidly changing characteristics of the 'human enterprise' – if I can call it that – are an important feature of the Anthropocene narrative.

So where is the Anthropocene going? Can we quickly change the trajectory of the Earth System away from its current pathway towards Hothouse Earth and onto a Stabilized Earth pathway? There is no clear answer to that question, but perhaps the various attempts to answer it can be grouped into two very broad, contrasting approaches. One is that technology is the solution – switching to renewable energy systems, smart grids, electrified transport systems, high-tech agriculture and so on – will create a sustainable future. Economies can grow and we can become wealthier, but decoupling will reduce our imprint on the Earth System. The other broad pathway is that we require a much deeper transformation, one that is based on a fundamental shift in core values – degrowth, less consumptive lifestyles, from 'wealth' to 'well-being', living much simpler but more satisfying lives, reconnecting with the biosphere, and so on. As of yet, there is no clear answer to these questions, and opinions and debates continue. Probably the only sure thing we can say about the future is that it hasn't happened yet.

JM: Taking stock then, do you see grounds for optimism?

WS: I think we are at a critical point in human history. There are grounds for both optimism and pessimism. The pessimism is fuelled by the power of the incumbents (e.g. the fossil fuel industry) and the conservative political ideologies that hang on to power. Breaking this toxic power structure can seem impossibly hard at times. On the other side of the coin, social tipping points are notoriously difficult to foresee and predict.

JM: And yet 2030 is fast approaching and 2050 is sooner than we like to think. We cannot, seemingly, afford to wait and must begin to provide answers and we need governments to begin to act – to mobilize akin to 'war-footing', as it has been put.[15] The rhetoric around COP26 makes much of this urgency. Moreover, whatever uncertainty pertains, given we are talking about high impact and irreversible processes there seems to be a policy asymmetry situation that the precautionary principle implies, but politics does not always fully embrace: it is better to overrespond rather than under since the consequences of underreaction are surely greater?

WS: But there appears to be mounting pressure across many societies for fundamental change. This, of course, gives one hope for the future. For me, a critical question is timing. There are tipping points in the Earth System and we could be approaching a planetary tipping point that could lead to Hothouse Earth and a dismal future for humanity. So it is a race against time. Can we transform our societies (and ourselves) fast enough to avoid a Hothouse Earth future? That is the critical question, and nobody knows the answer, but it will depend on us – the values that we hold and the choices that we make.

Notes

1. For further information and access to Professor Steffen's work visit:
   https://en.wikipedia.org/wiki/Will_Steffen
   https://climate.anu.edu.au/about/people/academics/professor-will-steffen
   https://www.stockholmresilience.org/meet-our-team/staff/2009-08-24-steffen.html
2. Note from JM: see Ripple et al. (2020, 2021) and "The Climate Emergency: 2020 in Review": https://bit.ly/3nk4QXt
3. Note from JM, the original full list of 9 Earth system processes each with a boundary, parameters, measurement status and comparison to a pre-industrial level (phrased here in terms of foci for potentially adverse effects) comprises: 1. Climate Change; 2. Rate of biodiversity loss; 3. Nitrogen cycle/Phosphorous cycle – jointly comprising the biogeochemical flow boundary; 4. Stratospheric ozone depletion; 5. Ocean acidification; 6. Global freshwater use; 7. Change in land use; 8. Atmospheric aerosol loading; 9. Chemical pollution (Rockström et al., 2009, p. 473). For tipping points discussion see also Lenton et al. (2008) and Lenton et al. (2019).
4. Note from JM: see, for example, Steffen et al. (2011); Robin and Steffen (2007); Crutzen and Steffen (2003). See also Waters et al. (2015) and Zalasiewicz et al. (2010).
5. Note from JM: see, for example, Steffen et al. (2018, p 2016, 2015, 2005).
6. Note from JM: see the 10 year summary of UNEP emissions gap reports for the general trend increase in global emissions (Christensen & Olhoff, 2019).
7. Note from JM: this, of course, does then raise the issue of what fully circular means and whether this is possible (which is a different issue than whether it is unreasonable for corporations to address the problem of pollutants in good faith).
8. Note from JM: see IPBES (2019), note also there is considerable debate regarding the use of standard economic theory to provide commensurable values as the basis of policies to protect, preserve and use ecosystem 'services', as the recent UK Dasgupta Report indicates.

9. Note from JM: Visit Race to Zero at: https://unfccc.int/climate-action/race-to-zero-campaign
   And for the Climate Ambition Alliance see: https://cop25.mma.gob.cl/en/climate-ambition-alliance/

10. Note from JM: moreover, (and noting Professor Steffen's previous comments on the climate planetary boundary) in the 'Trajectories of the Earth System' paper, Steffen and colleagues suggest that Paris climate targets may be insufficient to prevent a Hothouse Earth pathway: "This analysis implies that, even if the Paris Accord target of a 1.5°C to 2.0°C rise in temperature is met, we cannot exclude the risk that a cascade of feedbacks could push the Earth System irreversibly into a 'Hothouse Earth pathway. The challenge that humanity faces is to create a "Stabilized Earth" pathway that steers the Earth System away from its current trajectory toward the threshold beyond which is Hothouse Earth. The human created Stabilized Earth pathway leads to a basin of attraction that is not likely to exist in the Earth System's stability landscape without human stewardship to create and maintain it. Creating such a pathway and basin of attraction requires a fundamental change in the role of humans on the planet." (Steffen et al., 2018, p. 3). For similar concerns see Hansen et al. (2017); Bradshaw et al. (2021).

11. Note from JM: this is the subject matter of many of the contributions to the original special issue of *Globalizations*. See the introduction, Gills and Morgan (2020b). See also Lamb et al. (2020); Røpke (2020); Oreskes and Conway (2010).

12. Note from JM: compare Daly (1997) and Nordhaus (1991).

13. Note from JM: for indicative range see, for example, Hickel and Kallis (2020); Parrique et al. (2019); Dyke et al. (2021); O'Neill et al. (2018); Moore (2015); Asefi-Najafabady et al. (2020); Keen (2020); Spash (2020); Gills and Morgan (2020a).

14. Note from JM: see McNeill (2001).

15. Note from JM: see, for example, Newell and Simms (2020) on 'just transition' and also some of the essays in the edited collection Fullbrook and Morgan (2019).

Disclosure statement

No potential conflict of interest was reported by the author(s).

References

Asefi-Najafabady, S., Villegas-Ortiz, L., & Morgan, J. (2020). The failure of integrated assessment models as a response to 'climate emergency' and ecological breakdown: The emperor has no clothes. *Globalizations*. Advance online publication. https://doi.org/10.1080/14747731.2020.1853958

Bradshaw, C., Ehrlich, P., Beattie, A., Ceballos, G., Crist, E., Diamond, J., Dirzo, R., Ehrlic, A., Harte, J., Harte, M., Pyke, G., Raven, P., Ripple, W., Saltré, F., Turnbull, C., Wackernagel, M., & Blumstein, D. (2021). Underestimating the challenges of avoiding a ghastly future. *Frontiers in Conservation Science*, https://www.frontiersin.org/articles/10.3389/fcosc.2020.615419/full

Christensen, J., & Olhoff, A. (2019). *Lessons from a decade of emissions gap assessments*. UNEP.

Crutzen, P., & Steffen, W. (2003). How long have we been in the Anthropocene era? *Climatic Change*, 61(3), 251–257. https://doi.org/10.1023/B:CLIM.0000004708.74871.62

Daly, H. (1997). Forum, georgescu-roegen vs. solow/stiglitz. *Ecological Economics*, 22(3), 261–266. https://doi.org/10.1016/S0921-8009(97)00080-3

Dyke, J., Watson, R., & Knorr, W. (2021). Climate scientists: concept of net-zero is a dangerous trap. *Social Europe*. 27 April. https://www.socialeurope.eu/climate-scientists-concept-of-net-zero-is-a-dangerous-trap

Fullbrook, E., & Morgan, J. (2019). *Economics and the ecosystem*. World Economic Association Books.

Gills, B. K., & Morgan, J. (2020a). Global climate emergency: After COP24, climate science, urgency, and the threat to humanity. *Globalizations*, *17*(6), 885–902. https://doi.org/10.1080/14747731.2019.1669915

Gills, B. K., & Morgan, J. (2020b). Economics and climate emergency. *Globalizations*. Advance online publication. https://doi.org/10.1080/14747731.2020.1841527

Hansen, J., Sato, M., Kharecha, P., von Schuckmann, K., Beerling, D. J., Cao, J., Marcott, S., Masson-Delmotte, V., Prather, M. J., Rohling, E. J., Shakun, J., Smith, P., Lacis, A., Russell, G., & Ruedy, R. (2017). Young people's burden: Requirement of negative CO_2 emissions. *Earth System Dynamics*, *8*(3), 577–616. https://doi.org/10.5194/esd-8-577-2017

Hickel, J., & Kallis, G. (2020). Is green growth possible? *New Political Economy*, *25*(4), 469–486. https://doi.org/10.1080/13563467.2019.1598964

IPBES. (2019). Summary for policymakers of the global assessment report on biodiversity and ecosystem services of the inter-governmental Science-policy platform on biodiversity and ecosystem services. Bonn: Author. https://ipbes.net/sites/default/files/inline/files/ipbes_global_assessment_report_summary_for_policymakers.pdf

IPCC. (2018). *Global warming of 1.5°C: Summary for policymakers*. IPCC. https://www.ipcc.ch/site/assets/uploads/sites/2/2019/05/SR15_SPM_version_report_LR.pdf

Keen, S. (2020). The appallingly bad neoclassical economics of climate change. *Globalizations*. Advance online publication. https://doi.org/10.1080/14747731.2020.1807856

Lamb, W., Mattioli, G., Levi, S., Roberts, J., Capstick, S., Creutzig, F., Minx, J., Muller-Hansen, F., Culhane, T., & Steinberger, J. (2020). Discourses of climate delay. *Global Sustainability*, *3*(e17), 1–5. https://doi.org/10.1017/sus.2020.13

Lenton, T., Held, H., Kriegler, E., Hall, J., Lucht, W., Rahmstorf, S., & Schellnhuber, H. (2008). Tipping elements in the Earth's climate system. *Proceedings of the National Academy of Sciences of the USA*, *105*(6), 1786–1793. https://doi.org/10.1073/pnas.0705414105

Lenton, T., Rockström, J., Gaffney, O., Rahmstorf, S., Richardson, K., Steffen, W., & Schellnuber, H. (2019). Climate tipping points too risky to bet against. *Nature*, *575*(7784), 592–595. https://doi.org/10.1038/d41586-019-03595-0

McNeill, J. (2001). *Something new under the sun*. Penguin.

Moore, J. (2015). *Capitalism in the Web of life*. Verso.

Newell, P., & Simms, A. (2020). How did we do that? Histories and political economies of rapid and just transitions. *New Political Economy*. Advance online publication. https://doi.org/10.1080/13563467.2020.1810216

Nordhaus, W. (1991). To slow or not to slow: The economics of the greenhouse effect. *The Economic Journal*, *101*(407), 920–937. https://doi.org/10.2307/2233864

O'Conner, T. (2020). Emergent properties. *Stanford Encyclopedia of Philosophy*, https://plato.stanford.edu/entries/properties-emergent/

O'Neill, D., Fanning, A., Lamb, W., & Steinberger, J. (2018). A good life for all within planetary boundaries. *Nature Sustainability*, *1*(2), 88–95. https://doi.org/10.1038/s41893-018-0021-4

Oreskes, N., & Conway, E. (2010). *Merchants of doubt*. Bloomsbury.

Parrique, T., Barth, J., Briens, F., Kerschner, C., Kraus-Polk, A., Kuokkanen, A., & Spangenberg, J. H. (2019). Decoupling debunked. *European environmental bureau*. https://eeb.org/library/decoupling-debunked/

Ripple, W., Wolf, C., Newsome, T., Barnard, P., & Moomaw, W. (2021, January 6). The climate emergency: 2020 in review. *Scientific American*. https://www.scientificamerican.com/article/the-climate-emergency-2020-in-review/

Ripple, W., Wolf, C., Newsome, T., Barnbard, P., & Moomaw, W. (2020). World scientists' warning of a climate emergency. *BioScience*, *70*(1), 8–12. https://doi.org/10.1093/biosci/biz152

Robin, L., & Steffen, W. (2007). History for the anthropocene. *History Compass*, *5*(5), 1694–1719. https://doi.org/10.1111/j.1478-0542.2007.00459.x

Rockström, J., Steffen, W., Noone, K., Persson, Å., Chapin, F. S., Lambin, E. F., Lenton, T. M., Scheffer, M., Folke, C., Schellnhuber, H. J., Nykvist, B., de Wit, C. A., Hughes, T., van der Leeuw, S., Rodhe, H., Sörlin, S.,

Snyder, P. K., Costanza, R., Svedin, U., … Foley, J. A. (2009). A safe operating space for humanity. *Nature* *461*(7263), 472–475. https://doi.org/10.1038/461472a. https://www.nature.com/articles/461472a.pdf

Røpke, I. (2020). Econ 101—In need of a sustainability transition. *Ecological Economics, 169*, Article 106515 https://doi.org/10.1016/j.ecolecon.2019.106515

Spash, C. (2020). The economy as if people mattered: Revisiting critiques of economic growth in a time of crisis. *Globalizations.* Advance online publication. https://doi.org/10.1080/14747731.2020.1761612

Steffen, W., Grinevald, J., Crutzen, P., & McNeill, J. (2011). The anthropocene: Conceptual and historical perspectives. *Philosophical Transactions of the Royal Society A, 369*(1938), 842–867. https://doi.org/10.1098/rsta.2010.0327

Steffen, W., Richardson, K., Rockström, J., Cornell, S. E., Fetzer, I., Bennett, E., Biggs, R., Carpenter, S., de Vries, W., de Wit, C., Folke, C., Gerten, D., Heinke, J., Mace, G. M., Persson, L. M., Ramanathan, V. Reyers, B., & Sorlin, S. (2015). Planetary boundaries: Guiding human development on a changing planet *Science, 347*(6223), 736–746. https://doi.org/10.1126/science.1259855

Steffen, W., Rockström, J., & Costanza, R. (2016). How defining planetary boundaries can transform our approach to growth. *Solutions.* https://thesolutionsjournal.com/2016/02/22/how-defining-planetary-boundaries-can-transform-our-approach-to-growth/

Steffen, W., Rockström, J., Richardson, K., Lenton, T. M., Folke, C., Liverman, D., Summerhayes, C. P. Barnosky, A. D., Cornell, S. E., Crucifix, M., Donges, J. F., Fetzer, I., Lade, S. J., Scheffer, M. Winkelmann, R., & Schellnhuber, H. J. (2018). Trajectories of the Earth System in the anthropocene *Proceedings of the National Academy of Sciences of the USA, 115*(33), 8252–8259. https://doi.org/10 1073/pnas.1810141115

Steffen, W., Sanderson, A., Tyson, P., Steffen, W., Sanderson, R., Tyson, P., Jäger, J., Matson, P., Moore, B. Oldfield, F., Richardson, K., Schellnhuber, H., Turner, B., & Wasson, R. (2005). *Global change and the Earth System: A planet under pressure.* Springer.

UN. (2015). *Paris agreement.* UN. https://unfccc.int/sites/default/files/english_paris_agreement.pdf

UNFCCC. (1992). *United Nations Framework Convention on climate change.* UN. https://unfccc.int/files/essential_background/background_publications_htmlpdf/application/pdf/conveng.pdf

Waters, C., Zalasiewicz, J., Summerhayes, C., Barnosky, A., Poirier, C., Gałuszka, A., Cearreta, A., Edgeworth, M., Ellis, E. C., Ellis, M., Jeandel, C., Leinfelder, R., McNeill, J. R., Richter, D. d., Steffen, W., Syvitski, J. Vidas, D., Wagreich, M., Williams, M., … Wolfe A. P. (2015). The Anthropocene is functionally and stratigraphically distinct from the holocene. *Science, 351*(6269), Article 2622. https://doi.org/10.1126/science aad2622

Zalasiewicz, J., Williams, M., Steffen, W., & Crutzen, P. (2010). The new world of the anthropocene *Environmental Science & Technology, 44*(7), 2228–2231. https://doi.org/10.1021/es903118j

Postscript, an end to the war on nature: COP in or COP out?

Barry Gills and Jamie Morgan

ABSTRACT

In this editorial postscript, we return to a primary theme of this special issue on Economics and Climate Emergency. We elaborate on some aspects of, and reasons why we need, urgent and radical transformative change. We briefly update the trends affecting climate change and ecological breakdown, assess the need for an end to the 'war on nature', which resists a dichotomy between our species and nature and make some comments on the COP process and ways forward which resist 'trasformismo', while embracing the need for just transitions, degrowth and practices rooted in such concepts as 'transversalism'.

On this planet a great number of civilizations have perished in blood and horror. Naturally, one must wish for the planet that one day it will experience a civilization that has abandoned blood and horror; in fact … I am inclined to assume that our planet is waiting for this. But it is terribly doubtful whether we can bring such a present to its hundred or four-hundred-millionth birthday party. And if we don't, the planet will finally punish us, it's unthoughtful well-wishers, by presenting us with the Last Judgment. (Walter Benjamin)

Prophecies often come true as anti-climaxes, the predictions themselves having set the stage too well – serving to acculturate as well as alarm, introducing first and then effectively normalizing the possibility of events that would have seemed, not so long ago, unthinkable. (David Wallace-Wells, 2021)

Introduction

Given the extended period over which the essays for this Special Issue on Economics and Climate Emergency were written and first published online, we thought it appropriate to add a final editorial commentary, to review the significance of recent climate science and renew our call for urgent radical transformative action (Gills, 2020; Gills & Hossieni, 2021). We wish to begin, however, by saying something about our intentions when we decided to organize this project. Our main aim was to critique the dominant mainstream Economics paradigm (often referred to somewhat loosely by the term neoclassical and typically associated with neoliberalism) and to expose its function as a causal driver of the global climate emergency and ecological crisis. Thus, for example, we invited Steve Keen and a number of other economists to contribute critiques of mainstream economics. In our view, it is strategically vital to 'overturn' the dominant paradigm in the field of Economics, and to create and propagate a radically different paradigm and a new standard curriculum for the teaching of the field. This new paradigm should reflect whole systems thinking, Earth system science, and abandon false dichotomies including the supposed separation of humanity from nature (Biermann, 2021), and politics from economics, while moving to a postgrowth and post GDP measured understanding of what constitutes 'wealth creation' and human well-being and future peace and security.

The essays written for this special issue were composed and published online over a two year period. During this short period, we have witnessed an intensification and acceleration of the conjoint crises of global climate change and ecological breakdown (or 'biosphere degradation'). This entails more frequent and intense 'extreme weather events' around the globe; widespread fires and deforestation; increased emissions of methane; and increased polar ice melting, including in Greenland and West Antarctica. Warnings based on the science have grown evermore severe. The use of the term 'collapse' to refer to potential societal or civilizational failures in the coming decades has now become mainstream, while the official responses in terms of real policy commitments and actual greenhouse gas emissions cuts remain woefully inadequate to prevent potentially catastrophic scenarios from becoming future reality.[1] Myriad actors have at least rhetorically taken on board the need to plan to decarbonize, or to achieve 'net zero' status but much of this lacks concrete plans, clear implementable policy or immediate consequences (as well as a realistic assessment of the nature of 'net').

Average global temperature continues to follow a general trend increase, as do the cumulative parts per million of CO_2 in the atmosphere on a global basis. In response, mass movements of protest and mobilization have rapidly grown across the world, demanding radical change to the status quo and emergency action on the climate crisis. It has tended to be the poorest and most vulnerable people in the world who suffer first and most severely from the global crisis, revealing deep inequalities and structural injustices in the existing global order. The failure of the existing state governance systems and global institutions to adequately address the climate emergency indicates the urgent historical need for radical transformation, or what is now widely referred to as 'system change'.

Moreover, over the short period since we began this project, the global Covid pandemic has struck, numerous economies have floundered, poverty, debt and inequality have increased, and great swathes of populations have suffered increased vulnerabilities and disruptions. The triple crisis of capital, climate, and Covid, and their intimate interrelationship, is now apparent to everyone. The existing global system, and indeed our present form of civilization, is entering a period of 'implosion' (Gills, 2020). This too follows a trend, according to work by Earth system scientists over the last two decades or so, 3, then 4, and now likely 6 of 9 'planetary boundaries' have been transgressed (Steffen & Morgan, 2021). This risks a host of feedback amplification problems as well as transitions that are irreversible according to any reasonable timeline.

Amongst the recent scientific reports documenting the progress of the crisis, the eleventh UNEP emissions gap report was published, revealing yet another set of dire statistics for greenhouse gas emissions (UNEP, 2020). The situation is severe enough to cause many in the scientific community to organize and the Alliance of World Scientists have reiterated the extreme risks and urgent imperative for action commensurate to the reality of climate emergency (Ripple et al., 2021a, 2021b). The IPCC, meanwhile, collates and publishes material in cycles, culminating in a synthesis 'Assessment Report' (AR). The IPCC is currently in its 6th cycle, and the AR6 synthesis report is due in 2022. However, the IPCC recently released a report from Working Group 1 ('physical basis') which provides detailed measurements of the actual extent of greenhouse gas emissions and unfolding global climate patterns (IPCC, 2021). This makes it very clear that in all 5 of its scenarios, within the next two decades global warming reaches or exceeds the 1.5°C goal of the Paris Agreement, regardless of how radically governments and corporations now cut greenhouse gas emissions, albeit the authors make every effort not to convey the impression that our situation is irredeemable.

In any case, according to the IPCC report, 'low likelihood' but potentially high impact or 'extreme events', including the possibility of 'abrupt responses and tipping points of the climate system' are now becoming more likely as global heating continues. This includes processes such as Antarctic ice sheet melt, forest dieback, and slowing of the Atlantic Meridional Overturning Circulation (AMOC) oceanic flow (the conveyor which brings warm waters north in the Atlantic). Among the further consequences are continued trends of ocean acidification, and sea-level rise, which will be 'irreversible for centuries'. Humanity is currently on course for the IPCC 'intermediate' and 'high' emissions scenarios, which could produce warming of 2.7°C to 3.6°C by 2100 respectively.

We are thus heading towards the catastrophic end of previous anticipations of possible futures even though in recent years the key measure of 'climate sensitivity' (the rate of heating per doubling of CO_2) has narrowed for core scenarios; and it is worth noting that over the years the general direction of travel has been (eventually – given there have been debates regarding differences between immediately observable effects and long term consequences for the balance of modelling of climate change) towards worst cases based on the full array of interdependencies and effects on climate systems and the biosphere. This is mainly because explicable but otherwise uncertain effects are taking hold – creating a problem of known unknowns and surprise. As a recent paper in *Earth System Dynamics* notes, while various particular processes are 'well-understood' it remains unclear how 'interdependencies' will unfold and with what consequences, though 'domino effects' and tipping points can be at least conjectured within current computational constraints (Wunderling et al., 2021).[2] The anticipation is that these exacerbate adverse effects – and because of inherent limitations *modelling* may ultimately underestimate effects. In any case, some consequences are being observed *quicker* than expected, such as changes to temperature variation in the Antarctic, the fragmentation of ice shelves and the subsequent rate of loss of ice sheets from land to sea.

Still, according to the IPCC report the 'good news' is that, in the most ambitious low emissions scenario, with emissions cuts made to achieve 'net zero' and the removal of further CO_2 from the atmosphere (i.e. 'negative emissions'), the global climate might eventually stabilize after 20 years, and heating fall back to 1.4°C by 2100. Depending on the category of measure at present, humanity emits around 40 billion tonnes of CO_2 per annum. Under the 'very low' emissions scenario from the IPCC (to achieve 1.4°C by 2100) that will need to fall to 5 tonnes per annum by 2050. As Ed Hawkins, one of the authors of the IPCC report states, 'Every bit of warming matters. The consequences get worse and worse and worse as we get warmer and warmer and warmer. Every tonne of CO_2 matters.'[3]

The 'good news', furthermore, is tempered and this speaks to the need for the most urgent and radical of action. With assistance from members of Scientist Rebellion a leaked report has emerged from sources within the IPCC – Mitigation (Group III) (CTXT, 2021).[4] This is the group responsible for analysis of how to reduce emissions and mitigate impacts. The final report will not be published until March 2022, that is, long after vital decisions have been made at the next 'Conference of the Parties' (COP). In that leaked report, the authors state that emissions must peak globally *before* 2025 and reach net zero between 2050 and 2075. Concomitantly, no new coal or gas-fired plants should be built and existing ones should be wound down before their normal time of decommissioning, growth in global consumption of energy and materials (which remains the main cause of increase of greenhouse gases) must be reduced, which requires a 'massive transition in the consumption of materials around the world' (CTXT, 2021). Significantly, they also note it is possible to address extreme poverty around the world without exacerbating the global heating crisis – given that 'the largest emitters are the richest' and the richest 10% emit ten times more than the poorest 10%.

The leaked report endorses what amounts to a degrowth strategy and suggests that:

> In scenarios that contemplate a reduction in energy demand, mitigation challenges are significantly reduced, with less dependence on CO_2 removal (CDR), less pressure on land and lower prices of carbon. These scenarios do not suppose a decrease in well-being, but rather a provision of better services. (cited in CTXT, 2021)

Cited measures to be taken include both legislative acts and civil society mobilization and protest.

There are in addition various other endorsements by scientists of what are essentially degrowth pathways. For example, a recent article in *Nature Communications* advocates the benefits of planning a stabilization or decrease in energy and materials use, in recognition that continued unbridled growth without damage to the planetary environment is impossible (Keyber & Lenzen, 2021).

And as we return to below, then there is 'Glasgow' and the (as many of its participants now suggest) critical moment of COP26 … In terms of the planet taken as a whole there has been a gulf between the rhetoric and reality of the combined action of governments for decades. Gaming, denial, delay, and deferral in terms of actions commensurate to the problem have dominated. And so here we are in a situation where our species' future well-being and perhaps even survival now rests, in part, upon the ability of governments to rise above particular interests and recognize that there can be no particular interests if we do not act in our collective interest. That means taking the necessary decisions to change course *immediately* and to rapidly accelerate the scope and speed of action across the planet. This, in turn, requires (however one thinks about the nature of historic responsibility, since the planet doesn't care either way) greatest action from those who are currently in a position to make the majority of material difference – China, the USA, EU, Australia, Japan, Russia, Brasil … (e.g. Smith, 2020).

One thing seems certain, what 'we', i.e. the whole of humanity, do to respond to climate emergency and ecological breakdown during the present decade of the 2020s is absolutely pivotal. Our collective actions now seem likely to determine the future prospects of humanity for centuries to come. The radical urgency of now is present. An 'age of adaptation' looms, and an era of politics of tipping points ensues (Lewis, 2021). As the recent IPCC report concludes, we urgently need transformational change, across myriad processes and behaviours, at all levels from individual, to national, regional and global. We need to redefine and transform our way of life. Politics and policy in the coming decades will be compelled to debate and organize sweeping adaptations and mitigation, as the progress of the global climate crisis increasingly threatens our existing infrastructure, built environment, and food system with obsolescence (e.g. heat domes and melting power cables, extreme drought and flooding, widespread fires) In short, as global heating increases, our existing infrastructure, built environment, and agricultural and forestry systems will be rendered 'unfit for purpose' and will become more prone to potentially calamitous system failures. We need to redesign our civilization.

An end to the war on nature?

Industrial consumer capitalism has taken the form of an undeclared war on nature. If we look to adverse consequences for the planet on which we live this statement scarcely warrants defending today. Every new data point regarding rising tonnes of carbon in the atmosphere and thinning top soils on the Earth, every report of yet another square metre of the planet brought under the sway of human habitation, modification or extraction, speaks to this undeclared war ... And every new drought, forest fire and flood, every disappearing ice sheet, every oceanic algae bloom, every tangle of plastic, every poisoned river, every industrial fishing trawler, every species brought to extinction, lends credence to this undeclared war.

It does not require capitalism to be the only thing for this war to be real, it does not require other forms of socio-economic organization to be guiltless, it does not require an absence of countervailing initiatives in some places (clean air acts, taxes and targets for this or that problem, investment in and adoption of 'green technologies', changes to consumer behaviour etc.) for the existence of this war to be true in totality.[5] Nor is capitalism a dirty word (even if it invites us to dirty the planet from pole to pole). It is simply the term for our dominant way of organizing an economy and we need to be clear about what the consequences of this collective activity have been on a global basis (even if some countries, corporations, peoples and places are more responsible than others) since the industrial revolution and since the further 'great acceleration' of climate and ecological harms over the last half century (McNeill, 2001; Moore, 2015). Whatever one thinks of their various positions on issues such as how to value 'natural capital' and its implications for asset formation and exploitation, influential Earth system scientists such as Johan Rockström generally affirm that the root cause of our present climate and ecological crises is humanity's 'overexploitation' of nature and that this involves a 'mode of development' that now has a planetary extent. Global extractivism has expanded immensely over the past several decades, placing extreme stress on essentially every ecosystem and region of the planetary web of life and we may face a 'ghastly future' (Bradshaw et al., 2021).[6]

One might say the evidence hides in plain sight, but 'hides' seems inappropriate now, whatever the metaphor was intended to convey. In any case, we cannot continue to be reckless of obvious consequences. What has become equally obvious is that this is not a 'war' our current form of social order can win. It has been said many times but bears repeating, socio-economies depend on flows of energy and materials, they are 'metabolic' and their processes are subject to thermodynamics (e.g. Spash & Guisan, 2021). Energy is neither created nor destroyed (the first law) but in use it is dissipated or disordered (the second law), which we call entropy and this is the direction of travel of the totality of systems, but it is a tendency that any individual system can offset by drawing on another. Hence, human systems create order by drawing in and using up energy sources in order to transform one thing into another, but at the expense of energy dissipation and waste into the greater environment. Until the industrial revolution this was, historic empires notwithstanding, mainly a localized, slow and relatively low impact set of effects. Today, however, it is an industrial and consumer system built around continual expansion, built around intensive and extensive growth, an accumulation system, measured according to exchange values in a circular flow of income. Within this industrial and then consumer system, technology and fossil fuel use led to a whole new order of energy exchange, resource use and waste creation. From this has emerged a series of industrial revolutions (chemical, electrical, digital etc.), beginning in some countries but with a globalizing drive and from all of this has emerged the world as we know it: a place of marvels, but equally a system that has manifestly failed to learn the lesson that one cannot expand (the

ECONOMICS AND CLIMATE EMERGENCY

extraction and consumption of resources drawn from the web of life) without limit on a finite planet. To mix metaphors this is to cut off the branch on which we sit or hole the boat in which we float.

The overwhelming weight of evidence suggests that the global collective of economies cannot 'decouple' economic activity from energy and resource use sufficiently to allow that economic activity to continue at its current scale and intensity (which already far exceeds the regenerative capacity of the Earth) and that it cannot do so in a way that would facilitate economic activity on the basis of *continual* global economic growth (Hickel & Kallis, 2020; Parrique et al., 2019). Decarbonization is just one among many challenges and in the end no socio-economy can 'dematerialise' in any meaningful sense. How to address the problem 'as is' is already acute, as William Rees recently noted:

> Many analysts ignore the sheer scale of the required transition. The IPCC emissions reduction schedule requires reductions of ~7% year assuming we began in 2021. In the absence of carbon capture and storage, this would mean substituting for 7% of fossil fuel use. Consider that in 2019 fossil fuels contributed 492.34 Ej (136,761.11 Twh) to global primary energy production (84%). Seven percent of this is 34.46 Ej or 9573.3 Twh. If we assume a conversion ratio of 2.47:1 for wind and solar (W&S) energy (i.e., 1 unit of wind/solar energy = 2.47 units of fossil energy when converted to electricity), we would need 3875.8 Twh of new W&S electricity in just the first year. However, the total amount of W&S electricity generated in 2019 was 2153.7 Twh (equivalent to <4% of supply). In short, to meet the IPCC Paris target (-7% emissions per year) we need to build 1.80 (3875.8/2153.7) times the entire multi-decade cumulative global stock of wind and solar installations in the first year alone. Repeat the process in subsequent years. This is impossible. In any event, building out a renewable energy infrastructure at this pace would itself blow emissions limits; and even if it could be done (coupled with 100% carbon capture) the world would still have an overshoot crisis. (Energy data from BP Statistical Review of World Energy 2020). (Rees, 2021, p. 105, fn 6)

The precision and technical details of Rees's calculation are less important than the general point made. There is no victory over nature if our species insists on continual material growth, on treating the planet as a place of rapacious and relentless resource extraction and as a site for endless disposal of our waste products. Moreover, while the IPCC may be right to suggest we need a response equivalent to mobilization for war, the very language of war speaks to a meaning frame which seeks to master the world rather than take our place in it as one species among many. Recognition of this does not require us to idealize nature according to some bucolic fantasy or fictive past, it does not require us to reify nature or dichotomize 'man' and 'nature' (we must frame our thinking differently, e.g. Biermann, 2021), but it does require us to accept that commodifying nature is not just metaphor, it is a material reality which is counterproductive to the survival and ultimate flourishing of our species.[7] From this flows the ineluctable conclusion that civilization *must* change.

Rational accommodation to evidence is not surrender, but rather survival through cultural learning. As most of us know and as the news cycle increasingly informs us, governments have finally begun to acknowledge that we are in a climate emergency and that ecological breakdown is widespread. They have also started to acknowledge the broader significance of this. For example the UK House of Commons Environmental Audit Committee recently stated:

> To reverse the trend of biodiversity loss requires urgent transformative change. This cannot be achieved simply through using natural resources more efficiently. Total material consumption in developed economies needs to be reduced, nature needs to be accounted for in economic decision making and governments and businesses need to take pre-emptive and precautionary actions to avoid, mitigate and remedy the deterioration of nature. Alternatives to GDP urgently need to be adopted as more

appropriate ways to measure economic success, appraise investment projects and identify sustainable development. (UK Environmental Audit Committee, 2021)

This is a small step towards recognizing the underlying causes of our current predicament and as the previous section suggested, such acknowledgements can now be found in many places. But they are very far from a coordinated global, timely and practical set of solutions to climate emergency and ecological breakdown. The recent IPCC *Global Warming of 1.5°C* report (IPCC, 2018) has seemingly galvanized many powerful actors and the UN has organized the Climate Ambition Alliance to encourage countries to increase the ambition of their 'nationally determined contributions' under the Paris Agreement and has launched the 'Race to Zero' campaign to feed this through to cities, regions and businesses.[8]

Paris, of course, evokes the role of the United Nations Framework Convention on Climate Change (UNFCCC). The UNFCCC was established in 1992 and the Conference of the Parties (COP) process has been a key feature since 1995. As Will Steffen notes, the focus of the climate convention is insufficient to encompass all aspects of our current crises and yet the COP process is a vital component in any solution (Steffen & Morgan, 2021). As previously noted, at the time of writing, COP 26 hosted in Glasgow by the UK government (in partnership with Italy) was fast approaching and will quickly come and go. It is a cliché to say that these are 'days of decision' but the rhetoric of the COP process now reflects this cliché. The question is whether rhetoric will become reality (see Newell & Taylor, 2020). The UK Prime Minister, Boris Johnson, is no one's idea of an eco-activist and his introduction to COP 26 highlights a basic tension:

> As the world looks to recover from the impact of coronavirus on our lives, livelihoods and economies, we have the chance to build back better. Our Ten Point Plan will help deliver a green industrial revolution – by investing in clean energy, transport, nature and innovative technologies–creating hundreds of thousands of jobs in the process. Leading the world in tackling and adapting to climate change is a major economic opportunity for the UK, that will create new skilled jobs across the country as well as export opportunities for our firms. (UK Government, 2021)[9]

For wealthy countries and their governments, the climate emergency is an economic opportunity, one which invites responses according to the logic of an accumulation system energized by global competition between countries and through corporations and financial institutions. For poorer countries and their governments, this logic still applies, but climate emergency appears first more as economic threat than opportunity, since it seems to imply denial of the same basis of 'development' travelled by advanced capitalist countries. It is this fragmented sense of competitive concerns that must be disentangled if our species is to respond adequately to the crises it now confronts. As Andrew Sayer memorably puts it 'The dream of "green growth", with capitalism delivering sustainability, is like selling guns to promote peace' (Sayer, 2015, p. 341).

As we suggested in the previous section the case for smaller less impactful economies and transition to a 'postgrowth' world is gaining traction and there are numerous strands and contributions and continual development of argument and policy across an array of positions, such as social-ecological economics and degrowth (e.g. Demaria et al., 2013; Hickel, 2020; Kallis, 2018; Liegey & Nelson, 2020; Spash, 2020).

'Transversalism' and 'Deep restoration' rather than 'trasformismo'

To conclude, the many essays in this special issue and the many others published in *Globalizations* (e.g. Spash & Hache, 2021), including the recent special issue titled 'It's About Time: Climate

Change, Global Capital and Radical Existence' (e.g. Jasanoff, 2021), and the work of a growing community of scholars and activists (e.g. Polluters Out, 2020; Stay Grounded, 2021) speak to various aspects of the issues we have highlighted in this editorial postscript.[10] As Peter Newell's work argues and his latest book *Power Shift* confirms, the change we need must distinguish transformation from 'trasformismo' (Newell, 2021). Trasformismo is a term drawn from Gramsci. It refers to co-option that undermines or subverts change (greenwashing and so on) and its typical companion term is 'passive revolution' or strategies that advocate gradual change but default to vested interests or power preserving strategies that continually fall short of what is needed by deferring significant change into some notional future. One does not need to be a Marxist in order to appreciate how these terms resonate with our experience of the last few decades (Oreskes & Conway, 2010). Capitalist states are characterized by their simultaneous functions of reproducing the conditions for continued (and expanded) accumulation, while being held responsible for the mitigation or partial correction of the adverse social and environmental consequences of that same system of production and consumption (e.g. Ioris, 2014).

While we need governments to act and policy coordination through initiatives such as the COP process are vital, they are not sufficient and we cannot depend on them. Political pressure and grassroots changes from below are just if not more important. And transformation has many parts. These may sometimes be disparate but can be given a direction of travel. To begin with we need something better than the current sustainable development goals (Weber, 2017), something which begins from debt jubilee and which stops systematically taking from the poor in ways that produce and reproduce poverty and structural inequality within and across countries (Hickel et al., 2021). Without this there will always be motives for neoliberal varieties of 'development' within the prison cell of debt servicing. A change here provides a precursor to financing other changes and the combination might underpin the implementation of 'just transitions' at the global and local level (Newell & Simms, 2020).

With just transition comes the possibility of a feasible 'good life for all *within* planetary boundaries' (O'Neill, 2018; O'Neill et al., 2018). But for this to occur we need also to encourage critique of forms of theory and practice that invite complacency. As the many essays in this special issue suggest, we need to unlearn in order to move forward and nowhere is that more important than in terms of the role of mainstream economic theory. Moreover, we need to stop putting faith in technofixes that continually invite us to delay taking urgent action in the here and now (Dyke et al., 2021; Morgan, 2020). The COP process, however, is currently heavily invested (in both senses of the term) in technofixes, rather than consistently recognizes that technology is merely an aspect of a *differently founded* future, one that recognizes 'enough is enough' (Dietz & O'Neill, 2013). Ultimately, we need to move past the 'bullshit' (Stevenson, 2021) and we need to start unmaking the future we are currently making.[11]

As one of us has previously written, we 'are living in a time of exception. A time when the existing order is open to question' (Gills, 2020, p. 577). The triple conjuncture of climate change and ecological breakdown, global pandemic and neoliberal economic globalization speak to a Great Implosion, and while the pandemic will eventually end, responses to it have created a precedent. Governments can mobilize to address imminent crisis. 'Deep restoration' is possible. 'The time we had grown accustomed to feel and were socialized to understand as normality, and to regard as the only reality (i.e. the linear time of capitalist modernity) is now suddenly exposed as only one stream of time' (Gills, 2020, p. 578). But for this to be achieved we need new ways of thinking. 'Transversalism' is one possibility. Rather than co-option:

Transversalism aims at consolidating political coalitions and achieving ideational accommodation between social groups … it does not imply uniformity or a general theory of social emancipation … [it] consists of the following elements: (1) recognition of diversity and difference, (2) dialogue (deliberation across differences), (3) systemic self-reflection, (4) intentional openness (intention to explore the reality of the Other), (5) critical awareness of the intersectional nature of power relations that affects interconnections, and finally (6) commitment to creating alterity through hybridization and creolization of ideas and actions. (Gills & Hossieni, 2021)

That other worlds are possible does not dis-embed our species from the material world. The very need for us to develop a different way of living is because we need a different relationship to the environment on which we depend. Transversalism is simply a tentative guide for praxes and there are likely many similar, since it does no more than recognize decisions need to be made, populations need to mobilize, and action needs to be taken. Now. This can be democratic or it can follow a more ominous and increasingly authoritarian route if states and corporations do not match rhetoric to reality and our civilizations slide towards the dystopia science fiction has popularized.

Notes

1. The Kyoto protocol defined the GHGs as: Carbon dioxide (CO_2), Methane (CH_4), Nitrous Oxide (N_2O), Hydro-fluorocarbons (HFC), Perfluorocarbons (PFC), Nitrogen Trifluoride (NF_3) and Sulphur Hexafluoride (SF_6).
2. To be clear this creates a whole set of issues regarding the tendency to rely on modelled findings given the models cannot cope with fundamental uncertainty and it is highly debatable whether they can overcome this if it is an intrinsic aspect – as highly constrained scenarios, however, they provide a resource for prudential conduct (if placed in the context of further and fundamental uncertainty).
3. Ed Hawkins, Reading University, UK, cited in New Scientist, 9 August, 2021 'Earth will hit 1.5C climate limit within 20 years, says IPCC Report'.
4. See: https://scientistrebellion.com
5. See, for example, Richard Smith's work on China which makes the case that China's engine of growth does not reduce only to 'market drivers of capitalism' but rather also involves 'statist-nationalist extra-economic drivers' leading to 'overproduction, over construction, overdevelopment, profligate resource consumption and wanton dumping and venting of pollutants' (Smith, 2020, pp. xxi–xxii). And according to Smith: "For more than a century the US was the world's largest CO_2 emitter by far. But its emissions declined from their peak of 7,370 million Mt CO_{2e} (metric tons of CO_2 equivalent) in 2007 to 6,457 million Mt CO_{2e} in 2017, reflecting the ongoing replacement of coal-fired power plants with solar, wind and lower-emissions natural gas energy sources. The emissions of the European Union countries have also trended downward over the past three decades from 5,654 million Mt CO_{2e} in 1990 to 4,206 million Mt CO_{2e} in 2017. To be sure, these declines are far from sufficient to reverse global warming – they aren't even enough to meet their commitments to the 2015 Paris Agreement on climate change – but at least they were declines. By contrast, China's carbon emissions have relentlessly grown, quadrupling from 3,265 million Mt CO_{2e} in 1990 to 13,442 Mt CO_{2e} in 2018 … [Though China is the world's biggest investor in and producer of renewable technologies across economic sectors it continues to build coal power production facilities and capacity] China isn't replacing fossil fuels with renewables so much as building more capacity of *both*. [And China's emissions have grown faster than its proportion of the global economy, China's emissions overtook the US in 2005 then] in just twelve years from 2005 to 2017 China's CO_2 emissions nearly double again to more than twice those of the US. Yet China's GDP was only 63% as large as the US GDP in 2017 … [While] Per capita CO_2 emissions surged past those of the EU six years ago and are now half those of the US (7.45 Mt CO_{2e} vs. 15.56 Mt CO_{2e} in 2018). Yet China's per capita GDP was just 15% that of the US in 2018 ($9,627 vs. $62,904)" (Smith, 2020, p. xiv). See also Gills and Morgan (2020).
6. Visit: www.exalt.fi

7. Note: the UNEP recently published *Making Peace With Nature* (UNEP, 2021), and while this has many useful arguments and suggested initiatives it also makes the case for a full cost accounting of nature and this involves some deeply problematic issues as Spash and Hache note (2021) in regard of the Dasgupta report.
8. For the climate ambition alliance, see: https://cop25.mma.gob.cl/en/climate-ambition-alliance/
   Visit Race to zero at: https://unfccc.int/climate-action/race-to-zero-campaign
9. See also: https://ukcop26.org and https://unfccc.int/process-and-meetings/conferences/glasgow-climate-change-conference
10. The list of included contributions includes: Gills and Morgan (2021a); Spash (2021a); Hickel (2021); Trainer (2021); Galbraith (2021); Spash (2021b); Keen (2021); Asefi-Najafabady et al. (2021); Gills and Morgan (2021b); Bacevic (2021); Koch and Buch-Hansen (2021); Dale (2021); Fox and Alldred (2021); Goodman and Anderson (2021); Egmose et al. (2021) and Steffen and Morgan (2021).
11. There are numerous sources here including the work of Heikki Patomäki (e.g. Patomäki, 2011).

Disclosure statement

No potential conflict of interest was reported by the author(s).

References

Asefi-Najafabady, S., Villegas Ortiz, L., & Morgan, J. (2021). The failure of Integrated Assessment Models as a response to 'Climate Emergency' and ecological breakdown. The Emperor has no clothes. *Globalizations*, *18*(7), 1178–1188. https://doi.org/10.1080/14747731.2020.1853958

Bacevic, J. (2021). Unthinking knowledge production: from post-Covid to post-carbon futures. *Globalizations*, *18*(7), 1206–1218. https://doi.org/10.1080/14747731.2020.1807855

Biermann, F. (2021). The future of environmental policy in the Anthropocene: time for a paradigm shift. *Environmental Politics*, *30*(1-2), 61–80. https://doi.org/10.1080/09644016.2020.1846958

Bradshaw, C., Ehrlich, P., Beattie, A., Ceballos, G., Crist, E., Diamond, J., Dirzo, R., Ehrlich, A., Harte, J., Harte, M., Pyke, G., Raven, P., Ripple, W., Saltré, F., Turnbull, C., Wackernagel, M., & Blumstein, D. (2021). Underestimating the challenges of avoiding a ghastly future. *Frontiers in Conservation Science*. https://www.frontiersin.org/articles/10.3389/fcosc.2020.615419/full.

CTXT. (2021). (Contexto Y Accion) 'El IPCC considera que el decrecimiento es clave para mitigar el cambio climatico.' Juan Bordera and Fernando Prieto, 7/08/21.

Dale, G. (2021). Rule of nature or rule of Capital? Physiocracy, ecological economics, and ideology. *Globalizations*, *18*(7), 1230–1247. https://doi.org/10.1080/14747731.2020.1807838

Demaria, F., Schneider, F., Sekulova, F., & Martinez-Alier, J. (2013). What is degrowth? From an activist slogan to a social movement. *Environmental Values*, *22*(2), 191–215. https://doi.org/10.3197/096327113X13581561725194

Dietz, R., & O'Neill, D. (2013). *Enough is enough*. Earthscan.

Dyke, J., Watson, R., & Knorr, W. (2021). Climate scientists: Concept of net-zero is a dangerous trap. *Social Europe*, April 27th. https://www.socialeurope.eu/climate-scientists-concept-of-net-zero-is-a-dangerous-trap.

Egmose, J., Jacobsen, S., Hauggaard-Nielsen, H., & Hulgard, L. (2021). The regenerative turn: on the re-emergence of reciprocity embedded in living ecologies. *Globalizations*, *18*(7), 1271–1276. https://doi.org/10.1080/14747731.2021.1911508

Fox, N. J., & Alldred, P. (2021). Economics, the climate change policy-assemblage and the new materialisms: towards a comprehensive policy. *Globalizations*, *18*(7), 1248–1258. https://doi.org/10.1080/14747731.2020.1807857

Galbraith, J. K. (2021). Economics and the climate catastrophe. *Globalizations*, *18*(7), 1117–1122. https://doi.org/10.1080/14747731.2020.1807858

Gills, B. K. (2020). Deep Restoration: from the Great Implosion to the Great Awakening. *Globalizations*, *17*(4), 577–579. doi:10.1080/14747731.2020.1748364

Gills, B. K., & Hossieni, S. A. H. (2021). Transversalism and transformative praxes: Globalization from below. *Cadmus*, forthcoming.

Gills, B. K., & Morgan, J. (2020). Global Climate Emergency: After COP24, climate science, urgency, and the threat to humanity. *Globalizations*, *17*(6), 885–902. https://doi.org/10.1080/14747731.2019.1669915

Gills, B. K., & Morgan, J. (2021a). Economics and Climate Emergency. *Globalizations*, *18*(7), 1071–1086. https://doi.org/10.1080/14747731.2020.1841527

Gills, B. K., & Morgan, J. (2021b). Teaching climate complacency: mainstream economics textbooks and the need for transformation in economics education. *Globalizations*, *18*(7), 1189–1205. https://doi.org/10.1080/14747731.2020.1808413

Goodman, J., & Anderson, J. (2021). From climate change to economic change? Reflections on 'feedback'. *Globalizations*, *18*(7), 1259–1270. https://doi.org/10.1080/14747731.2020.1810499

Hickel, J. (2020). *Less is more: How degrowth will save the world*. Penguin Random House UK.

Hickel, J. (2021). What does degrowth mean? A few points of clarification. *Globalizations*, *18*(7), 1105–1111. https://doi.org/10.1080/14747731.2020.1812222

Hickel, J., & Kallis, G. (2020). Is green growth possible? *New Political Economy*, *25*(4), 469–486. doi:10.1080/13563467.2019.1598964

Hickel, J., Sullivan, D., & Zoomkawala, H. (2021). Plunder in the post-colonial era: Quantifying drain from the global south through unequal exchange, 1960–2018. *New Political Economy*, https://doi.org/10.1080/13563467.2021.1899153

Ioris, A. (2014). *The political ecology of the state*. Routledge.

IPCC. (2018, October). *Global warming of 1.5°C: Summary for policymakers*. Author.

IPCC. (2021). The physical science basis summary for policy makers. Working Group 1 of the IPCC, IPCC 6th Assessment Report (AR6).

Jasanoff, S. (2021). Humility in the anthropocene. *Globalizations*, *18*(6), 839–853. doi:10.1080/14747731.2020.1859743

Kallis, G. (2018). *In defence of degrowth: Opinions and manifestos*. Uneven Earth Press.

Keen, S. (2021). The appallingly bad neoclassical economics of climate change. *Globalizations*, *18*(7), 1149–1177. https://doi.org/10.1080/14747731.2020.1807856

Keyber, L. T., & Lenzen, M. (2021). 1.5°C degrowth scenarios suggest the need for new mitigation pathways. *Nature Communication*, *12*, article 2676 (11 May). doi:10.1038/s41467-021-22884-9

Koch, M., & Buch-Hansen, H. (2021). In search of a political economy of the postgrowth era. *Globalizations*, *18*(7), 1219–1229. https://doi.org/10.1080/14747731.2020.1807837

Lewis, S. (2021). The climate crisis can't be solved by carbon accounting tricks. *The Guardian*, 3 March. https://www.theguardian.com/commentisfree/2021/mar/03/climate-crisis-carbon-accounting-tricks-big-finance.

Liegey, V., & Nelson, A. (2020). *Exploring Degrowth: A Critical Guide*. Pluto Press.

McNeill, J. (2001). *Something new under the sun*. Penguin.

Moore, J. (2015). *Capitalism in the web of life*. Verso.

Morgan, J. (2020). Electric vehicles: The future we made and the problem of unmaking it. *Cambridge Journal of Economics*, *44*(4), 953–977. doi:10.1093/cje/beaa022

Newell, P. (2021). *Power shift: The global political economy of energy transitions*. Cambridge University Press.

Newell, P., & Simms, A. (2020). How did we do that? Histories and political economies of rapid and just transitions. *New Political Economy*, https://doi.org/10.1080/13563467.2020.1810216

Newell, P., & Taylor, O. (2020). Fiddling while the planet burns? COP 25 in perspective. *Globalizations*, *17*(4), 580–592. doi:10.1080/14747731.2020.1726127

O'Neill, D., Fanning, A., Lamb, W., & Steinberger, J. K. (2018). A good life for all within planetary boundaries. *Nature Sustainability*, *1*(2), 88–95. doi:10.1038/s41893-018-0021-4

O'Neill, J. (2018). How not to argue against growth: happiness, austerity and inequality. Pp, 141–152 in Rose, H. and Henning, C. (eds.) *The good life beyond growth* London: Routledge.

Oreskes, N., & Conway, E. (2010). *Merchants of doubt*. Bloomsbury.

Parrique, T., Barth, J., Briens, F., Kerschner, C., Kraus-Polk, A., Kuokkanen, A., & Spangenberg, J. H. (2019) *Decoupling debunked*. European Environmental Bureau. https://eeb.org/library/decoupling-debunked/.

Patomäki, H. (2011). Towards global political parties. *Ethics & Global Politics*, *4*(2), 81–102. doi:10.3402/egp v4i2.7334

Polluters Out. (2020). Our demands. https://pollutersout.org/demands.

Rees, W. (2021). Growth through contraction: Conceiving an eco-economy. *Real-World Economics Review 96*, 98–118. http://www.paecon.net/PAEReview/issue96/Rees96.pdf.

Ripple, W., Wolf, C., Newsome, T., Barnard, P., & Moomaw, W. (2021a). The climate emergency: 2020 in review. *Scientific American*, January 6th. https://www.scientificamerican.com/article/the-climate-emergency-2020-in-review/.

Ripple, W., Wolf, C., Newsome, T., Gregg, J., Lenton, T., Palomo, I., Eikelboom, J., Law, B., Huq, S., Duffy, P. & Rockström, J. (2021b). World scientists' warning of a climate emergency 2021. *BioScience*, https://doi org/10.1093/biosci/biab079

Sayer, A. (2015). *Why we can't afford the rich*. Policy Press.

Smith, R. (2020). *China's engine of environmental collapse*. Pluto Press.

Spash, C. (2020). A tale of three paradigms: Realising the revolutionary potential of ecological economics *Ecological Economics*, *169*), article 106518. https://doi.org/10.1016/j.ecolecon.2019.106518

Spash, C. (2021a). The economy as if people mattered: Revisiting critiques of economic growth in a time of crisis. *Globalizations*, *18*(7), 1087–1104. https://doi.org/10.1080/14747731.2020.1761612

Spash, C. (2021b). Apologists for growth: Passive revolutionaries in a passive revolution. *Globalizations*, *18*(7) 1123–1148. https://doi.org/10.1080/14747731.2020.1824864

Spash, C., & Guisan, A. (2021). A future social-ecological economics. *Real-World Economics Review*, *96*, 220–233. http://www.paecon.net/PAEReview/issue96/SpashGuisan96.pdf.

Spash, C., & Hache, F. (2021). The Dasgupta Review deconstructed: an exposé of biodiversity economics *Globalizations*. Advance online publication. https://doi.org/10.1080/14747731.2021.1929007

Stay Grounded. (2021). A rapid and just transition of aviation. https://stay-grounded.org/just-transition/.

Steffen, W., & Morgan, J. (2021). From the Paris agreement to the anthropocene and planetary boundaries framework: An interview with Will Steffen. *Globalizations*, *18*(7), 1298–1310. https://doi.org/10.1080/ 14747731.2021.1940070

Stevenson, H. (2021). Reforming global climate governance in an age of bullshit. *Globalizations*, *18*(1), 86–102. doi:10.1080/14747731.2020.1774315

Trainer, T. (2021). What does degrowth mean? Some comments on Jason Hickel's 'A few points of clarifica tion. *Globalizations*, *18*(7), 1112–1116. https://doi.org/10.1080/14747731.2020.1860621

UK Environmental Audit Committee. (2021). Biodiversity in the UK: Bloom or bust? Report Summary London: UK Parliament https://publications.parliament.uk/pa/cm5802/cmselect/cmenvaud/136/136 summary.html.

UK Government. (2021). COP 26 explained. UK Government https://2nsbq1gn1rl23zol93eyrccj-wpengine netdna-ssl.com/wp-content/uploads/2021/07/COP26-Explained.pdf.

UNEP. (2020). *Emissions gap report* (11th ed.). Author.

UNEP. (2021). *Making peace with nature: A scientific blueprint to tackle the climate, biodiversity and pollution emergencies*. Author.

Wallace-Wells, D. (2021). How to live in a climate 'Permanent Emergency'. *The Intelligencer*, July 1.

Weber, H. (2017). Politics of 'leaving no one behind': Contesting the 2030 sustainable development goal agenda. *Globalizations*, *14*(3), 399–414.

Wunderling, N., Donges, J., Kurths, J., & Winkelmann, R. (2021). Interacting tipping points increase risk of climate domino effects under global warming. *Earth System Dynamics*, *12*(2), 601–619. doi:10.5194/esd-12 601-2021

Global Climate Emergency: after COP24, climate science, urgency, and the threat to humanity

Barry Gills and Jamie Morgan

ABSTRACT
This Special Editorial on the Climate Emergency makes the case that although we are living in the time of Global Climate Emergency we are not yet acting as if we are in an imminent crisis. The authors review key aspects of the institutional response and climate science over the past several decades and the role of the economic system in perpetuating inertia on reduction of greenhouse gas emissions. Humanity is now the primary influence on the planet, and events in and around COP24 are the latest reminder that we live in a pathological system. A political economy has rendered the UNFCCC process as yet a successful failure. Fundamental change is urgently required. The conclusions contain recommendations and a call to action now.

Understanding the Climate Emergency: climate science, urgency, and the threat to humanity

We live in a time of Climate Emergency. Nevertheless, our collective actions do *not yet* approximate a real understanding nor fully appropriate actions. We are *not yet* acting as if we are facing an urgent and life threatening Emergency. What does 'Climate Emergency' actually mean? According to David Attenborough:

> It may sound frightening, but the scientific evidence is that if we have not taken dramatic action within the next decade, we could face irreversible damage to the natural world and the collapse of our societies. (Attenborough, *Our Planet*)

History is written later, but the future is written now. Perhaps the central message of contemporary climate sciences consists in the realization that the entire planet is deeply interconnected. There are no isolated ecosystems. There are no ecosystems that are safe from the effects of climate change. All life on this planet is profoundly interrelated. What happens in one area of the globe has far reaching, but as yet insufficiently understood, effects upon and consequences for even far distant regions. The introduction to a recent Intergovernmental Panel on Climate Change (IPCC) Report states the urgency and magnitude of the challenges facing humanity as follows: 'Now more than ever, unprecedented and urgent action is required of all nations' (IPCC, 2018). According to the IPCC,

Pathways limiting global warming to 1.5°C with no or limited overshoot would require rapid and far-reaching transitions in energy, land, urban and infrastructure (including transport and buildings) and industrial systems … These system transitions are unprecedented in terms of scale … and imply deep emissions reductions in all sectors. (IPCC, 2018, p. 17)

In other words, the present Global Climate Emergency demands a profound historical transformation of our civilization. We have not only been pouring greenhouse gases (GHGs) into the atmosphere; we have been collectively exceeding the regenerative capacity of the earth's natural resources and ecological systems. Earth Overshoot Day, the day in the annual cycle when humanity's demands for resources exceeds the capacity for regeneration of those resources, has advanced by two whole months over the past twenty years. This year Earth Overshoot Day took place on 29 July 2019. It now requires the equivalent of 1.75 planets to sustain us. Humanity is damaging the whole system upon which our lives, and that of all other species depends.

On a global basis, July 2019 was the hottest month ever recorded. NASA data on global warming indicates that 17 of the 18 hottest years ever recorded in the past 136 years were during 2001–2018. Rather than decreasing, global emissions are actually increasing. Annual $GtCO_2$ emissions (Gigatonnes of carbon dioxide) have increased from less than 25 $GtCO_2$ in the year 2000 to well over 35 $GtCO_2$ during 2012–2018 and reached an all-time high in 2017–2018. Cumulative atmospheric concentrations of CO_2 in earth's atmosphere, measured at the Mauna Loa facility in Hawaii, have been steadily rising and are now over 407 ppm (parts per million). This level of concentration of CO_2 has not been seen for three million years. The threshold figure of 450 ppm has been used in climate science to represent a critical level above which the probability of keeping global temperature rise to below 2 degrees centigrade drops dramatically. The Paris Agreement at COP21 now aims for 1.5 degrees. Some recent studies argue that we are at risk of reaching the 1.5 degree threshold as early as 2030, primarily due to extremely complex interactions between a variety of factors. Neither 2 nor 1.5 degrees is a magic number. Even 1.5 degrees warming implies setting in motion numerous cumulative effects in the global climate system and on the natural environments and ecosystems that constitute the global web of life.

The Arctic is now heating much faster than the average for the planet. This is accelerating the rate of melting of Arctic ice cover. The reduction of sea ice cover has multiple effects on the global climate system. The loss of ice reduces the albedo effect whereby the heat from the sun is reflected back into space, thus keeping the planet cooler. As the polar sea ice and the glaciers melt at an accelerated rate (e.g. in Greenland in summer 2018) huge amounts of freshwater are released into the northern seas, which affects the Atlantic Meridional Overturning Circulation (AMOC), commonly known as the Gulf Stream. Measurements of the flow of AMOC have indicated that it has been slowing in recent years. If the AMOC were to be severely disrupted the consequences for the climate of Northern Europe and possibly the world as a whole could be severe. Recent measurements indicate that the Antarctic sea ice is melting at an accelerated pace and scope. Globally, some 90% or more of the world's glaciers are melting. This situation is particularly important in the Tibetan plateau and Himalayan region. The glaciers in that region are an essential part of the watershed for the great river systems of Asia: from North China to Pakistan. Those rivers are a water supply for 40% of the world's people.

In the past few months, we have witnessed an unprecedented wave of global fires. The fires across the circumpolar Arctic have dramatically increased, especially in northern Russia. Last year the largest source of deforestation on earth was not the cutting of trees but rather the burning of trees. The fires of the Amazon region are now at an alarming intensity, following the radical change in national government policies in Brazil under the Bolsonaro regime. If the fires in the Amazon continue, there is a risk that the whole forest system will be effected; triggering a retreat of the forests into dry Savannah, a process known as 'dieback'. The water cycle of vast areas would be dramatically altered even in far-away regions such as North America. Fires in the tropical forests of Central Africa are more numerous than in previous years and a cause of increasing global concern. Likewise, the annual fires in Indonesia.

Finally, there is the issue of 'tipping points'. These are thresholds of various types, which if breached imply a state change and these occur both globally and in diverse regions around the planet. Tipping points and thresholds involve complex feedback processes that are as yet insufficiently understood. Above all, according to a seminal study by Steffen et al. (2018) regarding trajectories in earth system dynamics, it is the interactions between the various tipping point zones (e.g. The Arctic; the Amazon forests; the AMOC; Antarctica) which may pose the greatest source of future climate change. These interactions between the various tipping point zones of the planet are vital. According to Steffen et al., there is a risk that if dramatic action on global warming does not occur in good time, the earth's climate system will undergo a state change, moving into a new mode which they have named 'Hothouse Earth'. This is a state of runaway and irreversible global warming. The consequences could include inducing societal collapse or even making the earth uninhabitable for humanity. Our own species would be part of the Sixth mass extinction in earth's history. Systems evolve, and as they do so they tend to hit upon a maintaining synchronization with perturbations – a slowly accommodating chaotic pathway. Accelerated anthropogenic interference at all scales is disrupting this producing cacophony out of symphony. All this is the meaning of 'Climate Emergency'.

The Anthropocene

Humanity is now the primary influence on the planet, and events in and around COP24 are the latest reminder that we live in a pathological system. Fundamental change is urgently required, but grasping what this means needs initial context, since climate change is just one component. Environmentally concerned scientists and social scientists have been saying for over 40 years that we are *making* a problem that we can collectively avoid, that the problem is eminently foreseeable and the sooner we take significant action the more likely it is that a manageable way of living can be hit upon.[1] The background has been relatively straightforward: the world population is increasing (albeit at a decreasing rate), resource use has continued to grow, and the combination of numbers and how we organize our socio-economies is leading to a collision course with natural systems based on *scale*, processes, and consequences. Economies industrialize, incomes grow, a middle class emerges, society changes, consumption becomes more widespread, the economy becomes service-oriented, and under the auspices of corporations, governments, and supranational organizations industrialization is shifted to other countries; there is continuous domestic economic expansion and this spreads to those other countries, which have in turn industrialized and who then seek to emulate the consumption pattern of 'advanced' countries.[2]

We have, caveats notwithstanding, *acted* as though there were no material limits to growth whilst modern life has rapidly modified the planet through deforestation, extension of intensive agriculture, industrial scale fishing, extraction of minerals, gas and oil, the proliferation of energy production, transportation, and manufacturing (much of it carbon dependent), and all tied to consumption patterns that treat our environment as a bottomless disposal site for plastics, pesticides, cosmetics, fertilizers, food waste, heavy metals, medicines and more. The unintended and yet *known* (understood, explained and cumulatively observed) consequences of such action has and continues to be water table depletion, eutrophication and rising toxicities in soil and air, desertification, rapid species extinction and general loss of biodiversity on land and sea, disruption and destruction of ecosystems, melting ice sheets, sea level rises, increasingly erratic weather patterns and extreme events, and generalized human-induced climate change tending to warm the planet on average.

To be clear, the direction of travel has been *obvious* and the human ingenuity required to obfuscate regarding the obviousness has been considerable (for example, Jacques, Dunlap, & Freeman, 2008; Oreskes & Conway, 2010).[3] If as much effort had been put into early resolution, steering humanity along a different path, there would be no need for this editorial. However, priapic capitalism has continued to ransack the planet and so here we are. Increasingly concerned, wondering what to do.

As alluded to in the introduction, according to the Global Footprint Network, 'Earth overshoot day' this year was 29th July. This is the day in the year on which humanity's demand for ecological resources and services exceeds the annual regenerative capacity of the Earth. This is two months faster than twenty years ago and requires 1.75 equivalent Earths (for seminal work see Wackernagel and Rees1996):

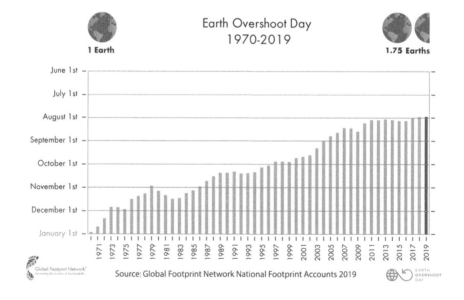

Source: Global Footprint Network National Footprint Accounts 2019

https://www.overshootday.org/newsroom/press-release-july-2019-english/

Much of this is captured by the United Nations Environment Programme (UNEP) in their periodic Global Environmental Outlook Reports.[4]

The UNEP was established in 1972 and there are now many domestic, regional, and global organizations whose remit has encompassed some or all of the problems stated above. Still, what is generically termed a 'Business as Usual' trajectory has dominated, so much so that we are now into territory where environmentally concerned scientists and social scientists are getting to say on multiple fronts and with no satisfaction, 'I told you so … '. Urgent action is required.

Where are we now and how did we get here?

The Intergovernmental Panel on Climate Change (IPCC) is the main source of collated findings of models on the emission of greenhouse gases (GHGs) and related aggregated data. In terms of volume, the main GHG is carbon dioxide (CO_2), though methane (CH_4) produces around twenty times the warming effect. An important measure of GHGs is parts per million (ppm) in the atmosphere. The natural range of atmospheric CO_2 ppm over the last 650,000 years has been 170–300 ppm and the pre-industrial point of departure is typically given as 280 ppm.[5] In May 2013 atmospheric CO_2 exceeded 400 ppm and, as noted in the introduction, in 2018 consistently exceeded 407 ppm which according to ice core tests is a level not seen in over 3 million years. The IPCC's baseline is the year 1750 though reliable data starts later. The atmosphere contains a combination of GHGs and by 2016, using as a comparative the 1880–1900 mean as the estimate for pre-industrial temperature, global mean average temperature had increased by 1.05°C (using a running mean calculated from 1970; see for example, Hansen et al., 2017). The current *linear* trend increase is estimated at 0.18°C on a decade basis. The point, however, is not the precision inherent in the quantities (given these emerge from variable data modelled in slightly different ways) but the collectively recognized tendencies manifesting in the relations. Adverse climate impacts are being felt *now*, something that the iconic heat map of the whole world (contrasted with the patchy red, orange, and blue of 1976) forcefully drove home during the heatwave of June 2018. The image of a brightly glowing ball was prominent in the press and the implication was clear, failure to curb global warming has been endemic.[6]

The United Nations Framework Convention on Climate Change (UNFCCC) was established following the Rio Earth Summit in 1992. According to Article 2 of the 1992 convention, the UNFCCC's stated goal is the 'stabilization of greenhouse gas concentrations in the atmosphere at a level that would prevent dangerous anthropogenic interference with the climate system' (UNFCCC, 1992, p. 4).[7] The phrasing is important – the focus is stabilized *prior* to dangerous anthropogenic interference. The basic climate science may have well developed conceptions of the direction of travel of warming, but there are different models and an emerging and developing understanding of different feedbacks in complex systems. This has been important in terms of the politics of climate policy tied to the political economy. Modern economies are predicated on growth, the fundamental constitution of those economies (energy production, much of the raw materials for manufacture – plastics and fertilizers, etc.) and the transportation networks in and between those economies have been carbon based. A line of least resistance perpetuation of the fundamentals of the socio-economic system has been the main tendency, and that tendency has exhibited a political fudge, conflating the increasing 'efficiency' of given resource use (less per $ unit GDP) with a gradual solving of the emissions problem. The dominant terminology has been 'relative decoupling' leading to 'absolute decoupling'. Since the point of departure of the climate challenge was stabilization prior to a dangerous threshold, a goal that need not and did not lead immediately to a halt on the growth of emissions, an exploitable ambiguity emerged.

Bear in mind that growth of emissions has two inflections for the metrics. GHGs are not calendar conscious in the way GDP is. They take many years to break down into other compounds or to be captured by natural processes. The atmospheric lifetime of CO_2 can be well over a century and CH_4 is more than a decade. There is, therefore, a distinction between the cumulative measure of emissions *in* the atmosphere and the annual level of emissions contributed *to* the atmosphere. The latter can be increasing or decreasing but still contributing to the former. Moreover, cumulative emissions lead to cumulative warming, which in turn affects the existing environment and thus the storage and release of GHGs, and this has impacts on GHG levels over and above the level of emissions from human sources in any given year. The relations are not necessarily linear, they are rooted in complex relations that have feedbacks and thresholds for transitions in systems, and this is also part of 'interference'. It is with this as background that the creation of the UNFCCC invoked the question, what is the level of 'stabilization'? However, this question has been addressed not only as science but as politics.

For the political economy, what is the level of 'stabilization' has translated into: how far can we continue to emit GHGs into the environment? The problem has been one of imposing limits on a socio-economic system that is not built for limits and actively resists them – it is disaggregated and intrinsically expansionary. States and corporations have had reasons to resist disruptive immediately costly (perhaps, though this is highly disputable, development *denying* to poorer countries) action and instead have opted to merely curb what they do, hoping that ultimate adverse consequences are (eventually by someone) prevented in a still ever-growing system. Emissions policy has been pursued in a framework that tacitly takes as its point of departure the question, when will our economy inform us that it is time to change? The substructure has been, how do we prevent harm to our economies (for which we demonstrably will sacrifice some of the environment)? The emissions focus has been, what is the measurable threshold beyond which we do not wish to go?

However, emissions are a byproduct of economic activity *not its focus,* so the immediate economic trigger for changes to the economic activity producing the emissions has actually been two types of cost: whether sufficient damage has been done and whether a threshold of resource depletion has been passed. Both these 'costs' affect resource pricing (including via correcting 'externalities'), and both are supposed to lead to signals that now is the time to invest or invest more and invent the technologies that fix this or that problem, and now is the time to decisively begin social redesign … These economic triggers have co-evolved with the institutional mechanisms developed to restrict the rate of growth of emissions.

There is a weird inversion here, a subtle shift from acknowledging that our economies are a primary source of the environmental-emissions problem and thus the location of much of what must be solved, to the prioritizing of the economy *over* the environment. The question *when will our economy inform us it is time to change* sounds rational, but it is rationally weird in terms of the practices and consequences we have cumulatively observed for a problem science recognized years in advance and knew in general was coming … It has tacitly encouraged dangerous delay because there is for some significant duration after recognition of the problem, always the next period in which emissions can fall or fall faster, there is always someone else who can do what needs to be done or can invent what will help, and this has subverted emissions policy – a problem compounded for many years because many of the most observable impacts are created in the current period but experienced later (heat-waves, drought, flooding …).[8] This has allowed, until recently at least, a kind of exploitable proactive complacency, where despite its obvious continued dependencies and the very fact it is expansionary economic growth has not been collectively recognized as *the* problem for emissions, but rather the unavoidable context of solutions and a source of those solutions. And yet the fundamental drive for expansion has consistently outpaced the particulars of incremental improvements in the provision of this or that …

Ultimately, deferment, blame shifting, and procrastination has dominated because these have been compatible with how we live and work and, by extension, with what has been imposed and tolerated or preferred. The very framing has involved an odd kind of recklessness that has become one aspect of continuing to do unsustainable things in what, since at least the Brundtland

Commission report of the mid-1980s, we have in self-congratulatory if illusory terms, themed the era of 'sustainable development' (WCED, 1987).[9] For 'developed' economies this has been the perpetuation of consumption-based economies and for 'developing' economies this has been a form of industrialization that has included commodity export provision for growth, outsourced or relocated manufacturing to feed developed country consumption (reducing the direct carbon footprint of wealthy importing states), and a huge industry in processing, storing, and sometimes just abandoning the waste products of developed countries.

As populations, for too long we have been encouraged to think that the environmental problem in general and the emissions problem in particular has been recognized and must, therefore, be in hand. But we have also been encouraged not to think *too* hard about the problem because, in any case, the marvels of capitalism include the creation and solving of problems and this is just another problem on the road to progress. The environmentally aware have been consistent critics, but the criticism has until recently had limited traction, not least because mainstream parties in most countries have typically co-opted the language of Greenpeace and domestic Green parties whilst diluting concrete action (typically opting for gradual, mainly voluntary and market conforming change that has been corporate led – not least carbon trading). In the meantime, the perpetual gamble has been that there will in fact always be at some point a technological solution to the problems created, and so there would be no need to opt for immediate and radical social change that prevents such problems manifesting. And yet the fatal flaw in this line of reasoning has been that capitalism is not a unified system of unproblematic progress. It is, rather, a complex interplay of power and interests. One of the problems to be solved for corporations and for countries has turned out to be environmentally concerned 'interference'. From this perspective, the question becomes: how to slow and subvert attempts to restrict, constrain, reform or transform their little part of the totality of globally expansive capitalism (even if there is also money to be made by green technology companies and sectors …). This has been the reality in which the UNFCCC call for 'stabilization' has been pursued. The continued growth of GHG emissions, despite formal recognition of the problem in 1992, has been one consequence of this. Some brief commentary on the institutional development provides some sense of this.

Institutional responses to climate change

The UNFCCC founding agreement includes a provision to create a body to discuss, develop, and review the Convention (UNFCCC, 1992, Article 7). After 1992 the UNFCCC began a series of regular conferences between countries to discuss the form solutions to emissions might take. The first 'Conference of the Parties' (COP) to the Convention took place in 1995 and began negotiations on target reductions (to be implemented as Protocols under Article 17). In 1997 COP3 in Japan resulted in the now well-known 'Kyoto Protocols': an initial 38 industrialized countries committed themselves to cut GHG emissions by 2012 to an average of 5.2% lower than a 1990 benchmark level. Detailed rules were finally adopted in 2001 at COP7 (the Marrakesh accords) and the Protocols were then intended to become binding in 2005, yet some mechanisms only became fully active in 2008.

Consider the context for what the Kyoto Protocols initially achieved: 5 years to agree targets should exist (1992–1997), another 4 years to agree actual targets (2001), another 4 years to initialize targets (2005) and another 3 years before the process of reduction began for some of the more technical mechanisms and components of the targets (2008), and this for a process to be formally completed by 2012 – i.e. 20 years after the beginning of the process. The Protocols, of course, were not all of what was happening in the world or under the Convention – economies were in any case becoming more efficient in the relative decoupling sense and individual governments were adopting some environmentally 'friendly' policies. But the *collective* global institutional framework to solve what is ultimately a planetary wide problem (emissions do not stop at borders and do not respect polities) was slow in its development in a way that the melting of glaciers has not been.

The Kyoto Protocols were initially targeted at the longstanding industrial economies of the time, the initial 'Annex 1' parties. This had little effect on developing countries like India or China, and the US did not ratify Kyoto early on under President George Bush junior. However, the Protocols did allow for a steadily increasing number of countries to become signatories and participate. By 2012, 192 countries were signatories (virtually all nations, though this did not necessarily place onerous binding commitments on them). The 2009 COP in Copenhagen was designated to develop a replacement agreement, but participants could not agree binding terms and targets, and so an extension to Kyoto was proposed in Doha and this has force from 2012 to 2020. It is during this period of extension that the Paris Agreement of 2015 was finally agreed at COP21.

Successful failures: from Kyoto to Paris to Katowice

Getting almost every country in the world to sign up to an agreement is a form of success, given the negotiating complexities of this. However, in the end results matter because you can't negotiate with the planet. You either do what is scientifically necessary or you don't. Kyoto and the COP process has so far been a successful failure. Complying with the Protocols and what has followed has not been the same as solving the problem that the UNFCCC or the process was intended to address; that is, the cumulative increase in GHGs that lead to global warming. Besides atmospheric ppm, GHGs are measured in Gigatonnes of Carbon (GtC) and Gigatonnes of CO_2 ($GtCO_2$) or a combined GHG CO_2 equivalent.[10] The creation of the UNFCCC did *not* result in a reduction in total annual emissions. Instead annual emissions steadily increased and numerous data sources confirm this. As we stated in the introduction, according to the Tyndall Centre, emissions have increased from an annual $GtCO_2$ of less than 25 in 2000 to more than 35 $GtCO_2$ every year 2012–2018. On some measures $GtCO_2$ now exceeds 40 and according to the UNEP, total $GtCO_2$ equivalent for 2017 was a record high of 53.5 (UNEP, 2018, p. xv). The rate of increase of $GtCO_2$ has markedly slowed since 2012 (and stalled in 2015), but this is very different than a significant fall in annual total emissions or any kind of reduction in cumulative emissions in the atmosphere (expressed as ppm). Combined annual emissions for all countries have increased by more than 60% this century and are far higher than they were in the Kyoto benchmark year of 1990.

To reiterate, the formation of the UNFCCC has manifestly not prevented increasing emissions. Countries and corporations have in combination essentially continued to emit as though it made sense to proceed up to the level of 'dangerous anthropogenic interference'. Over most of the duration of the UNFCCC the IPCC has maintained that it would be advisable to restrict atmospheric CO_2 to less than 450 ppm and warming to less than 2°C by the end of the century. The science of this is well developed and yet still allows for uncertainty. But this should not be misunderstood. It does not create leeway for a business as usual continuation of massive levels of emissions, though it does imply some ambiguity concerning what the *exact* level of 'safe' cumulative emissions will turn out to have been.

To reiterate, the climate is part of a broader complex system and the relation between atmospheric GHGs, warming processes and interrelated effects on land and sea is conditional. Climate scientists have different models and the IPCC collate these. Models express different scenarios and based on these the relation to outcomes is expressed probabilistically. This notwithstanding, the advice for decades has been to restrict cumulative emissions to less than 1000 GtC and the lower end of 3000 + GtCO$_2$ for the 2°C target. As of 2018 total cumulative emissions over the industrial period were estimated at approximately 600 GtC and more than 2000 GtCO$_2$.[11] The remaining quantities that it is 'safe' to emit within this 'carbon budget' before NO MORE can be emitted (unless captured or in relation to net falls) across the range of scenarios are relatively small in the context of the heavy dependence of our societies on carbon.[12] We are using up *this* budget at an alarming rate and actual emissions per year need to sharply reduce otherwise the budget will be exceeded much earlier than the end of the century and 2°C warming *will* also be exceeded.

This brings us to Paris. By the time of COP21 in Paris the weight of advice on the 2°C target had begun to shift. As we have noted several times, the models are conditional. By 2015 climate scientists were reporting that restricting emissions consistent with human-induced warming of 1.5°C was probably advisable. This then became part of the Paris Agreement. Article 2 (1a) states that parties to the Agreement will aim to strengthen the Convention by 'holding the increase in the global average temperature to well below 2°C above pre-industrial levels and pursuing efforts to limit the temperature increase to 1.5°C' (UNFCCC, 2015).

COP21 also included an invitation for the IPCC to report on the 1.5°C target. This special report was released in October 2018, and presented at the 48th session of the IPCC, just before COP24. The Report makes clear that an early and sustained attempt to reduce emission to achieve 1.5°C avoids a whole set of likely effects that might become ingrained if a 2°C target remained the goal. The Report states:

> Limiting global warming requires limiting the total cumulative global anthropogenic emissions of CO$_2$ since the preindustrial period, that is, staying within a total carbon budget (high confidence). By the end of 2017, anthropogenic CO$_2$ emissions since the pre-industrial period are estimated to have reduced the total carbon budget for 1.5°C by approximately 2,200 ± 320 GtCO$_2$ (medium confidence). The associated remaining budget is being depleted by current emission of 42 ± 3 GtCO$_2$ per year (high confidence). The choice of the measure of global temperature affects the estimated remaining carbon budget. Using global mean surface air temperature, as in AR5 [see IPCC fifth synthesis], gives an estimate of the remaining carbon budget of 580 GtCO$_2$ for a 50% probability of limiting warming to 1.5°C and 420 GtCO$_2$ for a 66% probability (medium confidence). Alternatively, using GMST [global mean surface temperature rather than air] gives estimates of 770 and 570 GtCO$_2$ for 50% and 66% probabilities, respectively (medium confidence). (IPCC, 2018, p. 14) [...] Pathways limiting global warming to 1.5°C with no or limited overshoot would require rapid and far-reaching transitions in energy, land, urban and infrastructure (including transport and buildings) and industrial systems (high confidence). These system transitions are unprecedented in terms of scale, but not necessarily in terms of speed and imply deep emissions reductions in all sectors. (IPCC, 2018, p. 17)

The IPCC Report translates achieving the target 1.5°C into a range where annual emissions reduce to *net zero* between 2040 and 2055. As the graphs below indicate, this is a radical shift, involving a situation where any additional emissions thereafter will have to be balanced or captured by technologies and managed natural processes:

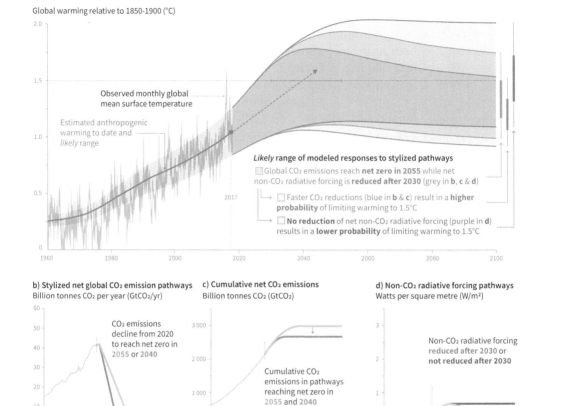

a) Observed global temperature change and modeled
responses to stylized anthropogenic emission and forcing pathways

b) Stylized net global CO₂ emission pathways
Billion tonnes CO₂ per year (GtCO₂/yr)

c) Cumulative net CO₂ emissions
Billion tonnes CO₂ (GtCO₂)

d) Non-CO₂ radiative forcing pathways
Watts per square metre (W/m²)

Faster immediate CO₂ emission reductions
limit cumulative CO₂ emissions shown in
panel (c).

Maximum temperature rise is determined by cumulative net CO₂ emissions and net non-CO₂
radiative forcing due to methane, nitrous oxide, aerosols and other anthropogenic forcing agents.

Source: IPCC (2018, p. 8).

To be clear, the IPCC projections indicate the need for major socio-economic change. The first step set out by the IPCC is a reduction in annual emissions of 45% by 2030 (IPCC, 2018, p. 12) compared with 25% for 2°C – and these figures are sensitive to current changes and delay. That is barely a decade, a startlingly brief period given what the general tendency has been. An IPCC Special Report on *Climate Change and Land* followed later (IPCC, 2019). It too emphasizes the unsustainable nature of current trajectories and the need for major shifts in land use and food consumption patterns.[13]

The immediate problem, however, is that though the Paris Agreement states a conditional 1.5°C target, the mechanism to achieve this is an aggregate of what parties to the Agreement *volunteer* to achieve. The Agreement does *not* begin by calculating the remaining carbon budget and then allocating it to parties as a maximum with some kind of formalized co-ordination system with accelerated reductions. Instead Article 4 requires parties to submit Nationally Determined Commitments (NDCs). NDCs are formulated for 5 year periods. The basic logic stated in and for the Paris

Agreement is that it is in member's interests to achieve their NDCs and to be ambitious in both subsequently setting and exceeding them. Furthermore, it is built into the Agreement that growing public awareness will tend to pressure governments, such that collectively the result achieves the Article 2 target (see Morgan, 2016). However, as the data so far suggests there is no sign of this actually happening.

The actual tendency since 2015 has been a slowdown in the increase in annual emissions and not a sustained decrease. The UNEP publishes periodic emissions gap reports, which set out current emission levels, the tendency and the difference between this and what is required to achieve the Convention target (2°C and now 1.5°C). According to the 9th emissions gap report, published November 2018, again just before COP24, current NDCs are FAR IN EXCESS of what would bridge the emissions gap by 2030:

> Current commitments expressed in the NDCs are inadequate to bridge the emissions gap in 2030. Technically, it is still possible to bridge the gap to ensure global warming stays well below 2°C and 1.5°C, but if NDC ambitions are not increased before 2030, exceeding the 1.5°C goal can no longer be avoided. Now more than ever, unprecedented and urgent action is required by all nations. The assessment of actions by the G20 countries indicates that this is yet to happen; in fact, global CO_2 emissions increased in 2017 after three years of stagnation. (UNEP, 2018, p. xiv) Global greenhouse gas emissions show no signs of peaking. Global CO_2 emissions from energy and industry increased in 2017, following a three-year period of stabilization. Total annual greenhouse gases emissions, including from land-use change, reached a record high of 53.5 $GtCO_2e$ in 2017, an increase of 0.7 $GtCO_2e$ compared with 2016. In contrast, **global GHG emissions in 2030 need to be approximately 25 percent and 55 percent lower than in 2017** to put the world on a least-cost pathway to limiting global warming to 2°C and 1.5°C respectively …. **Global peaking of emissions by 2020 is crucial** for achieving the temperature targets of the Paris Agreement. (UNEP, 2018: p. xv; bold added)[14]

Here the UNEP report calls for 55% rather than 45% reductions by 2030, but according to both the IPCC and UNEP reports, current NDCs are consistent with temperature rises of over 2°C by mid-century and 3°C by end of the century (IPCC, 2018: D.1.1, p. 20). Moreover, panel members acknowledge that their models are if anything conservative in terms of both impacts from warming and the actual rate of warming. The inclusion of 'fast' *and* 'slow' feedback loops, tipping-points and non-linearity for the interaction of anthropogenic effects and the natural system *could* lead to changes pushing the planet *irreversibly* into the 'hothouse Earth' trajectory set out by Steffen et al. (2018), even if emissions were reduced to levels currently consistent with 1.5–2°C warming. According to work by James Hansen, perhaps the most outspoken and prominent climate scientist during the last four decades, the safest option would be to not just halt cumulative emissions during the century but to reduce atmospheric ppm from its current elevated position to around 350 ppm (Hansen et al., 2017).

So, the situation is clearly urgent. Adverse climate change is happening now, emission levels are *not* falling, and major change is required to prevent changes that soon we will not be able to control. The IPCC is not a hotbed of radicalism populated by hyperbolic panic-mongers. They are ill-suited as harbingers of catastrophe. But they and others from the scientific community are now mapping out a possible future that includes: heatwaves, droughts, flooding, loss of landmass, an environment on land and sea hostile to many current species and in consequence, falling yields and rising crop failures, food and water insecurity, famine, loss of life from 'natural' disaster, a dive into poverty and escalating problems of mass migration. *This* is the future we are *currently* writing, one that raises the question of what kind of civilization will be around to write that history.

And so to COP 24, Katowice, Poland. The situation is extremely serious but this was not reflected in COP24. Each COP round of meetings and negotiations is followed by published 'decisions' (see also UNFCCC, 2018).[15] COP24 was notable for disagreement concerning how to respond to the IPCC report. Despite commissioning it, COP participants could not simply agree to universally 'welcome' or endorse the Report's findings. Instead this became a source of acrimony and the COP24 draft text merely thanks the IPCC for the Report and invites members to 'make use' of its information. The US still remains committed to its withdrawal from Paris and now Brazil has begun to signal the same. Moreover, many participants have mid-term commitments to carbon energy exploitation: fracking, transitions to gas, 'cleaner' coal, the race to exploit resources in the Arctic etc. (see Spash, 2016). More importantly, COP24 did not include any firm commitment to more 'ambitious' NDCs. It did, however, lead to collective agreement on how NDC achievement can be transparently assessed and measured, and it did also include some additional agreement on pledges and finance for the most climate vulnerable countries, if only over the first Agreement cycle 2020–2025.

COP24 was also the scene and focus of growing civil action and disobedience. However, for most of us, COP24 came and went in a flash – becoming one more in a long line of anxiety-inducing reports on the 'climate problem'. Until recently we experienced punctuated publicity. Consider this in the context of how the Paris targets have been positioned – predicated on public awareness and pressure. However, what has not been achieved so far is a consistent mobilization to make the climate problem core to politics, core to social action and civil society, and thus core to media reporting. There is a circularity here – a need for visibility characterized by continuity and consistency. Something has to change and that must be how we collectively mobilize *for* change. There are now signs of a more consistent press narrative spanning the news-cycle. Climate incidents are now often introduced as 'another instance of climate change' and this is a small positive.

However, as things stand in this time of rapid news-cycles, fake news and post-truth there are 3 incontrovertible facts we need to put before everything else:

(1) Human-induced climate change is real;
(2) The rate of change is such that there is only about 11 years to prevent irreversible and potentially catastrophic effects;
(3) There is currently not enough being done to prevent irreversible changes.

Conclusion: the Anthropocene and civilization in revolt?

Perhaps one of the central attributes of capitalist modernity is the tendency to replace faith in the spiritually miraculous with faith in a demonstrated track record of astounding socio-technological feats. Modern life is amazing (if sometimes spiritually hollowing). But the ultimate issue is not whether there are facets of the way we live that our species prefers and benefits from, but rather whether our *design* for life is feasible, whether this is *how* a population of 7 billion and more can live. The consequences of climate change are now being felt, this is not a problem of the future and not a problem for the future. Action is needed now. But how should this be framed? Clive Spash captures some of the activist dilemma:

> I was [recently] criticized by a member of the audience for painting too bleak a picture of policy on human-induced climate change. Apparently an approach was required that describes the opportunities and positive potential of stimulating future technologies and avoids noting the thirty years of international inaction and the structural links between economic growth and global greenhouse gas emissions increases. A

strategic concern appears to be that environmental messages need to be sold to people in friendly packaging, using psychology and marketing. This is reminiscent of the attacks on degrowth for being a term that will scare people off, leading to the suggestions that a better approach would be to use a French word or instead talk about flourishing potentials and dynamic equilibriums with nature. Environmentalists are chastised for 'negative framing' that is claimed to empower what it attacks (Raworth, 2015); so we should not mention being anti-capitalist and for degrowth, but nice things like doughnuts, that avoid scaring the Davos elite. Presumably opposing the nasty side of humanity – slavery, violence, torture, rape, pollution – should never be conducted in oppositional terms (e.g. against, anti, non) for fear of empowering the perpetrators? Harsh realities should be made soft. (Spash, 2018, p. 215)

The IPCC panel members and the 2018 Report are at pains to emphasize that it is not too late. Achieving the emissions reductions required to avoid 'hothouse Earth' is *technically* possible, and the IPCC provide four illustrative pathways (all emphasizing renewables, reforestation, environmental management, green infrastructure and massive investment in technologies, including carbon capture).[16] Equally, Raworth with her new 'doughnut' metaphor (2017) is not incorrect to argue a new way of thinking about the economy is needed. However, it is manifestly the case that the main impediment to change is our system of capital accumulation with its commitment to material growth of economies. This, as the evidence so obviously shows, creates both an escalating problem to solve and a whole set of interests continuously working to slow down solutions.

Moreover, it is implicit in all the current tendencies that global economic growth is incompatible with emissions reduction within the available timelines. Even if we accept for the sake of argument that there has been a 'Carbon Kuznets Curve' for some countries (whilst relocating some of their carbon consequences to other countries), then there is no good evidence that this is generalizable to the world (for the combination of production and consumption). If one includes Brazil, China, and India then a standard Carbon Kuznets Curve analysis extrapolating from what has happened in 'successful' countries indicates future 'turning points' at per capita income rates where the global carbon budget would already be exceeded before that level was reached. Though there have been attempts to make the case for 'Green Growth' there does not seem to be any plausible way to rationalize the evidence for this, even if one is otherwise committed to mainstream economic analysis, but especially if one is not (see for example, Morgan, 2017; Schroder & Storm, 2018). At worst, the concept of Green Growth has become one more way to encourage complacency (see Smith, 2016).

What is to be done, therefore, ought to start by accepting proper context. If we are to be committed to solving the emissions problem (and likely all the other aspects of the Anthropocene) then we have to accept material expansion (as growth) in the aggregate must stop and we must countenance degrowth as the rational course of action – our framework for what an economy can be and allow. To be clear, this does not mean an end to investment or opposition to technological change – economic progress. What it does mean is that we are going to have to accept different organizing principles in the form of social redesign and economic practices. The idea of survivable capitalism is going to have to give way to surviving current capitalism. We shouldn't think of this as a retrograde step (see Büchs & Koch, 2017). We need to start thinking about degrowth as responsible and not radical. We need to start thinking of it as the realistic option. And we need to accept it is going to require states to step up and start intervening in the economy in a way that is quite different than has been the case over the neoliberal period. New thinking on the state is already available from June Sekera and Mariana Mazzucato. However, states are not rational and capitalism is a system of political capture. For the IPCC Report's feasible suggestions to be realizable then we need to create sustained pressure in politics – making good on the claim that already frames the Paris Agreement. This is already beginning to happen. Greta Thunberg has become a globally visible figure and social movements such as Extinction Rebellion have added additional pressure to spaces long occupied by Greenpeace. There has already been a backlash in some parts of the press – reducing concern to Millenarian cultishness. This is distraction. Calls for transformation are neither histrionic nor virtue signalling.

As we emphasized at the outset of this essay, we live in the time of Global Climate Emergency. What we need now above all is to immediately begin to think and ACT as if it is a real EMERGENCY. Everything we do now, both individually and collectively, will matter. We are in a race against time. We must arrest the momentum drawing us closer to the critical tipping points and thresholds that once crossed would trigger runaway global warming. Every action at every level now matters greatly to the outcome and thus to determining our human future.

When only a few people make a small change perhaps it is not significant. When millions upon millions act however, that is social change. Everything we do NOT do now also matters. Inaction and passivity in the face of the realities of the Global Climate Emergency are the road to ruin, i.e. to climate catastrophe and societal collapse. We cannot allow this to be our future. It is time to act like the Climate Emergency is real. It is time to Act Now.

The IPCC Report with its focus on macro-changes requires associative action. There are things you can do and that we can all do. As an individual we internalize a sense of insignificance, which fosters inactivity as though we were powerless, and this is reinforced by a reflexive sense of hypocrisy that each act is not sufficient. But everything we do matters to some degree and every something is better than a nothing. Cumulatively and collectively this matters and there are multiple issue-areas that can be constructively pursued.

- The stubborn sources of individual emissions in developed economies are: private transport, aviation, household heating, and cooking (in relation to insulation and energy efficiency of homes) and consumption (food and goods). So, if this applies to you, make every possible effort to examine all aspects of your personal behaviour in relation to climate change impact. Practice low-impact living. Try to radically reduce your carbon footprint. Reduce or even eliminate travel by air. Reduce or even eliminate driving by cars using fossil fuels. Use public transport or shared transport wherever possible. Switch energy supplier to your home to renewables. Reduce personal consumption and waste, and reuse and recycle as much as possible. Reduce or eliminate consumption of beef in particular and other meats and dairy products (focus on local sources). Promote reforestation and conservation of forests locally and globally. Consume organic food and other organically grown products (e.g. cotton apparel) as much as possible.
- Act politically. Join social movements, civil society organizations, and political organizations dedicated to action to address global warming. Support and vote for ecologically aware political parties. Become better informed, become involved, take an interest in the mechanics of policy making rather than just the principles being espoused – communicate the understanding of climate science to others. Spread the concept of managed degrowth and the circular economy as rational and realistic. Investigate your links to global supply chains in all your activities and avoid ecologically destructive products and practices (e.g. palm oils grown on former rain forest destroyed for this production; soy products and beef grown on lands that were formerly rain forest …).
- Given that there has been progress in increasing renewable energy production from low and zero carbon sources, support policy efforts towards the electrification of all possible technologies that use power (transport, heating, home appliances, etc.), since this will progressively produce benefit from emissions reductions; support the creation of a new distributed energy landscape where residential and industrial and commercial consumption will be largely electric, and power is

generated and shared locally, enabled by new technologies balancing and optimizing usage, via the infrastructure of a smart interconnected network. Promote the transition by industry and transport to hydrogen fuel and renewable electricity sources. Support public investment and public and community ownership of electricity sources and support massive public investment in green energy production and green infrastructure (look for these policies, advocate them). Support investment in electrified public transport and advocate low cost or free public transport in cities.

- Act collectively to support policies that stop the current massive subsidies to fossil fuel interests. Support campaigns to divest from fossil fuels (e.g. by banks, universities, pension funds, investment companies, local governments …). Divest your personal savings from fossil fuel industry investments. Change your personal banking account: avoid banks heavily investing in fossil fuels and switch to banks divesting from fossil fuels and investing in sustainable alternatives (See: Banking on Climate Change, 2019; for list of worst offending banks).
- Support efforts to establish carbon taxes set at levels liable to create significant costs; accept that this will affect you (we) too in the short term but that it is necessary to facilitate transitions to carbon neutral alternatives; accept that states should exercise their authority to prohibit *some* actions we have got used to thinking are domains of private sector rights (where we express our preferences in markets); support the primacy of the collective interest and the common good before that of private interests.
- Seriously consider having fewer children or only one child. Support campaigns for funding for augmented Sustainable Development Goals (SDGs), including especially funding for education of girls and for family planning (that reduces the global birth-rate). (See: Drawdown.org) Support intellectual commons rather than intellectual property. Support technology transfer that facilitates rapid transition to reduce current emissions levels.
- Support radically increased collective funding for climate mitigation and adaptation with a focus on transfers to the most affected and vulnerable countries.
- Given that they are liable to become prominent if the Climate Emergency is exacerbated, take an interest in and provide support to collective transnational solutions to our planetary dilemma. We are ultimately global citizens and now more than ever one species.

Some of this is going to be disruptive. But it is time to move beyond states of denial. Time to overcome inertia, fears and doubts. Our house is on fire. If we watch and do nothing the outcome is predictable. The house will burn down. We need to and we must mobilize action now on an unprecedented level in order to meet the unprecedented and urgent challenges facing humanity in the Global Climate Emergency. We have a world to transform. Our collective future, and quite frankly our survival now depends on our own actions.[17]

Notes

1. Herman Daly, Ernst Schumacher, Donella Meadows, Kenneth Boulding, Robert Costanza, etc.
2. The pattern is, of course, *not* new to the last 40 years. What is new is the recognition of the cumulative consequences. Anyone who has read Marx and Engel's *Communist Manifesto* recognizes the pattern as a paraphrase and anyone familiar with world systems theory recognizes the longer degree of continuity and difference.
3. Al Gore and Naomi Klein have in well-known ways made the case that resistance to the evidence is systematic but in some ways subtle (e.g. Klein, 2014). Much of the argument is rooted in the subversion of skepticism. One begins from: 'no species has influenced their environment as rapidly or pervasively as humans'. However, the precautionary principle that this formally invokes is undermined by: (a) the data

problem mark one – 'this' has never occurred before so there is doubt about what will occur; how fast and how complex the interactions and consequences will be … (b) the data problem mark two – noted former changes occurred over very long periods, current observations are decades so the contrast allows for statistical anomaly and for the possibility *real* effects may be less or insignificant based on the appropriate contrastive comparative and timeline and/or they may be immersed in 'natural' processes … (c) future costs and uncertainty – since how we will do things in the future is *not certain* the subsequent effects cannot be adequately determined now; changing patterns of technology in the future will ultimately shape consequences, denying activity now may be unnecessary or even counterproductive to the wealth that solves problems later … These are all subversions that create complacency or trade on doubt to facilitate social recklessness rather than rational prudential conduct. Natural science by its very nature is cautious in its empirical claims and acknowledges the fallibility of its conceptual architecture and models. However, during the last 40 years there has been little dispute regarding the basic tendencies built into material relations (the chemistry and physics are not novel even if the applications are new) so there has been a subtle but *exploitable* difference between 'environmental effects' have been 'known' (if you continue to do x then degrees of y will result – the tendency based on the direction of travel of all of the factors) and 'proved'. The manipulation of doubt is also basic to the future costs problematic: essentially the argument hinges on the perpetual future capacity of technology to solve problems that we do not try to prevent now – the most basic of which is doing more of what we *know* is damaging (the aggregate socio-economic effects of the way we live), the argument simply facilitates continual deferment to the point where irreversible material consequences apply that we have not done enough to prevent and which we are then unable to respond to either because there is no possible technological fix or because we do not now have time (this is a deeply unstable argument since in economics it depends on price signals that theorists claim are proxies for recognizing thresholds of irreversibility – but why should a price encapsulate or convey this 'information' and even if it could why would we trust that it will when we already have the actual environmental science to guide us? Moreover, the whole frame of analysis subtly creates a technological dependence consciousness and thus reduces the way in which we are prepared to countenance and implement radical social redesign as an issue that can be disentangled from the merely technological).

4. GEO 6 was published 2019 and is available: https://www.unenvironment.org/resources/global-environment-outlook-6 The standard definition of carrying capacity is the maximum population size of a given species that an area can support without reducing its future capacity to support that species. Carrying capacity is a function of *both* the characteristics of the environment and the species and so is a contingent measure, especially for a global species such as humans who also adapt the environment to themselves.

5. See also: https://www.sciencemag.org/news/2019/04/new-climate-models-predict-warming-surge

6. This, of course, was not the first iconic image, there have been many previous; the gradual submersion of small islands, polar bears on melting ice rafts, etc; however the warming of the globe from space is a particularly powerful image – both abstract (invoking an evidential natural science frame of reference) and emotive.

7. With endnote 3 as context one should note Article 3(3):

    The Parties should take precautionary measures to anticipate, prevent or minimize the causes of climate change and mitigate its adverse effects. Where there are threats of serious or irreversible damage, lack of full scientific certainty should not be used as a reason for postponing such measures, taking into account that policies and measures to deal with climate change should be cost-effective so as to ensure global benefits at the lowest possible cost. To achieve this, such policies and measures should take into account different socio-economic contexts, be comprehensive, cover all relevant sources, sinks and reservoirs of greenhouse gases and adaptation, and comprise all economic sectors. Efforts to address climate change may be carried out cooperatively by interested Parties. (UNFCCC, 1992, p. 4)

8. See Hickel (2018), in a famous 1991 paper William Nordhaus, winner of the Swedish 'Nobel' Bank prize 2018 ('To slow or not to slow') argued firmly let's not be too eager to slow down global warming, because we don't want to jeopardize growth.

9. The report states:

The environment does not exist as a sphere separate from human actions, ambitions, and needs and attempts to defend it in isolation from human concerns have given the very word 'environment' a connotation of naivety in some political circles. The word 'development' has also been narrowed by some into a very limited focus, along the lines of 'what poor nations should do to become richer'. And this again is automatically dismissed by many in the international arena as being a concern for specialists, of those involved in questions of 'development assistance'. But the environment is where we live; and development is what we all do in attempting to improve our lot within that abode. The two are inseparable.

And defines sustainable development as: 'Meeting the needs of the present without compromising the ability of future generations to meet their own needs.'

10. 1 gigatonne of carbon = 1 billion tonnes. The CO_2 metric is 3.67 times the size of just carbon.
11. Note these do not all end up in the atmosphere, they are distributed between land sea and air depending on processes and cycles.
12. The Wikipedia entry for 'Emissions Budget' includes a useful table setting out a range of budgets targeted at 2°C and 1.5°C https://en.wikipedia.org/wiki/Emissions_budget
13. Agricultural land use is a major cause of emissions and climate change: noting the significant increase in the global population; that human use directly affects about 70% of the ice-free land surface; agriculture accounts for 70% of freshwater use; since 1961 per capita supply of meat and vegetable oils has doubled, 2 billion people are overweight (compared to 821 million undernourished) and 25–30% of total food produced is wasted; dryland (desertification) area has increased by average 1% per year since 1961
14. And:

The updates to this year's assessment result in changes of the GHG emission levels in 2030, compared with the 2017 Emissions Gap Report, consistent with limiting global warming to 2°C and lower. According to the new scenario estimates, emissions of all GHGs should not exceed 40 (range 38–45) $GtCO_2$ in 2030, if the 2°C target is to be attained with about 66 percent chance. To keep global warming to 1.8°C with about 66 percent chance, global GHG emissions in 2030 should not exceed 34 (range 30–40) $GtCO_2$. For a 66 percent chance of keeping temperature increase below 1.5°C in 2100 (associated with no or a low overshoot), global GHG emissions in 2030 should not exceed 24 (range 22–30) $GtCO_2$. (UNEP, 2018, p. xix)

15. https://unfccc.int/decisions_katowice
16. The technological solutions presuppose the efficacy of future iterations of technology at scale based on in-principle potential extrapolated from current demonstration – and this requires a leap of faith on their behalf.
17. Useful sites include: https://www.greenpeace.org, https://rebellion.earth, degrowth-world@lists.riseup.net, www.drawdown.org, https://www.ran.org, https://www.clivespash.org, https://www.greattransition.org/publication/economics-for-a-full-world

Disclosure statement

No potential conflict of interest was reported by the authors.

References

Amen, M., Bosman, M. M., & Gills, B. K. (2008). Editorial: The urgent need for global action to combat climate change. *Globalizations, 5*(1), 49–52. doi:10.1080/14747730701850886

Banking on Climate Change [Rainforest Action Network]. (2019, March). *Fossil fuel finance report card 2019.* San Francisco, CA: Author.

Büchs, M., & Koch, M. (2017). *Postgrowth and well being.* Basingstoke: Palgrave Macmillan.

Hansen, J., Sato, M., Kharecha, P., von Schuckmann, K., Beerling, D. J., Cao, J., … Ruedy, R. (2017). Young people's burden: Requirement of negative CO_2 emissions. *Earth System Dynamics, 8,* 577–616.

Hawken, P. (2016). *Drawdown: The most comprehensive plan ever proposed to reverse global warming.* London: Penguin.

Hickel, J. (2018, December). The Nobel Prize for climate catastrophe. *Foreign Policy.* Retrieved from https:// foreignpolicy.com/2018/12/06/the-nobel-prize-for-climate-catastrophe/

IPCC. (2018). *Global warming of 1.5°C: Summary for policymakers.* Geneva: Author.

IPCC. (2019). *IPCC special report on climate change, desertification, land degradation, sustainable land management, food security, and greenhouse gas fluxes in terrestrial ecosystems.* Summary for policymakers August 7th.

Jacques, P., Dunlap, R., & Freeman, M. (2008). The organisation of denial: Conservative think tanks and environmental scepticism. *Environmental Politics, 17*(3), 349–385.

Klein, N. (2014). *This changes everything: Capitalism versus the climate.* London: Simon & Schuster.

Morgan, J. (2016). Paris COP21: Power that speaks the truth? *Globalizations, 13*(6), 943–951.

Morgan, J. (2017). Piketty and the growth dilemma revisited in the context of ecological economics. *Ecological Economics, 136,* 169–177.

Oreskes, N., & Conway, E. (2010). *Merchants of doubt.* New York, NY: Bloomsbury.

Raworth, K. (2017). *Doughnut economics.* London: Random House.

Schroder, E., & Storm, S. (2018). Why 'Green Growth' is an illusion. INET Working Paper series.

Smith, R. (2016). *Green capitalism: The God that failed.* London: College Publications.

Spash, C. (2016). This changes nothing: The Paris Agreement to ignore reality. *Globalizations, 13*(6), 928–933

Spash, C. (2018). Facing the truth or living a lie: Conformity, radicalism and activism. *Environmental Values 27,* 215–222.

Steffen, W., Rockström, J., Richardson, K., Lenton, T. M., Folke, C., Liverman, D., … Schellnhuber, H. J. (2018) Trajectories of the Earth System in the Anthropocene. *Proceedings of the National Academy of Sciences of the USA, 115,* 8252–8259.

UNEP. (2007). *Global environmental outlook report 4.* New York, NY: Author.

UNEP. (2018, November). *Emissions gap report 2018* (9th ed.). New York, NY: Author.

UNFCCC. (1992, May 9). *United Nations Framework Convention on climate change.* New York, NY: Author

UNFCCC. (2015, December 12). *Adoption of the Paris Agreement and Annex: Paris Agreement.* Paris: Author

UNFCCC. (2018, December 14). *Katowice texts.* Katowice: Author.

Wackernagel, M., & Rees, W. (1996). *Our ecological footprint: Reducing human impact on the earth.* Gabriola Island, BC: New Society Publishers.

WCED. (1987). *Report of the world commission on environment and development: Our common future* New York, NY: United Nations.

Fiddling while the planet burns? COP25 in perspective

Peter Newell [ORCID] and Olivia Taylor

ABSTRACT

With fires, storms, social protests, and climate strikes sweeping the world, 2019 should have been a tipping point in how the world responds to global heating. This was the backdrop to the COP25 climate change summit which took place in Madrid in December 2019. This paper assesses the outcomes of the meeting and the path towards the critically important meeting in Glasgow at the end of 2020. It analyses and explains the key points of contention over levels of ambition, the rules which should govern global carbon markets and sensitive issues such as loss and damage associated with the impacts of climate change. The analysis is situated within a broader geopolitical and economic context of right-wing populism, deepening forms of marketization and financialization of responses to climate change and against a background of a world increasingly feeling the effects of the climate crisis.

1. Introduction

Every year since the ratification of the UN Framework Convention on Climate Change in 1994, parties to the treaty host a Conference of the Parties (COP) to review progress and chart next steps. Rarely are they considered a success given the increasing shortfall between what the scientific community calls for by way of action and what governments commit themselves to. But hopes for a more positive and ambitious outcome in late 2019 rested on a confluence of growing evidence of the alarming impacts of climate change, waves of protests from the school strikes to Extinction Rebellion, the fact numerous governments and councils around the world have declared a climate emergency, and the publication of a spate of recent scientific reports spelling out what is at stake. As if to underscore the gravity of the situation and the need for urgent action, the backdrop to the conference was provided by climate chaos sweeping the world. From bushfires in Australia, forest fires in Indonesia and wildfires in California to the deliberate burning of Amazonian rainforests in Brazil, record temperatures in India and record-breaking storms in the Caribbean, the message could not have been clearer. Yet none of this could seemingly shake the world's leaders from their intransigence and collective inability to address arguably the most pressing issue the world faces today (Amen, Bosman, & Gills, 2008; Gills & Morgan, 2019).

More than 23,000 people, including 8775 observers, duly attended the longest-ever UN climate conference (COP25), running past its agreed deadline by two days, mirroring delegates' collective failure to stick to agreed emissions reduction targets. Delegates met amid not only a world on fire, but waves of protest and populism conspiring to make things even more difficult. Although

Brazil was the original confirmed host of COP-25, the far-right government of Jair Bolsonaro withdrew the offer to host shortly after the Brazilian election, reflecting Brazil's transition from being an important proponent of climate action to occupying a position of climate pariah. After Brazil withdrew, Chile immediately offered to host the COP in partnership with Costa Rica. But mere weeks before the COP was expected to begin in Santiago, an unprecedented wave of social unrest spurred by rising social inequalities, forced Chilean President Sebastian Piñera to withdraw Chile's offer to host the conference. Spain, a country subject to its own fair share of protests and upheavals in recent years, offered to host at the last minute in Madrid. This last-minute shift of the COP to a new country on a new continent raised additional barriers to participation for both poorer states and hundreds of civil society organizations, including social movements and indigenous peoples that had invested heavily in public mobilizations around the COP. The omens were not good.

Yet three months before the COP, the UN Secretary General Antonio Guterres sought to build momentum for enhanced action by convening a Climate Action Summit in New York in September 2019. Despite the emergence of an 'Ambition alliance' of countries committed to raising their national commitments (Nationally Determined Contributions) or achieve carbon neutrality by 2050, the Summit ended with none of the high-emitting countries committing to increase their ambition prior to the end of 2020. In the meantime, it was reported emissions set a new record in 2018, and again in 2019. Just three years since the signing of the Paris accord, no major industrial nation on Earth is on track to honour the commitments it made (Morgan, 2016; Spash, 2016) and yet the widely reported message from the IPCC SR15 was that we have less than a decade to cut global emissions in half to safely avoid catastrophic warming (Wallace-Wells, 2019). The chasm between what the best available science suggests is required to address the issue and the commitments, currently on the table in countries' voluntary Nationally Determined Contributions (NDCs) could not be greater (UNEP, 2019).

A quick glance around the world's political leaders charged with tackling this issue gives some indication of why progress is so pitifully slow. We have a conjuncture in which Presidents Trump in the US, Bolsanaro in Brazil, Putin in Russia, and Prime Ministers Modi in India, Morrison in Australia and Johnson in the UK have all either explicitly doubted the scientific basis of climate change, or actively sought to scupper more aggressive action to address it. It is hard to think of a set of leaders less disposed to provide the sort of bold, ambitious, multilateral responses now required of us.

Given this situation, there are legitimate questions being raised about the very future viability of this way of doing climate politics. Besides the general delaying tactics of these leaders which, especially when combined, can serve as a veto coalition on greater ambition, a key issue is how to prevent the more active and explicit sabotage of the process by a small group of oil-exporting countries willing and able to hold the world hostage to their desire to protect the profit flows of oil majors such as Saudi's Aramco. Attention has focused on delegates attending UNFCCC negotiations that are in the pay of oil companies and able to stall progress of the negotiations by challenging the science and adopting delaying tactics in bad faith. For example, at COP25 over 40 Gulf state delegates were current or former employees of fossil fuel companies (Collett-White, 2019). In other words, they are using veto power to block progress towards the stated aim of the negotiations and have a clear material interest in slowing progress wherever possible.

This is just one of the procedural inequities which continue to dog the climate regime. Saleem Huq, long-term advisor to the Least Developed Countries grouping, recently declared the negotiations are no longer fit for purpose for developing countries (Huq, 2019). There have been longstanding critiques of process inequalities around the unequal size of delegations and sharp inequities in access to scientific and legal expertise, which manifested themselves again in Madrid as some vulnerable and developing countries were excluded from back room discussions on the issue of carbon market rules (see below). But added to this is the politics of brinkmanship which entrenches these inequalities in representation. As Huq (2019) puts it:

> COP25 was the longest COP ever, having gone on for two extra days (and nights) beyond the originally planned twelve days. This tendency, now standard practice at COPs, to take the negotiations into overtime for a day or more is not only extremely inefficient, but is also deeply unfair to the most vulnerable developing countries whose delegates cannot stay on. Thus, the decisions made in the last hours of extra time are invariably detrimental to their interests and by the time they get home and see the final text they see their words have disappeared.

Ensuring that future negotiations ensure an adequate and proper voice from those in the frontline of climate change, without further privileging polluter elites, is a critical challenge to address if the entire COP architecture is not to risk further jeopardy.

2. Raising ambition

A familiar note of disappointment and despondency, as well as increasing anger, surrounded the end of the summit. Countries failed to agree on many of the hoped-for outcomes, including rules to set up a global carbon trading system and the means to channel new finance to countries facing the impacts of climate change, about which more below. The Chilean presidency wanted to use COP25 to galvanize political leadership, but it failed to leverage the biggest emitters into action.

Invigorated by the US withdrawal from the Paris agreement and rising nationalism at home, Brazil, Australia, and Saudi Arabia, defended loopholes and opposed commitments to enhance climate action. Countries agreed in Paris in 2015 to revisit their climate pledges by 2020. But many countries were pushing for all countries to submit more ambitious climate pledges before 2020 to improve upon their current commitments. Countries such as China, India, and Brazil opposed placing any obligation on countries to submit enhanced pledges, arguing it should be each country's own decision. They also insisted on the delivery of finance and support promised by rich countries before 2020 as a precondition to any discussion on enhancing their current targets.

As talks reached their final days, tensions grew after a draft decision removed any call for countries to 'update' or 'enhance' their climate plans by 2020. Instead, it only invited them to 'communicate' them in 2020 – a far weaker form of language which put no obligation on enhanced ambition. Eventually, pushback led to some stronger language being reinserted which urges countries to consider the gap between existing commitments and what is needed to limit warming 'well below 2C', with a view to 'reflecting their highest possible ambition'. Indeed, 80 countries have already signalled plans to enhance their climate pledges this year. But to put those pledges in context, these countries represent only 8% of global emissions (Duyck & Lennon, 2019). Likewise, in the final text, countries agreed to hold pre-2020 roundtables. The outcomes of these pre-2020 roundtables will also be rounded up in a report in 2021, which will in turn feed into a review on progress towards meeting the Paris Agreement's goal. But it did not specifically say whether the results of these roundtables would feed directly into the global stocktake set to occur in 2023 under the Paris agreement.

State leadership was thin on the ground. But some European countries, emboldened by the demands of widespread public mobilizations and youth activists, sought to ensure the integrity of the Paris Agreement. The European Commission said it would present a plan to enhance the bloc's 2030 target to at least 55% by summer 2020. Indeed, the European Union was the only major emitter to make a significant announcement during COP-25 as Ursula von der Leyen, the newly appointed President of the European Commission, communicated its vision for a European

Green Deal. Released halfway through the COP, the Commission's economy-wide plan includes the ambition to make Europe the first 'carbon neutral continent' through a series of measures addressing all key sectors of the economy.

Two small wins perhaps were the approval of a new *Gender Action Plan* and a work plan for the *Local Communities and Indigenous Peoples Platform*. The COP successfully reviewed and renewed the UNFCCC Gender Action Plan, adopting a five-year roadmap to promote gender equality in the implementation of climate action. The new work plan promises to contribute to increasing the mainstreaming of gender across all climate action, including through increased capacity-building and the implementation of climate-just solutions. The Parties also endorsed the initial 2-year work plan of the *Local Communities and Indigenous Peoples Platform*, a body operationalized in 2017 in which representatives from governments and Indigenous Peoples organizations have seats with equal footing. The work plan provides a detailed roadmap for the increased recognition of the value of traditional Indigenous Peoples' knowledge for designing and implementing climate action, as well as how to increase the participation of Indigenous Peoples in climate policies, including in the implementation of NDCs.

Seen in context, however, these were minor victories. Closing the meeting, COP25 President Carolina Schmidt said the agreements reached were 'not enough to address the urgency of the crisis on climate change'. 'The world is watching us,' she warned, calling on countries to 'strengthen political will and to accelerate climate action at the pace that the world needs. The new generations are waiting for more from us, we have the obligation of being up to this task', she added (Farand, 2019). Yet as Jennifer Morgan, executive director of Greenpeace International, reflected: 'I have never seen the divide between what is happening between the inside of these walls and the outside so large' (Farand, 2019). The UN Secretary General expressed his disappointment regarding the outcomes, by suggesting that 'the international community lost an important opportunity to show increased ambition on mitigation, adaptation, and finance to tackle the climate crisis'. Even for a diplomat, it is hard to think of a greater under-statement.

3. The strange non-death of carbon markets

As with many other areas of environmental policy, climate policy has since the mid-1990s been increasingly subject to market disciplines and the increasingly hegemonic notion that market mechanisms provide the optimal and most effective way of delivering improved environmental outcomes (Newell & Paterson, 2010). In 1997 the Kyoto Protocol brought into being a global carbon market mechanism (the Clean Development Mechanism (CDM)) and regional schemes, most notably the EU Emissions Trading Scheme, followed suit. Despite their very limited success, the march towards the expansion of market-based approaches continues unabated. Colin Crouch's (2011) enquiry into the strange non-death of neo-liberalism, could equally apply to carbon markets whose recent 'alive but dead' status has seen them likened to 'zombie markets' (Newell & Lane, 2016).

This drive was given a key boost by Article 6 of the Paris Agreement which opened the way for a new wave of carbon market activity. A new Sustainable Development Mechanism will allow emission reduction credits to be traded on an open carbon market across countries, cities, and businesses, in contrast to the current CDM which operates more as an inter-state credit transfer mechanism between countries in the global North and South. Some countries, including Australia, Brazil, and India, want to be able to use old, unspent CDM credits in the new system. But many countries are concerned that allowing carryover could flood the market with cheap credits that do not represent real emissions reductions, undermining the integrity of the entire system. This is because

CDM credits represent emissions cuts made well before 2020, the year the Paris Agreement formally begins, and there are serious doubts in any case over whether many CDM-registered projects have even driven real emissions cuts.[1] The question of how to deal with CDM credits, potentially amounting to more than a billion tonnes of CO_2, became a big point of contention. The lion's share of these carbon credits are held by a handful of countries, particularly China, India, and Brazil. China alone has an estimated half a billion tonnes equivalent of credits, while India has around 100 million tonnes. Similarly, if Australia, which holds about 400 million tonnes of credits, (equivalent to $100 million) were allowed to count these credits against its Paris target, it will meet half of the target to cut emissions by 26–28% below 2005 levels by 2030 (Bhushan, 2019) taking pressure off the need for an urgent move away from coal mining for example.

Article 6 was then the hot topic of COP-25. As the main unfinished piece of the Paris Rulebook on how the markets will function in practice following COP24 in Katowice, the Chilean Presidency and Parties arrived in Madrid keen to finish Article 6 as the primary outcome of this COP. Negotiations largely focused on two concerns: avoiding double counting through the application of adjustments and strong accounting rules, and disallowing the carryover of Kyoto Protocol credits to countries' commitments under Paris. With tensions breaking out yet again on different parts of the rulebook, however, no outcome was agreed. In the end, a mere two paragraphs summed up plans to continue talks in 2020. These acknowledged the draft texts from this year's negotiations as a basis for future talks, meaning countries will not have to start from scratch. However, none of the texts secured a consensus. Australia and Brazil continued to push for a system with loopholes which allowed initial double counting of emissions reductions and the trading of Kyoto-era credits, while others suggested this would undermine the entire market. Indeed, a group of 31 countries led by Costa Rica signed up to the 'San Jose principles', a set of minimum standards for ensuring the integrity of the global carbon market. Negotiated at pre-COP discussions, these eleven principles set forth minimum standards to be met by the Article 6 rules centred on preserving environmental integrity and emphasizing the need to ensure that Article 6 activities actually increase ambition and lead to emissions reductions.

Amid long-standing controversies over the social and environmental impacts of previous projects supported under the CDM, indigenous and human rights groups have long called for the new mechanism to ensure that the projects it funds do not harm local communities (Newell, 2014). They have pushed for the new carbon market rules to require projects to respect human rights, protect indigenous peoples and other vulnerable groups, consult meaningfully with local communities and set up an independent grievance programme for projects that fail to do these things. While elements of these were in initial drafts discussed at the beginning of the talks, successive drafts removed several of them. The current draft text has no mention of human rights, asking only that projects shall 'avoid negative environmental and social impacts'. Incredibly, it merely states that consultations should take place 'where consistent with applicable domestic arrangements' and that further safeguards could be reviewed by 2028. As Erika Lennon, senior attorney at the Center for International Environmental Law (CIEL) put it, the texts are 'woefully inadequate' in regards to protecting people on the ground from harm caused by activities under the new market mechanisms (Timperley, 2019). Strategically, this outcome might constitute a partial short-term victory, however, because the creation of bad rules would have left open the possibility of accounting loopholes leading to double counting of emission reductions, carryover of previous Kyoto credits, and human rights abuses. These have been avoided, for now. Experience from the Kyoto mechanism demonstrates that once rules are developed, governments rarely, if ever, upgrade them later to fix loopholes. Thus, if bad rules had been adopted, they would have locked in very weak forms of safeguards of social and environmental integrity (Duyck & Lennon, 2019). Former UK clean energy minister Claire Perry O'Neill, who, until her recent dismissal, was set to lead the talks at the next COP in Glasgow said 'We will pull no punches … in getting clarity and certainty for natural carbon markets and will work with everyone including the private sector for clear rules and transparent measurement' (Timperley, 2019). Yet most of the contentious issues look likely to be re-opened at the Glasgow COP in 2020.

4. New sites of financialization

Finance, and who pays for what and from which sources, has been a mainstay of climate change negotiations from the very start. Battles over 'new and additional' finance for mitigation and adaptation and increasingly loss and damage (as we will see below) are nothing new (Timmons Roberts & Parks, 2007; Bulkeley & Newell, 2010). What has come to the fore, however, are growing attempts to financialize responses to address climate change. From crop insurance to weather derivatives and catastrophe bonds, there are now a number of initiatives aimed at creating financial opportunities out of markets for adaptation and resilience (Isakson, 2015).

Indeed, insurance programmes have become a rare site of consensus as an avenue for delivering finance, in part because of a preference for insurance-based approaches among G7 governments, and in part because a focus on existing channels neatly avoids the controversial topic of new and additional finance. Between negotiators from Japan, Norway and the US there was agreement that sovereign risk transfer facilities, such as CCRIF (the Caribbean Catastrophe Risk Insurance Facility), which mixes parametric insurance and regional risk pooling across governments, could be scaled up. The InsuResilience Global Partnership for Climate and Disaster Risk Finance and Insurance Solutions is also seen as a key avenue for scaling and delivering finance that was particularly supported by Japan during the negotiations. The InsuResilience partnership was launched in 2017 by the G7 countries to provide climate risk insurance for 400 million people in developing countries by 2020, through a range of existing insurance schemes at all levels (such as CCRIF) and supporting research and delivery projects.[2] The partnership held its 3rd annual forum at COP, this year with a particular focus on the Caribbean and Latin America. Supporters contend that initiatives such as sovereign risk transfer can help countries to manage their exposure to climate extremes and disasters by spreading the risk over a long period of time and pooling risk within regions. Moreover, it is argued that the process of generating an insurance product can be useful in identifying areas of climate risk while localized pricing structures can signal areas of unsustainable development, for example where properties in risk areas become too expensive to insure (Jarzabkowski et al., 2019).

In practice though, there is very limited evidence that insurance schemes incentivize risk and vulnerability reduction in developing countries. There are a number of serious limitations to insurance-based approaches, in particular, the costs of premiums in the face of escalating severity and frequency of extreme events. Insurance has always been an expensive climate risk management intervention, more so than either credit or savings schemes, while the level of pay-out is inherently constrained by the premiums that countries or donors can afford (Hillier, 2018). However, during COP25 this was brought into particularly sharp focus by the recent pay-out of the CCRIF scheme after Hurricane Dorian hit the Bahamas in September.[3] The total amount paid to the government of the Bahamas was $12.8 million USD, a drop in the ocean in comparison to estimates of total damage – at $3.4 billion USD (Inter-American Development Bank, 2019).

It is particularly striking that during the same week as insurance-based approaches were being praised at the COP, the UN Under-Secretary-General for Humanitarian Affairs and Emergency

Relief Coordinator, Mark Lowcock, was sounding a note of caution on insurance-based approaches, citing the meagre pay-out received in the Bahamas, as well as failures to incentivize risk reduction.[4] Thus, regardless of whether or not new and additional finance can be provided, discussions about whether existing delivery systems are suitable for the climate emergency should also have been on the agenda. Can systems such as CCRIF be usefully scaled up, from what is effectively a small-scale fiscal resilience system for governments, to a climate risk management system? Or should we instead be looking to grant and aid-based approaches, or alternatives such as regional solidarity funds? Unfortunately, the negotiations failed to deliver substance on these issues: political expediency won out over reflection about the effectiveness of the initiatives being proposed.

Another feature of the growing financialization of responses to climate change is the shift, notable in the lead up to COP-25, towards 'nature-based solutions' as a way of addressing the climate crisis. These even received their own track for discussion at the UN Secretary General's summit in September 2019. COP-25 saw numerous side events on both land and marine 'nature-based solutions', hence this being dubbed the 'blue COP': a reference to 'blue carbon' and the role of marine ecosystems in storing and regulating the flow of carbon. However, what began as an attempt to acknowledge the very real and important linkages between biodiversity and climate change, and to acknowledge the critical role that land and ecosystems can play in solving the climate crisis, has started to become co-opted. This was most evident at an event featuring speakers from large oil companies discussing the importance of nature-based solutions. These developments demonstrate the increasing risk that the term 'nature-based solutions' promotes both an agenda linked to the further commodification of nature, while also being used by fossil fuel industries as a way to avoid transforming their business models. This concerning shift will have to be carefully monitored as the Standing Committee on Finance considers funding for nature-based solutions, and as the Green Climate Fund, the main body for overseeing the multilateral financing of climate change, develops guidance for its land and forestry sectors, and as the negotiations on Article 6 continue with the potential for land to be used for offsets as part of the market mechanisms (Duyck & Lennon, 2019; Newell & Taylor, 2018).

5. Justice for current and future damage

For many least developed countries in the frontline of the effects of climate change, despite having contributed very little to the problem, discussions about loss and damage assume ever-growing importance (Roberts & Huq, 2015). The collective failure of the international community to bring down greenhouse gas emissions over the previous decades means we are now entering a world of real loss and damage due to human-induced climate change that is clearly attributable to the emissions of greenhouse gases.

A Warsaw International Mechanism on Loss and Damage (WIM) was established in 2014, but has never garnered momentum to provide new finance to cover climate losses. COP-25 was mandated to conclude the review of it. Yet as Huq (2019) argues,

> The failure of COP25 to allow the Warsaw International Mechanism on loss and damage to have an implementation and financing arm as demanded by the vulnerable developing countries, was an indicator of how out of touch with reality the negotiations have now become.

Vulnerable countries were seeking the establishment of a new financial facility under the WIM to channel new and additional loss and damage finance to countries facing climate emergency. However, richer countries that bear most historical responsibility for climate change are extremely wary of language around loss and damage finance for obvious reasons. The US was particularly resistant to any discussion about new areas of work, even for existing funds. Moreover, the key issue of whether the WIM should be put under the Paris Agreement body or the general COP was resolved in favour of the US. The US pushed strongly for it to remain outside the COP, which it does in the current draft. This means the US is not affected by the WIM after it leaves the Paris Agreement while continuing to remain a party to the convention and shaping its development.

This move to slow discussions of loss and damage assumed particular irony against the background of the declarations from a number of governments around the world of a climate emergency, which acknowledge that the mitigative measures taken up to this point are not sufficient to limit climate impacts. In fact, the frequency and severity of extreme climate events experienced this year led some to argue that this COP was the year in which disaster risk reduction (DRR) and humanitarian sectors should meet to find solutions together, having now surpassed the limits of mitigative and adaptive action. As Harjeet Singh from Action Aid put it; 'What we call loss and damage in climate parlance is nothing but humanitarian situations that are being created by climate change .... In fact, this particular COP is largely for the humanitarian community.'[5] Indeed, there were hints of progress around the creation of an expert group which could allow space for more conversations on how and by what means loss and damage funding could be provided and a newly formed 'Santiago network' will lead more work on how to minimize, avoid and recover from loss and damage, catalysing the initiatives already taking place. Yet with neither a fund nor a financial mechanism established to channel support for loss and damage, developing countries have been left without remedy as they face the mounting costs of climate inaction by the largest emitters.

While developed countries often point to humanitarian assistance as a means to provide support for the damages caused by extreme weather events, this support remains grossly inadequate and fails to cover the costs associated with slow onset events. The decision adopted in Madrid reflected this, with the inclusion of several references to the 'importance of scaling up the mobilization of resources to support efforts to avert, minimize and address loss and damage associated with the adverse effects of climate change'. Additionally, the decision also mandates the WIM to work with relevant bodies including the Green Climate Fund to facilitate access to international finance for projects addressing loss and damage and mandated the establishment of a WIM expert group on action and support. But with no reference to adequate, new or additional funding, the call to scale up finance was considerably weakened and the final text removed all reference to any developed country obligations on finance. With no outcome on long-term finance, discussion of the next long-term goal is scheduled to start at COP 26.

Beyond the narrower but critical question of loss and damage, the need for more adaptation finance was a constant theme as countries work to adapt to the rapidly changing climate. The link to the negotiations was most clearly seen in the discussion around the share of proceeds of Article 6 carbon trading activities that would go to the Adaptation Fund. While Parties largely agreed on having a share of proceeds from the mechanism going to the Adaptation Fund (in a similar manner to what the CDM currently does), they debated how much this contribution should be. Ultimately, the final text put forward included a share of proceeds at the same 2% rate as the CDM currently contributes to the Adaptation Fund. During COP25, the Adaptation Fund also received almost USD 90 million in pledged funding with new pledges from Germany, Switzerland, Norway, Poland, Ireland, and the three regional governments of Belgium that joined Sweden, Spain, and Quebec who had previously announced contributions.

Justice issues were not only addressed inside the negotiating rooms of the Madrid COP, however. There were vibrant and sustained protests inside and outside the negotiations. Hundreds of people, including many youth strikers, occupied the main plenary hall to highlight the inadequacy of the progress of climate negotiations. Together with Indigenous leaders and other civil society groups, they demanded that richer industrialized countries 'step up and pay up' for the damage caused to communities suffering from increasingly severe climate disasters. Following the protest, security barred civil society members from the UN Climate Talks and de-badged Observers (350.org., 2019). We can expect many more such protests in the run up to and during this year's Glasgow COP.

6. Towards Glasgow

With so little agreed in Madrid, the stakes will now be even higher for the Glasgow COP. This will now have the challenge of finding a resolution to the rules which will govern future carbon markets at the same time as galvanizing countries to submit upgraded climate pledges. Moreover, another discussion is set to begin on the promised new global climate finance goal to be made by 2025 which has to be higher than the $100bn per year promised from 2020 to 2025. In the light of the lack of progress on additional finance described above, this is a tall order.

Let us end though with one or two glimmers of hope amid the stalemate, delaying tactics, leadership failures and a desperate commitment to business as usual by the world's most powerful states.

The first is the growing momentum around what is referred to as supply-side policy: policies which actually get to the root of the problem by leaving fossil fuels in the ground (Erickson, Lazarus, & Piggot, 2018). In the run up to the COP, moratoria were announced on new oil exploration and production by a number of countries including New Zealand, France, Costa Rica and Belize. In November 2019, California, the third-largest oil-producing state in the US, blocked new fracking pending further scientific review. Leading Democratic candidates for President have also put forward plans to ban fracking and stop coal, oil and gas production on public lands. The wave of divestment from fossil fuels also grows ever bigger. On December 9, the $24 billion Norwegian insurance giant Storebrand divested from fossil fuels, joining more than 1,000 institutions worth over $17 trillion who have made some form of fossil fuel divestment commitment and in December 2019 the Swiss parliament announced it would be looking at divesting the $800 billion Swiss National Bank. The European Investment Bank announced that it will cease all fossil fuel financing including gas from 2022 onwards. And in the wake of the COP, ex-Irish Prime Minister Mary Robinson[6] in a speech to the UN Security Council backed calls for a Fossil Fuel Non-Proliferation Treaty (Newell & Simms 2019) that have gained the support of a number of politicians and civil society leaders.

Though not on the official agenda, therefore, fossil fuel production and fossil fuel companies were the elephant in every room at COP25. As some activists noted,

> for the first time in the United Nations space you can say the f-words in polite company. We're of course talking about 'fossil fuels.' The 2015 Paris Climate Agreement ran 16 pages, but didn't mention the words 'fossil fuels' 'coal,' 'oil,' or 'gas' once. That's a striking omission considering the central role that fossil fuels play in contributing to the climate crisis. (Abreu & Henn, 2019)

Indeed, nearly two-thirds of the greenhouse gas emissions contributing to global warming come from the production and burning of coal, oil, and gas. This glaring omission is perhaps less surprising in light of decades of sustained lobbying by some of the most powerful companies in the world (Newell & Paterson, 1998). Even the Madrid COP was sponsored by major companies with direct fossil fuel ties, including Iberdrola and Endesa (Spain's biggest corporate greenhouse gas polluter). But the demand coming from civil society and indigenous groups that we must 'keep it in the ground', is finally penetrating the political process, evidence perhaps of the increasing traction of what some scholars call 'anti-fossil fuel norms' (Green, 2018). When the UN secretary general opened COP25 he said, 'we simply have to stop digging and drilling', 'something that would have gotten him thrown out of the building just a few years ago' (Abreu & Henn, 2019).

The case for such policies, scientifically and morally, seems unquestionable. A series of important new reports were released at the talks in Madrid showing why this is the case. According to the *Production Gap* Report by the UN Environment Programme and leading research institutions (SEI et al., 2019), governments are planning to produce 120% more fossil fuels by 2030 than would be consistent with limiting warming to 1.5C. That conclusion was backed up by the report *Oil, Gas, and Climate: An Analysis of Oil and Gas Industry Plans for Expansion and Compatibility with Global Emissions Limits*, also released at COP25, that showed how oil companies are planning to invest $1.4 trillion in new oil and gas extraction projects between 2020 and 2024. 85% of the expanded production is slated to come from the US and Canada. This would lock in 148 gigatonnes of cumulative carbon dioxide emissions, equivalent to building over 1,200 new coal-fired power plants. Combined with increasingly vocal civil society demands to address this obvious anomaly, an accelerating wave of climate litigation, and support from the UN Special Rapporteur on Human Rights and the Environment and other leading international figures, supply-side climate policy may finally have arrived.

A second ground for hope, is the momentum from below (Bond, 2012) and beyond the UN which is seeking to bridge the gaping disconnect between the world of climate negotiations on the one hand, characterized by vested interests, political intransigence and sharp inequities in participation and representation and mired in bureaucracy and, on the other, the actions of cities, communities, social movements and businesses in acting in spite of government inaction. The UN climate regime's Global Climate Action lists 17,284 actors representing 25,961 actions on climate change.[7] This includes initiatives such as C40 and the Carbon Neutral Cities Alliance, the Transition Town movement and the growth of community energy and the work of businesses adopting 'science-based targets' to align their corporate strategies with the goals of the Paris agreement.[8] Indeed, some of the main drivers of the transition to a zero-carbon economy may come from factors like the falling costs of solar energy and the un-affordability of fossil fuel subsidies as much as from conscious climate policy interventions on the part of states.

Momentum for strengthened forms of transnational climate governance has been growing over the last decade (Bulkeley et al., 2014) and often seeks to fill governance gaps left by state inaction. Though it is important not to romanticize this, or suggest in any way that it offers a substitute for state action, when governments often still play a key role in orchestrating such initiatives (Hale & Roger, 2014), in so far as this generates pressure, raises ambition and shares and socializes the collective responsibility for addressing climate change, it can form an important part of collective responses.

In the end though, broader forms of public and social pressure will be key to raising the ambition of governments, corporations, and cities. It will determine whether climate change becomes an electoral issue and a focus for media and public debate, whether the fossil industries continue to see their social licence to operate diminish and whether social mobilization is able to penetrate elite politics and push back against incumbent actors and interests. The likelihood it can do this of course will be magnified by the way the climate crisis continues to draw attention to itself through extreme weather events and disruptions to everyday life that increasingly and unfortunately constitute the 'new normal'.

Notes

1. The technical term is additionality: whether the paid for emissions reductions are 'additional' to those which could have occurred without the project.
2. https://www.insuresilience.org/about/
3. https://www.ccrif.org/news/bahamas%E2%80%99-insurance-policy-ccrif-triggers-following-hurricane-dorian
4. https://reliefweb.int/report/world/mark-lowcock-under-secretary-general-humanitarian-affairs-and-emergency-relief
5. Action Aid – Harjeet Singh – https://www.thenewhumanitarian.org/news/2019/12/02/why-cop25-matters-emergency-aid-sector
6. https://www.theelders.org/news/multilateral-solutions-are-vital-tackling-global-challenges-we-face
7. https://climateaction.unfccc.int/
8. https://sciencebasedtargets.org/

Acknowledgements

We are grateful to the editor and reviewer of an earlier version of this article.

Disclosure statement

No potential conflict of interest was reported by the author(s).

ORCID

Peter Newell ⓘ http://orcid.org/0000-0002-5371-7668

References

350.org. (2019). *Protesters kicked out of COP25, stripped of badges*. Retrieved from https://350.org/civil-society-kicked-out-of-cop25/?akid=109819.1099932.8U6Imk&rd=1&t=7

Abreu, C., & Henn, J. (2019). *Finally saying the F-words at UN climate talks*. December 16th. Retrieved from https://www.climatechangenews.com/2019/12/16/finally-saying-f-words-un-climate-talks/

Amen, M., Bosman, M., & Gills, B. (2008). The urgent need for global action to combat climate change. *Globalizations, 5*(1), 49–52.

Bhushan, C. (2019). *COP 25: Failure of talks shows countries willing to sacrifice future of planet.* December 18th. Retrieved from https://www.financialexpress.com/opinion/cop-25-failure-of-talks-shows-countries-willing-to-sacrifice-future-of-planet/1797038/

Bond, P. (2012). *Politics of climate justice: Paralysis above, movement below.* Scottsville: University of KwaZulu-Natal Press.

Bulkeley, H., Andonova, L. B., Betsill, M. M., Compagnon, D., Hale, T., Hoffman, M. J., … Vandeveer, S. D. (2014). *Transnational climate change governance.* Cambridge: CUP.

Bulkeley, H., & Newell, P. (2010). *Governing climate change.* Abingdon: Routledge.

Collett-White, R. (2019). *COP25: Over 40 Gulf state delegates are current or former employees of fossil fuel companies.* December 13th. Retrieved from https://www.desmog.co.uk/2019/12/13/cop25-over-40-gulf-state-delegates-are-current-or-former-employees-fossil-fuel-companies

Crouch, C. (2011). *The strange non-death of neoliberalism.* Cambridge: Polity.

Duyck, S., & Lennon, E. (2019). *A process on the brink of collapse confronts a world on the move.* Global Gas and Oil Network.

Erickson, P., Lazarus, M., & Piggot, G. (2018). Limiting fossil fuel production as the next big step in climate policy. *Nature Climate Change, 8,* 1037–1043.

Farand, C. (2019). *Irreconcilable rift cripples UN climate talks as majority stand against polluters.* Retrieved from https://www.climatechangenews.com/2019/12/15/irreconcilable-rift-dominates-un-climate-talks-majority-stand-polluters/

Gills, B., & Morgan, J. (2019). Global climate emergency: After COP24, climate science, urgency and the threat to humanity. *Globalizations,* doi:10.1080/14747731.2019.1669915

Green, F. (2018). Anti-fossil fuel norms. *Climatic Change, 150,* 103–116.

Hale, T., & Roger, C. (2014). Orchestration and transnational climate governance. *Review of International Organizations, 9,* 59–82.

Hillier, D. (2018). *Facing risk: Options and challenges in ensuring that climate/disaster risk finance and insurance deliver for poor people* (Oxfam Briefing Paper). Retrieved from https://oxfamilibrary.openrepository.com/handle/10546/620457

Huq, S. (2019). For the vulnerable, UN climate talks are no longer fit for purpose. *Climate Home News,* December 17th. Retrieved from https://www.climatechangenews.com/2019/12/17/vulnerable-un-climate-talks-no-longer-fit-purpose/

Inter-American Development Bank. (2019). *Assessment of the effects and impacts of hurricane Dorian in the Bahamas.* Washington, DC: IDB. Retrieved from http://idbdocs.iadb.org/wsdocs/getdocument.aspx?docnum=EZSHARE-1256154360-486

Isakson, R. (2015). Derivatives for development? Small-farmer vulnerability and the financialization of climate risk management. *Journal of Agrarian Change, 15*(4), 569–580.

Jarzabkowski, P., Chalkias, K., Clarke, D., Iyahen, E., Stadtmueller, D., & Zwick, A. (2019). *Insurance for climate adaptation: Opportunities and limitations.* Rotterdam and Washington, DC: Global Commission on Adaptation. Retrieved from www.gca.org

Morgan, J. (2016). Paris COP21: Power that speaks the truth? *Globalizations, 13*(6), 943–951.

Newell, P. (2014). Dialogue of the deaf? The CDM's legitimation crisis. In B. Stephan & R. Lane (Eds.), *The politics of carbon markets* (pp. 212–236). London: Routledge.

Newell, P., & Lane, R. (2016). The political economy of carbon markets (with Richard Lane). In T. Van de Graaf, B. Sovacool, F. Kern, & M. Klare (Eds.), *The Palgrave handbook of the international political economy of energy* (pp. 247–269). London: Palgrave.

Newell, P., & Paterson, M. (2010). *Climate capitalism.* Cambridge: CUP.

Newell, P., & Paterson, M. (1998). A climate for business: Global warming, the state and capital. *Review of International Political Economy, 5*(4), 679–703.

Newell, P., & Simms, A. (2019). Towards a fossil fuel non-proliferation treaty. *Climate Policy.* doi:10.1080/14693062.2019.1636759

Newell, P., & Taylor, O. (2018). Contested landscapes: The global political economy of climate smart agriculture. *Journal of Peasant Studies, 45*(1), 80–88.

Roberts, E., & Huq, S. (2015). Coming full circle: The history of loss and damage under the UNFCCC. *International Journal of Global Warming, 8*(2), 141–157.

SEI, IISD, ODI, Climate Analytics, CICERO, and UNEP. (2019). *The production gap: The discrepancy between countries' planned fossil fuel production and global production levels consistent with limiting warming to 1.5° C or 2°C.* Retrieved from http://productiongap.org/

Spash, C. L. (2016). The changes nothing: The Paris Agreement to ignore reality. *Globalizations, 13*(6), 928–933.

Timmons Roberts, J., & Parks, B. (2007). *A climate of injustice: Global inequality, north-south politics, and climate policy.* Cambridge: MA: MIT Press.

Timperley. (2019). *COP25: What was achieved and where to next?* Retrieved from https://www.climatechangenews.com/2019/12/16/cop25-achieved-next/

UNEP. (2019). *Emissions gap report.* Nairobi: UNEP.

Wallace-Wells, D. (2019). *U.N. climate talks collapsed in Madrid. What's the way forward?* December 16th. Retrieved from http://nymag.com/intelligencer/2019/12/cop25-ended-in-failure-whats-the-way-forward.html

Democratizing global climate governance? The case of indigenous representation in the Intergovernmental Panel on Climate Change (IPCC)

Pedram Rashidi and Kristen Lyons

ABSTRACT

Indigenous communities have a particular stake in climate and energy developments, and have come to occupy a central role in both the movement toward decarbonization of industrial societies and renewable energy transition. Yet they remain underrepresented and excluded from climate policy processes. This paper critically evaluates the case of the Intergovernmental Panel on Climate Change (IPCC) to foster inclusive decision-making, with a specific focus on the place of Indigenous peoples in these processes. We demonstrate the ways in which the IPCC provides limited voice for Indigenous peoples in the Panel's deliberations. We argue the IPCC's disregard for Indigenous knowledges – and Indigenous peoples – arises from a configuration of structural problems within the governance of decarbonization and the politics of knowledge production. We conclude the IPCC faces on-going challenges in supporting the democratic functioning of climate decision-making, including in upholding Indigenous peoples' internationally recognized human rights as political actors.

Introduction

There is growing interest in the role that Indigenous peoples – and Indigenous Knowledges (hereafter 'IKs') – can play in the context of climate change. In this paper, we take a critical look at how Indigenous peoples and their laws, cultures, practices and knowledges, are approached and represented in this space. To do this, we look into reports generated by the main body of climate change research, the Intergovernmental Panel on Climate Change (IPCC). The IPCC was established in 1988, and is the only international institution that is tasked to provide a comprehensive and multidisciplinary corpus of knowledge to document, and respond to, the challenge of climate change. The IPCC reports are widely believed to be the most authoritative assessment of climate change available for policy makers, experts, and the general public (Hughes, 2015; Hughes & Paterson, 2017; Hulme & Mahony, 2010; Vasileiadou et al., 2011).

There is now some scholarly recognition of the neglect of IKs in the IPCC assessment processes, and of the limited scope for Indigenous peoples' participation in its deliberations. Scholars have shown that the Panel is biased towards the use of scientific and technical disciplines (Bjurstrom & Polk, 2011; Corbera et al., 2016; Hiramatsu et al., 2008; Hulme & Mahony, 2010), and generally neglects IKs. Ford et al. (2012; 2016a), for example, analysed Working Group II's contribution to the Fifth Assessment Report on climate change impacts, adaptation, and vulnerability, finding an underrepresentation of Indigenous expertise and limited coverage of Indigenous issues. They also identify inadequate critical engagement with the diversity and complexities of Indigenous knowledge systems. Their work points to structural issues in the politics of knowledge that have constrained Indigenous participation in the process of knowledge production. Adding to this critique, Suliman et al. (2019) demonstrate the state-centric architecture of the IPCC's global climate governance model fails to respond to the needs and interests of non-state actors, including Indigenous peoples. The outcome of this deepens Indigenous peoples' under-representation, or inclusion as 'objects' of global climate governance.

Despite this growing literature, there has been no in-depth study of the structural forces that work to limit Indigenous input into the formulation of authoritative knowledge on climate change. This paper contributes to nascent literature in this space with a diagnostic study of barriers to Indigenous engagement within the IPCC. Drawing from a content analysis of a selection of the Panel's reports, this paper demonstrates the IPCC's misrepresentation of Indigenous peoples and IKs. In so doing, we show that IKs are positioned as sources of information that may supplement science. Indigenous peoples are also situated as vulnerable to climate change, rather than actors who may be empowered by the tools of their own knowledge systems. To do this, we demonstrate that the main problem with Indigenous representation (or lack thereof) in the IPCC is not the day-to-day politics of exclusion; rather, it is the configuration of structural problems that have their roots in the history of the IPCC as a governing institution that has emerged within the context of European colonial science expansion (see Whyte, 2017). Overall, we argue that the epistemological and ideological forces shaping the structure of international knowledge institutions, such as the IPCC, allow for the inclusion of only a limited range of knowledge in their assessment processes. We conclude the IPCC must untangle these structural limits of its model of colonial global environmental governance to remedy its neglect of IKs, and invite on-going debate about pathways to reform.

Our paper begins with a brief background on relevant science, environmental governance and Indigenous Knowledges literature, which provides the context for our analysis of the IPCC. It then proceeds with the content analysis of selected IPCC reports. Based on our content analysis, we critically explore the way(s) the IPCC has come to construct IKs. Finally, we examine key underlying assumptions the IPCC draws upon in approaching Indigenous peoples and their knowledges which, we argue, results in such construction of IKs.

Science, environmental governance and Indigenous Knowledges

Our approach to the analysis of the IPCC is informed by historical legacies that shape the contemporary workings of science, science institutions and knowledge production. We therefore begin with some scene setting, locating our analysis within histories that bind the expansion of Western science with the colonial project, as well as considering the legacies of this for contemporary environmental governance, including global climate governance, the focus of this paper.

Western scientific expansion occurred alongside processes of modernization, developmentalism and colonization. The Scientific Revolution brought new ways of knowing the world, and with outcomes that sidelined, enclosed and/or co-opted, non-European knowledges. Harding (2008, p. 38) describes this demarcation project as bifurcating knowledge claims; between that valued as 'rational science', versus its 'irrational', or 'savage', 'nonscience' counterpart. This colonial project –

grounded in technocratic and developmentalist structures of domination – also enabled the expansion of Eurocentric science and scientific institutions, while at the same time sidelining Indigenous peoples (see Whyte, 2017).

Turning to contemporary environmental challenges, scientific and technical approaches remain central to both politics and governance, with scientists frequently positioned as 'experts' alongside the scientization of environmental decision making (Bäckstrand, 2004; Weingart, 1999). This is evident in the growth of science-based solutions to environmental problems. The expansion in global carbon offset initiatives, such as Reducing Emissions from Deforestation and Forest Degradation (REDD+), are exemplars of such technological-fixes that ground solutions to the challenge of climate change within a dominant modernist framework[1] (Hannigan, 1995). These development interventions position rational science-based decision making as best placed to address environmental problems. The IPCC is a product of this paradigm. Its politics of knowledge production was positioned from inception[2] as a scientific endeavour that would draw upon (mostly Northern-based) experts to generate technical – and market-based – solutions to the global[3] challenge of climate change.

The emergence of new forms of environmental and public health risks, and other kinds of uncertainties, however, have also challenged the conventional (and exclusive) role of science in decision making. Reflecting this tension, contemporary approaches to environmental problems are frequently characterized by the inclusion of a diverse array of actors as part of deliberative forms of environmental governance (see Dryzek, 2002). This participatory turn has widened the scope of what counts as knowledge, as well as who is recognized as a legitimate knowledge bearer. The proliferation of locally-driven 'bottom-up' approaches reflects the plurality of knowledges that are now recognized as part of environmental decision making (Bäckstrand, 2004).

This deliberative turn has occurred alongside growing international recognition of the rights of Indigenous peoples, including recognition of the right to self-determination and participatory rights in the global climate regime (Lindroth & Sinevaara-Niskanen, 2013), including the UN Declaration on the Rights of Indigenous Peoples (UNDRIP). Yet despite this recognition, Smith (2007, p. 200) explains 'Indigenous peoples and their counterhegemonic discourse are masked and marginalized', the outcome of which provides only limited possibilities for their voices to be heard within the IPCC.

Indigenous Knowledges can be taken to include those modes of knowledge belonging to communities, peoples, and nations that are identified with Indigeneity (Watson, 2014). For Semali and Kincheloe (1999, p. 3), IKs reflect 'the dynamic way in which the residents of an area have come to understand themselves in relationship to their natural environment and how they organize that folk knowledge of flora and fauna, cultural beliefs, and history to enhance their lives'. Agrawal (2002) avoids separating IKs from Western sciences on the basis of simple, universal criteria. Rather, he asserts that what we know today as IKs have interacted with Western knowledge since at least the fifteenth century, and on this basis – and given that both are based on systematic empirical observation – there is no strict division between Western and Indigenous knowledges. Yet IK's do have a distinctively holistic character: ultimately, as Latulippe and Klenk (2020, p. 10) assert, 'Indigenous knowledge is inextricably linked to Indigenous self-determination, rights and responsibilities, which includes respect for the obligations of all beings of creation, not only human'.

Research methodology

Our paper seeks to illuminate the political agency of Indigenous peoples in the context of global climate governance, and how Indigenous observations and responses to climate change are represented in IPCC reports. To do this, we adopt a method of content analysis. All references to Indigenous knowledges and peoples in IPCC reports have been surveyed. Given the volume of the reports, only the two latest assessment reports – i.e. the Fourth Assessment Report (IPCC, 2007a, 2007b, 2007c; hereafter 'AR4, 2007') and the Fifth Assessment Report (IPCC, 2013, 2014a, 2014b; hereafter 'AR5, 2014') – and the latest two Special Reports – i.e. 'Climate Change and Land' (IPCC, 2019a) and 'The Ocean and Cryosphere in a Changing Climate' (IPCC, 2019b) – were selected for analysis. These selected reports contain much larger numbers of references to Indigenous peoples and IKs as compared to the previous IPCC reports.[4]

To conduct the analysis, all references to the terms 'indigenous', 'aboriginal', 'native', 'indigeneity', 'indigenous knowledge', 'traditional knowledge', 'traditional ecological knowledge', and 'local knowledge' were identified. To ensure the extracted texts were representative of their respective sectional context, the paragraph, section, and chapter of those texts were systematically identified and compiled. The extracted text was then reviewed to answer the following questions:

- How are IKs approached or viewed?
- How are IKs evaluated?
- What roles, characteristics, and intellectual capacities are given to Indigenous peoples? And how are they represented and engaged with?

A summary of the analysis is shown in Table 1. The summary is accompanied by quotations from the reports that exemplify the authors' assumptions about the value of IKs for understanding and responding to climate change. Italics are added to call attention to key phrases. The full data comprising all coded and categorized extracted texts from the IPCC reports can be provided upon the request.

How the IPCC constructs 'Indigenous peoples' and 'Indigenous Knowledges'

Overall, despite the increasing recognition of the value of IKs in recent IPCC reports (e.g. IPCC, 2019a, 2019b), the analysis conducted of relevant IPCC documents – a summary of which is reported in Table 1 – demonstrates the IPCC fails to recognize IKs as knowledge systems parallel to, albeit different from, Western science. IKs are treated primarily as *sources* of *data* or *information* that can *supplement* science if they prove *useful*. This representation also prompts the question: How has the IPCC come to construct Indigenous peoples and their knowledges in such ways?

To answer this question, we begin by outlining the historical context from which the IPCC emerged. This helps elucidate the ways the Panel currently operates. We then identify several key institutional and epistemic assumptions that drive the assessment processes, thereby generating certain understandings of Indigenous peoples and IKs. We then show how the IPCC operationalizes its techno-scientific episteme through its determination of who counts as an expert and what counts as expertise.

IPCC: historical background

Discourses concerning climate change have been constructed predominantly in scientific and techno-economic terms. Environmental change has been recognized and recorded for millennia around the world, mainly at the local level. However, climate change as we know it today has exclusively developed within the Western scientific paradigm. It built on the work of the early nineteenth

Table 1. Summary of the reports analysis.

Questions	Summary of analysis	Extracted sample text from the IPCC reports
How are Indigenous Knowledges viewed in the reports?	In IPCC reports IKs are primarily assumed to be no more than *supplementary* to science, i.e. they have no status by themselves as independently authoritative worldviews or systems of knowledge. It is assumed the only way of including IKs in the dominant climate change discourse is to *incorporate* them into science and policy.	• 'The idea of usable knowledge in climate assessments […] requires the inclusion of local knowledge, including indigenous knowledge, to *complement* more formal technical understanding generated through scientific research' (AR4-WGII: 832). • 'Indigenous knowledge can *supplement* scientific knowledge in geographic areas with a paucity of data […]' (AR5-WGIII: 165). • '[…] recognizing and incorporating local knowledge and indigenous knowledge is increasingly emphasized in successful policy implementation' (IPCC, 2019a, p. 638).
How are IKs evaluated?	IKs in IPCC reports are often regarded as merely important *sources* of *information* or *data*, rather than as independent knowledge systems. The reports use 'indigenous knowledge' in the singular form as if all are essentially the same, and the variations are inconsequential, and glossing over the actual diversity of the knowledges of Indigenous peoples.	• 'There is recent recognition of the *untapped resource* of Indigenous knowledge about past climate change which could be used to inform adaptation options' (AR4-WGII: 523). • 'Indigenous knowledge is an important *resource* in climate risk management and is important for food security in many parts of the world' (AR5-WGII: 520). • '[…] actions are most successful when […] using local knowledge and Indigenous knowledge' (IPCC, 2019b, p. 30).
What roles, characteristics, and intellectual capacities are given to Indigenous peoples? And how are these groups represented and engaged with?	In the reports indigenous peoples are generally assumed to be passively *vulnerable* to climate change and incapable by themselves of adapting to it. They are thus assumed to be in need of help from the 'developed world'.	• 'Special attention needs to be given to indigenous peoples with subsistence livelihoods and groups with limited access to information and few means of adaptation' (AR4-WGII: 248). • 'most vulnerable to climate change including indigenous peoples and local communities, women, and the poor and marginalised' (IPCC, 2019a, p. 28) • 'Some valuable experience has been gained recently on […] involvement of *vulnerable* or marginalized groups such as indigenous peoples … ' (AR5-WGII: 1227).

century natural philosophers who pioneered the scientific investigation of the dynamics of the Earth's climate (Hulme, 2009) and later evolved with the help of computer modeling in the second half of the twentieth century. Furthermore, as Cox (1996) argues, from the 1970s the world economy began to transform, shifting the power nexus for environmental politics. Multinational corporations and international financial institutions emerged as the primary agents of economic development, while states took on the role of attracting global investors to advance their development priorities. The rise of non-state actors was largely limited to powerful economic agents (i.e. multinational corporations, international organizations, individual entrepreneurs, etc.) while others, including Indigenous groups, remained on the margins, both domestically and in international forums.

Within that context, global environmental governance was largely shaped by international epistemic communities that promoted global-scale science (Miller, 2004) and transnational economic forces that pursued economic growth to maintain the existing liberal global order (Bernstein & Pauly, 2012). In this highly politicized environment, the IPCC was established as an *inter-governmental* panel by states and tasked to provide a clear scientific view on climate change and its potential environmental and socio-economic impacts. From the outset, the Panel positioned itself as an inter-state scientific body with a rigorous peer-review process that could only be applied to (modern Western) scientific research. Consequently, other forms of knowledge were left in the categories of non-scientific information. The embedded 'scientism' in the IPCC has emerged through historical processes in which Western understandings of climate change and institutions that have defined it are co-produced (Miller, 2004). This history demonstrates a notable lack of discussion of colonialism and its impacts on both Indigenous peoples and anthropocentric climate change discourses (Whyte, 2017).

IKs as supplementary to science and 'useful' sources of information

As shown in the report analysis, the IPCC views IKs as supplementary to science, meaning their inclusion as 'knowledge' is possible only through their integration into scientific literature. Our analysis also demonstrates that the IPCC regards IKs as under-used resources (AR4-WGII: 139) which could be valuable to complement the work of scientists and planners (AR4-WGII: 456), especially to increase the effectiveness of climate change adaptation programmes (AR5-WGII: 26). The utility of IKs is therefore contingent on their suitability for calibration as scientific knowledge, thereby improving the efficacy of policy models (AR5-WGII: 844). The Panel goes as far as viewing the whole bio-cultural heritage of Indigenous peoples as 'an irreplaceable bundle of teaching on the practices of mitigation and sustainability' (AR5-WGIII: 255).

To better understand how the IPCC has come to view Indigenous peoples and their knowledges in such an explicitly utilitarian way, one needs to appreciate the broader historical-scientific context. This valuing of IKs only in relation to scientific knowledge demonstrates legacies of the demarcation project that occurred as part of the early spread of European science (see Harding, 2008).

IKs have long been approached in an instrumental and utilitarian manner and evaluated and defined on the basis of their usefulness for scientific and economic practices. To facilitate their usability, IKs have been conceptualized as unitary knowledge systems that are shared equally across all members of any community. That essentialism has generated a notion of IKs as 'given' and 'pristine' knowledge that is 'simply waiting to be tapped into' (Briggs, 2005, p. 107). Given this understanding, it is not surprising there is an increased appetite on the part of academics, government agencies, international organizations, and corporations for access to 'reservoirs' of IKs that are potentially useful for environmental conservation (cf. Verran, 2002).

The epistemological forces that press towards the integration of IKs into science reveals a tendency to treat IKs as an 'intellectual product' that can be isolated from its social context so as to make it a useful addition to the scientific corpus (Nadasdy, 1999). This process of scientization, which reproduces IKs through the logic of development and the epistemic filter of science, creates fragments of IKs that are able to be used as supplements to science (Agrawal, 2002). Such a utilitarian approach is not only damaging and exploitative, it also reconstructs IKs in objective and abstract ways that break linkages with their place of origin and their populations.

There are at least two consequences of this reductionist view of IKs: First, the utilitarian view denies the status of IKs as independent authoritative knowledge systems and reduces them to data and information to be used by scientists. From this perspective, climate change can only be imagined from the perspective of Western science. Yet that construction ignores the strong historical evidence that many Indigenous peoples have systematically observed, recorded, and responded to such changes from their own perspectives (Berkes, 2017, pp. 171–192; Nunn & Reid, 2016; Nyong et al., 2007).

Second, such a utilitarian approach to IKs has been a major stimulus for bioprospecting and rent-seeking activities aimed at accessing economically valuable ecological knowledge held by Indigenous communities. This has opened up 'new frontiers for commercial exploitation' of both Indigenous peoples and their habitats (Schroeder, 1999, p. 2). The widely used Clean Development Mechanism of the UNFCCC, a project that aims to appropriate the carbon sink capacity of many Indigenous peoples' lands to offset industrial emissions of the global north; and the 'green developmentalism' (McAfee, 1999) of the World Bank in the Mekong Dam project that led to unprecedented socioecological damage (Goldman, 2005), each exemplify global regimes that prepare the way for utilitarian and exploitative moves on Indigenous peoples' resources. The workings of the IPCC can be seen as part of this new eco-economic mode of governance.

Indigenous peoples as vulnerable populations

The construction of IKs in IPCC reporting as databases of potentially useful information defines those knowledges as archives, and as therefore static, and belonging to the past. In so doing, Indigenous peoples are rendered unreservedly vulnerable, and as unable to adapt to a changing climate. This concept of vulnerability to climate change is a key theme in the IPCC assessment reports, where Indigenous peoples are generally assumed to be the most vulnerable amongst all populations to experience the worst climate change. They are thus deemed as requiring special attention from developed countries. Entangled with that is the Panel's focus on how Indigenous communities are isolated by their low rates of literacy (AR5-WGII: 630). Sometimes they are even put in the same category as the poor, children or disabled persons (AR5-WGII: 1227; IPCC, 2019a, p. 28).

It is undeniable that climate change is posing an unprecedented challenge to Indigenous peoples across the world; however, presuming them to be simply vulnerable not only contradicts historical facts but devalues their collective knowledge. Indigenous peoples survived many cycles of natural environmental upheaval and climate change for millennia before European colonialism began (see discussions on Pacific Islands in Campbell, 2009, and on African Sahel in Nyong et al., 2007). The presumption of vulnerability also reinforces a false association of oral cultures with illiteracy, ignoring the ways many oral Indigenous traditions carry centuries, if not millennia, of knowledges and experiences (see for example, Nunn & Reid, 2016).

Vulnerability is thus exposed as a social construct that, in the IPCC reports, is implicitly defined according to measures of development. The extent to which Indigenous peoples are assumed to be vulnerable is as much subjective as factual. Thus, anticipated sea level rise in the current century is deemed threatening for the Maldives, Tuvalu, and Kiribati. Yet, how well those vulnerable nations may be able to respond to climate change impacts is highly contested (see Sulamin et al., 2019). Ross Garnaut, a prominent economist who led the Australian government's review on climate change in 2008, proposed a solution for inundated island countries in the form of mass migration.[5] But for many affected populations, leaving their ancestral lands is not an option. They believe they will survive this crisis as they have overcome past naturally caused climatic changes (Mortreux &

Barnett, 2009). For example, Petheram et al. (2010) found that for the Yolngu people of North East Arnhem Land in Australia, climate adaptation practices were not limited to mass migration and proposed mechanical solutions. To them, staying strong; maintaining cultural, physical, and emotional health; passing down knowledge and tradition as a means for survival; close observation of the environment; and kinship support and practices of sharing are as important.

It is evident that framing climate adaptation as 'vulnerability-reduction' affects how climate change is known and addressed by and for Indigenous peoples. What seems to dominate scientifically based socioeconomic responses to climate change is a linear model of impacts and adaptation. Climate is treated as an external system that generates threats; societies are social structures that are unevenly vulnerable to climatic impacts. Possibilities for adaptation around the world thus can be captured in a universal schematic of degrees of climatic threat and units of vulnerability. This linear cause–effect-response model, from one perspective, serves the technocratic elites who seek to contain climatic threats within existing institutional frameworks (Taylor, 2015, xii, 32). From another perspective, it is able to depict many parts of the world as dangerous (disaster-prone and poverty-stricken), with inhabitants who are culturally inferior, incapable, and mere victims (Bankoff, 2001).

The symptoms of climate vulnerability might be predominantly physical (e.g. the physical effects of sea level rise). However, the underlying causes of vulnerability are economic, social, and political, and many of these causes are embedded in adaptation and development programmes (Cardona, 2004). In the case of the Canadian Arctic, Haalboom and Natcher (2012) report that the Inuit's displacement by the government was rationalized by their inability to rely any longer on wildlife resources. They were thus urged to resettle and adopt an industrial wage-earning lifestyle. When they did, the Inuit not only lost control over their land and resources but were represented as vulnerable to social and ecological change and became dependent on government support. In a similar way, the IPCC's construction of Indigenous peoples as vulnerable may create a justification for further development interventions.

Underlying assumptions in the institutional design and practices of the IPCC

Since its establishment, the IPCC's commitment to scientific practice on the one hand, and increasing attention to IKs on the other, has driven it toward further recognition of IKs. However, as our content analysis illustrated, such recognition has occurred from a particular standpoint, wherein IKs were approached in a utilitarian way and Indigenous peoples were represented in ways that lack agency – (thereby resonating with familiar colonial narratives that portray them as passive, vulnerable, victim, etc.). In this section, we now examine key underlying elements the Panel draws upon as it operationalizes its approach to Indigenous peoples and IKs. Drawing from prior research and our analysis, we demonstrate key ideologically-loaded institutional assumptions and practices that ground its assessments: consensus-building, policy relevance, and the construction of climate experts and expertise.

Consensus-building

The universal rationality of science requires that the same rules and standards apply to all scientific practices; this, in turn, facilitates epistemic consensus (Kuhn, 1962, p. 11). This looks attractive from a policy perspective, as broader consensus, supposedly, promises greater public trust (Beck et al., 2014) and political legitimacy (Dryzek & Niemeyer, 2006). The IPCC has been open and explicit about its commitment to scientific practice and its aim to generate a scientific consensus around climate change (Hulme & Mahony, 2010).[6],[7] In fact, from the beginning, one goal for establishing such an institution was to build consensus for political action within the international community (Bodansky, 1992, p. 63).

The logic of consensus-building utilized in the IPCC assessments ignores the fact that reaching epistemic consensus between knowledge claims from science and IKs – without 'translating' one to the other – seems extremely difficult, if not impossible. This difficulty lies in the fundamental differences between most Indigenous knowledge systems and Western modern science: one is oral, the other is written; one is place-based, the other is universal; one is monist, the other is dualist, and so on (see Aikenhead & Ogawa, 2007). The history of colonialism presents how the West has consistently, from a positional superiority, translated others' cultures and knowledges (including those of Indigenous peoples) through the filter of science (Chakrabarty, 2000, pp. 3–23; Said, 2003, p. 7). This has resulted in a process whereby one side (the West), appropriates and exploits the other side's (Indigenous peoples') cultures and resources.

In response to such compulsion for consensus-building, many have argued in favour of dissent as part of a more pluralistic and deliberative epistemic practice (Longino, 2002). Solomon (2006) suggests that a situation of dissent can offer more informative outcomes and produce better decisions than narrowly consensually-based ones, provided that all competing knowledge claims have shown empirical success. She notes that dissenting positions can often produce insights that could be lost via consensus building. For example, the Kogies of Colombia have a system of allocating permits for planting specific crops according to lineage affiliation and the revelations of divination (*sewa*) (Reichel-Dolmatoff, 1982). This cannot be rendered into knowledge recognizable by modern agricultural science and any attempt to construe it as knowledge supplementary to science would strip the Kogies' agricultural practice of any insight it might have for other Indigenous groups living in similar ecologies and cultures.

Similarly, scholars who have studied the IPCC have pointed to the consensus approach in the Panel as a weakness, rather than strength (Hulme, 2010; Jasanoff, 2010; Van der Sluijs et al., 2010). They argue that the IPCC has not only excluded a diversity of perspectives, differences, and ambiguities on climate change; it has also, unwittingly, concealed both scientific and political dissent, further politicizing climate science (Hulme, 2010; Jasanoff, 2010; Van der Sluijs et al., 2010). Furthermore, given the existing global power structure, a consensus-based approach in practice leads to imposing worldviews, ideologies, and epistemologies drawn from the global North onto the South (Turnhout et al., 2016). In this context, Ford et al. (2016a) referred to the emphasis on consensus in the IPCC as a homogenizing force that is insensitive to diverse cultures and ways of knowing, including those of Indigenous peoples. Making a sort of consensual science that aspires to perfect universality weakens understanding of many aspects of climate change impact and response potential that are place- and culture-specific.

Policy-relevance

To assert their political neutrality and thereby gain legitimacy, knowledge institutions such as the IPCC claim their work is 'policy-relevant' and never 'policy-prescriptive'. Contemporary scholars of science studies have challenged this claim by arguing that science and policy are co-produced, and thus, such a separation is artificial (Jasanoff, 2004; Miller, 2004). A further and more pressing issue here is whose policies the work of the IPCC is intended to be relevant for. This needs to be understood in view of the overall directives of the IPCC.

From a scientific perspective, the IPCC is tasked with assisting global climate governance by researching and recommending the best ways to manage global mean temperature. From the perspective of the dominant policy-making paradigm, which is set to employ rational and techno-economic means of analysis (Miller & Robbins, 2007, pp. 465–479), the IPCC's climate policy recommendations must be techno-economic. The link between the two perspectives is well established and appears as the backbone of global climate governance: To curb temperature rises, global GHG emissions must be contained below a certain limit. To operationalize that, GHG emissions targets must be incorporated in an economic system, so the self-regulation and efficiency inherent in the market, as well as technological innovation, contain emissions under the specified safe maximum level. The Kyoto Protocol's flexibility mechanisms, including international offsetting and the CDM, are essentially built on this premise. In establishing such a techno-economic system of governance, the areas of expertise deemed relevant have proliferated to include, for example, all subfields of environmental economics and finance. Knowledge institutions such as the IPCC have therefore turned to experts in those disciplines to produce their assessment reports.

Policy relevance is necessarily selective. Turnhout et al. (2016, p. 67) note that 'the construction of policy relevant knowledge is a political act that involves choices about the preferred audiences of knowledge and the types of policy actions that may follow from this knowledge'. Thus, the IPCC's commitment to policy-relevance has the effect of reasserting the existing epistemic supremacy of techno-science, rendering Indigenous voices and concerns unheard. This arises out of a configuration of structural problems that have their roots in the inability of technocratic institutions to accommodate diverse perspectives and worldviews. The policy relevance imperative for international institutions such as the IPCC facilitates such exclusion.

Researchers engaged directly with Indigenous communities provide numerous examples of mismatches between their understandings and the knowledge frameworks employed by the IPCC. Boillat and Berkes (2013), for example, report that Indigenous Quechua farmers in Bolivia think the underlying causes of climate change are the bad things people do and their lack of respect for Quechua customs. Similarly, according to Tschakert (2007), villagers of the Old Peanut Basin in Senegal see the loss of tradition, the lack of respect for nature, and deforestation as the key causes of climate change. Villagers of Eastern Tibet, who traditionally understood weather entirely as a local phenomenon governed by local deities, attribute recent severe weather conditions and environmental changes to the deities' anger at their 'neglect of religious duties or breach of taboos' (Byg & Salick, 2009, p. 165).

Central to these claims is the contention that it is change in human values and behaviour toward nature that requires attention. Temperature rise is only a symptom of this greater problem for many of those communities. Yet, current policy paradigms are structurally dismissive of such Indigenous perspectives unless they are translatable to scientific facts and proved to be useful supplements that support associated policies. The institutions that attempt to make knowledge about climate change relevant to existing policies only reinforce the systemic exclusion.

Expert and expertise

The composition of IPCC authors also reflects the Panel's techno-scientific epistemic premises. In selecting authors, the IPCC determines who counts as an expert and what counts as expertise. Corbera et al. (2016) demonstrated the dominance of scientific and economic disciplines in IPCC Working Group III (AR5), with authors predominantly from the Global North. Similarly, the analysis of Ford et al. (2012) showed that only nine out of 309 authors of IPCC Working Group

II (AR5) had publishing records in climate change and Indigenous studies. However, such scientization of expertise obscures the strongly political nature of the IPCC and its selection processes. As Wynne and Lynch (2015) argue, the credibility of scientists as experts goes beyond the boundaries of science, as they are treated also as authorities on questions that have cultural, ethical, political, and legal implications.

Miller (2004, p. 47) contends that the Panel has constructed a discourse that frames climate change as a global risk, and, to manage this risk, 'offered a model of global politics in which experts and expert knowledge, as politically neutral agents, were accorded significant power to define problems of global policy'. The result is a circular dynamic in which the IPCC exerts power through its assessment reports by legitimizing certain global policy institutions. In return, 'the articulation of what counts as good science will depend heavily on political institutions for support and legitimacy' (Miller, 2004, p.65).

The definition of expertise used by the IPCC, then, cannot be seen merely as a technical task. It is also a political practice that excludes those holding different worldviews. Filer (2009) describes this political practice of exclusion in the production of the Millennium Ecosystem Assessment (MA). He notes that the MA conceptual framework may at first appear to be open to diverse ways of knowing insofar as it includes cultural and religious advocacy that could affect the consumption of ecosystem services. However, the institutional necessity for establishing 'a global form of expert consensus within a specific set of environmental policy regimes' leaves no space for the inclusion of others who are not considered as experts (Filer, 2009, pp.87–88). An exclusive epistemic community in the MA comprised scientists, environmental economists and utilitarian ecologists, similar to that found in the IPCC (Carey et al., 2014; Corbera et al., 2016), has led to the oversimplification of social and cultural complexities (Filer, 2009). Within the epistemic settings of international institutions such as the UNEP, the International Council for Science, and the IPCC, neither can Indigenous knowledge holders be regarded as experts, nor can IKs meet the criteria for bona fide sources of expert knowledge.

Conclusions

This paper has demonstrated that the IPCC is structurally resistant to drawing upon non-Western and non-science-based knowledge systems, more specifically, those of Indigenous peoples. Reporting on a qualitative content analysis of selected Panel's reports, we have demonstrated that IKs are treated by the Panel as supplementary to science-based knowledge, and are addressed only insofar as they may be seen as sources of additional data. The IPCC's commitments to consensus-based policy-relevant, and expert-led knowledge production render IKs without status as independently authoritative knowledges. IKs are only deemed relevant in relation to their capacity to bolster Western scientific knowledge. This whole process, therefore, appears to implicitly disempower Indigenous peoples. The chapter outlines of the Sixth Assessment Report that is due to be released in 2021–2022, do not indicate a major shift in this regard.

The instrumental engagement with IKs is a symptom of a deeper structural problem that extends beyond the work of the IPCC. Scholars who have studied other international environmental organizations and regimes demonstrate similar patterns in the exclusion of Indigenous voices. These include, for example the UNFCCC (Ford et al., 2016b; Shawoo & Thornton, 2019); the Kyoto Protocol (Smith, 2007); the Millennium Ecosystem Assessment (Filer, 2009); and the Intergovernmental Science-Policy Platform on Biodiversity and Ecosystem Services (IPBES) (Turnhout et al., 2014) Similarly, these organizations have evidenced considerable inertia in creating mechanisms to alter their assessment processes in ways that might facilitate genuine engagement with Indigenous peoples. This resistance occurs against a backdrop of wider progress in international engagement with Indigenous peoples, as seen within the United Nations Permanent Forum on Indigenous Issues (UNPFII) and recognition of Indigenous struggles, such as through the adoption of the 2007 United Nations Declaration on the Rights of Indigenous Peoples (UNDRIP). Despite these – and other – international advancements in the legal recognition of Indigenous peoples' rights, the entanglement of agendas for economic development across global climate governance with colonial legacies sets the scene for an extractivist relationship between the IPCC and Indigenous peoples.

The IPCC has come a long way from its first publication in 1990 with only a handful of general references to Indigenous peoples, to its recent publications (IPCC, 2019a, 2019b), wherein the Panel acknowledged the limitations of Indigenous involvement in IPCC assessments (IPCC, 2019b, p. 263) and suggested knowledge co-production for including IKs (IPCC, 2019b, pp. 103–105). However, the structural barriers that are, for instance, driven by the IPCC's strict scientific standards – a source of credibility for the Panel – treats IKs as bundles of information and depoliticizes Indigenous engagement with science. For example, in many instances, the Panel positioned Indigenous peoples as one group of 'stakeholders' next to private sector actors (IPCC, 2019a, p. 62). This ignores centuries of (neo) colonialism that entailed all sorts of deliberate attempts to assure Indigenous peoples not hold any agency and never gain self-determination. Within such a historical context, there is a legitimate concern about the contemporary 'Indigenous turn' to be another form of exploitation to unfairly share the burden of responsibility for ecological disaster with Indigenous peoples. Such attempts are not only problematic on ethical grounds, but also question the feasibility of dominant policies for a democratic transition to a low carbon society that requires fundamental shifts from existing economic and development activities.

Meaningful institutional modifications to the IPCC that facilitate equal exchanges and build trust between Indigenous knowledge holders and non-Indigenous experts may be more effective. More research will be required to understand the dynamics and effectiveness of such reforms. It is also clear from our analysis that more foundational work is required to enrich existing environmental research. International organizations, such as the IPCC, must find ways to deploy more innovative knowledge paradigms and research methods as part of their work. While this paper has focused on diagnosing the structural barriers to Indigenous engagement in the IPCC, it also urges debate about the pathways to reform.

Meantime, we should not lose sights of the many ways in which Indigenous peoples worldwide are engaging in action for climate justice. Their activities sit at, and go beyond, the limits of formal climate governance mechanisms. Working in this way, Indigenous peoples are not just pointing to the alternatives to reform within international organizations. More fundamentally, they are asserting their inalienable rights to respond to colonially-induced environmental change, and their agency in driving self-determined responses.

Notes

1. The threat of the REDD+ scheme unified and mobilized Indigenous peoples' on climate policy like never before – providing a powerful example of the Indigenous climate justice movement – with outcomes that effectively prevented its full inclusion as a UN recognized offset (Long et al., 2010). More broadly, REDD+ provided a unified platform for a wide range of justice-based resistance movements, and ground in Indigenous rights and self-determination (Suiseeya, 2017).

2. The IPCC was established in 1988 to provide assessments that influence both the UNFCCC and Kyoto Protocol, neither of which mention Indigenous peoples (see Suliman et al., 2019).
3. We note here the affect of this 'global' discourse in silencing and/or obfuscating power relations, as well as privileging state interests. As an organizing principle for international negotiations, the 'global' narrative also has a significant impact in rendering invisible the local and Indigenous peoples, a theme we return to in our analysis below.
4. For example, a simple word search in the IPCC's First and Second Assessment Reports shows only a handful of references to Indigenous-related issues, in comparison to hundreds of references to the same issues in AR4, AR5, and IPCC (2019a, 2019b).
5. http://www.radioaustralia.net.au/international/radio/onairhighlights/ross-garnaut-writes-off-pacific-states-on-climate-change.
6. http://www.ipcc.ch/organization/organization.shtml.
7. https://www.ipcc.ch/pdf/supporting-material/EM_Potential_Studies_web.pdf.

Disclosure statement

No potential conflict of interest was reported by the author(s).

Funding

The author(s) reported there is no funding associated with the work featured in this article.

References

Agrawal, A. (2002). Indigenous knowledge and the politics of classification. *International Social Science Journal*, *54*(3), 287–297. https://doi.org/10.1111/1468-2451.00382
Aikenhead, G., & Ogawa, M. (2007). Indigenous knowledge and science revisited. *Cultural Studies of Science Education*, *2*(3), 539–620. https://doi.org/10.1007/s11422-007-9067-8
Bäckstrand, K. (2004). Scientisation vs. civic expertise in environmental governance: Eco-feminist, eco-modern and post-modern responses. *Environmental Politics*, *13*(4), 695–714. https://doi.org/10.1080/0964401042000274322
Bankoff, G. (2001). Rendering the world unsafe: 'vulnerability' as western discourse. *Disasters*, *25*(1), 19–35. https://doi.org/10.1111/1467-7717.00159

Beck, S., Borie, M., Chilvers, J., Esguerra, A., Heubach, K., Hulme, M., Lidskog, R., Lövbrand, E., Marquard, E., Miller, C., Nadim, T., Neßhöver, C., Settele, J., Turnhout, E., Vasileiadou, E., & Görg, C. (2014). Towards a reflexive turn in the governance of global environmental expertise. The cases of the IPCC and the IPBES. *GAIA - Ecological Perspectives for Science and Society*, *23*(2), 80–87. https://doi.org/10.14512/gaia.23.2.4

Berkes, F. (2017). *Sacred ecology* (4th ed.). Routledge.

Bernstein, S., & Pauly, L. (2012). *Global liberalism and political order: Toward a new grand compromise?* State University of New York Press.

Bjurstrom, A., & Polk, M. (2011). Physical and economic bias in climate change research: A scientometric study of IPCC third assessment report. *Climatic Change*, *108*(1-2), 1–22. https://doi.org/10.1007/s10584-011-0018-8

Bodansky, D. (1992). Managing climate change. *Yearbook of International Environmental Law*, *3*(1), 60–74. https://doi.org/10.1093/yiel/3.1.60

Boillat, S., & Berkes, F. (2013). Perception and interpretation of climate change among Quechua farmers of Bolivia: Indigenous knowledge as a resource for adaptive capacity. *Ecology and Society*, *18*(4). https://doi.org/10.5751/ES-05894-180421

Briggs, J. (2005). The use of indigenous knowledge in development: Problems and challenges. *Progress in Development Studies*, *5*(2), 99–114. https://doi.org/10.1191/1464993405ps105oa

Byg, A., & Salick, J. (2009). Local perspectives on a global phenomenon—climate change in Eastern Tibetan villages. *Global Environmental Change*, *19*(2), 156–166. https://doi.org/10.1016/j.gloenvcha.2009.01.010

Campbell, J. (2009). Islandness: Vulnerability and resilience in Oceania. *Shima: The International Journal of Research Into Island Cultures*, *3*(1), 85–97.

Cardona, O. D. (2004). The need for rethinking the concepts of vulnerability and risk from a holistic perspective: A necessary review and criticism for effective risk management. In G. Bankoff, G. Frerks, & D. Hilhorst (Eds.), *Mapping vulnerability: Disasters, development and people* (pp. 56–70). Routledge.

Carey, M., James, L., & Fuller, H. (2014). A new social contract for the IPCC. *Nature Climate Change*, *4*(12), 1038–1039. https://doi.org/10.1038/nclimate2442

Chakrabarty, D. (2000). *Provincializing Europe: Postcolonial thought and historical difference*. Princeton University Press.

Corbera, E., Calvet-Mir, L., Hughes, H., & Paterson, M. (2016). Patterns of authorship in the IPCC Working Group III report. *Nature Climate Change*, *6*(1), 94–99. https://doi.org/10.1038/nclimate2782

Cox, R. (1996). A perspective on globalization. In J. Mittelman (Ed.), *Globalization: Critical reflections* (pp. 21–30). Lynne Rienner Publishers.

Dryzek, J. (2002). *Deliberative democracy and beyond: Liberals, critics, contestations*. Oxford University Press.

Dryzek, J., & Niemeyer, S. (2006). Reconciling pluralism and consensus as political ideals. *American Journal of Political Science*, *50*(3), 634–649. https://doi.org/10.1111/j.1540-5907.2006.00206.x

Filer, C. (2009). A bridge too far: The knowledge problem in the millennium assessment. In J. Carrier & P. West (Eds.), *Virtualism, governance and practice: Vision and execution in environmental conservation* (pp. 84–111). Berghahn Books.

Ford, J., Maillet, M., Pouliot, V., Meredith, T., Cavanaugh, A., and IHACC Research Team. (2016b). Adaptation and indigenous peoples in the United Nations framework convention on climate change. *Climatic Change*, *139*(3-4), 429–443. https://doi.org/10.1007/s10584-016-1820-0

Ford, J., Vanderbilt, W., & Berrang-Ford, L. (2012). Authorship in IPCC AR5 and its implications for content: Climate change and Indigenous populations in WGII. *Climatic Change*, *113*(2), 201–213. https://doi.org/10.1007/s10584-011-0350-z

Ford, J. D., Cameron, L., Rubis, J., Maillet, M., Nakashima, D., Willox, A. C., & Pearce, T. (2016a). Including indigenous knowledge and experience in IPCC assessment reports. *Nature Climate Change*, *6*(4), 349–353. https://doi.org/10.1038/nclimate2954

Goldman, M. (2005). *Imperial nature: The World Bank and struggles for justice in the age of globalization*. Yale University Press.

Haalboom, B., & Natcher, D. (2012). The power and peril of "vulnerability": approaching community labels with caution in climate change research. *Arctic*, *2012*, 319–327. http://doi.org/10.14430/arctic4219

Hannigan, J. (1995). The postmodern city: A new urbanization? *Current Sociology*, *43*(1), 151–217. https://doi.org/10.1177/001139295043001011

Harding, S. (2008). *Sciences from below: Feminisms, postcolonialities, and modernities.* Duke University Press.

Hiramatsu, A., Mimura, N., & Sumi, A. (2008). A mapping of global warming research based on IPCC AR4. *Sustainability Science, 3*(2), 201–213. https://doi.org/10.1007/s11625-008-0058-9

Hughes, H. (2015). Bourdieu and the IPCC's symbolic power. *Global Environmental Politics, 15*(4), 85–104. https://doi.org/10.1162/GLEP_a_00323

Hughes, H., & Paterson, M. (2017). Narrowing the climate field: The symbolic power of authors in the IPCC's assessment of mitigation. *Review of Policy Research, 34*(6), 744–766. https://doi.org/10.1111/ropr.12255

Hulme, M. (2009). *Why we disagree about climate change? Understanding controversy, inaction and opportunity.* Cambridge University Press.

Hulme, M. (2010). Problems with making and governing global kinds of knowledge. *Global Environmental Change, 20*(4), 558–564. https://doi.org/10.1016/j.gloenvcha.2010.07.005

Hulme, M., & Mahony, M. (2010). Climate change: What do we know about the IPCC? *Progress in Physical Geography: Earth and Environment, 34*(5), 705–718. https://doi.org/10.1177/0309133310373719

IPCC. (2007a). *Climate change 2007: The physical science basis.* CUP.

IPCC. (2007b). *Climate change 2014: Impacts, adaptation, and vulnerability.* CUP.

IPCC. (2007c). *Climate change 2007: Mitigation of climate change.* CUP.

IPCC. (2013). *Climate change 2013: The physical science basis.* CUP.

IPCC. (2014a). *Climate change 2014: Impacts, adaptation, and vulnerability.* CUP.

IPCC. (2014b). *Climate change 2014: Mitigation of climate change.* CUP.

IPCC. (2019a). *Climate change and land.* In Press. www.ipcc.ch

IPCC. (2019b). *The Ocean and Cryosphere in a changing climate.* In Press. www.ipcc.ch

Jasanoff, S. (2004). *States of knowledge: The co-production of science and social order.* Routledge.

Jasanoff, S. (2010). Testing time for climate science. *Science, 328*(5979), 695–696. https://doi.org/10.1126/science.1189420

Kuhn, T. (1962). *The structure of scientific revolutions* (3rd ed.). The University of Chicago Press.

Latulippe, N., & Klenk, N. (2020). Making room and moving over: Knowledge co-production, Indigenous knowledge sovereignty and the politics of global environmental change decision-making. *Current Opinion in Environmental Sustainability, 42*, 7–14. https://doi.org/10.1016/j.cosust.2019.10.010

Lindroth, M., & Sinevaara-Niskanen, H. (2013). At the crossroads of autonomy and essentialism: Indigenous peoples in international environmental politics. *International Political Sociology, 7*(3), 275–293. https://doi.org/10.1111/ips.12023

Long, S., Roberts, E., & Dehm, J. (2010). Climate justice inside and outside the UNFCCC: The example of REDD. *The Journal of Australian Political Economy, 66*, 222–246. https://search.informit.org/doi/10.3316/ielapa.833621482268969

Longino, H. (2002). *The fate of knowledge.* Princeton University Press.

McAfee, K. (1999). Selling nature to save it? *Biodiversity and Green Developmentalism. Environment and Planning D: Society and Space, 17*, 133–154. https://doi.org/10.1068/d170133

Miller, C. (2004). Climate science and the making of a global political order. In S. Jasanoff (Ed.), *States of knowledge: The coproduction of science and social order* (pp. 46–66). Routledge.

Miller, C., & Robbins, D. (2007). Cost-benefit analysis. In F. Fischer, G. Miller & M. Sidney (Eds.), *Handbook of public policy analysis: Theory, methods, and politics* (pp. 465–480). CRC Press.

Mortreux, C., & Barnett, J. (2009). Climate change, migration and adaptation in Funafuti, Tuvalu. *Global Environmental Change, 19*(1), 105–112. https://doi.org/10.1016/j.gloenvcha.2008.09.006

Nadasdy, P. (1999). The politics of TEK: Power and the "integration" of knowledge. *Arctic Anthropology, 36*(1/2), 1–18.

Nunn, P., & Reid, N. (2016). Aboriginal memories of inundation of the Australian coast dating from more than 7000 years ago. *Australian Geographer, 47*(1), 11–47. https://doi.org/10.1080/00049182.2015.1077539

Nyong, A., Adesina, F., & Elasha, B. (2007). The value of indigenous knowledge in climate change mitigation and adaptation strategies in the African Sahel. *Mitigation and Adaptation Strategies for Global Change, 12*(5), 787–797. https://doi.org/10.1007/s11027-007-9099-0

Petheram, L., Zander, K., Campbell, B., High, C., & Stacey, N. (2010). 'Strange changes': Indigenous perspectives of climate change and adaptation in NE Arnhem Land (Australia). *Global Environmental Change, 20*(4), 681–692. https://doi.org/10.1016/j.gloenvcha.2010.05.002

Reichel-Dolmatoff, G. (1982). Cultural change and environmental awareness: A case study of the Sierra Nevada de Santa Marta, Colombia. *Mountain Research and Development*, 2(3), 289–298. https://doi.org/10.2307/3673093

Said, E. (2003). *Orientalism*. Penguin.

Schroeder, R. (1999). Community, forestry and conditionality in the Gambia. *Africa*, 69(1), 1–22. https://doi.org/10.2307/1161075

Semali, L., & Kincheloe, J. (1999). Introduction. In L. Semali & J. Kincheloe (Eds.), *What is Indigenous knowledge? Voices from the academy* (pp. 3–58). Falmer Press.

Shawoo, Z., & Thornton, T. F. (2019). The UN local communities and Indigenous peoples' platform: A traditional ecological knowledge-based evaluation. *Wiley Interdisciplinary Reviews: Climate Change*, 10(3), 575. https://doi.org/10.1002/wcc.575

Smith, H. (2007). Disrupting the global discourse of climate change: The case of indigenous voices. In M. Pettenger (Ed.), *The social construction of climate change: Power, knowledge, norms, discourses* (pp. 197–216). Ashgate.

Solomon, M. (2006). Groupthink versus the wisdom of crowds: The social epistemology of deliberation and dissent. *The Southern Journal of Philosophy*, 44(S1), 28–42. https://doi.org/10.1111/j.2041-6962.2006.tb00028.x

Suiseeya, K. (2017). Contesting justice in global forest governance: The promises and pitfalls of REDD+. *Conservation and Society*, 15(2), 189–200. https://doi.org/10.4103/cs.cs_15_104

Suliman, S., Farbotko, C., Ransan-Cooper, H., Elizabeth McNamara, K., Thornton, F., McMichael, C., & Kitara, T. (2019). Indigenous (im)mobilities in the anthropocene. *Mobilities*, 14(3), 298–318. https://doi.org/10.1080/17450101.2019.1601828

Taylor, M. (2015). *The political ecology of climate change adaptation*. Routledge.

Tschakert, P. (2007). Views from the vulnerable: Understanding climatic and other stressors in the Sahel. *Global Environmental Change*, 17(3-4), 381–396. https://doi.org/10.1016/j.gloenvcha.2006.11.008

Turnhout, E., Dewulf, A., & Hulme, M. (2016). What does policy-relevant global environmental knowledge do? The cases of climate and biodiversity. *Current Opinion in Environmental Sustainability*, 18, 65–72. https://doi.org/10.1016/j.cosust.2015.09.004

Turnhout, E., Neves, K., & de Lijster, E. (2014). 'Measurementality' in biodiversity governance: Knowledge, transparency, and the intergovernmental science-policy platform on biodiversity and ecosystem services (ipbes). *Environment and Planning A: Economy and Space*, 46(3), 581–597. https://doi.org/10.1068/a4629

Van der Sluijs, J., Van Est, R., & Riphagen, M. (2010). Beyond consensus: Reflections from a democratic perspective on the interaction between climate politics and science. *Current Opinion in Environmental Sustainability*, 2(5-6), 409–415. https://doi.org/10.1016/j.cosust.2010.10.003

Vasileiadou, E., Heimeriks, G., & Petersen, A. (2011). Exploring the impact of the IPCC assessment reports on science. *Environmental Science & Policy*, 14(8), 1052–1061. https://doi.org/10.1016/j.envsci.2011.07.002

Verran, H. (2002). A postcolonial moment in science studies: Alternative firing regimes of environmental scientists and aboriginal landowners. *Social Studies of Science*, 32(5-6), 729–762. https://doi.org/10.1177/030631270203200506

Watson, I. (2014). Re-centring first Nations knowledge and places in a terra nullius space. *AlterNative: An International Journal of Indigenous Peoples*, 10(5), 508–520. https://doi.org/10.1177/117718011401000506

Weingart, P. (1999). Scientific expertise and political accountability: Paradoxes of science in politics. *Science and Public Policy*, 26(3), 151–161. https://doi.org/10.3152/147154399781782437

Whyte, J. (2017). *Girls into science and technology: The story of a project* (Vol. 16). Taylor & Francis.

Wynne, B., & Lynch, M. (2015). Science and technology studies: Experts and expertise. In J. Wright (Ed.), *International encyclopedia of the social & behavioral sciences* (pp. 206–211). Elsevier Ltd.

Climate and food inequality: the South African Food Sovereignty Campaign response

Vishwas Satgar 🄭 and Jane Cherry

ABSTRACT
This article focuses on climate and food inequalities while highlighting food sovereignty responses. It provides an analysis of climate inequalities ramifying through the world today. At the same time, food inequality is conceptually clarified as a counter approach to food security. It is argued that food inequality is consistent with the case for food sovereignty. Moreover, the combination of climate and food inequalities also highlight the complexity of climate crises and the challenges they pose for food regimes. The article further highlights the emergence of the food sovereignty response and systemic alternative. Taking this further is a case study of the transformative politics of the South African Food Sovereignty Campaign and its constitutive approach to various forms of power from below.

Introduction

Climate change is increasingly being recognized as one of the major issues facing humanity in the twenty-first century. As greenhouse gas emissions cause planetary changes and rising global temperatures, extreme weather events, and climate shocks are increasing, including heat waves, droughts, and flooding. During 2015 the World Meteorological Organization confirmed that the planetary temperature has increased by 1°C since the industrial revolution. This climate change fact has also been confirmed by the 2018 special report of the UN-IPCC, *Global Warming of 1.5°C* (IPCC, 2018). In addition, each of the last three decades has been successively warmer at the Earth's surface than any previous decade since 1850, while in the northern hemisphere, the period from 1983 to 2012 was likely the warmest 30-year period in the last 14,000 years (Intergovernmental Panel on Climate Change [IPCC], 2014a, p. 2). Global anthropogenic CO_2 emissions have risen too, increasing since the pre-industrial era, driven largely by economic growth, and are now higher than ever. This has brought to the fore climate inequalities which cannot be grasped with narrow economic approaches to inequality, including generic human causality associated with Anthropocene analytical frameworks. This article argues for recognizing particular forms of climate inequality while affirming a much more multi-dimensional approach to studying inequality.

Alongside but linked to the climate crisis is a growing global food crisis. This is a systemic crisis which undermines the food needs of a billion hungry people, has contributed to widespread food insecurity and has caught at least two billion people in the web of a dietary transition based on cheap and fast food, resulting in obesity and a host of attendant diseases such as sugar diabetes and heart failure. The food crisis is also a water crisis in many parts of the world. According to the International Water Association, almost four billion people lack proper access to water and at least 5.5 billion drink untreated water (Cosgrove, 2013). The scale of the food and water crisis cannot be comprehended by epistemic approaches that merely reproduce these crises. Food insecurity is a striking example in this regard. It is a conceptual and analytical framework taken up by development studies, food studies, and policy makers but it is a framework that is embedded in a narrow problem-solving approach within the parameters of a carbon-centred, globalized, and corporate-controlled food system. This article challenges this framework by making the case for understanding the food crisis as reflective of food inequality.

This article describes notable impacts of climate change on vulnerable countries and populations globally, and then turns to focus on South Africa. The recent El Niño-induced drought in South Africa, from 2014 till the present, has been exacerbated by climate change and has affected the national economy, but also local communities and the country's agro-economic system, as it has led to increased unemployment, negative impacts on upstream economic activities, and increased hunger. Despite forewarning that the El Niño would exacerbate low rainfall in an already arid country, the South African national, provincial, and local governments have failed to mitigate the impacts. Cape Town's drought, in particular, made international news headlines as a major city approaching 'Day Zero' as it experienced the worst drought in 30 years. If the recent droughts are a window into South Africa's future, government's failure to respond timeously indicates a lack of political will, coordination, and planning. This demonstrates that we cannot depend on international or national processes to mitigate forthcoming climate shocks. If these avenues will continue to fail us, what are the alternatives?

We argue that key pathways to confront the climate crisis involve building viable, just and ecocentric societies, alternatives and practices as part of the deep, just transition. The emergence of food sovereignty discourses and movements are a crucial source of inspiration in this regard. A florescence of international practices, initiatives and alliances are foregrounded in this article. However, the article focusses on the South African Food Sovereignty Campaign (SAFSC) as a case study that seeks to unify grassroots struggles for food sovereignty. An important element of its struggle is also climate justice. As the SAFSC undertakes its campaigning, we argue that it is building alternative avenues of people's power by showing that another democratic, solidaristic, climate justice food system is possible. It does this by advancing transformative practices from below which are constitutive of new forms of power while building concrete and embedded pathways for food systems in communities, villages, towns, and cities. These pathways are about laying the basis for a food sovereignty system that deepens the just transition to sustain life in a climate-driven world.

Carbon capitalism and climate inequality in the world

Today the global scientific consensus on climate change affirms three important facts. First, human-induced climate change is contributing to a heating planet through greenhouse gas emissions. Carbon emissions commenced about 150 years ago with the industrial revolution and the use of coal then later oil and gas. For the past fifty years, scientists have observed the hockey-stick curve in carbon emissions, sometimes referred to as the golden spike. Today carbon emissions are accelerating despite the science on climate change. Second, we are at a planetary increase of 1°C since the industrial revolution, at a global scale. With increasing carbon emissions, we are fast heading to a 1.5°C overshoot in the next few decades, which is dangerous for feedback loops and runaway global warming. This means systems collapses are very likely for water and food. Moreover, the global average of

1°C is already being surpassed in some localities. For instance, Johannesburg is 0.2°C hotter than the global average (Carbon Brief, 2018). Third, and according to the United Nations, we have the next 12 years – until 2030 – to bring down greenhouse gas emissions to at least 45% or 50% of 2010 levels and to net-zero emissions by 2050.[1] The great transition beyond the current carbon civilization is a crucial imperative.

In this context, the dominant interpretative and analytical framework used to explain climate change is the idea of the Anthropocene. Climatologists, geologists, and earth scientists are increasingly using this category as a geological marker to highlight the advent of a new period in Earth's history in which humans are a geological force shaping the planetary conditions of life. We are departing from the 11,000 years of a relatively stable climate in the Holocene period. This is the no-analogue state of human history; we are changing the climatic conditions of planet Earth in adverse ways that will undermine human and non-human life. While the notion of the Anthropocene and general causal explanation of human-induced climate change is useful, it fails to appreciate the inequalities that are imbricated in this socio-ecological transformation. More particularly it fails to recognize how financialized carbon capitalism and imperial practices are causing our life worlds' heating (Satgar, 2018c). At the same time, most studies on inequality merely take into account income metrics, mainly through studies done by economists. Climate change and food crises prompt us to think about the multidimensionality of inequality while also thinking about its causal mechanisms within a global and historic context (Therborn, 2013). Placing both climate change and food inequality within such a multi-dimensional approach provides us with a richer understanding of how inequality is patterned and reproduced in the context of globalized carbon capitalism.

Starting with climate change, there are three crucial inequalities informing this challenge. The first inequality relates to the historic climate debt owed by industrialized countries and carbon corporations to the global south. For more than 150 years, the global north has been in the vanguard of carbon emissions and carbon capitalism. At the same time, seven major oil corporations (infamously known as the Seven Sisters) have controlled global oil supply for the greater part of the twentieth century. They have profited from historical carbon extraction and sales and are not being held accountable for their role in causing the climate crisis. Hence, the principle of common but differentiated responsibility in the UN climate negotiations rings hollow. Since the Paris Climate Agreement, which reaffirms the goal of limiting global temperature increase to well below 2-degrees Celsius and pursuing efforts to limit the increase to 1.5 degrees, every country is now responsible for climate change despite historical emissions and responsibilities. Moreover, despite Paris Agreement commitments, there has been little change towards reducing carbon emissions and therefore limiting temperature rise. The Climate Action Tracker (2018) shows that if all governments were to achieve their Paris Agreement commitments, the world would still likely warm by 3°C, which is twice the 1.5°C limit they agreed on in Paris. Ironically, not all governments are responsible for a heating world, both historically and in the current period.

The second inequality in terms of greenhouse gas emissions relates to who is responsible for continuing greenhouse gas emissions through carbon extraction. Today, the US has eclipsed even Saudi Arabia and Russia in terms of carbon extraction. This is spurred on by the fracking boom and Trump's policy support for carbon capitalism. At the same time, the US per capita carbon footprint far outstrips other countries. In the world today there are 26 private international oil corporations and 24 state owned oil companies (23 of these are in the global south, with the exception of Norway) that feature amongst the top 50 fossil fuel corporations in the world (Carroll, in press). Merely by focusing on fossil fuel (oil) extraction, the picture emerging here is that international oil companies and some public companies are at the forefront of carbon extraction and burning. However, climate responsibility can also be attributed to other industries. Researchers have measured contributions of industries' historical emissions to global surface temperature rise. Findings suggest that nearly two thirds of total industrial carbon dioxide and methane emissions can be traced to 90 major industrial carbon producers (83 producers of coal, oil, natural gas, and 7 cement manufacturers) (Heede, 2014).

The second largest contributor to greenhouse gas emissions is the global carbon food regime. Some estimates suggest that the global food regime contributes 20–30% of all human-associated greenhouse gas emissions (Garnett, Smith, Nicholson, & Finch, 2016). While emissions from agriculture and associated land-use change account for 24% of human-made emissions (IPCC, 2014b; Smith et al., 2014), 14.5–19% of this comes from livestock alone (Herero, 2016; Reisinger & Clark, 2017). Packaging, retail, transport, processing, food preparation, and waste disposal contribute an additional 5–10% of global greenhouse gas emissions (Garnett et al., 2016). Not only is the food industry causing climate change, but it will also be very hard hit by climate variability. This is a point we will elaborate further below.

The third inequality relates to climate change induced shocks. These shocks not only affect the natural environment, but have drastic social and economic consequences which affect poorer countries and populations more severely, and also reproduce inequality. Climate change induced shocks are increasing, and so are their indirect and direct impacts. For example, heat waves, wild fires, hurricanes, and droughts of increased frequency and intensity are ushering in an increased risk of diseases, death, and destruction. While many of these shocks indiscriminately affect entire communities, the consequences of climate change (and related disasters) are not distributed uniformly within communities. Individual and social factors such as class, age, gender, ethnicity, geography, language, and education lead to differential vulnerability and capacity to adapt to the effects of climate change. The extremely vulnerable people are typically poor and live in the least developed countries that are prone to more than one type of weather disaster, such as floods, droughts, and storms as well as gradual environmental degradation such as sea-level rise or desertification (Global Humanitarian Forum, 2009).

It is the poor that are disproportionately affected by both direct and indirect effects of climate change. Direct effects include injury, illness, displacement, and deaths from heat stress, drought, floods, and increased frequency of intense storms. Indirect effects of climate change include malnutrition and undernutrition, the spread of infectious disease vectors, food insecurity, illness due to increased air pollution and aeroallergens and mental health disorders from social and political instability. Population displacement from sea-level rise and conflict associated displacement also leads to further downstream impacts such as conflict situations and mental disruptions due to social network disruption. Children, in particular, are likely to be at increased risk of mental health effects from climate change (McMichael & Lindgren, 2011). In terms of direct effects, when assessing deaths due to climate-related disasters, one analysis shows that natural hazards strike countries regardless of national income, but the severity of the impacts are directly related to income and development levels. This is particularly evident for disaster mortality. On average, 327 people died per disaster in low-income countries from 1995 to 2015, almost five times more than the average toll in high-income countries (CRED and UNISDR, 2016). Coupled with biophysical sensitivity and socio-economic exposure of poor nations to climate change, impacts on food security and human health for these countries generally exceeds that of wealthier nations (Füssel, 2010, p. 597).

We are already witnessing how poorer countries are being hit the worst as temperatures have risen over the last three decades and as the number of extreme weather events has increased. For example, the Global Climate Risk Index analyses the quantified impacts of extreme weather events, both in terms of fatalities and economic losses that have occurred. Using this index, the study looks at past extreme weather events between 1996 and 2015 and notes Honduras, Myanmar, Haiti, Nicaragua, the Philippines, and Bangladesh as the countries most affected during this period in terms of exposure and vulnerability to extreme events. During the year 2015, Mozambique, Dominica, and Malawi were at the top of the list. The report also notes that the continent of Africa will be severely affected by climatic events, with 4 African countries ranking amongst the 20 countries worldwide during 2015 (Kreft, Eckstein, & Melchior, 2016). In 2018, the cost of the 10 deadliest climate shocks has been estimated at US$84.8 billion (Drugmand, 2019). Kerala, India, experienced one of the worst floods in its history during 2018 and this has been estimated to have cost US$3.7 billion. While the US has been experiencing climate-induced devastation through wild fires and hurricanes, it is a much wealthier society than, say, Kerala. Global economic inequality is going to limit the ability of poorer countries and societies to rebuild themselves after devastating climate shocks.

Globalized food regimes, food inequality, and climate change

Over the past three decades of global neoliberalization and restructuring of capitalism, food regimes have also been remade to be more externalized (Holt-Gimenez, 2017, pp. 175–212). Privatization of seed systems, liberalization of agricultural sectors and increasing globalization of retail has made the global food regime much more unstable and prone to shocks. Large transnationals have been increasing their control of national food regimes. Between 2006 and 2008, 2011, from 2014 to 2016, and in 2018, there have been various shocks to the globalized food regime. Most analysts have identified multiple causal factors implicated in these shocks. These range from oil price increases, shifts to biofuel production, droughts, and financial speculation, amongst other factors. Between 2014 and 2016, the crisis that rocked the global food regime was largely regionalized and mainly in sub-Saharan Africa, due to the El Niño-induced drought (Lamble & Graham-Harrison, 2016; Mathiesen, 2015). In 2018 it was the price of crude oil which spiked at US$80 a barrel (Vaughan, 2018). The first shock (2006–2008) led to several food riots in different countries and the second shock (2009–2011) fed into the revolutions of the 'Arab Spring'.

The normative response to these systemic food crisis dynamics has been more food security interventions. This is due to the fact that in global policy discourses and development and agrarian studies, the notion of food security has occupied a hegemonic place. Food security has evolved with thousands of meanings over the past few decades. The Food and Agricultural Organization is the progenitor of the official discourse on food security. Its most recent definition of food security is this: 'Food security exists when all people, at all times, have physical and economic access to sufficient, safe and nutritious food that meets their dietary needs and food preferences for an active and healthy life' (FAO, 1996).

This technocratic discourse has various epistemic and methodological limits from a food inequality perspective. First, food inequality recognizes that despite aggregate food output in a country, income levels and distribution would determine whether food is available to most citizens. Food security discourse merely proclaims that a country can feed itself but in reality this falls very short. Those with low or no income cannot benefit from the food security of a country. For instance, South Africa is a country that constantly declares itself food secure yet 6.85 million people experienced hunger in 2017, while 12 million had limited access to food (StatsSA, 2018). In short, food inequality highlights how structural barriers exist to prevent the realization of food needs. Second, how one measures food inequality goes beyond a technical measure of caloric levels. Caloric levels is a quantitative measure which assumes food choice is equalized in the food market. The FAO definition of food security also upholds such an assumption when asserting the notion of 'food preferences'. Yet, food inequality will ask if a poor person has the same food choices and access to quality food as a rich person. Third, food inequality has a normative aspect to it, that is, food equality. Food equality cannot be realized through the existing carbon and capitalist food regimes, which are premised on food inequality. The challenge of food equality invites and frames the need for systemic alternatives. Hence, food inequality has a resonance with, and supports discourses on, food sovereignty.

Food inequality in the world is widespread. A profit driven, globalized, and carbon-based food regime is creating an extremely food insecure world, imposing unhealthy food choices, limiting access to water as a public good and contributing to greenhouse gases. The IPCC (2018) special report is explicit in the trajectories that it maps out. A planet heating at 1.5°C and increasing to 2°C will experience major stresses, risks, and even the collapse of most food sources (IPCC, 2018, pp. 238–240). Climate shocks will exacerbate food inequalities. More specific projections for climate change vulnerabilities have also shown that there is increasing evidence for the link between extreme El Niño events and global warming, and the occurrence of such events could double in the future owing to climate change (Cai et al., 2014). What is more, as we turn to look at regions that are highly dependent on agriculture, we can expect that they will be especially sensitive to climate change as it has the potential to undermine agricultural production. As the growing-season temperatures climb, this can have dramatic impacts on agricultural productivity, farm incomes, and food insecurity. Battisti and Naylor (2009, p. 240) note that by the end of the twenty-first century there is a high probability (greater than 90%) that growing seasons in the tropics and subtropics will exceed the most extreme seasonal temperatures that were experienced from 1900 to 2006, while in temperate regions, 'the hottest seasons on record will represent the future norm in many locations' (Battisti & Naylor, 2009, p. 240). These extremes are already being felt in African regions such as the Sahel and in South Africa.

The food sovereignty response internationally

In response to the multiple crises facing societies, including climate and food inequality, there has been a surge in alternatives. One notable movement of resistance is *La Via Campesina* (the way of the peasants), an international peasant organization which promotes food sovereignty and defends small-scale farmers and agroecology. *Via Campesina* is comprised of more than 200 million family farmers, peasants, landless people, rural workers, indigenous people, rural youth, and rural women from 182 organizations internationally who have joined together in a global alliance to promote food sovereignty (Via Campesina, 2016). In 1996 *Via Campesina* declared the need for an alternative to food security, the ideology that dominated the global development apparatus and corporate-controlled food regimes. Food sovereignty has since featured in various declarations and has travelled into academic discourses, policy debates, agrarian reform programmes, alliance building, and campaigning in different parts of the world.[2] In short, food sovereignty affirms the importance of a political economy critique of current approaches to food systems; it highlights the importance of transformative alternatives that are controlled by small-scale producers and consumers to ensure healthy and culturally appropriate food; and it is about aggregating power from below to build movements.

Within food sovereignty practice, agroecology is a key tool that small-scale farmers use to cool the planet as it offers an alternative to large-scale industrial agriculture. While large industrial farms use a scorched-earth mentality when managing farm resources – for example, monocultures, no trees, and no wildlife – small-scale farmers are very effective stewards of natural commons and the soil as they utilize a broad array of resources eco-centrically, their farming systems are diverse, and they incorporate and preserve significant biodiversity within their farms. By doing so, they not only reduce land degradation and cool the planet but are also more adaptive and resilient to climate change, including droughts, hurricanes, temperature changes, and shifting planting dates (Rosset, 2011). Another international example of food sovereignty is the Alliance for Food Sovereignty in Africa (AFSA). It is a broad alliance of 30 different civil society actors who are fighting for food sovereignty and agroecology on the continent. AFSA was formed at the UN Framework Convention on Climate Change Conference of Parties 17 in Durban, South Africa, in December 2011 and at their launch, they released a report emphasizing that Food Sovereignty can cool the planet while feeding the world and regenerating ecosystems (AFSA, n.d.).

A powerful international example of food sovereignty in practice in a city is in Detroit, USA, where women are transforming vacant land to create a community-based food system. Here activists construct urban farms as safe spaces for communities, which operate as creative, public outdoor classrooms where they nurture activism and challenge the racial and class-based barriers to access healthy food, while at the same time transform their communities into safe and green spaces (White, 2011). Detroit also has a food policy council which has a strong focus on using agriculture to remediate Detroit's 70,000 vacant properties (Hoover, 2016). Rural social movements have shown us that dismantling the industrial agrifood complex and restoring local food systems must be accompanied by the construction of agroecological alternatives that meet the needs of the vulnerable and hungry (those left out of the current industrialized food system) (Altieri & Toledo, 2011). The Detroit example shows what is possible in urban spaces. In South Africa, as we discuss in the next section, a campaign including both rural and urban actors has emerged to construct these food sovereignty alternatives.

South African carbon capitalism and the drought (2014 onwards)

South Africa's mining and industrial development were carbon intensive since the discovery of coal in the late nineteenth century. Coal was entrenched as the main energy source for apartheid-era development and has continued under ANC rule. Coal as a source of cheap energy skewed South Africa's economy, to the point where, structurally, South Africa's core productive sectors are centred on a minerals-energy complex that has been highly concentrated (Fine & Rustomjee, 1996). In the recent period, this articulated with finance as part of neoliberal restructuring of the South African economy. Today, South Africa's minerals-energy-finance complex has plans to build some of the largest coal-fired power stations in the world and is locked into a coal-based energy path for the next few decades; this is despite South Africa's commitments in the Paris Climate Agreement. Moreover, Eskom, the state parastatal propelling South Africa's coal-driven agenda, has a monopoly on the generation and supply of electricity. Its debt at over R420 billion threatens to also bring down the South African fiscus. Eskom is the major obstacle to a socially owned renewable energy path for South Africa.

South Africa was ranked the 14th highest greenhouse gas emitter in 2015 (UCS, 2018). Its per capita ranking for carbon emissions is above the average for the G20 countries, which together produce 75% of the world's greenhouse gas emissions, and includes developing country giants such as China and India (Marquard, 2017). South Africa's highly industrialized food system is also producing its fair share of greenhouse gas emissions. For example, agriculture contributes 6.1% of South Africa's greenhouse gas emissions (Gütschow, Jeffery, Gieseke, & Gebel, 2018), and while this includes emissions from livestock, it does not account for greenhouse gas emissions from pesticide production, energy, land use, land-use change, and transport in the food system.

There is evidence of national and local changes in the rainfall and temperature climatology of South Africa over at least the past five decades. This is based on several analyses of weather-station data from the South African Weather Service, the Agricultural Research Council and internationally developed and maintained climate data sets. These data sets have shown the following trends: in terms of studies on historical data for temperature trends,

> South Africa has been warming significantly over the period 1931-2015. Strong warming trends have been observed in the drier western parts of the country (North and Western Cape) and in the northeast (Limpopo and Mpumalanga, extending southwards to the east coast of KwaZulu-Natal), where the observed rate of warming has been 2°C per century or even higher – more than twice the global rate of temperature increase. (DEA, 2017, p. 11)

At the same time, South Africa is naturally prone to droughts. At times, extreme droughts that persist over several years can be triggered by the El Niño Southern Oscillation (ENSO), explained by Baudoin et al. (2017: p. 128) as 'a quasi-periodic invasion of warm sea surface waters into the central and eastern tropical Pacific Ocean, returning at least once in any ten-year period'. From 2014, South Africa experienced the combined effects of a strong El Niño and a severe drought. The effects of this El Niño-related drought have lasted for several years. National authorities quantified it as the worst drought in 23 years (Baudoin, Vogel, Nortje, & Naik, 2017). Others argue it is the worst since the 1930s. South Africa's average rainfall for the 112-year period from 1904 to 2015 was 608 mm, while 2015 had an annual total of only 403 mm. This is the lowest ever recorded (De Jager, 2016). During this period six provinces were declared drought disaster areas, namely Kwa-Zulu-Natal, Limpopo, Mpumalanga, the Free State, North-West province, and the Northern Cape. By January 2017 this increased to eight of the nine provinces, excluding only Gauteng (Baudoin et al., 2017). Other regions in Southern Africa, namely Zimbabwe, Swaziland, Zambia, and Lesotho, were also impacted on by the drought as they suffered reductions in crop yields and resultant increases in maize prices (WFP, 2016; cited in Davis-Reddy, Vincent, & Mambo, 2017).

Temperatures during this period were also among the hottest recorded in South Africa over the past 10 years. The drought compounded South Africa's food inequality. The drought and high temperatures impacted on agriculture negatively. The sectors most severely affected were maize, wheat, and sugarcane, as well as beef and mutton production. The bulk of maize (83%), wheat (53%), and sugarcane (73%) are produced under non-irrigated dryland conditions which rely on natural rainfall, making them especially vulnerable to periods of drought (AgriSA, 2016). The loss of agricultural output due to the drought led to a technical recession in 2018 and was registered in very low GDP performance in the South African economy, which was already reeling from various macroeconomic pressures.

Despite South Africa's advanced and world-leading legislation for disaster risk reduction (the National Disaster Management Act of 2002), and forewarning of El Niño conditions by the South African Weather Service in August 2015, months before the impacts were felt, South Africa's government failed to swiftly implement the risk-preparedness measures that it should have. Instead, risk management strategies were reactionary and only took place after the consequences of the drought were felt and farmers were harshly hit (Baudoin et al., 2017).

As in the international picture, climate change is already hitting South Africa – especially vulnerable populations – through extreme weather shocks such as droughts, flooding and heat waves. As mentioned, before the drought (2014 onwards), there were 14 million hungry people in the country. The drought exacerbated hunger, but the state has not tracked this. Instead, food inequality in South Africa has increased to crisis levels. Despite a seemingly efficient food system, South Africa's farming sector is particularly vulnerable to climate change and variability, which has further potential to wreak havoc with more frequent climate shocks.

Climate and food inequality in South Africa

The impact of the drought on hunger can be analysed by looking at food prices. The Pietermaritzburg Agency for Community Social Action (PACSA) shows how the drought and high temperatures had a significant effect on food prices. Foods in the baskets of low-income households were hard hit from November 2015 – when the drought started to impact on the prices on the supermarket shelves. The overall price inflation from September 2015 to September 2016 was 15.1%. The impact of the drought on the 'big foods' was stark. Big foods are those foods which households prioritize on their shopping lists and include maize meal, rice, cake flour, white sugar, and cooking oil. These foods' prices increased by 25%. Maize alone increased by 32.2% year on year. PACSA also notes how women and children are at the greatest risk of food price increases because they absorb this inflation in their bodies – 'they eat last and their plates are least diverse' (PACSA, 2016, p. 3).

This burden on the poor has been witnessed time and again during the drought and through stories of government's mismanagement of water resources. Cape Town's Day Zero approach, for example, promoted disciplinary demand management and fear. This led to a squeeze on households and communities that were already suffering from water insecurity. The burden and cost were also shifted to poor communities as water management devices and punitive tariffs were implemented. The drought in Cape Town has resulted in the further commodification of water for poor households. Agriculture and businesses, on the other hand, were let off the hook (Satgar, 2018b). In addition, job losses during the drought were another shock for the vulnerable. For example, between July and September 2017, 25,000 job losses were already reported in the agricultural sector.

Regions in South Africa most vulnerable to exposure to extreme events and climate change and variability do not always overlap with the most vulnerable populations. In addition, vulnerability to climate change and variability is intrinsically linked with social and economic development. The Western Cape and Gauteng provinces, with high levels of infrastructure development, high literacy rates, and a low share of agricultural GDP, are lower on the vulnerability index, whereas the most vulnerable regions – Limpopo, Kwa-Zulu Natal, and Eastern Cape – are those with a high number of small-scale farmers, high dependency on rain-fed agriculture, high land degradation, and highly populated rural areas where the majority of the population relies on agriculture for their livelihoods (Gbetibouo & Ringler, 2009). The recent drought started in 2014 by ravaging through rural communities in the province of Kwa-Zulu Natal. From then on, rural South Africa was devastated by the drought. Livestock was depleted by adverse conditions related to the drought.

The poor have limited opportunities and, as a result, are disproportionately affected by the negative impacts of climate change. This is especially true as climate change will directly affect the sectors which the poor are dependent upon, namely agriculture, water supply, ecosystems, and biodiversity (Turpie & Visser, 2013), but also because it will affect the natural commons that many rural communities are dependent on. Both subsistence and commercial farming have been and will be affected by climate change, but, compared to commercial agriculture, smallholder farmers are less adapted to climate change and do not usually have access to financial instruments such as credit and insurance to hedge against climatic risk, thereby leaving the poor and marginalized exposed and more vulnerable (Turpie & Visser, 2013). The state has also been unresponsive to the needs of small-scale farmers and this has been revealed in the course of the drought.

Another concern is mismanagement of government funds and water resources through state corruption. This creates climate inequalities in the context of droughts. Mike Muller (2017), shows how a lot of what is being presented as 'radical economic transformation' in South Africa at a national level is simply state capture by a corrupt elite. The shenanigans of the former water and sanitation minister, Nomvula Mokonyane, in South Africa's water sector have little to do with radical economic transformation and are more about the enrichment of a new elite. Nomvula Mokonyane has spent two years changing the rules on and governance of the expansion of the Vaal River system so that a broader array of companies could compete for contracts. Newspaper reports have told of huge contracts given to political friends (Masondo, 2016) – for example, R4 billion in the Limpopo Province alone – and there have been many questions about the province's performance as Limpopo remains one of the worst performing provinces with 60% of its households suffering long interruptions in water supply in 2015 (Muller, 2017). Essentially, the drought in South Africa further exposed state constructed inequalities, related to corruption, and the lack of adequate water resources for poor rural households.

In response to these crises (increasing hunger, climate shocks, and related inequality), there has been a rise in resistance and a push for an alternative food system. First rural social movements, and now urban ones too, are embracing the concept of food sovereignty as an alternative to a crisis-ridden, globalized, carbon-based, and corporate-controlled food regime.

The food sovereignty response in South Africa

The food sovereignty alternative has found variegated roots in South Africa since *Via Campesina's* championing of this idea. Agrarian sector organizations, food justice organizations, climate justice, and solidarity economy actors have all championed a food sovereignty thrust. However, in 2014, after a coalition of organizations from these various sectors held consultations in all nine provinces and these deliberations culminated in a right-to-food conference at the end of that year, it was agreed that the dominant food regime was in crisis and there was a need for a national platform to champion the food sovereignty alternative (COPAC, 2014). In these deliberations, the onset of the drought in 2014 was already registered. The SAFSC emerged in early 2015 as a national campaigning platform to facilitate a loose convergence of organizations (movements, community organizations, NGOs, trade unions, and networks). In total, just over 50 organizations have converged around the SAFSC platform since its formation. The alliance base continues to grow around different interventions made by the SAFSC.

Food sovereignty politics as transformative politics

The SAFSC is part of the second cycle of post-apartheid resistance. The first was from 1994 to 2001 and threw up various oppositional movements like the Treatment Action Campaign, the Anti-Privatization Forum, and the Landless People's Movement. Many of these movements had to contest hegemonic ANC rule. The second cycle of post-apartheid resistance begins after these movements ebb, from 2007 onwards, and as new social forces began to emerge on the South African scene searching for national responses to the crisis of ANC-led neoliberal rule. The SAFSC is part of this second cycle alongside the Right to Know campaign, the One Million Climate Jobs campaign, new independent trade union movements, and various anti-corruption forces that have come to the fore.

The SAFSC epitomizes a new mode of politics that is beyond reform (managing the system) or revolution (violently destroying the system). It represents an attempt to build a new popular imagination, activist capacity, and actual pathways for an alternative: a food sovereignty system. This is fundamentally about systemic change led from below by small-scale food producers, consumers, and citizens. In the South African context, it has meant translating the idea around four critical axes. The first has been about viewing the food crisis as a systemic crisis rather than merely a technocratic food problem that reinforces the existing food system or a narrow agrarian challenge. South Africa has had a racialized agrarian transition predicated on land dispossession. However, while land justice is a crucial part of food sovereignty struggles, this is not about securing land to reproduce the existing system. Rather it is about locating land and wider food struggles in the struggle for an alternative food system that straddles urban and rural spaces. This has become a necessary desideratum in the context of the climate crisis. Intellectually, this has also meant developing political economy critiques of the corporate-controlled food system as a whole and at the level of production, consumption, finance, and ecology (COPAC, 2015), while also being alive to the need to imagine and work with systemic alternatives that could build the logic of food sovereignty. In the South African context this has meant working with ideas like solidarity economy, climate jobs, and water commoning, for instance (Bennie, 2014; Bennie & Satgoor, 2018; Jara, 2014).

The second axis has been about capacity building for transformative activism. Such a form of activism requires mastering new forms of power – structural, movement, direct, and symbolic – and how to constitute these forms of power. We will elaborate on this below.

The third axis has been to develop actual food sovereignty practices that meet people's needs. SAFSC campaigning has thus actively attempted to confront the limits and contradictions of the existing food system while building grassroots pathways. This has meant building pathways in communities, villages, towns, and cities to end hunger (Cherry, 2019, p. 195; SAFSC, 2017a, p. 8). Moreover, SAFSC has recognized that a key pillar of food sovereignty is to ensure climate justice. As such, SAFSC has also taken the drought very seriously through its campaigning interventions and this entailed confronting high food prices and water challenges and raising the needs of small-scale producers.[3]

The fourth axis has been about attempting to contest, transform and reclaim the state to advance democratic systemic reform for food sovereignty (Satgar, 2019, pp. 154–159). Democratic systemic reform is different from market-centred regulation that builds the power of corporations or top-down, state-centric regulation that builds state power. Such a mode of regulation is about affirming people's power from below to transform society through systemic alternatives and logics. In this regard, the SAFSC has effectively shifted discourses in the South African Human Rights Commission (SAHRC) to the point where the Commission recognizes food sovereignty as a crucial approach, alongside food security, for realizing the right to food in the country.[4] Moreover, the People's Parliament convened in 2017 by the SAFSC and the adoption of People's Food Sovereignty Act on this platform explicitly provide an example of people-driven regulation to ensure seeds, land, water, production, consumption, democratic planning and that the state's role conforms to the imperatives of citizens' power (SAFSC, 2018a). Put differently, if there were political forces in power willing to challenge corporate dominance of the food system and its limits, then the SAFSC has demonstrated what this could entail through the People's Food Sovereignty Act.

Climate justice and the drought

SAFSC's commitment to climate change campaigning and against the drought is evident from its launch, where it was agreed that climate change would be one of the four campaigning priorities for 2015. In the same year, the Hunger Tribunal was co-hosted with the SAHRC, trade unions, and religious organizations. This provided a crucial platform to highlight existing lived experiences of hunger, and also connections were made to the drought in testimonies (Bennie & Satgoor, 2018; SAFSC, 2015).

In May 2016, SAFSC, together with other climate justice organizations, hosted three days of activism to connect the food and climate crisis to the social and environmental injustices of extractivism (Bennie & Satgoor, 2018). One of these days of action included a national people's drought speak-out and bread march. At the speak-out, farmers, the hungry, and community organizations came together to discuss the impacts of the drought on their livelihoods and communities. The memorandum from the march notes the following about the food system and the drought that South Africa was experiencing from 2014:

> We believe South Africa's food system is unjust, unfair, unethical and unsustainable. The current food price shock, El Niño-induced drought and carbon emissions due to coal burning are all connected and are revealing the limits of a corporate controlled and government supported food system. We need a transformed food system that gives control of the food system to the people through a food sovereignty pathway and an alternative now to realize the right to food. (SAFSC, 2016a, p. 1)

During the speak-out, the following inputs from farmers were noted (SAFSC, 2016a, p. 2):

- Small -scale farmers were struggling before the drought but the drought has worsened things, including financial problems;
- there is a lack of effort on governments part to mobilize communities;
- government is failing to assess small-scale farmer needs adequately such that food parcels even for livestock are not sufficient;
- there is no clear response on how to bring back cultivation of food crops;
- water management is revealing serious weaknesses with some support for boreholes and pumps but most are not getting adequate support for sustainable water management;
- there is no government policy thinking on how to mitigate impacts beyond the immediate effects of the drought; and
- increasing food prices are hurting even farming households.

The SAFSC also expressed the following demands (SAFSC, 2016a, p. 3):

- That the price of all staples fall to affordable levels;
- that government must declare the drought a national disaster with special measures taken to ensure food and livestock production for subsistence and small-scale farmers is recovered;
- to reject GMO seeds, including drought tolerant maize, and these should not be part of government support;
- the government should take part in a people's climate justice movement led process to learn lessons from this drought, including the importance of independent and permanent community-based food sovereignty forums and a serious review of the Disaster Management Act;
- an immediate transition out of coal mining and a lifting of the ceiling on renewable energy in the Integrated Resource Plan; the development of a national renewable energy parastatal, and the development of a domestic renewables industry as part of creating climate jobs;
- an increase in the social grant in the short term to ameliorate the impacts of food inflation, as opposed to spending on nuclear power, and the social grant to be replaced by the development of a basic income grant policy for South Africa;

- the democratization of water management plans in municipalities and for these to become people driven and owned;
- a review of all water licenses given to mining corporations to ensure compliance and where necessary to revoke such licenses if sustainable water use standards are not met;
- farming land must be protected from mining.

Other campaigning initiatives to promote food sovereignty and with a focus on the drought and climate change include a documentary about the link between climate change and hunger, created by the Cooperative and Policy Alternative Centre (COPAC, a vibrant SAFSC partner) and shared with SAFSC alliance partners as a campaigning tool to raise awareness about hunger and climate change among communities. The short animation is titled: 'The hidden story behind hunger: Why we need food sovereignty and climate justice' (COPAC, 2016).

COPAC also developed an activist tool on water sovereignty in response to the current climate and drought crisis, entitled *Building people's power for water sovereignty: an activist guide* (COPAC, 2017). In addition, an animation was put together titled *Water is ours: it's time to fight for water sovereignty*,[5] and this was circulating in various communities and freely downloadable from the SAFSC webpage. During 2018, COPAC and SAFSC hosted a discussion with parliament on the drought, where activists in the SAFSC and other water crisis organizations presented their challenges to representatives from the portfolio committee on water and sanitation. The programme of the engagement also included a presentation by SAFSC on the water guide and the People's Food Sovereignty Act. Through grassroots engagements, the use of the water sovereignty tool in local communities and engagements with SAFSC alliance partners and wider social forces, a consensus is emerging to develop the Climate Justice Charter for South Africa (see Satgar, 2018b). The impact of the drought, its impact on food prices, and the scientific evidence at hand about worsening climate change have necessitated this intervention.

Constituting new forms of subaltern power

Through its campaigning at different levels, and the development of a transformative activist orientation, SAFSC has and is promoting different forms of power, and in doing so, creating awareness about the crises in the food system, how capitalism is at the root (of hunger, and climate change), and how people's grassroots responses provide a way out of the hunger and drought crisis. At the same time, the campaign is also providing insight into how to establish a new food system and also push back the power of corporations who currently dominate South Africa's food system. Below we elaborate on four different forms of power that SAFSC is promoting through its campaigning. For heuristic and analytical purposes, these forms of power are distinguished; however, in practice, they are interrelated to reinforce and strengthen each other. Moreover, these forms of power have a class and popular belonging; these forms of power are rooted amongst the subaltern including the working class, the landless, the hungry, the wageless majority, and citizens confronting climate ecocide.

Symbolic power

Symbolic power is about the values, principles, vision, and practices that an ideal represents. It is about symbolic actions that provide glimpses of these values and provide hope, but also living examples to show that an alternative food system based on values of food sovereignty, including democratic control of the food system, is possible (COPAC, 2015, p. 41). SAFSC has promoted symbolic power through a number of its activist-convened events, research, activist tools, and campaign media. This includes exposing activists and the public to gardens, small-scale farming, bee keeping, composting practices, seed banking, actual food sovereignty pathway building, and solidarity economy practices through consumer and farming cooperatives.[6] Through these symbolic reference points, people are able to learn about food sovereignty alternatives – both theoretical and practical – including agroecology, water sovereignty, and seed saving. They are also spaces in which to share stories of success with each other, understand challenges and explore alternatives to current practices and beliefs. These symbolic examples are avenues for inspiration and ideas, the building of solidarity and instilling hope that these alternatives do work and are possible.

Direct power

Direct power involves methods to create awareness about food sovereignty among the public; for example, influencing the public through mass campaigns, mass marches, and awareness raising (COPAC, 2015, p. 41). Direct power has been constituted as SAFSC members have undertaken a hunger tribunal, a picket outside the *Sunday Times* newspaper to draw attention to its silence on food alternatives, a picket outside the Johannesburg Stock Exchange against corporate control of the food system, a bread march, drought speak-outs, visits to government departments to hand over the People's Food Sovereignty Act and engagement with parliament, and meeting with communities around the water and climate justice charter process.[7] SAFSC has also engaged the media through its events, and aims to educate the public about the crisis in the food system and the food sovereignty alternatives through its campaigns. Part of drawing attention to the Climate Justice Charter process was a recent call (SAFSC, 2018d) by SAFSC and more than 60 organizations to the president and the speaker of the South African parliament to convene an emergency sitting of the national parliament to deliberate on the UN-IPCC 1.5°C report and its implications for South Africa's climate policy and deep, just transition. Failure by the president and the speaker to respond to this call has provoked the SAFSC and all supporting organizations to call for mass resistance (see SAFSC, 2018e).

Movement power

Movement power involves bringing together different actors, and networks to create a broad activist base and space for convergence (COPAC, 2015, p. 41). The different sectors and forces that SAFSC aggregates represent movement power. This is not about building a member-driven movement that is hierarchical but is rather about a horizontal platform that enables initiative from various participating organizations. This is a loose convergence that builds capacities and network effectiveness through activist schools, local food sovereignty forums, farmer to farmer networking, seed sharing, sharing research, producing an activist driven newsletter[8] and co-creating a knowledge commons for all converging in the space. The SAFSC has hosted three national food sovereignty festivals that have also deepened the knowledge commons. Several activist tools, both training and learning tools, have been developed that are also grounding knowledge commoning.[9] Activist social media presence is another way by which movement power is encouraged as 'followers' have easy access to knowledge and awareness about SAFSC's and food sovereignty alternatives, events, and practices.

Structural power

Structural power is about building pathways from below, including alternative production, consumption, financing, and living patterns (COPAC, 2015, p. 41). It is about showing how people can meet their needs through food sovereignty practices, including seed saving, agroecology, water management, and local food markets, for example, and scaling these up.

SAFSC's campaigning priority since the beginning of 2018 has been to build food sovereignty in towns, villages, and cities to strengthen practices and promote alternatives that meet people's needs directly. There are already existing examples of structural power, and these serve as inspiration to others in the campaign. For example, Magda Campbell is a small-scale agroecological farmer who farms on the land of Beacon School for Learners with Special Education Needs. At this school, she teaches the children and community how to grow food. She also sells her vegetables through local distributors (SAFSC, 2016c).

Another example is the Wits Food Sovereignty Centre (SAFSC, 2017b). The memorandum that was handed over to Wits University management after the 2016 national bread march in Johannesburg was taken further. After further engagements, Wits signed a memorandum of agreement with COPAC to advance strategies and practices to bring about the first eco-centric university in South Africa. This entails advancing zero hunger, zero carbon emissions, and zero waste as part of the everyday functioning of the university. The Wits Food Sovereignty Centre is a pilot project through which to achieve these eco-centric practices and includes the creation of an eco-demonstration space, an organizing space for food sovereignty pathways and space of dignity for food-stressed students (including communal kitchens, eating, and cultural spaces and food gardens on campus). The first communal kitchen has been established, a pilot garden (running for 3 years) will now be replicated on 21 more sites at the university, and fundraising continues for 2 more communal kitchens. The Wits pathway will serve as a springboard into the inner city. Already a forum has been established with more than twenty inner city farmers and plans are underway to establish a food sovereignty market at Wits.

A third example is Ethical Co-op, food cooperative marketed online and based in Cape Town. Ethical Co-op was formed in 2005. The co-op provides ethically produced goods, including a range of fresh produce from local farmers to customers around Cape Town. Over the years it has actively built a successful relationship between its consumers and several small-scale farmers. Ethical Co-op is promoting food sovereignty in local spaces in Cape Town as it supports local farmers who work with nature to produce their food (Magda Campbell mentioned above also sells her produce through the cooperative), and links them to customers who value nutrition and the environment. Through its practices, it is demonstrating that an alternative food system is possible in Cape Town (Cherry, 2019).

Challenges

There are several challenges confronting the food sovereignty journey and campaign in South Africa. First is the capture of the South African post-apartheid state by corporate interests, including agrarian capital. Three examples stand out. The first is the dedicated Act of 1997 for Genetically Modified Organisms. The second is a recent push to ensure seed saving is criminalized through new plant breeders' legislation. The third is the corporate control of the food chain from farm to consumer via food corporations and retail giants. Placing food sovereignty on the national agenda requires confronting the state-agrarian capital relationship to open space for this alternative to emerge. Creative and innovative activist interventions have happened through SAFSC activism including its own

People's Food Sovereignty Act (a political hack), developing food sovereignty pathways from below, directly engaging society and winning over the SAHRC. However, much more has to be done to shift the state from below. The Climate Justice Charter process led by COPAC and SAFSC is going to be crucial to shift relations of force and power towards food sovereignty. It will place food sovereignty centrally into narratives and discourses to advance the deep, just transition.

The second challenge is to widen, deepen, and strengthen local food sovereignty pathways in communities, villages, towns, and cities. Crucial pilot sites and practices are taking root in urban and rural spaces. There is a crucial food sovereignty impulse on the ground. However, this has to be scaled up to demonstrate the symbolic power of food sovereignty. This means local food sovereignty systems, alliances, and transformative politics have to come to the fore in a more widespread way. Climate determinism will be a spur to this, but at the same time, an agency from below has to keep the strategic initiative to ensure such pathways take root to mitigate climate shocks. More droughts will occur, climate and food inequalities will worsen, but a food sovereignty response can become the counter-hegemonic response from below if many more pathways take root. The symbolic power and actual examples of these experiences will become common sense.

The third crucial challenge is movement building. The SAFSC has avoided institutionalizing itself as a top-down movement. The past four years of campaigning have equipped its activist base with tools, capacities, imagination, and practices. This was merely a phase of sharing, learning, and solidarity. The next few years will determine whether the SAFSC can and should institutionalize itself beyond a loose network. If local food sovereignty pathways and alliances take root this would become a crucial precondition for a national SAFSC institutional structure. However, the modalities of this will be shaped from below. Linked to this would be active learning from international experiences and solidarities.

Conclusion

Climate change is also about climate and food inequality or climate injustice. These are new inequalities that will test and further strain our societies. South Africa's drought has revealed the creation of such inequalities, in the context of a country already defined by yawning income inequality. Climate shocks are going to worsen for South Africa. The challenge is to overcome its addiction to carbon capital, particularly coal, and advance a deep, just transition. Central to making this happen is transforming South Africa's food system, both to bring down emissions and to create the eco-centric resilience to meet the food needs of society. Food sovereignty is emerging as a crucial systemic alternative in this context and in different parts of the world. The SAFSC is pioneering crucial activist interventions in this regard, including defining a new transformative politics that conceives of and champions food sovereignty as a systemic alternative from below, defining new forms of constitutive power, building concrete pathways from below to realize food sovereignty in local spaces and advancing an agenda for democratic systemic reform. There are many challenges to overcome on this journey but the food sovereignty alternative is without a doubt necessary for a climate-driven world and South Africa. It is central to a transitional compass.

Notes

1. The recent International Panel on Climate Change report highlights this challenge. See IPPC (2018).
2. See Magdoff and Tokar (2010). They highlight in this volume how food sovereignty has emerged at the frontlines of agricultural and food crises. Andree, Ayres, Bosia, and Massicotte (2014) show how food sovereignty has become central to theory, policy and contentious politics about food in different parts

of the world. Williams and Holt-Gimenez (2017) show how the US Food Sovereignty Alliance works across various communities.

3. See SAFSC newsletters documenting the bread march and speak-out (SAFSC, 2016b), and COPAC's (2017) activist tool on water sovereignty.

4. The SAHRC co-hosted a hunger tribunal with SAFSC in 2015 to receive testimony from South African citizens. In 2018, the SAHRC set up a Section 11 committee to advise it on the right to food, which included representation from the SAFSC. Section 11 Committees are advisory structures comprised of experts from different institutions and disciplines, who advise the Commission on matters and interventions relating to a particular right, in this case the right to food.

5. English and Xhosa versions are available at SAFSC (2018c).

6. See Bennie and Satgoor (2018) and Satgar (2019).

7. All of these activities have been documented in SAFSC newsletters. See www.safsc.org.za.

8. By the end of 2018, 12 newsletters had been produced.

9. This includes a solidarity economy activist guide, a worker cooperative guide, a food sovereignty activist guide, a seed saving guide, a water sovereignty activist guide, a land-use guide and two animations, one on hunger and another on water sovereignty. All these guides can be accessed at www.safsc.org.za.

Disclosure statement

No potential conflict of interest was reported by the authors.

ORCID

Vishwas Satgar ⓘ http://orcid.org/0000-0003-4572-9797

References

AFSA. (n.d.). *What is Afsa?* Retrieved from https://afsafrica.org/home/what-is-afsa/

AgriSA. (2016). *A raindrop in the drought: Report to the multistakeholder task team on the drought – AgriSA's status report on the current drought crisis.* Centurion: AgriRSA. Retrieved from https://www.agrisa.co.za/wp-content/uploads/2016/03/Agri-SA-Drought-Report_CS4.pdf

Altieri, M., & Toledo, V. (2011). The agroecological revolution in Latin America: Rescuing nature, ensuring food sovereignty and empowering peasants. *Journal of Peasant Studies, 38*(3), 587–612.

Andree, P., Ayres, J., Bosia, M. J., & Massicotte, M.-J. (2014). *Globalisation and food sovereignty: Global and local change in the new politics of food.* Toronto: University of Toronto Press.

Battisti, D. S., & Naylor, R. L. (2009). Historical warnings of future food insecurity with unprecedented seasonal heat. *Science, 323,* 240–244.

Baudoin, M., Vogel, C., Nortje, K., & Naik, M. (2017). Living with drought in South Africa: Lessons learnt from the recent El Niño drought period. *International Journal of Disaster Risk Reduction, 23,* 128–137.

Bennie, A. (2014). Linking food sovereignty and the solidarity economy in South African townships. In V. Satgar (Ed.), *The solidarity economy alternative: Emerging theory and practice* (pp. 249–278). Pietermaritzburg: University of KwaZulu-Natal Press.

Bennie, A., & Satgoor, A. (2018). Deepening the just transition through food sovereignty and the solidarity economy. In V. Satgar (Ed.), *The climate crisis: South Africa and global democratic eco-socialist alternatives* (pp. 293–313). Johannesburg: Wits University Press.

Cai, W., Borlace, S., Lengaigne, M., Rensch, P., Collins, M., Vecchi, G., … Jin, F. (2014). Increasing frequency of extreme El Niño events due to greenhouse warming. *Nature Climate Change, 4*, 111–116.

Carbon Brief. (2018). *Mapped: How every part of the World has warmed and could continue to warm*. Retrieved from https://www.carbonbrief.org/mapped-how-every-part-of-the-world-has-warmed-and-could-continue-to-warm

Carroll, W. (in press). Fossil capital, imperialism and the global corporate elite. In V. Satgar (Ed.), *New US imperialism and the BRICS – global rivalry and resistance*. Johannesburg: Wits University Press.

Cherry, J. (2019). More ethical than Ethical: Ethical food co-operative's conversion to a worker co-operative. In V. Satgar (Ed.), *Co-operatives in South Africa* (pp. 186–215). Pietermaritzburg: University of KwaZulu-Natal Press.

Climate Action Tracker. (2018). *Warming projections: Global update, December 2018*. Retrieved from https://climateactiontracker.org/documents/507/CAT_2018-12-11_Briefing_WarmingProjectionsGlobalUpdate_Dec2018.pdf

COPAC. (2014). *Inter-provincial dialogue on the right to food: Gauteng, Limpopo and North-west province*. Johannesburg: Cooperative and Policy Alternative Centre and Foundation for Human Rights. Retrieved from http://copac.org.za/files/Inter-provincial20Dialogue20on20the20Right20to20Food20Conference20Report.pdf

COPAC. (2015). *Food sovereignty for the right to food – a guide for grassroots activism*. Johannesburg: Author.

COPAC. (2016). *The hidden story behind hunger*. [online video]. Retrieved from https://www.youtube.com/watch?v=AYHybn0QdYA

COPAC. (2017). *Building people's power for water sovereignty: An activist guide*. Johannesburg: Author. Retrieved from https://www.safsc.org.za/wp-content/uploads/2017/11/Water-Guide-Final-Web_colour.pdf

Cosgrove, B. (2013). Assessing the future of water. *Options Magazine, Summer 2013*. Retrieved from http://www.iiasa.ac.at/web/home/resources/mediacenter/FeatureArticles/Water-Meeting-Report.en.html

CRED, & UNISDR. (2016). *Poverty and death: Disaster mortality 1996-2015*. Centre for Research on the Epidemiology of Disasters and United Nations Office for Disaster Risk. Retrieved from http://cred.be/sites/default/files/CRED_Disaster_Mortality.pdf

Davis-Reddy, C. L., Vincent, K., & Mambo, J. (2017). Socio-economic impacts of extreme weather events in Southern Africa. In C. L. Davis-Reddy, & K. Vincent (Eds.), *Climate risk and vulnerability: A handbook for Southern Africa* (2nd ed.) (pp. 30–46). Pretoria: CSIR.

De Jager, E. (2016). SA rainfall in 2015 the lowest on record – SAWS. *Politicsweb*. Retrieved from http://www.politicsweb.co.za/documents/sa-rainfall-in-2015-the-lowest-on-record-saws

DEA. (2017). *National climate change adaptation strategy: Republic of South Africa. 2nd draft for public comments*. Pretoria: Department of Environmental Affairs. Retrieved from https://www.environment.gov.za/sites/default/files/reports/nationalclimate_changeadaptation_strategyforcomment_nccas.pdf

Drugmand, D. (2019). Climate costs in 2018: Top 10 disasters cost $85 billion. *Climate Liability News*. Retrieved from https://www.climateliabilitynews.org/2019/01/03/climate-costs-2018/

FAO. (1996). *Rome declaration on World Food Security and World Food Summit Plan of Action: World Food Summit 13-17 November 1996, Rome, Italy*. Rome: Food and Agriculture Organisation.

Fine, B., & Rustomjee, Z. (1996). *The political economy of South Africa – from minerals-energy complex to Industrialisation*. London: Hurst.

Füssel, H.-M. (2010). How inequitable is the global distribution of responsibility, capability and vulnerability to climate change: A comprehensive indicator-based assessment. *Global Environmental Change, 20*, 597–611.

Garnett, T., Smith, P., Nicholson, W., & Finch, J. (2016). *Food systems and greenhouse gas emissions (Foodsource: Chapters)*. Food Climate Research Network, University of Oxford. Retrieved from https://www.foodsource.org.uk/chapters/3-food-systems-greenhouse-gas-emissions.

Gbetibouo, G. A., & Ringler, C. (2009). *Mapping South African farming sector vulnerability to climate change and variability: A subnational assessment*. Discussion paper presented where, what institution, department and city. Retrieved from http://citeseerx.ist.psu.edu/viewdoc/download?doi=10.1.1.435.1924&rep=rep1&type=pdf

Global Humanitarian Forum. (2009). *Human impact report: Climate change – the anatomy of a silent crisis.* Geneva: Author. Retrieved from http://www.ghf-ge.org/human-impact-report.pdf.

Gütschow, J., Jeffery, L., Gieseke, R., & Gebel, R. (2018). *The PRIMAP-hist national historical emissions time series (1850-2015).* V. 1.2 [Dataset]. GFZ Data Services. Retrieved from https://doi.org/10.5880/PIK.2018.003

Heede, R. (2014). Tracing anthropogenic carbon dioxide and methane emissions to fossil fuel and cement producers, 1854-2010. *Climatic Change, 122,* 229–241.

Herero, M. (2016). To reduce greenhouse gases from cows and sheep, we need to look at the big picture. *The Conversation, 21 March.* Retrieved from https://theconversation.com/to-reduce-greenhouse-gases-from-cows-and-sheep-we-need-to-look-at-the-big-picture-56509

Holt-Gimenez, E. (2017). *A foodie's guide to capitalism.* New York, NY: Monthly Review Press and Food First Books.

Hoover, B. M. (2016). White spaces in black and Latino places: Urban agriculture and food sovereignty. *Journal of Agriculture, Food Systems, and Community Development, 3*(4), 109–115.

Intergovernmental Panel on Climate Change [IPCC]. (2014a). *Climate change 2013: The physical science basis.* Cambridge: Cambridge University Press. Retrieved from https://www.ipcc.ch/site/assets/uploads/2018/02/WG1AR5_all_final.pdf

Intergovernmental Panel on Climate Change [IPCC]. (2014b). *Climate change 2014: Working group III contribution to the fifth assessment report of the intergovernmental panel on climate change.* Cambridge and New York, NY: Cambridge University Press. Retrieved from https://www.ipcc.ch/site/assets/uploads/2018/02/ipcc_wg3_ar5_full.pdf

Intergovernmental Panel on Climate Change [IPCC]. (2018). *Global warming of 1.5°C.* An IPCC special report on the impacts of global warming of 1.5°C above pre-industrial levels and related global greenhouse gas emission pathways, in the context of strengthening the global response to the threat of climate change, sustainable development, and efforts to eradicate poverty. Intergovernmental Panel on Climate Change. Retrieved from https://www.ipcc.ch/site/assets/uploads/sites/2/2018/12/SR15_Chapter3_Low_Res.pdf

Jara, M. (2014). The solidarity economy response to the agrarian crisis in South Africa. In V. Satgar (Ed.), *The solidarity economy alternative: Emerging theory and practice* (pp. 227–248). Pietermaritzburg: University of KwaZulu-Natal Press.

Kreft, S., Eckstein, D., & Melchior, I. (2016). *Global Climate Risk Index 2017: Who suffers most from extreme weather events? Weather-related loss events in 2015 and 1966 to 2015.* Berlin: GermanWatch. Retrieved from https://germanwatch.org/sites/germanwatch.org/files/publication/16411.pdf

Lamble, L., & Graham-Harrison, E. (2016). Drought and rising temperatures 'leaves 36m people across Africa facing hunger.' *The Guardian,* 16 March. Retrieved from https://www.theguardian.com/environment/2016/mar/16/drought-high-temperatures-el-nino-36m-people-africa-hunger

Magdoff, F., & Tokar, B. (2010). *Agriculture and food in crisis.* New York, NY: Monthly Review Press.

Marquard, A. (2017). South Africa and the G20: Where do we stand on greenhouse gas emissions. *UCT News, 11 July.* Retrieved from https://www.news.uct.ac.za/article/-2017-07-05-south-africa-and-the-g20-where-do-we-stand-on-greenhouse-gas-emissionsa

Masondo, S. (2016). R170m and still no water. *City Press, 14 March.* Retrieved from https://city-press.news24.com/News/r170m-and-still-no-water-20160314

Mathiesen, K. (2015). El Niño could bring drought and famine in West Africa, scientists warn. *The Guardian,* 21 May. Retrieved from https://www.theguardian.com/environment/2015/may/21/el-nino-could-bring-drought-and-famine-in-west-africa-scientists-warn

McMichael, A. J., & Lindgren, E. (2011). Climate change: Present and future risks to health, and necessary responses. *Journal of Internal Medicine, 270*(5), 401–413.

Muller, M. (2017). South Africa's water sector: A case study in state capture. *The Conversation, 1 December.* Retrieved from https://theconversation.com/south-africas-water-sector-a-case-study-in-state-capture-69581

PACSA. (2016). *PACSA food price barometer.* Annual report. October 2016. Pietermaritzburg: Pietermaritzburg Agency for Community Social Action. Retrieved from https://www.pacsa.org.za/images/food_barometer/2016/2016_PACSA_Food_Price_Barometer_REDUCED.pdf

Reisinger, A., & Clark, H. (2018). How much do direct livestock emissions actually contribute to global warming? *Global Change Biology, 24*(4), 1749–1761.

Rosset, P. (2011). Food sovereignty and alternative paradigms to confront land grabbing and the food and climate crises. *Development, 54*(1), 21–30.

SAFSC. (2016a). *Unite against hunger: National people's drought speak out and bread march memorandum.* Johannesburg: South African Food Sovereignty Campaign. Retrieved from http://www.safsc.org.za/wp-content/uploads/2016/05/SAFSC-memorandum.pdf

SAFSC. (2016b). Drought speak out and National Bread march. *SAFSC Newsletter 4, August.* Johannesburg: South African Food Sovereignty Campaign. Retrieved from https://us11.campaign-archive.com/?u= 6eb374fe9b580101982b7b47c&id=8bd02d0687&e=f7ba6dc34f

SAFSC. (2016c). Food sovereignty festival and future of SAFSC. *SAFSC Newsletter 6, December.* Johannesburg: South African Food Sovereignty Campaign. Retrieved from https://us11.campaign-archive.com/?u= 6eb374fe9b580101982b7b47c&id=aff41669c7&e=f7ba6dc34f

SAFSC. (2017a). The debate continues while we build from below: Extended NCC meeting outcomes on way forward for SAFSC. *SAFSC Newsletter 8, July/August.* Johannesburg: South African Food Sovereignty Campaign. Retrieved from https://mailchi.mp/b0e329b0cd96/safsc-newsletter8-campaign-updates?e= f7ba6dc34f

SAFSC. (2017b). A food sovereignty victory: The food sovereignty research centre at Wits University, *Newsletter 9, November/December.* Johannesburg: South African Food Sovereignty Campaign. Retrieved from http://www.safsc.org.za/wp-content/uploads/2019/01/SAFSC-newsletter-9-.compressed.pdf

SAFSC. (2018a). *People's Food Sovereignty Act. No.1 of 2018.* Johannesburg: South African Food Sovereignty Campaign. Retrieved from https://www.safsc.org.za/wp-content/uploads/2017/11/FS-Act-no.1-of-2018.pdf

SAFSC. (2018b). *Climate justice charter process.* Retrieved from https://www.safsc.org.za/climate-justice-charter-process/

SAFSC. (2018c). *Animation: Water is ours (English and IsiXhosa versions).* Retrieved from https://www.safsc. org.za/animation-water-is-ours-english-and-isixhosa-versions/

SAFSC. (2018d). *Open letter to president Cyril Ramaphosa.* Retrieved from https://www.safsc.org.za/wp-content/uploads/2018/10/Open-Letter_Emergency-sitting-of-Parliament-updated.pdf

SAFSC. (2018e). *Press release: Call for civil resistance against ANC government's blanket of secrecy around climate science and our possible extinction.* Retrieved from https://www.safsc.org.za/wp-content/uploads/2018/ 10/Press-Release_Parliament_31Oct.pdf

Satgar, V. (2018a). The climate crisis and systemic alternatives. In V. Satgar (Ed.), *The climate crisis: South Africa and global democratic eco-socialist alternatives* (pp. 1–27). Johannesburg: Wits University Press.

Satgar, V. (2018b). Light a fire under SA's climate policy. *Mail & Guardian, 13 April.* Retrieved from https:// mg.co.za/article/2018-04-13-00-light-a-fire-under-sas-climate-policy

Satgar, V. (2018c). The anthropocene and imperial eco-cide. In V. Satgar (Ed.), *The climate crisis: South Africa and global democratic eco-socialist alternatives* (pp. 47–67). Johannesburg: Wits University Press.

Satgar, V. (2019). With, against and beyond the state: A solidarity economy through a movement of movements. In V. Satgar (Ed.), *Co-operatives in South Africa: Advancing solidarity economy pathways from below* (pp. 140–163). Pietermaritzburg: University of KwaZulu-Natal Press.

Smith, P., Bustamante, M., Ahammad, H., Clark, H., Dong, H., Elsiddig, E. A., … Bolwig, S. (2014). Agriculture, Forestry and Other Land Use (AFOLU). In O. Edenhofer, R. Pichs-Madruga, & Y. Sokona (Eds.), *Climate change 2014: Mitigation of climate change. Contribution of working group III to the fifth assessment report of the intergovernmental panel on climate change* (pp. 811–922). Cambridge: Cambridge University Press.

StatsSA. (2018). General Household Survey 2017. *Statistics South Africa.* Retrieved from http://www.statssa. gov.za/publications/P0318/P03182017.pdf

Therborn, G. (2013). *The killing fields of inequality.* Polity: Cambridge and Malden.

Trenberth, K. (2018). Climate change and wildfires – how do we know if there is a link?' *The Conversation, 10 August.* Retrieved from https://theconversation.com/climate-change-and-wildfires-how-do-we-know-if-there-is-a-link-101304

Turpie, J., & Visser, M. (2013). *The impact of climate change on South Africa's rural areas; submission for the 2013/14 Division of Revenue, Financial and Fiscal Commission,* Cape Town: Financial and Fiscal Commission.

UCS. (2018). *Each country's share of CO2 emissions.* Union of Concerned Scientists. Retrieved from https:// www.ucsusa.org/global-warming/science-and-impacts/science/each-countrys-share-of-co2.html#.XBjq12g zY2y

UNFCCC. (1992). *United Nations Framework Convention on Climate Change.* Rio de Janeiro 1992. Retrieved from https://unfccc.int/resource/docs/convkp/conveng.pdf

Vaughan, A. (2018). What are the factors driving up the price of crude oil? *The Guardian*, 17 May. Retrieved from https://www.theguardian.com/business/2018/may/17/what-are-the-factors-driving-up-the-price-of-crude-oil

Via Campesina. (2016). *Organisational brochure*. Retrieved from https://viacampesina.org/en/la-via-campesina-organisational-brochure-edition-2016/

White, M. M. (2011). Sisters of the soil: Urban gardening as resistance in Detroit. *Race/Ethnicity: Multidisciplinary Global Contexts*, 5(1), 13–28.

Williams, J. M., & Holt-Gimenez, E. (2017). *Land justice: Re-imagining land, food, and the commons in the United States*. Oakland, CA: Food First Books.

The global south, degrowth and The Simpler Way movement: the need for structural solutions at the global level

Sarah MacKay (iD)

ABSTRACT
In a recent edition of *Globalizations*, Hickel and Trainer discuss the degrowth and The Simpler Way movement in regard to the global South. This author contributes a different point of view to the discussion using the world-systems analysis and highlights that to have any successful movement able to address global challenges, the differences between the South and North in terms of economic and political systems must be considered. Many South countries have rentier oligarchic systems, which require Western researchers to be more cautious about what they propose in terms of transitions. Furthermore, an effective solution for global challenges must go beyond behavioural or national strategies and be structural at the global level. This author claims that complete economic and political independence of the South from the capitalist world-economy is the only solution that can address global environmental and inequality challenges and should be considered as a long-term vision by degrowth and the TSW movement.

This paper provides a few comments on the previous articles written for the special issue of *Globalizations* 'Economics and Climate Emergency', by Jason Hickel (2021a) and Ted Trainer (2021b), in regard to degrowth and The Simpler Way (TSW). It includes some views from a person from the global South, with some sociological tunes. It is important to clarify at the outset that the two articles mainly examined here are not comprehensive accounts of degrowth or TSW. The literature is much broader than the two articles discussed.

Degrowth is both a political movement and an academic discourse with various strands. It is 'a critique of growth ... [and] signifies ... a desired direction, one in which societies will use fewer natural resources and will organize and live differently than today. 'Sharing', 'simplicity', 'conviviality', 'care', and the 'commons' are primary significations of what this society might look like' (D'Alisa et al., 2014, p. 33). TSW is a degrowth project (Morgan, 2020) and refers to 'working for transition from consumer society to a simpler, more cooperative, just and ecologically sustainable society' (Trainer, 2016, para. 1).

The degrowth and TSW movements provide important possibilities to address global challenges, including environmental challenges and global inequalities (Hickel, 2017a; 2019; Trainer, 2020). Some advantages of these movements include their critiques of the global development indicators, their questioning of global capitalism, their critiques of conventional development models, and their emphasis on lifestyle change, as well as their attention to injustices in regard to the global South (Hickel, 2017a; Trainer, 2021a, 2021b).

Scholars of the degrowth movement, including Hickel (2017a, 2021b), Hickel et al. (2021), Kallis (2011), and Morgan (2020), have considered exploitation, its underpinning structural conditions and global inequalities between South and North. For example, Hickel (2017a) criticized the World Bank's discourse in which the problems of the global South countries are because of their poor policies and institutions and instead looked at their problems as a relational issue connected with the world system. Criticizing global dominant measurements of poverty, inequality, and development, Hickel (2017b) highlighted increasing inequalities and compared the core and periphery of the world system in terms of wealth and power.

The degrowth movement also highlights that if we follow degrowth strategies in the global North, all people, including poor nations, can achieve a good life within planetary boundaries (Hickel, 2019). Using a world-systems analysis is another strength of degrowth movement (Hickel, 2021a). The TSW movement also offers useful ideas to address overconsumption and environmental challenges through simpler lifestyles and through taking action rather sooner than later (Trainer, 2020). However, this paper articulates two specific constructive critiques arising from the content and focus of the contributions to the special issue.

First, global inequalities bring different positions, different structures, and different priorities for the South and the North, which require different strategies and interventions for each. The claim of this author is that we need to scrutinize the differences more and how these differences may affect the implications of these movements. Morgan (2020), in his review of Kallis et al.'s (2020) book, 'The case for degrowth', notes that degrowth needs to be different for different placings in the world. Still, more caution is needed concerning strategies and implications are different for many parts of the global South compared to the North. To be clear, Hickel (2019) and Hickel and Kallis (2020) discuss different strategies for the South and the North: poor nations need a different development model, while the North needs to decrease/stop growth moving to post-capitalist models. I suggest there is a danger this may be overly general and idealistic, given the power dynamics in many global South countries.

Hickel (2021a) does elaborate on how the global South should go through a post-development phase, for example through the mobilization of its governments to bring fairer labour and raw material prices to the South. This author, however, believes these implications are not realistic and effective, given the conditions of the global South. In the following sections, I discuss impediments to these strategies, which may prevent them from working.

Second, I would argue that effective strategies should target structural changes at the global level, not only at the national level or behavioural level. Although the degrowth movement mentions structural changes, solutions mainly remain at the national and state policy level, for example, modification of taxing system or financial system. Moreover, although behavioural and micro-local changes are necessary, as suggested by TSW movement, they are not enough, especially for the global South.

Trainer (2011; 2020) acknowledges global inequalities and the importance of national and global structural changes and criticizes existing governments. However, his work does not provide structural strategies to address challenges like global corporate production, extractivism, and global inequalities. Trainer's (2020) emphasis is different. He argues that as structural forces are against major changes and as the condition is urgent, we should quickly move on with behavioural and localized interventions, including a community ecology approach and lifestyle changes. Although these interventions are necessary, they are not enough and they might not be a priority for the most vulnerable groups of the global South, including internally displaced individuals, those who live in poverty, or those who live under fragile states, such as Yemen, Libya, and Afghanistan. In addition, the lack of attention to structural changes may exacerbate the condition by perpetuating the status quo. The most relevant work I found in the degrowth literature that discusses global structural strategies is Hickel's, '*The anti-colonial politics of degrowth*'. In this paper, Hickel (2021b) highlights that 'degrowth is … a demand for decolonization' (Hickel 2021b, p. 1).

To reiterate, the critique discussed here is not of the degrowth and TSW movements in their entirety or of their motives, but rather of the implications of the two special issue articles. To clarify the critique, a global-level theory is required, and I would argue the most relevant theory explaining world conditions is world-systems analysis developed by Wallerstein. We live in one interconnected but differentiated world system. I would like to share a metaphor of a ship to clarify my point. This is not a perfect metaphor, but it is helpful. Current conditions of the world system resemble a huge multi-level ship, which is gradually sinking in the ocean. The people of the global South (not governments) are settled in the lower levels of this ship and many of them are already drowning in inflation, unemployment, wars, nation-wide collapse, unmet basic needs, limited welfare systems, and low purchasing power. People of the global North are located in the upper levels and the richest 1% of the world, as well as governments (North and South) are on the forward of the deck. Increasing production, extraction, population growth, and consumption make the ship heavier, and as the ship sinks, more people find their head below water.

Structural differences between the global South and the global North

There are significant differences between the global North countries and the global South that make it difficult to provide one solution that fits all. I do not talk about inequalities, which is commonly discussed in the global South literature; I mean economic and political structural differences. One critique of Trainer's work (2021a, 2021b) is that he does not seem to differentiate solutions for the global North and global South, yet these are two different contexts. Hickel (2021a), however, does distinguish between the South and North; still, his recommendations for the South remain imperfect. The significant differences between the North and South are the result of their specific position in the global capitalist world system (Frank, 1966; Wallerstein, 2004). While the North is positioned as core of the world system, the South plays the role of periphery or semi-periphery (Wallerstein, 2004). Although both global South and North are a part of the capitalist world-economy, they contribute differently to this world system (Wallerstein, 2004). Differences are in terms of economic systems and political systems. Capitalism and industrialization in the global South are dependent and underdeveloped (Cobb & Diaz, 2009; Ghosh, 2019). Political systems are also different in terms of the type and function of government. It is not simple, therefore, to prescribe what has worked or may work in the global North to the South. The context is different and we need different interventions. To be successful, any global movement should consider these differences.

I will talk particularly about the Middle East and North Africa, as I am familiar with these. Countries in these areas mainly have rentier states and economies (Achcar, 2013); that is, they survive based on rent, derived from oil and gas. Contemporary colonization (neocolonialism) of the global South is not limited to resource extractivism, cheap labour, and atmospheric colonization (Dorninger et al., 2021; Hickel, 2021a, 2021b). Amin (2016) and Kinzer (2007) articulate how the global North governments have used political interventions, including coups, to bring weak and reactionary states into power in the South to enable the North to manipulate them for their economic interests easily.

For example, after the Arab Spring uprising in Egypt, some Western governments supported and brought the Muslim Brotherhood (MB) to power. MB avoids presenting any social or economic programmes for people's well-being and readily accepts neoliberal policies. In this sense, it serves the interests of the global North as a comprador of imperialism (Amin, 2016).

Many Middle Eastern and North African governments are well known for human rights violations and corruption (Amnesty International, 2021; Transparency International, 2021) and oligarchic capitalism is dominant. Most of the wealth and power are owned by a small group of people (particularly ruling autocrats) and their families and friends (Baumol et al., 2008). It is important to bear in mind that in this kind of capitalism, the main goal is not economic growth but the welfare of leaders and patronage (Baumol et al., 2008). Achcar (2013) describes this as 'crony or nepotistic capitalism,' and Amin (2016) as 'comprador capitalism'. The economic system is for the benefit of a few people who are connected to the ruling autocrat while also serving the interests of global neoliberalism. In such a system, national social or economic development goals are not a priority to be pursued by the government (Achcar, 2013; Amin, 2016; Baumol et al., 2008). The main characteristic of such economic systems is extreme unequal income distribution (Baumol et al., 2008).

Clearly, difference matters for what one might expect degrowth and TSW movements to achieve in the global South. Controlled, dependent, and unstable political and economic systems, which are in high degrees contingent on the fluctuations and decisions made in core countries represent serious barriers to local organizations and democratic transitions along degrowth or TSW lines – i.e. strategic achievement of goals. In the meantime, the South also affects the North by increasing environmental disasters, refugee influx, and security issues.

Critique of degrowth and TSW strategies

We cannot trust in political and economic systems of the South

I disagree with both Hickel (2021a) and Trainer (2021a) to some extent regarding the development of the global South, but for different reasons. Stopping development/growth in the global South (Trainer, 2021a), while keeping the existing political and economic systems would be associated with more dependency, (neo)colonization, and humanitarian crises. The global South is not currently independent enough to be able to address their basic needs. They need to achieve practical independence from current power relations and develop more effective representative political and economic systems. Although Hickel (2021a) underlines the need for some kind of growth in the global South to ensure needs are met, more clarification is required regarding what kind of growth and under what conditions. Hickel (2021a) argues that the global South needs to develop through fair prices of labour and raw materials. The global South needs an end to the links between extraction-rents, aid, and debt. Development should be distinguished from the production of superfluous and luxury products and focus on the global South developing through meeting its own food and welfare needs.

Hickel (2021a) suggests that governments of the South can organize collectively to address injustices in prices of their resources and labour. Citing Amin's (1987) delinking notion, Hickel (2021a) adds that global South governments may refuse to submit their development policy to the capitalism of the global North. Yet, these governments are the result of the capitalist world system and are not capable of or committed to addressing their national development issues, nor to contributing to global ecological improvements. It seems unlikely that they would join any movement oriented to establishing justice.

Building on Baumol et al. (2008)'s work, I would suggest that achieving positive development goals under rentier corrupt states and oligarchic economic systems is unlikely and the situation may simply lead to more raw material extraction, environmental damage, unaddressed needs of the majority, as well as national inequalities. The current governments and economic systems in much of the South serve the global polarizing expansion of capital. They are part of the problem; instead of considering them as a change agent who may help address the problem, they must go. Considering global South governments as agents of change is one common mistake of Western discourses.

The need for more structural solutions

TSW highlights the necessity of modifying lifestyles and systems to reduce consumption and encourage low-impact, more frugal living (Trainer, 2021a). I agree that this is useful for improving human well-being and quality of life, as well as decreasing consumption, waste, and environmental damages (Grinde et al., 2018; Trainer, 2021a). However, while I support the idea of ecovillages, localized, and community-based projects, these are not structural solutions for global environmental challenges and global inequalities. For example, how can ecovillages and localized practices address issues like the global North's transfer of hazardous wastes (Frey, 2003) to the global South (which are nonregulating countries in terms of environmental policies)? How can they solve the over-extraction of raw materials by large corporations? Can these projects address macro-scale economic and political insufficiencies in the global South countries?

Additionally, ecovillages or community-based projects are vulnerable in the context of the global South. Such projects do not work in a vacuum; they are dependent on the outside world. In broken unstable conditions of the global South, political and economic fluctuations can affect ecovillages and localized projects, especially if they are not supported by broader political institutions. Furthermore, these projects work based on local people's ownership. How can we expect people in some countries, such as Western and Central African countries, to have successful ecovillages or localized community-based projects when France controls much of their natural resources, national monetary reserves, utilities, and agriculture (Jabbar, 2013; Koulibaly, 2008; Spagnol, 2019)? Can we expect changing lifestyles through community-based projects to be a priority for these countries where people have minimum control of their own natural resources or money? Or for the countries that experience state collapse or civil war, or struggle with many internally displaced populations?

As pointed out by Trainer (2021a, 2021b), the magnitude of the problem is great and there should be radical change in systems and lifestyles. However, I am sceptical about the kind of radical change that he mentions. First, moving to localized community-based agricultural projects worldwide, as mentioned by Huber (2021), cannot address the needs of the existing population. Second, changing lifestyles should be systematic since they are mainly rooted in social structures (Sobel, 2013). That is, if social structures change appropriately, this will result in constructively modified lifestyles.

I am not going to deny the importance of human agency, education, cultural work, and awareness-raising. But changing lifestyles is not radical enough to address global challenges. As long as the system produces the possibility of consumption and excess encouraged by debt and advertising, we cannot blame people for using them. Still, many global South countries do not have credit cards or widespread loan systems offered to people, which automatically decreases their purchase power and consumption level.

Recommendations

I have several suggestions following from my previous points.

First, clearly, multiple strategies at all levels are needed and to be welcomed, so long as these are working towards the same goals (as Demaria et al. (2013) and Kallis et al. (2020) have previously discussed). Decreasing high-impact consumption, modifying lifestyles and distinguishing between sources of emissions and wastes – what are they produced in pursuit of? – in both the global South and North are necessary.

There are many useful policy foci offered by the degrowth movement: setting caps on resource use with the goal of decreasing growth by rich nations, encouraging local community ecosystems, imposing system modification inducing taxation, reducing working hours, redirecting resources to public services, etc. (Hickel, 2019; Hickel & Kallis, 2020; Kallis, 2011). To return to my previous metaphor, these slow the sinking of the ship. However, sooner or later, the ship is still going to sink unless more is done to integrate effective, global structural strategies in the degrowth agenda, and these, in turn, must take account of contextual differences between the global South and North. For example, TSW may consider some kind of a global networking of ecovillages that may replace existing governments in the long run.

Second, most of the challenges we now face are the result of the capitalist world-economy or, as mentioned by Hickel (2021b), are connected to (neo)colonialism. More structural solutions at the global level require also change in political and economic power relations in both the global North and the global South – a new phase of decolonization. Although the South went through the first phase of independence and decolonization during the 19th and 20th centuries, it was mainly to eradicate the physical presence of the core countries. In this period, colonization changed to neo-colonization, which is a hidden and more dangerous form. Without decolonizing and independence of the South, unequal exchange imposed by the North, oligarchic economic systems, and authoritarian and corrupt South governments will prevent any movement aimed at addressing global challenges from success.

Decolonization and independence of the South would decrease the North's over-extraction of raw materials, as well as exploitation of cheap labour, resulting in less production by the global North. Furthermore, the global South is unlikely capable of extracting such big amounts of raw materials and is likely unable to produce large-scale complex products (Allen, 2011). Therefore, as a result of the decolonization of the South, production and, consequently, consumption are going to decrease in both the global North and South, resulting in more reasonable lifestyles.

There may be trade-offs here and the global South is likely to continue to be economically poorer than the North. But a system that dismisses dependency and the dehumanizing aspects of broken, corrupt economics and politics provides a sounder basis for subsequent progress in both climate-ecological terms and those of human well-being.

Conclusion

The author of this paper believes that without complete decolonization and independence of the global South, the degrowth movement and variations such as TSW will be ineffective and any solutions to climate emergency will be temporary. Collaboration of both the global North and South is crucial. Awareness-raising, particularly in the South, is necessary. As Paulo Freire (1996) states in the *Pedagogy of the Oppressed*, 'submerged in reality, the oppressed cannot perceive clearly the "order" which serves the interests of the oppressors' (p. 62).

As pointed out by Huber (2021), movements in the global South are not very familiar with degrowth concepts. They do not see direct connections between these and their political and economic struggles. To disseminate degrowth, the benefits of the movement for their emancipation from corrupt governments and broken economic systems must be clearer and better developed. Of course, emphasizing structural issues does not undermine the scope for agency among people. Global South intellectuals and social activists have a responsibility to apply critical thinking to solutions and knowledge offered from the global North, as these may not be necessarily relevant to the South's conditions. As many in the degrowth movement avow, this can only enhance the movement. I hope more scholars from the global South join the discussion.

Acknowledgements

I would like to thank Dr. Barry Gills, Dr. Jamie Morgan, and Dr. Jason Hickel for their comments that significantly improved the argument.

Disclosure statement

No potential conflict of interest was reported by the author(s).

Funding

The researcher received no financial support for the research, authorship, and/or publication of this article.

ORCID

Sarah MacKay 🆔 http://orcid.org/0000-0002-8761-1490

References

Achcar, G. (2013). *The people want: A radical exploration of the Arab uprising*. University of California Press.

Allen, R. C. (2011). *Global economic history: A very short introduction*. Oxford University Press.

Amin, S. (1987). A note on the concept of delinking. *Review, 10*(3), 435–444. http://www.jstor.org/stable/40241067

Amin, S. (2016). *The reawakening of the Arab world: Challenge and change in the aftermath of the Arab spring*. NYU Press.

Amnesty International. (2021). *Human rights in Middle East and North Africa – Review in 2020*. https://www.amnesty.org/en/location/middle-east-and-north-africa/report-middle-east-and-north-africa/

Baumol, W., Litan, R., & Schramm, C. J. (2008). *Good capitalism, bad capitalism, and the economics of growth and prosperity*. Yale University Press.

Cobb, C. W., & Diaz, P. (2009). *Why global poverty? A companion guide to the film "The end of poverty?"*. Robert Schalkenbach Foundation.

D'Alisa, G., Demaria, F., & Kallis, G. (2014). *Degrowth: A vocabulary for a new era*. Routledge.

Demaria, F., Schneider, F., Sekulova, F., & Martinez-Alier, J. (2013). What is degrowth? From an activist slogan to a social movement. *Environmental Values, 22*(2), 191–215. https://doi.org/10.3197/096327113X13581561725194

Dorninger, C., Hornborg, A., Abson, D. J., Von Wehrden, H., Schaffartzik, A., Giljum, S., Engler, J.-O., Feller, R. L., Hubacek, K., & Wieland, H. (2021). Global patterns of ecologically unequal exchange: Implications for sustainability in the twenty-first century. *Ecological Economics, 179*, article number 106824. https://doi.org/10.1016/j.ecolecon.2020.106824

Frank, A. G. (1966). The development of underdevelopment. *Monthly Review, 18*(4), 17–31. https://doi.org/10.14452/MR-018-04-1966-08_3

Freire, P. (1996). *Pedagogy of the oppressed*. Continuum.

Frey, R. S. (2003). The transfer of core-based hazardous production processes to the export processing zones of the periphery: The maquiladora centers of northern Mexico. *JWSR Editorial Policy, 9*(2), 317–354. https://doi.org/10.5195/jwsr.2003.236

Ghosh, B. N. (2019). *Dependency theory revisited*. Routledge.

Grinde, B., Nes, R. B., MacDonald, I. F., & Wilson, D. S. (2018). Quality of life in intentional communities. *Social Indicators Research, 137*(2), 625–640. https://doi.org/10.1007/s11205-017-1615-3

Hickel, J. (2017a). Is global inequality getting better or worse? A critique of the World Bank's convergence narrative. *Third World Quarterly, 38*(10), 2208–2222. https://doi.org/10.1080/01436597.2017.1333414

Hickel, J. (2017b). *The divide: A brief guide to global inequality and its solutions*. Windmill Books.

Hickel, J. (2019). Is it possible to achieve a good life for all within planetary boundaries? *Third World Quarterly, 40*(1), 18–35. https://doi.org/10.1080/01436597.2018.1535895

Hickel, J. (2021a). What does degrowth mean? A few points of clarification. *Globalizations, 18*(7), 1105–1111. https://doi.org/10.1080/14747731.2020.1812222

Hickel, J. (2021b). The anti-colonial politics of degrowth. *Political Geography, 88*, article number 102404, 1–3. https://doi.org/10.1016/j.polgeo.2021.102404

Hickel, J., & Kallis, G. (2020). Is Green growth possible? *New Political Economy, 25*(4), 469–486. https://doi.org/10.1080/13563467.2019.1598964

Hickel, J., Sullivan, D., & Zoomkawala, H. (2021). Plunder in the post-colonial era: Quantifying drain from the global South through unequal exchange, 1960–2018. *New Political Economy, 26*(6), 1–18. https://doi.org/10.1080/13563467.2021.1899153

Huber, M. T. (2021). The case for socialist modernism. *Political Geography, 87*, article number 102352, 1–3. https://doi.org/10.1016/j.polgeo.2021.102352

Jabbar, S. (2013). *How France loots its former colonies*. https://thisisafrica.me/politics-and-society/france-loots-former-colonies/

Kallis, G. (2011). In defence of degrowth. *Ecological Economics, 70*(5), 873–880. https://doi.org/10.1016/j.ecolecon.2010.12.007

Kallis, G., Paulson, S., D'Alisa, G., & Demaria, F. (2020). *The case for degrowth*. Polity Press.

Kinzer, S. (2007). *Overthrow: America's century of regime change from Hawaii to Iraq*. Macmillan.

Koulibaly, M. (2008). *Les servitudes du pacte colonial* [The servitude of the colonial pact]. NEI.

Morgan, J. (2020). Degrowth: Necessary, urgent and good for you. *Real-World Economics Review*, (93), 113–131. http://www.paecon.net/PAEReview/issue93/Morgan93.pdf

Sobel, M. E. (2013). *Lifestyle and social structure: Concepts, definitions, analyses*. Elsevier.

Spagnol, G. (2019). *Is France still exploiting Africa?* Institut Européen des Relations Internationales. https://www.ieri.be/en/publications/wp/2019/f-vrier/france-still-exploiting-africa

Trainer, T. (2011). The radical implications of a zero growth economy. *Real-World Economics Review, 57*(1), 71–82.

Trainer, T. (2016). The Simpler Way. https://thesimplerway.info/

Trainer, T. (2020). Simpler way transition theory. *Real-World Economics Review, 93*, 96–112.

Trainer, T. (2021a). De-growth: Some suggestions from the Simpler Way perspective. *Ecological Economics, 167*, article number 106436, 1–6. https://doi.org/10.1016/j.ecolecon.2019.106436

Trainer, T. (2021b). What does degrowth mean? Some comments on Jason Hickel's 'A few points of clarification'. *Globalizations, 18*(7), 1112–1116. https://doi.org/10.1080/14747731.2020.1860621

Transparency International. (2021). *Corruption perceptions index*. https://www.transparency.org/en/cpi/2020/index/nzl

Wallerstein. (2004). *World-systems analysis*. Duke University Press.

Climate justice and sustained transnational mobilization

Paul Almeida

ABSTRACT

Samir Amin's final essay called for the creation of a new international organization of progressive social forces. Here I review evidence from twenty-first century transnational movements germane for understanding the likelihood of the emergence of such an international organization and the issues and sectors most likely to facilitate coalitional unity. More specifically, the ecological crises identified by Amin in the form of global warming and climate change have created an unprecedented global environmental threat capable of unifying diverse social strata across the planet. The climate justice movement has already established a global infrastructure and template to coordinate a new international organization for confronting neoliberal forms of globalization. Pre-existing movement organizing around environmental racism, climate justice in the global South, and recent intersectional mobilizations serve as promising models for building an enduring international organization that will represent subaltern groups and have a substantial impact on world politics.

Samir Amin, a leading scholar and co-founder of the world-systems tradition, died on August 12, 2018. Just before his death, he published, along with close allies, a call for 'workers and the people' to establish a 'fifth international' [https://www.pambazuka.org/global-south/letter-intent-inaugural-meeting-international-workers-and-peoples] *to coordinate support to progressive movements. To honor Samir Amin's invaluable contribution to world-systems scholarship, we are pleased to present readers with a selection of essays responding to Amin's final message for today's anti-systemic movements. This forum is being co-published between* Globalizations [https://www.tandfonline.com/rglo], *the* Journal of World-Systems Research [http://jwsr.pitt.edu/ojs/index.php/jwsr/issue/view/75] *and* Pambazuka News [https://www.pambazuka.org/]. *Additional essays and commentary can be found in these outlets.*

Introduction

The transition to the neoliberal form of global capitalism in the late twentieth century corresponded with a variety of novel forms of resistance at the local, national, and international levels of political life (Almeida & Chase-Dunn, 2018). Neoliberalism produces new models of unequal development (Amin, 1976) between the capitalist core and periphery as well within nation states along with a host of tensions and threats motivating popular movements. These struggles will likely intensify as we move into the third decade of the new millennium. At the local level, collective action centres on everyday forms of resistance and grassroots struggles over racism, land grabbing, mining and mega development projects (Almeida, 2019). At the national level, opposition to neoliberalism manifests in the form of social movement campaigns against a bundle of economic liberalization policies that include austerity cuts, free trade agreements, privatization, de-regulation, and labour flexibility laws (Silva, 2009; Walton & Seddon, 1994). At the transnational level, opposition to international capital is most pronounced in the global economic justice movement, the World Social Forums, and, increasingly, the movement for Climate Justice, which is the focus of this essay.

In past decades, sociologists theorized that global capitalist accumulation would create its own self-induced limits through the depletion of natural resources, pollution, and environmental destruction (Gould, Pellow, & Schnaiberg, 2004; Rudy, forthcoming; Schnaiberg, 1980). Amin (2018) also referred to the ecological crisis of the twenty-first century in his final essay. James O'Connor (1988) conceptualized these processes as the 'second contradiction of capitalism', a contradiction in addition to the capitalist crisis of overproduction. In this perspective, advanced forms of capitalist accumulation undermine the necessary material requisites for systemic reproduction by destroying the ecological bases for continuous and expanded industrial activities on a global scale, leading to a crisis of underproduction. More recently, scholars contributing to these debates incorporate carbon emissions and global warming as an 'ecological rift' caused by global capitalism (Foster, Clark, & York, 2011; Moore, 2015).

The most recent scientific reporting suggests that the outlook for continued global warming is dire. Instead of a reduction in carbon emissions since 2017, there was a global increase of 1.6% in 2017 and 2.7% in 2018. (Dennis & Moody, 2018). Moreover, the past four years (2015–2018) have seen the warmest documented mean global temperatures on record, while the twenty warmest years on record have occurred over the past twenty-two years (World Meteorological Organization, 2018). The environmental challenge of global warming and climate change produced by neoliberal capitalism in the twenty-first century has also generated a massive transnational movement – the movement for climate justice. Environmental justice and climate justice combine threats of environmental degradation with concerns about inequality and the larger impacts on people with fewer resources and disadvantaged populations (Bullard, 2005; Pellow, 2017).

Ecological threats provide a major incentive for collective action in that failure to mobilize in the present will likely lead to worsening environmental conditions (Almeida, 2018; Johnson & Frickel, 2011). Earlier conservation movements (often involving more privileged social strata) organized in waves of environmentalism since the late nineteenth century against ecological threats associated with the expansion of industrial capital (Gottlieb, 1993). The movement to resist the environmental threat of climate change traces its origins back to the late 1980s and early 1990s. In the late 1980s, climate scientists and environmental NGOs started to push international organizations and nation states to take action based on meteorological and atmospheric studies that demonstrated a clear trend in global warming and its likely negative consequences. The United Nations established the Intergovernmental Panel on Climate Change (IPCC) to begin scientific discussions about how to reduce greenhouse gas emissions (Romm, 2018). Concurrently, a global network of environmental NGOs emerged to pressure the U.N. to propose a binding international climate accord – the Climate Action Network (CAN) (Brecher, 2015). During the United Nations Earth Summit on sustainability in Rio de Janeiro, Brazil in 1992, the United Nations Framework Convention on Climate Change (UNFCC) was established as an intergovernmental forum to work on reducing global warming (Caniglia, Brulle, & Szasz, 2015). In 1995, the UNFCC forum also set up annual meetings to move toward a global climate treaty to decrease carbon emissions – the Conference of Parties (COP). Throughout the 1990s and early 2000s the global climate movement to reduce greenhouse gases was concentrated in advanced capitalist countries and largely worked through the institutional channels of these U.N. bodies via the participation of environmental NGOs. This period has been referred to as 'mobilization from above' (Brecher, 2015).

Beginning in the mid-2000s, the climate justice movement became more contentious, organizing rallies and marches across the globe. The use of more non-institutionalized tactics rose in tandem with the lack of progress within the U.N. system to enforce past agreements and hold countries accountable for CO2 emissions. Already by 2005 the mass climate justice movement could mobilize simultaneous demonstrations in cities across several continents. The climate justice movement peaked in 2014 and 2015 by holding global days of protest in most of the world's countries and mobilized another large campaign in September of 2018 (Almeida, 2019). The movement has gained tremendous momentum in 2019 with the rise of Extinction Rebellion and Fridays for the Future promoting hundreds of actions across the globe. This global reach marked the transnational climate justice movement as one of the most extensive social movements on the planet.

The emphasis here is on the organizational infrastructure that has made the transnational climate justice movement so extensive and its prospects for future mobilization and lasting and effective coordination of popular organizations and movements. I examine the role of the global economic justice movement and the anti-war movement in providing the organizational and experiential bases for planetary mobilization against climate change. These are empirically based assessments to understand the likelihood of building a sustained international organization of progressive and subaltern forces along the lines envisioned by Amin (2018).

The global justice movement

The global justice movement took off in the late 1990s shortly after the establishment of the World Trade Organization (WTO) in 1996. The movement quickly developed an innovative organizational template for mobilizing mass protests on a transnational level. The coordinating template involved mobilizing a series of actions at the focal conference/summit/financial meetings while simultaneously holding dozens of solidarity actions across the globe (Almeida & Lichbach, 2003). This transnational organizing model is referred to by activists as a 'global day of action' (Wood, 2004). The global justice movement was a response to the neoliberal form of global capitalism that had been taking shape since the 1980s with a heavy emphasis on free trade and deregulation of social protections. The emerging global justice movement began to take advantage of the rise of internet communication technologies (ICTs). Beginning with international financial meetings in Europe in the late 1990s and the 1999 WTO conference in Seattle (Smith, 2001), the global organizational template was widely adopted. Indeed, by the turn of the twenty-first century the global justice movement had organized over 15 transnational campaigns per year with over 200,000 participants (Lichbach, 2003).

The organizational template invented by the global justice movement involves holding a large set of protests at the site of an international event along with simultaneous solidarity protests around the world (Almeida & Lichbach, 2003). By the early 2000s, the global justice movement had expanded the simultaneous protests to every continent. This would become the main form of transnational opposition to global capitalism in the twenty-first century (Wood, 2012). After the WTO meetings in Seattle, at least a half dozen global days of protest took place between 2000 and 2003. These included the IMF/World Bank meetings in Prague in September 2000, the G8 conference in Genoa in 2001, the WTO ministerial in Doha, Qatar in November 2001, and the fifth WTO Ministerial in 2003 in Cancun, Mexico (Juris, 2008). The global justice movement brought a wide coalition of different groups into their global days of action campaigns – youth, labour unions, human rights, environmentalists, LGBTQ groups, indigenous activists, feminists, peace, anarchists and etc. They united around the idea of protecting social citizenship and environmental rights that had been granted by nation-states in the twentieth century and now were under threat from neoliberal deregulation.

The global justice movement spilled over into the global anti-war movement in 2003 with demonstrations against the U.S. invasion of Iraq[1] and into the climate justice movement by the mid-2000s (Fisher, 2007; Hadden, 2014). At the same time, the issues and networks involved in the global justice movement continued via the World Social Forum process and ongoing mass demonstrations outside G20 meetings, as well as the global day of action in October of 2011 at the height of the Occupy Wall Street campaign. If there is to be a sustained progressive international movement in the twenty-first century it will probably coalesce around the climate justice movement and will further develop and augment the global days of action template.

Networks of transnational activists began to piece together the first Global Days Action to reduce carbon emissions in 2005 and 2006. These global networks came out of the alter-globalization and anti-war movements of the early 2000s to now battle climate change (Bond, 2012). They were joined by coalitions such as the Campaign against Climate Change and the transnational environmental NGOs such as Friends of the Earth and Greenpeace (Foran, 2014). By 2009, the climate justice movement reached 92 nations in the days of global action leading up to COP 15 in Copenhagen with the assistance of more assertive coalitions such as Climate Justice Action and Climate Justice Now! and greater representation from the Global South.[2] In the 2010s, web-based NGOs such as 350.org and Avaaz took a leadership role as brokers in coordinating the large mobilizations in 2014 and 2015 leading up to the Paris Climate Agreement. The 2014 and 2015 global days of climate action reached up to 75 percent of all countries on the planet with at least 1.5 million participants. Fridays for the Future and Extinction Rebellion are currently sustaining similar campaigns across the globe.

The increasing participation from countries across the world in the transnational climate justice actions, including from the global South, is remarkable. This loosely coupled global infrastructure provides a basis for future rounds of progressive collective action. The next steps for solidifying this infrastructure would be to continue to coordinate global summits and forums with representatives from the participating groups in the global days of action. Past examples of this approach include the World People's Summit on Climate Change and the Rights of Mother Earth held in Bolivia in 2010 following the worldwide mobilizations associated with COP 15 (Smith, 2014) and the World Social Forums. The Bolivia Summit called for ecological reparations for the Global South and an immediate and drastic reduction in carbon emissions.

Perhaps most pressing would be to increase the rate of summits and forums that bring together representatives from the climate justice coalition. The impressive scale of the transnational mobilizations over the past ten years is still limited by the vast amount of time between the launching of global days of action campaigns, even though much traditional organizing takes place on the ground in the interim periods. To overcome the 'flash activism' nature of these campaigns and to build the necessary level of solidarity among diverse groups, classes, and sectors for a long-term and capacious anti-systemic movement (Amin, 1990; Ciplet, Timmons Roberts, & Khan, 2015), climate justice activists will need to continue to find avenues and mechanisms for more frequent forums and mobilizations that can maintain and accelerate the momentum of a truly planetary movement.

The increasing intensity of climate change as an existential threat does create relatively more favourable conditions for international unity and avoids the sectarianism and fragmentation discussed by Amin (2018) in previous attempts at building a socialist *internationale* or permanent global organization of progressive sectors and groups. The threat is imminent and global, providing urgency and aligning common interests, the basic building blocks of sustained collective action (Almeida, 2019). At the same time, a number of pre-existing social and economic divisions will need to be given heightened recognition to build enduring transnational coalitions across the lines of race, class, gender, and colonial status. The environmental justice movement against ecological racism (Bullard, 2005), the Cochabamba Climate Change conference (Bond, 2012), and the current mass mobilizations fostering intersectional alliances (Luna, 2016; Terriquez, Brenes, & Lopez, 2018) offer some of the most promising models to incorporate within the larger global climate justice movement. With global warming disproportionately harming billions of the world's poor and excluded by global capital, the climate justice movement cannot continue to be directed by relatively privileged strata in the global North or South. Chase-Dunn and Reese (2007) also demonstrate that previous progressive parties organized on a global scale were initially able to coordinate simultaneously in the global periphery and capitalist core with membership from a variety of social sectors, including peasants and the urban working-class. The transnational climate justice alliance may also build internal cohesion by mobilizing against the xenophobia, authoritarianism, and climate change deniability of rightwing populism.

Notes

1. One of the largest protests in world history took place on 15 February 2003 against the impending U.S. invasion of Iraq. Nearly 800 cities in eighty countries participated against initiating a war on Iraq using the Global Days of Action template.
2. The terminology of the world-system perspective divides the Global South into the periphery and the semiperiphery.

Disclosure statement

No potential conflict of interest was reported by the author.

References

Almeida, P. D. (2018). The role of threat in collective action. In D. Snow, S. Soule, H. Kriesi, & H. McCammon (Eds.), *Wiley- Blackwell companion to social movements* (2nd ed., pp. 43–62). Oxford: Blackwell.
Almeida, P. D. (2019). *Social movements: The structure of collective mobilization.* Berkeley: University of California Press.

Almeida, P. D., & Chase-Dunn, C. (2018). Globalization and social movements. *Annual Review of Sociology, 44*, 189–211.

Almeida, P. D., & Lichbach, M. I. (2003). To the internet, from the internet: Comparative media coverage of transnational protest. *Mobilization, 8*(3), 249–272.

Amin, S. (1976). *Unequal development: An essay on the social formations of peripheral capitalism*. New York, NY: Monthly Review Press.

Amin, S. (1990). The social movements in the periphery: An end to national liberation? In S. Amin, G. Arrighi, A. Gunder Frank, & I. Wallerstein (Eds.), *Transforming the revolution: Social movements and the world-system* (pp. 96–138). New York, NY: Monthly Review Press.

Amin, S. (2018). It is imperative to reconstruct the Internationale of workers and peoples. *International Development Economic Associates (IDEAs)*. July3, 2018. Retrieved from http://www.networkideas.org/featured-articles/2018/07/it-is-imperative-to-reconstruct-the-internationale-of-workers-and-peoples/

Bond, P. (2012). *Politics of climate justice: Paralysis above, movement below*. Cape Town: University of Kwa Zulu Natal Press.

Brecher, J. (2015). *Climate insurgency: A strategy for survival*. Boulder, CO: Paradigm.

Bullard, R. (2005). *The quest for environmental justice: Human rights and the politics of pollution*. San Francisco, CA: Sierra Club Books.

Caniglia, B., Brulle, R., & Szasz, A. (2015). Civil Society, social movements, and climate change. In R. Dunlap & R. Brulle (Eds.), *Climate change and Society* (pp. 235–268). Oxford: Oxford University Press.

Chase-Dunn, C., & Reese, E. (2007). The world social forum: A global party in the making? In K. Sehm-Patomaki & M. Ulvila (Eds.), *Global political parties* (pp. 53–92). London: Zed Press.

Ciplet, D., Timmons Roberts, J., & Khan, M. R. (2015). *Power in a warming world: The new global politics of climate change and the remaking of environmental inequality*. Cambridge, MA: MIT Press.

Dennis, B., & Moody, C. (2018). 'We are in trouble.' Global carbon emissions reached a new record high in 2018. Washington Post, December 5, 2018.

Fisher, D. (2007). Taking cover beneath the anti-bush umbrella: Cycles of protest and movement-to-movement transmission in an era of repressive politics. *Research in Political Sociology, 15*, 27–56.

Foran, J. (2014). 'Get it done!' The global climate justice movement's struggle to achieve a radical climate treaty. Unpublished ms. University of California, Santa Barbara, Dept. of Sociology.

Foster, J. B., Clark, B., & York, R. (2011). *The ecological rift: Capitalism's war on the earth*. New York, NY: New York University Press.

Gottlieb, R. (1993). *Forcing the Spring: The transformation of the American environmental movement*. New York, NY: Island Press.

Gould, K. A., Pellow, D. N., & Schnaiberg, A. (2004). Interrogating the treadmill of production: Everything you wanted to know about the treadmill but were afraid to ask. *Organization & Environment, 17*(3), 296–316.

Hadden, J. (2014). Explaining variation in transnational climate change activism: The role of inter-movement spillover. *Global Environmental Politics, 14*(2), 7–25.

Johnson, E. W., & Frickel, S. (2011). Ecological threat and the founding of US national environmental movement organizations, 1962–1998. *Social Problems, 58*(3), 305–329.

Juris, J. (2008). *Networking futures: The movements against corporate globalization*. Durham: Duke University Press.

Lichbach, M. I. (2003). The anti-globalization movement: A new kind of protest. In M. G. Marshall & T. R. Gurr (Eds.), *Peace and Conflict 2003* (pp. 39–42). College Park, MD: Center for International Development and Conflict Management, University of Maryland.

Luna, Z. T. (2016). 'Truly a women of color organization': Negotiating sameness and difference in pursuit of intersectionality. *Gender and Society, 30*(5), 769–790.

Moore, J. W. (2015). *Capitalism in the web of life: Ecology and the accumulation of capital*. London: Verso Books.

O'Connor, J. (1988). Capitalism, nature, socialism a theoretical introduction. *Capitalism Nature Socialism, 1*(1), 11–38.

Pellow, D. N. (2017). *What is critical environmental justice?* London: Polity Press.

Romm, J. (2018). *Climate change: What everyone needs to know*. Oxford: Oxford University Press.

Rudy, A. (Forthcoming). On misunderstanding the second contradiction thesis. *Capitalism, Nature, Socialism*.

Schnaiberg, A. (1980). *The environment: From surplus to scarcity*. Oxford: Oxford University Press.

Silva, E. (2009). *Challenges to neoliberalism in Latin America*. Cambridge: Cambridge University Press.

Smith, J. (2001). Globalizing resistance: The battle of Seattle and the future of social movements. *Mobilization*, 6(1), 1–21.

Smith, J. (2014). Counter-hegemonic networks and the transformation of global climate politics: Rethinking movement-State Relations. *Global Discourse*, 4(2–3), 120–138.

Terriquez, V., Brenes, T., & Lopez, A. (2018). Intersectionality as a multipurpose collective action frame: The case of the undocumented youth movement. *Ethnicities*, 18(2), 260–276.

Walton, J., & Seddon, D. (1994). *Free markets and food riots: The politics of global adjustment*. Oxford: Blackwell Publishers.

Wood, L. J. (2004). Breaking the bank & taking to the streets: How protesters target neoliberalism. *Journal of World-Systems Research*, 10(1), 69–89.

Wood, L. J. (2012). *Direct action, deliberation, and diffusion: Collective action after the WTO protests in Seattle*. Cambridge: Cambridge University Press.

World Meteorological Organization. (2018). *WMO provisional statement on the state of the global climate in 2018*. New York, NY: United Nations.

Deep Restoration: from The Great Implosion to The Great Awakening

Barry Gills

We are living in a time of exception. A time when the existing order is open to question.

In this short essay for *Globalizations* I wish to make some initial reflections in response to the present 'triple conjuncture' of global crises. This triple conjuncture is an interaction among three spheres or vectors of global crises, together constituting a crisis of capitalist world order. The three spheres of the global crisis are: climate change and ecological breakdown; a systemic crisis of global capitalism and neoliberal economic globalization; and the current global pandemic of covid-19. The three spheres are deeply interrelated and now rapidly interacting. Their combined effects will bring radical systemic transformation.

What do these crises represent? How do we understand the meaning and causes of this comprehensive global crisis? Long established patterns have produced all three vectors. None of them are simply short-term phenomena. The mentalities, structures and practices that have produced the global climate change and ecological crisis are the deepest historically, but these have accelerated and widened in their destructive tendencies dramatically over the past few decades. That recent increase in scale and acceleration in the speed and extent of such destructiveness is closely related to the onset and deepening of neoliberal economic globalization over the past few decades, which has been a crucial driver of the climate change and global ecological crisis. The present pandemic is to some extent a consequence of decades of environmental degradation, and increasing destruction and intrusion by human beings into numerous ecological systems. Now, all the cumulative entropic tendencies of historical time are being combined and compressed into the present. The world as we know it is literally breaking down. We are living in The Great Implosion.

But we have the greatest capacity for reflexive learning and communication in human history. Radical transformative praxis is both a product of this history, and the only hope for the future. As the existing order begins to disintegrate a new social order must be built through deploying our collective radical imagination. We shall need new forms of collective human consciousness; a new type of global social covenant; new forms of appropriate technology; and new forms of appropriate lifestyle.

The most existentially threatening of the three crises in the long term is the climate change and ecological crisis: which itself is accelerating and deepening as a consequence of neoliberal economic globalization. As the current pandemic eventually recedes we must refocus our attention on addressing the climate change and ecological crisis with all urgency, and act together decisively to reduce global green house gas emissions by half by the year 2030. The fiscal and monetary response of numerous governments to the present pandemic may well be a factor leading to a similar and even larger emergency response to the global climate change crisis. The precedent has now been set for governments to mobilize resources in the midst of an imminent crisis that threatens the human security of their population. The pandemic is at present further accelerating a crisis in global capitalism: triggering steep economic contraction; rise in bankruptcies; sequential and large debt crises; very high unemployment; increasing poverty … Long-term crisis tendencies have been building in the global system before and after the great financial crisis of 2008. The ratio of debt to GDP at global level is now at its highest level in history, and years of quantitative easing combined with austerity measures have weakened the capacity of both states and society to cope with a new global financial crisis. Serious disruption of globalized production and supply chains caused by the pandemic would be amplified in a systemic financial crisis, with severe damage to all economies and especially to those in the global south still over dependent on natural resource extraction and primary commodity export.

The contraction in economic activity, however, in general reduces local and global levels of pollution, e.g. the steep reduction in private travel, especially flying, brings some needed reduction in carbon dioxide, nitrous oxide, and even carbon monoxide emissions … thus slowing the rate of increase of cumulative GHGs in the atmosphere. The pandemic shutdown of polluting industries has graphically illustrated both the horrific extent of daily 'normal' pollution to the planet by our economic activity, while at the same time paradoxically showing us exactly how quickly and dramatically we could (and should) reduce global emissions to address the global climate emergency.

The combination of all three crises brings the hitherto accelerating linear time of modernity into deceleration, into a pause. This space provides a time of awakening … to the deep malaise of our civilization. This awakening will generate a realization of common interests, producing social compassion and mutual aid. The crisis is producing a realization that a different social reality is possible. Where the experience of collective being starts to take precedence over egoistic individualism.

In conclusion, these are my hopes for deep restoration: how in the midst of deepening global crises there will emerge transformation:

A deep restoration of the spiritual inner life of humanity: towards a post materialistic philosophy. A deep restoration of the awareness of the necessity for maintaining ecological balance within the context of earth system dynamics. A deep restoration of the ethics of harmony with the web of life, including not only all species of creatures but also with the water, the oceans, the forests, and the soils of the earth, in which we are deeply embedded and mutually interdependent. A deep restoration of the Culture of Peace, including social peace, founded on bonds of kindness and mutual respect; and the final realization of international peace. This global culture of peace will be a historical necessity in the near future, as the great implosion of the existing capitalist world order produces ever greater danger and an urgency to refocus our resources on preserving life and transforming our life. Global de-militarization and disarmament will be a necessary part of this transformation, producing a new type of world order based on cooperation and mutual support. A deep restoration of the spirit of human solidarity and unity. New forms of social solidarity and global solidarity and internationalism are emerging: we must move now rapidly towards a post nationalist mentality, based on our common human interests. A deep restoration of the idea and practices of the Commons: strengthening the principle of collective interests to take full precedence over egoistic individualism. The idea of the commons in the 'economy' and in society will bring into being a new form of economy, embedding greater equality and democracy, with decentralized democratic decision making, and post-patriarchal equality throughout society.

The time we had grown accustomed to feel and were socialized to understand as normality, and to regard as the only reality (i.e. the linear time of capitalist modernity) is now suddenly exposed as only one stream of time. And that Time is now decelerating … giving us pause. Time to stop. Time to think. Time to awaken. A different reality is possible. It is we who must respond to the crisis and collectively create a different future.

Index

Note: Page numbers followed by "n" denote endnotes.

For Product Safety Concerns and Information please contact our
EU representative GPSR@taylorandfrancis.com Taylor & Francis
Verlag GmbH, Kaufingerstraße 24, 80331 München, Germany